THE IRWIN
HANDBOOK OF
TELECOMMUNICATIONS

FOURTH EDITION

THE IRWIN HANDBOOK OF TELECOMMUNICATIONS

JAMES HARRY GREEN

McGraw-Hill

New York San Francisco Washington, D.C. Auckland Bogotá
Caracas Lisbon London Madrid Mexico City Milan
Montreal New Delhi San Juan Singapore
Sydney Tokyo Toronto

Library of Congress Cataloging-in-Publication Data

Green, James H. (James Harry)
    The Irwin handbook of telecommunications / by James Harry Green.—4th ed.
      p. cm.
    ISBN 0-07-135554-5
    1. Telecommunication systems—United States. 2. Business enterprises—United
States—Communication systems. I. Title.

TK5102.3.U6 G74 2000
621.382 21—dc21   99-044782

McGraw-Hill

A Division of The **McGraw-Hill** *Companies*

1 2 3 4 5 6 7 8 9 0 DOC/DOC 0 9 8 7 6 5 4 3 2 1 0

ISBN 0-07-135554-5

This book was set in 10/13 Palatino by Carlisle Publishers Service.

Printed and bound by R. R. Donnelley & Sons Company.

McGraw-Hill books are available at special quantity discounts to use as premiums and sales promotions, or for use in corporate training programs. For more information, please write to the Director of Special Sales, Professional Publishing, McGraw-Hill, Two Penn Plaza, New York, NY 10121-2298. Or contact your local bookstore.

This publication is designed to provide accurate and authoritative information in regard to the subject matter covered. It is sold with the understanding that neither the author nor the publisher is engaged in rendering legal, accounting, or other professional service. If legal advice or other expert assistance is required, the services of a competent professional person should be sought.

> *—From a Declaration of Principles jointly adopted by a committee of the American Bar Association and a Committee of Publishers.*

This book is printed on recycled, acid-free paper containing a minimum of 50% recycled, de-inked fiber.

CONTENTS

As one who has worked in this industry for about a third of the life span of the telephone, I find the rate of technical progress fascinating. Following the invention of the telephone, a few milestones resulted in a major shift in the direction of telecommunications. In 1891, a Kansas City undertaker named Almon B. Strowger invented the first dial-controlled telephone switching machine, which ushered in the beginnings of automation. Lee DeForest's invention of the vacuum tube in 1906 led to repeaters and carrier telephony, which enabled telephone conversations to span continents and oceans. Electronic switching in 1965 near the end of telephone's first century marked a major breakthrough. For the first time, a computer program instead of electromechanical relays and switches controlled calls, and new features could be installed by upgrading a program instead of rewiring the central office. Ironically, at the time the first electronic switching system went into effect, the Bell System still had manual cord boards in operation—Strowger's invention didn't always cost justify itself in rural areas where the telephone exchange could still be operated manually.

Before the breakup of the Bell System, telecommunications was in a technology-push situation rather than demand-pull. Most developments originated in the Bell Labs and were released to the field only after they were thoroughly tested. Development cycles of 4 or 5 years were not uncommon. Then in the late 1970s came a fabulous development that is invisible to most people, but which has revolutionized telecommunications: fiber optics. Bell Laboratories did most of the research on fiber and the lasers that make information transfer possible, but other companies rapidly picked up on the technology, and demand exploded. Fiber optics was probably the first real demand-pull product that hit the telecommunications market.

Fiber optics is still, by far, the most dynamic and influential of all the telecommunications technologies. In a little more than two decades, strands of fiber have girdled the world and its capacity is practically unlimited. Production equipment can reach speeds of 10 gigabits per second (Gb/s) now, and that is still not the top limit. Dense wavelength division multiplexing divides the medium into 40 different "colors," each capable of carrying a 10-Gb/s signal. Undersea cables have, for all practical purposes, replaced satellites as transcontinental telephone media, but satellites are experiencing a new rebirth with low earth-orbiting vehicles that eliminate the delay inherent in geosynchronous devices. These make it possible to place a telephone call from virtually any place on the face of the earth.

New technology has flourished since divestiture, but perhaps a better indicator of the wisdom of the consent decree that broke up the Bell System is the fact that all parties remained dissatisfied. The regional Bell Operating Companies chafed at the long-distance restrictions the agreement imposed upon them. The interexchange carriers (IXCs) complained about access charges, which they deemed excessive, and a host of would-be competitors complained about the local monopoly. Congress entered the picture and, responding to multiple pressures, created the Telecommunications Act of 1996. The act uses both carrots and sticks to reshape the local telephone market from government regulation to competition. At the time this is written, the Telecommunications Act has resulted in few of its intended outcomes. Business subscribers in larger cities all have options for local dial tone provided they purchase enough lines to make it worth the while of competitive local exchange carriers (CLECs) to serve them.

Few residences have a choice of telephone service, but they are still saddled with increased costs. The Telecommunications Act requires carriers to contribute to a Universal Service Fund to subsidize rural and low-income consumers. Congress decided that schools, libraries, and rural health care organizations were also entitled to subsidies. The carriers passed their increased costs through to consumers in the form of surcharges and directly allocated costs, even while they were enjoying reduced access charges. The act required that local telephone numbers be portable between carriers, the costs of which are being pushed directly onto consumers who don't even enjoy the possibility of reduced rates from competitive carriers. The impact of these regulatory fiats has been negative for most consumers even though it may prove beneficial in the long run.

Mergers and acquisitions have changed the landscape in ways that we can't begin to grasp yet. The seven regional Bell Operating Companies have dwindled to four—probably three by the time you read this. GTE will merge into Bell Atlantic, which already has absorbed Nynex. Southwestern Bell has assimilated Pacific Telesis and Ameritech. US West announced its intention to join in a "union of equals" with Global Crossings, a Bermuda-based firm that has a corporate history stretching all the way back to 1997. Global Crossings has already acquired Frontier Communications and the undersea cable operations of Cable and Wireless, a British firm. Before the deal could be consummated, Qwest, another newcomer to the industry, offered a more attractive proposition. As this is written, regulatory approval is still pending.

After flirting briefly with British Telecom, MCI, which was a major player in triggering the collapse of the Bell System, allowed itself to be acquired by WorldCom, another corporate newcomer. The MCI WorldCom combination, which is the second largest IXC in the United States, is attempting to get approval to aquire No. 3 Sprint.

AT&T, which fought to keep its manufacturing and customer premises equipment business intact at divestiture and then launched a hostile takeover of NCR, suddenly dismantled its empire of its own volition. After setting free NCR and spinning off its manufacturing operations into Lucent Technologies, AT&T then set about to acquire Teleport Communications Group, a competitive local exchange carrier, and TCI and Media One, two of the country's largest cable providers, with the announced intention of delivering Internet and telephone services over cable. On the European continent, Deutsche Telekom and Telecom Italia have joined forces. Will all of these mergers and acquisitions work to the benefit of the users? The room for doubt is more than ample.

Much has been written about the convergence of voice and data. Accompanied by loud fanfare, products are beginning to appear, but the technology is yet in its infancy. A host of other products is appearing on the horizon and potentially will further alter the shape of telecommunications, but it's too early to tell. Wireless has the potential to break some of the stranglehold that the incumbent local exchange carriers (ILECs) have by virtue of their cable plant. At the same time, the ILECs are attempting to deploy a variety of digital subscriber line techniques to relieve some of the bottlenecks users experience in accessing the Internet. Cable companies, led by AT&T's acquisition of TCI, hope to grab some of the market for both dial tone and Internet access as they upgrade their older coaxial systems to fiber optics.

Another dramatic development was the cell phone, which happened about the same time as fiber optics. The development cycle of this product was astounding: the concept was born in 1947—before it was technically feasible. The Bell System demonstrated its feasibility in the 1970s, but the FCC camped on it for years, reluctant to grant the airwaves to a monopoly. Finally, they settled on a duopoly. Half of the frequency spectrum was awarded to the traditional wireline carrier in each market. The other license was granted to competitors for the asking. As cellular hit the market, demand exploded and the cost of cell phones dropped, but the legislated competition didn't do much else for the consumer. The FCC learned from its mistakes and divided the market more intelligently with personal communications services (PCS). Instead of a duopoly, the band is divided into six segments, and the FCC auctioned off the spectrum.

The Internet itself is nothing short of phenomenal, and it is just getting started. It is sparking not only information and entertainment pastimes, it is also fueling a whole new way of doing business, and offering ways for companies to link themselves together by building secure tunnels through a chaotic and insecure network.

All of this makes plenty of grist for a book that has the aim of helping people to make sense of the confusion. With the possible exception of health care, no other industry in the world has undergone such a radical and wrenching change in the past 20 years.

And more is yet to come.

James H. Green

When the first edition of this book, *The Dow Jones–Irwin Handbook of Telecommunications*, was published, the telecommunications world was a much different place. AT&T had just been broken up, equal access was gradually coming online, and the telecommunications giants were jockeying for position in the new competitive environment. AT&T's 22 Bell Operating Companies had been formed into seven regional holding companies that were testing their freedoms from centralized control. Little had been written about how the North American telecommunications system functioned. I felt, at the time, that divestiture would generate confusion for managers who suddenly found themselves needing to know more about how telecommunications networks functioned and how the pieces were integrated. To fill the need for a reference on how to manage telecommunications technology, a companion volume, *The Irwin Handbook of Telecommunications Management*, was published 2 years later.

Unquestionably, the confusion still exists, and the pace of change is accelerating. Since the third edition was published, the Internet has exploded, bringing the most far-reaching effects of any telecommunications development in our lifetimes. The "information superhighway" is no longer theoretical. The underlying technologies have been developing for decades and now they are converging into a network that is compelling in its simplicity and in its ability to link people with a cost and convenience that changes the foundation of our lives. Commerce is shifting to the Internet, altering conventional methods of doing business. Teaching and learning methods are changing, entertainment patterns are shifting, time spans are compressed as we no longer have to wait for information delivery, and even traditional telephone service is moving from the confines of narrow-band copper wire to broadband facilities.

The Handbook of Telecommunications has undergone regular revisions to keep pace with the changes in the industry. The third edition was written during the period when the Telecommunications Act of 1996 was passed, but its effects had not been felt. Now, competitive local service is available in most metropolitan areas and prices are dropping for multiline businesses. The structure of the telephone business is being challenged as voice and data converge over packet networks and cable television providers offer dial tone and Internet access over their facilities. The industry has evolved from staid predictability into one where chaos reigns. My aim in writing this book is to provide, in language that anyone with an interest in the subject can understand, an overview of how each of the telecommunications technologies works. Obviously, some very complex concepts have been simplified. Each chapter would easily require several volumes for a full treatment. For those who want more detail, the bibliography lists many excellent books on the subject.

With this edition, much is changed besides just an update to include new developments. First, in addition to the primary audience of business telecommunications managers, several colleges and universities have used this book as a text. Consequently, with this edition, an instructor's manual is available through normal university channels.

The second change involves giving the book a more international flavor. The first three editions dealt primarily with the North American network. While this is still the primary focus, additional emphasis has been given to international issues. Where the technology and terminology differ in other countries, these are discussed.

Over the course of four editions, the references to proprietary protocols and interfaces are gradually giving way to International Telecommunications Union standards. Most chapters reference the predominant standards applying to the technology under discussion. Standards have always been a wild card in the world of telecommunications, and the problem isn't getting better. The permutations and combinations of standards aren't quite infinite, but they are coming close and new ones are announced regularly. The Internet hasn't helped. Ironically, although the growth of the Internet was fueled by internet protocol (IP), the most open standard of all, its shortcomings have inspired a barrage of modifications, some open and some proprietary.

The structure of the book is modified somewhat from the third edition. It is divided into the same five parts as in previous editions, corresponding to major divisions in telecommunications equipment. The introductory chapter in Part One covers both voice and data. The remainder of Part One is devoted to concepts that are common to the industry. In Part One, we discuss voice and data fundamentals, pulse code modulation, outside plant, structured wiring, local area network principles, and the other building blocks of telecommunication networks.

Part Two covers circuit switching concepts. It begins with a discussion of signaling followed by three chapters that explain in overview how local and toll switches function. Circuit switching has been at the heart of the telephone industry for more than a century. Although it is being challenged by packet switching, it retains a stability and service quality that packet technologies cannot yet provide.

Part Three covers transmission equipment. Separate chapters discuss the fundamental technologies of fiber optics, microwave radio, satellite transmission, cellular and PCS radio systems, and video. Video has evolved the least of all telecommunications technologies over the past half century. Although color has been added, television signals still use the same techniques that they did when the first broadcast stations went on the air, but that is about to change. High-definition television is just entering the market, and as with other technologies the signals are changing to digital. Digital cable transmission systems will begin to compete with the conventional telephone system for carrying Internet and telephone traffic.

Part Four discusses customer premise equipment. We begin with an explanation of station equipment, followed by key telephone equipment and private branch exchange (PBX). Ancillary equipment, such as automatic call distribution, voice processing, and computer-telephony integration, are covered in separate chapters. Other chapters discuss electronic messaging, facsimile, and Centrex, which is the central office equivalent of a PBX.

Part Five pulls together the building blocks we have discussed in the earlier chapters into completed and functioning networks. This part illustrates the tremendous variety of alternatives that are available and discusses how and where they are applied. We begin this part with the discussion of enterprise networks, which is a blanket term covering the type of network large organizations use to link the company together. Following that, other chapters cover broadband protocols such as switched multimegabit data service, gigabit Ethernet, Fibre Channel, and fiber distributed data interface. We discuss frame relay, asynchronous transfer mode, the integrated services digital network, and wide area data networks. Other chapters deal with internetworking and convergence, which is one of the hottest topics in the industry today. The book concludes with a discussion of network management systems and how they are used to enable humans to cope with the complexity. The final chapter in the book looks ahead a few years with a view of where telecommunications technology is headed.

Readers of previous editions will find that some information has been omitted to make space for new developments. Previous editions included a buyer's guide at the end of each chapter and an appendix listing addresses and telephone numbers of telecommunications manufacturers and service providers. With the number changes that result from new area codes, these lists are frequently outdated. Therefore, we have instead included a list of Web sites of the telecommunications firms that we were able to identify. This list is posted on Pacific Netcom's Web site where it will be kept updated. Manufacturers who have been omitted from this list may send me an e-mail (*harry@pacificnetcom.com*) and you will be added. The list in Appendix A does not include distributors, software developers, and the like, but the Web site does. We hope to develop this into a comprehensive list of telecommunications-associated organizations.

As a guide to decoding the countless acronyms that have crept into the telecommunications vocabulary, this book contains an appendix that should be helpful. Appendix B lists the principal acronyms and what they stand for. In addition, a glossary is provided that defines terms that are used in this book. We have endeavored to either define the term in context, in the glossary, or both.

Some material, primarily transmission principles and an explanation of how to use network design formulas and techniques were to some degree duplicated in *The Handbook of Telecommunications Management*. These are omitted from this volume, and will be updated in the third edition of that book. In previous editions we've included an explanatory section on the fundamentals of electricity that are necessary for understanding some of the technical concepts presented in the book. That information is also omitted from this edition, but it is available for download along with other white papers on Pacific Netcom's Web site, which may be found at *www.pacificnetcom.com*. We also invite readers to offer corrections or suggestions for changes on the same Web site.

LIST OF FIGURES

LIST OF TABLES

PART ONE

Principles of Telecommunications Systems

CHAPTER 1

A Brief History of Telecommunications

The first century of telephone development was uninspiring, controlled by a staid Bell System that drove vehicles that were painted a slightly different shade of green than army trucks. Technological progress was slow, but service was stable and predictable. Government regulation was designed with low cost and universal service in mind. The FCC and the Bell companies negotiated depreciation rates for equipment in a process that tended to keep equipment in service until long after it was technologically obsolete. Even though the telephone industry began with wide-open competition, the principle of regulated monopoly served well in America as an alternative to the government ownership that prevailed in most of the rest of the world.

Then, in a series of court cases, AT&T's monopoly collapsed, and the result reverberated around the world as postal, telephone, and telegraphs (PTTs) gradually privatized their telephone systems to keep pace. Not coincidentally, the collapse of the monopoly coincided with the rise of the semiconductor industry. No longer was the design and manufacture of telecommunications equipment specialized. The electromechanical apparatus that served the industry for its first century was displaced by equipment that shares its technology with the computer industry. Half of the companies producing telecommunications equipment today weren't even formed when the first edition of this book was published in 1986. The Internet was the exclusive terrain of a selected group of users and experimenters, and most of today's transport control protocol/internet protocol (TCP/IP) experts hadn't even heard that term then. In 1986 a router was something you used to gouge holes in wood, and a bridge was used for crossing streams.

If someone were setting out today to build a new telecommunications infrastructure, it wouldn't much resemble what we have in place. The industry has well over a century of history, and several key events during that time have shaped the industry into the structure it has today. Governments have by no means been passive participants. In most of the world the government owns most, or all, of the telephone system, operating it as part of PTT operations. In most of North America ownership has been private, except for a short time during World War I when the U.S. government nationalized the telephone system. Nationalized telecommunications systems are now rapidly becoming a thing of the past. Governments are recognizing that their information systems must be freed from the sluggish responsiveness that often results from public management. Consequently, many of the major European and Asian economies have either privatized their telecommunications systems or are in the process of doing so.

In this chapter we will examine the major events that have shaped telecommunications as it is today. Much of this will focus on the United States, which has led the rest of the world in information system and telecommunications development. We will also look at some of the standards and regulatory agencies that develop and promulgate standards and otherwise shape the industry.

A SHORT HISTORY OF THE BELL SYSTEM

No organization in the world has influenced telecommunications to the degree that the Bell System did. The Bell System traced its roots back to Alexander Graham Bell's invention of the telephone in 1876, and survived for nearly 110 years until the Department of Justice broke it up in 1984 following a protracted antitrust case. For six decades prior to the 1984 dissolution of the Bell System, American Telephone and Telegraph Company (AT&T) operated as a regulated monopoly, but it wasn't always so.

The early days of the telephone were characterized by freewheeling and open competition. Following expiration of Bell's patents in 1893, small companies cropped up in every locale to provide switching services. The process was manual, handled from switchboards such as the one shown in Figure 1-1. Subscribers signaled the central office by lifting the receiver or turning a crank. The operators recognized the request for service by a lighted lamp on the switchboard or a magnetic flap that dropped down when ringing current was detected. By the turn of the twentieth century, some 4000 independent telephone companies served the United States, representing about 40 percent of the telephones in the country. AT&T, which was incorporated in 1885, owned the rest. During the first 35 years following Bell's invention of the telephone, AT&T acquired franchise rights to provide telephone service in most of the metropolitan areas of the United States.

The Principle of Regulated Monopoly

Finally, concerned about AT&T's monopolistic tactics, the Department of Justice stepped in. In 1913 AT&T signed an agreement with the Department of Justice that it would refrain from purchasing any more independent telephone companies. This agreement, called the Kingsbury Commitment, left the country with the configuration that persists today: a core metropolitan area in most major cities that

FIGURE 1-1

A 1926 Toll Switchboard

Property of AT&T Archives. Reprinted with permission of AT&T.

traces its roots back to the Bell System. A non-Bell company often serves the suburban areas.

In 1918, in the middle of World War I, the federal government nationalized the Bell System. For a brief 1-year period, the nation's telephone system was under government control. The AT&T president at the time, Theodore N. Vale, proposed to the government the principle of regulated monopoly. In exchange for freedom to retain the telephone system in private ownership, Vale agreed to submit AT&T and its operating companies to government regulation. The theory was that utilities, such as water, electricity, and telephone, were natural monopolies. The public interest would not be served in having duplicated facilities because the additional investment required would drive prices up. Furthermore, utilities rely on the public right-of-way to deliver service, and the needs of the public are not well served by having multiple utilities digging up the streets and installing pole lines.

At the conclusion of AT&T's negotiations with the government, the principle of regulated monopoly was established as an alternative to government ownership, at least in the United States and most of Canada. Regulation was divided into two parts. The Interstate Commerce Commission regulated the interstate portions of telephone service while the intrastate elements were left to the states. Some states formed statewide regulatory agencies, while others left regulation to municipalities.

ICC regulation continued until 1934, when Congress passed the original Telecommunications Act. This act, among other provisions, established the Federal Communications Commission, and gave it responsibility for regulating interstate communications. In addition, the FCC was charged with regulating the use of the airwaves.

Universal Service and Subsidies

It is important to understand that, during this period of regulation, the operation of the nation's telephone system was driven by a quest for universal service. The value of every telephone, the argument went, was enhanced by the number of telephones that could be reached. It was logical, therefore, for urban users, where the cost per subscriber was low, to subsidize high-cost rural users. Also, it was logical for basic service rates to be kept low and to be subsidized by optional services. The method of pricing services was pegged to the value to the subscriber, and had little to do with the carriers' cost of providing it.

Under regulation, the telephone companies and the utility commissions shared several joint objectives. For one, the cost of basic service would be held to a minimum, with revenues made up through discretionary services. Since a large portion of the carriers' expense was depreciation, the regulatory commissions had every incentive to keep this expense low, which they could do by extending the service life. In fact, the service lives for various classes of plants that would be assumed for depreciation purposes were negotiated between the FCC, the carriers, and the state utility commissions. The telephone companies retained equipment in service for decades, which was possible in an era of relatively slow innovation.

Another way of keeping basic rates down was to load costs on discretionary services. The utility commissions and local exchange carriers (LECs) negotiated through public hearings for a prescribed return on investment. After the return on investment was approved, the commissions and LECs decided how to allocate the consequent revenue requirement to various services, generally keeping basic residential rates as low as feasible. Business rates were pegged at three or four times residential rates even though the cost of providing service was not that different. Services such as trunk hunting and later push-button dialing demanded rates far in excess of the cost of providing them. Extension telephones, colored telephones, and even coiled handset cords commanded premium prices, contributing revenues to the LEC.

The discretionary service that bore the majority of the subsidy was long distance. Practically all long distance inside the United States was carried by AT&T's Long Lines Division. The method of subsidy was subtle. The FCC prescribed a rate of return on invested capital for Long Lines. The LECs, both Bell and independent, billed the customers for the long-distance calls. The revenue was placed in a settlement pot that Long Lines administered. At the end of the settlement period, each company withdrew enough money from the pot to enable it to recover its costs and to earn on its invested capital at the same rate the FCC authorized AT&T to earn. If earnings fell below the authorized level, the carriers lived with the shortfall until the FCC authorized a rate increase. Fortunately, increasing efficiency kept rates stable. Telephone rates increased at a rate much lower than the cost of living, and over the years long-distance rates dropped because of increasing efficiency.

One of the subtle elements in the long-distance subsidy was the manner by which the LECs established their cost of providing long-distance service. Most of their plant investment was involved in providing both local and toll service. All of this equipment, from local switching systems to outside plant to telephones and PBXs, was regulated at the time. The question was how the costs were allocated between local and toll. These were determined by separations studies in which the LECs determined the percentage of usage of various plant equipment for toll calls. The local exchange commissions had an incentive to attribute as much of the investment as possible to interexchange toll, because the LECs recovered those costs from the toll settlement pot. Toll revenue reduced the LECs' total revenue requirement, which in turn helped hold local rates down. It also, incidentally, helped to impede innovation. Under the regulatory environment, equipment was often left in service long after it had become technologically obsolete.

This environment served the nation until the late 1960s, when several events led to the eventual collapse of the Bell System as it was then structured. The regulatory era not only kept local service affordable, it kept telephone technology under tight, unified control. Virtually all telephone innovation during this period emanated from Bell Laboratories. With the vertically integrated Bell System, the entire path from research and development through delivery to the consumer was under Bell control. The standards that were set at the time were Bell standards and were not subject to outside review.

The First Antitrust Suit

In the years following World War II, the telephone system went through a dramatic expansion. The Bell System laced the nation with coaxial cable and microwave networks to fill a flourishing demand for telephone services. Many of the telephone exchanges were still manual, and these were gradually replaced using electro-mechanical switching equipment. In 1948, Bell Laboratories announced the discovery of one of the landmark technological developments of history—the transistor—and gradually began perfecting it to serve the telephone industry. Its lower power drain and increased reliability were of inestimable value to the industry.

In 1949, the Department of Justice filed an antitrust suit against the Bell System, charging it with unlawful monopoly. The government was concerned with the vertical integration of the Bell System. Figure 1-2 shows the organization of the Bell System at the time. Of particular concern was Western Electric, which was AT&T's manufacturing arm. At the time, some of the equipment Western Electric manufactured had nothing to do with telecommunications. Furthermore, the suit alleged that Western Electric charged high prices to the Bell companies, which were recovered in excessive costs to consumers.

After a prolonged court case, the antitrust suit was settled in 1955 by a consent decree. This decree, which was known as the Final Judgment, permitted AT&T to retain Western Electric, but required Western Electric to divest itself of distribution to outside companies and noncommunications manufacturing. With few exceptions, Western Electric's sales were to be confined to the Bell System.

FIGURE 1-2

Simplified Organization of the Predivestiture Bell System

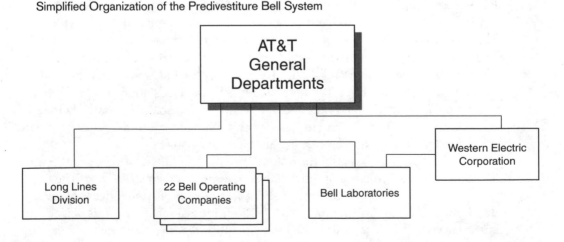

Perhaps most significant, Bell Laboratories was required to license its technology to outside firms. Had this not happened, it is interesting to speculate what might have been the worldwide impact had the Bell System retained exclusive rights to the transistor.

Bell System Manufacturing

It is also important to understand the relationships between the various Bell System entities. AT&T's General Departments were responsible for providing operational advice and assistance to the Bell Operating Companies (BOCs). In exchange, the BOCs were required under their License Contract to pay up to 2 percent of their gross revenues to AT&T. These revenues went to support the General Departments, which did methods work, and to fund the fundamental research portion of Bell Laboratories.

In an unusual arrangement, Bell Laboratories operated under dual ownership with AT&T owning half and Western Electric the other half. Western Electric, in turn, was owned by AT&T. The arrangement may seem deceptive, but it had a definite purpose. Product-oriented research in Bell Labs was part of the developmental cycle and Western Electric recovered the cost in the price of products. Bell Labs' fundamental research and development and research into operational matters was done on behalf of the BOCs and was funded by License Contract payments. Thus, Bell Labs could invent the transistor under License Contract funding, develop an electronic switching system under product-oriented funding, and then develop techniques to administer the switch under the License Contract. In the end, revenues from telephone subscribers ultimately paid the costs since, with few exceptions, Western Electric's customers were the Bell Operating Companies.

Against this background, many other manufacturers produced telecommunications equipment. Companies such as Stromberg Carlson, ITT, and Automatic Electric (a GTE subsidiary) produced switching equipment. Motorola, Farinon, NEC, Raytheon, and numerous other manufacturers produced microwave. ITT, Lenkurt, NEC, and host of other manufacturers produced transmission equipment. The BOCs purchased some of this equipment, but for the most part the independent companies and the international market comprised the market for other manufacturers. Internationally, giants such as Siemens, Alcatel, and Ericsson dominated the telecommunications equipment market. Except for sales to the government and sales to independent telephone companies that needed Western Electric equipment to connect to the BOCs, Western Electric's sales were confined to the Bell System.

By the 1970s another phenomenon was occurring. In earlier years telecommunications equipment manufacturing was highly specialized. Except for some equipment, such as microwave, that was in general commercial use, telecommunications gear was a composite of specialized components. Even electronic switching systems, the first of which was developed in 1965, used highly specialized computers that were designed for reliability that commercial computers and operating systems could not provide.

In the 1970s the transition from an analog to a digital world began to accelerate. With it came a host of manufacturers that were capable of using commercial and special integrated circuit components to develop communications equipment. Schools and universities began to teach technology that had heretofore been largely confined to the telephone industry. Data processing, which had been centralized, became increasingly decentralized, driving a demand for better means of data communications. The telephone network had been developed for voice communications. For data to survive in an analog voice-grade world, it had to emulate a voice signal, which is the role of the modem. Slow, error-prone circuits shackled users, further driving the need for an improved communications system.

Against this backdrop, manufacturers complained to the Department of Justice that the Bell System market was a closed entity because they found it almost impossible to compete with Western Electric. The difficulty, they claimed, was not so much that Western Electric's products were superior or their prices lower, but that AT&T directed the BOCs to buy exclusively from Western Electric.

Interconnection

A second complaint from manufacturers and users alike was the Bell System's policy on interconnection of so-called foreign attachments. A foreign attachment was any device that the BOC did not furnish under tariff. It included anything from long telephone cords to modems and extension telephones, which were then the exclusive property of the BOC. The Bell tariffs flatly prohibited foreign attachments, reasoning that since the BOCs were responsible for the quality of service, they needed to control the devices that were connected to the network. In addition to quality, the Bell companies argued that foreign attachments could interfere with the service to other subscribers on the network or harm workers, who might be subjected to unsafe voltages.

These restrictions against connection of foreign attachments held until 1968, when a radio dispatch company known as Carter Electronics Company, operating out of Dallas, complained to the FCC about Southwestern Bell's tariff restrictions. Mr. Carter's customers often asked him to pass messages from the radio terminal to telephone users on the landline. Carter developed a simple device that later became known as Carterphone to connect callers through directly. Southwestern Bell ordered the attachment to be removed, and the two companies ended up in court. Carter prevailed and the result was gradual dismantling of the interconnection tariffs.

The FCC ordered the BOCs to permit interconnection through a special coupler known as a protective coupling adapter (PCA). The couplers were intended to prevent harm to the network and workers, but still manufacturers and users complained about what they perceived as an unnecessary cost. The FCC established a registration program, which still continues to be in effect. Before any device, including LECs' own devices, can be connected to the telephone network in the United States, the manufacturer must obtain independent certification that its devices comply with the technical requirements of the network.

Long-Distance Restrictions

The third complaint that Department of Justice attorneys heard was that the Bell monopolies prevented others from competing to provide long-distance service. In the late 1960s, a company known as Microwave Communications, Inc. built a microwave link from Chicago to St. Louis and began leasing private line service. A customer with offices in the two cities could contract with MCI to provide lines tying their telephone systems together. AT&T filed a case in court that accused MCI of unlawfully providing a service that infringed on its monopoly. The argument wasn't entirely without foundation. AT&T had been granted license to operate a regulated monopoly, and, as such, was required to provide service to all comers. A company such as MCI was under no such obligation, and therefore could "cream-skim" the most lucrative customers, thereby raising costs for those remaining. The argument was not persuasive to the FCC, however, and in 1970 they declared that it was in the public interest for MCI to compete for private line service.

As was the case with Carter's customers, MCI's customers also wanted connection to the public switched telephone network (PSTN). To accommodate them, MCI ordered local telephone lines from Illinois Bell and Southwestern Bell and connected them to the network, as shown in Figure 1-3. Now, customers in either city could dial a local 7-digit telephone number, dial in a personal identification number (PIN), and connect to a user in a distant city by dialing its 10-digit number. AT&T subscribers, meanwhile, were automatically identified whenever they dialed 1+ calls. This arrangement was not indicative of any anticompetitive intent per se; it was simply the way the network was designed.

AT&T again complained to the FCC, stating that MCI's arrangement was in direct competition with its message telephone service, and was therefore unlawful. AT&T's argument against this type of service was twofold. First was the cream-skimming contention. The second related to AT&T's obligation to subsidize basic exchange rates. MCI could undercut AT&T's rates because they weren't required to provide any such subsidy. Again, after a bitter court battle, MCI prevailed and the FCC ordered AT&T to permit interconnection. The BOCs filed tariffs that allowed this access, which was ultimately called Feature Group A. Connect time was metered on both originating and terminating calls. This charge was to compensate the LECs for the cost of access to the local exchange network.

After winning this court battle, MCI was still dissatisfied with the Feature Group A arrangements. The transmission quality was inferior to AT&T's connection because an extra two-wire local loop was switched on each end of the circuit. The volume was inferior and MCI's circuits were more subject to impairments

FIGURE 1-3

Predivestiture Connection to the Local Network

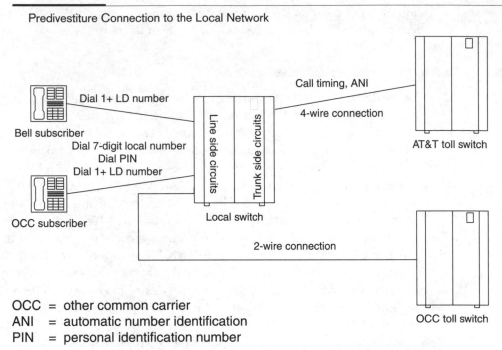

OCC = other common carrier
ANI = automatic number identification
PIN = personal identification number

such as echo. Callers could not be identified automatically as they could with AT&T's configuration and the local network did not signal the start and completion of each call. This meant that MCI had to use so-called software call timing. After a call had been ringing for a certain number of seconds, charging began whether it was answered or not. This resulted in overcharges on some calls and undercharges on others. Other long-distance vendors entered the market and echoed MCI's viewpoint.

The Second Antitrust Case

In 1975 the Department of Justice, responding to the complaints from the long-distance, interconnect, and manufacturing industries, filed a second antitrust against AT&T, alleging unlawful monopoly. The case dragged on until 1982, when it was abruptly settled by another consent decree. This decree, which was called the Modified Final Judgment (modifying the 1955 Final Judgment), contained a number of landmark provisions. The BOCs were spun off into seven separate regional companies that later became known as regional Bell Operating Companies (RBOCs). They were prohibited from manufacturing equipment and from providing telecommunications services outside artificial regions known as local access transport areas (LATAs). They were required to open their procurement to all manufacturers. In addition, they were ordered to provide equal access to the local exchange network to all long-distance carriers. This meant that AT&T would no longer have a technical advantage over other long-distance carriers. While the rest of the network was to transition gradually from regulation to competition, the local exchange network remained a regulated monopoly. The BOCs could offer customer premise equipment (CPE) only through a fully separated subsidiary that could not use local service to subsidize CPE.

AT&T retained its manufacturing arm, Western Electric, and its Long Lines division. It was also permitted to offer CPE without regulation, since this would be a competitive market. The FCC would closely regulate Long Lines until such time as it had substantial competition. Bell Laboratories was split into two parts. The half that had supported Western Electric's manufacturing remained with AT&T. The other half, which conducted research and development, was formed into a corporation known as Bell Communications Research (Bellcore). Bellcore was jointly owned by the seven RBOCs. Bellcore remained under RBOC ownership until 1998, when it was sold and later renamed to Telcordia Technologies.

Although the state utility commissions retained regulatory authority over the intrastate business, the FCC and the Department of Justice retained tight control over the provisions of the Modified Final Judgment. The court assigned itself the job of ensuring that the parties lived up to the provisions of the Modified Final Judgment.

Exchange Network Access

The provisions of the Modified Final Judgment left an interesting financial arrangement for enabling the RBOCs to recover the cost of providing interexchange carriers (IXCs) with access to the local exchange network. AT&T was no longer to be the sole supporter of the local exchange subsidy. All carriers and all users were subjected to the new concept of access charges. The FCC administered the interstate access charge provisions of the LECs' tariffs. They decreed that access charges would be paid in two elements. One would be a per-line charge of $6.00 a month for businesses and $3.50 for residences. All users paid this fee as a cost of originating and terminating long-distance calls, whether any such calls were placed or not. The second element was a usage-based fee that the long-distance carriers paid to the LECs.

Exchange access costs were high enough that large users bypassed the LEC with private line circuits directly to the IXC. Smaller users could not justify the cost of bypass, so these access costs were high. The local exchange portion of long-distance telephone calls was often more than the interexchange part, even though the interexchange mileage was many times greater. As a result, IXCs complained about the high cost of exchange access. They contended that exchange access, which was the largest single cost that most IXCs had, was overpriced. With minor changes, however, the shared access cost arrangement lasted through the passage of the Telecommunications Act of 1996.

The Telecommunications Act of 1996

The main thing that can be said about the telecommunications environment in the United States through the early 1990s was that with the possible exception of large business users, who were enjoying low long-distance costs, none of the participants was happy. Local service costs had more than doubled, even for large users. The LECs detested the LATA restrictions, which put them at a competitive disadvantage in providing service. LATAs were (and still are) confusing for users and in many cases impose unnecessary complications. For example, if a user wishes to contract with an RBOC to provide data service in two LATAs, it is necessary to bring an IXC into the picture to provide the network-to-network interface. IXCs railed against access charges, and numerous carriers wanted to break the LECs' monopoly on local exchange service. The RBOCs also wanted out from under the prohibitions against manufacturing, and wanted to be free of local rate regulation.

Recognizing that the Telecommunications Act of 1934 had serious shortcomings in the modern environment, Congress stepped into the picture. Under intense lobbying from all the would-be participants, they finally passed the Telecommunications Act of 1996. The text of the act is available for download from the FCC's Web page, which is listed in Appendix A.

About the best that can be said for the act is that it's good enough for government work. Congress was beset by pressures from groups with conflicting interests who could not easily be satisfied. Congress clearly recognized that if the local exchange was subject to competition, consumers who lived in high-cost areas and who spent little for telecommunications service would be disregarded by competitive carriers. Therefore, the act created a universal service fund (USF) that would be used to subsidize low-income consumers and rural telephone companies. Then, in a grand political gesture, another class of users was added to the list of those entitled to subsidy: schools, libraries, and rural hospitals.

The act starts from the assumption that the most effective way to regulate telephone service is through competition. Recognizing that it would be impractical to deregulate telephone service immediately, the act provides for gradual deregulation as the regulated entities meet certain criteria. The BOCs provide the vast majority of the telephones in the United States. Since they were the target of the antitrust action of the Department of Justice, Congress treated them differently in the act than they did smaller nondominant carriers. Under the act, local service can be offered by a variety of companies including IXCs, cable television (CATV) companies, electric power companies, and other utilities in competition with the LECs. If users change service providers, they are permitted to keep their telephone numbers through a process known as local number portability (LNP).

A major issue was how to keep rural rates from increasing. Competitive carriers would naturally focus on large businesses as their primary targets. Large businesses tend to be in large urban areas, so the result would be competitive pressures in urban areas, but little or no competition in rural areas. Congress directed the FCC to devise a system of subsidizing rural and low-income users under the USF. The FCC established a Federal-State Joint Board on Universal Service to recommend specific guidelines and rules for administering the provisions of the act.

The outcome of the recommendations of the Joint Board was a series of changes that became effective in 1998. All telecommunications service providers are required to pay a portion of their revenues into the USF. The subscriber line access charge for businesses was raised by approximately 50 percent, but left alone for residences. Usage-sensitive access charges for the IXCs were reduced, but all IXCs are required to pay a per-line flat fee into the USF. The IXCs, in turn, immediately passed along the charges to their customers. The result is a massive increase in telecommunications costs for all users.

The so-called e-rate funding for schools, libraries, and hospitals came under intense fire from opponents who believe the Joint Board and the Schools and Libraries Corporation had gone further than Congress intended with the subsidies. Four years after the passage of the act, some competition has resulted, but the LECs' monopoly is still largely intact. At issue is which carriers are required to pay the fees. The LECs have argued vigorously that Internet service providers (ISPs) should support universal service, but as of this writing the FCC has declined to subject ISPs to making USF contributions. Also, ISPs are not required to pay access charges for voice calls over their networks even if these are connected to long-distance calls over the Internet.

After completing the Telecommunications Act, which contained far more provisions than listed here, Congress tossed the ball to the FCC to administer what they created. The LECs are permitted to offer inter-LATA long-distance service upon state utility commission recommendation, and after they have demonstrated to the FCC and the courts that they have substantial competition in their areas. Several states have recommended freeing their LECs to provide long-distance service, but at press time no ex-Bell companies had been granted this authority.

From a consumer standpoint, the act has been mostly negative. Virtually all carriers have passed along the costs of their USF contributions directly to the end users. The schools, rural hospitals, and libraries that were added to the list of USF beneficiaries have been subjected to an incredible array of bureaucratic rules and regulations as the bodies charged with administering the plan have vacillated. Since every telecommunications consumer in the nation is paying additional costs, the universal service fund has amounted to a tax increase that happens to be administered through telecommunications bills. The effect is about the same if the federal excise tax on telecommunications had been increased, except that it is much more difficult to administer.

Competition is gradually finding its way into the local exchange network. Reduced costs are available, but only to a narrow range of subscribers. As expected, competitive local exchange carriers (CLECs) have gone after the most lucrative customers, which are those with large quantities of telephone lines. These customers can enjoy some substantial rate decreases compared to incumbent local exchange carriers' (ILECs) offerings. The ILECs, in most cases, are not free to drop their tariff rates to meet the competition. Therefore, the inevitable result will be reduced profitability for the ILECs and increased costs for consumers in less profitable areas.

We have not lived with the Telecommunications Act of 1996 long enough to begin to foresee its effects. Congress has passed many acts that have unintended and unforeseen consequences, and this one will be no different. The unprotected class is, ironically, the majority of the population of the United States: the individual residential telephone consumer. Little in the act bodes well for that class, at least in the near term, but most have not felt any adverse effects yet. In the long term, alternatives, such as multiple services over cable television, may provide better options, but for now, the individual consumer is likely to pay more for less. Long distance is a case in point. The consumer who places few long-distance calls receives rates that border on price gouging. Trusted names are no longer dependable when it comes to charges for telephone calls that the carriers deem unprofitable.

Furthermore, we run the risk of degrading service quality in the name of free and open competition. Numerous options are becoming available to send voice calls over data networks. Consumers may opt for these services to save money, but every voice call has two parties, only one of which is paying for the call. Many users do not realize it, but telephone transmission objectives are based on subjective factors that relate to user expectations. Throughout the history of the industry these expectations have been steadily rising. Some factors, however, have crept in that we accept in the name of convenience. Cell phones are a case in point. The quality of many calls is poor, but we accept it to have the benefits. The same may eventually be true of landline phone calls as they migrate to networks that lack the quality of service standards of today's telephone network.

STANDARDS

For the first 100 years or so of the telephone industry, standards were largely proprietary. The Bell System set its own standards. In many cases these were not published to the industry at large, but gradually it yielded to governmental pressure to license its technology and publish its interface specifications. The International Telecommunications Union (ITU), which is a United Nations agency, published standards through its consultative committees. The Consultative Committee on International Telephone and Telegraph (CCITT) handled telecommunications standards and the Consultative Committee on International Radio (CCIR) worked out the international agreements on use of the airwaves. These two groups have since been renamed ITU-T and ITU-R, respectively.

ITU standards are advisory rather than obligatory. The Bell System worked through ITU where it was in its interests to do so. Where it was not, it developed its own standards, many of which turned out to be incompatible. For example, the North American and European digital carrier formats are incompatible. Also, the interoffice signaling format that the Bell System adopted was incompatible with the international standard signaling system no. 7. This incompatibility was not solely due to the intransigence of the Bell System. Because it was free to develop its own protocols, it was able to move more rapidly than the ITU, which had to satisfy many more diverse interests, including the PTTs and the equipment manufacturers. The Bell System worked with ITU on these standards, but diverged after it became unwilling to wait for the process.

Data standards, in the meanwhile, were also proprietary. The Bell System developed the transmission standards for devices such as modems. Early modems bore such designators as 202A and 212C, and as these became obsolete, CCITT designators replaced them. Manufacturers, such as IBM, developed the proprietary data protocols by which computers communicated. Their bisynchronous (bisync) protocol was one early system. IBM later replaced it with their systems network architecture (SNA), which remains one of the chief protocols in operation. SNA is the model for the ITU's open systems interconnect (OSI) model, which is the foundation for nearly all current protocols. Data protocols were strictly proprietary in the early days, which meant that a company with market power could make it difficult for its competitors. Gradually, IBM opened the specifications for SNA, so other manufacturers could begin offering equipment that interoperated with it.

Proprietary standards work to the advantage of the developer, but they have distinct disadvantages for users. For one thing, no proprietary protocol meets all needs. SNA, for example, is designed for mainframe computers used by companies with large, centralized networks. As minicomputers came on the market, they generally applied the American Standard Characters for Information Interchange (ASCII) protocol through networks of multiplexers. The major problem with proprietary protocols is that the users are handicapped by the lack of interoperability. One of the oldest communications devices in the world is the facsimile machine, but facsimile languished for years. Not until CCITT published Group 3 fax standards in the early 1980s did facsimile become the mainstream technology that it is today.

Unfortunately, the need for standards and the need for technical progress sometimes conflict because standards often are not set until the technology has been proven in practice, and the only way to prove the technology is through extensive use. Therefore, when it comes time to set a standard, a large base of installed equipment is already in place designed to proprietary standards. The policies of many standards-setting organizations preclude their adopting proprietary standards, even if the manufacturer is willing to make them public. Also, competing manufacturers are represented on the standards-setting bodies, which is an incentive for bodies to not accept proprietary standards. As a result, even after standards are adopted, a considerable amount of equipment exists that does not conform to the standard.

A good example of this is in the V.90 standards developed for data transmission at 56 kilobits per second (kb/s) over analog telephone lines. Two competing manufacturers developed products to support 56-kb/s transmission, and began manufacturing in advance of the standard. 3Com Company developed a product known as X2. Lucent Technologies and Rockwell International collaborated on a technology they called K56Flex. Some of the modems manufactured under these two competing standards may be upgraded to the new standard, but neither is compatible with V.90, the ITU-T standard that finally emerged.

How Standards Are Developed

The field of players in the standards process is vast, and sometimes not closely coordinated. There are four key stages that occur in moving a standard from conception to adoption:

- ◆ Conceptualization
- ◆ Development
- ◆ Influence
- ◆ Promulgation

In the United States, just about anyone can conceptualize the need for a standard. Before development begins, however, some recognized body must accept responsibility for the task. For example, local area network standards could have been developed by several different organizations; the Institute of Electrical and Electronics Engineers (IEEE) accepted the task. The Electronics Industries Association (EIA) is another organization that has developed many standards that the American National Standards Institute (ANSI) has accepted.

The development of a standard is usually assigned to a committee within the organization. If the committee is not broadly represented across interest groups, the standards work may never begin. Participation is largely voluntary, and is usually funded by the standards influencers, which are the companies or associations with the most to gain or lose. Governmental organizations also wield influence in the standards process. Companies with vast market power also fill the role of standards influencers. Often, their influence is enhanced because they have already demonstrated the technical feasibility of the standard in practice.

The standards promulgators are the agencies that can accredit standards and produce the rules and regulations for enforcing them. In the United States ANSI is the chief organization that accredits standards developed by other organizations such as IEEE and EIA.

Standards Organizations

Many organizations and associations are involved in the standards process. The following is a brief description of the role of the most influential of them.

International Telecommunications Union (ITU)

The International Telecommunications Union (ITU) was formed in 1865 to promote mutual compatibility of the communications systems that were then emerging. The ITU, now a United Nations–sponsored organization to which 160 countries belong, distributes international standards. The two principal groups of interest to telecommunications are the ITU-T (telecommunications) and ITU-R (radio). ITU does its work through study groups that work in 4-year time increments. After a 4-year session, the study groups present their work to a plenary assembly for approval. Plenary assemblies coincide with leap years.

In some countries where a state-owned agency operates the telecommunications system, ITU recommendations bear the force of law. In other countries compliance is largely voluntary, although the motivation to accept standards is so great that most proprietary systems do not survive long on the market.

International Standards Organization (ISO)

The International Standards Organization (ISO) is an association of standards-setting organizations from the various nations that participate in the process. In the United States, ANSI is the ISO representative and advisor to the U.S. State Department on ITU standards. The most familiar ISO standards in the telecommunications industry are the standards that support the open systems interconnect (OSI) model.

International Electrotechnical Commission (IEC)

The International Electrotechnical Commission (IEC) accredits standards on much the same basis as ISO. IEC promulgates electrical standards, in contrast to ISO standards, which are primarily logical.

American National Standards Institute (ANSI)

The American National Standards Institute (ANSI) is the standards body in the United States that promulgates standards of all types, not just information processing and telecommunications. ANSI is a nongovernmental, nonprofit organization comprising some 300 standards committees. The ANSI X.3 committees handle information-related standards, and the T1 committees handle telecommunications standards. Both consumers and manufacturers are represented on ANSI committees, and cooperating trade groups that follow ANSI procedures do much of the work. The Institute of Electrical and Electronics Engineers (IEEE) and the Electronics Industries Association (EIA) are two prominent organizations that promulgate standards through ANSI.

Industry and Professional Associations

Three of the most important industry and professional associations are IEEE, EIA, and the Telecommunications Industry Association (TIA). EIA has produced many standards that are important to the telecommunications industry. For example, most data terminal devices use the EIA-232 interface standard in their interconnection with circuit equipment. More recently, EIA collaborated with TIA to produce commercial building telecommunications wiring standards, which are discussed in Chapter 7.

IEEE is a professional association that has had an important effect on standards activities such as the local area network standards that its 802 committee developed. These standards, discussed in more detail in Chapter 8, use the framework of ISO's Open Systems Interconnect model and ITU-T protocols to develop local network alternatives. IEEE is also responsible for metropolitan area network standards that most LECs are now deploying.

Other associations include the United States Telephone Association (USTA); the Corporation on Open Systems (COS), an industry group that is promoting open architectures; the Computer and Business Equipment Manufacturing Association; the Exchange Carrier's Association; the Open Software Forum; and in Europe, the Standards Promotion and Applications Group (SPAG).

The Importance of Standards

In the years before the FCC and the courts opened AT&T's network to interconnection and competition, users could avoid compatibility problems by turning the responsibilities over to the LEC (except in data communications where incompatible protocols were a frequent problem). Now that the LECs no longer own station equipment and long-distance networks are a complex combination of common carrier and private facilities, compatibility is a concern of almost every user. The need for compatibility thrusts the issue of standards to the forefront because users' options are limited if the manufacturers' interfaces are proprietary and not made publicly available.

We run another considerable risk in today's market of deteriorating service quality. We have already experienced this as LECs have shed experienced staff in an effort to remain profitable. Even though installation and repair service have deteriorated, LECs' transmission and switching quality have remained high, and even improved. Since divestiture, the LECs have eliminated most of the obsolete electromechanical switching systems, and IXCs and LECs have converted their trunking facilities to fiber optics. Signaling System 7 sets up calls in a fraction of the time the older in-band signaling required. So far, the technical quality of service has increased dramatically while the administrative quality has deteriorated.

CHAPTER 2

Introduction to Voice Communications

The next two chapters in this book offer an overview of voice and data networks. For now, most countries have two separate and distinct types of network. The public switched telephone network (PSTN) is a circuit-switched network. Connections are dialed up, a circuit or series of circuits are assigned to the call for the duration of the session and are returned to a pool of circuits when one of the parties hangs up. The data counterpart of the PSTN is the Internet. Anyone who has access to the Internet anywhere in the world can exchange data with any other user. Increasingly, voice is also carried over the Internet, although less reliably and with less convenience than over the PSTN.

The essence of a voice network is deceptively simple. Users want easy and economical access. Once connected to another user, they want adequate volume and low noise. The PSTN has evolved over many decades to provide just that. It is easy to use, and nearly anyone can afford it. Its value is enhanced by the fact that we can reach nearly anyone in the world with a telephone call. The ease of setting up a call means that it is also usable for data. In fact, when the enormous volume of faxes and calls to the Internet are considered, a high percentage of the PSTN is used for data. Although the PSTN is usable for data, however, it isn't ideal because the circuits are optimized for voice. When data users try to transmit a large file across a voice circuit, the amount of time it takes is directly proportional to the size of the file because voice circuits have fixed bandwidth.

Many data sessions aren't switched, so the PSTN isn't ideal for them since long-distance connections are charged by the minute. As a result, the earliest data networks used nonswitched connections. Instead of switching circuits together, the carriers wired them together physically, forming a circuit the industry calls a *dedicated* circuit. Although dedicated circuits are not usage-sensitive, they still have the fixed bandwidth restrictions of the PSTN. To make up for these shortcomings, several types of data networks have emerged. Most data networks were private until the recent explosive growth of the Internet.

As we will discuss in Chapter 3, the Internet is capable of handling both voice and data, as is the PSTN. For reasons that will be explained, the two types of networks remain separate and an understanding of each is essential. Industry uses the term *convergence* to describe the eventual merger of voice and data into a single network. Convergence will not be an event. It is an evolutionary process that will take place gradually over many years—perhaps many decades. This chapter will look at circuit-switched networks as primarily intended for voice although they carry an enormous amount of data.

THE PUBLIC SWITCHED TELEPHONE NETWORK

To the user on the end of a telephone, the PSTN looks like a single entity—a black box with telephone lines that somehow mysteriously get connected to one another. It is a tribute to the inventive genius of the thousands of scientists, engineers, and technicians who design, install, and maintain the many parts of the network that its complexity is hidden so well that users don't have to know any more about the network than how to dial and answer telephone calls. In reality, however, the network is composed of countless assemblies of circuits, switching systems, radio and fiber-optic systems, signaling devices, and telephone instruments that act as part of a coordinated whole even though they are owned by many companies with no organizational connection to one another. Every day, the industry adds brand new devices to the network, and they must function with other devices that were designed and installed more than 30 years ago.

The word "network" has become an ambiguous term. It can describe the relationship of a group of broadcasting stations or a social fabric that binds people of similar interests. In telecommunications the usage is somewhat more specific, but the precise meaning of the term must be derived from context, and this can be confusing to those outside the industry. In its broadest sense a telecommunications network is a combination of all the circuits and equipment that enable users to communicate. All the switching apparatus, trunks, subscriber lines, and auxiliary equipment that support communication can be classified as elements of the network. In another sense, the word narrows to mean the circuits that interconnect the inputs and outputs of a switching system. At the circuit level a third meaning describes the interconnection of components to form a filter or level-reducing attenuator. The only way the ambiguity can be dealt with is to become familiar enough with the technology to take the meaning of the term from its context.

The direct interconnection of two stations meets the definition of a network in the strictest sense of the word, but this is a restrictive kind of private network because it lacks accessibility. In a broader sense public voice networks provide the capability for a station to reach another station anywhere in the world without the need for complex addressing. The same, unfortunately, cannot yet be said for data networks.

To understand the systems discussed in this book, it is necessary to understand how they fit as part of a coordinated whole. This chapter discusses the major building blocks of the telecommunications network without explaining how or why they work. Many of these building blocks are used by both voice and data systems. Many terms are introduced and explained in detail only later in the book. You are cautioned that despite its origins in scientific disciplines, the vocabulary of telecommunications is frequently highly ambiguous, and the meaning of many of its terms must be taken from context. Therefore, when we use terminology, we will define it in context to clarify its meaning.

Just as the human body can be viewed either as a unit or as an assembly of systems such as digestive, respiratory, and circulatory, the telecommunications network can be understood from its systems. We will first discuss the major systems in broad terms, and in subsequent chapters examine them in greater detail.

THE MAJOR TELECOMMUNICATIONS SYSTEMS

Figure 2-1 shows the major classes of telecommunications equipment and how they fit together to form a communications network. In the telecommunications industry, as with the computer industry, the manufacturers often set the standards, and compliance with equipment standards set by others is voluntary. In the past few years, international standards-setting organizations have been more active, so we are now threatened by too many, rather than too few, standards. Unlike the systems of the human body, the systems in telecommunications are not tightly bound. Each element in Figure 2-1 is largely autonomous. The systems exchange signals across the interfaces to create the telecommunications network.

Customer Premise Equipment

Located on the user's premises, *station* or *terminal* equipment is the only part of the telecommunications system the users normally contact directly. This equipment includes the telephone instrument itself, and the wiring in the user's building that connects to *local exchange carrier* (LEC) equipment. For our purposes, station equipment also includes other apparatus such as *private branch exchanges* (PBXs), multiple-line key telephone equipment used to select, hold, and conference calls, videoconferencing equipment, and other voice devices that customers normally own. Customer premise equipment has two primary functions. It is used for intraorganizational communication within a narrow range, usually a building or campus, and it connects to private or common carrier facilities for communication over a wider range.

Subscriber Loop Plant

The *subscriber loop*, also known as the *local loop*, consists of the wire, poles, terminals, conduit, and other outside plant items that connect customer premise equipment to

FIGURE 2-1

The Major Classes of Telecommunications Equipment

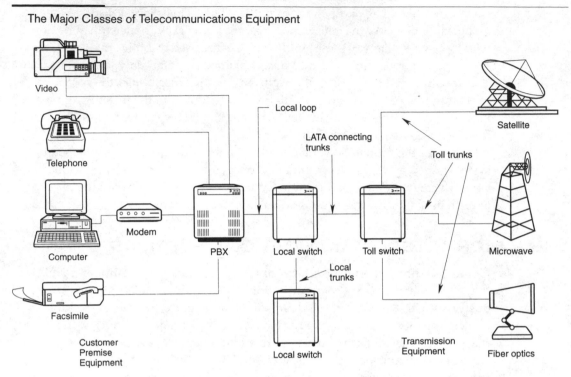

the LEC's central office. Before deregulation, LECs had a monopoly on the local loop. Now alternatives are becoming available. For some services it is possible to transport information over cable television, and in other cases to use facilities such as microwave radio or fiber optics to bypass LEC equipment. A class of common carrier known as an alternate access carrier (AAC) provides such service in most major metropolitan areas. AACs and LECs as well as some CATV companies offer service over fiber optics–based facilities. The local loop is shared between voice and data equipment.

Local Switching Systems

The objective of the telecommunications system is to interconnect users for the duration of a session. These connections are either dialed by the user, or the connections are wired in the LEC's central office and remain connected until the service is discontinued. This latter kind of circuit is called a *private line* or a *dedicated line.* The industry uses the term *provisioning* to refer to the process of setting up circuit groups.

The local switching office (often called an *end office* or *Class 5 office*) is the point where local loops terminate. Loops used for switched services are wired to computer-driven systems that can switch to other loops or to *trunks*, which are channels to other local or long-distance switching offices. Loops used for private line services are directly wired to other loops or to trunks to distant central offices. Until recently, local switching was a monopoly service of the LECs, but the Telecommunications Act of 1996 opens local switching to *competitive local exchange carriers* (CLECs).

Interoffice Trunks

Because of the huge concentrations of wire that converge in local switching offices, there is a practical limit to how many users can be served from a single office or *wire center*. Therefore, in major metropolitan areas, the LECs strategically place multiple central offices according to population density, and connect them with *interoffice trunks*. Central offices exchange signals and establish talking connections over these trunks to set up paths corresponding to telephone numbers dialed by the users.

Tandem Switching Offices

As the number of central offices in a region increases, it becomes impractical to connect every office to every other office with trunks. For one thing, the number of groups of trunks would be unmanageable. Also, some central offices have too little traffic demand between them to justify the cost of directly connected trunks. To address these issues, the telephone network is equipped with *tandem switches* to interconnect trunks. *Local tandem switches* connect local trunks together, and *toll tandem*, also called *interexchange tandem, switches* connect central offices to interexchange trunks leading outside the free calling area. A special type of tandem switch known as a *gateway* interconnects the telephone networks of different countries when their networks are incompatible.

Privately owned tandem switches also may interconnect circuits under the control of a single organization. Before the breakup of the Bell System, the telephone companies owned the toll tandem switches. Now, with multiple *interexchange carriers* (IXCs) offering service, each carrier connects tandem switches to the end office or to an LEC-owned *exchange access tandem*.

Interexchange Trunks

LECs divide their serving areas into classifications known as *exchanges*. Most exchanges correspond roughly to the boundaries of cities and their surrounding areas. Interexchange trunks that connect offices within the local calling area are known as *extended area service (EAS) trunks,* while those that connect outside the local calling area are called *toll trunks*. Trunks that connect the LEC to an IXC are called *interLATA connecting trunks*. The term LATA stands for *local access transport area.* It is the area within which the ex-Bell operating companies are permitted to carry long-distance calls under the terms of the consent decree that broke up the Bell System in 1984.

Transmission Equipment

The process of transporting information in any form, including voice, video, and data between users, is called *transmission* in the telecommunications industry. The earliest transmission took place over open wire suspended on poles equipped with crossarms and insulators, but that technique has now all but disappeared. For short ranges, some trunks are carried on pairs of copper wire, but most trunks now are carried on fiber optics. For longer ranges, interoffice and interexchange trunks are transported primarily over fiber optics, with microwave radio and satellites used to a limited degree. *Multiplexing* equipment divides these backbone transmission facilities into voice channels.

FUNDAMENTALS OF MULTIPLEXING

The basic building block of the telephone network is the *voice-grade* communications channel occupying 300 to 3300 Hz of bandwidth. *Bandwidth* is defined as the information-carrying capacity of a telecommunications facility. The bandwidth of a voice-grade channel is far less than the bandwidth of high-fidelity music systems that typically reproduce 30 to 20,000 Hz, but for ordinary voice transmission this bandwidth is entirely satisfactory. For the first six or seven decades of telephony, open wire or multiple-pair cables were the primary transmission medium. At first, each pair of wires carried one voice channel. However, these media (known as *facilities* in telecommunications vernacular) have enough bandwidth to carry multiple channels. Today's fiber-optic equipment, for example, can carry more than 100,000 voice channels on a single pair of fibers.

The telecommunications industry has always invested heavily in research and development. Much of it has been directed toward how to superimpose an increasing amount of information on a single transmission medium. The process for placing multiple voice or data channels over one facility is known as *multiplexing.*

Frequency Division Multiplexing

With the development of the vacuum tube in the 1920s, a form of multiplexing known as *carrier* became possible. The earliest carrier systems increased the capacity of a pair of wires by frequency division multiplexing (FDM). Broadcast radio is an example of FDM in action (except that it does not allow two-way communications). In an FDM carrier system, as Figure 2-2 shows, each channel is assigned a transmitter-receiver pair or *modem* (a term derived from the words modulator and demodulator). These units operate at low power levels, are connected to cable

FIGURE 2-2

Frequency Division Multiplexing System

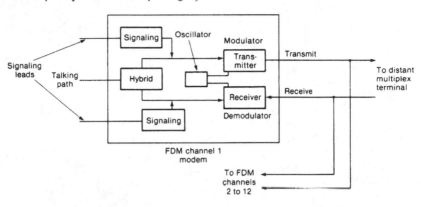

rather than an antenna, and therefore do not radiate as a radio does. Otherwise, the concepts of radio and carrier are similar. FDM carrier systems were once the backbone of the telecommunications network, but most have been replaced by digital multiplexing systems today.

Time Division Multiplexing

Although FDM is an efficient way of increasing the capacity of a transmission medium, the techniques used for its manufacture do not lend themselves to large-scale integration in special chips. Therefore, time division multiplexing (TDM) has replaced FDM. In TDM, shown conceptually in Figure 2-3, the voice is digitized and inserted on the transmission medium in 8-bit segments. Instead of the bandwidth of the transmission medium being divided into frequency segments, each user has access to the full bandwidth of the system for a stream of time slots that repeats 8000 times per second. The capacity of the transmission medium is so great that users are not aware that they are sharing it. Chapter 5 describes the concept of time division multiplexing in more detail. The only portion of a telephone connection today that is analog is the telephone instrument itself and the pair of wires connecting it to the central office. Some analog switching systems remain in service, but they are being replaced by digital switches as budgets permit. Users can obtain end-to-end digital connections by subscribing to *integrated services digital network* (ISDN) service as discussed later.

Higher-Order Multiplexing

The basic building block of both analog and digital multiplexing systems is the *group*. A group has 12 voice-grade circuits combined into a band of analog frequencies, or into a stream of digital data. Groups are formed in equipment called

FIGURE 2-3

Time Division Multiplexing System

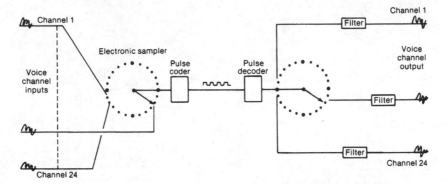

a *channel bank*. Digital channel banks in North America derive 24 circuits and are known as a *digroup*. Higher-order multiplexing combines the output of channel banks into hundreds and thousands of circuits that can be transmitted over broadband facilities such as coaxial cable, microwave radio, and fiber optics.

Data Multiplexing

When data communications people speak of multiplexing, they are usually using it in a different sense than voice people. Data multiplex equipment will be discussed in Chapter 4. For now it is important to know that the term "multiplex" must be understood in context because it is an ambiguous term.

ANALOG AND DIGITAL TRANSMISSION CONCEPTS

When people speak into a telephone instrument, the voice actuates a transmitter to cause current flowing in the line to vary proportionately or *analog*ous to the changes in sound pressure. Because people speak and hear in analog, there was, until a few decades ago, little reason to convert an analog signal to digital. Now, there are four primary reasons digital transmission has replaced analog in most parts of the network:

1. Digital equipment is less expensive to manufacture than analog.
2. An increasing amount of communication takes place between digital terminal equipment such as computers.
3. Digital transmission provides higher quality in most respects than analog.
4. Digital signals can be compressed to occupy a fraction of the bandwidth an analog signal requires.

The higher quality of digital signals results from the difference in the methods of amplifying the signal. In analog transmission, an audio amplifier known as a *repeater* boosts the signal, together with any noise on the line. With digital transmission, regenerators detect the incoming bit stream and create an entirely new signal that is identical to the original. If a digital signal is regenerated before noise causes errors to occur, the result is a channel that is practically noise-free.

The system for generating and transmitting telephone signals digitally is known as *pulse code modulation* (PCM). A PCM device samples the voice 8000 times per second, converts each sample to an 8-bit digital word, and transmits it as a 64-kb/s bit stream over a line interspersed with signals from other channels. Repeaters spaced at appropriate intervals regenerate the signal. In North America this technique results in a 1.544-megabit-per-second (Mb/s) digital signal known as T1, which is the basic building block of the North American digital hierarchy. Most other parts of the world use a 32-channel voice system with a 2.048-Mb/s signal known as E1.

The theory of PCM is not new—an IT&T scientist in England developed it in 1938. Though the system was technically feasible then, it was not economical because of the high cost of the electronics needed to make the analog-to-digital conversion. With the invention of the transistor, the development of solid-state electronics, and particularly large-scale integration, the economics shifted in favor of digital transmission. Telephone sets in which the voice is digitized in the instrument are common in PBXs. Presently, digital telephone sets are not widely used in public telephone networks for technical and economic reasons, but the drawbacks will disappear in time as users move to ISDN. ISDN is the architecture that is being used to upgrade the local network, which has changed little in its basic architecture since the invention of the telephone.

SWITCHING SYSTEMS

For many applications requiring communications between points, dedicated point-to-point circuits are desirable. Usually, however, the real value of a telecommunications system is in its ability to access a wide range of users wherever they are located. This is the role of telephone switching systems.

Early Switching Systems

The earliest switching systems were manually operated. Telephone lines and trunks were terminated on jacks, and operators interconnected lines by inserting plug-equipped cords into the jacks. In 1891 a Kansas City undertaker named Almon B. Strowger patented an electromechanical switch that could be controlled by pulses from a rotary dial. The Strowger system, also known as *step-by-step*, has been replaced by modern electronic switching systems in most parts of the world. Step-by-step's distinguishing feature was that electrical pulses created by a dial directly controlled the motion of the switches. The switching system had no intelligence, and limited ability to vary the destination of the call. This limitation, coupled with high maintenance cost, led to common control switching.

Common Control Switching Offices

All switching offices have a common characteristic: they contain a limited amount of equipment that many users share. With manual and step-by-step systems, all the equipment used to establish a talking path remained connected for the duration of the call. As technology advanced, it became evident that keeping all the equipment occupied for the duration of the call was not the most economical way to switch. More importantly, it was also inflexible. As a call progressed through the switching system, if it encountered a blockage, the system was incapable of rerouting the call to a different path. It could only signal the user to hang up and try again. These drawbacks were overcome by use of *common control.*

Common control switching equipment sets up the talking path through a switching fabric, and releases when the connection is established. The common control equipment is not called on again until the connection is to be taken down. In this respect, common control equipment serves a function similar to the manual switchboard operator. Although common control equipment is more complex than directly controlled switching, it is also more efficient and much faster.

When contrasted to step-by-step where the user builds a connection gradually with pulls of the dial, under common control the user transmits dial or tone pulses into a circuit that registers the digits. An advantage of this method is that when dialing is complete, logic circuits can inspect the digits, determine the destination of the call, and choose an alternative route if all trunks in the preferred route are busy. This capability, known as *alternate routing,* is a characteristic shared by all modern switching systems.

The earliest common control equipment, introduced in the 1920s, was a system known as *panel,* followed about two decades later by the *crossbar* system. The systems take their names from the method of interconnecting lines and trunks.

Computer-Controlled Switching Systems

Common control offices used electromechanical relays in their logic circuits. Relays have an electronic counterpart, the *logic gate.* Both gates and relays are binary logic devices. That is, they are either ON or OFF, and if a decision can be reduced to a series of "yes/no" responses to outside conditions, both logic gates and relays can perform the same functions.

The electronic equivalent of a common control central office was a natural outgrowth of computer and switching technology. Early electronic switching systems (ESSs) used wired logic, that is, they were not programmable. In the middle 1960s the age of the stored program control (SPC) central office was born. The no. 1 ESS, which is still in use today, has a reed-relay switching fabric driven by a software program. The switching fabric of the no. 1 ESS is analog, although the control is a digital computer.

The no. 1 ESS was manufactured by Western Electric, which has evolved into Lucent Technologies through a series of reorganizations. No. 1 ESS equipment was not widely used outside the United States, but similar systems were made by other manufacturers. Today, these analog switching systems are obsolete; new switching systems are digital.

Digital Central Offices

When large-scale integrated circuits were perfected in the 1970s, it became technically feasible to develop a digital switching fabric to replace the analog electronic network in SPC central offices. The current state of the art of central office technology has a digital switching fabric controlled by a programmable central processor. Most modern switching equipment, ranging from small PBXs to large toll tandem switches that can handle thousands of trunks, uses this technology. Now, further research is under way to develop even less costly switching systems, capable of switching light streams directly rather than electrical pulses. As we will explore in more detail in Chapter 12, digital switches match efficiently with digital transmission systems. By contrast, an analog switching system must convert signals to digital to send them across the digital transmission network.

NUMBERING SYSTEMS

Switching systems route calls between themselves and selected terminating stations by *addressing*. Station addresses consist of a country code, an area code, and a telephone number. The exact structure of the numbering plan varies with the country, but the pattern is compatible worldwide. Without controlled assignment of telephone numbers, the telephone system could not function. In this section we will look briefly at how telephone numbering operates.

The Switching Hierarchy

The telephone numbering system is geographically oriented and hierarchical. The highest tier in the hierarchy is the country code. Below that, countries are assigned a second-tier code that is known as an area code or numbering plan area (NPA) in North America. This level covers a geographical area, and is not duplicated anywhere else in the country. The area code is divided into central office areas that are also unique within certain limits. Until 1995, a 0 or 1 as the second digit identified the NPA. Several forces have converged to exhaust the pool of available numbers, so on January 1, 1995, the new North American Numbering Plan was introduced. This plan permits any digit from 0 to 9 in the second position. Area codes were once unique within a geographical area, but recently state commissions have begun to select *overlay area codes* in preference to requiring area code changes when they have exhausted capacity. With an overlay area code, two or more codes cover the same geographical area. This requires callers to dial 10 digits to make a local call.

The next level is the central office code or prefix. In most parts of the world a central office code is a unique geographical area. In the United States, however, the Telecommunications Act of 1996 required LECs to support number portability as a way of promoting competition in the local network. Since users are reluctant to change telephone numbers, the lack of number portability would dampen enthusiasm for switching from one LEC to another. Therefore, within limits, users are free to change carriers and retain their previous number. This means that the central office code is no longer a reliable indicator of geographical location.

The lowest tier on the PSTN switching hierarchy is the *end office,* also known as a *Class 5* office. The latter designation referred to the lowest level of a five-level hierarchy AT&T used before divestiture. Now, long-distance networks tend to be flat, although most long-distance connections route through one or more tandem offices, which connect toll trunks together. Trunks between switching systems are classified as either *high-usage* or *final* trunks. High-usage trunks can be established between two offices if the traffic volume justifies it. Common control switching systems contain routing algorithms to enable them to select the appropriate group of trunks, always attempting first to connect to a distant central office over a high-usage trunk. Calls progress from system to system until the terminating office is reached. Systems route calls by exchanging signals over an external data network known as *Signaling System 7* (SS7).

INTEREXCHANGE CARRIER ACCESS TO LOCAL NETWORKS

In those countries that have privatized their telephone systems and opened the long-distance network to competition, two classes of carrier have developed. The LEC interfaces local subscribers, and depending on the regulations within the country, either may or may not handle long distance. The IXC carries traffic over the wider area. The user presubscribes to an IXC. The LEC routes long-distance calls so the selected IXC can complete the calls over its network. The caller accesses the toll network by dialing an access code, often "1." The LEC looks up the identity of the calling party through a process known as *automatic number identification* (ANI) and forwards it to the IXC.

In countries with a competitive long-distance system, the access afforded all carriers is identical; that is, it provides ANI, accurate call timing, and transmission quality equal to that provided for the LEC's own customers. In North America callers can dial any IXC by dialing a code preceding the call. The carrier access code is 101*XXXX*, where *XXXX* is a number assigned to the IXC.

PRIVATE TELEPHONE SYSTEMS

Many organizations operate private telecommunications systems. These systems range in size from small PBXs to the Federal Telephone System (FTS), which is larger than the telecommunications systems in many countries. Private networks normally must be connected to the public network so users can place calls to points that the private network does not cover, and so people outside the private network can reach them. This is done by connecting to an end office through connections switched through a PBX or through private tandem switching systems.

Private network operators design their networks to transmission and numbering plan criteria similar to networks operated by the LECs. There is no reason that private systems must conform to the nationwide numbering plan. If they do not, however, the result is often a dual numbering system, one for calls placed on the private network, and another for calls placed on the public network.

SUMMARY

This chapter has covered voice networks in overview. In the next chapter we will examine data networks in overview and discuss how two parallel network systems are emerging. It is important to recognize that although voice and data are separate at this time, they are converging, at least to some degree, down to the desktop level. It is also important to understand that except for the desktop devices and switching systems, data and voice share the same facilities. The fiber-optic backbones, multiplexed with synchronous optical network (SONET), carry voice and data signals with few distinctions. In Europe, SONET is known as the synchronous digital hierarchy (SDH). In this book we will generally refer to it as SONET/SDH.

One cannot help being awed by the intricacy of the world's telecommunications system. The complexity is evident from this brief overview, but it becomes even more impressive as the details emerge. The marvel is that the system can cover such a vast geographical area, can be administered by hundreds of thousands of workers, contain countless pieces of electrical apparatus, and still function as reliably as it does. As we discuss these elements in greater detail, the techniques that create this high-quality service will become more understandable.

CHAPTER 3

Introduction to Data Networks

Chapter 2 discussed voice networks, making limited reference to data networks although both use the same underlying transmission media. The data counterpart of the PSTN is the Internet. The Internet can be accessed through Internet service providers (ISPs) by anyone in any country that supports it.

The Internet did not start out to be a public network. The Department of Defense in the 1960s funded the early development of the Internet as a way of communicating with research agencies and manufacturers. The first implementation, developed by the Advanced Research Projects Agency (ARPA), was known as ARPAnet. The network was designed to enable computers to communicate with each other rapidly and simply over leased telecommunications lines. The protocol that was developed was known as TCP/IP, which stands for transport control protocol/internet protocol.

The contrast between the Internet and the PSTN is significant. The Internet consists of two classes of device: hosts and gateways. A *host* is a computer, and a *gateway* is a specialized computer to enable hosts to access other hosts. As the Internet expanded, a different device, known as a *router*, was used as a gateway. Figure 3-1 shows how an internet is used to connect various networks and subnetworks.

In 1994 the Department of Defense decided to turn the operation of the Internet over to private business. Until that time the use of the Internet was limited to a handful of users compared to today. The Internet had three major applications that were used by academics and researchers. These were Telnet, which enables users to log onto a remote computer over the Internet; file transfer protocol (FTP), which enables users to transfer files between computers; and simple mail transfer protocol (SMTP), which is used for e-mail. The development of hypertext transfer protocol (HTTP) and the World Wide Web caused the Internet to boom. No longer was it necessary to use obscure Unix commands across the network. Web browsers and graphical user interfaces brought millions of users into the Internet for the first time.

FIGURE 3-1

Internetworking Architecture

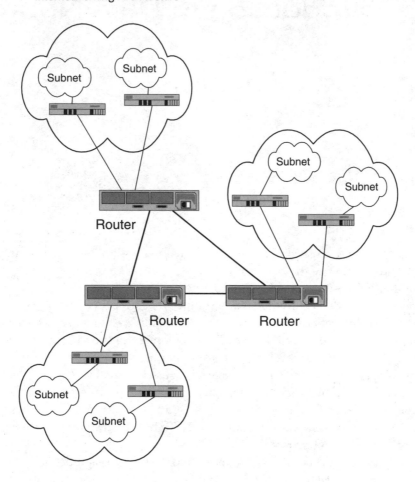

Ironically, although the Internet is a data network that does not lend itself well to fixed bandwidth circuits, most of the access today is through the PSTN. For many users this is a matter of convenience rather than choice. Anyone who has a telephone and a modem can access an ISP, but the limited bandwidth of a telephone circuit means it takes a long time to download large files. This situation is temporary for those who can afford dedicated access. Alternatives, such as asymmetric digital subscriber line (ADSL) and cable modems, are becoming available to increase the bandwidth to the ISPs.

A few words of notation are in order before we discuss data networks. In most data networks information is sliced into bite-sized fragments. These fragments may be very short. In asynchronous transfer mode (ATM) the fragments are

53 bytes long and they are known as *cells*. In other types of networks data is sliced into longer *frames* and in yet other networks the data unit is a *packet*. All of these terms have specific meanings in certain types of networks, but the industry is generally casual about terminology and assumes that the user can take the meaning from context. One term that is widely used is the *packet*. In a packet-switched data network the word "packet" has a specific meaning, but many people refer to cells and frames as packets. To be unambiguous about our meanings, we will usually use the general term *protocol data unit* (PDU) to refer to a data unit that could be a cell, packet, or frame, depending on the type of network it is used in.

It is also important to distinguish between the Internet and an internetwork. The Internet, which is represented with a capital "I," is a public network owned by many different companies. An internet with lower-case "i" is a private network that is architecturally similar to the Internet, but is not accessible to the public.

STRUCTURE OF THE INTERNET

Until quite recently, both voice and data networks were based on voice circuits. With few exceptions, voice sessions are switched either through the PSTN or through a private switch such as a PBX. Some data sessions are, by their nature, switched but most data sessions use the voice network only as a matter of convenience. Voice sessions have characteristics that make them significantly different than data sessions. For one thing, the bandwidth of a voice channel is optimized for the purpose. Providing extra bandwidth to a voice session doesn't add value to the user. In a data session, however, extra bandwidth may be extremely valuable because it allows information to flow across the network in a much shorter period of time.

Another key difference between voice and data lies in the process of setting up a session. Voice calls have a single worldwide addressing scheme that consists of a country code, area code, office code, and line number. Different countries use varying quantities of digits for these, but the basic pattern is geographically oriented. Data addresses, on the other hand, have nothing to do with geography unless they are using the PSTN to handle the session. Public data addresses such as internet protocol (IP) are organizationally related. Both the PSTN and the IP addressing schemes are hierarchically organized, but there the similarity ends. A large organization, for example, that has a class A IP address has a range of addresses it can use for host computers all over the world. Anyone looking at the first three digits of the IP address would know that they belong within that organization's hierarchy. Obviously, whether you place a telephone call over the PSTN or send an e-mail message to a desktop computer, the information must reach a physical location, but the way in which it gets to that address is totally different over the Internet compared to how it gets there over the PSTN.

If a user in Los Angeles is calling another user in New York City over the PSTN, the called user's address is something like 213-223-1234. A combination of circuit switching machines finds a route through the network that leads from Los Angeles to New York, and generates a fixed path for the duration of the session. If the call happens to be going to London instead, the calling party adds a country code and the circuit-switched network boosts the call eastward to England.

By contrast, if the same user wants to send an e-mail message to a desktop computer somewhere in the world, the real address of that computer is not even known, and if it was, it would be meaningless to the user sending the e-mail. The computer is equipped with a network interface card (NIC) that contains a permanently assigned address that has nothing whatsoever to do with geography. In fact, the computer could move from New York to London and the address in the NIC would remain the same. In order for the Internet to find that computer the address must be translated. It begins by defining the computer as a member of a *domain*. A domain in data network terms consists of one or more networks that are linked together.

Companies register their domain names with the Internet Network Information Center. Every device on the network is equipped with logic on where to find its domain name server (DNS). DNSs are installed within internal networks and on Internet service providers' (ISP) networks. A device trying to reach another device on the network sends a query message that reaches the DNS serving the domain. That server returns the IP address to the originator, which usually caches the information for use in future transactions. Within the subnet, a server maps the IP address to the hardware address in the NIC.

IP addresses are four-part numerical addresses with each part separated by a period or dot. For example, 123.24.13.65 would be a valid IP address. Unlike a telephone number, which is fixed by geography, the above IP address can be located anywhere in the world. IP addresses are not easy to remember, but domain names are. Since the addresses are not geographically arranged, a large domain such as IBM.com can have its addresses spread throughout the world. As long as the DNS knows where to find the domain, internal servers can locate the name to the left of the @ sign. The details of how this happens aren't important in this part of the discussion, but it *is* important to understand that the Internet and the PSTN are two completely different types of networks. It is also important to understand that although the PSTN was primarily designed for voice traffic and the Internet was specifically designed for data, either network can carry the other type of traffic.

We need to make it clear that while we speak of the Internet or the PSTN, neither of these is a single monolithic network. The PSTN consists of many circuit switches in many different countries owned by hundreds of public and private organizations, and interconnected by millions of miles of circuits traveling over fiber optics, satellites, microwave radio, and twisted pair wires owned by many other entities. By the same token, the Internet is far from a monolithic entity. Its backbone circuits ride over the same fiber-optic and satellite routes that support the PSTN, but these are not subdivided into voice channels. Instead, the bandwidth is allocated based on demand. Instead of circuit switches, the Internet uses powerful routers to boost packets from the origin to the destination. In the telephone network, a connection is set up between the originating and terminating parties. The Internet, on the other hand, is connectionless. Each packet is launched with originating and terminating addresses and the routers forward it to the destination. If a router is unable to handle a packet for some reason, it is permitted to discard it. Discarded packets don't cause a problem for applications because higher-order protocols running in the host arrange to resend the lost information.

TYPES OF DATA NETWORKS

Where the PSTN operates with switched circuits, data networks operate with virtual circuits. A *virtual circuit* is one that is defined in the network software. The path doesn't occupy a fixed hardware circuit. Neither is it restricted to a fixed bandwidth. The amount of bandwidth allocated to a data circuit can vary based on demand. This is important since many of today's applications require a lot of bandwidth for a very short time, and then none.

Take, for example, the case of a physician reading a digitized x-ray of a patient across town or even in another country. The x-ray may contain 1 million or more bytes even after it is compressed. To download this file over today's analog networks, using the fastest modem available, would take nearly 5 minutes. Over the full bandwidth of a T1 circuit it would take a little over 5 seconds, which isn't bad, but you can't readily dial up a T1 connection, hold it for a few seconds, and release it. Our physician needs the ability to access a broadband circuit, hold it long enough to transfer the file, and pay only for the bandwidth used.

The Internet is the data equivalent of the public switched telephone network. It is public and you can reach anyone on the Internet provided they have arranged for service with an ISP. The ISP is the Internet's equivalent of the LEC in the PSTN. The Internet is far from being the only alternative for data communications. Networks can be interconnected with leased telephone circuits. At one time, these were the only alternative available, but over the past few decades several other alternatives have evolved. One is the public data network (PDN), which is a packet-switched network. Packet networks are also known as X.25 networks, named after the access protocol. You can connect data devices over a PDN, generally paying by the number of packets you send. PDNs were developed at a time when the circuits interconnecting their nodes were analog with a high error rate. Each node in the PDN checks to be sure the packet has been received correctly before forwarding it to the next node. Generically, most public wide area data networks are connected as a mesh, as shown in Figure 3-2.

Public data networks were popular until the middle-to-late 1980s. By then, fiber optics had been installed throughout most of the industrialized world. The

F I G U R E 3-2

A Mesh Network

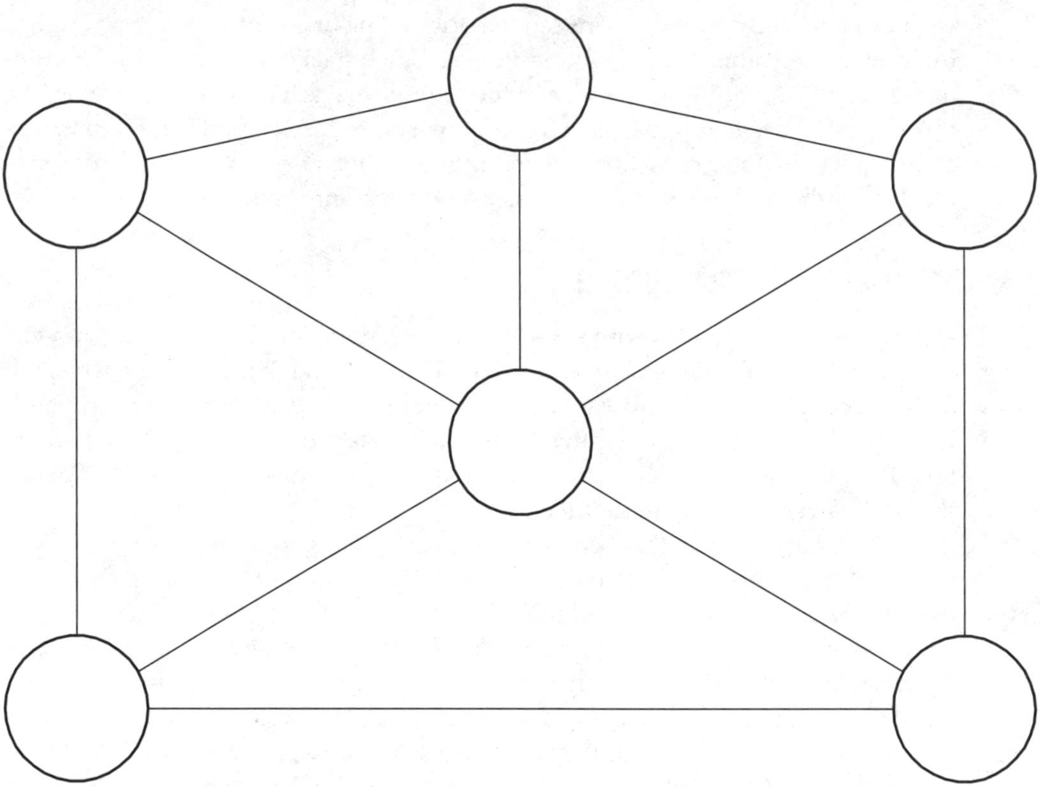

error rate on fiber-optic facilities is much lower than it is on analog facilities, so the extra time delay caused by link-by-link error correction was unnecessary. A service known as *frame relay* emerged to take advantage of high-quality fiber-optic circuits. Frame relay consists of nodes and high-speed interconnecting trunks, but unlike X.25, it does no error correction at all. In fact, a frame relay network does not even guarantee that packets will be delivered. Under certain conditions the network may simply discard packets that have been marked as discard-eligible. This does not mean that a network deployed over frame relay is unreliable because higher-order protocols take care of correcting errors and replacing discarded packets.

Users connect to frame relay nodes over access circuits, the bandwidth of which is selected by the customer. Architecturally, a frame relay and a packet network look alike. They consist of high-speed computer nodes connected with circuits, but there the similarity ends. The frame relay network offers much greater bandwidth than X.25 and has a different pricing structure, as we will discuss in Chapter 4.

Another type of network is an IP network, so called because the IP protocol is used for routing PDUs between nodes. An IP network also looks, at first glance, like a packet network, except that the nodes are routers with circuits of varying amounts of bandwidth connecting them. IP networks can be composed of private or public facilities as the designer chooses. Networks known as virtual private networks (VPNs) can be deployed over IP networks, using a variety of facilities, including the public Internet in full or in part.

In their initial implementations, IP networks had no method of ensuring quality of service. As we will see in the next section, quality of service has different meanings in voice and data networks. In an effort to develop quality of service standards to permit voice and video to be carried on data networks, another type of network was developed: asynchronous transfer mode (ATM). We will discuss ATM in more detail later, but for now, suffice it to say that the PDU of ATM is a cell with a 48-byte payload and a 5-byte header to steer it through the network. These short cells can be switched with a minimum of processing overhead, which results in a network that supports time-sensitive media such as a voice and video as well as media such as data that can tolerate lower quality of service.

If we were building a network to handle one type of information, the network could be reasonably simple. In fact, this is the case with the PSTN. Its primary purpose was, and remains, switching voice traffic. If data needs to ride on the PSTN, the data signals must be made to resemble voice signals, which is exactly what happens in a modem or fax machine. The reason the PSTN works so well for voice is because voice is predictable in terms of bandwidth required and volume. Data is also predictable if you're dealing with only one application, but there is an enormous difference between requirements of different data applications. For example, an agent operating a terminal in an airline ticket booth has a requirement that bears almost no resemblance to someone working at a personal computer connected to a LAN and surfing the World Wide Web. When we begin adding multimedia applications, such as attaching voice and video clips to an e-mail message or reviewing a CAT scan on a remote terminal, it is easy to see that data applications lose their predictability. The voice network is no longer satisfactory because it has fixed bandwidth and many data applications may require no bandwidth at all for a period of time, and then put a sudden demand on the network. For this reason, different types of networks have emerged.

QUALITY OF SERVICE

To understand the convergence of voice and data, it is important to examine the differences between the two in terms of service quality requirements. In a voice connection we care about two things: how easy it is to set up the call and how intelligible the call is after it is set up. Intelligibility is a function of volume, noise, and distortion. We also care about being cut off in the middle of a connection, but cutoffs are rare these days. Fast call setup is desirable, but unless we're using an automatic dialer, speed of setup is limited by how fast we can move our fingers across the dial and how quickly the switching system connects the call. In data terms, what seems like fast call setup to a human may be totally unacceptable to a data application that may be able to complete the whole transaction in the time it would take to dial a call. In terms of intelligibility, we expect the voice on the other end to be recognizable and easy to understand. Voice call quality is subjective. What might be sufficient volume to one person is barely audible to hearing-impaired individuals. Quality-of-service (QoS) variables in the voice network are developed using subjective criteria. The design objectives of the network were developed to establish a grade of service consisting of a noise and volume combination that at least 80 percent of the users would classify as good or better. A combination of volume and noise is used because the lower the noise, the more we can tolerate a low-volume connection and vice versa.

When we send data over a voice network, a connection that is perfectly adequate for voice may be unusable for data. Short static pops don't bother a voice connection much, but they may render a data connection unusable. At the same time, things that don't bother a data connection can be detrimental to voice. If the data network discards or delays packets, the user may see that as response time that is slower than usual, but half a second here or there is scarcely noticeable in most applications. Voice and video, on the other hand, are severely impaired by end-to-end delay, which is called *latency,* and by variations in packet arrival, which are known as *jitter.*

To understand the effects of latency and jitter, assume that the human voice is sliced into packets of a few syllables, routed across the network, and reassembled in a buffer at the distant end. If the packets reach the far end with precise spacing between them, they can be buffered, reassembled, and presented to the receiving user as a continuous stream with no interpacket spacing. If, however, something occurs in the backbone network that prevents the packets from arriving precisely spaced, they began to pile up in the buffer awaiting the arrival of the next group of packets. The buffer delays the packets and absorbs the additional space so the user isn't affected. As long as the buffer doesn't fill up and overflow, the user sees the effect as latency. If the buffer does fill up, however, the network must either let the packets begin to flow out with increased spacing between them or discard them. In either case, the effect is a drop in quality that the user will perceive immediately. To provide quality-of-service in a computer network that is carrying isochronous traffic, the network must identify time-sensitive packets. Voice and video must be given priority to ensure that jitter and delay are kept within acceptable limits.

Studies by the ITU and others indicate that if round-trip delay of a voice signal is 300 milliseconds (ms) or less, most users will be unaware of it. Delays of 500 ms are undesirable, and delays over 800 ms render the circuit unusable.

To recap, voice and video are almost polar opposites from data with respect to what they need from a network. Data is far less sensitive to delay and jitter than voice, while voice is insensitive to small amounts of noise. Voice gains no advantage from bandwidth in excess of the standard circuit, while many data applications require bandwidth in bursts.

WHY CONVERGENCE?

Given these differences, it is natural to ask why we bother to integrate voice and data. For many users the answer is that data integration makes no sense because they have no data entry requirements beyond those that can be handled on a standard push-button dial. The number of such users is rapidly diminishing, however, as thousands of new users each day began to access the Internet. As they begin to download data from the World Wide Web, the limitations of voice circuits become painfully obvious. The industry's immediate solution is the asymmetrical digital subscriber line (ADSL), which is a form of voice and data integration on a local loop that we will discuss in Chapter 32.

For other users, the advantages lie in the application. The worldwide business model has changed dramatically over the past few years. Voice always remains an absolute requirement for all organizations, but data applications that were just a dream a few years ago are mainstream today. Office workers are equipped with PCs, PCs are connected to LANs, and LANs are interconnected worldwide. Companies need to connect to their suppliers and customers and to traveling or work-at-home employees. These connections are made on dedicated and dial-up sessions over the PSTN, the Internet, and a variety of public networks.

Electronic commerce is ramping up quickly as a few pioneers point the way. In the past, businesses have exchanged a few standard business forms such as in voices, purchase orders, bills of lading, and the like over electronic data interchange (EDI). EDI is complex to implement, and has been slow to catch on, but a new form of commerce over the Web is growing rapidly. As consumers begin to shop on the Web, the shortcomings of dial-up connections will become intolerable for many.

Businesses, in particular, consist of interconnected islands of local networks, and they have both voice and data requirements. Whether they are connected via the public Internet or a private internet, the cost is fixed and incremental capacity can be added for a small amount of money. Voice connections across the wide area are usage-sensitive in all but a few instances. Even though the cost is a fraction of what it was a few years ago, it still is substantially more than the cost of putting voice over data networks.

Equipment for putting voice over IP networks takes advantage of voice characteristics, one of which is that voice tends to be half-duplex—that is, it flows in only one direction at a time. This half-duplex mode means that half of the bandwidth during any two-way conversation is unused at any instant. Also, the typical voice conversation has many silent periods. While silent periods are not great, in data terms they are long enough to squeeze in several packets. Since voice over IP equipment both compresses and packetizes the voice, it makes more efficient use of bandwidth than circuit switching. Voice is first digitized using techniques described in Chapter 5, and then it is compressed to about 8 kb/s, which is one-fourth of the bandwidth of a digital voice channel. Next, it is sliced into packets for transmission on the data network. Silent periods are compressed out at the sending end and reinserted at the receiving end. Quality is somewhat lower than toll-quality voice, but the cost is a fraction of the PSTN for many applications.

Voice over IP has numerous applications that will begin gradually, but catch on as users become accustomed to it. One potential application is an affinity network. In many parts of the world immigrants from one country cluster into communities. Calls back to the home country are costly, but an affinity network can be created to allow callers to dial into a gateway over the local PSTN, connect to a gateway in the other country over the Internet, and terminate through the distant PSTN. Quality will not be ideal, but the cost reduction will compensate.

A second application is the Web-enabled call center. Customers who are attracted by information they read on a company's Web page can click on an icon to set up a voice over IP connection to a live agent. The customer and the agent may be able to see each other on a video display as well as talk to one another over the Web. This application is attractive because it doesn't require a gateway.

For businesses, the branch office application is perhaps the most appealing use of voice over IP. Assuming that the branch office needs to be connected to headquarters, frame relay is usually the most cost-effective way to do it. Tunneling through the Internet is also possible, but many companies avoid it because of security problems. In either case a router with voice over IP capability can provide voice paths in addition to data. The voice connections may not be as good as the PSTN, but for internal communications they are acceptable, and the cost is minimal.

Voice over IP will be discussed in greater detail in Chapter 38.

STANDARDS

As discussed in Chapter 1, the ITU is responsible for promulgation of both voice and data standards. With respect to the Internet, a group known as the Internet Architecture Board develops and approves Internet standards.

The Internet started out as an open association of interested individuals who experimented with protocols, and put them out on the network for peer review. As the Internet developed, the Internet Architecture Board was formed to coordinate standards development. Individuals may propose standards and improvements through a request for comments (RFC) process. The board appoints one of its members as the RFC editor, who publishes the RFCs. Standards are reviewed by the Internet Engineering Steering Group, with appeal to the Internet Architecture Board, and promulgated as international standards by the Internet Society. The RFC editor is responsible for preparing and organizing the standards in their final form.

The Board establishes numerous task forces, the primary one of which is known as the Internet Engineering Task Force (IETF). Details on the IETF's operation are available on its home page, which is listed in Appendix A. The IETF is an open international consortium of individuals interested in the evolution and operation of the Internet. The IETF is subdivided into working groups, which are organized by subject matter. Area directors, who are members of the Internet Engineering Steering Group (IESG), manage the working groups. The IETF meets three times per year.

The result of this process has been remarkably successful. Other networks, in particular the PSTN and proprietary networks such as IBM's Systems Network Architecture, have evolved in closed laboratories and have reached the public domain through a slow licensing process, if at all. The openness of the Internet, combined with the eagerness of countless companies to profit from it, has resulted in a network that is able to absorb rapid change, but is nearly overwhelmed by the variety of choices that are emerging.

CHAPTER 4

Data Communications Principles

Data communications is not as new as most people might think. Samuel F.B. Morse invented the telegraph, which was a data communications device, in 1844. The telegraph, and its successor the teletypewriter, played an important part in communications for the first century of their existence, but these early communications systems were used for messaging, which is a far cry from today's needs. Just a few years ago most people had never had their hands on a computer. Today they use computers regularly at work and at home for applications that weren't even dreamed of back in the days of Western Union telegrams and the railroad telegraph. Although messaging is still important, the focus has shifted to e-mail over the Internet. From the office to the home to the classroom, many of us are hands-on data communicators when we surf the Web, use automatic teller machines, or transfer funds between bank accounts over the telephone.

Just a few years ago personal computers were rare, and the Internet was the province of a handful of intellectuals in universities, government agencies, and large companies. Most people had no idea what a modem was or why they would ever need one. Now, desktop computers are selling for well under $1000, hard-drive capacities run into the multigigabits, and the applications are un-limited.

Meanwhile, we are left with a network that is part analog and part digital, and the issue of how best to carry out data communications remains very much alive. Data is far more complex than voice from a user's standpoint and is likely to remain so for several reasons. First, data demands a precision that is totally un-necessary in voice communication. A voice session has so much redundancy that a few audible noise bursts on an analog circuit or thousands of missing bits in a dig-ital circuit have little effect on the intelligibility of the message. If the message is garbled, the receiving party simply asks the sender to repeat, and both parties are satisfied, unless the noise is excessive, in which case they hang up and try another circuit. With data, on the other hand, a single missing bit can cause a serious problem, and every effort is made to get error-free transmission.

The second difference is the proliferation of standards in data communications. The major computer manufacturers have developed proprietary networking protocols, and although progress is being made toward developing international standards, proprietary standards are still in common use. Many international standards are in use today, but the dozens of options and alternatives make data communications complex, and the setup is usually left to the experts.

Telecommunications and the computer are partners in a marriage that is changing the way people store, access, and use information. The merger of the computer and telecommunications makes possible many applications, including the Internet, automatic teller machines, airline reservation systems, and credit card verification networks. The telephone network was designed and constructed for voice, however, which means that the computer, a digital device, must either use a separate digital network or adapt to the analog portions of the voice network.

This chapter is the first of several in this book that deal with data communications. This chapter sets the foundation, and deals primarily with legacy data networks. We will discuss how data travels across a circuit, how errors are corrected, and how the major components of a data network function and interact. We will discuss how data devices work around the limitations of the analog portions of the network, and how voice and data live together in a mixed environment. Later chapters discuss advanced data protocols and equipment.

DATA COMMUNICATIONS FUNDAMENTALS

The objective of a data communications network is to provide devices with a communication path that makes the complexities of the network and the disruptions that can occur transparent to the user. Some applications can tolerate an occasional error, which is defined as any pattern of received bits that is not identical to the transmitted pattern. Most applications, however, require absolute data integrity. As shown in Figure 4-1, a host computer may have both directly attached and remote terminals. With the short, secure connections of a directly attached device, errors are rare, but not unheard of. When the circuit extends across town or across a continent, data errors will occasionally occur. A major objective of a data network, therefore, is to present the host computer with an error-free data stream.

The devices in a data network that originate and receive data are collectively called *data terminal equipment* (DTE). These can range from computers to simple receive-only terminals. DTE is coupled to the telecommunications network by *data circuit–terminating equipment* (DCE), which includes devices that convert the DTE output to a signal suitable for the transmission medium. DCE ranges from line drivers to complex modulator/demodulators (modems) and multiplexers.

The basic information element processed by a computer is the binary digit, or bit. A *bit* is the smallest information element in the binary numbering system and

FIGURE 4-1

Data Network Showing Locally and Remotely Attached Terminals

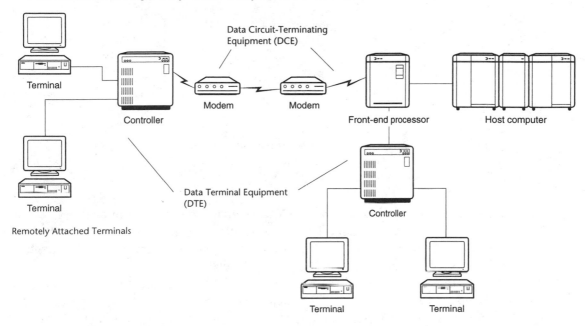

is represented by the two digits, 0 and 1, corresponding to two different voltage states within the DTE. Processors manipulate data in groups of 8 bits known as *bytes* or *octets*. Within the computer's circuits, bytes travel over parallel paths that may be extended to output ports for connection to peripherals such as printers.

The range of parallel ports is limited to a few feet. Although the range can be extended with electronic regenerators, extending eight circuits in parallel over long distances is uneconomical because one circuit would be required for each parallel path. Therefore, most DTE is equipped with an interface to convert the 8 parallel bits into a serial bit stream, as Figure 4-2 shows. This serial bit stream can be coupled to telecommunications circuits through a modem or line driver, or directly to circuits up to about 1 kilometer (km).

Coding

The number of characters that can be encoded with binary numbers depends on the number of bits in the code. Early teletypewriters used a five-level code called *baudot* that had a capacity of 2^5 or 32 characters. A five-level code limits communications, because there are insufficient combinations to send a full range of upper and lower case plus special characters. In the baudot code, upper and lower case

F I G U R E 4-2

Parallel and Serial Data Conversion

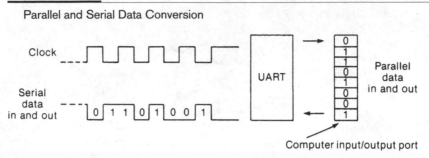

UART = Universal Asynchronous Receiver/Transmitter

are indicated by shift characters. The receiving device continues in upper- or lower-case mode until it receives a case-shifting character. If it misses a shift character for some reason, the transmission will be garbled, because special characters are shifted numeric characters in the baudot code.

To overcome this limitation, a seven-level code known as the American Standard Code for Information Interchange (ASCII) was introduced. This code, shown in Table 4-1, provides 2^7 or 128 combinations. In ASCII transmissions, although 7 bits are used for characters, 8 bits are transmitted. The eighth bit is used for error detection as described later.

Several other codes are used for data communications. The most prominent is the Extended Binary Coded Decimal Interchange Code (EBCDIC), which is shown in Table 4-2. EBCDIC is an 8-bit code, allowing a full 256 characters to be encoded. It is used extensively in IBM applications.

Code compatibility between machines is essential. Because EBCDIC and ASCII are both widely used, code conversion will be required in some applications. Most intelligent terminals can be programmed for code conversion, but with nonprogrammable terminals, external provisions are necessary. This can be a separate code converter or a value-added function of the network.

Data Communications Speeds

Speeds in data communications are measured in bits per second (b/s) or some multiple: kilobits (kb/s), megabits (Mb/s), gigabits (Gb/s), terabits (Tb/s), and so on. Early data applications were limited by the speed at which an operator could type or toggle a telegraph key. When punched paper-tape teletypewriters were developed, the operator could type offline, and then send at the full speed of the device. Teletypewriters using the baudot code around the time of World War II ran at 60 words per minute, which was roughly 30 b/s. Today, backbone circuits on the Internet routinely run at speeds up to 10 Gb/s.

TABLE 4-1

American Standard Code for Information Interchange (ASCII)

$b_7\, b_6\, b_5$ $b_4\, b_3\, b_2\, b_1$	000	001	010	011	100	101	110	111
0000	NUL	DLE	SP	0	@	P	`	p
0001	SOH	DC1	!	1	A	Q	a	q
0010	STX	DC2		2	B	R	b	r
0011	ETX	DC3	#	3	C	S	c	s
0100	EOT	DC4	$	4	D	T	d	t
0101	ENQ	NAK	%	5	E	U	e	u
0110	ACK	SYN	&	6	F	V	f	v
0111	BEL	ETB	'	7	G	W	g	w
1000	BS	CAN	(	8	H	X	h	x
1001	HT	EM	)	9	I	Y	i	y
1010	LF	SUB	*	:	J	Z	j	z
1011	VT	ESC	+	;	K	[	k	{
1100	FF	FS	,	<	L	\	l		
1101	CR	GS	-	=	M	]	m	}
1110	SO	RS	.	>	N	^	n	~
1111	SI	US	/	?	O	_	o	DEL

Where data communications are carried over a voice-grade telephone line, the bandwidth of the voice channel limits the speed. The bandwidth of a voice channel is 300 to 3300 hertz (Hz). With sophisticated modems operating under ideal conditions, a voice-grade line may support up to 56 kb/s. In practice, the bandwidths achieved are usually lower. Where wider bandwidths are required, special service or digital circuits must be obtained over private facilities or through common carrier tariffs.

Two terms used to express the data-carrying capacity of a circuit are *bit rate* and *baud rate*. Bit rate and baud rate are often used interchangeably, but to do so is not technically accurate. The bit rate of a channel is the number of bits per second the channel can carry. For example, with complex modulation schemes, a voice-grade channel may carry up to 56 kb/s provided one end of the connection is digital and both ends are using the V.90 modem protocol. The baud rate of a channel describes the number of cycles or symbols per second the channel can handle. The 3000-Hz bandwidth of a voice channel can pass a 2400-baud signal with the extra bandwidth used for guard bands between signals. If the data is encoded at 1 bit/Hz, the channel is limited to 2400 b/s. Higher bit rates are transmitted by encoding more than 1 bit/Hz. A 19,200-b/s signal can be carried on a voice-grade channel, for example, by encoding 8 bits/Hz. The latest versions of high-speed modems using the V.90 modulation method use higher baud rates, which will work on some, but not all voice channels, depending on the total bandwidth available and the absence of impairments.

TABLE 4-2

Extended Binary Coded Decimal Interchange Code (EBCDIC)

Bits 8765 ↓ \ 4321 →	0000	0001	0010	0011	0100	0101	0110	0111	1000	1001	1010	1011	1100	1101	1110	1111
0000	NUL	SOH	STX	ETX	PF	HT	LC	DEL			SMM	VT	FF	CR	SO	SI
0001	DLE	DC1	DC2	DC3	RES	NL	BS	IL	CAN	EM	CC		IFS	IGS	IRS	IUS
0010	DS	SOS	FS		BYP	LF	EOB	PRE			SM			ENQ	ACK	BEL
0011			SYN		PN	RS	UC	EOT					DC4	NAK		SUB
0100	SP										¢	.	<	(	+	¦
0101	&										!	$	*	)	;	¬
0110	-	/									¦	,	%	_	>	?
0111											:	#	@	'	=	"
1000		a	b	c	d	e	f	g	h	i						
1001		j	k	l	m	n	o	p	q	r						
1010			s	t	u	v	w	x	y	z						
1011																
1100		A	B	C	D	E	F	G	H	I						
1101		J	K	L	M	N	O	P	Q	R						
1110			S	T	U	V	W	X	Y	Z						
1111	0	1	2	3	4	5	6	7	8	9						

PF Punch Off
HT Horizontal Tab
LC Lower Case
DEL Delete
SP Space

PN Punch On
EOT End of Transmission
BYP Bypass
LF Line Feed
EOB End of Block

UC Upper Case
RES Restore
NL New Line
BS Backspace
IL Idle

PRE Prefix (ESC)
RS Reader Stop
SM Start Message
Others Same as ASCII

F I G U R E 4-3

Data Modulation Methods

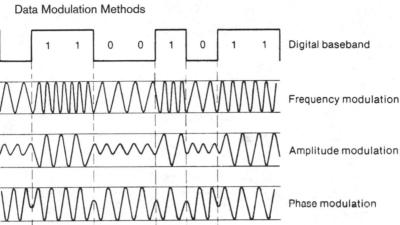

Modulation Methods

A data signal leaves the serial interface of the DTE as a series of *baseband* voltage pulses, as Figure 4-3 shows. Baseband means that the varying voltage level from the DTE is impressed without modulation directly on the transmission medium. Baseband pulses can be transmitted over limited distances from the serial interface or over longer distances by using a *limited distance modem* or a *line driver* that matches the serial interface to the cable.

For transmission over voice-grade channels, a modem modulates the pulses into a combination of analog tones and amplitude and phase changes that fits within the passband of the channel. The digital signal modulates the *frequency*, the *amplitude*, or the *phase* of an audio signal, as Figure 4-3 shows. Amplitude modulation by itself is the least used method because it is susceptible to noise-generated errors. It is frequently used, however, in conjunction with frequency and phase changes. Frequency modulation is an inexpensive method used with low-speed modems. To reach speeds of more than 300 b/s, phase-shift modems are employed.

Quadrature Amplitude Modulation

Modems use increasingly complex modulation methods for encoding multiple bits per hertz to reach speeds approaching the theoretical limit of a voice-grade circuit. Since an analog channel is nominally limited to 2400 baud, or symbols per second, to send 9600 b/s, for example, 4 bits/Hz must be encoded. The resulting 2^4 encoding yields a total of 16 combinations that each symbol can represent. High-speed modems use *quadrature amplitude modulation* (QAM) to send multiple bits per hertz. In QAM two carrier tones combine in quadrature to produce the modem's output signal. The receiving end demodulates the quadrature signal to recover the transmitted signal. Each symbol carries one of 16 signal combinations. As Figure 4-4

FIGURE 4-4

Signal Constellation in a 16-Bit (2^4) Quadrature Amplitude-Modulated Signal

Corresponding Plot Points

Possible Signal
Combinations

0000
0001
0010
0011
0100
0101
0110
0111
1000
1001
1010
1011
1100
1101
1110
1111

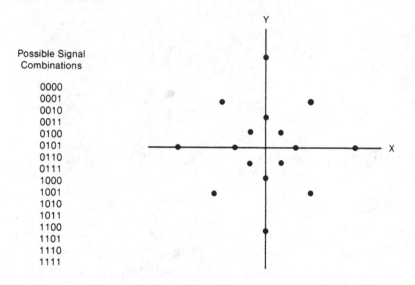

shows, any combination of 4 bits can be encoded into a particular pair of X-Y plot points, which represent a phase and amplitude combination. This combination modulates the carrier signals. This two-dimensional diagram is called a *signal constellation*.

The receiving modem demodulates the signal to determine what pair of X-Y coordinates was transmitted, and the 4-bit signal combination passes from the modem to the DTE. If line noise or phase jitter affects the signal, the received point will be displaced from its ideal location, so the modem must make a best guess about which plot point was transmitted. If the signal is displaced far enough, the receiver makes the wrong guess, and the resulting signal is in error.

Even higher rates can be modulated, with each additional bit doubling the number of signal points. A 64-QAM signal encodes 2^6 bits per symbol, and a 128-QAM signal results in 2^7 combinations, bringing the signal points closer together and increasing the susceptibility of the modem to impairments. As discussed later, the performance of the modem can be improved by using forward error correction to process the incoming bit stream.

Trellis-Coded Modulation

Trellis-coded modulation (TCM) is a more reliable method of encoding data signals. In a 14,400-b/s modem, for example, data is presented to a TCM modulator in 6-bit groups. Two of the 6 bits are separated from the signal, and a code bit is added. The resulting signal is two groups, one 3-bit and one 4-bit. These are combined, and the resulting 2^7 bits are mapped into a signal point and selected from a 128-point signal constellation. Since only 6 of the 7 bits are required to transmit the original signal, not all the 128 points are needed to transmit the signal, and only certain patterns of signal points are defined as valid. If a line impairment results in an invalid pattern at the receiver, the decoder selects the most likely valid sequence and forwards it to the DTE. TCM reduces the signal's susceptibility to line impairments, but, as discussed later, some means of correcting errors must be added to the session.

Full- and Half-Duplex Mode

Full-duplex data systems transmit data in both directions simultaneously. *Half-duplex systems* transmit in only one direction at a time; the channel reverses for transmission in the other direction.

Full-duplex circuits use separate transmit and receive paths on a *four-wire* circuit, or a *split-channel modem* on a *two-wire* circuit. Two- and four-wire circuits refer to the type of facility that the local and interexchange carriers furnish. In the interexchange portion circuits are inherently four-wire, and the two directions of transmission travel over separate paths. It is possible, however, to lease two-wire local loops, in which case the two directions of transmission must be combined in a single path for transmission and reception.

Split-channel modems provide the equivalent of four-wire operation by dividing the voice channel into two segments, one for transmit and one for receive. The 2400-baud bandwidth of a channel limits a full-duplex modem to 1200 b/s in each direction when straight frequency modulation is used. Modems with more sophisticated modulation are available at higher cost to provide 2400-b/s full-duplex communication over two-wire circuits using the ITU V.22 *bis* modulation method, 9600 b/s using V.32, 14,400 b/s with V.32 *bis*, 33,600 b/s with V.34 modulation, and 56 kb/s with V.90 modulation.

Synchronizing Methods

All data communications channels require synchronization to keep the sending and receiving ends in step. The signal on a baseband data communications channel is a series of rapid voltage changes, and synchronization enables the receiving terminal to determine which pulse is the first bit in a character.

The simplest synchronizing method is *asynchronous,* sometimes called stop-start synchronization. Asynchronous signals, illustrated in Figure 4-5, are in the one or *mark* state when no characters are being transmitted. A character begins with a start bit at the zero or *space* level followed by 8 data bits and a stop bit at the one level. The terms mark and space are carried over from telegraphy, where current flowed in the line to a teletypewriter to hold it closed when it was not receiving characters. Current loop lines have largely disappeared from public

FIGURE 4-5

Asynchronous Data Transmission

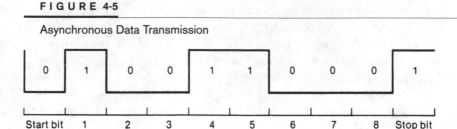

FIGURE 4-6

Synchronous Data Transmission (IBM SDLC Frame)

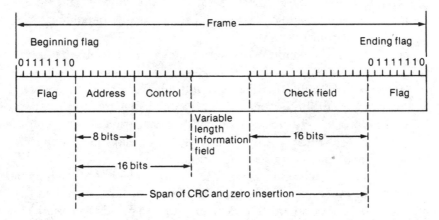

networks because they generate noise. Some asynchronous terminals, however, op-·erate in a current loop state because their range is greater than the range of EIA serial interfaces.

Asynchronous signals are transmitted in a character mode; that is, each character is individually synchronized. The chief drawback of asynchronous communication is the extra 2 bits/byte that carry no information. These noninformation bits are called *overhead*.

To reduce the amount of overhead, data can be transferred in a *synchronous* mode, as illustrated in Figure 4-6. Synchronous data is sent in a block mode with information characters sandwiched between header and trailer records. The header and trailer contain the overhead bits; the information bits are transferred in multiples of 8 bits. A clock signal that the modem extracts from the incoming bit stream keeps the two devices in synchronization.

The drawbacks of synchronous signals are their complexity and their lack of standardization. Variables in the data block, such as block length, error-checking routine, and structure of the header and trailer records, are functions of the protocol. *Protocols*, which are discussed in the next chapter, are handshaking signals that devices go through to establish their readiness and ability to communicate.

Although many protocols are standard, such as high-level data link control (HDLC) recommended by ITU, many data manufacturers have proprietary and incompatible protocols.

Whereas asynchronous data terminals can communicate with each other if the speed, code, and error-checking conventions are identical, synchronous terminals require protocol compatibility and intelligence in the DTE or terminal controller. Synchronous data communications systems have offsetting advantages of greater throughput and the ability to use sophisticated error-correction techniques that are not compatible with the character mode of transmission.

Error Detection and Correction

Errors occur in all data communications circuits. Where the transmission is text that people will interpret, a few errors can be tolerated because the meaning can be derived from context. In many applications, such as those involving transmission of bank balances, computer programs, and other numerical data, errors can have catastrophic effects. In these applications nothing short of complete accuracy is acceptable. This section discusses causes, detection, and correction of data communications errors.

Causes of Data Errors

The type of transmission medium and the modulation method have the greatest effect on the error rate. Any transmission medium using analog modulation techniques is subject to external noise, which affects the amplitude of the signal. Atmospheric conditions, such as lightning, that cause static bursts can induce noise into data-carrying analog radio and carrier systems. Relay and switch operations in electromechanical central offices, switching to standby channels in microwave, fiber optics, and carrier systems all cause momentary interruptions that result in data errors. Changes in the phase of the received signal, which can be caused by instability in carrier supplies or radio systems, also can cause errors because the modem is incapable of determining accurately which of many possible signal patterns was transmitted.

Any communications circuit is subject to errors during maintenance actions and external damage or interruption by vandalism. Even local networks within a single building are subject to occasional interruptions due to equipment failure or human error. Whatever the causes, errors are a fact of life in data circuits. The best error mitigation program is a design that reduces the susceptibility of the service to errors. Following that, the next most important consideration is to design the application to detect and correct the errors.

Parity Checking

The simplest way of detecting errors is *parity checking*, or *vertical redundancy checking* (VRC), a technique used on asynchronous circuits. In the ASCII code set, the

FIGURE 4-7

Character Parity

	BIT 8	BIT 7	BIT 6	BIT 5	BIT 4	BIT 3	BIT 2	BIT 1
ASCII a		1	1	0	0	0	0	1
Even Parity	1	1	1	0	0	0	0	1
Odd Parity	0	1	1	0	0	0	0	1

eighth bit is reserved for parity. Parity is set as odd or even, referring to the number of 1 bits in the character. As Figure 4-7 shows, DTE adds an extra bit, if necessary, to cause each character to match the parity established for the network.

Most asynchronous terminals can be set to send and receive odd, even, or no parity. When a parity error occurs, the terminal registers some form of alarm. Parity has two drawbacks: there is no way to tell what the original character should have been, and worse, if an even number of errors occurs, parity checking will not detect the error at all. Therefore, parity is useful only for showing that an error occurred; it is ineffective when transmission accuracy is required.

In terminals operating at 300 or 1200 b/s or more, characters arrive so fast that it is difficult to determine which character was in error when the parity alarm was registered. DTE can be programmed to flag an error character by substituting a special character, such as an ampersand, in its place. The error can be corrected by communication with the sending end. In today's data networks, parity is of little value, and is turned off in many networks.

Echo Checking

Over full-duplex circuits, errors can be detected by programming the receiving device to echo the received characters to the sending end. This technique, called *echo checking*, is suitable for detecting errors in some forms of text. It is, however, subject to all the drawbacks of proofreading; it is far from infallible. Besides, an error in an echoed character is as likely to have occurred on the return trip as in the original transmission so the receiver may have the correct character but the transmitter believes it was received in error. At 300 b/s, a reader can keep up with echoed characters, but with machine transmission at 1200 b/s or more it is impossible to read with any degree of reliability. The DTE can be programmed to make the echo check automatically, but correcting errors is just as difficult as with parity. Echo checking is widely used in asynchronous computer and terminal combinations.

Most dial-up modems in use today have built-in error correction using the V.42 error-correction standard. File transfers over dial-up lines also use error-correcting protocols to ensure data integrity. Several protocols such as X-modem, Kermit, and so on are widely supported by telecommunications programs and value-added carriers for end-to-end error correction. These protocols operate on an *automatic repeat request* (ARQ) much the same as synchronous error-correcting protocols, which are described in the next section. Most popular telecommunications software packages support one or more of these protocols. They are required for transfers of binary files and are easy to use; the user specifies the file to be up- or downloaded. The protocol automatically takes care of the transfer, signaling the user when the transfer is completed. The need for error-correcting protocols has almost been eliminated by the use of graphical user interfaces that allow the user to drag and drop files across a network or attach them to an e-mail message.

Cyclical Redundancy Checking

Most synchronous data networks use cyclical redundancy checking (CRC). All the characters in a data frame are processed against a complex polynomial that always results in a remainder. The 16-bit remainder is entered in an error check block that is transmitted following the data block. The synchronous frame illustrated in Figure 4-6 contains a CRC field in the trailer record.

At the receiving end, the frame is processed against the same polynomial to create another CRC field. If the locally created CRC field fails to match the field received in the frame, the protocol causes the block to be retransmitted. The probability of an uncorrected error with CRC is so slight that it can be considered error-free. Synchronous data-link protocols acknowledge which frames have been received correctly through a process that is described later. If a frame is not acknowledged, the sending end retransmits it.

When a frame is received in error, it makes no difference how many bit errors were received; the entire frame must be retransmitted. Therefore, the block error rate (BLER) is the best measure of the quality of a data link. BLER is calculated by dividing the number of errored blocks or frames received over a period of time by the total number of blocks transmitted. A device, such as a front-end processor or a protocol analyzer, can compute BLER.

Forward Error Correction

When the BLER of a circuit is excessive, *throughput,* which is the number of information bits correctly transferred per unit of time, may be reduced to an unacceptable level. The error rate can be reduced by a technique known as *forward error correction* (FEC). In FEC systems, an encoder on the transmitting end processes the incoming signal and generates redundant code bits. The transmitted signal contains both the original information bits and the additional bits. At the receiving end, the redundant bits are regenerated from the information bits and compared with the redundant bits that were received. When a discrepancy occurs, the FEC circuitry on the receiving end uses the redundant bits to generate the most likely bit combination and passes it to the DTE. Although FEC is not infallible, it reduces the block error rate and the number of retransmissions.

Throughput

One critical measure of a data communications circuit is its throughput, or the number of information bits correctly transferred per unit of time. Although it would be theoretically possible for the throughput of a data channel to approach its maximum bit rate, in practice this can never be realized because of overhead bits and the retransmission of errored frames. The primary factors that limit the throughput of a data channel are as follows:

◆ *Modem speed.* Within a single voice channel, modems at speeds up to 56 kb/s can be accommodated.

◆ *Half- or full-duplex mode of operation.* With other factors equal on a private line circuit, full-duplex circuits have greater throughput because the modems do not have to reverse between transmitting and receiving.

◆ *Circuit error rate.* The higher the error rate, the lower the throughput.

◆ *Protocol.* Protocol includes the quantity of overhead bits and method of error handling such as selective retransmission or "go back N," which are discussed later.

◆ *Overhead bits.* Overhead bits include start and stop bits, error checking, and forward error correction bits.

◆ *Size of data block.* The shorter the data block, the more significant the overhead as a percentage of information bits. When the data block is too long, each error requires retransmitting considerable data. The proper block length is a balance between time consumed in overhead and in error retransmission.

◆ *Propagation speed of the transmission medium.*

The throughput of a data channel is optimized by reaching a balance between these variables using complex formulas.

DATA NETWORK FACILITIES

A *facility* is the generic term used to describe the combination of local loops and long-haul circuits that support communications. For data applications that require nearly full-time use of a channel between fixed points, dedicated, or private line, facilities are the most economical. Many applications, however, require switching because they transmit data between multiple points or send only a few short messages each day.

The variety of data communications applications means that no single facility type is universally suitable. For example, the following types of applications illustrate the need for a variety of facilities:

◆ *Interconnected local area networks.* Nearly every office worker today has a desktop computer, and most of these are connected to a LAN. Multilocation companies interconnect their LANs so users can easily share files, use e-mail, and access public networks such as the Internet.

◆ *Automatic teller machines.* These devices are available in nearly all banks and in many public locations such as shopping centers and airports. They demand perfect transmission, high security, and rapid response. The transactions are short and even a heavily used machine makes use of only a fraction of the data-carrying capacity of a circuit.

◆ *Credit card verification.* Nearly every retail establishment has a credit card machine, and many of these verify each transaction. The applications vary from large department stores with dozens of terminals to small remote stores with a single seldom-used terminal. For the former a high-speed dedicated line is needed; for the latter a dial-up line is more cost-effective.

◆ *Single host that supports multilocation terminals.* This application is typical of many large businesses such as airlines, banks, and order bureaus that use a mainframe computer linked to terminals over wide area networks. Since input is from a keyboard, the data rate is limited to typing speed, yet near-instantaneous communication is required. This application requires a network of shared lines to reduce circuit costs.

◆ *Point-of-sale terminals.* Large department stores with multiple locations are typical of this application. Data is transmitted at high speed, but each terminal is used only a fraction of the time. High security and perfect accuracy are essential.

◆ *Electronic mail.* Several nationwide carriers, such as AT&T and MCI, offer electronic mail services to the public. The messages can originate from, and be retrieved from, any residence or business in the nation. The dial-up telephone network is the most practical facility to support this kind of application except for large users who need a real-time connection.

◆ *Surfing the World Wide Web.* Web communications are usually asymmetric with a small upstream request from the user to the Web that results in a large downstream response. Asymmetric facilities such as ADSL are ideal.

Private line networks can be provided over all-digital facilities, but for the next several years most dial-up data communications will be handled over analog voice facilities. ISDN facilities are available in most locations, but their additional expense has led most users to stay with analog. Many applications do not use the full capacity of a circuit, so the only economical way they can be implemented is by sharing the capacity of the circuit. Generally, the facilities they share can be classed as one of seven types: point-to-point, multidrop, circuit-switched, message-switched, packet-switched, frame-switched, or cell-switched. These are explained briefly here, and are discussed in more detail in later chapters.

FIGURE 4-8

Point-to-Point Circuits

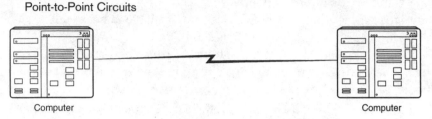

a. Computers directly connected with a point-to-point circuit

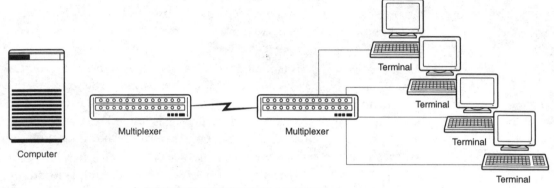

b. Point-to-point circuit shared with a multiplexer

Point-to-Point Circuits

A *point-to-point circuit*, shown in Figure 4-8, is directly wired between the stations on the network. Point-to-point circuits are cost-effective for high-speed communications between two processors but are expensive for most keyboard applications. For slower or keyboard-driven applications, the circuit capacity can be shared by subdividing it with a *multiplexer*, which is discussed later. Figure 4-8*b* shows the configuration of a multiplexer used for sharing a circuit.

Low-speed point-to-point voice-grade circuits are known in the industry as 3002 circuits, following the nomenclature used in AT&T and LEC tariffs. Voice-grade analog circuits can carry data from the slowest speed up to 19.2 kb/s. Higher speeds may be possible, but probably won't be guaranteed by the carrier. With data compression, even greater speeds can be carried if the data is not already compressed by the application. Digital circuits can carry data at 2.4, 4.8, 9.6, 19.2, 56, and 64 kb/s. Digital circuits are not technically voice-grade, but they can be used to carry either voice or data.

Multidrop Circuits

The simplest point-to-point circuits connect directly between two stations that share exclusive access to the circuit. More complex configurations are *multidrop cir-*

FIGURE 4-9

A Polled Multidrop Circuit

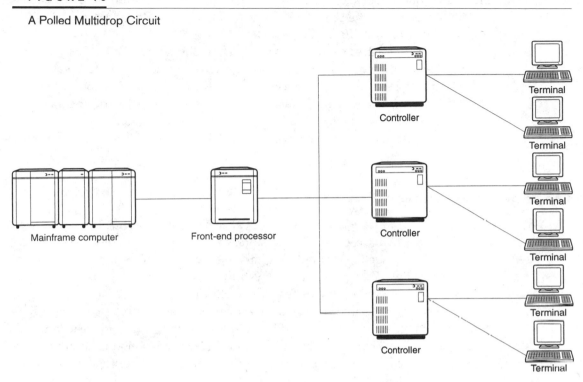

cuits, as shown in Figure 4-9, in which a station can transmit only when polled. The host computer or an attached unit called a *front-end processor* does the polling. The processor sends a polling message to each station in turn. If the station has traffic, it sends it. Otherwise, it responds negatively. The central unit also sends output messages to the remote stations.

The intelligence to respond to polling messages is sometimes built directly into the terminal. In other configurations the terminals connect through a controller. A polling system keeps circuits fully utilized. Much circuit time is consumed with polling messages and negative responses, however, and these messages, which add to the overhead, do not contribute to information flow. In a widely distributed network, where no single station takes up more than a fraction of the circuit time, a multidrop circuit is an effective way of sharing capacity. Automatic teller machines often use this type of circuit.

Circuit Switching

In a circuit-switched network, a central switch is connected to stations in a star configuration. Communication is between the stations and the switch, or the switch establishes circuits between two or more stations. The stations signal the switch to set up the connection, and when the stations have sent their traffic, they signal the switch to disconnect the circuit. The switch can be a data PBX, a voice/data PBX, or a telephone central office.

In circuit-switched networks, the circuits to the stations (called *loops*) are not fully utilized. When the circuits are short, the cost of idle time is acceptable, but with long circuits costs may be excessive if usage is light. Utilization can be improved by using a hierarchical network. In a hierarchical network, the switch is placed close to the stations so the circuits can be short and less costly. The more costly long circuits between the switches (called *intermachine trunks*) are engineered for a higher occupancy rate.

Message Switching

Message switching networks are sometimes called *store-and-forward*. Stations home in on a computer that accepts messages, stores them, and delivers them to their destination. The storage turnaround time can be either immediate for interactive applications or the message may be delayed for forwarding when circuits are idle, rates are lower, or a busy device becomes available.

In its earliest form, message switching existed as a torn tape system. Teletypewriter messages were punched into paper tape by a perforator. The tape was torn at the end of the message and transmitted over another circuit, sometimes after being clipped to the wall and stored for a time. Magnetic storage media made paper-tape systems obsolete, but the principle remains of receiving messages, formatting them, storing them (if only for an instant), and forwarding them to another location. Message switches route and queue messages, clearing them to their destinations at the scheduled delivery times according to the priority the sender establishes.

Store-and-forward networks include private networks and both domestic and international Telex. Access may be through public value-added networks, such as MCI Mail, AT&T Mail, or electronic mail offered by one of the online services such as CompuServe or America Online. Most networks offer speed and code conversion and may also offer protocol conversion.

Packet Switching

A *packet-switched network* has control nodes that host the stations, as Figure 4-10 shows. In a packet network, nodes are interconnected by sufficient trunks to support the traffic load. Data travels from the station to the node in *packets,* which are data frames with additional header records appended. The node moves the packet toward its destination by handing it off to the next node in the chain. Nodes are controlled by software, with algorithms that handle congestion and determine the route to the next station. In contrast to a circuit-switched network, where circuits are physically switched between stations, a packet-switched network establishes *virtual*

FIGURE 4-10

A Packet-Switched Network

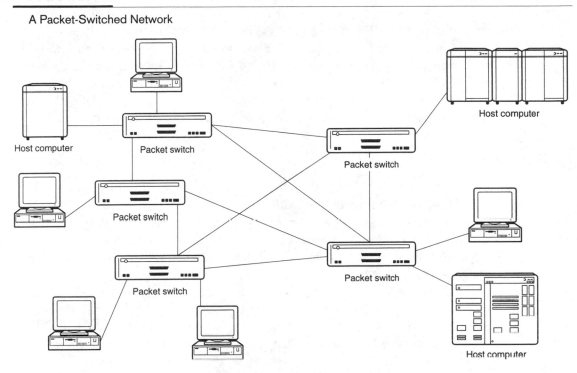

circuits between stations. A virtual circuit is one that appears to the user as if it exists, but it exists only as a defined path through a shared facility. Virtual circuits are of two types. In a *permanent virtual circuit* mode, the routing between stations is fixed and packets always take the same route. In a *switched virtual circuit* mode, the routing is determined with each packet.

Frame Relay

The architecture of a frame relay network is similar to a packet switching network, but with some significant differences. Packet networks were designed in the 1970s when the network was largely analog and error rates were high. Frame relay networks were designed in the late 1980s when digital networks operating over fiber-optic facilities were common. Where a packet network checks for errors between each pair of nodes, frame relay networks do not check for errors. Instead, it is up to the end devices to check for and correct errors. As we will discuss in the next chapter, a frame is a lower protocol level than a packet, and imposes less overhead on the network.

The method of charging on frame relay networks is also different. Packet networks typically base their charges on kilopackets transmitted. Frame relay network costs are not usage-sensitive. Instead, the cost of the network is based on the cost of the access circuit, the speed of the access port, and the committed information rate (CIR) of carrying data between stations. The CIR is the mini-mum rate the network guarantees to carry. It allows the information rate to burst up to the speed of the access port if capacity is available.

A user could, for example, purchase a 64-kb/s access circuit and port, but choose a lower CIR, such as 16 kb/s. The network would guarantee to carry at least 16 kb/s. If capacity was available, the network would carry data up to 64 kb/s. If capacity was not available, the network can mark frames as discard-eligible, carry them if capacity permits, but discard them to prevent overload.

Cell Relay

Cell relay, the most significant example of which is asynchronous transfer mode (ATM), is a combination multiplexing and switching protocol. The architecture of the network is similar to a packet network except the nodes are high-speed switch-ing devices instead of packet store-and-forward devices. Data is sliced into short cells, 48 bytes in ATM, and forwarded across the network with a short header, which is 5 bytes in ATM.

ATM is used in both private and public networks. Unlike other data pro-tocols, cell relay is designed to be used in both voice and data networks. It is used in *broadband* networks, which are high-speed networks used for multime-dia applications including imaging, voice, data, video, and other bandwidth-consuming applications.

DATA COMMUNICATIONS EQUIPMENT

An effective data communications network is a compromise involving many vari-ables. The nature of data transmission varies so greatly with the application that designs are often empirically determined. The network designer arrives at the most economical balance of performance and cost, evaluating equipment alterna-tives as discussed in this section.

Terminals

Terminals can be grouped into three classes—dumb, smart, and intelligent. They are also categorized as synchronous and asynchronous or ASCII terminals. This section discusses the characteristics of terminals and how they differ.

Dumb Terminals

Dumb terminals are so called because they have no processing power. They are not addressable and, therefore, cannot respond to polling messages. They have no error-correcting capability and so are most often located near the host computer, or they operate behind a controller or multiplexer that has addressing and error-correction capability.

Smart Terminals

Smart terminals are nonprogrammable devices, but they are capable of addressing and can be used on a multidrop line. Unlike asynchronous terminals that transmit one character at a time, smart terminals can often store data in a buffer and transmit in block mode. In block mode the terminal can detect errors and, through an ARQ process, retransmit errored blocks. A smart terminal contains only limited processing capability. For example, it may have limited editing capability, but it relies on the host for processing.

Intelligent Terminals

An intelligent terminal contains its own processor and can run application programs. The most common type of intelligent terminal is the personal computer (PC), although PCs do not always operate in intelligent terminal mode.

An intelligent terminal, being capable of running application programs on its own, provides better line utilization than dumb and smart terminals. Certain tasks can be delegated from the host to the terminal, which reduces the amount of data that flows between the two. It is important to note that some kind of communications software must run in an intelligent terminal. By changing applications software, the operator can function with different applications on the host.

Terminal Emulation

As the prices of desktop computers have fallen over the past few years, many companies have replaced terminals with desktop computers. Depending on the application program running on the computer, it can emulate any of the three classes of terminal.

Since a serial (EIA-232) port is a standard feature of most desktop computers, it is simple for a computer to emulate an asynchronous terminal. Telecommunications software ranges in features from simple dumb terminal emulation to full-featured intelligent terminal applications. In the latter category, a desktop computer can upload and download files from and to its own disk, select and search for files on the host, and even interact with the host without a human attendant.

Interaction with a synchronous host is considerably more complex. Not only is the protocol specialized and more difficult to implement, the physical interface is likely to be something other than EIA-232; coaxial cable and twinax are common. In such a case, terminal emulation requires placing an interface board in a desktop computer's expansion slot and running emulation software in the computer. Emulation boards and software are available for most of the popular synchronous protocols such as IBM's Synchronous Data Link Control (SDLC).

Modems

Since the early 1980s, modems have undergone a striking evolution. To discuss modems, it is useful to classify them as dial-up and private line. In the latter category,

FIGURE 4-11

ITU-T V.35, EIA-449, and EIA-232 Interfaces

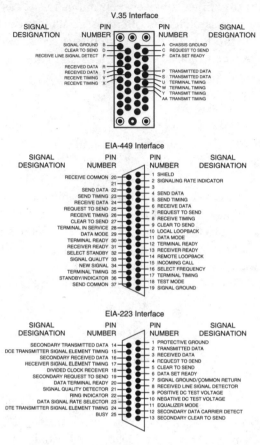

V.35 Interface

SIGNAL DESIGNATION	PIN NUMBER		PIN NUMBER	SIGNAL DESIGNATION
SIGNAL GROUND	B		A	CHASSIS GROUND
CLEAR TO SEND	D		C	REQUEST TO SEND
RECEIVE LINE SIGNAL DETECT	F		F	DATA SET READY
RECEIVED DATA	R		P	TRANSMITTED DATA
RECEIVED DATA	T		S	TRANSMITTED DATA
RECEIVE TIMING	V		U	TERMINAL TIMING
RECEIVE TIMING	X		W	TERMINAL TIMING
			Y	TRANSMIT TIMING
			AA	TRANSMIT TIMING

EIA-449 Interface

SIGNAL DESIGNATION	PIN NUMBER		PIN NUMBER	SIGNAL DESIGNATION
RECEIVE COMMON	20		1	SHIELD
	21		2	SIGNALING RATE INDICATOR
			3	
SEND DATA	22		4	SEND DATA
SEND TIMING	23		5	SEND TIMING
RECEIVE DATA	24		6	RECEIVE DATA
REQUEST TO SEND	25		7	REQUEST TO SEND
RECEIVE TIMING	26		8	RECEIVE TIMING
CLEAR TO SEND	27		9	CLEAR TO SEND
TERMINAL IN SERVICE	28		10	LOCAL LOOPBACK
DATA MODE	29		11	DATA MODE
TERMINAL READY	30		12	TERMINAL READY
RECEIVER READY	31		13	RECEIVER READY
SELECT STANDBY	32		14	REMOTE LOOPBACK
SIGNAL QUALITY	33		15	INCOMING CALL
NEW SIGNAL	34		16	SELECT FREQUENCY
TERMINAL TIMING	35		17	TERMINAL TIMING
STANDBY/INDICATOR	36		18	TEST MODE
SEND COMMON	37		19	SIGNAL GROUND

EIA-223 Interface

SIGNAL DESIGNATION	PIN NUMBER		PIN NUMBER	SIGNAL DESIGNATION
SECONDARY TRANSMITTED DATA	14		1	PROTECTIVE GROUND
DCE TRANSMITTER SIGNAL ELEMENT TIMING	15		2	TRANSMITTED DATA
SECONDARY RECEIVED DATA	16		3	RECEIVED DATA
RECEIVER SIGNAL ELEMENT TIMING	17		4	REQUEST TO SEND
DIVIDED CLOCK RECEIVER	18		5	CLEAR TO SEND
SECONDARY REQUEST TO SEND	19		6	DATA SET READY
DATA TERMINAL READY	20		7	SIGNAL GROUND/COMMON RETURN
SIGNAL QUALITY DETECTOR	21		8	RECEIVED LINE SIGNAL DETECTOR
RING INDICATOR	22		9	POSITIVE DC TEST VOLTAGE
DATA SIGNAL RATE SELECTOR	23		10	NEGATIVE DC TEST VOLTAGE
DTE TRANSMITTER SIGNAL ELEMENT TIMING	24		11	EQUALIZER MODE
BUSY	25		12	SECONDARY DATA CARRIER DETECT
			13	SECONDARY CLEAR TO SEND

there is risk of incompatibility between modems of different manufacture, although today most modems are built to ITU standards. In the dial-up category, modems have almost become a commodity, they are manufactured to international standards, and prices have dropped to a fraction of their former level.

The primary issues in selecting modems are the features and protocol to purchase. Proprietary modem standards have often been in effect, but with the approval of the new V.90 standard, almost any modem should be able to communicate with another. The interface between DTE and the modem is standardized in most countries, with the predominant interfaces being the EIA-232, EIA-449, and ITU V.35. Figure 4-11 illustrates these interfaces. EIA and ITU standards specify the functions of the interface circuits but do not specify the physical characteristics of the interface connector. Connectors have been adopted by convention; for example, the DB-25 connector has become a de facto standard for the EIA-232 interface. Not all the 25 pins of the DB-25 are necessary in most applications. Therefore, many manufacturers use fewer pins as a way of conserving chassis space. The DB-9, a 9-pin connector, has become common in personal computers. The physical connector is only a minor problem to users because units can be easily interconnected with adapters if they are electrically compatible.

Dial-Up Modems

Like other telecommunications products, modems have steadily become faster, cheaper, and smarter. The ready availability of inexpensive personal computers has expanded the demand for modems, and where a few years ago 9600-b/s modems were the state of the art, they are now obsolete. V.34 modems, which operate at 36,600 b/s, are a minimum standard, with V.90 modems becoming the norm.

The Hayes command set is a proprietary group of instructions that is effectively a de facto standard for communicating with a modem. The modem receives commands from the DTE preceded by the letters AT. The modem translates these into instructions to handle functions such as dialing a number and hanging up when the session ends. Matched with telecommunications software, dial-up modems enable users to upload and download files, converse with databases, access packet switching networks, exchange files, and perform other functions that once required a highly trained operator.

Dial-up modems either plug into a desktop computer expansion slot or are self-contained devices that plug into the computer's serial port. Most modems support the V.42 error-correction protocol and are, therefore, useful between devices that lack error-correction capability. Most modems also implement V.42 *bis* data compression, which, on V.34 modems may result in a data transfer rate approaching 100 kb/s.

The switched telephone network carries a considerable share of asynchronous data communication. Therefore, many modem features are designed to emulate a telephone set. The most sophisticated modems, in combination with a software package in an intelligent terminal, are capable of fully unattended operation. Modems designed for unattended, and many designed for attended, operation include these features:

- ◆ Dial-tone recognition
- ◆ Automatic tone and dial pulse dialing
- ◆ Monitoring call progress tones such as busy and reorder
- ◆ Automatic answer
- ◆ Call termination

Dial-up modems operate in a full-duplex mode. When two modems connect, they go through an elaborate exchange of signals to determine the features the other modem supports. Such features as error correction and compression are examined. High-speed modems test the line to determine the highest speed with which they can communicate.

The V.90 Standard

An ordinary telephone circuit is designed to support voice communications, and has inherent characteristics that limit its bandwidth. For years engineers believed that 33.6 kb/s was the maximum speed that a voice-grade circuit could carry. With the popularity of the Internet, companies began seeking ways to increase modem speeds. Engineers began reasoning that in virtually every telephone connection, most of the circuit is digital, and that only the local loop from the central office to the user's premise is analog.

As we will discuss in Chapter 5, every time a circuit undergoes an analog-to-digital conversion, a bit of the quality is lost. If the connection could be digital all the way, except for the loop on the modem user's end of the circuit, only one analog conversion would take place, and the majority of the connection would be digital. Several companies began experimenting with an approach to increase modem speed. Compatible modem protocols would be used at each end of the connection, but the portion of the circuit from the central office to the Internet service provider would be digital.

At first, different manufacturers developed competing protocols, but early in 1998 ITU-T approved the V.90 standard. Although 56 kb/s is possible, simply equipping both the user and the ISP with V.90 modems doesn't mean that it will always be achieved. Poor-quality phone lines and the presence of multiple analog-to-digital conversions will limit speed. Users who are unable to reach full speed with V.34 modems are not apt to achieve higher speeds with a V.90 modem. Note also that V.90 modems are asymmetric. They download at speeds up to 56 kb/s, but are limited to 33.6 kb/s in the upstream direction.

Private Line Modems

Like dial-up modems, private line modems have dropped in price and improved in functionality, but there is such a diversity of features that they have not reached commodity status, and probably never will. Analog private lines are rapidly becoming a thing of the past, and private line modems are replaced by their digital equivalents, so little additional development work is being conducted. Different manufacturers use proprietary formats to encode the signal, compress data, and more important, communicate network management information.

Private line modems can be classed as synchronous or asynchronous, as half- or full-duplex, and as two- or four-wire, with the latter being the most common. When synchronous modems are used at speeds above 4800 b/s, they may require *line conditioning* from the common carrier. Line conditioning is not available on the switched voice telephone network, but most manufacturers offer modems equipped with *adaptive equalization*, which is circuitry that automatically adjusts the modem to compensate for irregularities in the telephone channel. Adaptive equalization substitutes for line conditioning and enables the use of 9600 b/s or higher on a voice-grade private line.

Circuit throughput can be improved by using data compression, a system that replaces the original bit stream with a stream that has fewer bits. With data compression techniques and adaptive equalization, it is possible to operate at 19.2 kb/s or higher over nonconditioned voice-grade lines.

The following is a list of the most important features of private line modems. Not all manufacturers use these terms to describe their equivalent features.

Adaptable Inbound Rate   On multidrop circuits where the modems contain adaptive rate capability, one drop suffering from impairments can bring the speed of the entire line down to the speed of the worst-case drop. With adaptable inbound rate, each modem establishes its own rate with the host and transmits at the maximum supportable speed.

Adaptive Line Rate Capability   This feature enables a modem to sense line conditions and adjust its transmission speed to the maximum speed the line will support.

Fast Reversal   In half-duplex circuits, the modem flip-flops between send and receive. The time required to reverse itself is an important factor in determining throughput. A fast reversal modem minimizes turnaround time.

Internal Diagnostics   With this feature the modem automatically runs real-time diagnostics and displays information about its status. Some models also display the condition of the communications facility.

Loop-Around   Forcing the modem into a loop-back configuration can help a technician isolate line troubles. Most modems permit looping the analog and digital sides of the signal to isolate whether a problem is on the line, in the modem, or in the DTE.

MNP Error Control   The Microcom Network Protocol has become a widely accepted method of obtaining data integrity and data compression on asynchronous lines. Modems equipped with MNP monitor incoming data for errors and request retransmission of errored frames. This protocol is standardized as ITU-T V.42.

Modem-Sharing Capability   A modem-sharing unit separates the transmission line into two or more channels, providing multiple slow-speed channels without the use of a multiplexer. For example, a modem with a bandwidth of 9600 b/s could support four 2400-b/s channels.

Network Management   Many proprietary network management systems collect information from modems and other devices in real time. The modem provides a narrow channel for transmitting network management information, such as analog line parameters, back to the host for continuous line quality evaluation. With this capability, the network administrator or network management software can test, monitor, and reconfigure the modem from a central site.

Reverse Channel Capability   In half-duplex applications, it is sometimes desirable to send a small amount of information in the reverse direction. For example, it may be necessary to interrupt a transmission. Reverse channel capability provides a narrow band of frequencies for slow-speed operation in the reverse direction, while the forward direction transmits wider band data.

Signal Constellation Generator   The bit patterns of the modem's signal constellation are brought out to test points for monitoring with external test equipment.

Special-Purpose Modems

The market offers many modems that fulfill specialized requirements. This section discusses some of the equipment that is available.

Alarm-Reporting Modem   This class of modem has connections for dry alarm contacts from external devices. It may also monitor the ASCII bit stream of a channel looking for particular bit patterns. When these occur, the modem dials a predetermined number.

Digital Subscriber Line (DSL)   DSL devices transmit data over a standard analog subscriber line. In some applications, for example, asymmetric digital subscriber line (ADSL), voice and data are transmitted simultaneously on the same line.

Digital Simultaneous Voice and Data (DSVD)   This new technology enables PC users to share collaborative applications and voice conversation simultaneously over a single standard telephone line using a V.34/V.FC modem. The use of digital voice compression allows additional bandwidth for simultaneous data transmission.

Dial Backup Modems   A dial backup modem contains circuitry to restore a failed leased line over a dial-up line. The restoral may be automatically initiated on failure of the dedicated line. The modem may simulate four-wire private line over a single dial-up line, or two dial-up lines may be required.

Fiber-Optic Modems   Where noise and interference are a problem, fiber-optic modems can provide high bandwidth at a moderate cost. Operating over one fiber-optic pair, these modems couple directly to the fiber-optic cable.

Limited Distance Modems (LDM)   Many LECs offer limited distance circuits, which are essentially a bare nonloaded cable pair between two points within the same wire center. LDMs are inexpensive modems operating at speeds of up to 19.2 kb/s. Where LDM capability is available, the modems are significantly less expensive than long-haul 19.2-kb/s modems.

F I G U R E 4-12

Time Division Multiplexing

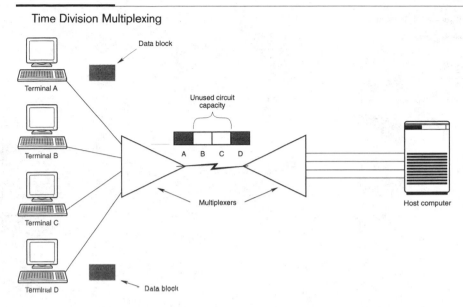

Data Service Unit/Channel Service Unit (DSU/CSU)

A DSU/CSU connects DTE to a digital circuit. It provides signal conditioning and testing points for digital circuits. For example, the bit stream out of a data device is generally a unipolar signal, which must be converted to a bipolar signal for transmission on a digital circuit. The CSU/DSU does the conversion, and also provides a loop-back point for the carrier to make out-of-service tests on the circuit. Operating at 56 and 64 kb/s, DSUs are full-duplex devices. They are available for both point-to-point and multidrop lines.

Multiplexers and Concentrators

Many data applications, by their nature, are incapable of fully using a data circuit. Rather than flowing in a steady stream, data usually flows in short bursts with idle periods intervening. To make use of this idle capacity, data *multiplexers* are employed to collect data from multiple stations and combine it into a single high-speed bit stream.

Data multiplexers are of two types, *time division multiplexers* (TDMs) and *statistical multiplexers* (statmux). In a TDM, each station is assigned a time slot, and the multiplexer collects data from each station in turn. If the station has no data to send, its time slot goes unused. TDM operation is illustrated in Figure 4-12.

A statmux, illustrated in Figure 4-13, makes use of the idle time periods in a data circuit by assigning time slots to pairs of stations according to the amount

FIGURE 4-13

Statistical Multiplexing

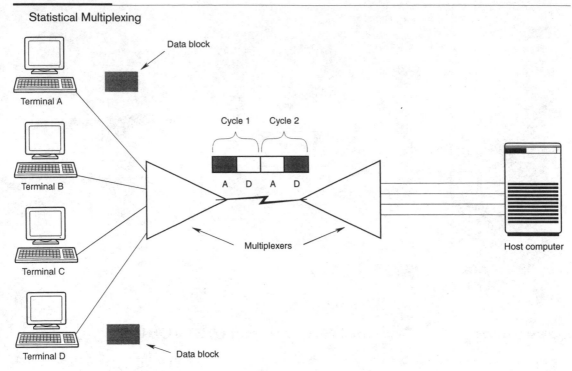

of traffic they have to send. The multiplexer collects data from the DTE and sends it to the distant end with the address of the receiving terminal.

Statistical multiplexers improve circuit utilization by minimizing idle time between transmissions. They are more costly than TDMs and must be monitored to prevent overloads, with stations added or removed to adjust the load to the maximum the circuit will handle while meeting response time objectives.

A *concentrator* is similar to a multiplexer, except that it is usually a single-ended device. At the terminal end, devices connect to the concentrator exactly as they would connect to a multiplexer, and the concentrator connects to the facility. At the host end, the facility is routed directly into the host or front-end processor. A concentrator matches the characteristics of the host processor.

The primary application for multiplexers is in data networks that use asynchronous terminals. Since many of these devices cannot be addressed and have no error-correction capability, they are of limited use by themselves in remote locations. The multiplexer provides end-to-end error checking and correction and circuit sharing to support multiple terminals. Although multiplexers are still available, they are being displaced by local area networks linked over digital circuits.

Multiplexer Features

Alternate Routing   Multiplexers with alternate routing capability can transmit data around network congestion and circuit failures.

Terminal-to-Host Mapping   With this feature, users can log onto a network and address any host. The multiplexers determine the route.

Network Management Capability   With this feature, a remote network management system can monitor the network through an interface into the multiplexers. It is possible to perform such functions as determining system status, changing port assignments, and diagnosing trouble.

Integrated CSU/DSU   Many multiplexers have a built-in CSU/DSU, which eliminates the need for a separate outboard device.

Packet Switching Equipment

Packet switching can be implemented on either public or private networks. A device known as a packet assembler/disassembler (PAD) creates the packets on the sending end and disassembles them at the receiver. The PAD accepts a data stream from the DTE and slices it into packets of a length that the network designer determines. The packets are handed off to a packet node, which terminates the circuits and routes packets to the destination. The nodes may be specialized computers or devices that closely resemble multiplexers. The interface between the PAD and the packet node is ITU X.25. The standard does not establish the protocol between nodes, so networks are assembled from nodes with proprietary routing protocols.

Packet networks are usually interconnected in a mesh configuration with at least two alternate routes for handing off traffic. The network uses one of several routing algorithms, which Chapter 34 discusses, to deliver packets to the next node. The transmission is checked for errors in each link and packets are sequenced and handed off to the PAD. The PAD disassembles received packets and presents the original bit stream to the receiving device.

A packet switching network is robust compared to other data communications facilities. Because of its alternate routing capability, the network can usually survive a link failure, although throughput may be diminished. The end-to-end transmission delay through a packet network is usually greater than through a multiplexer network because of the processing time required in each node. Packet networks were developed for a time when circuit error rates were high and speeds were low. With today's digital circuits, packet switching technology is giving way to techniques such as frame relay, which use routers or frame relay access devices. Some observers believe that packet switching in its present form will probably not survive long beyond the turn of the century.

Frame Relay Access Device

Many users employ routers to access frame relay networks. Routers are expensive compared to simple frame relay access devices (FRADs). The FRAD connects to a network, such as Ethernet, and conditions the frames for connection across the network. The primary difference between a FRAD and a router is that the FRAD is incapable of making routing decisions. Its purpose is simply to connect a network to a frame relay network, and not to make routing decisions.

Ancillary Equipment

This section discusses the ancillary equipment that is available on the market to aid the user in assembling unique applications.

Protocol Converters

When incompatible devices must be used on the same data network, it is often necessary to use a protocol converter. The most common conversion is between synchronous and asynchronous devices. For example, an ASCII to SDLC converter can be used to enable asynchronous terminals to function on an IBM network. Protocol converters to enable asynchronous and synchronous devices to communicate with X.25 networks are also available. Special types of protocol converters known as gateways are often used to interconnect incompatible networks. A gateway physically connects to each network and implements all the protocol functions of each, making the incompatibility transparent to the users. Gateways also enable local area networks to interface with host computers.

Dial Backup Units

Dial backup capability, which provides continuity of service if a dedicated line fails, is either contained in a modem or provided as a stand-alone device. A dial backup unit normally requires two dial lines to provide the equivalent of full-duplex private line capacity. The service may be established manually, or the dial backup unit may monitor the dedicated line and automatically switch with a short interruption in service when a failure occurs.

Multidrop Bridges

Multidrop circuits are established by *bridging* multiple point-to-point lines. A bridge terminates each line in its characteristic impedance and may provide amplification to make up for bridging losses. The LEC or IXC often provides bridging, but it also may be installed on the customer's premises. Customer premises bridging is effective when a network of T1/E1 private lines is available and in a campus environment where twisted-pair cable supports multiple controllers. It is important to understand that this type of bridge is different from bridges used in local area networks. A LAN bridge is used to extend the range of a network.

APPLICATIONS

Unlike voice applications, which usually can be handled by equipment vendors and common carriers with little participation by the customer, data applications require direct involvement of the manager. Few applications have a single design alternative. It is usually possible to design an array of solutions to any problem, with the principal trade-offs being ease of use, first cost, ongoing cost, maintainability, and survivability in case of failure. The manager needs a fully defined set of requirements and objectives to select the most effective alternative. This section discusses some important considerations in evaluating data communications services and equipment.

Standards

ANSI, EIA, and ITU are the principal standards agencies affecting data communications equipment used in the United States. Although much of the data communications equipment being manufactured today conforms to ITU standards, some older nonconforming equipment is in use. Many data communications systems operate under proprietary protocols such as IBM's Binary Synchronous Communication (BSC) and Synchronous Data Link Control (SDLC).

Evaluation Considerations

This section discusses considerations in evaluating the major items of data communications equipment. Some factors, including the following, are common to all classes of equipment:

- Compatibility with standards
- Compatibility with existing equipment
- Support of the manufacturer and its representatives
- Compatibility with network management systems

Evaluating Network Alternatives

The first question to ask in evaluating network facilities is whether the application requires a switched or dedicated circuit network. Circuit switching is advantageous where the simple addressing scheme and universal connectivity of the PSTN is required. Consider circuit switching whenever multiple short sessions to widely distributed terminal points are required. With switched virtual circuits available for ATM and frame relay, they may be a suitable substitute for circuit switching in some applications.

The application usually determines the type of network. If you are expanding an existing network, the choice is usually clear: continue to grow the network with an extension of existing services.

In a new network or when the existing network must be redesigned, the protocol used by the application may determine the shape of the network. Multidrop networks are feasible when the host computer uses a polling protocol and usage on the network is light. When usage is high, point-to-point circuits may be required. Host computers that use asynchronous terminals usually require point-to-point circuits and statistical multiplexers or connection to an X.25 network. Increasingly, Ethernet is used in lieu of serial ports on the host. If the computer is a member of a LAN, a router provides the interface to the LAN. Routers can be interconnected by point-to-point circuits, but when the circuit complexity grows, frame relay networks become cost-effective. If the bandwidth required is T1/E1 or less, frame relay is an obvious choice. ATM is often not feasible at bandwidths below T3/E3, but lower bandwidth implementations are effective for branch offices in an ATM network.

Message switching is used in some private networks. Most new applications will likely use one of the other alternatives as this technology becomes obsolete.

Evaluating Modems

The following are the most important considerations in choosing a modem.

Dial-Up versus Private Line   Although some modems are designed for both dial-up and private line uses, most models are designed for one or the other. Units that are designed for both are more expensive than single-purpose units.

Standards Compatibility   Most of today's modems conform to one or more ITU standards, older Bell standards, or both. An important consideration in standards compatibility is what form of data compression and error-correction capability the modem supports. ITU V.42 and V.42 *bis* standards provide error correction and compression.

Modem Reversal Time   Half-duplex modems require a finite time to reverse the line from send to receive. This variable is specified as turnaround time or RTS/CTS delay. Fast reversal modems have delay times of less than 10 ms. Other modems may have reversal times as high as 100 ms.

Modulation Method   The modulation method normally will be a function of the ITU or Bell compatibility specification if the modem conforms to one of those standards. Since nearly all dial-up modems conform to a standard, the modulation method depends on speed. Private line modems may follow a proprietary modulation scheme, but most will be phase-shift keying (PSK), quadrature amplitude modulation (QAM), or trellis-coded modulation (TCM).

Speed   Next to standards compatibility, speed is the primary factor in selecting a modem. Generally, the higher the speed, the higher the price. To save money, choose the lowest speed that meets response time and throughput requirements.

Operating Mode   Modems operate in either full- or half-duplex mode, synchronous or asynchronous. The application often drives the mode. For example, IBM's bisync protocol is inherently half-duplex synchronous. Dual-mode modems are available and are generally more expensive than single-mode modems.

Equalization Method   Most modems are equalized to match the characteristics of the transmission facility. Equalization is either fixed or adaptive. The latter is more expensive, but it may enable the modem to function over an unconditioned line, which saves recurring costs on leased circuits.

Diagnostic Capability   Most external modems display the status of the line and major signal leads on the front panel. More elaborate models display status information on alphanumeric readouts. The most elaborate private line modems include network management information that can be linked to a diagnostic center.

Evaluating Multiplexers and Concentrators

Multiplexers can be classified in several ways. First is the time division versus statistical multiplexer classification. Statistical multiplexers are divided into two classes, high-end multiplexers that support multiple lines and 30 or more ports and can wrap around line failures, and low-end units that simply permit multiple devices to share a single line. This section discusses evaluation considerations of multiplexers and concentrators.

Line Speed   Most multiplexers on the market can support 9600-b/s analog and digital lines. Higher speeds, including 19.2, 56, and 64 kb/s, are available. An important factor is whether the multiplexer can be upgraded to higher speeds by replacing a card.

Number and Speed of Ports Supported   The multiplexer must be evaluated based on the number of EIA input devices it can support. Also, the speed of the input ports is important. In some multiplexers, port contention permits multiple input devices to contend for access to a group of ports, which effectively increases the port capacity of the system.

Redundancy   High-end multiplexers have redundant power supplies and processors, which make them less vulnerable to equipment failures.

Protocol Support   Multiplexers usually support asynchronous devices. Some applications require support of other protocols such as SDLC and BSC. Some multiplexers support X.25 connections from packet assembler/disassemblers (PADs) and X.25 connections to a packet node.

Security   Multiplexers may require users to log in and enter a password, adding a second level of security to the host environment.

Network Management Capability   The multiplexer may be required to support a network management protocol such as SNMP (simplified network management protocol) to simplify the task of managing the network and its resources.

Evaluating Packet Switching Equipment

Evaluation considerations for packet switching equipment and multiplexers are equivalent. The factors discussed in the preceding section should be considered, plus these.

Absolute Delay   Absolute delay affects throughput. The more nodes a signal traverses, the greater the delay and the lower the throughput. A packet switch vendor should be able to quote the absolute delay through its packet switching equipment.

Access Method   Packet networks are accessed by one of three methods: dial-up to a PAD located on the vendor's premises, a dedicated circuit to a vendor-supplied PAD, or an X.25 connection from the user's PAD to the node. The link between the user's premises and the node may not be protected from errors in the first two access methods. Unless an X.25 circuit from the premises to the node is employed, an error-correcting protocol between terminal devices may be required.

CHAPTER 5

Pulse Code Modulation

All telephone sessions begin as an analog signal. In the majority of the cases, the analog voice signal is converted to digital for the bulk of its journey to the other end of the connection. The analog portion of the connection may be as short as the length of the handset cord, with the analog-to-digital conversion done in the telephone instrument. This is the case with most PBXs and all ISDN sessions. If the customer premises equipment has an all-analog connection to the central office, voice travels to the central office as an analog signal. If the central office is digital, the voice is converted in the switching system's line circuit. If the switching system is analog, the voice is converted in the trunk circuit and travels to a distant central office as a digital signal. The process for converting between digital and analog is known as *pulse code modulation* (PCM), which is the fundamental building block of today's switching and transmission systems.

Alec Reeves, an ITT scientist in England, patented the PCM method of converting analog voice signals to digital in 1938. Although the system was technically possible then, it wasn't economically feasible. Pulse generating and amplifying circuits required vacuum tubes and their size and power consumption consigned PCM to the shelf for another 20 years. Following the development of the transistor, PCM became commercially feasible in the 1960s, and with the development of large-scale integration in the following decade, cost, size, and power consumption continued to drop, even in the face of high inflation.

Today, digital technology has all but replaced analog technology in transmission systems and is rapidly replacing it in switching systems. Virtually all new central offices, PBXs, and even most key systems use digital technology. The advantages are substantial. Analog circuits do not lend themselves well to integrated circuitry, whereas digital circuits use the same manufacturing techniques that have resulted in dramatic cost reductions in electronic devices. Digital switching systems can interface with digital multiplexing systems directly without the need for an analog-to-digital conversion.

Digital circuits are also less susceptible to noise. In analog circuits, noise is additive, increasing with system length, but in a digital carrier the signal is regenerated at each repeater. Over a properly engineered system, the signal arrives at the receiving terminal with quality unimpaired and a bit error rate several orders of magnitude less than analog. Furthermore, digital signals can be compressed into a fraction of their original bandwidth, while analog signals occupy a fixed amount of bandwidth.

DIGITAL CARRIER TECHNOLOGY

The basic digital multiplexing system is known as T carrier. The name came from the Bell System's carrier designation system, which assigned letters to each successive model that Bell Laboratories designed. The T1 carrier system used in North America consists of 24 channels, each of which occupies a bandwidth of 64 kb/s. A T1 digital carrier system samples a voice signal, converts it to an 8-bit coded digital signal, interleaves it with 23 other voice channels, and transmits it over a line that regenerates the signal approximately once per mile on twisted-pair copper wire. The European version, known as E1, uses the same sampling method, but applies 32 channels to the line, of which two channels are used for signaling. Although this discussion refers to voice channels, the T1/E1 signal is channelized only if the terminating equipment does so. The entire bandwidth of the T1/E1 signal can be used between devices such as routers, which are used to interconnect LANs. Other devices such as T1/E1 multiplexers can divide part of the bit stream into voice channels and part into a wider channel for LAN interconnection.

T1/E1 also can be transmitted over digital radio and over fiber optics with regenerators spaced at wider intervals. The digital signal is encoded and decoded in a digital central office or on one of several types of terminal devices. A *channel bank* combines 24 or 32 voice and data circuits into a T1/E1 bit stream. A *T1/E1 multiplexer,* which is described later, breaks the bit stream into smaller increments than a channel bank and supports both voice and data signals. T1/E1 lines can be directly connected to digital PBXs and a variety of other devices such as key systems and automatic call distributors.

A digital signal is developed by a five-step process, consisting of the following:

- ◆ Sampling
- ◆ Quantizing
- ◆ Encoding
- ◆ Companding
- ◆ Framing

Sampling

According to Nyquist's theorem, if an analog signal is sampled at a rate twice the highest frequency contained within its bandwidth, enough intelligence is retained

FIGURE 5-1

Voice Sampling

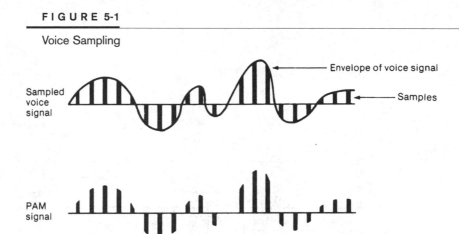

in the samples to reconstruct the original signal. The range of human hearing is approximately 20 to 20,000 Hz, but the frequency range in a voice signal is much narrower. Communications channels filter the voice to a nominal bandwidth of 4000 Hz (actually 300 to 3300 Hz). Therefore, a sampling rate of 8000 times per second is sufficient to encode a voice signal for communications purposes. A PCM system does exactly this. The output of the sampling process is a *pulse amplitude modulated (PAM) signal*, shown in Figure 5-1.

Quantizing, Encoding, and Companding

The amplitude of the pulses from the sampling circuit is encoded into an 8-bit word by a process called *quantizing*, which is illustrated in Figure 5-2. The 8-bit word provides 2^8 or 256 discrete steps, each step corresponding to the instantaneous amplitude of the speech sample. The output of the encoder is a stream of octets, each representing the magnitude of a single sample.

The quantizing process does not exactly represent the amplitude of the PAM signal. Instead, the output is a series of steps, which, as shown in Figure 5-3a, does not precisely represent the original waveform. The error is audible in the voice channel as *quantizing noise*, which is present only when a signal is being transmitted. The effects of quantizing noise are greater with low-amplitude signals than with high. To overcome this effect, the encoded signal is compressed to divide low-level signals into more steps and high-level signals into fewer steps, as shown in Figure 5-3b. When the signal is decoded at the receiving terminal, reversing the compression process expands it. The combination of expansion and compression is called *companding*. In the United States companding follows a formula known as *mu law* coding. In Europe, the companding formula is a slightly different form known as *A law* coding. Although the two laws are incompatible, they differ only

FIGURE 5-2

FIGURE 5-2

Quantizing

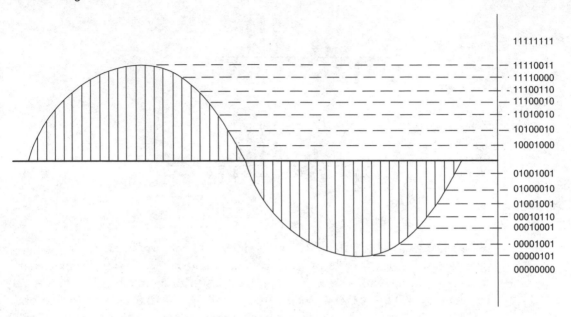

slightly. ITU-T recommendation G.711 defines the standard for both algorithms and the process for converting between them.

Framing

The PCM voice signal is encoded in the terminating device and merged with other voice channels. Each channel generates a bit rate of 64 kb/s (8000 samples per second × 8 bits, or 1 byte, per sample). The 24 channels in the North American system produce the frame format shown in Figure 5-4. A single framing bit is added to the 192 bits that result from the 24 8-bit bytes. A 193-bit frame, 125 microseconds (μs) in duration, results. The frame repeats 8000 times per second for a total line rate of 1.544 Mb/s. The framing bits follow a fixed pattern of zeros and ones throughout 12 frames. This repetitive sequence of 12 frames is called a *superframe*. The 1.544-Mb/s rate results from the following:

8,000	samples per second
× 8	bits per sample
64,000	bits per channel
× 24	channels
1,536,000	bits per second
+ 8,000	framing bits per second
1,544,000	bits per second total

F I G U R E 5-3

Companding in a PCM Channel

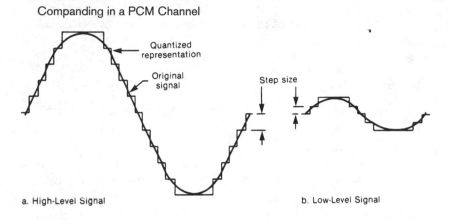

a. High-Level Signal   b. Low-Level Signal

F I G U R E 5-4

PCM Frame

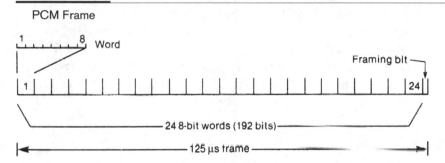

This system of multiplexing is known as *byte interleaved multiplexing*. It is also referred to as *synchronous multiplexing*. The terms synchronous and asynchronous are somewhat overused in telecommunications, and can result in confusion when applied to devices as diverse as an asynchronous terminal and asynchronous transfer mode, or ATM. Nevertheless, it is important to understand that the T carrier modulation scheme results in a bit stream in which any individual channel can be detected simply by its position in the transmission frame, which is a multiple of 8 bits. Each byte position in the transmission frame is called a *time slot*, and the process is known as *time division multiplexing* or TDM.

European digital carrier systems, which are known as E1 systems, use the same 64-kb/s channel bit rate but multiplex 32 rather than 24 channels for a 2.048-Mb/s bit rate. Of the 32 channels, 30 are used for information channels, one channel is used for frame alignment, and one for signaling. Companding and bit rate differences make North American and European digital carrier systems incompatible. This incompatibility was of little consequence when the systems were developed in the 1960s because they would not be interconnected. With the development of undersea fiber-optic cable, however, the issue of end-to-end connectivity of incompatible systems became a significant problem. This incompatibility came to be one of the driving forces behind SONET/SDH, which is discussed later in this chapter.

Bit-Robbed Signaling

T1 carrier's original purpose was interoffice trunking in metropolitan areas. Analog carrier systems required, with a few exceptions, outboard devices to signal over the channel. Since signaling is a binary function, it was feasible to use a portion of the T carrier signal itself to convey the ON- or OFF-hook status of the channel. See Chapter 11 for further discussion of how signaling systems work.

The original digital channel banks used the least significant bit in every sixth frame for signaling. This technique is known as *bit robbing*. Within a superframe, the bit that is robbed from the sixth frame is called the *A bit*, and the one that is robbed from the 12th frame is called the *B bit*. The distortion resulting from bit robbing has no effect on voice signals or data signals that are modulated with a modem. The forced errors render a circuit unusable, however, for a 64-kb/s digital data signal. Therefore, devices that are designed to operate over superframe lines use only 7 of the 8 bits. At a sampling rate of 8000 samples per second, this leaves a usable signal of 7×8000 or 56 kb/s. Special data channel units provide direct digital access to the usable bandwidth.

Extended Superframe

Within a superframe, the framing bits synchronize the channels and signaling, but otherwise carry no intelligence. Also, the signaling bits reduce the data-carrying capacity of a T1 channel by 8000 bits per second. As the LECs and IXCs convert to common channel signaling between central offices, the in-band signaling capability of T1 is no longer required. *Clear channel* capability, which is one of ISDN's features, eliminates the bit-robbed signaling and introduces a revised T1 format known as *extended superframe* (ESF). Under ESF, the 8000-b/s framing signal, also called the Fe channel, is multiplexed to provide 2000 b/s for 6-bit cyclical redundancy checking (CRC) on the bit stream. A 4000-b/s facility data link (FDL) is used for end-to-end diagnostics, network control, and maintenance functions such as forcing loopback of a failed channel. The remaining 2000 b/s are used for framing and signaling. ESF is supported by ANSI as the T1.403 standard.

The CRC code operates in the same manner as data-link error detection, which is discussed in Chapter 4. It does not, however, correct errors; it only detects them. The CRC code is calculated at the source and then again at a terminal or intermediate point. If an error is detected, the equipment can flag the fault before a hard failure occurs. The receiving equipment calculates the performance of the facility from the CRC results and stores it or sends the information back to the originating equipment over the FDL.

ESF requires that terminating equipment and repeaters be compatible. Some ancillary equipment, such as the channel service unit (CSU), which is described later, can be designed to operate under either SF or ESF rules. In contrast to SF, which uses a line-coding scheme known as *alternate mark inversion*, ESF uses *bipolar with 8-zero substitution* (B8ZS) as its line-coding method, and this method is discussed later.

DIGITAL TRANSMISSION FACILITIES

The basic digital transmission facility is a T1/E1 line, which has an office repeater at each end feeding twisted-pair wire, with digital regenerators spaced every 6000 feet (ft). The function of the office repeater is to match the output of the channel bank to the impedance of the line and to feed power over the line to the repeaters. The line repeaters regenerate the incoming pulses to eliminate distortion caused by the cable. The 6000-ft spacing was selected to install repeaters in manholes, which are placed at 6000 ft intervals to match the spacing of load coils in voice frequency cables.

Digital signals in North America are applied to twisted-pair wire in groups of 24, 48, and 96 channels called T1, T1C, and T2. T1 signals originate in channel banks, digital central office switches, T1 multiplexers, PBXs, and other T1-compatible devices. The higher bit rates of T1C and T2 are developed by higher-order multiplexing as described later. Digital signals also can be applied to fiber optics, microwave radio, satellite, or coaxial cable for transmission over longer distances.

Digital Timing

T1/E1 signals are synchronized by loopback timing, in which synchronizing pulses are extracted from the incoming bit stream, as discussed in a later section. The PCM output of the terminating device is encoded in the bipolar format that is described later. The transition of each 1-second bit is detected by the repeaters and the receiving terminals and is used to keep the system in synchronization. If more than 15 consecutive zeros are transmitted on a digital facility, the receiving end may lose synchronization. To prevent this, the channel bank inserts a unique bit pattern that is detected by the receiving end and restored to the original pattern. This technique, called *bit stuffing,* is used by digital carrier systems to prevent loss of synchronization.

The T1/E1 Carrier System

Figure 5-5 is a block diagram of a T1/E1 carrier system. The primary elements of the system are the channel banks and the repeaters. The other elements, the distributing

FIGURE 5-5

Block Diagram of a T1 Carrier System

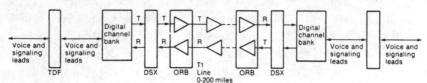

TDF - Trunk Distributing Frame
DSX - Digital Signal Cross-connect Frame
ORB - Office Repeater Bay
  T - Transmit
  R - Receive

FIGURE 5-6

Block Diagram of a PCM Channel Bank

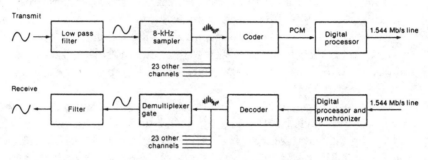

frame and digital cross-connect frame, are provided for ease of assignment and maintenance. In this diagram channel banks are used for the purpose of illustration, but most T1/E1 circuits today are terminated in a device other than a channel bank. PBXs, T1/E1 multiplexers, routers, and other devices that use the full bandwidth of a T1/E1 are diminishing the use of channel banks.

Channel Banks

A T1 channel bank consists of 24 channels called a *digroup*. Some manufacturers package two digroups in a 48-channel framework. The 48 channels share a common power supply and other common equipment. Figure 5-6 is a block diagram of a digital channel bank. The channel bank has a metal framework with backplane wiring designed to accept plug-in common equipment and channel units.

A variety of plug-in channel units are available to provide special transmission functions. Numerous signaling options are available. Foreign exchange (FX) service is a combination of special signaling and transmission service. It is used by LECs to connect a telephone line in one exchange to a station located in another. FX channel units are equipped for direct connection to metallic loops and have provisions for ringing telephones and for adding gain to long loops.

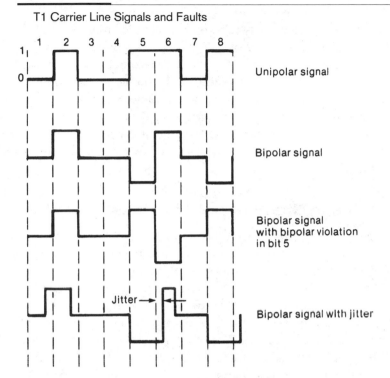

FIGURE 5-7

T1 Carrier Line Signals and Faults

Program channel units replace two or more voice channel units and use the added bit stream to accommodate a wider channel for use by radio and television stations, wired music companies, and other applications that require a wide audio band. Program channels with 5-kHz bandwidth replace two voice channels, and 15 kHz units replace six voice channels.

T Carrier Lines

T1/E1 carrier lines can be extended on twisted-pair wire for about 200 miles, although most private and common carrier applications are considerably shorter because longer circuits are usually deployed over radio or fiber-optic facilities. A superframe T carrier line accepts a *bipolar* signal from the connected device, as shown in Figure 5-7. A bipolar signal, also called *alternate mark inversion*, assigns 0s to a zero voltage level. One signals are alternately ± 3 volts (V). The bipolar signal offers two advantages. First, the line signaling rate is only half the data rate of 1.544 Mb/s because in the worst case where a signal composed of all 1s, the signal would alternate at only 772 kb/s. The second advantage is the ability of a bipolar signal to detect line errors. If interference or a failing repeater adds or subtracts 1-second bits, a bipolar violation results, which indicates a fault in a T carrier system. A bipolar violation occurs when two 1 bits of the same polarity arrive in sequence.

Clear channel capability requires the T carrier system to support any pattern of bits, including long strings of 0s. ESF systems replace the straight bipolar signal with a coding scheme known as bipolar with 8-zero substitution (B8ZS). In this system, any string of eight 0s is replaced with an intentional bipolar violation at the fourth and seventh bits. The receiving equipment, normally the channel service unit, detects the bipolar violation and replaces it with a string of eight 0s. The B8ZS coding scheme is not compatible with earlier T carrier lines, but most modern regenerators, office repeaters, channel service units, and connecting equipment are ESF compatible.

Office Repeaters and Channel Service Units

An office repeater terminates the T1/E1 line at each central office. In the receiving direction, the office repeater performs normal regenerator functions, but it is passive in the transmit direction. Its transmit function is to couple the bipolar signal to the line and to feed power to the line repeaters. A special type of repeater called a channel service unit (CSU) terminates the customer end of a T1/E1 line that feeds customer premises. Unlike a DDS signal where a DSU is required to convert the line signal from bipolar to the unipolar signal required by the terminal equipment, the T1/E1 device produces the bipolar signal. Increasingly, the CSU function is built into the channel bank or the multiplexer. The CSU fulfills the following functions:

- Terminates the circuit, including lightning and surge protection.
- Regenerates the signal.
- Loops the digital signal back to the originating end on command.
- Monitors the incoming line for bipolar violations.
- Generates a signal—usually all 1s—to maintain synchronization on the line if the terminal equipment fails.
- Maintains the 1s density requirement of the line.
- Provides signal lamps and line jacks for testing and monitoring.
- Provides line build-out (LBO) if necessary.

Line Repeaters

Line repeaters are mounted in apparatus cases, which are watertight for mounting on poles and in manholes. Repeaters, shown in a block diagram in Figure 5-8, perform these functions:

- Amplify and equalize the received signal.
- Generate an internal timing signal.

FIGURE 5-8

Block Diagram of a T1 Repeater

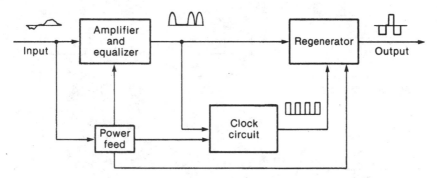

- ◆ Decide whether incoming pulses are 0s or 1s.
- ◆ Regenerate pulses and insert them in the correct output time slot.

Incoming pulses are received in one of three states—plus, minus, or zero. If the incoming pulse exceeds the plus or minus threshold, the repeater generates a 1 output pulse. Otherwise it registers a 0. Phase deviations in the pulse, which are additive along a T carrier line, are known as *jitter*. Excessive jitter, as illustrated in Figure 5-7, can cause errors in data signals. Errors occur when the receiver in a repeater or a terminal incorrectly interprets the incoming signal.

The transmit and receive paths of T1/E1 signals must be isolated to prevent crosstalk coupling. If excessive crosstalk occurs between the high-level pulses of a repeater's output and the low-level received pulses of adjacent repeaters, errors will result. These are prevented by assigning the transmit and receive directions to separate cables, to partitions within a specially screened cable, or to separate binder groups within a single cable. Cable binder groups are explained in Chapter 6.

T1C and T2 lines operate on the same general principles as T1 lines except that their bit rates are higher and greater isolation between the pairs prevents crosstalk. Design rules for these systems require either a screened cable, which contains a shield to separate transmit and receive pairs, or separate transmit and receive cables.

T1/E1 Carrier Synchronization

When a T1/E1 carrier is used in a private network that carries end-to-end digital signals, it is important that the network be kept in synchronization. To understand why, consider the timing diagram shown in Figure 5-9. If the clock of one terminal device runs slightly faster or slower than the clock at the other end, a point will be reached where an extra bit will be inserted or a bit will be lost, and the frame will lose synchronization momentarily. This condition is known as a *slip*.

FIGURE 5-9

Slip in Digital Transmission

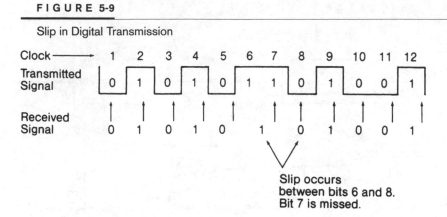

Slip occurs
between bits 6 and 8.
Bit 7 is missed.

Slips have a negligible effect on voice circuits, but the loss of a transmission frame causes errors in data circuits. The data system corrects the errors, but an excessive error rate causes frequent resends and a deterioration of response time. To prevent slips and consequent data errors, the entire digital network must be kept locked in synchronization.

In a private network of only two devices linked by T1/E1, one device is configured as the master and the other is a slave. A precise clocking rate is not important because the slave extracts clocking from the 1-second bits in the received signal to maintain synchronization. The more nodes that are added to the network, the more critical the provision of a master clock becomes. When the network is connected to a common carrier network, as with a long distance service, it is vital that the entire network slave from the common carrier because the carrier is tied to a higher level in the national clocking structure.

Nationally, digital network synchronization is maintained through a four-level hierarchy of clocks. ANSI standard T1.101 defines the four levels, which are known as stratum 1 through stratum 4 timing levels. Stratum 1 clocks use highly accurate oscillators using cesium and rubidium clocks with a maximum drift of 1 $\times$ 10^{-11}. Stratum 2 clocks, which are used in common carriers' toll centers, are slightly less accurate—1 $\times$ 10^{-10} in the short term (1 day)—but if synchronization with the stratum 1 clock is lost, it will still maintain an acceptable amount of stability. Stratum 3 and stratum 4 are less stable and generally depend on synchronization from higher levels to maintain an acceptable degree of performance. Private network equipment generally contains stratum 3 or 4 clocking.

THE DIGITAL SIGNAL HIERARCHY

Digital signals from a T1/E1 source are multiplexed to higher rates. Figure 5-10 shows the bit rates of the North American digital hierarchy. T1/E1 signals are ap-

FIGURE 5-10

North American Digital Signal Hierarchy

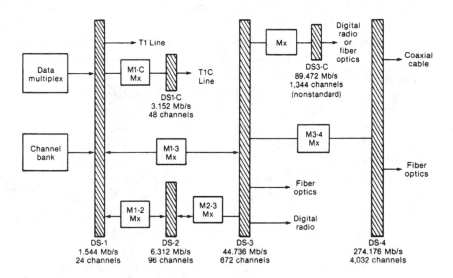

plied to a standard repeatered line. Higher-rate signals are applied to wire, coaxial cable, fiber optics, and digital microwave radio. The European hierarchy begins by multiplexing 32 signals of 64 kb/s each into an E1 line at 2.048 Mb/s. The E1 line is also known as CEPT-1. An E2 signal consists of four E1s for a line rate of 8.448 Mb/s. Four E2s form an E3 at 34.368 Mb/s, and four E3s form an E4 at 139.264 Mb/s. Obviously, the North American and European hierarchies do not mesh comfortably despite their use of the same sampling rate.

A family of multiplexers raises the basic digital group to higher bit rates. Multiplexers are designated according to the digital signal levels with which they interface. For example, an M1-3 multiplexer connects DS-1 to DS-3. An M1-3 multiplexer accepts 28 DS-1 inputs and combines them into a single 45-Mb/s bit stream. (The bit stream is 45.736 Mb/s, but it is commonly called 45 Mb/s in the industry.) Multiplexer output can be directly connected to a digital radio or to a fiber-optic system.

The DS-4 signal was designed to feed T4 coaxial cable. Before T4 was used to any significant extent, however, lightwave systems came on the market. Lightwave systems can easily support 274 Mb/s, but their bandwidth can transport much higher bit rates. Manufacturers began producing transmission equipment with bandwidths far in excess of DS-4, but in the absence of a standard, the transmission rates and overhead bits used for maintenance were proprietary. This set of circumstances led to the development of the synchronous optical network (SONET/SDH) standards, which are discussed in a later section.

T3/E3 Service

The highest level of the North American digital hierarchy that came into widespread use was the T3, which consists of 28 DS-1s. A T3 usually combines DS-1s through an M1-3 multiplexer, although they can be combined in a digital cross-connect system as discussed later. A T3 signal is 45.736 Mb/s that can be subdivided in any way the customer chooses. If it is multiplexed into voice channels, it supports 672 uncompressed voice channels. Most carriers offer T3/E3 at a cost considerably lower than the cost of separate T1/E1s. T3/E3, therefore, is attractive to large organizations that have multiple T1/E1s for access to the IXC or for broadband data transmission. T3/E3 bandwidth is too great to deliver over twisted-pair wire the way T1/E1 is. It requires fiber optics, which means that it is not universally available.

Unlike T1/E1, which is a synchronous multiplexing system, T3 is asynchronous. It is formed by combining seven DS-2 signals. Since the DS-2 signals are separate, they may get out of synchronism. To correct synchronization problems, T3 uses bit stuffing. As a result, it is difficult to extract individual DS-1 or DS-0 signals from the T3 bit stream. If, for example, an organization has T3 connecting three or more sites and wishes to drop DS-1 or DS-0 signals at an intermediate point, the DS-3 signal is broken down into its constituent T1s with M1-3 multiplexers connected back to back. This problem is resolved with SONET/SDH, which is discussed in a later section.

Fractional T1/E1

Digital service users have, until recently, been faced with two alternatives: leasing service one channel at a time or leasing full T1/E1 or T3/E3 lines. With the advent of fractional T1/E1, a wider choice is available. For example, AT&T's fractional T1 offering, Accunet Spectrum of Digital Services (ASDS), provides service at 56, 64, 128, 256, 512, and 768 kb/s. Other vendors offer fractional T1/E1 in multiples of 64 kb/s. The basic building block is the DS-0 channel. Higher bandwidths are available for services such as slow-speed digital conferencing, high-speed data, and local area network bridging.

Technically, fractional T1/E1 is little different from a full T1/E1. The IXC subdivides an existing T1/E1 channel with a digital cross-connect system (DCS) or an add-drop multiplexer (ADM). Until the LECs file fractional tariffs, the local loop portion of the service requires the bandwidth of a full T1/E1 service though less than a full T1/E1 is used. One cost-effective way for many companies to obtain fractional T1/E1 is to bring data channels in over the same T1/E1 that carries incoming and outgoing long-distance service. At the customer's premises, the T1/E1 is connected to an ADM to separate the voice and data channels. The voice channels are connected directly to the PBX and the data channels to a computer or multiplexer.

SYNCHRONOUS OPTICAL NETWORK/SYNCHRONOUS DIGITAL HIERARCHY (SONET/SDH)

The original T1 hierarchy was developed long before lightwave transmission was practical. In fact, Bell Laboratories worked for years on buried waveguide as an alternative to microwave, which was then the prevalent method of wide-area transmission. When fiber optics proved practical in the mid-1970s, work on waveguide ceased, and dozens of companies began producing lightwave products. The standards at the time were well developed up through T3, but beyond that, higher bandwidths were obtained only by multiplexing DS-3 signals to higher bit rates, and feeding them into lightwave transmission systems using proprietary multiplexing schemes.

The proprietary systems had a distinct disadvantage: equipment at both ends of the circuit had to be of the same manufacture. The Bell System's manufacturer, Western Electric, sold most of its equipment to the BOCs. When it was necessary for independent telephone companies to interface the BOCs, they purchased Western Electric equipment, but emerging IXCs, such as MCI, had limited interest in buying equipment from their chief competitor. To fulfill the need for a "midspan meet," and for other technical reasons, it became clear that a standard was needed. The result was SONET/SDH.

SONET/SDH is a hierarchy of optical standards that is replacing the previous digital signal hierarchy. Theoretically, SONET has up to 192 levels, which correspond to a bit rate of nearly 10 Gb/s, but in practice only a few of the levels are defined. The basic building block of SONET is a byte or octet repeated every 125 μs, which corresponds to the 64-kb/s rate of T1 and E1.

The lowest level of SONET is STS-1, which has a line rate of 51.840 Mb/s. STS stands for synchronous transport signal. It defines the electrical characteristics of a SONET signal. The optical signal is characterized by optical carrier (OC) levels corresponding to the STS levels. Although the STS and OC designations are distinctly different, the industry tends to refer to SONET by its OC identification.

A further problem with the traditional hierarchy was its lack of compatibility between North American, Japanese, and European systems. The Japanese use a DS-0 and DS-1 hierarchy identical to the North American system, but different at DS-3 and above. Table 5-1 shows the defined OC and STS designations, together with the European synchronous digital hierarchy (SDH) classification. The SDH levels are known as synchronous transport module (STM). As Table 5-1 shows, an STM-1 and an OC-3 have the same line rate of 155.520 Mb/s. As a result, European and North American SONET/SDH signals are compatible at OC-3 and above.

It is important to note that although an OC-1 has more than enough bandwidth to carry a DS-3, it uses a multiplexing scheme that makes it easy to extract channels from the bit stream. As a practical matter, OC-3 is the lowest level used in transmission equipment, and then only for short distances since its bandwidth is a fraction of the capabilities of fiber optics. The most common levels in use today are

TABLE 5-1

SONET and SDH Line Rates

Electrical Level	Optical Level	SDH	Line Rate (Mb/s)
STS-1	OC-1		51.840
STS-3	OC-3	STM-1	155.520
STS-9	OC-9	STM-3	466.560
STS-12	OC-12	STM-4	622.080
STS-18	OC-18	STM-6	933.120
STS-24	OC-24	STM-8	1,244.160
STS-36	OC-36	STM-13	1,866.240
STS-48	OC-48	STM-16	2,488.320
STS-96	OC-96	STM-32	4,976.640
STS-192	OC-192	STM-64	9,953.280

OC-12 and OC-48. The use of higher levels such as OC-192 is stretching the capabilities of the equipment, but is not uncommon. Nothing suggests that OC-192 is the ultimate capacity of the fiber-optic transmission medium; in fact the history of the technology suggests that the limits have not yet been glimpsed.

In addition to resolving the midspan meet and international compatibility issues, SONET/SDH brings several other advantages to telecommunications. A major advantage lies in the fact that it is a synchronous system. As we discussed earlier, T1 is synchronous, but as it is multiplexed up to T3, it becomes bit-interleaved. As a result, it is difficult to extract a single DS-0 or DS-1 from the DS-3 bit stream. The most common way of doing that involves disassembling the DS-3 signal with an M1-3 multiplexer. SONET/SDH is like a T1/E1 carrier in that it is byte synchronous up to the highest multiplexing level. As a result, individual DS-1s and DS-0s can be extracted from the bit stream with relatively simple equipment that falls into the general category of add-drop multiplexing (ADM).

SONET/SDH is often deployed in a ring configuration with two fiber-optic pairs carrying service in opposite directions. The multiplexers are designed to detect a loss of signal and loop back over the protection pair. This provides automatic restoration with only a small loss of data.

SONET/SDH offers the following advantages:

- It offers bandwidths more commensurate with today's fiber-optic systems than the older digital signal hierarchy.
- It merges North American and European hierarchies at higher rates.
- It offers multivendor interoperability over fiber-optic systems. By contrast, non-SONET/SDH networks use a proprietary frame overhead that mandates equipment from the same manufacturer at both ends of a fiber-optic cable.

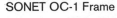

FIGURE 5-11

SONET OC-1 Frame

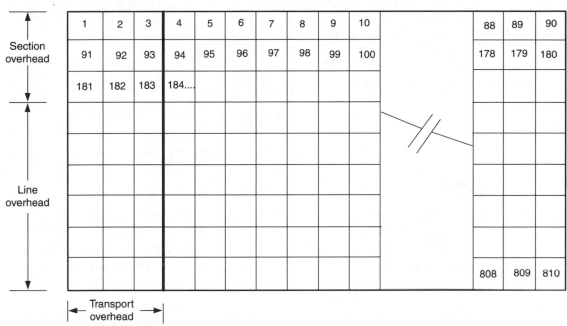

- It offers centralized end-to-end network management and performance monitoring
- Network costs are lower because SONET/SDH permits direct access to any signal level from DS-0 to the top of the hierarchy. It permits add-drop capability without the use of back-to-back multiplexers.
- It provides support for new switching standards such as ATM and B-ISDN.

SONET/SDH Framing

SONET/SDH begins with an 8-bit byte repeated every 125 μs, the same as the European and North American voice channel of 64 kb/s. The signal is transmitted in frames of nine rows and a variable number of columns. Figure 5-11 shows an OC-1 frame. Note that each row has 3 bytes of overhead plus 87 bytes of payload. Nine rows times 90 bytes per row equals a single SONET/SDH frame of 810 bytes, which is a 51.840-Mb/s OC-1 signal. Multiple OC-1 signals interleave to form the higher levels. At each level of the hierarchy, the payload and overhead bytes are exact multiples of OC-1. For example, an OC-3 signal has 270-byte rows, of which 9 bytes are overhead and 261 bytes are payload.

The overhead bits are used for operations, administration, maintenance, and provisioning (OAM&P) in four levels of SONET/SDH operations. These levels are the path, line, and section overhead signals plus the photonic layer. Note that these four levels are contained within the physical layer of the OSI model. SONET/SDH is a physical layer protocol that is concerned only with moving bits across a fixed path. It does not have any switching or routing capability. The four levels of the SONET/SDH signal are

- Photonic, which is concerned with the optical transmission path. Physically, the photonic layer consists of lightwave-terminating equipment, lasers, and photonic diodes.
- Section, which is concerned with monitoring and administration between regenerators.
- Line, which is concerned with monitoring and administration across the maintenance span.
- Path, which is concerned with end-to-end transmission.

Section overhead carries framing and error-monitoring signals that all devices on the line can monitor and process. Line overhead extends between central offices. It carries performance information plus automatic protection switching and control information. Path overhead provides performance and error information plus control signaling between the customer end points of a SONET/SDH network.

SONET/SDH is being used by LECs to deliver clear-channel DS-1 and DS-3 digital services between offices and directly to end users. Private network users also employ SONET/SDH over private and public fiber-optic systems. As bandwidth demand increases, SONET/SDH will likely be the physical layer technology that the LECs use to carry services from customer premises to the central office, where they can access a variety of services, including broadband ISDN. B-ISDN standards are not part of SONET/SDH, but the two standards are compatible. OC-3 forms the primary transport for the B-ISDN signal.

DIGITAL CROSS-CONNECT SYSTEMS

SONET/SDH takes care of one of the major issues the various carriers have in grooming digital signals. *Grooming* is the process of combining digital signals to make maximum use of the bandwidth in a particular circuit cross section. For example, suppose an IXC has elected to centralize its switching for a region in a particular city. To be cost-competitive with other IXCs in the T1/E1 access facilities, it establishes points-of-presence (POPs) for rating purposes in other cities. As multiple T1/E1s arrive at its central office from multiple customer premises, the IXC wants to combine these to form a DS-3 or higher level for transmission to a switching system located some distance away. These signals are combined to form a broadband signal that may be combined with signals from other cities to form an OC-3, OC-12, or higher-level signal. The equipment for combining and disaggregating digital signals is known as a *digital cross-connect system* or DCS. It is often referred to as a *digital access cross-connect system* or DACS.

Digital Cross-Connect Panel

Physical cross-connect positions are known as digital signal cross-connect (DSX) panels. A DSX-1, for example, is a DSX panel for DS-1 signals. The physical transmit and receive legs of the digital circuit are wired through jacks in this panel to provide test access and to enable the equipment to be patched to another T1/E1 carrier line to rearrange circuits and to transfer manually to a spare line when repeaters fail. The ability to patch to spare lines is a vital part of service restoration in common carrier applications and is provided in most central office installations. In private networks the DSX panel is useful for temporary rearrangement of facilities. For example, a T1/E1 facility might be used for a voice tie line during working hours and patched to a high-speed multiplexer for data transfer after hours.

Short-haul carrier systems converge in central offices in both private and common carrier networks for connection to long-haul facilities. If 24-channel digroups are connected through the office to a single terminating point, the incoming T1/E1 line is connected to the outgoing line with an express office repeater. If fewer than 24 channels are needed, or if channels from a single originating point must be split to separate terminating points, back-to-back channel banks or an add-drop multiplexer must be used to access the channels. Back-to-back channel banks are undesirable for several reasons:

- ◆ Cost of the channel banks.
- ◆ An added source of potential circuit failure.
- ◆ Labor cost of making channel cross-connections.
- ◆ Extra analog-to-digital conversions, which are a source of distortion.

For smaller networks, an add-drop multiplexer, which splits a certain number of channels out of the T1/E1 bit stream, can be used. For larger networks, the DCS is a specialized electronic switch that terminates T carrier lines without channel banks and grooms the individual channel bit streams or complete DS-1s to the desired output line.

Digital Cross-Connect System (DCS)

Unlike central office switching systems, which are used for temporary connections, a DCS establishes a semipermanent path for the bit stream through the switch. This path remains connected until it is disconnected or changed by programmed order or administrative action, known as provisioning in the telecommunications vernacular.

The DCS system eliminates most of the labor associated with rearrangement, eliminates extra analog-to-digital conversions, and offers a high degree of flexibility in rerouting circuits. Also, routing changes can be controlled from a central location over a data link. If the organization uses a mechanized database to maintain records of facility assignments, the same source that updates the database can drive the DCS assignments. DCS is a space-saving system because it eliminates the distributing frame blocks and wire required to interconnect the large numbers of voice frequency and signaling leads that back-to-back channel banks would require.

DCS is the key to implementing the intelligent digital network that is described in Chapter 31. Linked to the user's network control system, DCS allows the user to reconfigure the network to meet changes in demand or to accommodate changes that occur with time. For example, network capacity could be assigned to a voice switch during normal working hours and to a computer center for high-speed data transfer during off-hours.

Private network managers are increasingly becoming attuned to the problem of network restoral, a function in which DCS plays a key role. When a major switch node fails, a DCS system can quickly reroute traffic around the point of failure. It also increases the traffic carried by T1/E1 systems. Many of today's T1/E1 networks are only partially filled. With DCS it is feasible to combine channels to fill a T1/E1, although it may mean routing a circuit over greater distance than it would otherwise span.

Privately owned DCS systems are not the only alternative available to network operators who need DCS capability. Most large LECs offer DCS as a contracted or tariffed service. Since the T1/E1 lines may extend through the LEC's central office anyway, using a centralized DCS may make sense technically and economically. For example, part of a T1/E1 could be used for access to the IXC, with the remainder of the bandwidth used for Internet access. The principal issue in using a public versus a private DCS is the degree of control the LEC provides over the DCS facility. If the LEC allows the network operator full control over circuit configuration, the use of private versus common carrier DCS is primarily an economic issue.

T1/E1 MULTIPLEXERS

Channel banks are inflexible devices for subdividing the T1/E1 bit stream. Voice channels and data occupy a full 64 kb/s each, although the data channels may operate at lower speeds. A T1/E1 multiplexer is a more versatile device, combining multiple low-speed bit streams into a T1/E1 signal. Multiplexers can be equipped with plug-in cards to handle a wide range of bit rates. Cards are normally available to support low-speed terminals. Fractional T1/E1 cards can be connected to routers. Voice is accommodated by using straight PCM or is compressed into bandwidths as narrow as 8 kb/s for point-to-point service. Figure 5-12 shows how a network might be configured with a variety of T1/E1 multiplexer options and illustrates the T1/E1 divided into low-speed terminal connections, PBX tie lines, and the remaining bandwidth used to connect local networks through routers.

T1/E1 multiplexers are more expensive than channel banks. Some products cost two to four times the price of a channel bank, but multiplexers offer signifi-

FIGURE 5-12

T1 Multiplexer Used to Subdivide a T1 Line

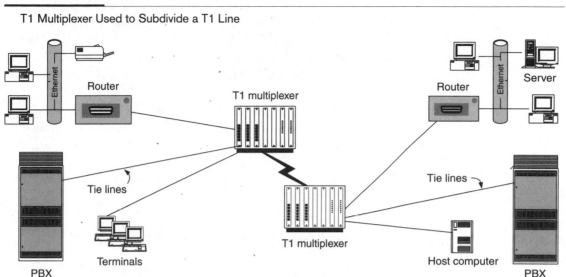

cantly increased functionality. Multiplexers can be networked to form an integrated voice and data network with alternate routing capability and sophisticated network management. Some multiplexers have the capability of monitoring multiple points in the network, reporting malfunctions and keeping the network manager supplied with usage and performance information from all the nodes. Another vital feature of many multiplexers is their ability to reroute circuits during failure or congestion. Two different systems are used to keep data flowing. A *table-based* system is composed of fixed routing tables that instruct the multiplexer how to act in the face of a failure. A *parameterized,* or rule-based, system develops a global view of the network and responds flexibly.

Add-Drop Multiplexers

T1/E1 multiplexers are decreasing in importance as networks are increasingly connected through routers. Still in frequent use, however, are add-drop multiplexers. An add-drop multiplexer is used to subdivide a T1/E1 line into two or more portions. An ADM normally has a straight-through T1/E1 connection that can be terminated in a PBX. It also has one or more V.35 connections that can be cabled to a router. One frequent use of an ADM is to split a T1/E1 line to the IXC so that part of the line is used for access to the IXC's long-distance network and the remainder to a data network such as frame relay or, in some cases, to the Internet. Most CSUs are available with add-drop capability. Since the T1/E1 line must be terminated in a CSU anyway, this method of obtaining add-drop capability is inexpensive.

VOICE COMPRESSION

Pulse code modulation uses an efficient encoding algorithm that provides excellent fidelity and clarity for a voice signal. Its use of bandwidth, however, is inefficient, and other coding methods can compress several voice channels into the same 64-kb/s bandwidth that a single PCM channel requires. Bandwidth costs are dropping, but transmission costs are still high enough that decreased circuit costs often repay the cost of the hardware to compress voice and, in some products, combine it with data. Voice compression is increasing in importance as voice over IP gains in popularity. Some compression methods are commonly enough used that they are virtually a standard. Others are proprietary, and may carry names such as vector quantization coding, high-capacity voice, and code-excited linear prediction (CELP).

Adaptive Differential Pulse Code Modulation (ADPCM)

ADPCM equipment compresses two PCM bit streams into a single bit stream that can be transmitted over T1/E1 carrier lines or applied to M1-3 multiplexers and transmitted over fiber-optic or radio facilities. An ADPCM transcoder encodes a digital signal at 32 kb/s rather than 64 kb/s, enabling transmission of 48 channels over a 1.544-Mb/s line.

ADPCM uses the same 8000-times-per-second sampling rate as PCM, but instead of quantizing the entire voice signal, it quantizes only the changes between samples. A circuit known as an *adaptive predictor* examines the incoming bit stream and predicts the value of the next sample. ADPCM encodes the difference between the actual sample and the predicted sample into 16 levels, which can be coded with a variable number of bits. The encoder adapts to the speed of change in the difference signal: fast for speechlike signals and slow for data signals. Figure 5-13 compares PCM and ADPCM, both of which result in a 1.544-Mb/s line signal.

ADPCM, which is covered by ITU-T recommendation G.726, can sample at various rates:

- ◆ Five bits = 40 kb/s
- ◆ Four bits = 32 kb/s
- ◆ Three bits = 24 kb/s
- ◆ Two bits = 16 kb/s

The most common implementation of ADPCM is 32 kb/s, which provides voice quality that is equivalent to full PCM.

ADPCM can use the bit-robbed signaling methods of PCM, but to do so presents two problems. First, the voice-compression techniques of ADPCM make it necessary to rob a bit from every fourth rather than every sixth frame. This makes ADPCM incompatible with the DS-1 signal format. Second, the robbed bit can de-

FIGURE 5-13

Comparison of Pulse Code Modulation and Adaptive Differential Pulse Code Modulation

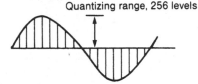

Quantizing range, 256 levels

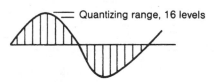

Quantizing range, 16 levels

Sampling: 8,000 times per second
Quantize: 256 levels/sample
Code: 8 bits/sample

8,000 samples/sec
x   8 bits/sample
x   24 circuits
1.536 Mb/s
+   8 Mb/s framing
1.544 Mb/s

Sampling: 8,000 times per second
Quantize: 16 levels/change
Code: 4 bits/change

8,000 samples/sec
x   4 bits/sample
x   48 circuits
1.536 Mb/s
+   8 Mb/s framing
1.544 Mb/s

grade data on a voice channel. To address this problem, the standard offers an optional 44-channel format, in which one channel of every 12 is devoted to signaling. Some manufacturers provide either 44- or 48-channel operation as options.

The primary disadvantages of ADPCM are the extra expense of the transcoder, which is required besides PCM channel banks, the inability of ADPCM to handle data reliably above 4800 b/s, and the loss of two voice channels per digroup for signaling. The data speed restriction is apt to be most critical with companies that need to send group 3 facsimile or V.32 or higher data over ADPCM circuits. The facsimile machines will automatically downshift to compensate for the lack of bandwidth, and transmission will take approximately twice as long. Several ADPCM products on the market provide 64-kb/s clear-channel capability by using two voice channels for high-speed data transmission.

Delta Modulation

Delta modulation is a less sophisticated method of signal compression than ADPCM. Delta modulation, also called *continuously variable slope delta* (CVSD), uses a 1-bit code to represent the voice frequency waveshape. If a sample is greater in amplitude than the previous sample, it transmits a one. If the sample is less, it sends a zero. These signals result in a code that represents the instantaneous slope of the voice frequency waveshape as Figure 5-14 shows.

The primary advantage of delta modulation is its ability to compress more voice channels into a bit stream at a lower cost than PCM, ADPCM, or other adaptive low bit-rate systems. A reasonably good quality signal can be obtained at 16 kb/s per channel. It is a simple and inexpensive method that several manufacturers support, although their products are not necessarily compatible.

FIGURE 5-14

Delta Modulation

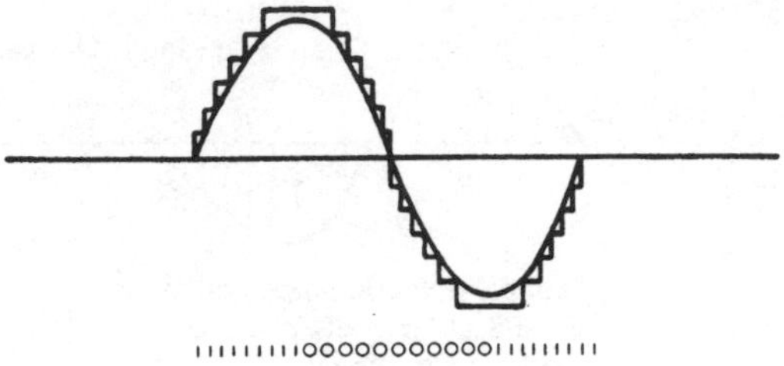

The main weakness of delta modulation is its inability to follow rapid changes in the voice signal. Fortunately, however, voice signals are predictable in their behavior, so the effect is not noticeable in most conversations. A second weakness of delta modulation is the inability of the system to handle direct data transmission through data port channel units or to transport high-speed data using modems.

Time Domain Harmonic Scaling

Several companies that make voice/data integration equipment use the time domain harmonic scaling (TDHS) algorithm. Voice is digitized and compressed by algorithms that remove redundancy and compress silent periods in a voice session. Most products that use this technology provide a combination of voice and data services over one or more 56-kb/s lines. Some products packetize the voice signal, which causes delay. Most users can tolerate a limited amount of delay, so the quality approaches that of a "toll grade" circuit.

Code Excited Linear Prediction

CELP technology provides higher compression ratios than many of the other algorithms while maintaining satisfactory voice quality. Numerous standard and proprietary variations of CELP are on the market with more coming in the future. ITU-T recommendation G.729 covers conjugate structure algebraic CELP. G.728 covers low-delay CELP. G.723.1, which is part of H.323 videoconferencing over IP, includes a 5.3- or 6.3-kb/s CELP. In addition, manufacturers have proprietary versions of CELP.

CELP operates in a manner similar to ADPCM in that the algorithms rely on analyzing the relationship between multiple voice samples. A "codebook" at each end stores samples, which are compared to find a match. The matched sample and deviation is transmitted across the circuit, where it is filtered with a model of the speaker's voice. Since this is a voice-based algorithm, modem signals are limited to about 1200 b/s with today's technology.

VOICE/DATA MULTIPLEXERS

Voice/data multiplexers are devices that enable a private line circuit to carry a combination of digitized voice and data signals. A sampling and compression algorithm, such as CVSD, digitizes the voice signals. The algorithms used in the products on the market are proprietary, so the same manufacturer must furnish the devices on each end of the circuit.

With fractional T1/E1 prices dropping, these devices are becoming increasingly popular. For a modest capital investment, from two to five voice channels can ride with data on a 56 kb/s circuit for no additional cost.

Currently available products compress voice signals into bandwidths as narrow as 4800 b/s. Some products vary the amount of data bandwidth available, expanding it when voice does not need it, and contracting it when the channel fills with voice signals. This strategy can slow data down when there is heavy voice traffic, but it keeps the bandwidth fully occupied when the demand exists. At night, when there is little voice traffic, the multiplexer can expand the data channel to occupy the entire bandwidth for high-speed data transfer.

The compression algorithm used by voice/data multiplexers will not handle high-speed modem data. Some systems provide automatic recognition of modem signals, a feature that also permits the multiplexer to pass facsimile traffic. Other products have integrated facsimile capability, which permits them to recognize a fax signal and allocate the necessary bandwidth.

APPLICATIONS

Digital carrier systems have wide application in both common carrier and private networks. Virtually all common carrier metropolitan and wide area networks use digital carriers today. Satellite common carriers also offer digital circuits, which are multiplexed with T1/E1 equipment. Private networks use T1/E1 for tie lines between PBXs, connection between routers, access to frame relay networks, and a variety of other uses. The following are some typical uses of T1/E1 in private network applications.

IXC Access   Use of analog private lines to access the IXC has virtually disappeared and has been replaced by T1/E1. Companies with a moderate amount of long-distance traffic can justify the cost of the T1/E1 to bypass the LEC's switching network.

Frame Relay Access   Frame relay is rapidly replacing fixed private lines as a means of linking data networks and as a means of accessing Internet service providers. Users have a choice of 56- or 64-kb/s private lines or T1/E1 lines for frame relay access.

Internet Access   To obtain bandwidth in excess of 56 or 64 kb/s, companies must use T1/E1 or a fraction thereof to access the ISP.

PBX Tie Lines   Most PBXs can interface with T1/E1 lines directly using plug-in cards that are less expensive than the equivalent number of analog trunk cards. PBXs also use T1/E1 for access to LEC's dial tone. Some LECs provide two-way direct inward dial trunks over T1/E1. Also, primary rate ISDN circuits are provided over ESF T1/E1s. CLECs deliver their dial tone almost exclusively over T1 lines.

Private Networks over SONET/SDH   Most LECs and alternate access carriers offer private networks on public SONET/SDH rings. As Figure 5-15 shows, a private network can be deployed over public SONET/SDH by using ADMs to add and drop bandwidth as needed.

EVALUATION CONSIDERATIONS

Standards

Bell Laboratories originally developed North American T carrier standards and licensed them to other manufacturers. Internationally, the ITU publishes digital carrier standards including T1, E1, and SONET/SDH. The American National Standards Institute (ANSI) develops digital standards through its T1 Committee and its six Technical Subcommittees that are advised and managed by the T1 Advisory Group (T1AG). The six subcommittees are

- ◆ T1A1 Performance & Signal Processing
- ◆ T1E1 Interfaces, Power, & Protection for Networks
- ◆ T1M1 Internetwork Operations, Administration, Maintenance, & Provisioning
- ◆ T1P1 Wireless/Mobile Services & Systems
- ◆ T1S1 Services, Architectures, & Signaling
- ◆ T1X1 Digital Hierarchy & Synchronization

Evaluating Digital Transmission Equipment

Originally, digital transmission equipment was used almost exclusively by common carriers, but most large companies now have T1/E1 service in their network. T1/E1 is widely used for tie lines between PBXs, for access to the IXC, and for access to data networks such as frame relay. The network user owns terminal equipment, and digital lines are implemented over common carrier or privately owned facilities. The criteria for evaluating digital transmission equipment are the same for both private and public ownership.

Availability of Special Service Features

T carrier channel banks and T1/E1 multiplexers can be equipped with a range of special-service channel units to match the user's requirements. Most private net-

FIGURE 5-15

Customer Locations Connected through SONET Rings

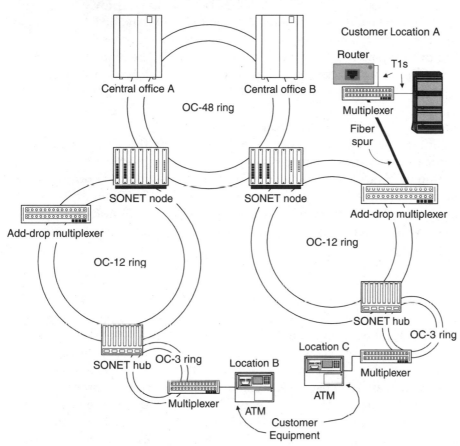

works will require data and foreign exchange channel units plus a variety of voice channel units to match the PBX or station equipment with which they interface. Compatibility with extended superframe should be considered for all equipment purchased. Even if ESF is not used now, it will be required for future applications.

Maintenance Features

The design and layout of a T carrier system has a substantial effect on the cost of administering and maintaining it. Channel banks and line equipment should be equipped with an alarm system that registers local alarms, which can be interfaced to telemetry or SNMP for unattended operation. Test equipment needed to keep the system operative also should be considered. Typically this is a bit-error-rate monitor, repeater test sets, a T1/E1 signal source, and extender boards to obtain access to test and level monitor points on the plug-in units.

The physical layout of the system should be designed to aid maintenance. Voice frequency and signaling leads should be terminated on a distributing frame. If multiple T carrier lines are terminated, DSX jacks should be provided.

Spare channel and common equipment plug-in units should be provided for rapid restoral, with quantities related to the number of units in service and the failure rate of the system. Carrier group alarm (CGA) may be required to lock out switching systems from access in case of channel bank failure. CGA should restore circuits automatically when the failure is corrected.

Backup Power

Most digital channel banks require −48V dc to match the storage batteries in telephone central offices. Converters to power the equipment from commercial alternating current sources are available. If continuous service during power outages is required, a battery plant should be provided. T1/E1 multiplexers that use random access memory to store the multiplexer configuration should be equipped with battery power to prevent loss of the configuration when the power fails.

Compatibility

T1 channel banks built for use in the United States are generally compatible with each other and with the standard T1 line format. CSUs can generally be applied without concern about compatibility. Any T1 multiplexer will be end-to-end compatible only with one of like manufacture unless it was specifically designed to be compatible with that of another manufacturer. Voice compression systems that follow ITU standards are usually compatible; other systems are proprietary and will be found incompatible with one another. Any system purchased today should be compatible with the ESF frame format or it will be obsolete before the end of its service life. Compatibility with fractional T1/E1 is also a concern in devices such as multiplexers and CSUs.

Evaluating T1/E1 Multiplexers

Several features are unique to T1/E1 multiplexers and should be considered along with the above factors:

- ◆ *Vendor support.* Multiplexers are normally deployed over a wide area and in locations where the company may not have staff. Vendor support is critical to minimize outage time.
- ◆ *Granularity.* This is the bandwidth of a single time slot and affects the ability of the multiplexer to use the total bandwidth of the T1/E1 signal.
- ◆ *Minimum bandwidth required.* Wide bandwidths may require submultiplexers to use lower-speed DTE. Some multiplexers provide narrow bandwidth channels that require no submultiplexing.

- *Data channel interface.* The multiplexer will normally support cards of different types to interface EIA-232, V.35, asynchronous, and other standard interfaces.

- *Bypass or nodal delay.* This variable refers to the propagation delay that occurs between nodes on a T1/E1 multiplexer network.

- *Rerouting capability.* This is the ability to reroute traffic automatically when the primary link fails. The routing method, table routing or parameterized routing, and the time required to effect a reroute are important.

- *Channel bypass and add-drop.* These capabilities may be required to enable flexible use of time slots.

- *Redundancy.* The amount of redundancy in the power supply and central logic improves reliability. Also, the type of redundancy in the power supply is important. Load-sharing supplies are more reliable than hot standby supplies, which must switch when the working supply fails.

- *Configuration backup.* Determine whether configuration is maintained in software or hardware. PROM (programmable ROM) tends to be inflexible; RAM (random access memory) is flexible but can be lost during power failures. If RAM is used, a backup method of restoring the configuration, such as booting from floppy disk or tape, should be provided. Also, nondisruptive reconfiguration, which is the ability to reconfigure channels without affecting other channels in service, is important.

- *Circuit trace.* This is the capability to trace the lines and nodes through which a circuit passes.

- *Network management.* This capability provides at least performance reporting, configuration management, and problem diagnosis. Consider whether the device is SNMP compatible.

- *Voice compression capability.* The type of modulation used for voice channels is important. Compression limits the speed of data and facsimile that can be transmitted over a voice channel.

- *Self-diagnostic capability.* The more capability the multiplexer has to diagnose its own trouble, the more rapid restoral will be.

Evaluating Channel Service Units

The following features should be considered in evaluating CSUs for T1/E1 or fractional T1/E1 service:

- *Diagnostic capability.* Loopback capability should be a feature of any CSU. Some CSUs permit more advanced testing, particularly when devices of the same manufacture are on both ends of the circuit. ESF-compatible circuits can take advantage of accumulated statistical information, which evaluates the overall health of the circuit. ANSI T1.403 standards establish the reporting capabilities of the CSU. A CSU that is not ESF compatible may not be compatible with T1.403 standards, and may or may not be capable of reporting line variables such as clock synchronization and framing errors.

◆ *Powering.* When CSUs were part of the network, they were usually powered from the T1/E1 line. The main reason for line powering was to use the CSU to maintain synchronization if the terminal equipment lost its power. Many LECs no longer furnish power, in which case the end user must provide power for the CSU.

◆ *Monitoring capability.* The CSU should contain 1s density and bipolar violation monitoring capability. Discrepancies should be reported to an outboard management system, displayed on panel lamps, or both.

CHAPTER 6

Outside Plant

Outside plant is the collection of cables, poles, conduit, and fiber optics that interconnects central offices and connects the local central office to the customer's premises. The link between the customer's premises and the local central office—the local loop—is the most expensive and the least technically effective portion of the entire telecommunications system. Wide bandwidth signals travel across the country in ribbons of fiber-optic cable, are digitally routed and switched, but finally must be converted to analog and piped to the customer over a pair of wires that may cut off any frequency higher than 4 kHz. Even though the local loop is far from ideal, together with its supporting conduit it is the most valuable asset the LECs have, and one that cannot easily be duplicated or replaced by their CLEC competitors. Furthermore, new technologies, such as the digital subscriber line (xDSL), are expanding the capacity of the local loop. The "x" in the acronym xDSL refers to any of the numerous DSL options, which are discussed in Chapter 32.

The local loop is referred to as the "last mile," and it consists largely of twisted-pair copper wire enclosed in large cables that are routed through a conduit, buried in the ground, or hung on poles to reach the end user. Except for metropolitan areas where many buildings are served by fiber optics, the local loop hasn't changed much over the years. Insulation has improved, cable sheaths have evolved from lead to nonmetallic, and improved splicing techniques have increased the productivity of the LECs. Much of the outside plant that once was aerial has migrated underground, which makes it less vulnerable to damage. Otherwise, a cable placed today is technically about the same as one placed in 1920.

The portion of outside plant that connects central offices has changed substantially over the past two decades. Local trunks are a critical part of maintaining customer service, so most trunk routes were constructed in underground conduit with manholes placed every 6000 ft. High-quality cables provided voice-grade trunks between offices. As the conduits filled, cable capacity was expanded with multiplex; at first analog, then with T carrier as digital multiplexing became feasible. Today, the conduit remains, but the copper wires are being replaced with fiber optics, which can expand the capacity of a conduit system almost indefinitely.

Although interoffice plant has changed significantly, the local loop has not kept pace in most LECs. The local loop is the choke point of telecommunications, and technology has many solutions to offer, most of which are not yet economically practical. The obvious approach is to replace copper with fiber optics. The raw material is unlimited, the bandwidth it delivers is far greater than most applications need, and fiber is immune to the noise and corrosion that sometimes attack copper cables. Eventually, today's copper cables will undoubtedly be replaced, but now it is impractical to do so for several reasons. First is the matter of simple economics. Fiber-optic cable has enormous bandwidth, but it must be multiplexed, and multiplexing equipment is expensive and must be housed somewhere. Then there is the matter of powering station equipment. Today's copper cable carries power to the customer premises, and with the power equipment in the central office, telephone service is effectively immune to commercial power failures. Since fiber-optic cable is nonconducting, station equipment must be locally powered.

A third drawback is the sheer magnitude of the task of replacing today's copper facilities. Where the type of service requires it, LECs are replacing copper plant with fiber, but extending fiber to millions of residences and small businesses is an enormous undertaking that must be justified by benefits, and the benefits are not yet great enough. Many observers believe that video-on-demand will be the technology that drives the conversion to fiber in the local loop. The industry has even given the technology the name FITL, an acronym for fiber in the loop, but it has yet to make a significant impact in the local loop except for fiber feeds to large businesses.

This chapter discusses how outside plant is constructed and deployed. The chapter includes a discussion on electrical protection, which is an issue that all private and public network managers must consider when metallic cable is used between buildings. Although this chapter primarily discusses the application of outside plant by LECs, the same fixtures are used for wire facilities in private networks. Also, because nearly every private network requires a local loop obtained from the telephone company, it is important for private network managers to understand the characteristics of the loop and how it affects the performance of the network.

OUTSIDE PLANT TECHNOLOGY

Outside plant (OSP), diagrammed in Figure 6-1, consists of the following components:

- Pole lines
- Conduit
- Feeder cable
- Distribution cable
- Terminals

FIGURE 6-1

Major Components of Outside Plant

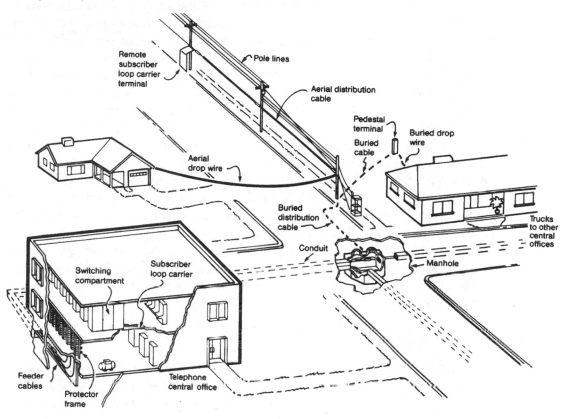

- ◆ Subscriber loop multiplex equipment
- ◆ Aerial and drop wire

Protection equipment and range extension devices located in the central office and on the user's premises are also included in this discussion though the LECs do not normally consider them as part of outside plant.

Supporting Structures

Most subscriber loops are routed from the user's premises to the telephone central office over twisted-pair cable, which is classified according to its supporting structure:

- ◆ Aerial cable supported by pole lines
- ◆ Underground cable supported by a conduit
- ◆ Buried cable placed directly in the ground without a conduit

Aerial cable is being discontinued as rapidly as economics permit because it is unsightly and vulnerable to storm damage. Aerial cable requires an external strength member to relieve tension on the conductors. Self-supporting aerial cable contains an internal strength member; all other cable requires an external *messenger* that is attached to poles. The messenger is a multistrand metallic supporting member to which cable is lashed with galvanized wire applied with a lashing machine. Down guys and anchors are placed at the ends and offsets in pole lines to relieve strain on the poles.

Underground cable is placed in conduit runs. Conduit is used for feeder cables wherever it is economically feasible. Empty conduit ducts are reserved for future expansion and to make it easy to replace the cable. The main limiting factor in conduit is the cost of digging up the street and trenching. Where the LECs place several cables simultaneously, or where future additions and rearrangements will be required, they also place empty conduit to avoid the expense of opening streets more than once. Manholes are located in conduit runs at intervals corresponding to the maximum length of cable that can be handled physically and at 6000-ft [1830-meter (m)] intervals to house T carrier repeaters and load coils.

Direct burial is often the preferred method for placing cable underground because it is less expensive than conduit. Buried cable is either placed in an open trench or plowed with a special tractor-drawn plow that feeds the cable underground through a guide in the plow blade.

Cable Characteristics

Twisted-pair cables are classified by the wire gauge, sheath material, protective outer jacketing, and the number of pairs contained within the sheath. Sizes available range from one- or two-pair drop wire to 3600-pair cable used for central office building entrances. The upper limit of cable size, which depends on wire gauge and the number of pairs, is dictated by the outside diameter of the sheath. Sheath diameter, in turn, is limited by the size that can be pulled through conduit, which is usually 4 inches (in) [10.54 centimeters (cm)] in diameter. Cables of larger sizes, such as 2400 and 3600 pairs, are used primarily for entrance into telephone central offices, which are fed by conduit in urban locations. Wire gauges of 26, 24, 22, and 19 American wire gauge (AWG) are used in loop plant. Cost considerations dictate the use of the smallest wire gauge possible, consistent with technical requirements. Therefore, the finer gauges are used close to the central office to feed the largest concentrations of users. Coarser gauges are used at greater distances from the central office as needed to reduce loop resistance.

Cable sheath materials are predominantly high-durability plastics such as polyethylene and polyvinyl chloride. Cable sheaths guard against damage from lightning, moisture, induction, corrosion, rocks, and rodents. In addition to the sheath material, coverings of jute and steel armor protect submarine cables. Besides the outer sheath, a layer of metallic tape, which is grounded on each end, shields the cables from induced voltages.

The twist of cable pairs is controlled to preserve the electrical balance of the pair. Unbalanced pairs are vulnerable to noise induced from external sources, so the twist is designed to ensure that the amount of coupling between cable pairs is minimized. This is done by constructing cable in units of 12 to 100 pairs, depending on the type of cable. Each unit is composed of several layers of pairs twisted around a common axis, with each pair in a unit given a different twist length.

Cable pairs are color coded within 50-pair *complements*. A color-coded string binder that is wrapped around the pairs identifies each complement. At splicing points, the corresponding pairs and binder groups are spliced together to ensure end-to-end pair identity and continuity. Cables can be manually spliced with compression sleeves or ordered from the factory cut to the required length and equipped with connectors.

Splicing quality is an important factor in preserving cable pair balance. Some older cables are insulated with paper and have been spliced by twisting the wires together. These older splices are often a source of imbalance and noise because of insulation breakdown and splice deterioration. To prevent crosstalk, it is also important to avoid splitting cable pairs. A split occurs when a wire from one pair is spliced to a corresponding wire in another pair. Although electrical continuity exists between the two cable ends, an imbalance between pairs exists, and crosstalk may result.

Cable splices are stored in above-ground closures and in aerial splice cases such as the ones shown in Figure 6-2. Cables must be manufactured and spliced to prevent water from entering the sheath because moisture inside the cable is the most frequent cause of noise and crosstalk. In a later section we will discuss methods of keeping cables impervious to moisture.

Loop Resistance Design

Outside plant engineers select the wire gauge to achieve an objective loop resistance. All telephone switching systems, PBXs, and key telephone systems are limited in the loop resistance range they can tolerate. The loop resistance a system can support is specified in ohms (Ω) and includes the following elements:

- Battery feed resistance of the switching system (usually 400 Ω)
- Central office wiring (nominally 10 Ω)
- Cable pair resistance (variable to achieve the design objective of the central office or PBX)
- Drop wire resistance (nominally 25 Ω)
- Station set resistance (nominally 400 Ω)

The cable gauge is selected to provide the desired resistance at the maximum temperature under which the system will operate. This method of design is called *resistance design.* Telephone central offices can signal over total loop resistance

FIGURE 6-2

An Aerial Splice Case

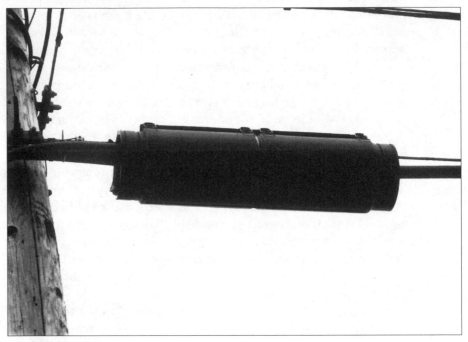

Photo by James Harry Green

ranges from 1300 to 1500 Ω or more; most PBXs have less, with many supporting ranges of 400 to 800 Ω. The range can be extended with subscriber carrier or range extension devices, which are described later. The range limitation of subscriber loops depends on the current required to operate PBX trunk circuits, DTMF dials, and the telephone transmitter. Range is also limited by the supervisory range of the central office, the range over which ringing can be supplied and tripped on answer (ring trip range), and the transmission loss of the talking path. Depending on the type of switching system, one of these factors becomes limiting and determines the loop design range.

A further consideration in selecting cable is the capacitance of the pair, expressed in microfarads per mile (μF/mile). Ordinary subscriber loop cable has a high capacitance of 0.083 μF/mile. Low-capacitance cable, used for trunks because of its improved frequency response, has a capacitance of 0.062 μF/mile. Special 25-gauge cable used for T carrier has a capacitance of 0.039 μF/mile.

Special types of cable are used for cable television, closed-circuit video, local-area networks, and other applications. Some types of cable are constructed with internal screens to isolate the transmitting and receiving pairs of a T carrier system. These types of cable are beyond the scope of this book; however, the reader should

FIGURE 6-3

Feeder and Distribution Service Areas

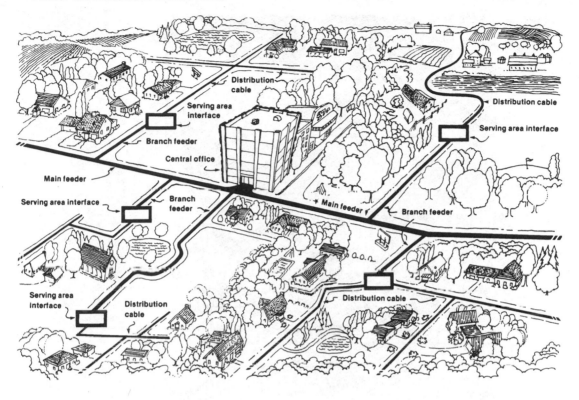

be aware that they exist and may be required for certain telecommunications applications such as high-capacity T carrier systems.

Feeder and Distribution Cable

Cable plant is divided into two categories in the local loop—*feeder* and *distribution*. Feeder cables route cable pairs directly to a serving area without intervening branches to end users. Feeder cable is of two types, main and branch feeders. *Main feeders* are large backbone cables that exit the central office and are routed, usually through conduit, to intermediate branching points. *Branch feeders* are smaller cables that route pairs from the main feeders to a serving area. Distribution cable extends from a serving area interface to the user's premises. Figure 6-3 shows the plan of a typical serving area.

Where enough pairs are needed in a single building to justify wiring an entire complement into the building, the interface between feeder and distribution plant is a direct splice. Otherwise, the interface may be a cross-connect cabinet similar to

FIGURE 6-4

Serving Area Interface Terminal

Photo by James Harry Green

the one shown in Figure 6-4 where provision is made to connect cable pairs flexibly between feeder and distribution plant. Distribution cable is terminated in *terminals* to provide access to cable pairs. Terminals may be mounted on the ground in pedestals, in buildings, on aerial cable messenger, or underground. Aerial or buried *drop wire* connects from the terminal to the protector at the user's premises.

To the greatest degree possible, feeder cables and distribution cables are designed to avoid *bridged tap,* an impairment shown in Figure 6-5. Bridged tap is any portion of the cable pair that is not in the direct path between the user and the central office. It has the electrical effect of a capacitor across the pair and impairs the high-frequency response of the circuit. Bridged tap can render DTMF dials and modems inoperative because of amplitude distortion, prima-

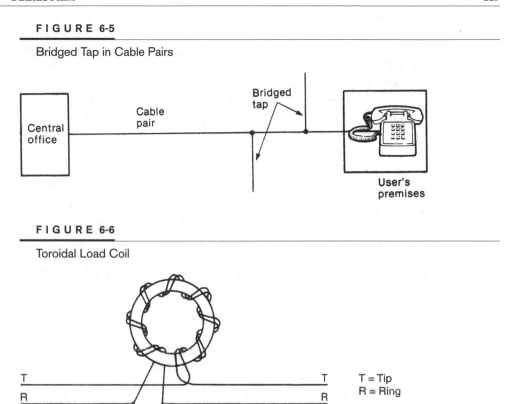

FIGURE 6-5

Bridged Tap in Cable Pairs

FIGURE 6-6

Toroidal Load Coil

rily at high frequencies. It can be detected by measuring the frequency response of a metallic circuit.

The frequency response of long subscriber loops is improved by *loading*. Load coils are small inductors wound on a powdered iron core as shown in Figure 6-6. They are normally placed at 6000-ft (1830-m) intervals on loops longer than 18,000 ft [5.5 kilometers (km)]. Load coils are contained in weatherproof cases that are mounted on poles or in manholes. Load coils cause the high-frequency response of a cable pair to drop off rapidly outside the voice band. Therefore, load coils must be removed from cable pairs that are required to support applications such as T carrier, xDSL, and limited distance modems.

ELECTRICAL PROTECTION

Whenever communications conductors enter a building from an environment that can be exposed to a foreign source of electricity, it is essential that electrical protection be used. Protection is required for two purposes—to prevent injury or death to personnel and to prevent damage to equipment.

Common carriers are responsible for protecting cables between their central offices and the user's premises. The type of protection provided is sufficient to prevent injury or death, but may not be sufficient to prevent damage to delicate telecommunications and computer equipment. Also, interbuilding cables may require protection, and the carrier will be responsible only if it provides and owns the cable.

Protection requirements are based on the **National Electrical Safety Code.**® Much of the information in this section is based on AT&T practices, which often are more stringent than the Code.

Determining Exposure

The first question that must be answered in determining electrical protection requirements is whether the cable is considered *exposed*. An exposed cable is one that is subject to any of the following hazards:

- ◆ Contact with any power circuit operating at 300 V root mean square (rms) or more from ground.
- ◆ Contact by lightning.
- ◆ Induction from a 60-Hz source that results in a potential of 300 V rms or more.
- ◆ Power faults that cause the ground potential to rise above 300 V rms.

Bearing in mind that safety considerations must not be compromised in designing a protection plan, it is natural to wonder why 300 V rms is chosen as the apparent threshold of danger. Actually, any shock that results in more than about 10 milliamps (mA) of current flowing through the body is painful. More than 20 mA is dangerous and more than 50 mA of current flow through the heart is likely to result in ventricular fibrillation, a condition that usually results in death.

The amount of current that flows through the human body in contact with electricity is unpredictable. It depends on the skin resistance (damp skin has a much lower resistance than dry skin), the body parts in contact (current flow between two fingers of the same hand is less dangerous than current flow between the two hands), and several other factors that circuit designers cannot control. Despite the danger that contact with less than 300 V can be fatal, this value is chosen because terminal equipment is designed to insulate the user from direct contact with electricity.

All cables with aerial sections should be considered exposed. Even though a short section of aerial cable may not be in proximity to power at the time it is constructed, aerial power may be added later and expose the cable. Therefore, it is advisable to protect all aerial cables, which include any cable that contains any pairs that may be exposed. For example, a 600-pair cable, only 25 pairs of which are connected to aerial cable, is considered exposed in its entirety. Buried and underground cables should be considered exposed unless one or more of the following conditions exist:

FIGURE 6-7

Zone of Protection Provided by Vertical Grounded Conductors

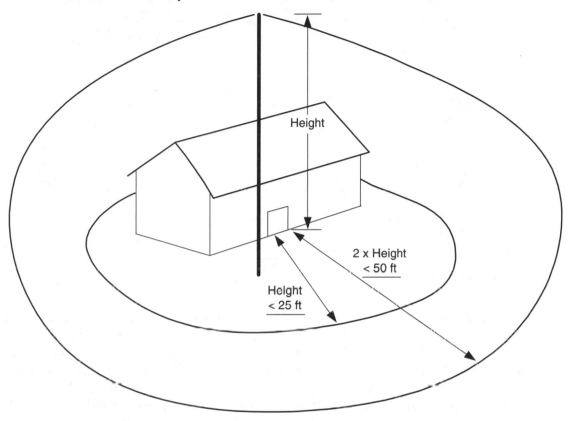

Height

2 x Height
< 50 ft

Height
< 25 ft

- ◆ There are five or fewer thunderstorm days per year and the earth resistivity is less than 100 meter-ohms (m-Ω).
- ◆ A buried interbuilding cable is shorter than 140 ft (43 m) and has a shield that is grounded on both ends.
- ◆ A cable is totally within a cone of protection because of its proximity to buildings or other structures that are grounded (see Figure 6-7).

In metropolitan areas, cables may be considered to exist under a *zone of protection* that diverts lightning strikes and shields the cable from damage. As Figure 6-8 shows, if a grounded shielding mast is 25 ft (7.6 m) high or less, a high degree of protection is afforded to objects within a radius equal to the height of the mast. A satisfactory degree of protection is also afforded to objects within a radius equal to twice the height of the mast if the mast is 50 ft (15.2 m) high or less. To illustrate, assume that a cable runs between two buildings, each of which is 50 ft high. Each building extends a zone of protection of 100 ft, which means that a

FIGURE 6-8

Protected Zone from Lightning Strike Using Rolling Ball Model for Structures Greater Than 50 Feet Tall

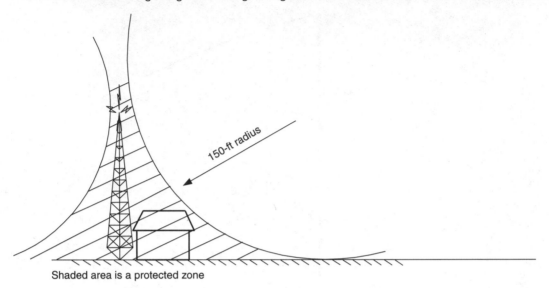

150-ft radius

Shaded area is a protected zone

cable 200 ft long would not be considered exposed to lightning. For structures higher than 50 ft, the zone of protection concept does not apply on the same basis as for lower structures. To conceive the protection zone that surrounds higher objects, visualize a ball 300 ft (91 m) in diameter rolled up against the side of the structure as in Figure 6-8. The zone of protection is shown as the shaded area in Figure 6-8. Note that the zone of protection applies only to lightning, not to power exposures. A cable also should be considered exposed to lightning, even though it is in an area that would otherwise be excluded by the earth resistivity and lightning requirements if it rises above the elevation of surrounding terrain—on a hilltop, on a tower, etc.

Normally, the ground is considered to be at zero potential, or the potential of the earth. In practice, the ground has some resistance, and when current flows through it, the ground potential can rise. The hazard of a ground potential rise from commercial power is most severe near a power substation, but ground potential rise can occur anywhere from a lightning strike.

Induction occurs when power lines and telephone cables operate over parallel routes. Under normal conditions, the magnitude of the induction is not so great as to constitute a hazard, but when telecommunications lines are unbalanced or when a fault occurs in the power line, the amount of induced voltage can rise to hazardous levels. This is not a concern in most private networks, but designers should be alert to the possibility of induction whenever power and telecommunications circuits share the same route, though they may not share a pole line.

Even though a circuit is protected to eliminate hazards to users, the equipment attached to it may be sensitive to foreign voltages. Since the equipment provider is in the best position to know of this sensitivity, requests for proposal and purchase orders should require the vendor to specify the level of protection required.

Protection Methods

Personnel and equipment can be protected from the hazards of unexpected contact with a foreign source of electrical potential by the following methods:

- Insulating telecommunications apparatus
- Shielding communications cables
- Grounding equipment
- Opening affected circuits
- Separating electrical and telecommunications circuits

This section discusses how each preventive measure is applied to telecommunications circuits.

Insulating Telecommunications Apparatus

Nearly all telecommunications circuits installed today are insulated with some kind of protective coating that serves as the first line of defense against accidental cross with a foreign voltage. Polyethylene, which is the insulation used with most copper cables, has a conductor-to-conductor breakdown value of from 1000 to 4000 V. Although this is enough to guard against a high value of foreign voltage, it is possible that the insulation will be damaged by the fault. A lightning strike or power cross may cause a burning effect that will destroy the insulation even if the voltage itself does not pierce the insulation.

Not only are the conductors insulated, but also most apparatus is constructed to insulate the user from foreign voltage. If the magnitude of the voltage is great enough to arc from the supply conductors to the chassis, however, the inherent insulation of the equipment may not be enough to protect the user from dangerous shock, and the equipment will be destroyed or heavily damaged. Although insulation is the first line of defense against the invasion of foreign potential, it alone is not enough to solve electrical protection problems.

Shielding Communications Cables

Cables can be shielded from lightning strikes by placing a grounded conductor above the cable so it intercepts the lightning strike. A grounded shield wire can be placed above aerial cable to serve the same function as a lightning rod serves on a building—it attracts the lightning strike to itself. Shield wires also can be buried

FIGURE 6-9

Station and Central Office Protection Equipment

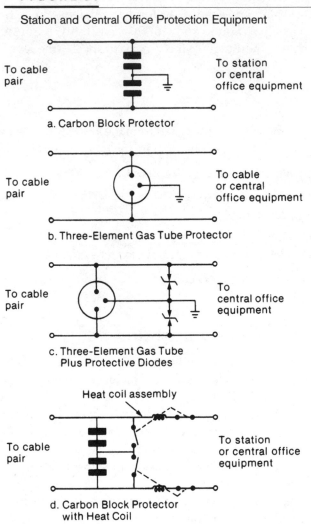

a. Carbon Block Protector

b. Three-Element Gas Tube Protector

c. Three-Element Gas Tube
   Plus Protective Diodes

d. Carbon Block Protector
   with Heat Coil

above a communications cable. If there is enough separation to prevent arcing between the shield and the cable, this method is effective.

Grounding Equipment

An important principle of electrical protection is to provide a low-impedance path to ground for foreign voltage. Both carbon and gas tube protectors, which are illustrated in Figure 6-9, operate on the principle of draining the foreign voltage to ground.

The simplest form of protector is the *carbon block*. One side of the carbon block is connected to a common path to ground. It is essential that the ground path be a known earth ground. In most buildings the grounding point for the power entrance is a suitable grounding point. A metallic cold-water pipe may be a satisfactory ground, but if the water system has any nonmetallic elements in it, the effectiveness of the ground may be lost. To ensure an effective water pipe ground, the pipe should be bonded to the power ground with a copper wire of at least #6 AWG.

The other side of the carbon block protector is open, with a mating block separated from ground by a narrow gap. The communications conductors are connected to the mating block. When the voltage rises to a high enough level to arc across the gap, current flows, the block fuses, and the communications conductors are permanently connected to ground. When a carbon block protector is activated, it is destroyed and must be replaced.

A *gas tube protector* may be connected between the communications conductors and ground. Like the carbon block protector, its purpose is to provide a low-impedance path to the ground for foreign voltage. The electrodes of the gas tube are farther apart than the carbon block electrodes, however, and they are contained in a glass envelope that is filled with an inert gas. When the breakdown voltage is reached, the gas ionizes and current flows until the voltage is removed. When the voltage is removed, the tube restores itself. Although gas tubes are more expensive than carbon blocks, the self-restoring effect may repay the additional cost. They are particularly effective in sensitive apparatus that is easily damaged by relatively low voltages.

Another type of grounding protector is the *heat coil.* A heat coil is a spring-loaded device that, when released, connects the communications conductors to ground. Heat coils protect against *sneak currents*, which are currents that flow from voltages that are too low to activate a carbon block or gas tube protector. The heating effect of the sneak current is sufficient to melt a low-melting-point metal that keeps the electrodes separated. When the metal is melted, the spring forces the electrodes together and the circuit is grounded until the heat coil is replaced.

Protectors cannot operate effectively unless they are connected to a good ground. It is essential that all protector frames and apparatus such as PBXs and key telephone systems be connected to a good ground, and that the ground be bonded to the power system ground or other known low-impedance ground.

Opening Affected Circuits

Everyone is familiar with the next method of protecting circuits and equipment, the fuse or circuit breaker. If the communications conductors are opened before they enter the building or before they reach the protected equipment, current cannot flow and damage the equipment or reach the operator. The LEC often installs a *fuse cable* between its distribution cable and the building entrance. A fuse cable is a short length of fine-gauge cable, usually 26 gauge. If the distribution cable is of coarser gauge, the fuse cable will open before the protected cable opens. To restore the circuits, a new fuse cable is spliced in. Although this is an inexpensive method of protection, it can be detrimental to good service because of the length of time required to replace the fuse cable.

A fuse, by its nature, takes time to operate. Current flows during lightning strikes tend to be very short, lasting less time than the duration of most lightning strikes. Therefore, fuse cables are effective against power crosses, but not against lightning.

Separating Electrical and Telecommunications Circuits

Another method of protecting from accidental crosses with electrical power is adequate spacing. Many buildings are served by buried power and telecommunications cables that share a joint trench. (Although joint trenches offer adequate spacing, joint power and telecommunications conduits are never acceptable.) The minimum acceptable separation between power and telecommunications circuits in a joint trench is 1 ft; more separation gives an additional measure of protection. The sharing of a joint trench with at least the minimum separation does not, of itself, create an exposure condition.

Each cable pair in a central office is protected in a frame, as described in Chapter 10. At the user's end of the circuit, protectors range from a simple single-pair device to multiple-pair protected terminals. Although station protectors are adequate to prevent injury to users, they are often inadequate to prevent damage to delicate electronic equipment. The owners of all devices connecting to the network, including modems, PBXs, key telephone systems, and answering recorders must be aware of the degree of protection offered by the telephone line and the ability of their equipment to withstand external voltage and current.

SUBSCRIBER LOOP CARRIER

Subscriber loop carriers are increasingly used to deliver multichannel service to large concentrations of users. Digital subscriber carriers operate over T1/E1 lines using either PCM or some form of voice compression. T1/E1 repeaters are placed at intervals to provide a line equivalent to that used for trunk carrier. The same spacing as load coil spacing is used so that repeaters can be located in manholes. Digital carrier operates effectively over either fiber optics or copper cable and provides excellent transmission quality. Current models of subscriber carrier offer a variety of plug-in units to support services, such as ISDN and xDSL, to subscriber locations that are outside the cable-pair range for these services.

A line concentrator, diagrammed in Figure 6-10, is similar to a subscriber carrier except that it is specifically designed for concentrated service and terminates multiple T carrier trunks to a larger number of subscriber lines to reduce the probability of a trunk being unavailable when a user requests service. Contrasted to concentrated subscriber carrier with a 2:1 concentration ratio, a remote line con-

FIGURE 6-10

Block Diagram of a Remote Line Concentrator

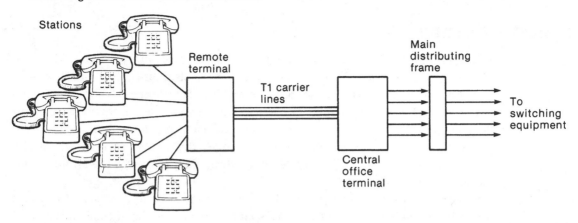

centrator may assign, say, 600 users to five T1 lines, a concentration ratio of 5:1. Concentrators are equipped with circuits to collect usage information that an administrator can use to avoid overloads. They must be engineered and monitored in the same manner as central office switching equipment.

Concentrators also may include circuitry known as *intracalling,* which enables users within the concentrator to connect to one another without using channels to the central office and back. Intracalling features require only one channel for the central office to supervise the connection. With intracalling, a concentrator may provide service between the users it serves even though the carrier line is inoperative. Without this feature, a carrier line failure disrupts all service to its users.

The term *pair gain* describes the degree to which subscriber carriers and concentrators increase the channel-carrying capacity of a cable pair. The pair gain figure of a carrier or concentrator is the number of voice circuits that are added above the single voice circuit that a cable pair supports. For example, a 24-channel digital subscriber carrier requiring separate transmit and receive pairs has a pair gain of 22. The families of single- and multiple-channel subscriber carriers and concentrators are called *pair gain devices.* A pair gain device has a central office terminal and a matching remote terminal with intermediate repeaters if required. The remote terminal is contained in a pole-mounted cabinet or a ground-mounted enclosure.

Pair gain devices provide better transmission quality than cable facilities. The transmission loss is fixed, normally at 5 decibels (dB) or less, despite the length of the system. Pair gain devices also provide quieter channels than the cable pairs they replace. An advantage of digital subscriber carrier is its ability to use special service channel units to provide services other than POTS. Pair gain devices must be powered from an external source, so backup battery power is required to maintain telephone service during power outages.

RANGE EXTENDERS

Another family of loop electronic devices is classified as *range extension*. Although these devices are normally mounted only in the central office, they are discussed here because they improve subscriber loop performance. Range extenders are single-pair devices that boost the line voltage and may include voice frequency gain. Battery-boost range extenders overcome the direct current loop limitations of the switching system and station equipment. Range extenders increase the sensitivity of the switching system line circuits in detecting dial pulses and the on-hook/off-hook state of the line.

A second type of range extender increases the central office sensitivity and feeds higher voltage to the station. This latter type boosts the normal 48-V central office battery to 72 V, which increases the line current when the station is off-hook, supporting greater DTMF dial range and providing greater line current to the telephone transmitter. If the voice frequency transmission range of the cable pair is limiting, range extenders with built-in amplification to boost the voice level can be used. These devices either contain a fixed amount of gain or adjust gain automatically in proportion to the line current.

CABLE PRESSURIZATION

LECs pressurize cables to keep moisture out of the cable. Pressurization should be considered in private networks when the cable is exposed to moisture for long distances. In a cable pressurization system, a compressor pumps dehydrated air into the cable. At terminals where pairs are exposed, the cable sheath is plugged with a watertight dam and air bypasses the dam through plastic tubing. A flowmeter at the source shows the amount of leakage. When leakage exceeds a specified amount, it indicates sheath damage, which must be located and repaired to ensure watertight integrity. When a cable run is long with multiple branches, low air pressure alarms help locate trouble.

APPLICATIONS

Loop plant is part of every network application. Even in private networks that bypass the local telephone company by routing circuits directly to an interexchange carrier, a connection may be made from the network terminal to the station over metallic cable facilities that must be designed as part of the total network. Increasingly, however, fiber-optic connections are available to large companies. Where available, fiber optics eliminates the transmission problems that are inherent with copper facilities. This section includes only electrical considerations. The evaluation of supporting structures involves mechanical considerations that are beyond the scope of this book.

Standards

With the exception of wire, which meets American wire gauge standards, outside plant is not manufactured to the standards of an independent agency. Manufacturers' specifications determine cable size, construction, and sheath characteristics. Outside plant is selected according to its specifications to meet the requirements of the application.

Evaluating Subscriber Loop Equipment

This section includes the principal considerations for both LECs and private network users for selecting metallic outside plant facilities.

Cable Structural Quality

Cable is selected to match the pair size and gauge required by the network design. The sheath must be impervious to the elements if it is mounted outside. Crosstalk and balance characteristics are of paramount concern. When cables support special applications such as local area networks and high-speed data transmission, the cable must meet the specifications of the equipment manufacturer.

Insulation resistance and direct current continuity measurements should be made on all new cables. On loaded cables, structural return loss, gain frequency response, and noise measurements should be made to ensure the electrical integrity of the cable. When cable facilities are obtained from a common carrier, these measurements also should be made when trouble is experienced.

Air Pressurization

Air pressurization should be considered on long cables and on any cable that carries essential services and is exposed to weather. The system should be equipped with a dehydrator, a compressor, a flowmeter, and a monitoring and alarm system to detect leakage.

Protection

All metallic circuits, both common carrier and privately owned, are subject to lightning strikes and crosses with external voltage. It is not safe to assume that the protection provided by the telephone company is enough to prevent damage to interconnected equipment. Private network users should determine the characteristics of the input circuits of their equipment and obtain external protection if needed.

CHAPTER 7

Structured Wiring Systems

Premises wiring has long taken a back seat to electronics in the quest for improved telecommunications technology. In the past, wiring systems were designed to the interface needed by the equipment and by the vendor's preference. The result has been a mix of quality and wire sizes—2 pair, 3 pair, 4 pair, 6 pair, 12 pair, and 25 pair have been common. Some low-quality wire is susceptible to crosstalk because little attention was paid to the amount of twist during manufacture. Different manufacturers have required different wiring types, including shielded twisted-pair and coaxial cable, for their apparatus. The lack of uniformity in station wiring was tolerable for voice, but when data devices became common the situation demanded standards. Conduits and raceways became clogged with special-purpose cabling, designation and labeling were haphazard, and new wire was often installed with older, undesignated wire left in place.

In the early 1990s the Electronic Industries Association (EIA) and the Telecommunications Industries Association (TIA) collaborated to develop standards for a structured wiring system. Wiring manufacturers had demonstrated that if wire is carefully manufactured and installed to high quality standards, it can support data rates in excess of 100 Mb/s over distances of up to 100 m. To obtain this kind of performance new standards were required. These standards, which are listed in Table 7-1, were developed and published to bring order from chaos. These standards do not have the same force as the **National Electric Code.**® Compliance is not, in most jurisdictions, required by local building codes, but any company planning a wiring system is well advised to follow the standard because it ensures compatibility with future equipment.

Structured wiring includes other media besides twisted-pair wire. Fiber optics and coaxial cable are covered in addition to both shielded and unshielded twisted-pair wire. The standards are voice and data oriented. Where video is planned, coaxial cable may be needed.

TABLE 7-1

EIA/TIA Wiring Standards

EIA/TIA-568	Commercial Building Telecommunications Cabling Standard
EIA/TIA-569	Commercial Building Standard for Telecommunications Pathways and Spaces
EIA/TIA-606	Administration Standard for the Telecommunications Infrastructure of Commercial Buildings
EIA/TIA-607	Commercial Building Grounding and Bonding Requirements for Telecommunications
EIA/TIA-570	Residential and Light Commercial Telecommunications Wiring Standard

Note: Global Engineering Documents is the primary distributor of all TIA and EIA technical documents. To purchase a document, call 1-800-854-7179, send a fax to 303-397-2740, or see the Web page listing in Appendix A.

This chapter presents an overview of structured wiring. Readers are referred to the standard itself for more detailed design information.

OVERVIEW OF STRUCTURED WIRING

As products move to open systems, equipment designs are based upon the assumption that the cable over which services will ride complies with standards. Anyone who chooses noncompliant cable runs the risk that equipment will not perform as expected. Structured wiring brings numerous benefits to the owner:

- ◆ Since manufacturers design their equipment to work on standard structured wiring, the owner is assured of compatibility with future applications.
- ◆ Problem detection and isolation are enhanced by a standardized layout and documentation method.
- ◆ It ensures that wiring is installed within recommended distance limits.
- ◆ The system promotes an efficient and economical wiring layout that technicians can easily follow.
- ◆ It eases the job of network segmentation by providing network interfaces for LAN hubs.
- ◆ Moves, adds, and changes are facilitated.

Most of these advantages are absent with nonstandard wiring systems. The advantages of structured wiring may be lost, however, with a substandard installation job. Unless wire is terminated in accordance with the manufacturer's instructions, the wiring system may fail to meet the specifications even though the hardware is manufactured to standards. Installation considerations include distance from sources of electromagnetic interference (EMI), bend radius, and the amount of twist that is unwrapped when terminating the cable to connectors. Bridged tap is not permitted.

Elements of a Structured Wiring System

A structured wiring system serving a multibuilding campus, as shown in Figure 7-1, is composed of the following elements:

- Equipment rooms (ER), which are building areas intended to house telecommunications equipment. Equipment rooms may also fill the functions of a telecommunications closet.
- Telecommunications closets (TC) are rooms in which wiring is terminated. A building may have multiple TCs.
- Backbone wiring (riser cable) is the wire that connects ERs to TCs.
- Work area (WA) is the user's workspace. Telecommunications outlets (TO) are located in the work area.
- Horizontal wiring is the wiring from the ER or TC to the work area.
- Entrance facility (EF) is the physical structure and cable connecting the main ER to the common carrier's facilities.

A major objective of a structured wiring system is to ensure that it is capable of supporting future broadband applications. Any transmission facility offers a trade-off between bandwidth and distance: with other factors equal, the greater the bandwidth requirement, the shorter the distance wire can support. Applications, such as fiber distributed data interface (FDDI) (100 Mb/s) and ATM (155 Mb/s), are designed to operate over either fiber optics or unshielded twisted-pair (UTP) wire. Structured wiring standards specify that horizontal wiring is limited to a maximum distance of 90 m, which yields a maximum UTP end-to-end length of 100 m including patch cords. Within this distance, the specifications of a properly manufactured and installed wiring system will support high-bandwidth applications that are designed for UTP.

The three main variables that are of concern with a structured wiring system are attenuation, impedance, and crosstalk. Attenuation is affected by the wire gauge, which is specified in the standard as 22 or 24 AWG, and by its capacitance, which is a function of the manufacture and type and structure of insulation. The characteristic impedance of the wire is affected by the same factors. Neither of these is likely to be affected greatly by the installation job, but the third characteristic, crosstalk, is highly dependent on good installation practice.

Crosstalk refers to the amount of coupling between adjacent wire pairs. The EIA/TIA standard specifies four-pair UTP to each workstation, so the wire has strict crosstalk specifications between pairs. It is measured by injecting a signal into one pair and measuring it on each of the other pairs. Crosstalk is referred to as near-end and far-end crosstalk (NEXT and FEXT). In wire installations, NEXT is the most important because at the near end the signal source is at its highest level, while the received signal is lowest, having been attenuated by the loss of the wire. In any

FIGURE 7-1

Campus Wiring Topology

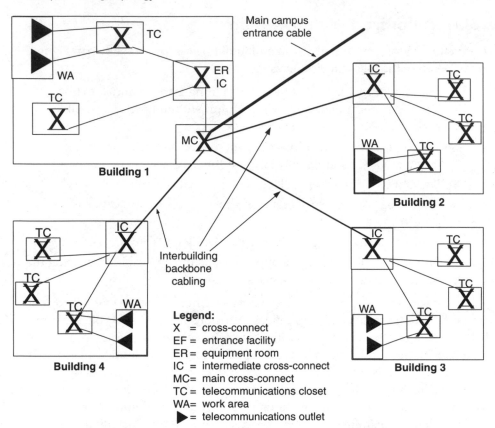

telecommunications circuit it is important that the ratio between the wanted and unwanted signal is at a maximum. Since the received signal level can be predicted from the output specifications of the transmitting end, it is possible to calculate the wanted-to-unwanted signal ratio by knowing the amount of crosstalk coupling.

The amount of crosstalk coupling is a function of both the wire itself and the telecommunications outlets in which it is terminated. Crosstalk is kept to a minimum in the wire by carefully controlling the length and tightness of twist. If the installer untwists too much wire to terminate it on the outlet or jack panel, the amount of isolation between pairs will be reduced.

EIA/TIA STANDARDS

Four parts of the EIA/TIA standards are of particular interest to telecommunications managers: wiring, pathways, grounding and bonding, and administration. The residential and light commercial standards may be of interest in branch offices.

TABLE 7-2

Characteristics of Unshielded Twisted-Pair Wire

	Unshielded Twisted-Pair Categories			
	Maximum Data Rate (Mb/s)	Attenuation (dB/1000 ft)	Capacitance (pF/ft)	NEXT*
Level 1 (variables not specified)				
Level 2	4	8 dB @ 1 MHz		
Category 3	10	30 dB @ 10 MHz	20	26 dB @ 10 MHz
		40 dB @ 16 MHz		23 dB @ 16 MHz
Category 4	20	22 dB @ 10 MHz	17	41 dB @ 10 MHz
		31 dB @ 20 MHz		36 dB @ 20 MHz
Category 5	100	32 dB @ 10 MHz	17	47 dB @ 10 MHz
		67 dB @ 100 MHz		32 dB @ 100 MHz

*NEXT = near-end crosstalk.

Wiring Standards

Wire is installed in a star configuration with horizontal wiring extending from the work area to the TC or ER with no splices or bridged tap. The standard recognizes four types of wire:

◆ Four-pair 100-Ω UTP

◆ Two-pair 150-Ω shielded twisted-pair wire (STP)

◆ 62.5- or 125-μm-graded index multimode fiber-optic cable

◆ 50-Ω coaxial cable

The standard calls for at least two four-pair UTPs to each WA; additional media are optional. Wire can be specified in a combination of levels and categories, as shown in Table 7-2. Levels 1 and 2 are older wire types that predate the standard. Level 1 is ordinary quad telephone wire that is suitable for telephone service, but not for data since it is not constructed to meet crosstalk specifications. Level 2 wire is defined by Underwriter's Laboratories (UL) as IBM type 3 cabling system. Under EIA/TIA specifications, wire is listed by category. The minimum wire to be installed to the WA is category 3. Category 4 wire is rarely installed. It is intended for 16-MHz token ring LANs, but since token ring installations may be upgraded to 100 Mb/s in the future, most companies install category 5 wire or higher as the data standard. Most companies install at least one category 3 for voice plus one or more category 5 for data. In most commercial installations one category 3 and one category 5 should be the minimum to be installed.

Users often ask why four-pair wire is recommended when the typical telephone system uses only one or two pairs, and both Ethernet and token ring use two pairs. The answer lies in future applications. Some high-speed LAN applications

T A B L E 7-3

EIA/TIA 568 Jack Wiring Standards

	T568A			*T 568B*	
Pair	Pin	Color	Pair	Pin	Color
1	4-5	BL/W-BL	1	4-5	BL/W-BL
2	3-6	W-O/O	2	1-2	W-O/O
3	1-2	W-G/G	3	3-6	W-G/G
4	7-8	W-BR/BR	4	7-8	W-BR/BR

Color codes: W = white, BL = blue, O = orange, BR = brown, and G = green.

such as 100VG-AnyLAN require four pairs, and all LANs are designed to use specific pairs out of the four-pair cable. The gigabit Ethernet standard 1000base T depends on category 5 wiring, and uses all four pairs. By using four-pair wire in a standard manner you can apply future applications to the wire without rewiring the jacks.

The telecommunications outlets in the work area must also meet the standards. Multiple outlets can be installed in those installations where multiple wire runs are terminated. The standard does not specify the physical jack arrangement, and a variety of configurations are available from different manufacturers. The wire is terminated on RJ-45 jacks. Most voice systems require one or two pairs. T adapters can be used to access spare pairs for additional ports for modems or other such applications.

The data pairs should not be used for more than one simultaneous application. LAN protocols such as Ethernet and token ring use two pairs, but putting a different application on the unused pairs can lead to data errors. Devices equipped with RS-232 or V.35 connectors can be connected to the TO with adapters.

The standard recommends two wiring patterns for jacks and patch panels: T-568A and T-568B. The two standards are shown in Table 7-3.

Shielded versus Unshielded Wire

For some applications, the bandwidth of UTP may not be sufficient. For these, the standard recognizes fiber-optic cable, shielded twisted-pair, and coax. Users often intuitively assume that STP is superior to UTP, but for most properly designed applications, it is not. Shielding is a metallic braid or layer of foil surrounding all or some of the conductors in the cable. The purpose of the shield is to reduce electromagnetic interference (EMI). The shield reduces EMI by attenuating the electrical energy radiated from the cable and minimizing energy coupled from outside sources. Shielding operates through one of two effects, the *field effect* or the *circuit effect*. The field effect theory holds that the shield reflects and absorbs the interfering waves. The circuit effect assumes that interfering signals generate a secondary

T A B L E   7-4

Comparison of Characteristics of Shielded and Unshielded Four-Pair Solid Conductor Twisted-Pair Wire

	Attenuation (dB/1000 ft)		Characteristic Impedance (Ω)	
	1 kHz	1 MHz	1 kHz	1 MHz
Shielded	0.43	9.4	500	65
Unshielded	0.41	6.1	600	105

field in the shield, canceling the original field. It is difficult to connect the shield to ground in some types of connectors so most shielded cables include a drain wire, which is in direct contact with the shield throughout the cable length.

The key to using UTP lies in balance. Network equipment that is designed to use UTP is designed for a balanced transmission medium. That means that it takes its signal across the two wires of a pair, or in some applications across the wires of two or four pairs. If an interfering signal is induced into the cable, the two wires of a pair will receive an equal voltage if they are twisted so they have equal exposure to the interfering signal. If the voltage on both wires is equal, the receiving device does not detect a voltage difference across the pair, so the interference has no effect. In practice, balance is not perfect, but the circuit has enough margin that it does not have to be.

Many organizations choose shielded wire for one of two convincing reasons: the equipment manufacturer specifies it, or it seems the most conservative approach. Both are rational reasons for using shielded wiring, but the reasons for avoiding it, if possible, are equally convincing. Shielded wiring is significantly more expensive than unshielded. It is more difficult to install and terminate, and it has higher loss. As Table 7-4 shows, shielding affects the electrical characteristics of the wire. The effects are not significant at voice frequencies, but at the higher frequencies typical of LANs, shielding can increase loss by 50 percent or more.

Some services are inherently unbalanced, which makes them susceptible to interference. The most frequently used DTE-to-DCE connection is EIA-232, which uses a common signal ground path for transmit and receive. This limits the transmission distance, which the specification lists as 50 ft. Many organizations violate this limit without encountering trouble, but manufacturers generally decline to support their products outside the limit.

To sum up the shielded versus unshielded question, most administrators should consult an expert on their particular installations before making the decision. A properly installed category 5 UTP system should support any future technology up to 100 Mb/s, and probably up to 155 Mb/s. Bear in mind, however, that the terminating equipment must be designed and manufactured with a high degree of balance. If the equipment specifies shielded wire, then the manufacturer's recommendations should be followed.

Connectors and Patch Panels

In the TC and ER, two methods are available for terminating wire: punch-down connectors and patch panels. The latter are preferred for data wiring, and the former for voice. Data wiring usually connects to a hub that is equipped with RJ-45 jacks, and hub ports can easily be connected to wire runs with patch cords. Cross-connects of category 5 wire should be avoided because it is difficult to make cross-connections and still retain category 5 compliance. Most manufacturers do not produce category 5 jumper wire because it is impossible to control its manufacture and installation to the degree that can be achieved with patch cords. Jumper wire is preferred for voice wiring, on the other hand, because it is less expensive and the typical voice connection is from horizontal wiring to riser cable. With the proper kind of administration system, the cross-connection in the TC remains in place after the service is disconnected.

Beyond Category 5

Category 5 wire is designed for applications up to 100 Mb/s. Many data protocols run faster than that speed, so that category 5 wire may not be able to support it. ATM runs at 155 Mb/s, and gigabit Ethernet runs at 1000 Mb/s, both of which are well outside the range of category 5 cabling. Accordingly, several manufacturers have been producing so-called enhanced category 5, which has superior crosstalk performance compared to standard category 5. Also, the industry is working on category 6 and category 7 wire, although the standards are not complete as of this writing.

The primary driver for increased performance is gigabit Ethernet, which requires wire to support bidirectional transmission on all four pairs. Category 6 wire is expected to specify an upper frequency range of at least 250 MHz, and will use the standard 8-pin jack as the interface. Category 7 will be fully shielded, and will use a new type of plug. Table 7-5 shows some of the proposed wire parameters that TIA is considering.

Telecommunications Pathways and Spaces

Every building supports one or more methods of running telecommunications wiring. The method is inherent in the design of the building itself, whether through the design, or lack thereof, by the architect. In a new building it is a grave error to leave the communications wiring method to chance. In older buildings designers could not foresee the impact of telecommunications, so wiring methods are often a compromise between utility and aesthetics.

EIA/TIA 569 standards cover commercial building telecommunications pathways and spaces. Figure 7-2 shows the elements of building pathways as described in the standard. The pathways include the conduit, floor cells, and cable

TABLE 7-5

Comparison of Category 5 Wire with Standards under Development

Parameter	Category 5	Enhanced Category 5	Category 6	Category 7
Frequency range (MHz)	1–100	1–100	1–250	1–600
NEXT (dB)	27.1	30.1	33.1	62.1
Attenuation (dB)	24	24	36	54.1
Attenuation to crosstalk ratio (dB)	3.1	6.1	−2.9	−3.1

troughs that support the backbone and horizontal cables. They also support entrance cables and pathways for the grounding systems. Standards are an excellent starting place for installing wiring in new buildings. In older buildings the wiring technicians often have to use what is available.

Fire codes also regulate pathway choices. In any building that uses air plenum space for wiring, the insulation must be plenum rated. Plenum cable uses a smokeless sheath such as Teflon to minimize toxic fumes in case of fire. Non-plenum wire can be installed in plenum spaces if it is enclosed in conduit.

Building codes also require that the length of outdoor cable sheath brought into the building not exceed 50 ft unless the cable is in conduit. For that reason, as well as for ease of rearrangement, the pathway provided for the building entrance cable should always be conduit if at all possible; otherwise it may be necessary to splice the cable near the entrance.

Conduit also facilitates placing the backbone cable. Campus backbone cable can be buried directly, but the major cost of installation is opening a trench. Placing conduit adds a small increment to the total cost. If space permits, good practice is to place an inner duct for future fiber-optic cable. It is also good practice to place empty conduit while a trench is open.

Horizontal cable is usually installed in four-pair increments. Twenty-five–pair cable is available in both category 3 and 5, and can be used effectively where multiple TOs are clustered. Horizontal cable is brought to the work area from the TC by one of the following pathways.

Ceiling Area Pathway   The area above a suspended ceiling is an excellent space for concealing horizontal wire. Wire must be fastened to the building structure, and not resting on the ceiling grid. Wire is brought into the work area through conduit stubbed into the ceiling, run in surface-mounted raceways, fished through walls, or placed in telepower poles.

Floor Cells   Many buildings are constructed with cells under the floor for power and telecommunications. Access into the cell is by core drilling. TOs are mounted in monuments that fasten to the floor.

FIGURE 7-2

Typical Commercial Building Wiring Topology

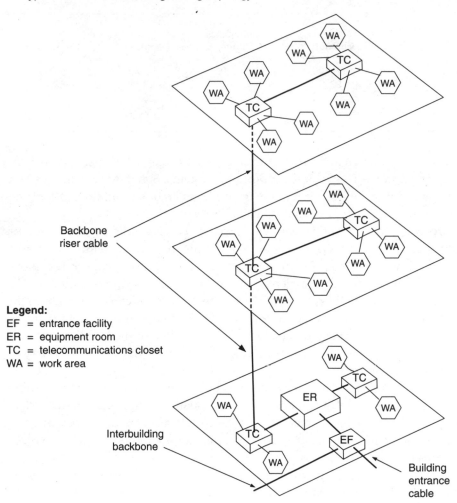

Legend:
EF = entrance facility
ER = equipment room
TC = telecommunications closet
WA = work area

Raised Flooring   Some buildings are equipped with raised flooring built on a metal framework. Cable is placed under the floor and brought into the work area through holes in the floor tiles.

Cable Trays and Raceways   Cable trays are an effective way of routing large quantities of wiring along both horizontal and vertical surfaces. Cable trays are particularly effective in warehouses, factories, and other areas where appearance is not important. Enclosed raceways can be surface-mounted to conceal wire. Surface-mounted raceway comes in a variety of colors to blend with the decor.

FIGURE 7-3

Cross-Connect Topology

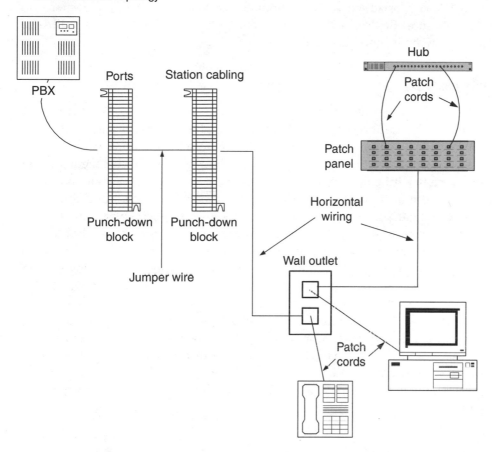

Telecommunications Closets

Telecommunications closets must be placed with close attention to the maximum horizontal and backbone wire lengths. Good practice limits the number of TCs while restricting the wire length to 90 m. Note that the locations must take into consideration the route the wire will follow to the work area so the maximum is not exceeded. TCs must be built large enough to provide adequate wall space for terminating horizontal and backbone cables. Many TCs also contain hubs, routers, and other active equipment that is often relay-rack mounted. Swing-out relay racks are available where space does not permit installing a floor-mounted rack. As with equipment rooms, telecommunications closets need to be well lighted and secure.

Telephone wiring is normally terminated on punch-down connectors. Closets that contain 10baseT or token ring hubs should have the wire terminated in patch panels as shown in Figure 7-3. Connections between the hub and the horizontal wiring are made with modular patch cords.

Work Area

The work area is the area in which telephone instruments and data workstations are installed. Horizontal wiring terminates in modular jacks. Connections are made into most devices with modular cords, but some devices that are EIA-232 equipped require a modular-to-EIA adapter.

Wire Administration

TIA/EIA 606 covers administration of telecommunications wire. To make it easy to administer, wire and terminations must be numbered, labeled, color-coded, and designated in a manner that is easy to follow. Before the standard was developed most wire installation companies had a preferred method of documentation, although many wiring systems have been installed with no documentation whatsoever. Separate designations are used for backbone, horizontal, and grounding paths. The standards are not the only way of designating wire plans, and the designations themselves have no effect on technical performance. In time, however, as companies adopt this standard, it will become the most cost-effective system to use because technicians will be familiar with it. Poorly documented wiring systems cause technicians to spend unnecessary time in toning and tracing. A properly documented system solves this problem.

The TIA/EIA 606 standard specifies the types of records that are to be kept. Records include required information and linkages and optional information and linkages. Linkages are the logical connections between identifiers and their corresponding records. Identifiers are the designations that are assigned to items of plant such as cables, manholes, conduits, and bonding and grounding locations.

Bonding and Grounding

Modern electronic equipment is sensitive to grounding. Resolving grounding deficiencies has cured many cases of erratic operation, unexplained noise, and periodic equipment failure. EAI/TIA 607 describes bonding and grounding requirements in commercial buildings. The standard specifies a single grounding point called the telecommunications main grounding bus bar (TMGB), with all equipment room and telecommunications closet grounds brought back to this point. The TMGB is bonded securely to the building's electrical power ground and to the building's metal framework.

Each TC and ER must contain a telecommunications grounding bus bar (TGB) that is connected to the TMGB over the telecommunications bonding backbone (TBB). The purpose of the TBB is to equalize, as far as possible, the ground potential of the various building locations housing telecommunications equipment. It is sized according to the size and structure of the building. The minimum size is #6 AWG, but it may be as large as #3/0 AWG. Each TGB also is bonded to the metal building frame with a #6 AWG wire. It is important that architectural drawings specify the installation of these grounding and bonding elements when a building is constructed, and that an electrical engineer specify the ground wire size.

NATIONAL ELECTRICAL CODE® (NEC)

The **National Electrical Code**® (NEC) specifies fire-resistance standards for communications cables to protect people and property from fire hazards. The code, covered by the *National Bureau of Standards Handbook H43*, addresses the methods of limiting the hazards of cable-initiated fires and cable-carried fires. The code requires that communications and signaling wires and cables in a building be listed as suitable for the purpose. The following summarizes the code requirements. Further information can be obtained by consulting the code itself.

Article 800 Communications

This article lists six categories of communications cables:

◆ CM cables for general-purpose use, except plenums and risers

◆ CMP cables for use in plenums

◆ CMR cables for use in risers

◆ CMX cables for residential use and for use in raceways

◆ CMUC cables for use under carpets

◆ MP cables for multipurpose use (must satisfy requirements for CM, CMP, and CMR)

Any cable used for telecommunications must be tested and listed as meeting the fire-resistance, mechanical, and electrical standards of the testing laboratory. The code requires that jumper wire be fire resistant. It also requires that equipment intended to be electrically connected to a telecommunications network is listed for the purpose. The NEC specifies requirements for separation between communications and power conductors, and states what types of cables can share raceways and closures.

APPLICATIONS

The type of telecommunications wiring should always be dictated by the application. In the past many buildings were constructed with inadequate attention to communications wiring and pathways. It may be difficult to bring these up to standard, but whenever rewiring is considered, the EIA/TIA standards should be followed. In any new building the wiring plan should be constructed as part of the building, and not left as an afterthought. A properly designed and installed structured wiring system can, and should, have a life of at least 10 years. The actual life

T A B L E   7-6

TIA/EIA Backbone Cable Distances [m (ft)]

Single-mode fiber	3000 (9840)
62.5- or 125-μm multimode fiber	2000 (6560)
UTP copper applications <5 MHz	800 (2625)

you will experience depends on how rearrangements are handled. If wiring runs through troughs in cubicles that are moved frequently, the wiring may have to be replaced well in advance of its service life. In buildings with fixed walls the telecommunications wiring should last as long as the electrical wiring and it should be installed with the same degree of forethought. The EIA/TIA standards remove the uncertainty equipment designers have had to contend with in the past. Building owners now can proceed with structured wiring, knowing that the wiring will be compatible with the applications.

In new buildings the telecommunications wiring design must be part of the building's architecture, just as the electrical wiring is. TCs and ERs must be located to keep backbone and horizontal wiring lengths within specified limits. Table 7-6 shows the recommended lengths of backbone cable. The design of a multitenant building is necessarily different than a single-tenant building. In a single-tenant building the backbone extends from the carrier's point-of-presence throughout the building. In a multitenant building each tenant may have its own backbone and a separate equipment room, depending on the amount of floor space and the number of floors it occupies. Where it is impossible to foresee future wiring requirements as, for example, in unoccupied space that hasn't been built-out, the designer must provide pathways to avoid building roadblocks that are expensive to overcome.

Category 5 wiring systems are often installed with the expectation of future applications, but immediately used on 10base T or token ring. These systems do not begin to test the ultimate capabilities of category 5 wiring, and even many hand-held testers cannot test wire to the limits of its specifications. To cope with this problem, owners are advised to consider extended performance warranties, which are offered by most of the major wiring manufacturers. These warranties, most of which run for 15 years, warrant that if the system fails to support a 100-Mb/s application, the manufacturer (not the vendor) stands behind the installation. This warranty, which may carry an additional cost, ensures that the installation meets the manufacturer's specifications. Since the manufacturer offers the warranty, it survives the potential demise of the vendor that installed it. Without a performance warranty, you are left with the manufacturer's materials warranty, which is of limited value considering that labor is usually more than half the cost of an installation.

FIGURE 7-4

Elementary School Wiring Layout

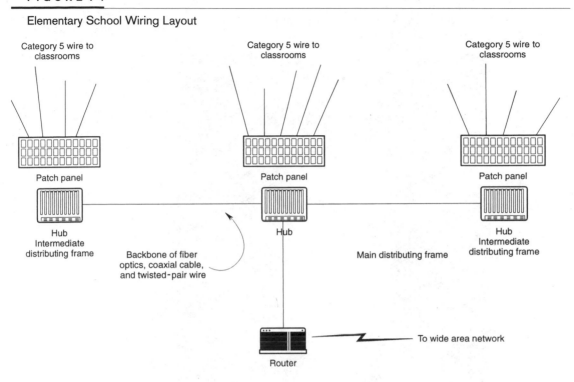

Standards

Structured wiring standards are published by EIA/TIA. The standards are listed in Table 7-1.

Case History: A Suburban School District

A large suburban school district with 1200 classrooms in 41 schools initiated a project to bring network connections to every classroom. The computers, video devices, printers, and other devices are used for instructional purposes. Each school has a connection to a backbone network over video channels provided by the cable television company connecting the schools to the administration building.

The schools in the district were built over a period stretching from the 1920s to the 1990s, which raises interesting problems in installing wiring. The typical elementary school is structured in three pods. In some schools the pods are in separate buildings, and in others they are areas of a single building. Middle and high schools are similarly constructed, except they have more pods. The typical cabling architecture for an elementary school is shown in Figure 7-4. Each school has a main distributing frame linked to one or more intermediate distributing frames by a backbone of

FIGURE 7-5

Telepower Poles Are a Convenient Way of Terminating Telecommunications Wire and
Power in Open Floor Areas

Photo by James Harry Green

UTP and fiber-optic cabling plus coaxial cable for video. The UTP is for voice services and the fiber optics for linking 10base T hubs in each frame location.

Two four-pair category 5 cables were run to two different locations in each
classroom, providing four-wire drops per classroom. To multiply the number of
ports available, eight-port minihubs were installed in each classroom. In addition,
one RG-6 coaxial cable was run to one of the two locations for video.

Since the schools were built over a considerable time span, different wiring
methods had to be employed. In schools with fixed ceilings, cable was run through
surface-mounted raceways. Breakouts from these raceways, usually installed near
the ceiling, were used to bring cabling into the classrooms through smaller raceways that terminated in matching boxes to hold the TOs.

In schools that were built with suspended ceilings, drops were either fished
down the walls, installed in surface-mounted raceways, or installed in telepower
poles. Many classrooms were built with open construction that did not permit
running and terminating wires on walls, so telepower poles, such as the one shown
in Figure 7-5, provided a good alternative.

CHAPTER 8

Data Communications Protocols

When diplomats speak of protocols they refer to the etiquette, customs, and procedures by which diplomats conduct political relations. In the telecommunications world protocols have a similar purpose. Devices exchange signals, sometimes called a "handshake," that establish the terms and conditions under which they will communicate. Unlike human beings who have the ability to adjust to an unfamiliar protocol, however, data devices are unable to communicate at all unless their protocols match within narrowly defined limits.

Protocol compatibility and standardization are the most important issues in data communications. Most major computer manufacturers have developed proprietary protocols that are incompatible with those of other manufacturers. Even standard protocols developed by international agencies, such as ITU's HDLC and X.25, provide multiple options and are not always compatible.

Incompatible protocols can communicate with each other through *protocol converters*. A protocol converter, also known as a *gateway*, communicates with both connecting protocols converting their languages. Certain value-added networks also offer protocol conversion. They communicate with the DTE using that DTE's own protocol, convert it to the network protocol, and transport it to the distant DTE in its own language. The incompatibility of protocols has long been a stumbling block in the path of full interconnectability of data networks. Although international standards have progressed significantly, the problems of incompatibility still remain.

The simplest protocols have been established by common usage. For example, every device that has a standard EIA-232 serial interface uses asynchronous protocol. It is universally accepted, and when the device is initialized with the proper speed, parity, stop bits, and data bits, it can communicate with any other device that is identically set up. Such simplicity is achieved at a price, however. As we have seen, the asynchronous protocol does not provide for such an important function as error correction. The lack of error correction was a serious drawback of the asynchronous protocol until development of file transfer protocols such as X-Modem, Kermit, and the like. Now, all modern asynchronous modems have built-in error correction using another protocol, Microcom's MNP, which is the international standard V.42.

The hundreds of different protocols in the data communications industry are at the root of traits that make data communications more complex than voice. Not only is the sheer number of protocols enormous, but most of them have options and variations that must be satisfied before devices can communicate. Many protocols are proprietary. The major computer manufacturers have proprietary networks derived from protocols of their design. Most have been released into the public domain or licensed to allow other manufacturers to interoperate, but the standard remains under the manufacturer's control.

This chapter discusses the kinds of functions data protocols perform, and the terminology that is common to most protocols. We will discuss the International Standards Organization's Open Systems Interconnect (OSI) model, which is at the heart of most current protocol designs. We will review two examples of protocols that are in common use today: transport control protocol/internet protocol (TCP/IP) and point-to-point protocol (PPP). These protocols are complex, and will be reviewed in concept as a way of illustrating how protocol functions are carried out. For a more detailed bit-level discussion of these and other protocols, readers are referred to publications listed in the bibliography. Subsequent chapters will discuss many other protocols in the context in which they are used.

PROTOCOL TERMINOLOGY AND FUNCTIONS

Data protocols may be implemented in firmware (a chip), software, or a combination of both. Just as computer programs are usually written in modules to simplify administration, layered protocols allow developers to write software to a clearly defined interface. Each layer has a defined function. If a function or specification changes, it isn't necessary to change the entire protocol stack; only the affected layer and its interfaces with other layers are changed.

A good example of layered protocols in action is found in LAN standards. These standards, which are discussed in more detail in Chapter 9, are designed to work at the first two layers of the OSI model. Hardware vendors can build network interface cards (NICs) to connect to any of the transmission media that LAN standards support (twisted-pair wire, fiber optics, coaxial cable, wireless, and so on). Network operating system developers, such as Novell, Microsoft, and others, develop higher-layer protocols that talk to any NIC. The card manufacturers provide software drivers to enable the functions in their cards to communicate with the network operating system across a protocol known as the *logical link control* (LLC).

LAN standards further illustrate how the protocol is deployed. The portion of the protocol that describes how the NIC communicates with the transmission medium is implemented in firmware. The card manufacturers use chips that implement the access protocol. The drivers and the network operating system are implemented in software. The result is a complete network that can be composed of NICs from one manufacturer, bridges or routers from another, a network operating system from a third manufacturer, and computers from a variety of companies. Although interoperability is not completely assured, manufacturers are able to design to known interfaces, and when problems occur the standard makes it easier to determine what corrective action is appropriate.

Protocol Functions

To continue with the analogy of a diplomatic protocol, the way people behave in a situation is dictated by a complex set of rules. Diplomatic protocols suggest who is seated next to whom, how officials of different ranks are to be addressed, what kind of response is appropriate to another's statement, who is introduced to whom, and other such niceties that govern diplomatic affairs. Data protocols dictate some of the same types of relationships. In this section we will discuss some of the major functions of protocols. In a layered protocol these functions are usually assigned to one layer, but the rules regarding this are not rigid. For example, every Ethernet NIC has an address embedded in firmware. That address permanently belongs to the station, and is not duplicated anywhere else in the world. That address is used to identify the station in intra-LAN transactions. If the LAN is connected to a distant LAN, the internetworking protocol is likely to be TCP/IP. IP, a higher-level protocol, uses an addressing scheme entirely different from that used on the LAN. Therefore, a station has two addresses, a permanent firmware address and an ad hoc IP address. In this section we will discuss the major functions of protocols without concern for where or how they are implemented.

Session Control   The major objective of interactions between protocols is to establish a session across a network. A session begins when devices establish communication, and ends when the communication terminates. In dial-up communications a session begins when parties establish a connection across the network, and ends when one party hangs up. In data communications a session may begin when a user logs on a distant computer, and ends when the user logs off. The protocol authenticates the parties before permitting communication to begin.

Data networks handle sessions in two distinct ways: *connectionless* and *connection-oriented*. In a connection-oriented protocol the devices have a physical or logical connection across the network; the connection is set up at the start of the session and remains for its duration. The connection can be circuit-switched as in the telephone network, or it can be a *virtual* connection, which is defined in a software path that shares bandwidth with other sessions.

A connectionless session is one in which data is launched into the network and delivered to the distant end based on its address. The postal service is an example of a connectionless operation. The user doesn't know or care how a letter gets to its destination provided it is delivered intact and in a timely manner. Each letter is individually addressed and handed to the post office for delivery to the addressee. Most LANs are also connectionless. A stream of information is launched onto the network. All stations copy the message but retain it only if they are the addressee. In a data network, connectionless operation means that each packet or frame must contain the address of the sending and receiving stations. In a connection-oriented session the packets or frames typically contain a path identifier, but do not need the address of either the sender or the receiver after the session is set up.

Communications Control   Protocols can be classified as peer-to-peer or master-slave. In the latter protocol the master controls the functioning of the data link and controls data transfer between the host and its terminals. All communication between slaves goes through the master. A peer-to-peer protocol does not use a controller, so devices can communicate with one another at will.

Link Management   After the session is set up, the protocol controls the flow of data across the data link.

Synchronizing   At the start of a session data devices exchange signals to determine such variables as the bit rate of the modems, whether compression or error correction will be used, and so on. Modems exchange signals to determine the highest speed at which they can exchange data, falling back to a lower speed if the circuit will not support the maximum.

Addressing   Every session requires an address to set up a connection if the protocol is connection-oriented or to route packets if it is connectionless. Not all protocols contain addresses. Many of them rely on higher or lower layers for addressing.

Routing   In data networks having multiple routes to the destination, the protocol determines the appropriate route based on variables such as cost, congestion, distance, and type of facility.

Data Segmenting and Reassembly   A continuous data stream from the source is segmented into frames, cells, or packets as appropriate and equipped with header and trailer records for transmission over the network. At the distant end the protocol strips the overhead bytes and reassembles the data stream for delivery to the receiver.

Data Formatting   The bit stream may require conditioning before transmission and restoration after reception. For example, conditioning could include encryption or compression.

Supervision   The protocol establishes a connection, determines how the session will be started and ended, which end will control termination of the session, how charging will be handled, and so on.

Flow Control   Protocols protect networks from congestion by sending signals to the source to halt or limit traffic flow.

Error Detection and Correction   Protocols check for errors, acknowledge correctly received data blocks, and send repeat requests when blocks contain an error. In the most primitive type of error correction, each packet is separately acknowledged, so the sending device must wait for an acknowledgment before sending another packet. More sophisticated protocols can acknowledge multiple packets using one of two types of acknowledgment. A *selective repeat* acknowledgment enables the receiving device to request specific packets to be repeated. In the *go-back-n* method the receiver instructs the sender to resend an errored packet and all subsequent packets.

Failure Recovery   If the session terminates unexpectedly, the protocol determines how to prevent the application from being corrupted.

Sequencing   If data blocks are received out of their original sequence, the protocol delivers them to the receiving device in the correct order.

Setting Session Variables   The protocol determines such variables as whether the session will be half or full duplex, network login and authentication, file transfer protocols that will be used, and so on.

THE OPEN SYSTEMS INTERCONNECT MODEL

The standardization efforts in protocols have resulted in layered protocols. A layer is a discrete set of functions the protocol is designed to accomplish. The International Standards Organization (ISO) has published a seven-layer protocol model, the Open Systems Interconnect (OSI) model, which is illustrated in Figure 8-1.

Controlling communications in layers adds some extra overhead because each layer communicates with its counterpart through header records, but layered protocols are easier to administer than single-layer protocols and provide greater opportunity for standardization. Although protocols are complex, functions in each layer can be modularized so the complexity can be dealt with separately by system designers. Layered control offers an opportunity for standardization and interconnection between the proprietary architectures of different manufacturers. Generally, the degree of standardization is greatest at the first layer, and becomes increasingly disparate in the higher layers. The seven OSI layers are defined next. Table 8-1 lists the OSI layers and some of the standards that apply to each layer.

FIGURE 8-1

International Standards Organization (ISO) Open Systems Interconnect Model

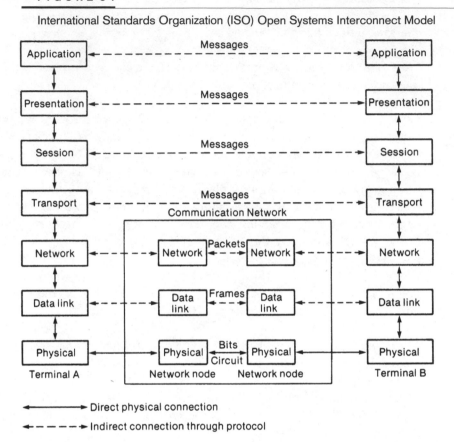

→ Direct physical connection

⇠ – – – –⇢ Indirect connection through protocol

Layer 1−Physical   The first layer describes the method of physical interconnection over a circuit. The physical layer contains the rules for the transmission of *bits* between machines and standardizes pin connections between DCE and DTE. The standards discuss modulation methods and multiplexing over the physical medium, which is wire, fiber optics, coaxial cable, or wireless. For example, EIA-232 is a common standard for serial-port connections. Its speed and distance limitations are overcome by using balanced interfaces such as EIA-422 or V.35. Two devices can communicate using nothing but the physical layer. For example, if the serial ports of two computers are connected through an adapter known as a *null modem,* they can send data to each other. The null modem connects the transmitting data and signaling leads of each computer to the corresponding receiving leads of the other.

Layer 2−Data Link   Data-link protocols are concerned with the transmission of *frames* of data between devices. The protocol in the data-link layer detects and corrects errors so the user gets an error-free circuit. The data-link layer takes raw data

TABLE 8-1

Representative Protocols of the OSI Layers

Layer	Common Standards
1. Physical	EIA-232
	EIA-422
	V.35
2. Data link	High-level data-link control (HDLC)
	Balanced link access procedure (LAPB)
	Designated link access procedure (LAPD)
	IEEE 802.2 logical link control
3. Network	X.25 packet level protocol
	Internet protocol (IP)
	Connectionless network protocol (CLNP)
	Address resolution protocol (ARP)
	IBM/SNA path control
4. Transport	Transport control protocol (TCP)
	User datagram protocol (UDP)
	Netware control protocol (NCP)
	ISO transport protocol
5. Session	ISO connection-oriented session protocol
	NETBIOS
	IBM/SNA data-flow control
6. Presentation	ISO connection-oriented presentation protocol
	Microsoft server message block protocol
	Netware file service protocol
7. Application	X.400 message-handling service (MHS)
	ISO file transfer, access, and management (FTAM)
	ISO office document architecture (ODA)
	ISO virtual terminal service
	Simple mail transfer protocol (SMTP)
	Virtual terminal (TELNET)

characters, creates frames of data from them, and processes acknowledgment messages from the receiver. When frames are lost or mutilated, the logic in this layer arranges retransmission. Protocols contain flags and headers so DTE can recognize the start and end of a frame. A frame of information, as Figure 4.6 shows, has flags to signal the beginning and ending of the frame, a header containing address and control information, an information field, and a trailer containing CRC bits for error correction. The principal international standard, high-level data-link control (HDLC), has numerous subsets, of which balanced link access procedure (LAPB) and designated link access procedure (LAPD) are common. The former is used in packet-switched data networks, and the latter as the access protocol for ISDN.

Layer 3—Network   The network layer forms a logical connection between source and destination nodes on a network. It accepts messages from the higher layers, breaks them into *packets*, routes them to the distant end through the link and physical layers, and reassembles them in the same form in which the sending end delivered them to the network. The network layer controls the flow of packets, controls congestion in the network, and routes between nodes to the destination. The X.25 protocol is a connection-oriented layer 3 protocol for access to a packet-switched data network. Internet protocol (IP) is one of the most widely used protocols in the world which, together with transport control protocol, forms a common language used in most internets. IP is a connectionless layer 3 protocol. Since TCP/IP predated the OSI model, its layer functions do not correspond directly to OSI.

Layer 4—Transport   The transport layer controls end-to-end integrity between DTE devices, establishing and terminating the connection. It segments data into manageable protocol data units (PDUs), and reassembles them at the receiving end. It is responsible for flow control, sequencing, and end-to-end error correction. If the lower layers have any shortcomings in their ability to deliver data with complete integrity, it falls to the transport layer to overcome them. Transport control protocol (TCP), which is discussed later in this chapter, is the most widely used transport layer protocol. User datagram protocol (UDP) is a connectionless protocol that is used by simple network management protocol (SNMP) and other functions that support connectionless sessions.

Layer 5—Session   The user communicates directly with the session layer, furnishing an address that the session layer converts to the address the transport layer requires. The conventions for the session are established in this layer. For example, the validity of the parties can be verified by passwords. The session can be established as a full-duplex or a half-duplex session. The session layer determines whether machines can interrupt one another. It establishes how to begin and terminate a session and how to restore or terminate the connection in case a failure interrupts the session. If a user attempts a file transfer, for example, the file must be opened, the data moved across the network, and the file closed at the end of the session. If anything happens to disrupt the transfer, the file could be left in limbo. It is the job of the session layer to ensure that the transfer is as orderly as if the distant device was directly connected to the host.

Layer 6—Presentation   This layer interprets the character stream that flows between terminals during the session. For example, if encryption or bit compression is used, the presentation layer may provide it.

Layer 7—Application   The application layer is the interface between the network and the application running on the computer. Examples of application layer functions now in use are ITU's X.400 electronic mail protocol and its companion X.500 directory services protocol. Message-handling service (MHS) is an important protocol for enabling X.400 e-mail systems to communicate. ISO's file transfer, access, and management (FTAM) is a protocol for managing and manipulating files across a network. Other protocols include virtual terminal (VT), which provides a standard terminal interface, and electronic document interchange (EDI), which uses the MHS platform for transferring electronic documents across networks.

The objective of the OSI reference model is to establish a framework that will allow any conforming system or network to connect and exchange signals, messages, packets, and addresses. The model makes it possible for communications to become independent of the manufacturer that devised the technology, and to shield the user from the need to understand the complexity of the network. It should be understood that although the OSI model can be used to develop standards, it is not a complete data-networking standard itself. At one point it was intended to become a complete network, but the industry gravitated toward TCP/IP, which has become the default internetworking protocol.

TRANSPORT CONTROL PROTOCOL/INTERNET PROTOCOL (TCP/IP)

TCP/IP is a collection of protocols that were developed beginning in the 1970s by the Department of Defense as a way of providing interoperability among equipment manufacturers. The protocols emerged from research that spanned three decades under the auspices of the Advanced Research Projects Agency (ARPA). The agency is now called the Defense Advanced Research Projects Agency (DARPA). ARPANET, as it was called in its early days, was a loosely confederated collection of networks operated by colleges, universities, and defense-related companies and agencies. Unlike OSI, TCP/IP is not a true international standard, although it is an open standard that is widely used internationally. The standard is administered through the Internet Engineering Task Force (IETF), which is a voluntary body. The IETF distributes its recommendations through Internet Requests for Comments, which are open to anyone. The IETF's Web page is listed in Appendix A.

In late 1989 the original ARPANET gave way to a network that has become the Internet. Internet is a collection of independent networks that are interconnected to act as a coordinated unit. Governmental agencies, military branches, educational institutions, and commercial companies operate the networks, but no single body has overall control. The protocols compensate for the unreliability of the underlying networks and insulate users from the need to understand the network's architecture and addressing scheme. The Internet has four primary purposes:

◆ To provide electronic mail service to the users.
◆ To support file transfer between hosts.
◆ To permit users to log on to remote computers.
◆ To provide users with access to information databases.

FIGURE 8-2

Comparison of TCP/IP to the OSI Model

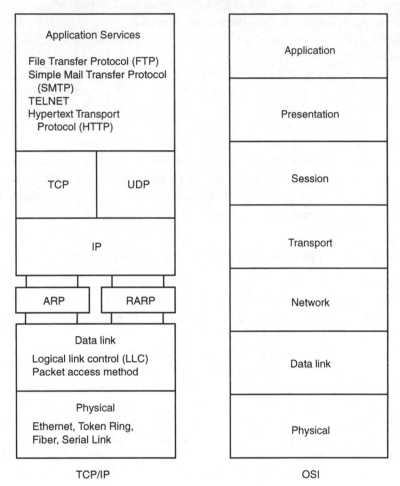

The primary application layer protocols that support these functions are simple mail transfer protocol (SMTP) for e-mail, file transfer protocol (FTP) for file transfers, TELNET, a protocol that allows users to log on a remote computer over the network and operate as if they were directly attached, and hypertext transport protocol (HTTP) to support database access through web browsers. FTP, SMTP, and TELNET correspond to FTAM, X.400, and VT in the OSI structure.

A TCP/IP internet fits in a three-layer framework atop the physical and data-link layers as shown in Figure 8-2. The application services layer defines the interface to the basic network, which consists of the transport control protocol and internet protocol. IP is a packet protocol that segments data so it fits within the packet-size limitations, and launches the packets into the network as datagrams. A *datagram* is a connectionless and unacknowledged packet. IP does not guarantee delivery of datagrams, nor does it guarantee error-free delivery. That is left up to the transport layer, which has two separate protocols. Besides TCP, which is a connection-oriented protocol, user datagram protocol (UDP) is connectionless. Figure 8-2 compares TCP/IP to the OSI model. The protocols do not correspond directly, and the boundaries between layers are not the same, but they share the layered concept in common. While OSI is not an operating protocol, TCP/IP is very much so, and in fact forms the foundation for a significant portion of today's data communications.

UDP is a greatly abbreviated version of TCP. It is used by simple network management protocol (SNMP), trivial file transfer protocol (TFTP), and versatile message transfer protocol (VMTP). Voice and video over IP also use UDP since they have no requirement for the error-correction capabilities of TCP.

In addition, the protocol family includes address resolution protocol (ARP) and reverse address resolution protocol (RARP), which are discussed later. Routing information protocol (RIP) is used by Unix-based computers for exchanging routing information, although it is inefficient and is being replaced by another routing protocol, open shortest path first (OSPF). Internet control message protocol (ICMP) reports on delivery of IP datagrams. It warns users when a destination is unreachable, and reports on how long it takes to reach a host or when datagrams exceed their time-to-live parameters. Internet group management protocol (IGMP) allows devices to be added and removed from address groups that use class D addresses, which are discussed later.

TCP/IP has evolved over the years to become increasingly sophisticated. Although no international standard-setting agencies sponsor TCP/IP, it is so widely used that it is universally supported. It has achieved the status of a common language between otherwise incompatible computers and will remain a de facto standard for the foreseeable future, particularly because it is evolving to meet new demands. TCP/IP is designed for operation on the Internet, but it is equally adaptable to communication within a closed network.

How TCP/IP Functions

TCP/IP became an important protocol because it was available at a time when the world needed a standard, and nothing else was available. The network structure has a simple three-level hierarchy. The lowest level is the *subnetwork* or *segment* as it is often called in LANs. Numerous subnetworks linked together, usually through switches or routers, comprise *domains*. Domains, in turn, are linked by an enterprisewide internetwork as shown in Figure 8-3. An IP network has two types of nodes: hosts and gateways. Although the initial gateways were built into computers, today routers handle the gateway function in most networks. A host is a source or destination of information such as a computer, printer, server, router, or other addressable unit. Gateways select routes to a host based on the address, which is unique for every device.

F I G U R E 8-3

Hierarchy of TCP/IP Networks

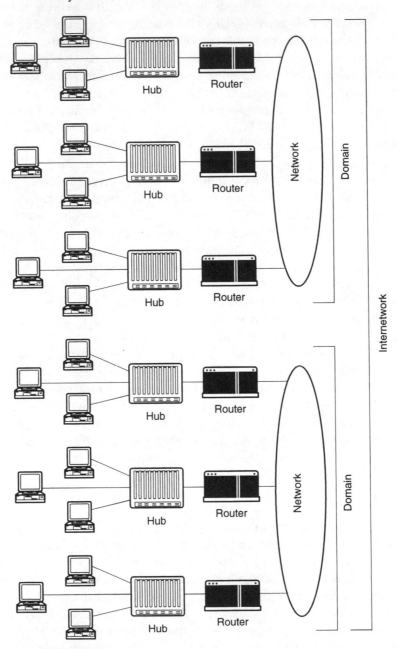

Gateways are of two types—core gateways and noncore gateways. Core gateways have, through routing tables, information about the structure of the network. Noncore gateways have incomplete routing information; they know the route to a core gateway but have no knowledge of routing beyond the core. From their routing tables, core gateways boost each packet toward its ultimate destination, handing it from gateway to gateway until the packet reaches a gateway that has direct connection to the addressee. A stream of packets can travel over different routes to the destination and can arrive out of sequence, mutilated, duplicated, or not at all. TCP's role is to ensure that any irregularities during the journey from source to destination are corrected.

The physical networks, which can be LANs, public networks such as frame relay, or private networks made up of individual circuits, are connected by the gateways. All devices on the network are given addresses that correspond to their physical position in the hierarchy. The hierarchical addressing scheme of TCP/IP is the key to efficient traffic flow. Networks can be broken into subnetworks with each device on the network having a unique address.

The operation of TCP/IP is straightforward. For example, assume the application is file transfer using FTP. The application transfers the file to the TCP layer, which adds a header and passes it to the IP layer. A router in the IP layer recognizes the destination from the address, segments the file into datagrams, and passes it over the physical network to the destination. The router determines the route from its internal tables based on the addressing structure. If the network is configured as a star, static routing works fine because only one path exists from a network to the world, but few networks are configured that way, so some form of routing algorithm is needed. Early systems used a protocol known as *routing information protocol* (RIP), but it proved to be inefficient in adapting to network configuration changes. The routing algorithm currently used in most networks is open shortest path first (OSPF), in which nodes need only know the shortest route to the destination.

IP is roughly analogous to the OSI network layer, but it has some important differences. First, it is a connectionless protocol, compared to X.25, which is connection-oriented. IP's protocol data unit is the datagram, which, as discussed earlier, is a unit of information carried through the network without assurance of delivery. Unlike OSI's data-link protocol, which ensures message integrity from link to link, IP lacks end-to-end error checking and acknowledgment. TCP takes care of those functions.

TCP is analogous to OSI's transport layer. Its function is to discipline an otherwise chaotic path through the Internet. TCP sets up a connection at the start of a session, and terminates it at the end. It performs end-to-end error checking, correction, acknowledgment, and flow control. It resequences packets that arrive out of sequence and communicates directly with the application program in the host. Some host operating systems include a TCP module.

TCP uses a *sliding window* form of flow control. When a session begins, the routers negotiate a factor that is the number of unacknowledged packets the receiving router will accept. For example, if the factor is set at eight, the router can acknowledge the correct receipt of up to eight packets, which allows the sending router to delete those packets from its buffer. If the receiving router's buffers begin to overflow, it returns with the acknowledgment a message reducing the size of the window. If it is capable of receiving more packets, it can enlarge the window.

The IP flow process gives the impression of being chaotic, which it is. The discipline in the network is administered by TCP, which has features built in to assure integrity despite the inherent unreliability of the IP protocol.

IP Addressing

The IP addressing system is both the strength and the weakness of the TCP/IP protocol. The address consists of four segments separated by a decimal, with each segment providing 255 addresses. A sample address would be 188.12.2.1. The addresses are carefully chosen to identify the network to which the device attaches as well as the address of the device itself.

IP addresses are composed of three parts: class, network portion, and host. The addresses are classed as A, B, C, and D. Class A addresses have 24 bits for hosts and 8 bits for networks, 1 bit of which identifies the network class, leaving 7 bits for network number. Therefore a maximum of 2^7 or 128 class A networks are available, each of which can have 2^{16} or 65,536 hosts. Class B addresses allocate 14 bits for host addresses and 16 bits for networks. Class C addresses have 8 bits for hosts and 21 bits for the network address. Class D addresses are multicast addresses. The actual quantities of networks and hosts are somewhat less than listed here because of certain reserved addresses. For example, binary addresses of all 1s are broadcast to all stations in a network.

The 32-bit address makes it difficult to connect IP to LANs, which have 48-bit addresses embedded in hardware. Address resolution protocol (ARP) enables a host to find the hardware address of its target given its Internet address. Address classes can be recognized from the digits in the first octet. Addresses from 1 to 126 are class A, 127 to 191 are class B, and 192 to 223 are class C. Table 8-2 shows the four classes of address, the address ranges, and the binary digits that start the address range. Class E addresses are experimental, and are not assigned at this point.

Although the theoretical addresses are enormous (2^{32}), the hierarchical nature of the system precludes using all of them. An expanded addressing method known as IPv6 (IP version 6) has been approved. The previous version is generally referred to as IPv4 to distinguish the versions. There was no version 5. IPv6 provides 128-bit addresses, which should be plenty to handle all conceivable devices that might connect to the Internet. Devices, such as hubs, routers, switches, and the like, must be modified to support IPv6. Consequently, the new format has been slow to catch on, particularly because version 4 addresses are not being exhausted as rapidly as once feared.

TABLE 8-2

Address Ranges of IP Classes

Address Class	Minimum	Maximum	Binary First Digits
A	1	126	1
B	128	191	10
C	192	223	100
D	224	239	1110
E	240	247	11110

TABLE 8-3

Internet Suffixes

Commercial	.com
Government	.gov
Organization	.org
Military	.mil
Network	.net

Networks that will never connect to the Internet are free to use any addresses they like, but any organization doing so should be aware that a future Internet connection may require changing existing addresses, which may be no small task. Internet addresses are assigned by the Internet Network Information Center (InterNIC), and their address is listed in Appendix A. Of the four segments of IP addresses, InterNIC assigns only the first segment in class A addresses, the first two segments in class B addresses, and the first three in class C addresses. The network administrator assigns the lower address levels. Anyone using TCP/IP is advised to obtain an address from InterNIC. Class A addresses are given only to the largest organizations, which can make efficient use of the lower-level addressing structure.

Numerical IP addresses are not particularly easy to remember, so the Internet has adopted a naming convention that is easy to use. Each user is assigned to a domain, which is the name of the company or service provider having direct connection to the Internet. The domain name is separated from a suffix by a period. A typical address might be jsmith@acme.com. Table 8-3 shows the common suffixes. The suffix is either functional (com, edu, and so on) or it is geographical (us, uk, jp, and so on). Users send messages across the Internet using the domain name, which must be translated into a numerical address. The translation function is assigned to domain name servers (DNS), each of which either knows about, or is able to find, a route to every connected domain. When a host needs to know an IP address from a domain name, it sends a message to the DNS, which reports back the whole IP address. Each Internet host has in its root directory the address of its DNS for its domain.

The dots between domain names are not directly related to the dots between the numeric address. The addresses are used for routing, which depends on the physical structure of the network, but address names are more related to the organization structure.

Address Resolution

When computers share a physical network, they are assigned a network address, which, in the case of LANs, is encoded permanently in the NIC. Even though the NIC contains the address, it isn't permanently associated with the address of the machine. For example, if a card fails and is changed, its physical address changes, but if the computer is a member of an internetwork, its IP address remains the same. Hosts and gateways must have a method of mapping IP addresses to physical addresses in order to send data across an internet. The objective of address resolution is to hide physical addresses and allow communication using only IP addresses. The problem is further complicated with Ethernet, which has a 48-bit address that cannot be encoded into the 32-bit IP address.

The solution to the problem is called *address resolution protocol* (ARP). When a host needs to know the physical address of a station, it sends a broadcast message requesting the physical address of a station with a given IP address. The station with that IP address responds with its physical address. The host that sent the ARP message retains the IP physical address mapping in cache memory to avoid the need to send repeated ARP messages. This is on the theory that when devices are in session, it is likely that multiple exchanges will take place.

A special case occurs with devices such as diskless workstations that are unable to store their IP addresses permanently. Before they can operate they must determine their IP address when all they know is their physical address. This is done through reverse address resolution protocol (RARP). At startup, such stations broadcast their physical address, asking hosts to respond with their IP address, which is contained in a table. Once this initial transaction is completed, the workstation is able to respond to ARP messages.

Dynamic Address Assignment

In large networks with thousands of devices, IP address assignment becomes a time-consuming chore. Each device must have an IP address, and if the device moves to a different subnet, the address changes. Furthermore, the ubiquitous laptop computers many move to different subnets several times per day, needing a different IP address each time. Static IP address administration is not only time-consuming, it consumes addresses, which are in short supply, and duplicate address assignment is always a risk.

The TCP/IP model specifies a protocol known as Bootp, which is intended to enable diskless PCs to request an IP address assignment from a server. This eliminates the need to visit each node to enter an IP address, but Bootp has a major drawback: once it assigns an address, it has no way of unassigning it if it is not used. Dynamic host configuration protocol (DHCP) maintains a pool of IP addresses. When a PC logs into a server, if it does not have an IP address, it is given one from the pool. The address has a definite expiration time so that addresses can remain inactive only for a limited time. DHCP saves administrative time, and conserves IP addresses that may be in short supply.

Gateways

Gateways are the key to a host's finding its way through the Internet. The host does not have to know the route to the destination; it needs only the route to the nearest gateway. Gateways contain routing tables that the programmer enters or that the gateway builds by querying neighboring gateways. A gateway has detailed routing information for all directly attached networks and knowledge of where to send traffic for remote networks. If a gateway is unable to identify an address, it broadcasts an ARP (address resolution protocol) message, which causes other gateways to aid in resolving the dilemma. Ultimately, if traffic cannot be delivered because there is no valid route to the destination, the network returns a delivery failure message to the originator.

Internet Protocol

The IP protocol routes information between devices. It is an unreliable, connectionless, best-effort, datagram protocol that delivers data across an internet. An unreliable protocol is one that does not guarantee delivery. Packets may be lost, discarded, delayed, delivered out of order, or duplicated, but the protocol does not detect the irregularity or inform the higher-layer protocols. The protocol is called best-effort because it tries to deliver packets, and does not discard them without a good reason.

IP routes packets and defines the rules under which hosts and gateways handle packets. It also defines the basic PDU of traffic passing across an internet, which is an IP datagram. An IP datagram is a simple PDU that contains a 28-octet header plus a data area that can be up to 65,535 octets long. The 28-octet header will be replaced by one that is 40 octets long when Ipv6 addressing arrives. The data area length is too long to allow the IP datagram to fit inside the maximum length frames of many networks. The maximum length permitted by a network is called its *maximum transfer unit* (MTU). For example, Ethernet has a maximum data field length of 1500 octets. When it is necessary to send an IP datagram across a network with a shorter MTU than the datagram's data field, the protocol divides the datagram into fragments and reassembles it at the destination.

IP is a *laissez-faire* protocol. The Internet lacks flow control and has no way of detecting duplicate, out-of-sequence, or lost packets. The gateways attempt to send messages over the shortest distance to the destination, but there is no assurance that a packet is always heading toward its destination. Every packet, therefore, contains a time-to-live field that has a maximum value of 255. Each router decrements the field by 1. If the time-to-live timer expires before delivery, the network discards the packet. This process prevents undelivered packets from traveling the Internet forever.

Internet control message protocol (ICMP) enables gateways and hosts to send messages over the Internet to other gateways and hosts to do functions that lower levels handle in the OSI model. For example, flow control is achieved by sending a source quench message to throttle back a host that is outstripping the recipient's ability to handle traffic. A destination unreachable message is returned when a route to the destination does not exist, and a time-exceeded message is returned when a packet is killed because its time to live has expired.

Transport Control Protocol

TCP is a connection-oriented guaranteed delivery protocol. It provides reliable end-to-end data delivery, and is also responsible for sequencing, flow control, deleting duplicate packets, and arranging delivery of missing packets. TCP can be used with a variety of networks, but its usual function is paired with IP to form TCP/IP. Its function is to receive messages from the application program and break them into packets, which may be further fragmented for transmission on the Internet. Datagrams are received at the destination and reassembled into the original message. TCP hosts, therefore, must contain adequate buffering to resequence packets. TCP provides positive acknowledgment of the receipt of packets from the distant end. The sender waits for the acknowledgment, and if it fails to arrive before a transmission timer has expired, it retransmits the packet. This may result in duplicate packets, so the receiving TCP host must be prepared to discard them.

TCP uses a sliding window protocol to control the session between two hosts. The receiving machine acknowledges the number of correctly sequenced packets it has received by sending the sequence number of the next packet it is prepared to accept. If its buffers have plenty of space, it opens the window further by sending a window message to the sender. When the buffer begins to overflow, it reduces the size of the window in its next acknowledgment.

POINT-TO-POINT PROTOCOL (PPP)

PPP was designed by the Internet Engineering Task Force to route multiple protocols over dial-up and dedicated point-to-point links. Most dial-up Internet programs support PPP in addition to the less-effective synchronous-line interface pro-

F I G U R E 8-4

Comparison of PPP to the OSI Model

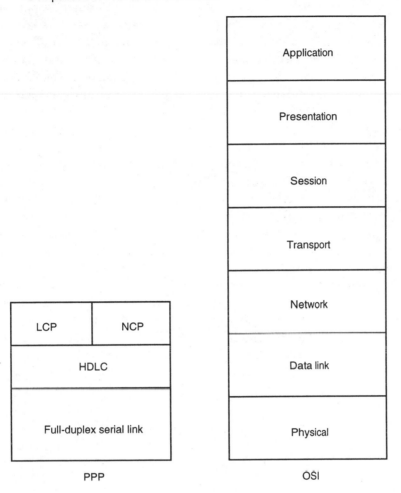

LCP	NCP
HDLC	Data link
Full-duplex serial link	Physical

PPP   OSI

tocol (SLIP). PPP permits interoperability of hosts, routers, and bridges over serial links. Various types of networks, such as Ethernet, token ring, Apple Computer's LocalTalk, and FDDI, can communicate simultaneously over serial links. Figure 8-4 shows how PPP compares to the OSI model.

The data-link control protocol is HDLC. Operating above HDLC are two higher-level protocols, link control protocol (LCP) and network control protocol (NCP). LCP is responsible for negotiating link options and authenticating the link between devices. Link negotiation can include frame compression, adjustment of frame size, and setup of link monitoring. The protocol also provides for compression of the address and control fields in the HDLC header to save transmission time.

Authentication is particularly important in dial-up applications compared to dedicated lines where the link remains intact until dismantled. PPP has two methods of authentication. The simplest is by password through the password authentication protocol (PAP). In this option the originator sends a password. The receiver either accepts the password or closes down the link. In the second, called challenge handshake authentication protocol (CHAP), the host transmits a challenge that contains a random character string to the distant station. The distant station responds with a calculated value using a private algorithm and the receiving station's identifier. The host looks up the station in a table, checks the response against the station's key, and either accepts or rejects the connection. The authentication can be repeated during the session if desired.

Once the link is established, the NCP provides a framework to enable the network layer protocols, such as IP or AppleTalk, to establish a connection. When the connection is established, data transfer can take place. A link quality monitoring protocol provides for checking link quality during the session. For example, link quality reports include the number of PDUs and octets that have been transmitted and received, plus a count of errored and discarded packets and correctly received octets. If quality is unacceptable, the protocol can decide when it is appropriate to terminate and reestablish the connection over another facility.

Although PPP operates as a leased-line protocol, the most common use is over networks that include dial-up connections. With the increasing use of dial-up access to Internet, especially by users with little or no data protocol experience, PPP has become increasingly important because of its ease of setup and use.

CHAPTER 9

Local Area Network Principles

Just as offices can no longer function without desktop computers, computers multiply their value when they are connected to a local area network. Without a LAN, people share files by passing floppy disks between machines, with the result that no one is quite sure which disk contains the latest version of a file. Furthermore, it wastes time to interrupt others to borrow a file, and many files are too large to fit on a floppy disk. LANs also make it easy to share expensive peripherals such as printers, plotters, and pools of faxes and modems.

LANs bring other benefits as well. They make productivity-enhancing features, such as electronic mail, scheduling, and Internet access, available to all users. They help administrators enforce uniformity, and, with internetworking equipment, they tie remote offices together so far-flung companies can make files and resources available worldwide. Compared to centralized computer systems, LANs offer scalability. You can add computing power in small increments compared to a mainframe or minicomputer where adding processing power usually means a major change. Also the variety of application software is a big factor in favor of PCs. LANs have become the glue that binds the office together and connects it to other offices.

LANs have reached their state of development today because an effective set of standards makes it possible for hardware and software developers to design to known interfaces. In this chapter we will discuss these standards and how the principal access protocols work.

When the Institute of Electrical and Electronics Engineers (IEEE) began developing LAN standards in its 802 committee in 1980, no one could foresee the impact of desktop computers. IBM had not announced its personal computer, the availability of which sparked an explosion in desktop computing. Fueled by ever-faster processors, cheap memory, and excellent software, desktop computers are now firmly entrenched, and the LANs bind them together. The two principal LAN standards developed by IEEE are 802.3 for Ethernet and 802.5 for token ring but as we shall see, standards have gone far beyond these.

Local area networks began with the modest objective of sharing facilities: files, expensive peripherals such as printers and plotters, and software applications. It wasn't easy to foresee additional requirements that have since emerged, including access to mainframe computers and connectivity to WANs. Also, no one could have realized that processing power and storage would become so inexpensive, that servers would replace many mainframes, and that bandwidth requirements for LANs would increase accordingly.

The networked desktop computer today is the rule rather than the exception, which was not the case a decade ago. LANs are shared-media systems, which provide the node with access to the full bandwidth of the network for a portion of the available time. Shared media LANs work well over a short range. They are intended to be confined to a building or, at most, a campus. Just as desktop computer users discovered their drawbacks as stand-alone devices, LAN users quickly discovered a need to communicate with other LANs. To accomplish this, remote bridges and routers were developed, and they are examined in a later chapter.

By definition, a *LAN* is a network dedicated to a single organization, limited in range, and connected by a common communication technology. This definition has important implications. Because the network is private, it can be specialized for a function. Security may be less critical than in wide area networks, and because the range is limited, a LAN can operate at high speeds without incurring the high costs of broadband transmission. Although LANs started out as narrow-range systems, their reach has expanded now to the point where wide area networks are increasingly networks of interconnected LANs.

In this chapter, the term *network* is used to mean a local area network as opposed to a wide area network or WAN. The various devices that connect to a network are referred to as nodes or stations. *Nodes* is the more inclusive term, which may comprise personal computers, servers, workstations, printers, routers, switches, and other active devices that are attached directly to the network. The term *station* is used to denote a programmable device, which may be a desktop computer or an engineering workstation. One other clarification of nomenclature is necessary. *Ethernet*, as discussed later, is a proprietary protocol developed in Xerox's Palo Alto Research Center. Together with their partners, Intel and Digital Equipment Company, Ethernet was offered to the 802 committee, which adopted the principles, but with enough variation that Ethernet and 802.3 are not compatible. The term Ethernet has stuck, however, and in keeping with industry practice, we will use it interchangeably with 802.3 even though it is not strictly accurate to do so.

LOCAL AREA NETWORK TECHNOLOGY

A LAN has the following characteristics:

◆ High speed that permits users to transfer data at speeds approaching or exceeding the rate of transfer from a directly attached hard disk.

- A restricted range—usually 2 kilometers (km) or less.
- An access protocol that permits nodes to share a common transmission medium.
- A network operating system that permits stations to address file and print servers as if they were directly attached.

Personal computers, printers, and other devices connect directly to a LAN through a network interface card. The original version of Ethernet used thick coaxial cable and contained some of the functions of the NIC in a separate transceiver, but most current LANs combine the functions in a single card. The functions of the NIC are

- Provides a physical interface to the transmission medium.
- Monitors the busy/idle status of the network.
- Buffers the speed of the attached device to the speed of the network.
- Converts the protocol of the attached device to the network protocol.
- Assembles the transmitted data stream into frames for transmission on the network and restores the frames into a data stream at the receiving end.
- Recovers from errors and collisions that result from simultaneous transmissions or other disruptions.

Data is formed into frames in LANs. The node delivers a data stream to the NIC, which accepts the responsibility for broadcasting it to the network. Any node on the network can receive any frame, but the NIC copies only the frames addressed to it.

LANs can be classified according to four criteria:

- Topology
- Access method
- Modulation method
- Transmission medium

Topology

Network topology is the pattern of interconnection of the network nodes. LANs use the same topologies as wide area and metropolitan networks: star, bus, ring, and branching tree. The original LAN topology is the bus, in which devices connect to a single circuit, as in Figure 9-1a. Frames are broadcast simultaneously to all devices on the bus. Most networks that use coaxial cable as the transmission medium use a bus topology.

Star networks, which are illustrated in Figure 9-1b, are the preferred topology in virtually all LANs that use twisted-pair wire or fiber optics to the desktop as the transmission medium. The EIA/TIA 568 wiring standards specify star wiring. The wire from the device is connected to a central hub. Multiple hubs often are interconnected to form a network of multiple stars. Electrically, the star network is identical to the bus.

FIGURE 9-1

Local Area Network Topologies

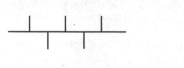

a. Bus topology

b. Star topology

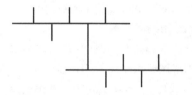

c. Branching tree topology

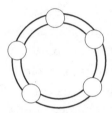

d. Ring topology

Branching tree networks, illustrated in Figure 9-1*c*, are often used in broadband LANs that employ cable television technology. The branching tree is electrically identical to the bus except that its branches are connected through properly designed impedance-matching devices. In a broadband LAN the transmit and receive directions of transmission are full duplex, occupying either separate cables or separate frequencies on a single cable.

The star, branching tree, and bus topologies function identically in IEEE 802 LANs: a node with data to send gains access to the network and broadcasts a frame of data that all nodes receive. The addressee retains the message; all other nodes discard it.

In a ring topology, illustrated in Figure 9-1*d*, all nodes are connected in series, and the frames circulate through each node. Each node receives the signal, regenerates it, and transmits it to the next node in order. Data flows in only one direction. The addressee copies the frame, but the frame continues to circulate until it returns to the sending node, which is the only node entitled to remove it from the ring. Other nodes act as repeaters that pass the frame but do not retain it.

Access Method

A key distinguishing feature of LANs is the method of providing the nodes with access to the network. Most LANs are connectionless, that is, no connection is formed between the communicating stations. In a connection-oriented network, such as circuit switching, nodes establish a connection by signaling over the network and trans-

FIGURE 9-2

Collisions in a Contention Network

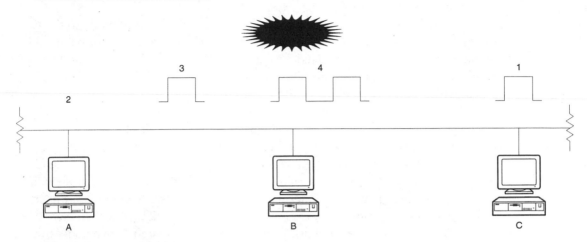

1. Station C begins to transmit.
2. Station A listens to network, but signal from C has not arrived.
3. Station A transmits.
4. Signals from A and C collide.
5. Station B detects the collision and transmits a jamming signal.
6. Stations A and C back off and wait a random time before retransmitting.

mitting a destination address to a central controller. The controller sets up a path or circuit between the sender and receiver. Because the circuits are dedicated to the parties that are connected, stations cannot interfere with one another after a session is established. By contrast, a shared-media LAN has only one path to handle high-speed data. The total capacity of the path, however, exceeds the transmission requirements of any node, so the fact of medium sharing is transparent to the nodes. Nodes are given exclusive access to the entire network for long enough to send a frame of data. LAN access methods are classified as contention or noncontention.

Contention Access

A *contention* network can be visualized as a large party line with all nodes vying for access. Contention networks have no central control. Instead, control functions are embedded in the NICs of all nodes. When a node has traffic to send, a function known as *media access control* (MAC) in its NIC listens to the network and, if it is idle, sends a frame of data.

It is not always possible, however, for the MAC to determine when the network is idle. A finite time is required for a signal to transit the length of the transmission medium. In LANs pulses typically travel at about three-fourths of the speed of light. Therefore, as Figure 9-2 shows, a node at one end of a LAN may begin to transmit without realizing that a node at the other end of the network has also begun to transmit. When simultaneous transmissions occur, the two signals collide, and are mutilated.

During the time it takes a pulse to travel from the sending node to the furthest nodes on the network, known as the *collision window,* nodes are blinded to potential collisions. In 1 km of coaxial cable the collision window is approximately 5 μs wide. Because of potential collisions, contention networks are restricted in diameter—the wider the network, the longer the collision window. The practical limitation in contention LANs operating at a data rate of 10 Mb/s is about 2 km. The 802.3 standards specify a maximum length of 500 m for a single coaxial segment, with up to five segments connected through a maximum of four repeaters.

The most common system for managing access and collisions in a contention network is known as *carrier-sense multiple access with collision detection* (CSMA/CD). CSMA/CD, which is used in Ethernet and IEEE 802.3, is a listen-before-transmit protocol. A node wishing to transmit monitors the network to determine whether any traffic is present. If the network is idle, it begins to transmit. If two nodes transmit simultaneously, their frames collide. The first node hearing the collision transmits a jamming signal. When the two transmitting nodes hear it, they immediately cease to transmit and wait for a random time. If nodes attempted to reaccess the network immediately following a collision, repeated collisions between the same two nodes would occur. To prevent repeated collisions, the protocol causes nodes to wait a random time before the next attempt. The procedures that nodes follow when a collision occurs are called their *backoff algorithm.*

Noncontention Access

CSMA/CD is known as a *statistical* access method, relying on the probability that its nodes will get enough share of the network to send their traffic in a timely manner. During heavy load periods access may be delayed, so CSMA/CD is not satisfactory for applications that rely on predictable network access.

A noncontention system, called *token passing,* introduces a form of control that overcomes the drawbacks of the free-for-all system used by CSMA/CD. A token is a unique combination of bits that circulates through the network following a predetermined route. When a node has data to send, it captures the token, transmits its message, and replaces the token on the network. Token passing is a *deterministic* system. If a node has traffic equal to or higher in priority than other traffic on the network, the control mechanism will allocate it a portion of the network's capacity.

The advantages of control are purchased at the price of greater complexity. One of the nodes in a token network must be equipped to initiate recovery action if the token is lost or mutilated, which can occur if a node fails or loses power at the time it possesses the token. Other functions required of the control node include the removal of persistently circulating frames, removal of duplicate tokens, control of priority, and addition and removal of nodes. Further complicating the process is

FIGURE 9-3

Token Ring Network

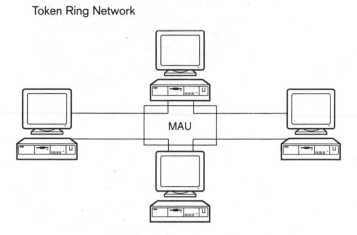

the need for a recovery routine if the control node fails. To avoid the impact of loss of the control node, all nodes are equipped with logic to assume control if necessary. Because of this greater complexity, token-passing NICs are more expensive than contention NICs.

Ring and bus topologies predominate in token networks. In a token ring, which is illustrated in Figure 9-3, each node receives each message and repeats it to the next node in turn. Sequencing is automatic; it always follows the same route in the same direction around the ring. As shown in Figure 9-3, although token ring networks are wired as a ring, the wire is configured as a star. Two pairs of wires terminate in a multinode access unit (MAU) in the center of the network. The MAU routes the token from port to port, and bypasses a port if its node is inoperative.

In a token bus network, messages are broadcast to all nodes simultaneously, but control follows a logical ring sequence, as illustrated in Figure 9-4. When a node acquires the token, it is permitted to broadcast a message, but the token can be passed to any other node without regard to its physical position on the network. Token bus networks are used primarily in manufacturing automation protocol (MAP) networks, and have no office application.

Modulation Methods

LANs use one of two methods to impose a data signal on the transmission medium. In the first, known as *baseband,* the signal is pulsed directly on the transmission medium in the form of high-speed, square-wave pulses of direct current voltage. *Broadband* systems use cable television technology to divide the transmission medium into frequency bands or channels. Each broadband channel can be multiplexed to carry data, voice, or video. Broadband networks are

FIGURE 9-4

Token Bus Network

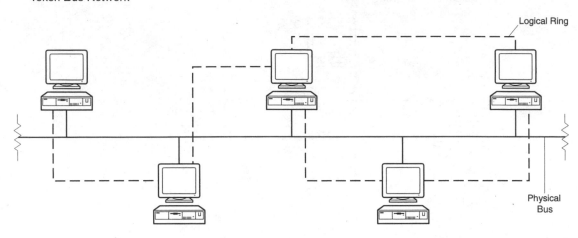

used in a few specialized applications, but the vast majority of LANs use base-band modulation.

Baseband and broadband networks accept identical data streams from the terminal, but they differ in the network access unit. In a baseband thick coaxial cable system, the NIC is coupled to a transceiver, which is a simple cable driver that matches the impedance of the cable and transmits pulses at the data transfer rate. In thin coaxial cable systems, the transceiver is built into the NIC. In a broadband network, the NIC connects to a *radio frequency (rf) modem*, which modulates the data to an assigned rf channel.

Baseband

The primary advantage of baseband is its simplicity. No tuned circuits or radio frequency apparatus is required. A baseband system has no active components aside from the NICs, hubs, and, in thick Ethernet systems, external transceivers. Only the cable is common to the network, making baseband less vulnerable to failure than broadband, which contains amplifiers and other active components.

A baseband network consists of nodes that contain NICs plugged into an expansion slot or built into the motherboard. The NICs accept a data stream from the application and form it into frames that are pulsed directly on the transmission medium. The transmission medium, discussed in a later section, can be unshielded or shielded twisted-pair copper wire, coaxial cable, fiber-optic cable, or wireless. In fiber-optic cable, data pulses drive a light transmitter, which turns a laser or light-emitting diode ON and OFF, corresponding to the 0s and 1s of the data signal. Wireless uses infrared or spread spectrum radio signals to carry the signal.

Broadband

Broadband networks use a coaxial cable and amplifier system capable of passing frequencies from about 5 to 400 MHz. Television channels each occupy 6 MHz, with the total cable supporting more than 60 one-way channels, which can be used for a LAN, video, or voice. The primary advantage of broadband over baseband LANs is their greater capacity. The equivalent of several baseband networks is derived by using multiple subcarriers for increased LAN channels, video, or in some cases, voice. Broadband LANs should not be confused with the use of the term broadband to describe high-speed transmission facilities. Chapter 33 discusses broadband networks such as FDDI, SMDS, and other high-speed technologies. These technologies use baseband modulation at high speeds to obtain the bandwidth needed for specialized applications such as imaging and multimedia.

Unlike baseband, where signals are broadcast in both directions simultaneously, broadband is inherently a one-way system because of its amplifiers. Bidirectional amplifiers are available, but the transmitting and receiving signals must be separated to obtain bidirectional transmission. The reverse direction is handled either by sending on one cable and receiving on another or by splitting the sending and receiving signals into two different frequencies. The first method is called a *dual-cable system*, and the second a *single-cable system*. *Headend equipment* couples the transmit cable to the receive cable in a dual-cable system and shifts the transmit frequency to the receive frequency in a single-cable system. Headend equipment in a single-cable system and amplifiers in all broadband systems are active elements; a failure can interrupt the network.

Devices in a broadband network connect to the transmission medium through rf modems that contain a transceiver tuned to the network transmit and receive frequencies. Two types of rf modems are available. *Fixed frequency modems* are tuned to a single frequency. *Frequency agile modems* can be shifted under direction of a central controller that connects nodes by selecting an idle channel, directing the two modems to the channel, and dropping out of the connection.

Baseband and broadband LANs are similar in most respects except for the frequency separation in a broadband network and differing methods of collision detection. Collisions are detected on a direct current basis in a baseband network, but because broadband networks are incapable of passing direct current, they employ a different method of collision detection. A common technique is for the sending node to listen for transmissions mutilated by collision. Another system of collision detection is the bit comparison method in which a series of bits is transmitted to acquire the network. If a collision occurs, the first section detecting the collision transmits a jamming signal on a separate channel. Throughput is reduced slightly by the increased overhead and the added length of the doubled cable.

When LANs were first developed, broadband appeared as if it would be an important method of implementing them. Since then, the simplicity of baseband LANs, primarily those using unshielded twisted-pair wire, has eliminated broadband LANs for all but a few specialized applications.

Transmission Media

All of the transmission media used in other networks—twisted-pair wire, coaxial cable, fiber optics, radio, and infrared—are employed in LANs. Radio and infrared are used for special applications; the other three are used for general LAN application. The choice of transmission medium is usually dictated by the application. Because of differing characteristics, the choice of system may be driven by the transmission medium required. The principal factors to consider are

- ◆ Presence of electromagnetic interference (EMI)
- ◆ Network throughput
- ◆ Bandwidth required
- ◆ Network diameter
- ◆ Multiple device access
- ◆ Cost
- ◆ Security

Twisted-Pair Wire

In the early LAN designs UTP was considered to lack the bandwidth and noise immunity needed for reliable operation over a reasonable distance. Recently, however, structured cable systems using precisely manufactured and carefully installed components have been standardized by EIA and TIA. Category 5 UTP has enough bandwidth to handle up to 155 Mb/s, which enables it to carry FDDI and ATM to the desktop. As a result, UTP has become the default medium. The IEEE designation for Ethernet running on UTP is 10base T.

The primary advantages of twisted-pair wire are cost and ease of installation. Wire is readily available from many vendors and can be installed by trained personnel with simple and inexpensive hand tools. It has enough bandwidth to handle data speeds of up to 155 Mb/s for distances of up to 100 m. See Chapter 7 for a discussion of structured wiring systems that support high-speed LANs. Wire is available in multiple twisted-pair cable, both shielded and unshielded, and in flat ribbons that can be installed under carpet. It is durable and capable of withstanding considerable abuse without damage, and with its sheath intact, it is impervious to weather. Equally important, voice systems use central switches that require wire runs to be brought to a central location. UTP for both voice and data can be placed simultaneously using the same pathways and reducing the cost of the installation.

Industry standard RJ-45 jacks and patch cords are used to connect the NIC to the transmission medium. Many NICs have two or three types of adapters on the card so the station can connect to UTP, thin coaxial, or thick coaxial through an attachment unit interface (AUI) connector.

Coaxial Cable

Coaxial cable, or "coax," is a good transmission medium for some LANs. It is inexpensive, has wide bandwidth, and can be installed by moderately skilled workers. Coax can support both high-speed data and video, and because it is widely used for cable television (CATV), it is readily available at moderate cost.

Coaxial cable has one or more center conductors surrounded by a shield of flexible braid or semirigid copper or aluminum tube, with an outer jacket of PVC or Teflon. When properly installed, the conductor is shielded from EMI and is reasonably impervious to weather. Special precautions are required to avoid unwanted effects in installing coaxial cables. In baseband networks, cables must be grounded in only one place; precautions are required to insulate connectors from the ground at unwanted places. Branching points in broadband coax must be equipped with splitters and directional couplers to avoid impedance irregularities. The bend radius of coax must be sufficiently wide to prevent kinking, which can cause an impedance irregularity.

Coax can be tapped with little difficulty, which is advantageous when adding nodes to a LAN without interrupting service. This means, however, that communications on the network are not entirely secure from unauthorized access. Refer to Chapter 20 for further discussion of CATV components.

The earliest versions of Ethernet, now known as 10base 5, operate on thick 50-Ω coaxial cable. Segments are limited to 500 m in length. Transceivers mount on the cable and connect to the network interface card through the attachment unit interface. This method of node attachment is effective for interconnecting large-scale computers or 10base T networks, but it is difficult to install in an office environment. The cable can be placed in suspended ceilings or in the wiring troughs of modular furniture, but it is difficult to administer, so it has been replaced as a backbone medium by fiber optics in most cases. The AUI-to-transceiver cable is limited in length to 50 m.

Some of thick Ethernet's deficiencies are resolved with thin Ethernet, which works on RG-58 cable. This cable is about the thickness of a pencil, and is easier to install. Thin Ethernet, also known as 10base 2, is daisy chained from node to node, as shown in Figure 9-5. Thin Ethernet segments are limited to 185 m in length, not 200 m as its 10base 2 designation would imply. The cable terminates directly on a BNC connector, which mounts on the NIC. A T connector is used to daisy chain the cable from one node to the next, with terminators placed on the end nodes.

Thin Ethernet is acceptable in an open work area where cable can be run easily from node to node: computer labs, for example. In an area with fixed walls, the cable must be looped down the wall and back up again to connect from office to office. The 185-m segment length can be reached quickly in such an environment. Thin Ethernet also has the disadvantage of being difficult to troubleshoot. If the cable is broken, all the nodes downstream (away from the server) are isolated.

Both thick and thin coaxial cable must be terminated on both ends in a 50-Ω terminator. An unterminated cable results in reflections that can disrupt the

FIGURE 9-5

Thin Ethernet Daisy Chains between Computers

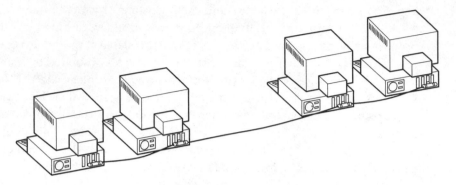

network. Another important factor is to ensure that the cable is grounded once, and only once.

Fiber Optics

Fiber-optic cable with its wide bandwidth can support data speeds far higher than those needed by most LANs. Fiber can be applied to single links between the workstation and a hub, or as a medium to connect hubs. Ethernet can be supported at 10 Mb/s over fiber by a *fiber-optic inter-repeater link* (FOIRL). A newer standard known as 10base F allows a fiber link to be used for up to 2 km between repeaters. The 10base F standard defines three types of fiber segments, as shown in Figure 9-6:

- *10base FL.* Fiber link segment
- *10base FP.* Star topology using a passive optical coupler at the hub
- *10base FB.* Fiber-optic synchronous backbone link

Fiber optics supports one of the three 100-Mb/s Ethernet options. Fast Ethernet, which is discussed later, operates over fiber optics under the 100base FX specifications. Fiber is the medium of choice for gigabit Ethernet, which is discussed in Chapter 33. Fiber is also the primary transmission medium used with fiber distributed data interface (FDDI), also covered in Chapter 33. Refer to Chapter 15 for additional information on lightwave.

Radio

As discussed in Chapter 19, spread spectrum radio is used for wireless LANs where bandwidth requirements are not great. Spread spectrum is an inherently secure mechanism for releasing nodes from the confines of a mounting cord. For

FIGURE 9-6

Fiber-Optic Links

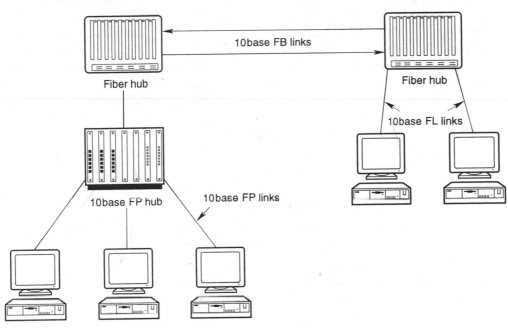

portable applications, such as personal digital assistants, spread spectrum radio is an effective medium that can penetrate walls and floors without the need to string wire. It is not, however, robust enough at this stage of development to replace wired media.

Microwave radio is inherently a point-to-point medium, and as such is useful for linking LANs. Microwaves travel in a straight line, so intermediate nodes can be linked only if they are on the path of the radio beam. Radio is useful where right-of-way is a problem, as in crossing obstructions and spanning moderate distances. It is also useful in connecting LANs.

Among its limitations, radio is not easily secured. It is impossible to prevent unauthorized detection of data signals over a microwave path, so when security is important, encryption is required. Frequency allocations are coordinated by the Federal Communications Commission (FCC) and may be difficult to obtain in crowded urban areas. Also, microwave is expensive to purchase, requires trained technicians to install and maintain, and is susceptible to interference from outside sources. Nevertheless, it is an economical way of interconnecting LANs, particularly where obstructions make it impossible to obtain right-of-way for fiber optics. Refer to Chapter 16 for additional information on microwave.

Light

Optical transceivers are available for the same kinds of applications as described above for radio. Point-to-point systems use infrared light transceivers operating over short line-of-sight distances such as crossing a street between two buildings. Distances are limited, and transmission is not completely reliable because light beams can be interrupted by influences such as fog and dust. Its application is limited to short distances where other alternatives are prohibitively expensive.

Some wireless LAN products use infrared light to connect nodes to a hub. Light is transmitted from the station to a centrally located infrared transceiver mounted on the ceiling or light is scattered throughout the coverage area. Infrared cannot penetrate walls, so its applications are strictly limited to line of sight.

LOCAL AREA NETWORK STANDARDS

Local area network standards originated in much the same way that other communications standards have been set. Manufacturers experimented with communications and access methods, developed proprietary techniques, and gradually demonstrated their feasibility. Early protocols were proprietary, limiting the compatibility between the network and existing equipment and that of other manufacturers. Ethernet is a case in point. Developed in the early 1970s by Xerox Corporation in its Palo Alto Research Center, Ethernet was offered for licensing at a nominal cost. Rarely, however, do proprietary systems become adopted as standards without modification. Ethernet was no exception.

The IEEE 802 Committee

In 1980, the Institute of Electrical and Electronics Engineers (IEEE) formed the 802 committee, which was charged with developing LAN standards. A few years earlier, Digital Equipment Company, Intel, and Xerox had collaborated to produce Ethernet. Ethernet was offered to the 802 committee as a potential standard. Several companies represented on the committee objected to a contention protocol as the sole standard, however, so eventually IEEE settled on the three standards that are discussed in this chapter. The 802 committee's objectives were to establish standards for the physical and data-link connections between devices, using the OSI model as the foundation. With this as a standard, other companies could develop higher protocol layers to form a complete network. The following requirements were established:

- ◆ Existing data communications standards were to be incorporated into the IEEE standard as much as possible.
- ◆ The network was intended for light industrial and commercial use.
- ◆ The maximum network diameter was set at 2 km.
- ◆ The data speed on the network was to be between 1 and 20 Mb/s.

T A B L E 9-1

802 Local Area Network Standards

802.1	Overview Document Containing the Reference Model, Tutorial, and Glossary
802.1b	Standard for LAN/WAN Management
802.1p	Specification for LAN Traffic Prioritization
802.1q	Virtual Bridged LANs
802.2	Logical Link Control
802.3	Contention Bus Standard 10base 5 (Thick Net)
802.3a	Contention Bus Standard 10base 2 (Thin Net)
802.3b	Broadband Contention Bus Standard 10broad 36
802.3d	Fiber-Optic InterRepeater Link (FOIRL)
802.3e	Contention Bus Standard 1base 5 (Starlan)
802.3i	Twisted-Pair Standard 10base T
802.3j	Contention Bus Standard for Fiber Optics 10base F
802.3u	100-Mb/s Contention Bus Standard 100base T
802.3x	Full-Duplex Ethernet
802.3z	Gigabit Ethernet
802.3ab	Gigabit Ethernet over Category 5 UTP
802.4	Token Bus Standard
802.5	Token Ring Standard
802.5b	Token Ring Standard 4 Mb/s over Unshielded Twisted-Pair
802.f	Token Ring Standard 16-Mb/s Operation
802.6	Metropolitan Area Network DQDB
802.7	Broadband LAN Recommended Practices
802.8	Fiber-Optic Contention Network Practices
802.9a	Integrated Voice and Data LAN
802.10	Interoperable LAN Security
802.11	Wireless LAN Standard
802.12	Contention Bus Standard 100VG AnyLAN

Note: This table lists only the major standards in the 802 series. Each standard has numerous subparts, many of which are omitted for clarity.

- ◆ The network standard was to be independent of the transmission medium.
- ◆ The failure of any device on the network was not to disrupt the entire network.
- ◆ There was to be no more than one undetected error per year on the network.

The committee concluded that Ethernet would not suffice as a single standard because of the potential of blockage under heavy load conditions. Therefore, the committee adopted three incompatible standards. For light duty, a bus contention network, 802.3, similar but not identical to Ethernet was selected. For applications where assurance of network access is needed, token passing bus (802.4) and ring (802.5) standards were selected. LAN protocols are connectionless, which means that frames are launched onto the transmission medium as unacknowledged frames. Connection-oriented protocols are available as options, but these are rarely used. Table 9-1 lists the 802 standards, which have expanded significantly since the initial project.

The 802 standards are developed around layers 1 and 2 of the OSI protocols and do not include all the functions of a complete network. The missing functions are provided by the network operating system (NOS), which operates between the user application and the logical link control layer of the 802 standards. The NOS controls access to the network through rights and permissions that are a function of the user's account. The NOS handles the following functions, which are discussed in more detail in a later section:

- Controls and regulates access to the network's resources including disk space and printers.
- Controls security, including rights and permissions to access files and directories.
- Contains network utilities for setting up user accounts, granting rights to files, controlling passwords and login scripts, setting up printers, and so on.
- Connects the user applications to the underlying transmission medium and access control.
- Detects and corrects errors and recovers from network failures.
- Manages the transfer of data across the network.

The layered protocol structure of the 802 standards means that any NOS can operate with any of the 802 standards by changing the NIC and software drivers. This architecture provides a great deal of flexibility and interoperability among applications and different manufacturers' products.

The IEEE 802.3 CSMA/CD Standard

The 802.3 standard is a CSMA/CD network intended for commercial or light industrial use. The specification supports baseband and broadband coaxial cable, twisted-pair wire, baseband fiber, and wireless. Although the terms 802.3 and Ethernet are often used interchangeably, there are differences between the two protocols. Both use CSMA/CD, but the frame structure is somewhat different, and the transmission media they support are not identical. Ethernet specifies only a 50-Ω coaxial cable medium; 802.3 supports 50-Ω coax, unshielded twisted-pair (UTP), fiber optics, and wireless. Despite the differences, the Ethernet term is used by the industry (and in this book) synonymously with 802.3. As another example, the terms fast Ethernet and gigabit Ethernet are widely used even though the original specification did not contemplate such speeds.

The 802.3 standards are identified by a three-part designation that specifies the data rate, modulation method, and, except for twisted-pair wire, the maximum segment length. Twisted-pair segments terminate in hubs, with the maximum length from the node to the hub, including patch cords, set as 100 m. Table 9-1

T A B L E 9-2

802.3 Media Designations

	Transmission Medium	Maximum Segment Length (m)	Connections per Segment
10base 5	RG-8 50-Ω coax	500	100
10base 2	RG-58 72-Ω coax	185	30
10base T	Category 3 UTP wire	100	12 per hub
10base FL	Multimode fiber	2000	NA

F I G U R E 9-7

IEEE 802 Standard Protocol Stack

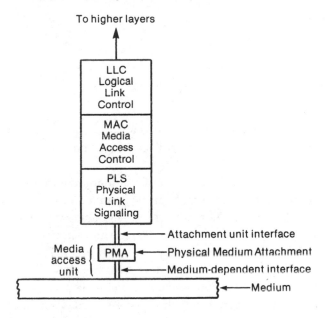

shows the shorthand designations for the 802 standards. Table 9-2 shows the essential characteristics of the coaxial, UTP, and fiber-optic standards.

Figure 9-7 illustrates the elements of 802.3. The link layer is divided into two sublayers—the logical link control (LLC) and the media access control (MAC)—which together correspond to the data-link layer in the OSI model. The 802.3 standard interacts with higher layers for error recovery and network control. The interface between the media access sublayer and the LLC transmits and receives frames and provides status information to forward to higher levels for error recovery. The

F I G U R E 9-8

802.3 Frame Format

Preamble (7)
Start frame delimiter (1)
Destination address (2 or 6)
Source address (2 or 6)
Length (2)
Data field (0-1500)
Pad (0-46)
Frame check sequence (4)

interface between the media access and the physical layers includes signals for framing, detecting, and recovering from collisions, and passing serial bit streams between the two layers.

The network is composed of cable segments that are a maximum of 500 m (1640 ft) long—the greatest distance that can be spanned efficiently at the maximum signaling rate of 20 Mb/s. As many as five segments can be interconnected through a maximum of four repeaters. The design rules specify that a signal between two nodes cannot traverse more than four repeaters. The repeaters sense carriers from both cable segments to which they are connected and also detect and avoid collisions. When a repeater detects a collision in one segment, it transmits a jamming signal to both segments to which it is connected. Two pairs of UTP are used for 10base T—one to transmit and one to receive. During transmission, the node listens to the receive pair for collisions.

The 802.3 frame, which is shown in Figure 9-8, must always be at least 64 octets long, and no more than 1500 octets in length. The reason for the frame lengths relates to the collision detection algorithm. If the frames are too short, a collision could escape undetected because the frame could have completed transmission before the collision could be reported back to the transmitting node. This would prevent hardware collision detection, and would require higher-layer protocols to compensate for the errors caused by the collision. Therefore, the frame includes a variable-length pad field to build out the frame length if necessary.

The IEEE 802.4 Token Bus Standard

A token bus LAN, illustrated in Figure 9-4, uses the same topology as CSMA/CD, but control flows in a logical ring. Although messages are broadcast as with CSMA/CD, control passes in sequence from node to node by means of a circulating token. Each node is programmed with the address of the preceding and succeeding nodes, and is programmed to recover if one node goes offline or fails.

Token passing allows a wider physical network diameter than CSMA/CD. The diameter can range from 1280 to 7600 m (4200 to 25,000 ft), depending on cable grade.

The MAC in a token bus performs many of the same functions that it does in CSMA/CD, such as address recognition and frame segmentation, but several functions are added to accomplish the more complex control. The primary functions of the MAC are to determine when its node has the right to access the medium, to recognize the presence of a token, and to determine when and how to pass the token to the next node. The MAC must be capable of initializing or resetting the network. It must be able to recognize when a token has been lost and to regenerate it when necessary. It also must be able to control the addition of a new node to the network and to recognize when a succeeding node has failed.

On the surface, token passing does not appear complicated, and if all goes well, the protocol has little work to do. Each MAC is programmed with the address of its successor and predecessor nodes. When it passes the token to its successor, it listens for the successor's transmission. If the successor fails to transmit, the MAC sends a second token and again listens for a response. If it hears no response, it assumes the next node has failed and transmits a message asking which node follows. Each MAC on the network compares its predecessor node number with the number contained in the "who follows" message. The node that follows the failed node responds to the message, and the failed node is bypassed. A similar process is required for a node to reinsert itself in the network.

The primary use for the token bus LAN is in industrial applications. The manufacturing automation protocol is the principal product using the 802.4 token bus. The protocol, which has no application in the office, is covered in books listed in the Bibliography.

The IEEE 802.5 Token Ring Standard

The token ring LAN, illustrated in Figure 9-3, is both a logical and a topological ring. Each node is a repeater, enabling greater diameter than bus networks. A token ring network is wired as a ring in a star topology, with a hub known as a multistation access unit at its center. MAUs are either passive or active devices that couple the twisted-pair wire of the side legs to the central ring. MAUs can be chained to broaden the scope of the ring. If the ring becomes overloaded, breaking the tie between MAUs and splitting a single ring into two or more rings segments it. Because each node repeats the data stream, failure of a node could disrupt the network. Therefore, the MAUs are equipped with trunk-coupling units to bypass a failed node automatically.

Tokens, which are three-octet fragments, contain a priority indicator. When a token circulates through a node that has traffic with a priority equal to or greater than the priority designator in the token, that node can seize the token and send priority traffic until a timer within its MAC, known as the *token-holding timer* (THT), expires. When the THT expires, the node generates a new token and passes it to the next node. In this manner, the network ensures that traffic is always transmitted up to capacity and that low-priority traffic is deferred.

One node on the ring is designated as the active monitor (AM) to supervise the network. The AM controls error recovery, detects the absence of a token or valid frames of data, and detects a persistently circulating token or frame. The AM sets an indicator on each frame, and checks the indicator to be sure a frame circulates only once. Although only one node is designated as the AM, all nodes contain its logic. If the AM fails, the node first detecting the failure assumes the role.

A token ring has three rules that are simple in concept, but complex to execute in the NICs:

- A node can transmit a frame only when it possesses the token.
- All nodes copy the frame, but only the addressee retains it, putting it back on the ring as it is received.
- Only the sending node (or the AM if the sending node should fail) is permitted to remove the frame.

The 802.5 protocol, like 802.3, does not correct errors. When any receiving node detects an error in a frame, it sets an error flag, which the sending node detects almost immediately. Upon detecting the error flag, the sending node begins to resend the frame, which can commence before the last of the errored frame is received.

Token ring runs at 4 and 16 Mb/s on six different wiring types, which are listed in Table 9-3. When the network was initially designed, it required shielded twisted-pair wire (STP), which is significantly more costly and more difficult to install than UTP. As wire quality improved, IBM, which designed token ring, supported the use of UTP on 4 Mb/s, but required STP on the 16-Mb/s LAN. Now UTP is supported for both 4 and 16 Mb/s, but STP is required for the backbone.

Token ring is a more robust network than Ethernet, but it is also more expensive. The NICs are more costly, and the MAUs are more expensive than Ethernet hubs. The cost of installation can be reduced considerably by using the UTP alternative. Category 4 wiring (see Chapter 7) is specifically designed to support 16-Mb/s token ring. Most companies install category 5, however, because it also supports FDDI and 100-Mb/s token ring, which is under development. Both of these are migration paths that require category 5 wire. Token ring is capable of greater throughput than Ethernet because of its more disciplined way of allocating

T A B L E 9-3

Token Ring Wiring Types

Wire Designation	Wire Type	Number of Pairs	Use
Type 1	STP	Two	Ring and lobe
Type 2	STP	Two data, four voice	Ring and lobe
Type 3	UTP	Four	Ring and lobe
Type 5	Fiber-optic	100 μm	Backbone
Type 6	Stranded	Two	Patch cable
Type 8	Flat	Two	Under carpet
Type 9	STP	Two	Short ring and lobe

Note: STP = shielded twisted-pair and UTP = unshielded twisted-pair.

network access. Where Ethernet is capable of about 60 percent utilization (throughput of about 6 Mb/s), token ring can approach 90 percent utilization. Most installations of token ring are in companies that use IBM hardware, while most other installations use Ethernet.

The 802.6 Metropolitan Area Network

The limited speed and range capabilities of LANs spawned the need for a standard network that can transmit data at speeds of 100 Mb/s or more over a range approximating the size of a metropolitan area. The 802.6 metropolitan area network, which Chapter 33 discusses, fulfills this requirement. Unlike LANs, which are intended for private use, the 802.6 network is intended for shared use over public rights of way.

HIGH-SPEED ETHERNET

Token ring networks have the option of 4- and 16-Mb/s network speeds, with a path for upgrading to FDDI if a higher data rate is needed. Standard Ethernet is fixed at a 10-Mb/s data rate, with throughput limited to about 6 Mb/s in normal operations. These limits dropped with the introduction of numerous enhancements to increase the speed of Ethernet—first to 100 Mb/s and next to 1 Gb/s. Fast Ethernet rapidly caught on in the market, so that it is now usually the default choice of companies installing LANs. The cost of dual 10-/100-Mb/s NIC cards is little more than the cost of single-speed cards. Even if hubs, switches, and other devices are running at 10 Mb/s today, the use of dual-speed cards makes the upgrade easier. Dual-speed hubs and switches are somewhat more expensive than 10-Mb/s units, but they enable the network manager to assign any device to any port without being blocked by speed considerations. Although FDDI is a

TABLE 9-4

Fast Ethernet Alternatives

	Speed (MB/s)	Cable Type	Number of Pairs
100base TX	100	Category 5 UTP or STP	Two
100base T4	100	Category 3, 4, 5 UTP	Four
100base FX	100	62.5- or 125-μm fiber	Two fibers
100VG AnyLAN	100	Category 3, category 5 fiber	Four
Full-duplex Ethernet	20	Category 3, category 5 fiber	Two
IsoEthernet	16.144	Category 3, category 5	Two

100-Mb/s alternative, it is significantly more expensive than fast Ethernet, and is used primarily for the backbone.

The alternatives, which are listed in Table 9-4, all use twisted-pair wire. Other than that, they have little in common. Although full-duplex Ethernet and isoEthernet are not technically classed as high-speed Ethernet, which runs at 100 Mb/s, they are included because they provide methods of carrying more data than 10-Mb/s options. Gigabit Ethernet is discussed in more detail in Chapter 33.

100base T

This network uses the same protocol and frame structure as standard Ethernet, but operates at 10 times the speed. It was adopted by IEEE in 1995 as 802.3u. Two different varieties are supported: 100base T4 and 100base TX. The attraction of the latter alternative is its simplicity. The protocols and the frames are the same as standard Ethernet. Dual-speed Ethernet cards, hubs, and switches are readily available. Use of these makes upgrade to 100 Mb/s easy, provided the cable infrastructure supports the increased speed. Any wire installed according to EIA/TIA 568 standards will support 100base T except for the reduced segment length discussed next.

The 100base T4 protocol is also attractive, although unlike standard Ethernet, which uses two of the four pairs in a category 3 wire run, 100base T4 uses all four pairs. Companies that installed nonstandard wire runs will have to upgrade the wire to use this alternative.

One drawback of fast Ethernet is its reduced network diameter. Where standard Ethernet supports a total diameter of 2.5 km, the 100base T alternatives have a 100-m repeater-to-node limit for UTP, with a limit of two hops per network. Both fast Ethernet alternatives use a different coding scheme than the Manchester coding that 10-Mb/s Ethernet uses. The 100base 4 protocol uses a scheme known as 8B6T. The 100base T and FX protocols use 4B/5B coding.

100VG AnyLAN

The VG in this protocol stands for voice grade. This method uses four pairs of category 3 wire to provide 100-Mb/s service. It does not use the standard Ethernet protocol. Instead, it uses an access process that eliminates collisions. The hubs poll the nodes in the order in which they are connected to see if they have traffic to send. Nodes respond with an indication of normal or priority traffic. The use of this protocol, which is called *demand access,* makes 100VG AnyLAN more suitable for multimedia and voice traffic, which are time-sensitive. Although the protocol has been accepted by ANSI as 802.12, it has not achieved a fraction of the popularity of 100base T.

Full-Duplex Ethernet

In its standard implementation, Ethernet is a half-duplex protocol. Since the original transmission medium was coaxial cable, full-duplex operation at baseband was impossible with the standard contention access method. With UTP, however, which uses separate wire pairs for transmit and receive, full-duplex operation is feasible if the traffic is run through a switch. The switch provides a separate segment for each node on the network, and since there is one segment per node, collisions are eliminated.

The value of full-duplex Ethernet comes when the application is full duplex. In networks that support such functions as word processing and spreadsheets, full-duplex operation offers little or no advantage because traffic is mostly one-way between station and server. In networks that support heavy database use where files are constantly being saved and retrieved, and the amount of traffic is approximately equal in both directions, full-duplex can come close to doubling the basic speed.

Isochronous Ethernet

A major disadvantage of standard Ethernet is its inability to handle time-sensitive traffic such as voice or video. One solution to this is isochronous Ethernet (isoENET), which combines standard 10base T with 6.144-Mb/s isochronous channels to provide a total of 16 Mb/s of bandwidth. Through the use of switching, this bandwidth can be made available to every user that is equipped with an isoENET hub. The 6.144 Mb/s of isochronous bandwidth can be subdivided into 96 ISDN B channels, one D channel of 64 kb/s, and a 96-kb/s maintenance channel. Circuits are set up and torn down using the Q.931 ISDN signaling protocol.

Isochronous Ethernet offers a solution to the problem of running voice and video over LANs, but it has not been popular for several reasons. First, 100-Mb/s networks are rapidly replacing 10-Mb/s Ethernets, which leaves isoENET out of the picture. Second, even faster network alternatives such as gigabit Ethernet are providing ever-increasing amounts of bandwidth at a reasonable cost. Third, the complexity of isoENET is greater than the benefits warrant for many users.

LAN Traffic Prioritization

A further development that may eliminate the need for IsoENET is the 802.1p specification for LAN traffic prioritization. This specification enables switches and routers to assign up to eight levels of priority to different classes of traffic. The highest priority is assigned to critical traffic such as routing table updates. Also assigned high priority are time-sensitive frames such as voice and video. These may move through the switch ahead of less critical traffic such as data frames. To implement 802.1p, switches must have buffer capacity to queue low-priority traffic while high-priority frames move ahead of it in the data stream.

GIGABIT ETHERNET

Fast Ethernet had scarcely made its mark on the user market before the industry began working on a protocol to increase the speed by another order of magnitude. The application for gigabit Ethernet is in the backbone, not to the desktop—yet. Its attraction as a backbone medium is the fact that its frame structure is nearly identical to 100- and 10-Mb/s Ethernets. The common frame structure means that relatively inexpensive components can be employed to link users and servers. By contrast, an ATM or FDDI backbone requires a protocol conversion, often through an expensive router, to connect Ethernet segments.

Gigabit Ethernet operates over a variety of media: single-mode fiber, multimode fiber, coaxial cable, and to a limited extent, twisted-pair wire. Gigabit Ethernet uses a coding method known as 8B/10B. It operates in a full-duplex mode for switch-to-switch connections. Figure 9-9 shows conceptually how gigabit Ethernet can be employed to link fast Ethernet networks.

NETWORK OPERATING SYSTEMS

By themselves, the 802 networks implement only the first two layers of the OSI model, and are incapable of complete communication. The higher protocol layers, which are needed to complete the network, are implemented in the network operating system. The following are the primary functions of the NOS:

- ◆ Capture calls to the computer's operating system from the application program and convert them to network operating system calls.

FIGURE 9-9

Gigabit Ethernet Backbone Switch

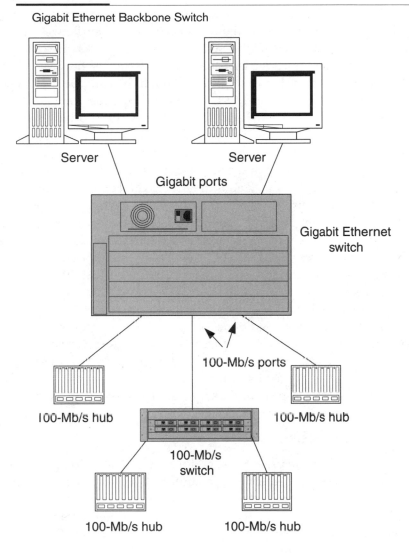

- ◆ Manage the hard disk in the file server to maximize the efficiency of information transfer between the network and the server.
- ◆ Manage security on the network, permitting users to offer their files for shared access and restrict them from unauthorized access.
- ◆ Designate and manage shared resources as if they were directly attached to the users' personal computers.
- ◆ Provide tools with which the network administrator can manage the network.

The concepts of redirection and virtual resources are important to understanding any NOS. The NOS interacts with the user's computer operating system. In the process of logging onto the network the interaction between the desktop device's operating system and the NOS defines virtual disk drives and printer ports. Virtual drives and ports act as if they were installed as hardware, but they actually exist on a server. For example, a PC might be equipped with one hardware line printer port, defined as LPT1. The NOS allows the administrator to provide the desktop computer with additional printers that do not exist as hardware. When the application program sends a document to the designated printer, the NOS intercepts the document and redirects it to the network printer.

File service works in the same manner. NOSs define various drive letters as a path to the file server's disk and underlying directories. The file server then behaves as if it was directly attached to the station. When the application program makes a file call, the NOS redirects it to the file server over the network.

To simplify the task of reaching various directories, the NOS allows you to establish virtual drives represented by an arbirtrary letter. For example, many LAN administrators set up directory space for each user. A virtual drive letter such as P for personal is defined as the path to each user's personal directory. After the user logs on with his or her login name, the P drive then leads directly to the personal directory.

NOSs can be classified as peer-to-peer or server-centric. A peer network enables all users to offer their resources for sharing. A server network concentrates the resources in one or more servers. Nothing prevents a peer network from using dedicated servers. If a station is not occupied, it can be designated as a server, offering its resources as print or file services, to other stations on the network.

Peer-to-Peer Networks

Peer networks enable users to share directories, disk space, printers, or other resources that are attached to their computers. If a directory is marked for sharing, other users have access to the files it contains. If a printer is marked for sharing, print jobs are spooled from the network to that printer. Except for early versions, peer network capability is inherent in Microsoft's Windows. Since the capability is there, it may be useful for sharing devices, such as special printers, that are attached directly to a personal computer.

Peer network operating systems are usable in small offices that do not have regular network management or a great concern for security. Users must, however, be trained to observe network discipline. For example, if users reboot or turn off their computers while other nodes are accessing a file or using a printer, the data or print jobs are likely to be corrupted. Normal file shutdown procedures inform users when others are attached to their computer, so if procedures are followed, the results are satisfactory.

Enforcing security on a peer network may be difficult. If all files are stored on a server, the network administrator can prevent users from accessing files by marking the directory as unshared. With some peer networks the entire directory is either sharable or not, in which case it is impossible to allow some users rights to access files while denying them to others.

Network statistics, which enable the administrator to check the amount of activity, collisions, and other such load indicators, are generally not provided by a peer NOS even if one station is dedicated as a file server. Although some companies operate peer networks successfully with numerous stations (roughly more than 20), most networks of this size will find it preferable to use a server. Unless a file server is used on a peer network, the probability of data loss is high because no one may be responsible for backing up all files. Without a dedicated server, it is difficult to be sure where the latest version of a file is stored because users can copy a file from another user's disk, modify it, and save it to their own hard disk. Peer network operating systems are best suited for small offices that cannot justify the cost of a server NOS.

Server-Centric Network Operating Systems

The server-centric network has various service functions such as file, print, fax, modem pool, and remote access centralized in one or more servers. A server NOS has significantly more administrative features than a peer NOS. The following are some of the administrative features that typical operating systems provide.

Control of File and Directory Access   Users are given rights to access files. Typical rights include:

- ◆ Who is authorized to access what files and with what level of rights.
- ◆ What shared resources are available and to what group of users.
- ◆ How security is managed to prevent unauthorized access and damage to files.
- ◆ What administrative tools are available to evaluate network performance, control access to the network, and add, move, and change nodes.
- ◆ What other networks are accessible and how access is controlled.
- ◆ What maintenance, statistical, and troubleshooting tools are available to alert managers to impending problems and assist in restoral when they occur.
- ◆ What utility programs are made available to the users and administrator.

The administrator can grant or revoke rights to directories or individual files. Files and directories can be hidden to conceal their presence from users who lack the appropriate rights.

User Groups   Users can be assigned as groups of users who have a common set of interests. Members can send messages, the supervisor can assign rights to selected files and directories, users can share exclusive use of a common printer, and so on.

Security Administration   The administrator can assign and control passwords, user IDs, and other means of regulating security. The administrator can force passwords of a particular length, and can force users to change passwords as needed.

Login Administration   Login procedures can be established for every user. These define virtual drives, set up port redirection for printers, send messages to the users, and with other commands allow the administrator to otherwise customize configurations for users and groups.

Printer Administration   The network administrator can identify stations as printer control stations. These stations can delete or move print jobs in queue, establish or change print priorities, pause the printer to change forms, and other such tasks concerned with printer management.

Administrative Tools   Many local area network users underestimate the amount of administrative effort it takes to keep a network operating. The network administrator is defined in software as the person who has the right to modify and control the rights of other users. In most networks, the rights approximate the following list, which is ordered by the degree of control the right provides, with the highest rights listed first. Each right has the rights of succeeding but not of preceding levels of authority:

- ◆ *Hidden.* The presence of the file or directory is itself concealed from unauthorized users.
- ◆ *Parental.* Has full control over any file in the directory.
- ◆ *Private.* Only users with parental rights can read files.
- ◆ *Modify.* Can change any file in the directory.
- ◆ *Read/write:* Can read any file or write any file in the directory but cannot modify existing files.
- ◆ *Read only.* Can read files in the directory but cannot add or change a file.

The operating system permits managers to create a tree-structured directory structure on the server. Files are contained in directories and subdirectories, and the network administrator can regulate rights at any level from a file up to the entire directory.

The operating system also provides statistical information that enables the administrator to isolate trouble and reconfigure the network as necessary. For example, the administrator needs to know the volume of traffic on the network and the frequency with which users encounter delays. Contention networks should show the frequency of collision. The operating system should inform the administrator of factors, such as the number of cache hits, that affect the operating efficiency of the file server.

Utility Programs   Most network operating systems also provide a set of utilities for performing the same sorts of functions that a user expects on a single-user operating system. Utility programs enable users to list directories, copy files, and perform other such functions. The network administrator has utilities to add and remove users, establish rights, change the classifications of files, and oversee the activities of the users. In most networks, administrators have utilities that allow them to create menus to insulate users from the operating system's command language.

OTHER LAN APPLICATION ISSUES

The foregoing factors are the principal issues involved in selecting and applying LAN technology. Several other issues must be considered, however, when deciding which product to purchase. These issues are discussed in this section.

Network Management

In larger networks consider the availability of a network management network system. Components installed on the network should be SNMP-compatible. More details on network management are provided in Chapter 39.

Internetworking

Most multisite companies connect their LANs with an internet. Internetworking raises several issues that affect the choice of NOS. Some peer protocols do not support TCP/IP, some protocols cannot be routed, and some network protocols are not supported by many routers. Refer to Chapter 37 for further information on internetworking.

Infrastructure Planning

The default transmission medium in LANs today is UTP. In some specialized situations thick or thin coax may be used, but 100base T, 10base T, or 16-Mb/s token ring running over UTP constitutes a majority of networks.

Companies that occupy multiple floors of a building or have multiple departments will probably segment the LAN using bridges, switches, or routers. The architecture of the system should be planned in advance to be certain that the infrastructure has been built to accommodate the necessary hardware. Planning is especially important when a structured wiring system is being installed.

It is always less expensive to install additional capacity in the horizontal and backbone wiring paths at the time of initial wiring than it is to add it later.

The minimum of two horizontal wiring paths specified by EAI/TIA 568 is not enough for many companies. It is difficult to look far enough in the future to predict bandwidth requirements, but fiber optics in the horizontal distribution system will probably be needed in most companies. Installing dark fiber at the time of twisted-pair installation saves the labor cost of adding it later.

Backbone Architecture

LAN architecture is flexible and it can often be rearranged by changing the equipment if the proper infrastructure is in place. In planning a LAN, determine whether a backbone, such as FDDI, will be used to link segments, or whether the segments will connect in a collapsed backbone. The choice affects the number of fibers in the backbone. Consider whether the company needs a virtual LAN architecture.

Network Speed and Throughput

Throughput, or *rate of transfer of information between nodes,* is an important issue with LANs as with any other network. LANs have high data-transmission speeds, generally ranging between 10 and 16 Mb/s, with FDDI and fast Ethernet networks operating at 100 Mb/s. Transmission speed should not be confused with throughput, however, which may be a fraction of the transmission speed. Throughput is limited by several factors in a LAN:

- ◆ Data transmission speed of the network.
- ◆ Overhead bits used by the network protocol.
- ◆ Time spent in collision and error recovery.
- ◆ Bandwidth of the transmission medium.
- ◆ Diameter of the network.

Throughput is predictable in token ring networks but is difficult to predict in contention LANs. In contention networks, throughput can be determined by a computer simulation or experimentally by loading the network to see how response time is affected. Although the network itself may have a high throughput, communication may be slowed because of characteristics of the file server, which is the principal device other stations wish to communicate with.

Throughput can be increased by using a faster protocol. LAN protocols operating at 100 Mb/s are available today. As the price of the hardware drops and as bandwidth demands increase, these faster protocols will replace standard Ethernet as the default network protocol.

Network Size or Diameter

All LANs have a limited diameter, which can be overcome with ancillary devices such as bridges, routers, and gateways. Designers must be careful in designing networks not to exceed the maximum diameter. Remember that the limiting factor is measured in cable feet, not in point-to-point distance. Designers must take into account routing that may add to the network diameter. Diameter can be extended with repeaters. Be careful to observe the design rule that states that no more than four repeaters can be connected between any two nodes.

Virtual LANs

The theory of LAN development is that a network may start as one or more large segments. As the network use grows, the network is subdivided into segments by bridging or routing. As long as the users on the segments remain in the same physical proximity, this method of segmentation works well. If a user moves to a location that is served by a different LAN segment, the benefits of segmentation may be lost because traffic from that node flows over both segments as well as the backbone. Furthermore, unless the hub offers port switching, hub ports may be unused because they are dedicated to a segment, and there may not be enough users physically located near enough to use the excess capacity.

The solution to this dilemma is known as a *virtual LAN*. Nodes in a virtual LAN are assigned to a switch that connects to a backbone network. Traffic from the nodes in a virtual LAN flows through the switches and the backbone, but does not overload segments to which the member does not belong.

Fault Tolerance

A fault-tolerant LAN is one that can handle irregularities in network operation while allowing users to continue processing or, at worst, to terminate their operation without losing data. Network irregularities fall into three categories, each of which may require a different recovery strategy: *faults*, which are software or hardware defects; *errors*, which are incorrect data; and *failures*, which are breakdowns of network components. End users do not distinguish between these three categories; their concern is the continued operation of the network.

Fault-tolerant LANs employ a combination of hardware and software, usually consisting of the following elements:

- ◆ An uninterruptable power supply to protect against alternating current power failure or at least permit a graceful shutdown.
- ◆ A duplicate file allocation table (FAT) kept on the disk.
- ◆ Software that logs what users were doing at the time of a crash and saves their files. For example, Novell fault-tolerant software provides a transaction log that helps bring a failed system back to the starting point.

- ◆ Redundant hardware, such as multiple disk drives that mirror each other so the second drive takes over when the first fails, mirroring servers, duplicated bridges, and redundant cabling. RAID (redundant array of independent drives) technology is even more fault tolerant because data is striped across multiple drives, any of which can fail without data loss.
- ◆ Applications software that stores information between saves.
- ◆ Careful backup procedures.

A key to fault tolerance is a network management system that alerts the administrator to impending problems by detecting minor faults before they grow into major problems. All the systems comprising fault tolerance come at a price, so the degree of fault tolerance a network is likely to have is a function of the willingness of management to pay for it.

CHAPTER 10

Common Equipment

Common equipment supports all classes of telecommunications. Common equipment, as covered in this chapter, includes:

◆ Relay racks and cabinets
◆ Distributing frames
◆ Ringing and tone supplies
◆ Alarm and control equipment
◆ Power equipment

RELAY RACKS AND CABINETS

Central office equipment, PBXs, ACDs, routers, hubs, patch panels, and other telecommunications equipment can be mounted in either cabinets or relay racks. In cabinetized equipment the interbay cabling is sometimes contained within the cabinet. In relay rack–mounted equipment the cabling is external and is supported by overhead cable troughs or run through raceways in the floor. Because of the quantities of cables involved and the need for physical separation in some cables, overhead racking is the most common method in both central offices and large PBXs. Cables can be run through closed cable trays, or in open ladder racks. The latter are generally less expensive than cable trays, and permit airflow around the cables.

The manufacturer's specifications must be followed for the type and layout of cabling to control noise and crosstalk in telecommunications equipment. As with outside plant cable the twist in interbay cable controls crosstalk and prevents unwanted coupling between circuits. Also, cables often must be run in separate troughs that are segregated by signal level and kept physically separated by enough distance that signals from high-level cables cannot crosstalk into low-level cables. For some types of cable, shielding is required to further reduce the possibility of crosstalk.

In central offices and PBXs alike, many critical leads have maximum lengths that cannot be exceeded. If lead lengths are exceeded, signal loss between components may be excessive, signals may be distorted, or timing in high-speed buses may be affected by propagation delay. Manufacturer's specifications must be followed rigorously with respect to lead length.

DISTRIBUTING FRAMES

Temporary connections or those requiring rearrangement terminate on cross-connect blocks mounted in distributing frames. Distributing frames also provide an access point for testing cable and equipment. The size and structure of a distributing frame are dictated by the quantity of circuits to be connected. Cabling to the central office equipment routes through openings at the top of the frame, fastens to vertical members, and turns under a metal shelf or mounting bracket that supports the cross-connect blocks. The cross-connect blocks are multiple metallic terminals mounted in an insulating material and fastened to the distributing frame. Equipment and lead identity is stenciled on the blocks.

Technicians make cross-connects by running "jumper" wire in a supporting wire trough. Between blocks, connections are made at the block by one of three methods. In the oldest method, rarely used in modern equipment, the wire is stripped and soldered to the block. The second type uses wire-wrapped connections in which the wire is stripped and tightly wrapped around a post with a wire-wrap tool. The third type of connection uses a split quick-clip terminal that clamps the wire and pierces the insulation as a special punch-down tool inserts it in the terminal. The punch-down method has several variations that operate on the same principle of piercing the insulation and gripping the wire against a metallic connection.

Some installations use modular distributing frames, such as the one in Figure 10-1, which keep the length of cross-connects to a minimum, and are often administered by a computer. In small installations distributing frame administration is not enough of a problem to require computer administration. In large centers with thousands of subscriber lines and trunks terminated in the office, however, distributing frame congestion becomes a significant problem as quantities of cross-connect wires are piled in troughs. In large installations it is important that the distributing frame be carefully designed and administered to keep the wire length to a minimum.

Large PBXs may use the same hardware as central offices, or they may use a wall-mounted backboard that holds 66-type blocks or 110 connectors. Wall-mounted frames are satisfactory in small installations. However, in PBXs with more than about 1000 stations the frame becomes too large to be administered efficiently because jumpers are long and wiring trough congestion becomes a problem. To relieve jumper congestion, hardware is available to mount wiring blocks on double-sided free-standing frames.

FIGURE 10-1

A Modular Distributing Frame Being Installed

Courtesy of Lucent Technologies, Inc.

Protector Frames

Incoming circuits that are exposed to power or lightning are terminated on protector frames. The protector module forms the connection between the cable pair
and the attached equipment. As described in Chapter 6, if excessive current flows
in the line, the protector opens the circuit to the central office equipment and
grounds the conductors. If excessive voltage strikes the line, carbon blocks inside
the protector module arc across to ground the circuit. Modules are manufactured
with gas tubes where these are needed to protect vulnerable central office equipment such as digital switches.

Combined and Miscellaneous Distributing Frames

Small installations use combined protector and distributing frames. The incoming cable pairs terminate on the protector frame, where they are cross-connected
to equipment that terminates on the distributing frame. In large central offices

the size of the frame may dictate separate protector and distributing frames. One or more distributing frames terminate trunks, switching machine line terminations, and miscellaneous equipment such as repeaters, range extenders, and signaling equipment. In offices large enough to need multiple frames, tie cables permit cross-connecting between cable and equipment terminated on different frames. Buildings with multiple floors require several distributing frames linked with tie cable.

RINGING AND TONE SUPPLIES

Common equipment includes ringing, dial-tone, call progress tone, and recorded announcement apparatus. In digital central offices many of these tones are generated by software, so no external equipment is needed. Electromechanical and analog electronic central offices require external supplies.

Ringing machines are usually solid-state supplies that generate 20-Hz ringing current at about 90 V. Dial-tone supplies with precisely generated tones are required. Busy-tone and reorder supply tones are generated in the same manner as dial tones. Recorded announcements are stored in digital form in solid-state memory or in analog form on magnetic tapes or drums. Most announcement systems contain multiple tracks for the several types of messages used in central offices.

ALARM AND CONTROL EQUIPMENT

Most telecommunications equipment has integral alarms in any circuit that can affect service. The extent and type of alarming varies with the manufacturer, but generally alarms draw attention to equipment that has failed or is about to fail, and direct the technician to the defective equipment.

Equipment alarms light an alarm lamp on the equipment chassis and operate external contacts that are used for remote control of the alarm and for operating external audible and visual alarms. Most central offices contain an office alarm system to aid in locating failed equipment. Alarms are segregated into major and minor categories to show the seriousness of the trouble; different tones sound to alert maintenance personnel to the alarm class and location. Besides audible alarms, aisle pilots and bay alarm lamps guide maintenance personnel to the room, equipment row, bay, and the specific equipment in trouble.

In offices designed for unattended operation, telemetering equipment transmits the alarms to a distant center over telephone circuits. The alarm remote is generally a slave that reports only the identity of the alarm point. The center typically is equipped with a processor and database that pinpoint the trouble and also may diagnose the cause. Some equipment, including most electronic switching systems, communicates with a remote that provides the equivalent of the local switching machine console. Other remote alarms report building status such as open door, temperature, smoke, and fire alarms.

Central offices designed for unattended operation frequently include control apparatus for sending orders from a distant location over a data circuit. For example, microwave and fiber-optic equipment usually have control systems that enable technicians to transfer working equipment to a backup channel. Offices equipped with emergency generators are frequently arranged for engine start and shutdown and transfer to and from commercial power.

The more extensive private telecommunications networks use central office techniques for reporting alarms and diagnosing trouble. Most PBX manufacturers support their systems with a remote maintenance and testing system that enables technicians to diagnose trouble remotely, and, sometimes, switch around failed apparatus. Alarm systems range from simply reporting a contact opening or closure over a circuit to more elaborate systems that report values to a remote center, support remote diagnostics, and maintain a trouble clearance database.

POWER EQUIPMENT

Most central office equipment operates from direct current, nominally −48 V, which is the typical voltage supplied by central office charging and battery plants. PBXs operate either on −48 V or on commercial alternating current. Figure 10-2 shows a battery plant and charging equipment in an AT&T toll office. PBX direct current power systems use a similar type of power plant, only smaller. Microwave equipment usually works on −24 V dc in radio stations and −48 V dc in central offices. Some central office equipment operates from alternating current and requires a direct current to alternating current converter, known as an *inverter*, to provide an uninterrupted power source during power failures. Alternating current–operated equipment includes tape and disk drives, computers, and other equipment that is not normally designed for direct current operation. Commercial uninterruptable power source (UPS) equipment, which we will discuss later, is an alternative family of equipment that contains a built-in battery supply.

Most central offices and PBXs in hospitals and other organizations that cannot tolerate system failures have an emergency generator to carry the load and keep the batteries charged during prolonged power outages. The emergency generator connects to the charging equipment through a power transfer circuit that cuts off commercial power while the generator is online. Offices lacking emergency power equipment often have circuitry for connecting an external generator.

Storage batteries use technology similar to automobile batteries. Lead acid and nickel cadmium cells are common, and some equipment uses batteries with a solid electrolyte called gel cells. Power is distributed from the battery plant to the central office equipment over *bus bars*, which must be designed large enough to carry current for the total equipment load. Bus bars connecting the batteries are visible in the foreground of Figure 10-2. To minimize the amount of voltage drop, batteries are installed as close to the equipment as possible.

F I G U R E 10-2

A Central Office Power Plant

Property of AT&T Archives. Reprinted with permission of AT&T.

Some types of central office equipment require voltage higher or lower than the nominal −48 or −24 V used by most equipment. These voltages are supplied by either a separate charging and battery plant or by using solid-state power converters. Except for very high current loads, power converters are the preferred method of supplying other voltages.

Uninterruptable Power Supplies (UPS)

Any telecommunications apparatus that operates from commercial alternating current power is vulnerable to failure from irregularities that cannot be predicted or controlled. The following are the principal types of commercial power irregularities:

- ◆ *Blackouts*, which are total failures of commercial power.
- ◆ *Brownouts*, which are reductions in voltage.
- ◆ *Surges*, which are momentary voltage changes.
- ◆ *Transients*, which are momentary open-circuit conditions.
- ◆ *Spikes*, which are sharp pulses of high voltage that rapidly rise and decay.
- ◆ *Frequency variations*, which are momentary or prolonged deviations from the nominal power-line frequency.

Many power-line irregularities have no effect, but others can damage equipment, interrupt service, or both. The severity of the problem varies with locale and season. In some parts of the United States outages happen so infrequently that protective measures are unnecessary. In other parts of the country outages are a regular occurrence, particularly in bad weather.

Equipment that can be categorized as *power-line conditioning* equipment removes spikes, transients, and surges. Blackouts and brownouts require some form of backup power. Equipment, such as computers, tape and disk drives, many PBXs, and most key telephone systems, operate from commercial alternating current. These are protected from failure by an uninterruptable power supply.

UPS devices come in a many sizes and capacities. Capacities range from enough to enable a small shared device, such as a file server, to shut down gracefully to ones with enough capacity to operate a mainframe computer, a PBX, and auxiliary equipment such as modems, multiplexers, and voice mail through a prolonged power outage. If the UPS does not have the capacity to operate through an outage, the protected device should have circuitry connected to an alarm port on the UPS and shut itself down. Some UPS supplies can dial a pager to notify the administrator of the power outage. Some supplies are SNMP-compatible so they can be monitored and controlled from a network management system.

UPS supplies are available in three general types: offline or standby power source, online, and line interactive.

Offline UPS

An *offline supply*, sometimes known as *standby power source or standby UPS*, monitors the power line and switches the load to its internal inverter when the power falls outside its limits. Figure 10-3 shows schematically how this type of supply works. The inverter converts direct current to alternating current. It connects permanently to a storage battery that charges from the alternating current source. The alternating current source carries the load, and on failure the load switches to the output of

F I G U R E 10-3

An Offline UPS

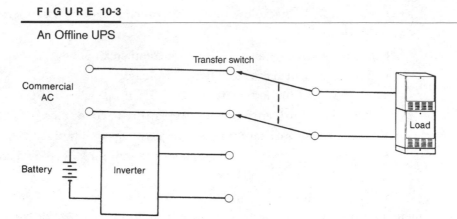

the inverter. A short break in power occurs when the load transfers. The break runs from 5 to 20 ms, which is short enough to keep most apparatus working. During brownout conditions, however, the switching time may be longer. Some offline UPSs have ferrite core transformers that provide a flywheel effect to keep power supplied to the load long enough to prevent any interruption. Many inexpensive offline UPS supplies lack line conditioning, have no frequency regulation, and provide limited or no surge and spike protection.

Online UPS

An online UPS, which is shown in Figure 10-4, supplies power continuously to the protected apparatus. The commercial power source keeps the UPS battery charged. When the power fails, the inverter continues to function without a break in power because the power is supplied directly from the inverter. The charging apparatus keeps the equipment completely isolated from power-line irregularities. Some types of online supplies have a dangerous flaw in that if the UPS itself fails, the load is isolated from the commercial source. When selecting equipment of this type, be certain that the unit has bypass circuitry to connect the protected equipment directly to the commercial source in case of UPS failure.

Line-Interactive UPS

A line-interactive UPS has some of the characteristics of both an online and an offline UPS. The protected equipment is powered from commercial power during normal conditions, but the UPS has circuits that can boost or reduce (buck) the voltage from the source. This technique provides voltage regulation, which the offline supply lacks. If the commercial supply fails, the UPS increases the amount of voltage boost in a time interval approaching that of an online supply.

FIGURE 10-4

An Online UPS

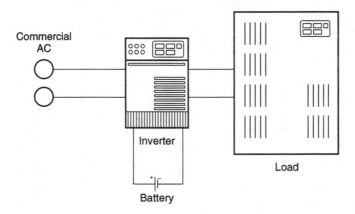

Commercial
AC

Inverter

Battery

Load

Battery Supplies

Both central office and PBX equipment that operates from direct current connects to a 48-V bus, as Figure 10-5 shows. A string of batteries connects between the bus and ground. Charging equipment keeps the batteries charged, and furnishes direct current power to the equipment. When commercial power is online, the charging equipment carries the central office load; the batteries draw only enough power to compensate for internal leakage and to filter noise on the power bus.

When commercial power fails, the equipment is unaffected because it draws its operating current from the battery supply. As the batteries discharge, the bus voltage drops. Equipment is designed with a tolerance for a variance in supply voltage. Under normal operation the −48-V bus is actually "floated" from the charger at approximately −52 V. Most central office equipment can tolerate a drop to 44 V or less without affecting equipment operation.

The length of time equipment can operate under power failure conditions depends on the current drain and the capacity of the batteries. For example, if equipment draws 10 amperes (A) and the battery string can supply 100 ampere-hours (A-h), the equipment could operate for 10 hours under power failure conditions. As a practical matter, it may operate for fewer than 10 hours because of reduced battery capacity, which is discussed later. The operating time under power failure conditions can be extended by three methods: paralleling battery strings, end cells, and emergency generators.

Paralleling Battery Strings

Connecting a paralleling battery string can extend battery capacity. Each string contributes its capacity to the load. For example, if three 100-A-h strings are connected in parallel, the total string will furnish approximately 300 A-h.

FIGURE 10-5

Central Office Power Plant

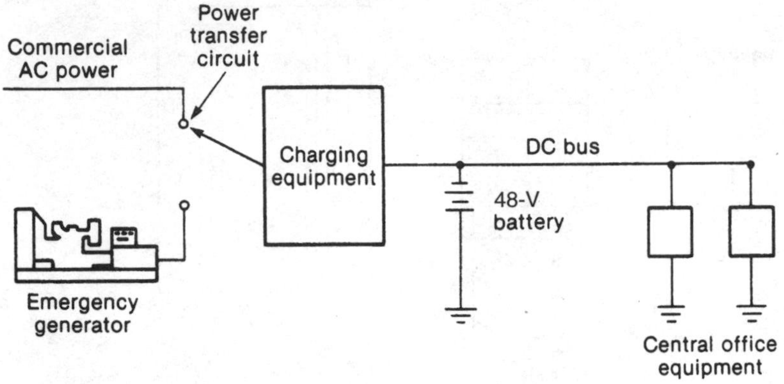

End Cells

As battery voltage begins to deteriorate, the voltage can be boosted by switching in auxiliary cells known as end cells. Switching apparatus, which is either manual or automatic, connects the end cells in series with the existing battery string so they contribute their voltage to the overall bus voltage. When end cells are not in use, they are switched out of the circuitry and an auxiliary charger keeps them charged.

Emergency Engine Generator

Common carriers and organizations, such as hospitals and public safety organizations, that require continuity of telecommunications service must use an auxiliary engine generator to furnish power. The generator connects through a transfer switch to the charging equipment. If a generator is available, less battery capacity is needed because the battery must furnish power only until the generator starts.

Battery Capacity

A storage battery has three principal elements: positive and negative plates, electrolyte, and the case. The plates, which are made of a metallic substance such as lead or nickel-cadmium, are suspended in electrolyte from the case, which is made of an insulating material. In contrast to automobiles, which normally have the negative pole grounded, in telecommunications equipment the positive pole is grounded to aid in preventing electrolysis. Some central office batteries have open cells, which require periodic maintenance to measure the specific gravity and add water. More recent telecommunications applications use sealed batteries. These batteries normally have a jellylike electrolyte that requires no maintenance.

Temperature has a significant effect on battery life and capacity. Battery capacity is highest during moderately warm temperatures, but as the temperature increases, battery life is shortened. Conversely, cooler temperatures extend battery life, but below freezing, battery capacity is greatly reduced.

To maintain the best balance between capacity and life, batteries should operate at approximately room temperature. Obviously, this is impractical in remote locations, such as repeater sites, that may be unheated and have no air conditioning. In such locations, batteries should be placed to minimize their exposure to temperature extremes. For example, they should be placed on the shady side of a building to reduce heat.

APPLICATIONS

Common equipment is separately engineered in central offices. In private networks the switching equipment supplier will usually engineer and furnish common equipment. This section discusses the primary considerations in evaluating common equipment in a local private network environment.

Standards

Common equipment is generally built to manufacturer's standards. The principal voltages used in central offices, −48 and −24 V, are accepted by convention, but are not regulated by telecommunications standards. The **National Electrical Safety Code**® and local codes apply to wiring commercial power to charging equipment, but the voltages used on central office equipment are too low to be considered hazardous.

Most central office equipment manufacturers in the United States follow the Bellcore Network Equipment Building System (NEBS) guidelines in their bay dimensions. Relay racks are standardized at 7, 9, and 11.5 ft in height and support equipment with 19- or 23-in-wide mounting panels. The mounting screw holes are also spaced at standard intervals. In other countries metric dimensions are used.

Evaluating Common Equipment

Evaluation considerations discussed in previous chapters are equally applicable to common equipment. As with all telecommunications equipment, high reliability is imperative. Compatibility is important with alarm and control systems, but with power, distributing frame, and cabling, compatibility is generally not a problem if the equipment meets the specifications of the manufacturer of the interfacing equipment.

Environmental Considerations

An early consideration in planning a telecommunications system is to provide the floor space and environment required for its operation. The manufacturer's recommendations should be followed with respect to heating, air conditioning, air circulation, cabling, and mounting. The primary considerations are provision of

- ◆ Administrative workspace
- ◆ Sufficient floor space for expansion
- ◆ Sufficient air-conditioning and heating capacity
- ◆ Ducts and raceways where required
- ◆ Separate power equipment room where recommended by the manufacturer
- ◆ Adequate security

Workspace

Equipment areas should provide a physical working environment with adequate space and lighting for equipment maintenance. The manufacturer should install equipment to its standards and should specify aisle space between equipment line-ups, lighting standards, and commercial alternating current outlets for powering test equipment.

Protection and Distributing Frames

Frame terminations should be provided for all equipment that requires rearrange-ment or reassignment. The primary considerations are the density of frame blocks and the amount of trough space provided for jumper wire. Block density is a trade-off between the amount of floor space consumed by the distributing frames and the difficulty of running multiple wires to small or congested blocks. Distributing frames should always conform to a plan that is designed to eliminate congestion and support productivity in placing and removing cross-connects.

All cable pairs exposed to lightning strikes or power cross should be pro-tected (see Chapter 6). This includes all pairs furnished by the LEC. The manufac-turer's recommendations should be followed with respect to gas-tube protection.

UPS Equipment

The primary criterion in evaluating UPS equipment is whether the supply is on-line, offline, or line-interactive. This can usually be determined by evaluating the manufacturer's specifications. If the supply has any transition time before it as-sumes the load, it is not an online supply. If it lacks any kind of power-line condi-tioning equipment, it is most likely an offline supply.

A second important evaluation criterion is the *crest factor ratio*. This factor evalu-ates the supply's capability of handling load peaks. Technically, it is the ratio between the nonrepetitive peak load the supply can provide and the linear rms (root mean square) load it supplies. The ratio should be at least 2.5, and the higher, the better.

The output wave shape is another evaluation factor. Commercial alternating current is a pure sine wave, and the more effective UPS supplies also furnish sine wave output. Less expensive supplies provide square wave output, which could affect the operation of the power supply in the supported equipment. If the vendor is unable to provide photos of the output wave, this factor is easy to evaluate by looking at the wave under load with an oscilloscope.

The amount of voltage regulation and the backup time are two more important factors in evaluating a UPS. The supply should maintain voltage within ±3 percent. The amount of backup time is determined by comparing the power drain of the protected equipment to the power furnished by the UPS, and how long the equipment is to be protected. A key telephone system or PBX normally is protected through the longest expected power outage. It may be necessary to power a file server or computer only long enough to allow a graceful shutdown since desktop devices are down anyway.

Batteries and Charging Equipment

Storage batteries are evaluated by their capacity, usually stated in ampere-hours, type of plate material, and electrolyte. Central office batteries are usually strings of individual cells, each having a nominal voltage of 2.17 V. The cells must be in leak-proof and crack-proof cases, preferably with a sealed electrolyte. Private telecommunications equipment batteries are usually purchased in 12-V increments. A 48-V string consists of four such batteries.

Manufacturers also specify batteries by their expected service life. Long-life central office batteries have sufficient plate material to last for up to 20 years with proper maintenance.

If a plant powers a switching system, it is important to ensure that it has enough spare capacity to power external transmission and signaling equipment. In a private network the provision of batteries depends on whether the network must remain in operation during power failures or whether it will be allowed to fail until the power is restored. The decision whether to provide an emergency generator depends on whether the battery reserve is enough to survive a long power outage.

Cabling

The number of leads cabled to the distributing frames is an important consideration in installing equipment. Apparatus, such as T1 carrier and NCTE, usually has many wiring options designed to fit special services. If not all leads are cabled to the distributing frame, the use of certain options may be precluded in the future unless the equipment is recabled. If unneeded leads are cabled to the distributing frame, however, extra costs will be incurred in cabling, frame blocks, and installation labor, and more frame space will be consumed by the extra terminations.

Also of importance is proper segregation of cables. For example, cables carrying low-level carrier signals usually are separated from high-level cables or the cables are shielded to prevent crosstalk. Data bus cables in many electronic switching systems must be isolated from other cables to prevent errors. The manufacturer's specifications must be rigidly adhered to in designing cable racks and troughs.

The manufacturer usually specifies maximum cable length. Most telecommunications equipment has critical lead lengths that must not be exceeded.

PART TWO

Circuit Switching Systems

CHAPTER 11

Signaling Systems

The objective of any circuit-switched network is to establish a connection between end users, to monitor the circuit while it is in use, to disconnect it when the users finish, and to compile information for billing the call. Users need to know nothing of how the network establishes the connection; they supply the destination address and let the system select the route. Processor-driven controllers, which are the brains of the network, determine the route over signal paths that are the nerve system. Signals travel between controllers either over the talking path or over separate data networks. Telecommunications networks have a variety of methods for setting up and taking down circuit connections, which we will discuss under the topic of signaling systems.

As with so many other telecommunications terms, signaling is somewhat ambiguous. The term is sometimes used to mean the method by which information is transported across data networks. In this vein, signaling refers to an information-encoding method such as alternate mark inversion, Manchester, or nonreturn to zero. In this book we will refer to this as *encoding* (which, in itself, can ambiguously mean an encryption method). Signaling will refer to the process of setting up circuits which, as we have seen, can be real or virtual. Virtual circuit setup is discussed in Chapters 4 and 32, which deal with data protocols and broadband. This chapter discusses signaling in circuit-switched networks. Bear in mind that circuit switching doesn't refer exclusively to voice, nor does packet switching refer exclusively to data transport. The methods of signaling and encoding are only loosely related to the type of information being carried.

Signaling can be separated into two categories: in-band and out-of-band. In-band signaling means that signals are carried over the same circuit that carries information during the session. Out-of-band signaling uses a separate network to carry the signals. The two most prominent out-of-band signaling systems are the D channel of ISDN (Chapter 32) and signaling system 7 (SS7), which is a separate *common channel* signaling network that we discuss in this chapter.

In-band signaling has several drawbacks that common channel signaling overcomes. The most significant drawback of in-band signaling for long-distance circuits is its susceptibility to fraud. As we will discuss later in the chapter, in-band tone signaling on toll trunks uses a 2600-Hz tone for transmitting supervisory signals. Toll thieves are able to defeat automatic message accounting systems by using devices that emulate signaling tones. Common channel signaling eliminates this form of toll fraud.

The second drawback is setup time. When circuits are built up with a series of signals over the circuit itself, the time required to set up the call is much longer than it takes to manage call setup end-to-end from a central computer network. Furthermore, conventional signaling lacks look-ahead capability. A circuit can be connected only to find that the call cannot be completed because the called number is busy. This is undesirable from the network owner's standpoint because uncompleted calls waste circuit time.

Another major benefit of common channel signaling is in the service options it supports. In Chapter 14 we mentioned virtual private voice networks, which are not feasible with conventional signaling. Common channel signaling supports credit card authorization, cellular phone roaming, intelligent network services, and custom local area signaling services (CLASS), which Chapter 13 discusses. Besides reducing call setup time, common channel signaling reduces the access charges that IXCs must pay LECs for circuit connect time. In addition, the IXCs' circuit utilization is improved by reducing holding time.

Signaling systems can also be classified by the method of exchanging signals: direct current (dc), tone, bit-robbed, and common channel. Direct current signaling is used in local loops. It was formerly used in metallic trunks, but few of these remain in service. Multifrequency tone signaling was once used on all long-distance circuits, but it has largely been replaced by SS7 now. Local loops and tie lines still use both direct current and tone signaling; the familiar dual-tone multifrequency (DTMF) signals are used in nearly all loops, including those served by T carriers. The bit-robbed T carrier signaling is a hybrid in-band system that is neither tone nor direct current signaling.

Signals can be grouped by the four functions they perform:

- *Supervising* is monitoring the status of a line or circuit to determine if it is busy, idle, or is requesting service. Supervision is a term derived from the function telephone operators performed in monitoring manual circuits on a switchboard. Manual switchboards displayed supervisory signals by an illuminated lamp on the keyshelf to show a request for service on an incoming line or an on-hook condition of a switchboard cord circuit. In the network, the supervisory signals are conveyed as voltage levels on signaling leads or the on-hook/off-hook status of signaling tones or bits.

- *Alerting* indicates to the addressee the arrival of an incoming call. Alerting signals are audible bells and tones or visual lights.

- ◆ *Call progress* signals, such as busy and reorder tones, inform the user of the status of the call setup process
- ◆ *Addressing* is the process of transmitting route and destination signals over the network. Addressing signals include dial pulses, tone pulses, or data pulses over loops, trunks, and signaling networks.

To illustrate these four functions, consider what happens when you lift a telephone handset to place a call. Lifting the handset sends a direct current signal that notifies the central office of your intention to place a call. The central office responds by returning dial tone and preparing its circuits to receive the address of the call's destination. As you press the DTMF buttons on the telephone, the central office registers the address, sets up the path, and sends an alerting signal in the form of a ringing signal to the called station. If the called station is busy, the central office sends a busy signal. If all circuits are busy, it sends a reorder or fast busy tone.

In this chapter we will discuss the various types of signals the telephone network uses to accomplish these functions of supervising, alerting, call progress, and addressing.

SIGNALING TECHNOLOGY

Except for ISDN users, switched connections over the telecommunications network today involve some analog signaling; even though most of the connection is digital, the subscriber loop remains analog and requires analog signals. Even when T carrier is used for the local loop, the addressing signals are, in most cases, DTMF. Supervisory signals using digital equipment are simple and inexpensive. As indicated in Chapter 5, it involves little more than robbing the lowest-order bit from every sixth frame, and using the binary status of this bit to signal the switching system or drive signaling leads in channel units.

When local networks are converted to ISDN, analog signaling is eliminated. Signals pass among IXC, LEC, and users as data messages. With today's signaling systems, when a station is busy, the signal stops at the end office (unless the user has chosen the call-waiting feature, which interrupts the call in progress). ISDN provides a separate out-of-band signaling channel that allows the network to send alerting messages to the user, where they can be displayed on the telephone. The user can choose how to handle the call without terminating or interrupting the original session.

Consider the general call state model shown in Figure 11-1. Call setup connects circuits together regardless of whether the signaling is in-band or out-of-band. Let us consider the differences between these two signaling methods.

In-Band Signaling

In the idle state, subscriber loops have battery on the ring side of the line and an open circuit on the tip. No loop current flows in this state. Signaling equipment attached to

FIGURE 11-1

General Call State Model

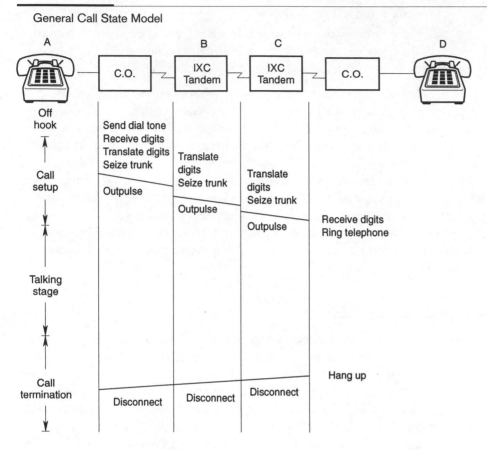

the trunks between the local offices and the toll office furnishes a 2600-Hz signaling tone, indicating idle circuit status. If the interoffice trunks are digital, signaling bits indicate the circuit status. With analog trunks the tone operates auxiliary single-frequency (SF) signaling sets that show the line status by changing the status of direct current voltages on their signaling leads.

The local central office continually scans the subscriber line and trunk circuits to detect any change in their busy/idle status. When station A lifts its receiver off the hook, current flows in the subscriber loop, signaling the local central office of A's intention to place a call. The central office responds by marking the calling line busy (a status indication), and returns dial tone to the calling party. Dial tone is one of several call progress signals that telephone equipment uses to communicate with the calling party. It conveys the readiness of the central office to receive addressing signals.

Station A transmits digits to the central office using either DTMF or dial pulses. The system registers the digits and translates them to the address of the terminating station D. The switching system looks in its database to determine which is A's primary IXC. Included in the switching system's address translation is a routing table that tells it the path to take to the destination. From the address, the system determines that the call must be passed to tandem B. The local switch at A checks the busy/idle status of trunks to office B, and seizes an idle trunk. If no trunks are idle, central office A attempts to find an alternate route. If none is found it returns a re-order or fast busy call progress tone to station A. When the switch seizes an idle trunk, the caller at A hears nothing except, perhaps, a faint click. If central office A has local automatic message accounting (LAMA) equipment, it registers an initial entry to identify the calling and called number, and to prepare the LAMA equipment to record the details of the call when D answers. If the office does not have LAMA, it sends the initial entry to a centralized AMA office over a CAMA trunk.

The trunk seizure removes the 2600-Hz SF tone from the channel or changes the signaling bits to show the change in status. Tandem office B, detecting the change in status, returns a signal, usually a momentary interruption in the signaling tone toward A. This signal, called a *wink*, signifies that B is ready to receive digits. Detecting the wink, central office A sends its addressing pulses toward B. These pulses are either dial pulses, conveyed by interrupting the SF tone, or, usually, *multifrequency* pulses, conveyed by coding digits with combinations of two out of five frequencies. Tandem office B continues to send an on-hook tone toward office A, and will do so until station D answers. At this point, office A has completed the originating functions, and awaits the completion of the call.

Tandem B translates the digits and picks a route to local central office D through tandem C, selects an idle trunk to tandem C, and seizes it. Tandem C, detecting the seizure, sends a start signal to tandem B, and prepares to receive digits. Tandem B detects the start signal and sends the digits forward. Tandem C repeats the process to local central office D. Office D tests the called station for its busy/idle status, and if busy, returns a busy tone over the voice channel. The calling party, recognizing the call progress tone, hangs up; the switches take the connection down. The originating switch adds no completion entry to the AMA record. If station D is idle, office D sends a 20-Hz alerting signal to ring the bell in D's telephone. It also returns an *audible ring* (another call progress tone) over the transmission path to the originating party. The line continues to ring until D answers, A hangs up, or the equipment times out.

When station D answers, central office D detects the change in status as line current begins to flow. This trips the ringing signal and stops the audible ringing. Office D changes the status of its signaling set toward C from on-hook to off-hook by interrupting the SF tone. C sends the off-hook signal to B, which transmits the off-hook signal to A. The AMA equipment registers call completion, indicating the time that charging begins.

When either party hangs up, the change in line current indicates a status change to its central office, which forwards the change to the other end by restoring the SF tone. Office A registers a terminating entry in the AMA equipment to

Signaling System No. 7 Architecture

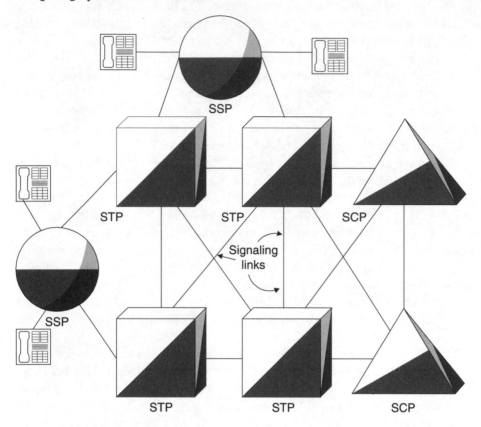

SSP = Service Switching Point

STP = Signal Transfer Point

SCP = Service Control Point

stop charging. The SF tones are restored to all circuits to show idle circuit status. All equipment then is prepared to accept another call.

This system, with minor variations that we will discuss later, can be used for signaling over both dedicated and switched circuits. Not all circuits use SF signaling, however. T carrier and common channel signaling are making SF signaling obsolete. SF signaling can be transmitted over a digital circuit, and often is when a digital link connects to an analog link. As mentioned earlier, SF and MF signaling have been replaced in nearly all circuits because of toll fraud and wasted circuit time during call setup.

Call Setup with Common Channel Signaling

Consider now how a call is handled under common channel signaling. To replace the in-band signaling equipment, common channel signaling uses a separate data communications network to exchange signals and route the calls. The architecture of SS7, which is the international common channel signaling system, is shown in Figure 11-2. We will discuss later how it works. *Service switching points* (SSPs) are software applications running in the central offices, and are linked via data circuits to *signal transfer points* (STPs), which are network nodes that act as hubs for signaling messages. STPs are linked to *service control points* (SCPs), which contain a database of network information that can be accessed by the network nodes.

Referring to the call setup model in Figure 11-1, assume that the stations are ISDN. An ISDN station at A sends a setup message over its D (data) channel to local central office A. The message includes the address of the terminating station D plus information about the call, such as the type of call it is. Call types can be data, voice, video, etc. The SSP in central office A selects the appropriate combination of B (bearer) channels based on the call type, and sends a data message to its STP. The STP sends a data message to the SCP's database to retrieve information about the originating and terminating stations. For example, the user's class of service indicates whether the called and/or calling stations are members of a virtual network, and whether the connection is switched or dedicated. The STP selects a route to the destination, allocates circuits, and sends connect messages to the switches.

Each stage of the call, ringing, connect, and disconnect, is signaled with a data message. The signaling network is fast enough that circuit connection can wait until the called party answers, further increasing circuit utilization.

E & M Signaling

By long-standing convention, signaling on interoffice circuits uses two leads designated as the E or recEive and the M or transMit leads for conveying signals. External signaling sets and the built-in signaling of T carrier channels use E & M signaling to communicate status to attached central office equipment. Signaling equipment converts the binary state of line signals (tone on or off for analog and zero or one for digital equipment) to actuate the E & M leads.

There are five different types of E & M signaling interfaces, but in the most common type the M lead is grounded when on-hook. Applying a -48-V battery to the M lead indicates an off-hook seizure. The E lead is open when on-hook; the signaling set applies ground to the E lead when it receives an off-hook signal from the distant end.

Direct Current Signaling Systems

Direct current signaling can be employed on metallic facilities, which include most subscriber loops and voice frequency interoffice trunks. The use of direct current signaling over metallic facilities is not mandatory. In some applications it is desirable to use tone signaling from end to end. The simplest status signal on the local loop occurs when the caller takes the telephone receiver off the hook, closing a direct current path between tip and ring and allowing loop current to flow. This system is called *loop start*. All subscriber loops that terminate in station sets use loop-start signaling.

All of us have experienced situations where we pick up the telephone to place a call and find that the line is already connected to an incoming call, but the bell hasn't rung. This condition, known as *glare*, occurs when both ends of a circuit are simultaneously seized. Glare is easy to resolve in ordinary telephone circuits (the parties both say hello), but it creates a problem in trunks. One way of preventing glare is by using one-way signaling on trunks. On small trunk groups the use of one-way trunks is inefficient from a traffic-carrying standpoint. Therefore, to accommodate two-way trunks, signaling and switching systems must prevent glare or resolve it when it occurs. In the worst case, when glare occurs, the equipment is unable to complete the connection, the circuit times out, and the user receives reorder.

Most PBXs connect to the central office over two-way trunks, and are therefore subject to glare. PBXs cannot use loop-start two-way trunks because the only indication the PBX has of a call incoming from the central office is the ringing signal, which occurs at 6-second intervals. For up to 6 seconds the PBX would be blinded to the possibility of an incoming trunk seizure. It could seize a circuit for outgoing traffic when the trunk was already carrying an incoming call that the PBX had not yet detected. To provide an immediate trunk-seizure signal toward the PBX, central office line circuits can be wired for *ground start operation*. With this option, the central office grounds the tip side of the line immediately upon seizure by an incoming call. By detecting the tip ground, the PBX is alerted to the line seizure before ringing begins. PBX users must specify to the LEC when ground start operation is required.

TRUNK SIGNALING SYSTEMS

In-band trunk signaling requires the built-in signaling of a digital carrier, or a separate SF set. Signaling systems are required to supervise the connection (single-frequency signaling) and to relay addressing signals (multifrequency or DTMF signaling). Although common channel signaling has largely displaced these, some in-band signaling remains in service.

Single-Frequency Signaling

The most common analog trunk signaling system is 2600-Hz single-frequency (SF) signaling, which is illustrated in Figure 11-3. The voice frequency leads from a carrier channel connect directly to the SF set. The SF set contains circuitry to change the state of the E & M leads in response to the presence or absence of the SF tone and to turn the signaling tone on and off when the switching system or other cen-

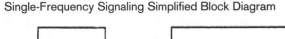

FIGURE 11-3

Single-Frequency Signaling Simplified Block Diagram

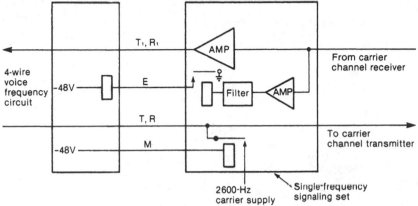

tral office equipment changes the status of its leads. The SF set blocks the voice frequency path toward the switching system while the signaling tone is on the channel. The user does not hear the tone, although short tone bursts are occasionally audible when one party hangs up.

One hazard of SF signaling is the possibility of *talk-off*, which can occur when the user's voice contains enough 2600-Hz energy to actuate the tone-detecting circuits in the SF set. Voice filters minimize the potential of talk-off, but the problem may occur, particularly to people with high-pitched voices.

Addressing Signals

Addressing signals between station and central office equipment use either dial-pulse or DTMF signals. DTMF pulses require a DTMF receiver in the central office to convert the tones to the addressing signals. Because DTMF pulses travel over the voice path, they can be passed through the switching system after the connection is established. This capability is required to send addressing and identification information to interexchange carriers that use exchange access feature group A. It is also useful for converting the telephone to a simple data-entry device.

Addressing signals are transmitted over trunks as DTMF, dial-pulse, or multifrequency signals, or over a common channel as a data signal. MF signals are more reliable and considerably faster than dial-pulse signals, but require a *sender* to transmit the pulses. MF senders use a 2-out-of-5 tone method to encode digits, as Table 11-1 shows. Digits are sent at the rate of about 7 digits per second, compared to the 10 pulses per second of dial pulsing. Since a dial-pulsed digit requires from 1 to 10 pulses plus an interdigital interval, MF pulsing requires substantially less time to set up a call than dial pulsing.

TABLE 11-1

Multifrequency Signaling Tone Frequencies

Tone Combination	Digit
700 + 900	1
700 + 1100	2
900 + 1100	3
700 + 1300	4
900 + 1300	5
1100 + 1300	6
700 + 1500	7
900 + 1500	8
1100 + 1500	9
1300 + 1500	0

COMMON CHANNEL SIGNALING

As discussed earlier, in-band signaling systems have four major drawbacks in interexchange networks:

1. They are vulnerable to fraud. In the 1970s, the loss of revenue to persons with devices that simulated in-band signaling tones was considerable, and was a prime motivating factor in developing common channel signaling.
2. In-band call setup takes several seconds.
3. Call setup consumes circuit time. A separate signaling network reduces call setup overhead. Not only is reduced call setup time important to the IXCs' competitive positions, it also represents a direct expense in the access charges paid to the LECs.
4. The fourth drawback is important to the market strategies of the IXCs: in-band systems are limited to transferring call setup and supervision information, and are therefore incapable of supporting virtual voice networks, which Chapter 31 discusses.

Common channel signaling is also important to the LECs' market strategies. It enables them to receive more revenue from CLASS services. Moreover, common channel signaling is required for local number portability, without which subscribers would have an inferior method such as remote call forwarding to avoid the necessity of changing numbers when changing LECs.

Common channel signaling uses a separate packet-switched network to pass call setup, charging, and supervision information. It also can access the carrier's database to obtain account information, such as features and points served, on a virtual network. The ITU has adopted signaling system no. 7 as the world standard common channel signaling system. The purposes of SS7 can be summarized as follows:

- *Improves call management.* The system handles call setup and disconnect. SS7 handles end-to-end call supervision, and call timing and billing.
- *Enhances network management.* SS7 is responsible for call routing and congestion control, functions that previously were handled by each switch in communication with a network management center. It provides status information to network elements and collects performance information.
- *Separates network control from hardware.* With other signaling systems, network control is embedded in the underlying hardware. SS7 is a control system independent of the circuits and transmission equipment that make up the network.
- *Supports ISDN.* Common channel out-of-band signaling is inherent in ISDN.
- *Supports user database.* SS7 provides database information to form virtual networks, provide enhanced services, and identify and verify callers.
- *Handles addressing and supervision.* Common channel signaling protocols carry line status, calling and called numbers, credit card numbers, and other such information through the network.
- *Supports 800 number portability.* When an 800 number is dialed, an SS7 message to a central database returns with the identity of the IXC.
- *Supports local number portability.* As discussed in Chapter 13, the advanced intelligent network feature in local central offices uses SS7 to relay to the originating switch the identity of the LEC that carries the call.

With in-band signaling, the process of setting up the talking path determines whether the path is operative since audible signals are passed over the channel that will be used for talking. With common channel signaling this test is not possible; therefore the equipment makes a separate path assurance test before connecting the call.

Signaling System No. 7 Architecture

Figure 11-2 shows the architecture of SS7. The system has three major components: the service switching point, the signal transfer point, and the service control point. The SSP is a software application in a tandem switch in the interexchange network, or an end office in the LEC network. The STPs are packet switching nodes, and the SCPs are databases of circuit, routing, and customer information. Each carrier has its own signaling network; the networks are interconnected to enable carriers to interoperate.

When the SSP receives a service request from a local end office or a user attached on a direct access line, it sends a service request to the SCP, and suspends call processing until it receives a reply. The SCP forwards the request to the STP over the packet network. The STPs are geographically dispersed redundant nodes that are interconnected over a high-speed packet network that is protected from failure by alternative paths. STPs are deployed in pairs so that the failure of one system will not affect call processing. STPs pass the call setup request to an SCP over direct circuits or by relaying it through another STP.

The SCP is a high-speed database that is also deployed in pairs, each having duplicates of the database. The database has circuit and routing information, and for customers that are connected through a virtual network, the database contains customer information such as class of service, restrictions, and whether the access line is switched or dedicated. The SCP accepts the query from the STP, retrieves the information from the database, and returns the response on the network. The response generally takes the same route as the original inquiry.

Signaling System No. 7 Protocol

SS7 uses a layered protocol that resembles the OSI model, but has four layers instead of seven. Figure 11-4 shows the protocol architecture compared to the OSI model. The first three layers are called the message transfer part (MTP). The MTP is a datagram service, which means that it relays unacknowledged packets. The MTP has three layers, which form a network similar to X.25. The functions of these layers are

- ◆ The *signaling data link* is the physical layer. It is a full-duplex connection that provides physical links between network nodes.
- ◆ The *signaling link layer* is a data link that has three functions: flow control, error correction, and delivering packets in the proper sequence.
- ◆ The *signaling network layer* routes messages from source to destination and from the lower levels to the user part of the protocol. Its routing tables enable it to handle link failures and to route messages based on their logical address.

The fourth layer is called the *signaling connection control part* (SCCP). It is responsible for addressing requests to the appropriate application, and for determining the status of the application. An application, for example, might be an 800 service request. The ISDN service user part (ISUP) relays messages to ISDN users. The user in this context refers to the interface with the end user's equipment and not to the user itself. The ISUP handles call setup, accounting and charging, and circuit supervision for ISDN connections.

PRIVATE LINE SIGNALING

Private or dedicated lines use all the types of in-band signaling discussed so far plus *selective signaling*, an in-band system for operation of certain private line switching systems. Some dedicated circuits use signaling identical with that used by the telephone network. PBX tie trunks and large private switched networks require all the signaling capabilities of the telephone network. Many private net-

F I G U R E 11-4

SS7 Protocol Architecture Compared to the OSI Model

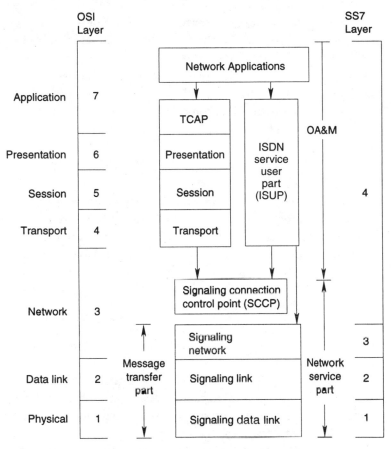

TCAP = Transaction Capabilities Application Part
OA&M = Operations, Administration & Maintenance

works use tie trunks with out-of-band signaling links. Some use SS7 between tandem switches, some use ISDN, and others use proprietary networking protocols, which most PBX manufacturers offer. Special dedicated circuits require signaling arrangements that use the same techniques and equipment as the telephone network, but have no direct counterparts in switched systems. Examples are

- ◆ *No signaling.* Some private lines require no signaling. Examples are data circuits that include signaling in the DTE and circuits that use microphones and speakers for alerting. Other examples of circuits requiring no signaling are program and wired music circuits.
- ◆ *Ringdown circuits.* In ringdown circuits a 20-Hz generator signal rings the bell of a distant station. The 300-Hz cutoff frequency of carrier channels

prevents 20-Hz ringing signals from passing over the channel. Ringdown circuits require equipment to convert the 20-Hz ringing supply to SF or E & M signals and vice versa. A similar circuit actuates ringing when the receiver goes off the hook. This type of circuit requires a loop-to-SF converter. The signal at the far end may activate a light instead of a bell by using additional converter circuits.

◆ *Selective signaling.* Some private line networks use a four-wire selective signaling system to route calls without the use of switching systems. Dial pulses generate in-band tones to drive a simple switch to build up a connection to the desired terminating point.

Coin Telephone Signaling

Coin telephones owned by the LECs use the dialing and ringing signals of ordinary telephones plus direct current signals that operate apparatus within the telephone to collect and return coins. Coin tones are also generated in the telephone to enable the operator to distinguish between coin denominations. Privately owned coin telephones are not connected to coin control circuits in the central office, and since supervisory signals are not repeated over the local loop, they must rely on internal circuitry for coin control, as discussed in Chapter 22.

APPLICATIONS

All public and private voice networks use signaling systems and equipment. Equipment used in public and private networks is identical and performs the same functions of alerting, addressing, supervising, and indicating status in both private and common carrier networks.

All major PBXs provide methods of network signaling to support features such as voice mail, automatic callback, and message lamp illumination across the network. The methods are proprietary, and although some vendors use signals that resemble international standards, signaling is not carried through to the LECs or IXCs.

Standards

Few published standards exist on the conventional single-frequency signaling system. Most standards have evolved by practice, and are followed by signaling equipment manufacturers. Internationally, most carriers use the ITU nos. 6 and 7 standards for common channel signaling and ITU nos. 4 and 5 line-signaling systems. These standards are of little concern to users because the IXCs administer them. In North America, carriers have adopted similar systems for SF and MF signals.

Evaluating Signaling Equipment

A circuit design is essential before selecting signaling equipment. So many alternatives exist for interconnecting signaling equipment that it is necessary to determine the most economical design to minimize signaling costs. The most economical configuration in digital systems is the use of the built-in equipment in the T carrier channel. Where built-in signaling is not included as part of the channel unit, external signaling converters are required. These units are often available with amplifiers contained in the same package, and are built into plug-in units that mount in a special shelf. The voice frequency and signaling leads are cabled to distributing frames, as discussed in Chapter 10, for connection to carrier and subscriber loop equipment.

Signaling compatibility is also an important consideration in acquiring signaling equipment. Compatibility is rarely a problem with respect to signaling equipment of different manufacturers. Signal frequencies, ringing frequencies, and E & M lead connections are universal with all manufacturers. However, the timing of signals, which is controlled by switching and transmission equipment connected to signaling sets, is a frequent cause of incompatibility, but this has little to do with the signaling equipment itself.

Another important consideration in evaluating signaling equipment is testing capability. Circuits have either end-to-end signaling or link-by-link signaling. End-to-end signaling is the easiest to test. If SF tones are used between both ends of a circuit, signaling status can be determined by listening to the tone over the voice channel or monitoring the signaling leads of a T carrier channel. The operation of the SF set is determined by measuring the electrical state of the E & M leads. With link-by-link signaling, the signals are extracted at intermediate points and connected by a pulse link repeater, which interconnects the E & M leads. In most private networks with station, PBX, and NCTE equipment furnished by the user, the local loop by the LEC, and the intercity circuits by an interexchange carrier, link-by-link signaling is the rule. For the user to diagnose signaling problems, testing capability is required to evaluate signaling in the station and NCTE.

CHAPTER 12

Circuit Switching Technology

In telephone terms, a *circuit* is any path that connects two or more users. In the first few years of the telephone's existence, circuits ran from point to point, and they were always connected over a physical facility such as a pair of wires. To solve the obvious impracticality of running a physical circuit between each pair of users that wishes to communicate, a circuit switch connects the output of one circuit, such as a telephone line or a trunk, to the input of another so information can be passed. Circuits can be direct between two switching systems or switched in tandem so users can reach the desired destination over a series of built-up connections.

In the early days of telephony, subscriber loops terminated in jacks, and operators used long patch cords to connect circuits. As the number of telephones grew, the size of the jack panels increased until it became impractical to switch circuits with plug-equipped patch cords. The next stage in the evolution of circuit switching brought manual cord boards. Circuits still terminated on jacks, but they were wired within reach of an operator, who sat at a fixed position that was equipped with several pairs of cords on the key shelf: key switches to control talking, monitoring, and ringing and lamps to show the on-hook/off-hook status of the circuits. Jacks were connected in multiple so that each circuit appeared in front of several operator positions. As antiquated as manual circuit switching seems, it survived in the public telephone network well beyond the middle of the twentieth century and still exists today in some countries.

Manual switching was fine when labor was cheap and the telephone was a rarity, but it was an obvious candidate for mechanization. In 1891, a Kansas City undertaker named Almon Strowger became convinced that telephone operators were reporting false busy signals on his line and connecting callers to wrong numbers, depriving him of business. He designed an electromechanical replacement for the operator and invented the switch that today bears his name. With

Strowger's invention, the automatic circuit switching system, which is the subject of this chapter, was born.

An effective switched telecommunications network has these attributes:

- *Connectivity.* Any station can be connected to any other station.
- *Ease of addressing.* Stations are accessed by sending a simple address code. Using that address, the network does translations and code conversions to route the call to the destination.
- *Interconnectability.* Network ownership rarely crosses national borders, and in the United States multiple ownership is the rule. For greatest utility, interconnection across sovereign or proprietary boundaries is required.
- *Robustness.* Networks must contain sufficient capacity and redundancy to be relatively invulnerable to overloads and failures and to recover automatically from failures that do occur. They must offer some form of flow control to prevent users from accessing the network when overloads occur.
- *Capacity.* Networks must support enough users to meet service demands.

To meet these requirements, networks employ three forms of switching: packet switching, in which traffic is divided into small segments and routed to the destination by nodes that are interconnected with circuits; message switching, in which traffic is stored and forwarded when a path to the destination is available; and circuit switching, in which users are interconnected directly by a path that lasts for the duration of the session. Message switching is practical only for data communications. Packet-switched voice is technically feasible and some systems use packet switching for voice traffic, but voice signals are time-sensitive. Any delay in forwarding packets is noticeable, and may impair effective communications. Therefore, time-sensitive media, such as voice and video, require different protocols than data. Circuit switching is also feasible for some data traffic, and a significant portion of the traffic carried by the public switched telephone network (PSTN) is dial-up data and facsimile.

NETWORK TERMINOLOGY

Network terminology is often confusing because of the ambiguity of the vocabulary. In this discussion of circuit networks the following terms are used:

- A *node* terminates trunks. In circuit-switched networks, nodes are circuit switching systems that are usually computer-controlled.
- *Trunks* are the circuits or links that interconnect nodes.
- *Stations* are the user terminal points in a network. Telephone instruments, key telephone equipment, data terminals, modems, and computers all fall under the station definition for this discussion.
- *Lines* are the circuits that connect stations to the nodes.

FIGURE 12-1

Direct and Tandem Trunks in Single-Level and Hierarchical Networks

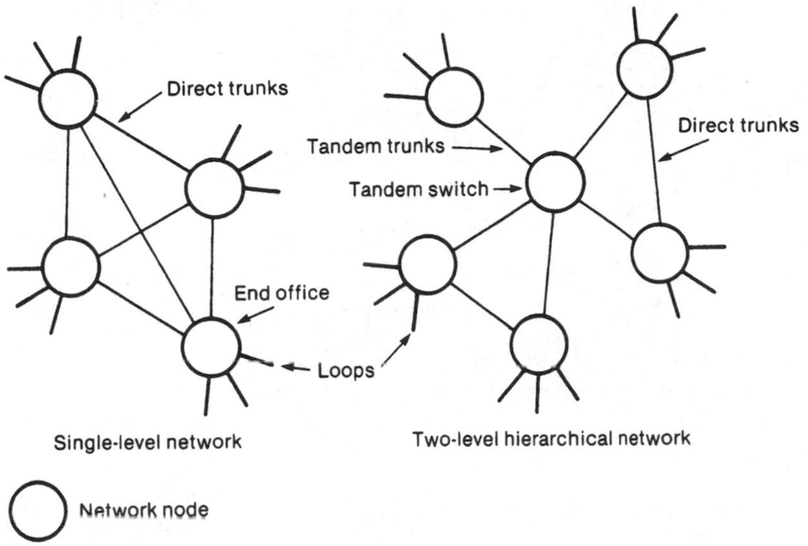

Single-level network   Two-level hierarchical network

Network node

NETWORK ARCHITECTURE

Networks can be connected in five basic topologies—ring, bus, branching tree, mesh, and star. Circuit-switched networks use the star and mesh topologies almost exclusively. Lines radiate from the central office to stations in a star topology, and the nodes are usually interconnected as a mesh. For survivability, the trunks that connect switching systems are often carried on self-healing fiber-optic rings.

The fundamental network design problem is determining how to assemble the most economical configuration of circuits and equipment based on peak and average traffic load, grade of service required, and switching, circuit, and administrative costs. It is practical to connect a few nodes with direct trunks between nodes, as Figure 12-1 shows. Direct connection is feasible up to a point, but as the number of nodes increases, the number of circuit groups increases as the square of the number of nodes, and the number of trunks soon becomes unwieldy. To control costs, a hierarchical network can be formed using tandem switches to interconnect the nodes.

The number of levels in a network hierarchy is determined by the network's owner and is based on a cost/service balance. In the past, the AT&T and Bell Operating Company networks were connected in a five-level hierarchical structure. With the increasing power and intelligence of switching systems, the hierarchical arrangement is giving way to a flat network structure, but in most networks each node has more than one path to the next node.

FIGURE 12-2

Block Diagram of a Switching System

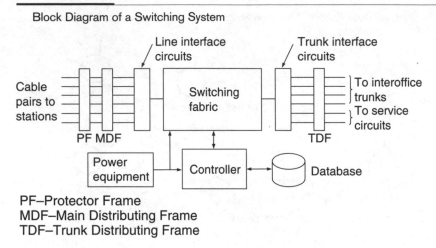

PF–Protector Frame
MDF–Main Distributing Frame
TDF–Trunk Distributing Frame

The Changing Network Environment

Telecommunications networks exist in an environment that is continually changing. Service demands are not constant—they vary by time of the day, day of the week, and season of the year. Demand is continually evolving in response to changing calling habits and business conditions. Competition and new technology have a substantial effect on cost and demand. Also, network design is always a compromise that seeks to balance the use of existing equipment with the provision of satisfactory service. Because of these diverse forces, any network is a complex of modern and obsolescent equipment that is continually being shrunk or expanded to meet demand. Even a new network assembled with the latest technology is soon made partially obsolete by technical advances.

The remainder of this chapter explains the characteristics of the switching equipment that serves telephone users. This technology is common to the three major classes of switching systems—local central offices, tandem switches, and PBXs, which Chapters 13, 14, and 24 discuss. The distinctions between these three types of switching systems are not absolute. A single system can serve any or all functions, depending on how it is programmed.

Switching System Architecture

All switching systems include the following elements, as shown in Figure 12-2:

- ◆ A *switching network,* or fabric, that connects paths between input and output ports.
- ◆ A *controller* that directs the connection of paths through the switching network. Direct-control switching systems, which we will discuss later,

do not employ a separate controller. The user controls the switch by dialing digits.

♦ A *database* that stores the system configuration and addresses and features of lines and trunks. In direct-control systems the database is not a separate element.

♦ *Line ports* that interface outside plant for connection to users. All local and PBX switching systems include line ports; tandem switches may have only a few specialized line ports.

♦ *Trunk ports* that interface with interoffice trunks, service circuits, and testing equipment.

♦ *Service circuits* that provide call progress signals such as dial tone, ringing, and busy tones.

♦ *Common equipment* such as battery plants, power supplies, testing equipment, and distributing frames.

Switching System Control

When a user signals a switching system with a service request, the switch determines the terminating station's address from the telephone number dialed and translates the number to determine how to route the call. Translation tables specify the trunk group that serves the destination, an alternate route if the first choice route is blocked, the number of digits to dial, any digit conversions needed, and the type of signaling to use on the trunk. Some switches lack translation capability. These systems, called *direct-control systems*, route calls only in direct response to dialed digits. *Common-control systems* include circuitry that enables them to make alternate routing choices; that is, when one group of trunks is blocked, another group can be selected. Electromechanical common-controlled switching systems use wired relay logic. Modern electronic switching systems use stored program control (SPC) controllers to direct call-processing functions. In central offices the controller is a special-purpose computer. In most PBXs, a commercial processor is the heart of the controller.

Switching Networks

Switching systems can be classified by type of switching network. Direct-controlled switching systems have inflexible networks that are directed to the destination by dial pulses. Most common-control and stored program control systems use one of four types of switching fabric:

♦ Crossbar analog

♦ Reed-relay analog

♦ Pulse amplitude modulated (PAM) analog

♦ Pulse code modulated (PCM) digital

Of these four types, nearly all currently manufactured systems use PCM switching fabric. The others are obsolete and are used only to grow existing systems. The basic function of the switching fabric is to provide paths between the input and output ports. Like all other design tasks, the network design objective is to provide enough paths to avoid blocking users while keeping costs under control. Crossbar switches use electromechanical relays for the switching medium and are more expensive than electronic switches, which employ digital logic circuits to provide and control the network paths. Electromechanical networks have some restrictions on the number of users that can be served at once. A network that contains fewer paths than terminations is called a *blocking network* because not all users can be served simultaneously.

A *nonblocking network* enables a connection to be made between any two ports independently of the amount of traffic. Nonblocking networks are not economically feasible with electromechanical switching systems because the cost of the network increases directly with the number of switch points. With digital networks where the switching medium is entirely solid state, nonblocking networks are not only economically feasible, they are common in PBXs.

Vendors frequently stress nonblockage as a selling point, but it is easy to exaggerate the importance of a nonblocking network, which can deliver a full 36 CCS of capacity to every station. (CCS, a measure of traffic intensity, is discussed in *The Irwin Handbook of Telecommunications Management*.) Not only is the need for this kind of capacity rare, it must be remembered that the switching network is but one element of the switching system; another element invariably arises to limit capacity. The phrase "virtually nonblocking" has evolved in the industry to describe a network that is not designed to be totally nonblocking but provides enough paths that users rarely find themselves blocked by the network. In switching terminology, the situation in which an incoming call cannot be connected to a port because of blockage in the switching network is called *incoming matching loss* (IML). The percentage of IML is a useful factor in evaluating the health of the system. In a nonblocking switch, the IML should always be zero. In a virtually nonblocking network the IML should rarely be anything but zero. In a switch with concentration and a satisfactory degree of load balance, IML should be a fraction of 1 percent.

A nonblocking switch network does not ensure that users will not encounter blockage because trunking is always designed to some level of blockage. If the switching system is configured without enough common equipment, users will encounter delays that they will interpret as blockage. For example, too few digit receivers result in slow dial tone. Switches are also subject to processor overloads, which can result in a variety of call-processing delays. Switches are rated by the number of busy hour call attempts (BHCA), which is the factor that describes the number of calls the system can handle during the peak hour of the day. The term "call attempt" may bear little relationship to the actual number of calls handled by the system. Not only are call originations counted as call attempts, but accesses to

F I G U R E 12-3

Nonblocking Switching Network

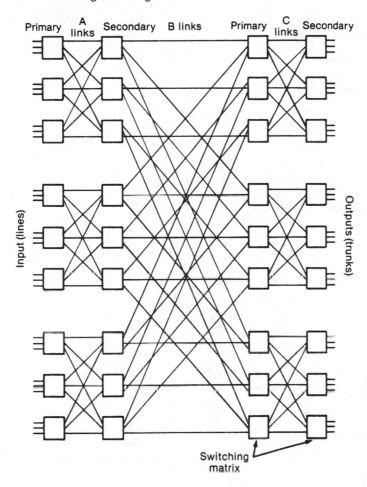

features such as call pickup, call transfer, and call waiting, which require attention by the central processor, count as call attempts in most switches.

Modern switching networks are wired in grids, as Figure 12-3 shows. Each stage of the grid consists of a switching matrix that connects input links to output links. Links, which are often called *junctors,* are wired between switching stages to provide a possible path from any input port to any output port. The network shown in Figure 12-3 is nonblocking because it has an equal number of input and output ports, and the number of possible paths equals the number of ports.

Many switching networks use concentration to reduce network cost. If the primary switch on the input side of the network has six input ports as in Figure 12-4, the network would have a 2:1 concentration ratio because only three of the six in-

F I G U R E 12-4

A Switching Network with a 2:1 Concentration

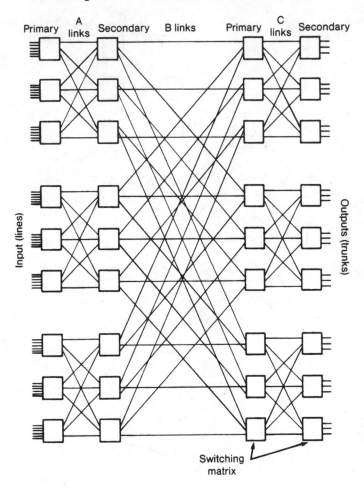

puts could be serviced simultaneously. Local central offices typically use a line-switch concentration ratio of 4:1 or 6:1. It should be understood that even though a switch may have a nonblocking switching fabric, it can still be blocked in the line-switch networks if these use concentration. Trunk switches usually use no concentration. LECs have typically found light usage on the part of residential subscribers and heavy usage by businesses. Business usage peaks during working hours and drops to low usage at night. With the popularity of the Internet, however, traditional traffic engineering assumptions must be reexamined. Residential subscribers may obtain a second line for Internet access and instead of an average call length of 4 minutes, the average may be 30 minutes or more. This results in unexpectedly high usage on trunks as well as the switching network, and is leading to the introduction of new services to shift the Internet load off the circuit-switched network.

The capacity of a switching network relates directly to the number of switching stages it has. The switching matrix is physically limited by the number of terminations it can support. To avoid blocking, the controller must have multiple choices of paths through the network. These paths are obtained by providing multiple switching stages so that each stage has enough choices that the probability of blocking is reduced to a level consistent with grade of service objectives.

EARLY SWITCHING SYSTEMS

The earliest type of switching system was a manual switchboard. Although these are obsolete today, many of the terms we use today originated with manual switchboards, which employed operators to make connections. An incoming signal, actuated by taking the receiver off the hook or turning a crank, operated a signal on the switchboard to notify the operator of an incoming call. The operator answered the call by inserting a plug in a jack, obtaining the terminating number, and inserting the matching plug in the jack of the called line or of a trunk to a distant office. Disregarding the cost of labor to operate a manual switchboard, it was efficient because the operators could make alternate routing decisions.

Many terms in common use today originated with the manual switchboard. Incoming calls to some switchboards were signaled by a hinged cap that covered the jack and dropped down when a ring arrived. The term *drop* has survived to signify the equipment toward the central office from the line. The operator's cord had three connections as Figure 12-5 shows—the tip, the ring, and the sleeve. The *tip* and the *ring* connected to the two sides of the subscriber's line, and this terminology survives today. The operator detected the busy or idle status of the line by touching the tip of the plug to the sleeve of the jack. If the line was busy at another position in the lineup, a click could be heard in the headset from the battery on the *sleeve*, which supervised the connection. The operator's reach imposed a practical limit on the number of lines that a single switchboard position could serve, so multiple positions were connected in parallel.

The operator monitored a connection by observing lamps on the switchboard console. A lighted lamp on the operator's keyshelf meant the line was on-hook; when the telephone was off-hook, the lamp was extinguished. The operator supervised the connection by watching the lamps. The term *supervision* survives today to describe the process, now entirely electronic, of determining when a party answers or terminates a call. Supervision not only directs the equipment to establish and take down a connection but also determines when to start and stop billing for the call.

As the telephone system expanded, it exceeded the practical limitations of manual operation. Mechanical switching systems were necessary to keep the costs under control and to contain the equipment in a reasonably sized area. The Strowger, or step-by-step, switch was an electromechanical device that followed pulses from the telephone dial to switch calls from an originating line to a terminating connector.

F I G U R E 12-5

Derivation of the Terms Tip, Ring, and Sleeve from an Operator's Switchboard Plug

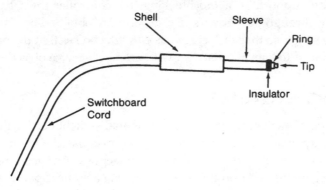

Two problems, permanent signals and calling party hold, plagued step-by-step offices. A *permanent signal* results when a user takes the receiver off the hook and leaves it off without dialing. The line equipment is seized and cannot be released except by manual intervention. Since the line equipment is shared, receiver-off-hook conditions can block other users from getting dial tone. A *calling party hold* condition occurs when the calling party fails to hang up. The switch train remains connected through to the called party, who cannot use the telephone until the caller releases the path.

Although step-by-step central offices are historically interesting, they are no longer suitable for service. They cannot make routing decisions. When a caller encounters a blockage, the switch can return only a reorder or a busy signal. The user must hang up and try again. The switch is slow, regulated by the speed of the telephone dial and depends on the number of digits in the dialed number and the dialing speed of the user. Step-by-step switches have limited features. They are incapable of providing modern enhancements, such as conferencing and call waiting, that make telephone service more valuable. They are electrically noisy, making them unsatisfactory for data transmission, and they require a lot of labor to keep them operating. Nevertheless, step-by-step switches served the world well for the first hundred years of the telephone's existence.

Common-Control Central Offices

Common-control switching systems employ electromechanical logic circuits to drive the switching network. These logic circuits are brought into a connection long enough to establish a path through the switching network, and then released to attend to other calls. Figure 12-6 is a block diagram of a crossbar common-control switching system. Note that calls are connected between line and trunk frames by a *marker*, which was an electromechanical computer that served as the brains of the crossbar system.

FIGURE 12-6

Block Diagram of a Crossbar Switching System

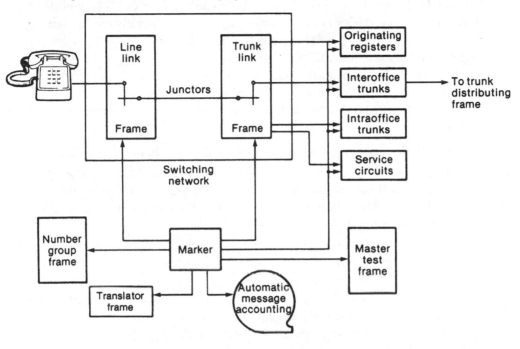

When a telephone goes off the hook, the marker connects the line to a *register*, which is a circuit that collects the dialed digits. After dialing is complete, the marker calls a *translator*, a device that stores routing and signaling information. If the translator informs the marker that the call is to a chargeable destination, the marker calls in automatic message accounting (AMA) equipment and records the initial entry. If the number is within the same office, the marker tests the status of the terminating number, and if busy, attaches the calling line to a busy signal trunk. If the called line is idle, the marker reserves a path through the network, connects the called number to a 20-Hz ringing trunk, and connects the calling number to an audible ringing trunk. When the called party answers, the marker removes audible and 20-Hz ringing and connects a path through the network. When the first party hangs up, the marker takes down all the connections. The process used in a crossbar switch is the same as today's electronic switches. The difference is in the fact that the switching fabric is digital today, and the marker is replaced by a processor that is controlled by a stored program.

The most significant advantage of common-control offices compared to direct-control offices is the flexibility of common control. If, for example, an office has direct trunks to another office but they are all busy, it can attach an outgoing call to an alternate route to a tandem office. This capability is designed into most networks.

Direct-circuit groups, called *high-usage (HU) groups,* are established to terminating offices if the traffic volume is sufficient to justify the cost. The capacity of HU groups is engineered to keep the circuits fully occupied during heavy calling periods. Overflow traffic is routed over tandem trunks that are more liberally engineered.

Crossbar offices are not bound by a fixed numbering plan that relies on the digits dialed to route the call. They can insert and translate digits, choose alternate routes to the destination, and offer *Centrex* service, which is a PBX-like service provided from the central office. Chapter 28 discusses Centrex.

The following characteristics are significant in common-control switching systems:

♦ Alternate routing capability offers flexibility in handling overloads.

♦ Crossbar offices require less maintenance than step-by-step offices because their internal circuitry has no wiping action to generate wear. Also, trouble indications are detected by the marker and recorded in a trouble recorder for analysis.

♦ Although crossbar offices are not as electrically noisy as step-by-step offices, relay and switch operations cause noise that can cause errors in switched data circuits.

♦ Common-control switches are vulnerable to total central office failure. When markers are all occupied or out of service, no further users can be served, even though idle paths are available.

♦ Common-control offices are much faster than step-by-step offices. Dial pulses are registered in shared circuits to avoid tying up equipment with slow users or long dial-pulse strings.

Stored Program Control

Stored program control (SPC) central offices have been in operation since 1965 and in either analog or digital form have essentially replaced their electromechanical counterparts. The primary economies of SPC offices lie in their lower maintenance cost and their ability to provide enhanced features that are impractical with electromechanical central offices. Analog SPC systems, diagrammed in Figure 12-7, use concepts similar to common-control electromechanical offices except that electronic logic replaces wired relay logic.

The central processor controls call processing. When service circuits detect an off-hook signal, the processor attaches a dial-pulse or DTMF receiver to the originating line. The receiver supplies dial tone and registers the incoming digits. The processor stores the details of the call in a temporary *call store memory.* Translation tables are stored in semipermanent memory. The processor establishes a path through the switching network, attaches 20-Hz ringing to the called party and an audible ringing trunk to the calling party. When the called party answers, the processor marks completion of the connection.

F I G U R E 12-7

Block Diagram of a Stored Program Switching System

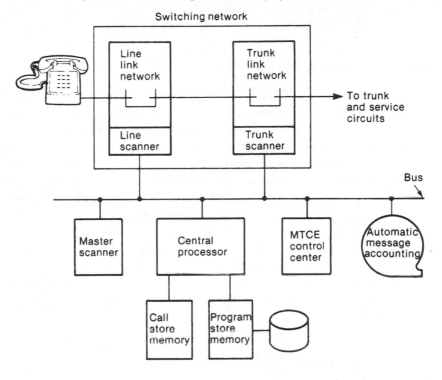

The central processor in SPC central offices is similar to that used in mainframe computers, but with some important differences. First, the SPC processor is not only fault tolerant; it is almost fail-safe. Although SPC central offices can fail, their design objective is no more than 1 hour's outage in 20 years, which is an outage tolerance several orders of magnitude better than that of most mainframe computers. Central office processors have extensive trouble-detection modules that are designed to ensure reliability. A second difference is in the nature of the processing task. Call processing is highly input/output intensive, with little requirement for arithmetic operations compared to commercial computers. Where a mainframe computer is overseeing several dozen peripherals, a central office processor is managing tens of thousands of individual terminals, any of which can spring to life at any time and demand service within a second or less.

Although call processing is similar to that in a common-control electromechanical office, the SPC processor offers much greater flexibility. The processor operates under the direction of a *generic program*, which contains the call-processing details. Features can be added by replacing the generic program with a new issue. Because of this factor, SPC systems are far more flexible than their electromechanical counterparts. The generic program contains special features that Chapters 13,

14, and 24 discuss. These can be activated, deactivated, or assigned to a limited group of users by making changes to the translation tables. SPC systems also can collect statistical information and diagnose circuit and system irregularities to a much greater degree than electromechanical systems.

Reed-Relay Switching Networks

Over the past two decades many changes have been made in SPC switching networks, which can be broadly classed as analog or digital. Most analog systems use reed-relay networks. A *reed relay* has contacts enclosed in a sealed glass tube and surrounded by a coil of wire. The contacts are closed by a short pulse of current and remain closed until opened by a second pulse. The switches are wired in a matrix of horizontal and vertical paths to establish a direct current circuit through the network. Call setup involves finding a path of reed relays from the originating line or trunk to the termination. The processor then directs a service circuit to pulse the contacts closed.

Many electronic switching systems in use in the United States today are analog switches using reed-relay networks; however, this technology is obsolescent and is rapidly being replaced by digital switching. Reed switches are more expensive to manufacture and require more maintenance than the digital networks that are replacing them. Analog systems are also incapable of supporting ISDN, which most LECs offer.

Pulse Code Modulated (PCM) Networks

The latest generation of switching systems uses PCM switching networks. PCM networks are similar in concept to the analog matrix, shown in Figure 12-3, with some important exceptions.

First, PCM networks connect the encoded signal over 8-bit parallel paths. The incoming serial bit stream from the line or trunk circuits is converted to an 8-bit parallel signal and assigned to a *time slot*. At the proper time-slot instant, all 8 bits of the input PCM signal are gated in parallel to the output port. The output circuits connect them to trunk and line circuits where they are converted to serial.

The second exception is in the mode of switching employed in PCM networks. Analog networks use *space division* switching exclusively. That is, input paths are physically connected to output links. Digital networks use a combination of space division and time division switching. Although the term "space division" implies a relay operation, the switches used in digital networks contain no moving parts. Integrated logic gates form the switching element to direct the PCM pulses from one path to another.

The other form of electronic switching is time division switching, which is implemented in a *time-slot interchange* (TSI) element (see Figure 12-8). A TSI receives digital pulses during one time slot, stores them for one processor cycle, and releases them during the proper time slot in the next cycle. Two stations can talk

FIGURE 12-8

Time-Slot Interchange

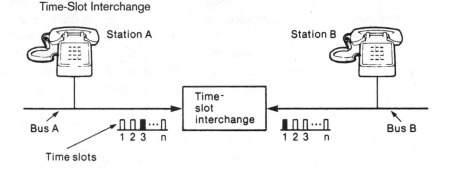

FIGURE 12-9

Time-Space-Space-Time Digital Switching Network

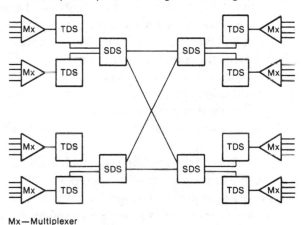

Mx—Multiplexer
TDS—Time Division Switch
SDS—Space Division Switch

through the switch if they are assigned to the same time slot. Time-slot assignments are made by the processor and released when the call terminates. The time-slot interchange process introduces an absolute delay of one processor cycle for each time division switching stage.

Practical digital switching networks contain a combination of space and time division switches. For example, Figure 12-9 shows a time-space-space-time (TSST) network. This is a four-stage network that is the functional equivalent of the space division networks of older analog switching systems.

Control Systems

Electronic switching systems are designed as *central control, multiprocessing,* or *distributed control.* In a central-control system, all the call processing is concentrated in a single location. A multiprocessing system has two or more processors that share call-processing functions. The sharing takes the form of dividing the call-processing load or assigning one set of functions to one processor and another to its mate. For example, one processor could handle call processing and the other maintenance. If either failed, the other could assume the entire load. The third method of control, distributed, uses multiple processors, each of which handles a designated part of the switch. For example, a separate processor might be assigned to each shelf or each frame.

The software that drives electronic switching systems falls into four categories. Although not all manufacturers use the same terminology, and there may be architectural differences between systems, the functions are contained in every SPC switch.

The *operating system* is the system that keeps the switch alive even though it is not processing calls. The operating system ties the elements of the switch together, takes care of input and output functions, and supervises the general health of the system. Closely tied to the operating system is the call-processing software, which in many systems is called the *generic program*. This software contains all the features of the switch and maps the connections through the switching fabric.

The third type of software is the *parameters*. These are a database that contains the types, quantities, and addresses of the major hardware components. By maintaining records of the busy/idle status of components, the processor sets up a path through the network, assigns it while a call is in process, and releases it when the call ends.

The fourth type of software is the *translations*, which are a database of how ports are assigned and what feature is assigned to each port. Each trunk and each station in a switching system is assigned through the translation tables, and the features associated with that port are defined within the table. For example, the trunks are translated as to location, signaling, and type. Stations are translated as to location, restrictions, and features.

Synchronization

Networks of digital switches must be closely synchronized to prevent transmission errors. If two interconnected systems do not have a common synchronizing source, their clocks will run at slightly different rates. This means that occasionally the receiving end will miss a bit or will sample the same bit twice, either of which results in a bit error in data transmission. These momentary losses of framing are known as *slips*. Slips have little effect on voice transmission, but their effect is detrimental to data.

Circuit-switched networks are kept in synchronization by slaving switches from a highly stable master clock known as the basic standard reference frequency (BSRF). Each central office has its own clock that can run freely with a certain degree of stability. The highest level clock below the BSRF is a stratum 1 clock, which has an accuracy of at least 1×10^{-11}. Three lower levels of clocking offer progressively less accuracy and lower cost. Timing passes down from each higher-class office to the offices that home on it. This type of synchronization is called *plesiochronous*. When clocking is lost from a higher-level office, lower-level devices run freely. The greater the differences in clocking between two such devices, the higher the number of slips that will occur. Clocking principles are discussed in Chapter 5.

Comparison of Digital and Analog Switching Networks

Digital switches have several advantages over their analog counterparts:

 ◆ The switching networks are less expensive to manufacture because of the ability to use low-cost integrated components.
 ◆ T1 or SONET circuits can interface the switching system directly. Analog switches must use channel banks to bring digital circuits down to voice frequency.
 ◆ Digital switches can support ISDN.
 ◆ Analog-to-digital conversions are reduced, which improves the quality of the connection.

Line, Trunk, and Service Circuits

All switching systems are equipped with circuits to interface the switching network to stations, trunks, and service circuits such as tone and ringing supplies. In some systems, these circuits are external devices. In other cases, they are integral to the switching equipment. For example, some digital central offices develop tones internally by generating the digital equivalent of the tone, so when it is applied to the decoder in a line or trunk circuit it is converted to an analog tone.

Line Circuit Functions

In a digital central office, line circuits have seven basic functions that can be remembered with the acronym BORSCHT. Analog central office line circuits require five of the seven functions; the hybrid and coding functions are omitted since they have two-wire switching networks. The BORSCHT functions are

 ◆ *Battery* feeds from the office to the line to operate station transmitters and DTMF dials.
 ◆ *Overvoltage protection* is provided to protect the line circuit from damaging external voltages that can occur during the time that it takes the protector to operate.
 ◆ *Ringing* connects from a central ringing supply to operate the telephone bell.
 ◆ *Supervision* refers to monitoring the on-hook/off-hook status of the line.
 ◆ *Coding* converts the analog signal to a PCM bit stream in digital line circuits.

♦ *Hybrids* are devices that are required in digital line circuits to convert between the four-wire switching fabric and the two-wire cable pair.

♦ *Testing* access is provided so an external test system can obtain access to the cable pair for trouble isolation.

In PBXs and digital central offices, line circuits reside on plug-in cards. Because much of the cost of the system is embedded in the line circuits, shelves are installed, but to defer the investment, line cards are added only as needed. In analog central offices, line circuits omit the analog-to-PCM conversion and the two- to four-wire conversion. Analog line circuits are permanently wired in frames that are connected to a distributing frame for cross-connection to the cable pairs.

Trunk Circuits

Trunk circuits interface with the signaling protocols of interoffice trunks to the internal protocols of the switching system. For example, in an SPC office a trunk is seized by an order from the central control to a trunk distributing circuit in the trunk frame. This seizure causes the trunk circuit to connect the battery to the M lead toward the carrier system. When a trunk is seized incoming, the ground on the E lead passes from the trunk circuit to a scanner that informs the controller of the seizure.

Service Circuits

All types of switching systems require circuits that are used momentarily in routing and establishing connections. These applications are briefly discussed so readers will understand how the services are obtained and applied in all types of switching systems.

Ringing and Call Progress Tone Supplies

All switching systems that interface with end users require 20-Hz ringing supplies generating approximately 90 V to ring telephone bells. In addition, switching systems require audible ringing supplies, busy tones operating at 60 interruptions per minute (IPM), and reorder tones operating at 120 IPM. In digital switching systems, these tones are generally created in firmware.

Recorded Announcements

Recorded announcements provide explicit information to the user when calls cannot be completed and tone signals are insufficient to explain the cause. For example, calls to disconnected numbers are connected to recorded announcements. When a transfer of calls is required, the system routes the incoming call to an intercept operator; otherwise, calls to nonworking numbers route to a recorder. Announcements are also used on long-distance circuits to indicate temporary circuit or equipment overloads. Often these are preceded by a three-tone code called *spe-*

cial identification tones (SIT) so automatic service observing equipment can collect statistics on ineffective dialing attempts.

Permanent Signal Tones

A *permanent signal* occurs when a line circuit is off-hook because of trouble or because the user has left the receiver off the hook. Permanent signals in trunk circuits occur because of equipment malfunctions or maintenance actions. Most switching systems use combinations of loud tones and recorded announcements to alert the user to hang up the phone. Permanent trunk signals are indicated by interrupting the supervisory signal at 120 IPM, which flashes the supervision lights attached to E & M leads in some signaling apparatus.

Testing Circuits

All end offices and some PBXs contain circuits that provide testing access to subscriber lines. These circuits connect the tip and ring of the line to a test trunk to allow a test position access to both the cable facility and, to a limited degree, the central office equipment.

All tandem switching systems, most end offices, and some PBXs also include trunk-testing circuitry to make transmission and supervision measurements on central office trunks. These circuits vary from 1004-Hz tone supplies that can be dialed from telephones served by the switching system to trunk-testing circuits that enable two-way transmission and supervision measurements on trunks. Chapter 14 discusses trunk-testing methods.

ACCESS TO THE LOCAL EXCHANGE NETWORK

Until AT&T's divestiture of its Bell Operating Companies (BOCs) on January 1, 1984, the telephone network in the United States was designed for single ownership in each exchange. In some countries it still is, but those countries that have deregulated the long-distance business provide access to multiple interexchange carriers (IXCs). Divestiture, which intended among other objectives to open long-distance telephone service to competition, has far-reaching effects that should be understood by telecommunications managers. This section discusses the architectures of local and long-distance telephone networks, how the interexchange carriers (IXCs) obtain local access, and the way IXCs sometimes bypass the local networks to provide service directly to end users.

Predivestiture Network Architecture

Until the mid-1970s, AT&T had a monopoly on long-distance telephone service in the United States. In most other countries the postal telephone and telegraph (PTT) had a monopoly on telephone service. The 22 BOCs that comprised AT&T and some 1500 independent telephone companies (ICs) owned the local network up to that time. The local exchange companies (LECs) furnished all local telephone service, most intrastate long-distance service, and a limited amount of interstate long-distance service. AT&T's Long Lines Division furnished most interstate service.

The network was divided into five classes of switching systems and their interconnecting trunks. Class 5 central offices, the lowest class in the hierarchy, were owned and operated by the LECs. Class 5 offices served subscribers directly. Higher-class offices were used for switching toll calls. Ownership of class 4 and higher offices was established by agreement between the parties; many of these systems were owned jointly before divestiture, reflecting their use for both intrastate and long-haul traffic.

The class 5 offices connected to higher-class offices over toll-connecting trunks now called *interLATA-connecting trunks*. The higher-class offices are interconnected by *intertoll trunks*. The LECs and the independent telephone companies, as negotiated by the parties, own interLATA-connecting trunks; AT&T and other IXCs own or lease the intertoll trunks. The FCC and the courts regulate the regional Bell holding companies, a situation that exists as of this writing, but which will diminish as the local network becomes more competitive.

Competition in the Long-Distance Network

In 1978, the FCC decided to permit other common carriers to offer switched long-distance telephone service in competition with AT&T. A key issue in the decision was how the carriers would obtain access to local telephone subscribers through class 5 offices. Because the network was designed for single ownership, it was impossible to give other carriers access identical to AT&T's without extensive redesign of the local central offices. The AT&T Long Lines circuits terminated on trunk ports in the central offices as did circuits to independent telephone companies. This trunk-side access was not suitable for multiple common carriers, however, because local central offices were not designed for customer-directed access to a carrier.

Under court order, the BOCs filed tariffs to provide IXCs other than AT&T access to the local network through line-side terminations in the central office. These tariffs were called the Exchange Network Facilities Interconnecting Arrangement (ENFIA) and were subsequently replaced by feature group tariffs that are discussed in a later section.

ENFIA A tariffs allowed IXCs' customers to access their long-distance network by dialing a seven-digit access number, identifying themselves with a PIN number, and then dialing the desired number. This arrangement had numerous disadvantages:

- ◆ The call setup string, which was as long as 22 digits, was more awkward than access to AT&T's network, which was reached by dialing 1.
- ◆ Automatic number identification is possible only over trunk-side connections. PIN number identification was susceptible to fraud.

◆ Line-side connections are inherently two-wire and provide inferior transmission performance compared to the four-wire terminations of trunk-side access.

◆ Answer and disconnect supervision are not provided over line-side connections. Call timing was handled in software, and was less accurate than AT&T's timing.

The BOCs filed another ENFIA tariff to improve access before divestiture. This tariff, ENFIA B (now feature group B), offers trunk-side access to the local switching system and most of the features of AT&T's access. The most notable exception to equal access under feature group B is that single-digit access was provided only to AT&T's network. Feature group B, which is still available, uses the code 950-10XXX where XXX is a three-digit code identifying the IXC, for access to the IXC's network. Although IXCs have now converted to equal access, feature group B continues to be used for terminating calls within a LATA and for access to the IXC for some services.

Equal Access

AT&T's agreement with the Department of Justice required the BOCs to provide access substantially equal to that given to AT&T by September 1986, except where it was not technically and economically feasible to do so. Equal access, called *feature group D*, gives all IXCs access to the trunk side of local switching systems. Users presubscribe to service from a preferred IXC and obtain access to that IXC by dialing 1. Callers reach other IXCs by dialing 101XXXX where XXXX is a nationwide access code to the particular carrier.

Equal access requires intelligence in the class 5 office to route the call to the required IXC trunk group. This required changes in the generic programs in SPC offices. Electromechanical offices required extensive redesign to provide equal access; usually they were replaced instead of being converted.

Many LECs provide equal access through a tandem switching system, as Figure 12-10 shows. An access tandem registers the dialed digits from the end office and, based on originating telephone number, routes the call to the selected IXC. Where the LEC provides access tandems, IXC trunks interfacing electromechanical central offices terminate on the tandem rather than the end office. The access tandem introduces some delay in call setup time, so it is advantageous for IXCs to use direct trunks to the end office where practical.

Local Access Transport Areas

The terms of the agreement between AT&T and the Department of Justice prohibit the LECs from transporting long-distance traffic outside geographical boundaries called *local access transport areas* (LATAs). The Telecommunications Act of 1996

FIGURE 12-10

Feature Groups A and D Access to the Local Exchange Network

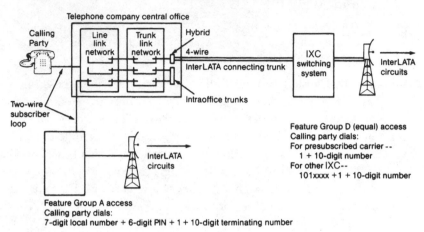

provides for the eventual lifting of this restriction, but at this writing all RBOC applications to provide interLATA toll have either been denied or are pending approval. LATA boundaries correspond roughly to Standard Metropolitan Statistical Areas defined by the Office of Management and Budget. State utilities commissions regulate traffic within LATA boundaries.

The North American Numbering Plan

The North American Numbering Plan underwent a significant transition on January 1, 1995, when the area-code structure of the number changed. The area code had always been identifiable from the digits 0 or 1 in the second position. Several factors, however, caused the supply of available area codes to exhaust in 1994. These factors included rapid growth of cellular telephone, paging, direct inward dialing, facsimile, distinctive ringing, and other applications that consumed numbers. As prefixes filled up, area codes were split, until the available supply of numbers was consumed.

The new numbering plan allows any digit from 0 to 9 in the second position. Equipment that once could distinguish an area code from a prefix had to be reprogrammed to comply with the new plan. The carrier access codes, which had previously been 10XXX, also reached exhaust about the same time. The access code of 101XXXX was added to increase the quantity of available codes.

The 800 number supply was also exhausted in 1995, resulting in the need for another code for reverse charging. The industry selected the area code 888 as the new toll-free number. IXCs began assigning these numbers as their supply of 800 numbers exhausted. The supply of 800 numbers lasted more than 20 years; 888 numbers exhausted in less than 4 years. The code 877 was assigned in 1998 to supplement 800 and 888 toll-free numbers.

International Dialing

Each country is free to adopt its own numbering structure for internal calls, but international dialing requires countries to conform to a dialing plan standardized by ITU. The ITU standard in the past specified a country code of up to three digits and a national significant number (NSN) of up to 11 digits. The total number of digits could not exceed 12. Effective January 1, 1997, the international dialing plan was expanded to 15 digits. The three-digit country code did not change, but the NSN can now be as many as 14 digits.

APPLICATIONS

Switching system applications and standards are covered separately by type of system in Chapters 13, 14, and 24.

CHAPTER 13

Local Switching Systems

Local switching systems, like all telecommunications products, have evolved with the availability of high-powered and inexpensive processors and memory. The earliest electronic switches used specialized processors and memory, but now many systems use commercial processors and random access memory (RAM), which reduces both cost and complexity. The LECs, CLECs, and cellular and PCS operators are the primary users of the switching systems discussed in this chapter, although some large organizations use modified or specially adapted local central office systems such as PBXs and tandem switching applications. The key to the application of a local switch lies in the features provided in its generic program. Hardware differences between local switches, PBXs, and tandem switches are not significant. Some manufacturers produce systems that can handle all three applications, with software changes and hardware variations determining whether the switch is a central office, a tandem, a PBX, or a cellular mobile telephone switching office (MTSO).

Central office switching systems are occasionally used as PBXs or tandem switches. With the right software, a local central office can function in any of the three applications. The primary differences between these applications are

- *Line circuits.* Tandem switches have few or no line circuits. PBX line circuits omit some BORSCHT functions, have less loop range, and use less expensive technology than central office line circuits.
- *Trunk circuits.* Central office and tandem switch trunk interfaces must meet identical requirements. PBX trunk interfaces are built for private network applications, have a narrower range of features than central office trunks, and are frequently two-wire compared to central office trunks, which are invariably four-wire.
- *Maintenance features.* Local central offices include features for subscriber line testing and maintenance. These features are usually omitted from

PBXs and tandem switching systems. Trunk maintenance features are usually more sophisticated in tandem switches than in either local central offices or PBXs. Both tandem and local switching systems have administrative, self-diagnostic, and internal maintenance features that exceed the capability of all but the most sophisticated PBXs.

♦ *Capacity.* With some exceptions, local central offices have greater capacity than all but the largest PBXs. The switching network capacity of local and tandem switches is generally equivalent.

DIGITAL CENTRAL OFFICE (DCO) TECHNOLOGY

DCOs fall into two categories: community dial offices (CDOs) that support unattended operation serving up to about 10,000 lines, and central offices designed for urban applications of 60,000 lines or more. The distinction between these categories is not absolute. Both use similar technology, but CDOs use an architecture that limits their line size. When the system exceeds this capacity, it must be replaced. The size of urban central offices, on the other hand, is limited primarily by the calling rate of the users. If the calling rate is low, some DCOs can support 100,000 lines or more, but with a high calling rate, the central processor or the switching fabric limits the capacity to fewer lines. As processing power continues to grow, central office switching capacity will grow with it. DCOs in operation today can handle more than 1,000,000 busy hour call attempts. Note that busy hour call attempts do not refer simply to the number of completed calls per line. Any time a line requires the processor's attention, such as initiating a call transfer or activating other enhanced services, it represents one or more busy hour call attempts.

Switching systems are enclosed in cabinets or mounted in relay racks. Since DCOs operate at high frequencies, electromagnetic radiation must be controlled, so all components that radiate are enclosed in shielded cabinets. A small system can be installed with little labor, although skilled personnel and special equipment are required to install and test the system. The interconnecting circuits in cabinet systems are prewired, and installation involves cabling the system to protector and distributing frames and to power and alarm equipment. Figure 13-1 shows the major components of a DCO.

Distributed Processing

The earliest SPC switches used a central processor for all call-processing functions. With the advent of high-powered microprocessors, many SPC systems now use distributed processing, in which a central processor links to distributed microprocessors over a data bus. The central processor controls the primary call-processing functions such as marking a path through the switching network. Processors or service circuits located in the line switch units control such functions

FIGURE 13-1

Major Components of a Digital Central Office

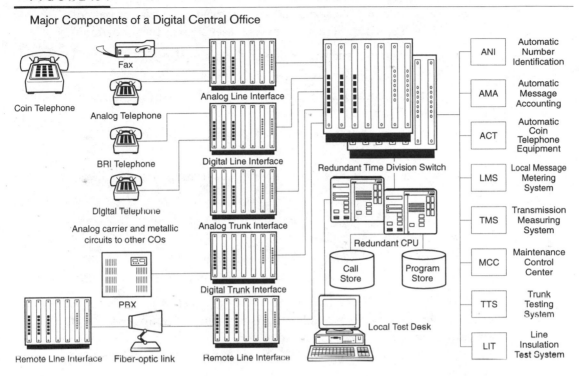

as line scanning, digit reception, ringing, and supervision, which require no access to the system's database.

DCOs must process packet-oriented data required by ISDN and signaling system 7 (SS7). Also, some DCOs are capable of supporting frame relay and X.25 packet switching. These functions are typically assigned to a peripheral processor that is bus-connected to the main processor.

SPC Central Office Memory Units

DCOs require three types of memory. The *generic program* provided by the manufacturer is common to all switching systems of the same type. It resides in *program store* memory and directs call processing. *Parameters* also reside in a program store database and are unique to the particular central office. The generic program uses parameters to find the quantities and addresses of peripheral equipment. Parameters are developed when the office is engineered and remain constant until the office is reengineered.

The second type of memory is the *data store,* which contains *translations.* Translations are unique to the office and are input by the system administrator to enable the generic program to identify working lines and trunks, to determine the features associated with lines and trunks, and to provide trunk-routing information for interoffice calls. Each line is assigned a record in the line translation memory. The line translation includes information about each user such as the following:

◆ Class of service such as residence, business, ISDN, PBX, Centrex, and so on

◆ Telephone number associated with the line

◆ Optional features such as call waiting, call forwarding, three-way calling, caller ID, and DTMF

◆ Status of the line such as working, temporarily disconnected, out of service, and so on

Trunk translations identify signaling and terminating characteristics of the trunk:

◆ Method of pulsing such as dial pulse or multifrequency

◆ Terminating office identity

◆ Type of signaling on trunk such as loop, E & M, and so on

◆ Use of trunk such as local, toll, service circuit, and so on

The third type of memory is the *call store*, which is temporary memory that the program uses to store details of calls in progress. Temporary memory is also used to store *recent change* information, which is line and trunk translations that have been added to the system but have not yet been merged with the semipermanent database.

Redundancy

Redundancy of critical circuit elements in the switching system provides local DCOs with reliability in the order of 1 hour's outage in 20 years of operation. This is not to imply that individual users experience that degree of reliability, because component and local loop failures can interrupt individual lines, but total failure of the central office is rare.

All local DCOs have duplicate central processors. In addition, other circuit elements that can cause significant outage, such as scanners and signal distributors, are duplicated. Redundant switching networks are usually provided in digital systems. In analog systems, the high cost and low probability of total network failure make redundant switching networks unnecessary. Other than network redundancy, the degree of duplication is similar in digital and analog systems.

Redundancy is provided on one of three bases:

◆ *Shared load* redundancy provides identical elements that divide the total load. When one element fails, the others can support service to all users, but during heavy loads a lower grade of service may be provided.

◆ With *synchronous* redundancy, both regular and duplicate elements perform the same functions in synchronism with each other, but only one element is online. If the online element fails, the standby unit accepts the load with no loss of service. Either unit can carry the entire office load alone.

◆ With *hot standby* redundancy, one unit is online, with the other waiting with power applied but in an idle condition. When the regular unit fails, the standby unit switches online with a momentary interruption.

The critical service considerations in evaluating redundancy are the degree to which the system diagnoses its own problems and initiates a transfer to standby and the degree to which a transfer results in a loss of service. With the first two forms of redundancy, little or no detriment to in-progress calls should be experienced. With the third form of redundancy, calls in progress are usually unaffected by a failure, but calls being established are often lost and must be redialed. When calls in progress are lost, many immediate reattempts can be expected with the possibility of temporary processor overload.

Maintenance and Administrative Features

DCOs include many features to monitor the system's health from a local maintenance control center (MCC) or from a remote location. These features enable the system to respond automatically to abnormal conditions. These features can be classified as fault detection and correction, essential service and overload control, trunk and line maintenance features, configuration management, and database integrity checks.

Fault Detection and Correction

The central processor continually monitors all peripheral equipment to detect irregularities. When a peripheral fails to respond correctly, the processor signals an alarm condition to the MCC and switches to a duplicated element if one is provided. The MCC interfaces maintenance personnel to the fault-detecting routines of the generic program. At the MCC, the central processor communicates its actions with messages on a CRT, a printer, or both. Depending on the degree of sophistication in the program, the system may register the fault indication or may narrow the source of the fault down to a list of suspected circuit cards. For unattended operation the MCC transmits fault information to a control center over a data link.

The processor also monitors its own operation through built-in diagnostic routines. If it detects irregularities, the online processor calls in the standby and goes offline. All such actions to obtain a working configuration of equipment can be initiated manually from the MCC or from a remote center. The ultimate maintenance action, which can be caused by an inadvertently damaged database or a program loop, is a restart or initialization. Initialization of the system is usually only done manually because it involves total loss of calls in progress and loss of recent change information.

Essential Service and Overload Control

Switching systems are designed for traffic loads that occur on the busiest normal business days of the year. Occasionally, peaks higher than normal yearly peaks occur. Heavy calling loads can occur during unusual storms, political disorders, and other catastrophes. During these peaks, the switching system may be overloaded to the point that service is delayed or denied to large numbers of users. Central offices include *line load control* circuitry that makes it possible to deny service to nonessential users so that essential users, such as public safety and government employees, can continue to place calls. Nonessential users are assigned to two groups. When line load control operates, one group is denied service while the other group is permitted to dial. The two groups are periodically reversed to give equal access to both groups. Central offices also may be equipped with features that control overloads in the trunk network. These features are discussed in Chapter 14.

Trunk Maintenance Features

Local central offices have varying degrees of trunk maintenance capability. The system monitors trunk connections in progress to detect momentary interruptions or failures to connect. For example, if a trunk fails during outpulsing, the unexpected off-hook from the far end causes dialing to abort. The system registers the failure and enters it on a trunk irregularity report, which technicians use to determine patterns in trunk trouble. The system marks defective trunks out of service and lists them on a trunk out-of-service list. When all trunks in a carrier system fail, the system detects a carrier group alarm, marks the trunks out of service in memory, and through its alarm system reports the failure to the MCC.

DCOs also include apparatus for offline trunk diagnosis. Trunk test systems, which Chapter 14 discusses, interface with distant central offices to measure transmission performance and to check trunk supervision.

Line Maintenance Features

Switching systems contain circuits to detect irregularities in station equipment and outside plant. Like trunk tests, these are made on a routine or per-call basis. On each call, many systems monitor the line for excessive external voltage (foreign EMF), which suggests cable trouble.

Line insulation tests (LITs) are made routinely during low-usage periods to detect incipient trouble. The LIT progresses through lines in the office on a preprogrammed basis and measures them for foreign voltage or low insulation resistance, which is low resistance between the tip and ring or from each side of the pair to ground. These tests detect outside plant troubles such as wet cable and terminal, drop wire, and protector problems.

Electronic switching systems can deal with permanent signals, which are caused by a telephone off-hook, cable trouble, or a defective station protector. Any of these irregularities places a short circuit on the line, and the line circuit attaches the line to a register, which furnishes dial tone and prepares to accept digits. If the central office could not protect itself, all its common equipment could become tied up with a single case of cable trouble, and other users would be blocked. Common-control and SPC offices, therefore, have the capability of dealing with permanent signals. First, the line is disconnected from the register and connected to a permanent signal holding trunk. Then the line is connected to a series of tones and recordings such as a recording that asks the caller to hang up the line. Then after a suitable interval, it may be connected to a progressively louder series of tones to attract the caller's attention. These are of no value during cable trouble, but identifying the lines connected to permanent signal holding trunks helps maintenance forces find which cable count is defective. Then the heat coils (see Chapter 6) can be removed to disconnect the cable from the central office until the fault is corrected.

Configuration Management

Portions of the central office configuration remain static until it is upgraded with additional circuit pack slots. When the office is upgraded, the configuration management system modifies the parameters to inform the switch of the presence of new equipment. Daily service order activity modifies the software to add new subscribers, delete disconnected ones, or change features. The configuration management system enables technicians to enter order activity through a terminal or through a file transfer.

As discussed later, the system samples call activity and reports traffic information such as call counts, call completions, and line, trunk, and feature usage. The system monitors CPU activity and reports grade-of-service measurements such as dial-tone delay and common equipment usage.

Database Integrity

Changes to a switching system's database of line, trunk, and parameter translations are made only after checks to ensure the accuracy of the input record and to ensure that existing records will not be damaged. Update of the database may be allowed only from authorized input devices, and then limited with password control to ensure that only qualified personnel may access the files. A copy of the database also may be kept offline in disk storage so it can be reinserted if the primary file is damaged or destroyed. The manner of ensuring database integrity varies with the manufacturer and is an important consideration in evaluating local switching systems.

Line Equipment Features

Line switch frames in DCOs are constructed modularly with several line cards concentrated into a smaller number of links to the switching network. The ratio of lines to links is the *concentration ratio* of the office. Two different architectures are employed in the line interface. In the coder/decoder (*codec*) per-line architecture, each line card contains a separate analog-to-digital converter. The 64-kb/s bit streams from multiple cards combine in a multiplexer into a high-speed bit stream and route to the switching matrix. In the shared codec architecture, the output of the analog line circuits is switched to a group of shared codecs. The former method, while more expensive, reduces the service impact of a single codec failure. The line card also provides testing access to the local test desk through a relay that transfers the cable pair to a testing circuit.

Line cards are produced in different varieties to provide features required by special types of subscriber equipment. The simplest card provides POTS (plain old telephone service) features to 2500-type telephone sets. Business class line cards provide features for ground-start (see Chapter 11) and coin signaling. DCOs equipped for digital Centrex (Chapter 28) require digital line cards that communicate with proprietary telephone sets. Message-waiting line cards are available to light lamps on telephones associated with LEC-provided voice mail. DCOs offering ISDN service (Chapter 32) require line cards supporting T and U basic-rate interfaces.

Transmission Performance

Because every line circuit in a digital switching system contains a hybrid circuit to convert between the two-wire line and the four-wire switching fabric, line circuit balance is of particular importance in a DCO. The variability of outside cable plant makes it difficult to design an economical line circuit to balance a wide range of cable pairs. Some manufacturers compensate by designing loss into the line circuit hybrid. The addition of loss to the line circuit is undesirable because it degrades transmission performance.

Distributed Switching

Planning for service expansion is a difficult proposition in fast-growing areas. New business or residential developments can spring up rapidly, putting a strain on switching and outside plant facilities. Instead of bringing the lines to the central office with more copper or fiber outside plant facilities, it is often more economical to move the front end of the switch to the users. Most DCOs are capable of remote switching. As most line switches have a concentration ratio of 4:1 or more, distributed switching reduces the number of circuits needed between the central office and the users. Use of a remote line switch reduces the need for range extension and gain devices because the line circuit is moved close to the user and linked to the central office with low- or zero-loss trunks.

Remote switches can be located miles from the main switch, delivering up-to-date services to rural subscribers. They are connected over fiber optics or copper cable. LECs can replace obsolete electromechanical systems in rural locations and offer services such as custom local area switching service (CLASS), ISDN, digital Centrex, and advanced intelligent networking without the cost of a total central office replacement.

FIGURE 13-2

Digital Remote Line Equipment

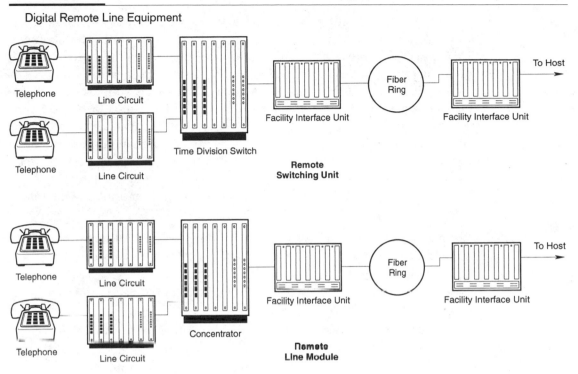

Remote line equipment comes in two general forms, as illustrated in Figure 13-2. The first, a remote line switch, contains a switching matrix. Calls within the module are switched through an *intracalling* link. A single circuit to the central office sets up and supervises the connection. The second form, a *remote line module*, contains no intracalling features. A call between two stations within the module requires two central office links. If the *umbilical*, or data link, to the central office fails, calling within a remote line switch is still possible, but a remote line module can neither place nor receive calls without the umbilical.

Intracalling is essential for replacement of remote CDOs. In case of failure of the umbilical, local subscribers require service to each other, and must have access to local emergency services. Survivability of the remote is enhanced by using a SONET-based fiber-optic ring architecture between the host and the remote, as shown in Figure 13-2.

Subscriber carrier, as described in Chapter 6, also can interface digital central offices. Subscriber carrier differs from a remote line module in that carrier usually does not include concentration. The number of lines served at the remote location is equal to the number of trunks from the remote to the central office. Digital central offices can interface directly to digital subscriber carrier without using a central office terminal.

Trunk Equipment Features

T1 interfaces to other central offices and to customer premises are provided on DS-1 trunk interfaces. Some DCOs offer higher-bandwidth trunk interfaces such as DS-3 and OC-3. Both AMI and B8ZS interfaces are required (Chapter 5). DCOs supporting primary rate ISDN require trunk circuits and software to support primary rate interface (PRI) toward the station. Most DCOs support nonfacility-associated signaling (NFAS), which permits one PRI D channel to support multiple B channels. See Chapter 32 for more details on this feature, which is also known as nB+D, where n is the number of bearer channels supported by one D channel. Special trunks interface with service circuits such as directory assistance, repair service, local test desk, and disconnected number intercept.

Trunk interface circuits must be capable of supporting multiple interoffice protocols including:

- *Feature group A.* FGA is a line-side interface to IXCs and subscribers. FGA is identical to any subscriber line, except that usage is measured both originating and terminating.
- *Feature group B.* FGB is a trunk-side interface to IXCs and subscribers.
- *Feature group D.* FGD is the equal access protocol. It permits subscribers to presubscribe to a particular IXC for all long-distance calls by dialing 1.
- *Signaling system 7.* SS7 is the out-of-band signaling protocol recommended by ITU and adopted by most LECs and IXCs. SS7 provides interoffice signaling over a separate data network, as discussed in Chapter 11.
- *In-band signaling.* As discussed in Chapter 5, signaling between central offices and between the central office and subscribers using a T1/E1 interface may use bit-robbed signaling to exchange on-hook and off-hook signals.
- *D-channel signaling.* PRIs between the central office and subscribers exchange signals over the D channel, and provide full 64-kb/s bandwidth on the subscriber circuits.

Dialable Bandwidth

Services such as videoconferencing and medical imaging require more bandwidth than is available on the 64-kb/s circuits that central offices provide. This leads to a need for inverse multiplexing to combine multiple channels. Some ISDN-equipped DCOs provide the capability of $N \times 64$ service, which enables the user to dial the amount of bandwidth needed. Most switching systems lack this capability, and most LECs have not begun to offer the service, but, depending on the cost and availability of alternatives such as ATM and SMDS, the service may become more widely available.

LOCAL CENTRAL OFFICE EQUIPMENT FEATURES

Local central offices contain peripheral equipment units that facilitate maintenance and special software features. The most significant of these features are listed in the following sections.

Alarm and Trouble-Indicating Systems

As central offices have progressed, alarm systems have evolved from simple visual and audible alarms to systems that include internal diagnostics. In early switching systems, technicians located trouble by alarm lights on the ends of equipment frames and on the individual equipment shelf. Crossbar offices punch alarm indications into trouble cards that provide information on the status of the circuits in use when an alarm occurs.

SPC offices have internal diagnostic capability; the degree of sophistication varies with the manufacturer. In addition to audible alarms and aisle pilots, trouble indications register on the maintenance console and can be printed. Alarms also can be sent to remote surveillance centers. The console operator sends orders to the system to transfer to backup equipment, make circuits busy, and perform other actions designed to diagnose trouble or obtain a working configuration of equipment. Some systems carry the diagnostic capability to the level of directing which circuit card should be replaced to clear the trouble.

Automatic Number Identification (ANI)

ANI automatically identifies the calling party for billing purposes. Single-party lines are identified from their line circuit. In electronic offices this is a table lookup function. In electromechanical offices, separate equipment translates the billed telephone number from the line equipment. On two-party lines the ANI equipment decides which party to bill by determining whether the station ringer is wired from the tip or the ring of the line to the ground. ANI should not be confused with calling line identification (CLID). The difference is explained later.

Automatic Message Accounting (AMA)

Automatic message accounting (AMA) equipment interrogates ANI equipment to determine the identity of the calling party. Where automatic identification is not provided, as with most four-party lines, the switching system bridges an operator on the line to receive the calling party's number and key it into the AMA equipment.

AMA equipment is classified as local AMA (LAMA), in which call collection is done in the local central office, or centralized AMA (CAMA). A CAMA office connects calling subscribers to a center where call details are recorded for all subtending central offices. AMA equipment records call details at each stage of a connection. The calling and called party numbers are registered initially. An answer entry registers the time of connection, and the terminating entry registers the time of disconnect. A common identifying number links these entries to distinguish them from other calls on the storage medium.

The storage medium is tape, disk, or solid-state memory. Call records are sent to distant data processing centers over a data-link or dial-up connection, or AMA circuits may be polled from the remote processing center. AMA equipment also registers local measured service billing details, sometimes called local call detail recording (LCDR).

Coin Telephone Interface

As described in Chapter 22, private organizations own coin telephones in some countries, in which case the telephone itself may provide all coin functions. In LEC-owned coin telephones, central office equipment is required to control the flow of coins. Three classes of coin operation are in use in various parts of the world:

+ *Dial tone first.* This class offers dial tone to the user without a coin so calls can be placed to operators and emergency numbers. When a call is placed to a chargeable number without a coin deposit, the central office signals the user that coins are required to complete the call.

+ *Prepay or coin first.* This class requires a coin deposit before dial tone is supplied. Calls to the operator and emergency numbers require a coin, which is returned after the call is completed. Prepay is largely obsolete because of its inability to handle emergency calls without a coin.

+ *Postpay.* The central office supplies dial tone to the phone, and a call can be placed to any number without a coin. However, a coin must be deposited before the parties can talk. This system, which is common in many countries, is rare in the United States.

Coin telephones are assigned to a separate class of service that provides access to special coin trunks. The coin trunk supports one of three classes of coin operation. Its function is to send coin collect and return signals to operate relays in the telephone to route the coin to the collection box or to the return chute.

For long-distance calls the coin interacts with the operator or automatic coin equipment to transmit tones corresponding to the value of the coins deposited. The operator controls the collecting and refunding of coins with switchboard keys that control the coin trunk. This gives the operator the ability to collect coins before the call is placed and to refund them if the call is not completed.

COMMON EQUIPMENT

Chapter 10 discusses equipment common to all types of central office equipment. This section describes how common equipment items provide external interfaces for the central office.

Power Equipment

Power equipment consists of a commercial alternating current entrance facility, a backup emergency generator, a −48-V direct current storage battery string, and battery-charging equipment. Emergency generators are provided in all metropolitan central offices. CDOs may be wired with an external plug to couple to a portable generator. In either case, the battery string has sufficient capacity to operate the office until emergency power can assume the load during a power failure.

The switching system connects to the battery plant with heavy copper or aluminum bus bars. Where higher voltages are required, separate battery strings are provided in some offices, but in most applications direct current converters raise the battery voltage to the higher voltage required by the equipment.

Trunks, subscriber lines, loop electronic equipment, and other central office equipment are wired to terminal strips mounted on protection and distributing frames. Distributing frames provide access points to the transmission and signaling leads and are used for flexible assignment of equipment to user services and to trunks. Equipment is interconnected by running cross-connects between terminals.

Local Measured Service (LMS)

Many telephone companies base their local service rates on usage. Flat-rate calling is often available, with LMS as an optional service class. With the LMS class of service, calls inside the local calling area are billed by number of calls, time of day, duration of call, and distance between parties. The method is similar to long-distance billing except that calls may be bulk-billed with no individual call detail.

Traffic Measuring Equipment

All central offices are engineered based on usage. Usage information is based on the number of times a trunk or line circuit is seized and the average holding time of each attempt. This information is collected by attaching software registers to the equipment to measure the number of times the circuit is seized and to measure elapsed time that the circuit is busy. The registers are periodically unloaded to a processing center for summary and analysis.

Most electromechanical central offices also provide dial-tone speed registers, which are devices that attach to line circuits, periodically go off-hook, and measure the number of times dial tone is delayed more than 3 seconds. Dial-tone speed is an important measure of the quality of local switching service.

Traffic measuring equipment can provide a variety of other data for administering the central office. For example, database statistical information is provided to update the availability of vacant lines and trunks. Point-to-point data collection enables the system administrator to detect the calling pattern of various subscriber lines to improve the utilization of the network by reassigning lines to different network terminations. Subscriber line usage (SLU) measurements enable the administrator to distribute heavy-usage lines among different terminations on the line switch frame to avoid overloading the line switch with several heavy users. The system makes service measurements to determine key indicators such as incoming matching loss (IML), which is the failure of an incoming call to obtain an idle path through the network to the terminating location.

Network Management

Many local offices have network management provisions to prevent overloads. For example, *dynamic overload control* automatically changes routing tables to reroute traffic when the primary route is overloaded. *Code conversion* allows the system to block traffic temporarily to a congested central office code. This feature enables the blocked system to take recovery action without being overwhelmed by ineffective attempts from a distant central office.

THE ADVANCED INTELLIGENT NETWORK (AIN)

LECs have long been hampered by the inability to react quickly to customer demands for specialized services. Until AIN the switching services the LECs offered were restricted to those provided by the particular central office manufacturer. If an LEC uses central offices from more than one manufacturer, the service offerings are not uniform across the serving area, but instead are confined to those offered in the wire center. New service offerings require the switching system manufacturer to upgrade the generic program, which may be unacceptable in this day of fast-moving competition.

AIN provides service based on customized logic located at centralized nodes in the network. Central offices use the SS7 network to communicate with the central nodes. Figure 11-2 shows the architecture of SS7. The service switching point (SSP) is a software application in the central office that communicates over SS7 links with a central database known as a service control point (SCP). The signal transfer point (STP) is a packet switch that routes SS7 messages through the network. The SSP determines when a call requires an AIN service based on variables such as the digits dialed or the class of service. This process is called *triggering*. When the SSP is triggered, it sends a message to the SCP asking for instructions. The SCP responds with a message that tells the switch how to handle the call. AIN can be conceived as similar to computer-telephony integration (CTI) offered by most PBX manufacturers. The switching system offers an interface that provides information and accepts instructions from an outboard computer. The features can be provided via data link from a central point to all compliant switches in the LEC's network.

Local Number Portability

One of the major conditions of the Telecommunications Act of 1996 is a requirement that LECs provide local number portability (LNP). Recognizing that subscribers would be inhibited from changing LECs if number changes were a condition, the act requires the incumbent LECs to provide a method of supporting number portability among carriers. The method that was developed is similar to the method used in toll-free number portability. A switch makes a call on a central database to determine which carrier handles the call. In the case of LNP, the existing SS7 and AIN infrastructure was used. There are three types of local number portability: (1) users can retain their directory number when changing services, (2) users can retain their number when changing local service providers, and (3) users can change location between central office serving areas.

A particular NPA/NXX is defined as portable upon bona fide request from a CLEC. At that point, every call placed from a line within that NXX triggers a message to the SCP. The SCP responds with a location routing number (LRN), which is a 10-digit number that identifies a switch in the network. The switch uses the LRN to route the call to the appropriate switch. SCP calls are not required for intraswitch calls.

LNP imposes some other requirements on the network in addition to call routing. One issue involves billing. In the past, long-distance billing has been based on airline mileage between the wire centers involved in the call. Distance calculations are made using vertical and horizontal (V&H) coordinates of each NPA/NXX combination. With LNP, the NPA/NXX is no longer a reliable indicator of physical location, so the LRN is appended to the call record.

LOCAL CENTRAL OFFICE SERVICE FEATURES

Local central offices provide a variety of service features that enhance call processing. In SPC offices, these are provided primarily by software. The following is a brief description of the principal features provided by most electronic end offices.

Call-Processing Features

Call-processing features allow the customer to recall the central office equipment by a momentary on-hook flash. The system responds with stutter dial tone to show that it is ready to receive the information. Each of these features is optional to the user, generally at extra cost. Many call-processing features that once were reserved for business use are now becoming popular with residential subscribers. As residential users increasingly subscribe to second lines and custom calling features, such services as call pickup and do-not-disturb are becoming popular. In addition, the following features are supported by most switching systems, although not necessarily offered by all LECs.

Three-way calling is a feature that allows the user to add a third party to the conversation by momentarily holding the first party while a third number is dialed. *Call transfer* is a similar feature that is exactly like three-way calling except one party can hang up, leaving the other two parties in conversation.

If a line equipped with *call waiting* is busy, the switching system sends a tone to signal that another call is waiting. The user can place the original call on hold and talk to the waiting call by flashing the switch hook. Most LECs offer a *cancel call waiting* feature that enables users to disable the service temporarily. This feature is important to anyone who uses a dial-up modem and wants to avoid having a modem call interrupted by call waiting. *Speed calling* is different from the other features in that a switch hook flash is not used. This feature gives the user the ability to dial other numbers with a one- or two-digit number.

Call blocking enables subscribers to prevent long-distance or other billed calls from being completed from their line.

Call forwarding enables the user to forward incoming calls to another telephone number. While this feature is activated, calls to the user's number route automatically to an alternative telephone number. When the user of a forwarded line picks up the telephone, the system sends stutter dial tone to show the forwarded status of the line. *Call forward remote access* enables the user to activate or deactivate call forwarding from a remote location.

Distinctive ringing allows the LEC to assign as many as four separate directory numbers to a single line. Using an adapter that responds to the unique ringing pattern, as discussed in Chapter 22, the user can route calls to a separate telephone, fax machine, modem, or other analog device.

Gab line is a feature that enables callers to dial a number to which multiple callers can be simultaneously connected. Some LECs use the gab line, which is popular with teenagers, as a revenue-generating feature.

Custom Local Area Signaling Services (CLASS)

Most LECs offer a suite of services known as custom local area signaling services (CLASS). CLASS services bring to residence and small business users features that are available in most PBXs. These additional features improve the service for the users and, in turn, generate more revenue for the LECs. Most CLASS features depend on SS7 for communication between central offices, and others are available only through ISDN. Some of the services require special telephone sets or external adapters to use them.

Initially, many of the CLASS services were assumed to be possible only with ISDN. With the large number of analog telephones in operation, the LECs had substantial motivation to make CLASS features available to analog subscribers. The result is analog display services interface (ADSI) protocol that allows many CLASS features to operate on an analog line. An ADSI-compatible telephone can communicate with the central office using analog tones. Unlike ISDN, which can inform you of a second call without any interruption to the call in progress, ADSI cannot send its information while a call is in progress. It sends caller ID between the first and second rings; if you pick up the telephone before the ID message is sent, caller ID will not be displayed.

The following discusses the principal CLASS features that are defined to date. Additional services will undoubtedly be defined in the future.

Anonymous Caller Rejection   This feature allows the subscriber to reject calls from callers who have blocked identification of their telephone number. Rejected calls are sent to a recorded announcement.

Automatic Callback   When activated by a caller who has reached a busy line, the central office lets the subscriber know when the called line is available, and automatically redials the called number unless canceled by the caller.

Automatic Recall   This feature enables a called party to initiate a call to the number from which the last call arrived, which lets the caller return a missed call. The central office announces the call before completion of call setup so the called party can decide whether to continue with the call or drop it.

Calling Name Delivery   The listed directory name of the calling party is delivered to a display on the customer's telephone.

Calling Number Delivery   This feature delivers the calling number to the called party. The number can be displayed on a special telephone set, or it can be linked to a database in a computer to give the call certain treatment before it is delivered to the called telephone. For example, the calling number could be used to retrieve a customer record from the database before sending the call to an agent position behind an automatic call distributor.

Calling Name and Number Blocking   This feature enables a calling party to block transmission of calling party identification. Blocking can be implemented on a per-call or per-line basis. To communicate with lines that have anonymous caller rejection, the user can dial a code to unblock the feature for that call.

Customer-Originated Trace   With this feature the called party can initiate a trace on the last call placed. The service is useful for tracing harassing or obscene calls. The calling number is not delivered to the customer, but is entered on a log at the LEC or a law enforcement agency.

Distinctive Ringing/Call Waiting   This feature enables a user to enter a list of numbers, calls from which are to be announced with a special ringing tone. If the user subscribes to call waiting, the call waiting tone is also distinctive.

Ring Again   This service allows station users who encounter a busy signal to request the network to alert them when the busy station becomes idle and to place the call automatically. When callers encounter a busy signal, if they flash the switch hook, the central office returns a special dial tone. The caller dials the ring-again code and can then use the telephone normally. When the called party hangs up, the central office signals the caller with a ring-again signal. If the caller picks up the handset, the central office places the call.

Selective Call Acceptance   This feature enables users to enter a list of numbers from which calls will be accepted. Calls from numbers not on the list route to an announcement and are rejected.

Selective Call Forwarding   This feature enables users to enter a call-screening list in the central office. Only calls from stations on the list are forwarded to another number. Calls from stations not on the list ring at the dialed number.

Selective Call Rejection   Users of this feature can enter directory numbers into a screening list. Calls from these stations will be routed to an announcement that states that the called party is not accepting calls. Calls from other stations will be routed through normally.

Signaling Systems and Calling Line Identification

Calling line identification (CLID) is often confused with automatic number identification (ANI). The difference between the two is rooted in how signaling is handled in local central offices. This section discusses the differences between the two, and explains when the delivered number may be identical in either case. The distinction is important to anyone who plans to capture calling numbers, whether for personal purposes or for business purposes such as routing calls in a call center.

Automatic number identification identifies the originating party's billing number, and cannot be blocked by the user. The ANI process sends the calling party's billing telephone number from the originating central office to the IXC, or retains it if the LEC is billing the call. The purpose of ANI is to bill long-distance calls. The IXC may deliver it to the called party for identification but that is not its primary purpose. The ANI number may be the directory number of the line that originates a call, but often the ANI is another number assigned for billing purposes. This is often the case with large businesses that have all charges billed to a single telephone number. The same business may have numerous trunks, each of which the LEC sends to the IXC as calling line identification. If the call comes from a PBX equipped with ISDN trunks, the station number may show as the CLID if the PBX is programmed to send station numbers to the central office, and if the central office is programmed to send it forward.

IXCs forward ANI to some accounts if the customer asks for, and sometimes pays extra for, the service. This feature enables the customer to use ANI for such purposes as calling up a computer screen from the database with an incoming call. Originating callers can block CLID in most jurisdictions, but they cannot prevent the IXC from forwarding the ANI over a toll-free trunk to the called subscriber. Note that ANI is provided to the customer only over T1 lines and not over regular telephone lines, which are used for switched-access toll-free service.

Signaling methods are different for ANI and CLID. The LEC can pass ANI to the IXC via in-band signaling over trunks that use multifrequency signaling. (See Chapter 11 for a discussion of signaling.) They can also pass ANI over an SS7 data link, and can pass it to the customer over PRI trunks. CLID is passed between LEC offices only by SS7 technology. It identifies the calling line's directory number, which may be the same as the billing number. The two numbers are usually the same for single-line residences, but different for multiline businesses. An SS7-equipped central office retains the CLID of both the originator and terminating party for later use if either party initiates subsequent calls between them using the special CLASS features. CLID is not used for billing.

CLID is usually transmitted on most calls carried on the LEC's networks. Where SS7 signaling has not been installed, CLID is not transmitted because it cannot be sent over multifrequency trunks. For CLID to work reliably, the LECs must have agreed to send line identification between their offices. LECs that are equipped for SS7 usually forward CLID to the IXCs, but the IXCs and cellular/PCS carriers sometimes do not forward CLID. Therefore, CLID is not received on every call. Also, CLID is not transmitted for users who have subscribed to nonpublished number service. These calls usually are identified with a message that indicates the line is a private number.

Voice Messaging Services

Most LECs offer centralized voice messaging service to their subscribers. Central office voice mail provides features similar to stand-alone voice mail offered by service bureaus. Message waiting is indicated by either message waiting lamps or stutter dial tone. With stutter dial-tone indication, if a message is waiting, the subscriber hears a burst of interrupted dial tone upon lifting the handset. Calls can cover to voice mail on busy, no answer, or call forward.

Voice messaging services can include services such as automated attendant and interactive voice response (IVR). Fax messaging, fax-on-demand, and fax overflow (calls to a busy fax number) services are also available in central office–based messaging services.

Centrex Features

Centrex is a PBX-like service furnished by LECs through equipment located in the central office (see Chapter 28). Usually the switching equipment is a partition in the end office called a *Centrex common block.* Centrex features allow direct inward dialing (DID) to a telephone number and direct outward dialing (DOD) from a number. For calls into the Centrex, the service is equivalent to individual line service. Outgoing calls differ from individual line service only in the requirement that an outgoing access code—usually 9—be dialed. Calls between stations in the Centrex group require four or five digits instead of the seven digits required for ordinary calls.

An attendant position located on the customer's premises is linked to the central office over a separate circuit. Centrex service provides PBX features without locating a switching system on the user's premises.

Emergency Reporting

In much of Europe the code 999 and in North America the code 911 is dedicated to fire, police, ambulance, and other emergency numbers. The local central office switches an emergency call over a dedicated group of trunks to a public safety answering point (PSAP). Calls can be routed over the switched network to the PSAP, but there is always a risk that calls will be blocked by normal telephone traffic, so dedicated lines are normally used. The PSAP is staffed with personnel who have been trained in emergency call–handling procedures. In North America emergency centers can be classified as basic 911 (B-911) or enhanced 911 (E-911).

The telecommunications equipment in a B-911 center can be as simple as key telephone service or calls can be delivered to an automatic call distributor (ACD). Emergency operators have features that enable them to trace calls and hold up a circuit to rering the calling party to obtain more information, but they cannot identify the caller. Almost all exchanges equipped for 911 provide coin-free dialing, which enables a caller to dial from a pay phone without a coin. The B-911 center also can force a disconnect on a 911 trunk that a caller is holding.

To provide calling party identification if E-911 service is used, the LEC or other bureau maintains a database of calling party information that is furnished to the PSAP. Besides the originating telephone number, the database furnishes name and address, the address of the nearest emergency facility, and identification of which facility has emergency jurisdiction. Besides automatic number and location identification, E-911 provides selective routing, which, for overlapping jurisdictions, routes the call to the appropriate PSAP.

Routing to Service Facilities

All central offices provide access to certain service facilities such as operator services and repair service bureau. All local switching systems also provide access to call progress tones—busy, reorder, vacant number tone, etc.—and recorded announcements for intercepted numbers and permanent signals. Some systems also provide access to local testing facilities.

Multiline Hunt

This feature, often called *rotary line group,* connects incoming calls to an idle line from a group of lines allocated to a user. In older central offices the numbers had to be in sequence; in electronic offices any group of numbers can be linked by software into a multiline hunt group.

Call Processing

Most DCOs use similar techniques for processing calls. The following is a short description of how calls typically are processed. The discussion assumes that the call originates and terminates in the same central office. The principal processing elements are

- *Scanners,* which are circuits that detect changes in states of lines and trunks.
- *Signal distributors,* which transmit signals from scanners to call-processing programs.
- *Registers,* which are circuits that furnish dial tone and accept and register dialed digits. Registers are normally dial pulse (rotary dial) or DTMF.
- *Generic program,* which is the call-processing instructions contained in the program store.
- *Call store,* which is the temporary scratch-pad memory used to store the details of calls in progress.
- *Data store,* which stores the line translations.
- *Time slots,* which, in a digital switch, are units of time reserved for the parties to share during a session.
- *Network or switching fabric,* which contains the time slots to make connections between lines and trunks.

A call is initiated when the calling party removes the receiver from the switch hook, which causes current to flow in the line. A line scanner detects the change in the state of the line and sends a signal through a signal distributor to the generic program, which marks the line busy in call-store memory and consults the data store about features and options available to the line. The processor marks a path through the network and reserves a time slot to a register.

The processor connects the line to a register and sends dial tone toward the line. The register receives tones or dial pulses and stores them in a call-store register. The processor consults the data store about the address of the called number. It marks the called line and reserves two time slots through the network—one for the originating party and one for the terminating party.

The called number connects to a ringing source. The calling number is connected to an audible-ringing source. The terminating line is monitored for ring trip, which is a short circuit on the line that indicates that the called party has answered. When the called party answers, the ringing and audible ring signals are removed, and the two time slots that were previously reserved are linked through the network. The connection is supervised for an indication that either party has gone on-hook. When either party hangs up, the processor restores the circuits, marks the time slots idle, and restores the call-store registers. The line status is changed in memory from busy to idle, and the call is terminated.

Calls outside the same central office are handled similarly, except that two switching systems are involved. Chapter 11 explains how signals are exchanged between two central offices. During call processing, many events other than those described here may occur. One party may flash the switch hook, which recalls the processor to send a second dial tone and to be prepared for another process such as conferencing to occur.

APPLICATIONS

Local exchange and cellular/PCS carriers use digital central offices almost exclusively, although a few have found their way into service as large PBXs. The selection of a digital switch is a complex process that depends on the maintenance strategies, service offerings, and cost objectives of the LECs. This section briefly describes the primary criteria used in selecting a DCO.

Standards

Few local switching system standards have been set by standards agencies. Subscriber line and trunk interface standards are published by EIA; the bulk of DCO performance criteria is a matter of matching the manufacturer's specifications to the user's requirements. Bell Communications Research (Bellcore—now Telcordia Technologies) publishes a comprehensive list of requirements that are available to all manufacturers and service providers. This publication, *Local Switching System General Requirements* (LSSGR), defines the features and technical specifications required of local central offices used in North America. LSSGR is not a standard; compliance by manufacturers is voluntary, but it is the most comprehensive publication available for local central office operation. The FCC specifies emission requirements in Part 15, Subpart J of its rules.

Grounding requirements are specified in Telcordia Technical Reference on Ground Arrangements, TR-EOP-00295. Most DCOs use a system ground that is isolated from the frame ground. Ground integrity is essential to system operation and for signaling.

Evaluating Digital Switching Systems

The primary criteria in evaluating a DCO are cost, features, compatibility, maintenance features, and the ability of the office to provide the desired grade of service. The complexity of a DCO makes the provision of maintenance features particularly important. The following is a list of the primary DCO evaluation criteria.

Maintenance Features and Reliability

DCOs must be designed to provide a high degree of reliability with duplicated critical circuit elements and high-grade components. All processors must be duplicated, preferably on a synchronous basis. The processor should be capable of full self-diagnosis. Overload control is essential, including automatic recovery from faults and discontinuing nonessential call-processing operations.

The system should be operable from a remote location except for changing defective circuit cards and running cross-connects. Manufacturers should provide an online technical assistance center to aid in solving unusual maintenance conditions. The system must be fully documented with maintenance practices, troubleshooting manuals, software operation manuals, office wiring diagrams, and a complete listing of database information.

The system should provide an interface to a local test desk for diagnosing subscriber line troubles. It also should have a complete suite of trunk tests to aid maintenance forces in diagnosing and correcting trunk faults.

Training and Documentation

The manufacturer must provide a full line of courses designed to train the user organization in designing, engineering, maintaining, and administering the system. A full range of installation, maintenance, and operating practices is required for system operation.

Transmission Performance

The central office should insert no more than 1 dB of loss into a line-to-line and 0.5 dB into a line-to-trunk or trunk-to-trunk connection.

Line Concentration

The system should be capable of providing line concentration ratios to match the expected usage. Line concentration ratios as low as 2:1 may be required in heavy-usage systems, with ratios as high as 8:1 acceptable in low-usage systems. Local switching systems are usually not designed to be nonblocking.

Environment

The system should operate under the temperature extremes that could occur with power, heating, or air conditioning failure. The normal operating temperature range of most central office systems is at least 10 to 30 degrees Celsuis (°C) [50 to 80 degrees Fahrenheit (°F)]. The amount of heat dissipation determines the size of air conditioning equipment required. Switching systems are also sensitive to relative humidity. They normally operate in a humidity range of 20 to 60 percent. Both temperature and humidity ranges are expressed as normal and short term. Short term means the equipment can operate under those conditions for specified periods of time. Short-term temperatures of 0 to 50° C (32 to 120°F) and humidity up to 80 percent are typical.

Earthquake Resistance

Survivability of any local switching system during earthquake conditions is essential—not only because of the expense of restoring damaged equipment, but also because the safety and well-being of the community depends on continued telecommunications service. Switching systems should be constructed and installed to meet the requirements of the seismic zone in which they are installed.

Multiclass Operation

A DCO should contain the software needed for all end-office functions. In addition, some applications require tandem software. If the DCO is used as a PBX, it must include the PBX features described in Chapter 24. Of major significance in PBX use is the ability to interface a local end office through the line side rather than the trunk side of the system.

Remote-Line Capability

A DCO should include remote-line capability to minimize range extension and subscriber-loop costs. The remote should contain intracalling capability when used in remote communities or a locale with a strong community of interest. The user will notice no difference in operation if a system lacks intracalling capability unless the link to the central office is severed. The DCO should also be capable of interfacing subscriber carrier at the T1/E1 level.

Capacity

The system should have the capacity to handle the traffic load for the expected life of the system. The system should also be capable of terminating the required number of lines and trunks. All central offices must have the capability of measuring and recording usage, whether with built-in or external equipment.

Conversion and Technical Support

Conversion to a new switching system is a major task that requires assistance from the manufacturer. Data from the old switch must be converted and loaded into the new. Technical assistance is required to engineer, install, and test the new system. Postinstallation support is needed from the manufacturer to assist with trouble diagnosis and emergency repair.

CHAPTER 14

Tandem Switching Systems

Common carriers and many private companies use tandem switching systems to build up long-distance connections by switching trunks together. Both local central offices and PBXs can be equipped to serve as tandem switches. If trunking requirements are light, the most economical way to switch trunks is through a PBX or an existing end office switch, but the market offers switching systems designed specifically for trunk switching applications. Tandem switching systems are the subject of this chapter.

The primary users of tandem trunk switching systems are

- LECs and CLECs that use tandem switches for switching local interoffice trunks.
- LECs that use tandem switches to provide IXC access to the LATA. These are known as *LATA tandems* or *access tandems*.
- IXCs, resale carriers, and debit-card companies that use tandem switches for access to their networks.
- Large government and business organizations that use tandem switches for private message and data networks.

The technologies used in these systems are similar; however, the size varies considerably from a few dozen trunks to systems equipped with more than 100,000 trunk terminations.

Long-haul trunk facilities are owned primarily by private carriers and furnished to end users as individual circuits, as bulk groups of circuits, or as bandwidth that can be channelized at the user's discretion. Some large organizations lease or own private facilities, but the majority of users obtain long-haul facilities through common carrier tariffs.

TANDEM SWITCH TECHNOLOGY

Tandem switch architecture is similar to local digital switch architecture except that a tandem switch has few, if any, line terminations. Otherwise, the typical tandem has a nonblocking switching fabric controlled by central or distributed processors. Digital trunks terminate in digital interface frames that couple incoming T1/E1, T3/E3, or SONET bit streams directly to the switching network. Peripheral equipment handles signaling and the central processor sets up a path through the switching network from the incoming time slot to an outgoing time slot that it assigns to an outgoing digital channel. Calls that cannot be completed because of trunk congestion or invalid dialed digits route to a tone or recorded announcement trunk. The digital switch acts as a large time-slot interchange device which, except for some delay, is transparent to the bit stream in the terminated circuits.

Power, alarm, and control circuits are similar to those discussed in Chapter 10. Maintenance and diagnostic circuits are important in tandem switches, which cannot tolerate extended failures because they account for significant amounts of revenue. All critical elements are fully duplicated to provide a high degree of reliability.

Digital switches designed for the public telephone network are equipped for signaling system 7 (SS7), which is an ITU common channel signaling standard. See Chapter 11 for a discussion of common channel signaling. The SS7 interface is a circuit that interprets incoming data messages and communicates them to the call processor. This out-of-band signaling method replaces the bit-robbed signaling built into T carrier.

Figure 14-1 shows how a tandem switch fits into the circuit switching scheme. Circuit groups of different types connect to end offices. As discussed in Chapter 2, feature group A trunks offer line-side access to end offices. Interstate feature group A connections provide usage-sensitive access to all locations in the LATA through the LEC's network. FGA connections are similar to foreign exchange (FEX) except that usage is measured in both directions. Feature group B connections offer trunk-side connections to the end-office switch. Feature group D (equal access) connections are technically similar to FGB except they are accessed through the LEC's office when the user dials 1. IXCs may use LATA-connecting trunks for direct access to the end office in lieu of connecting through a LATA tandem, which introduces call setup delay. Intermachine trunks (IMTs) interconnect tandems. Finally, some tandem switches support operator service positions, which are used for providing call setup assistance.

Tandem switches offer two kinds of dedicated access lines (DALs) to their customers. Analog DALs are analog private lines from the customer's premises either directly to the tandem switch or routed to an LEC end office where they are switched to the IXC. Analog lines are disappearing in favor of T1/E1 or T3/E3 facilities. Digital facilities are connected from the customer's premises to the tandem switch via LEC, alternate access carrier (AAC), or privately owned facilities such as microwave. The motivation for installing DALs is to bypass the LEC's local exchange facilities, reducing access charges.

IXC Tandem Switch Network

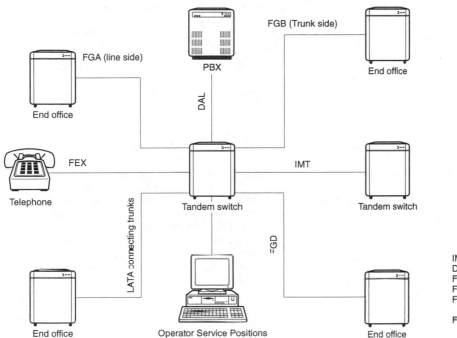

IMT= Intermachine trunk
DAL= Dedicated access line
FGA= Feature group A
FGB=Feature group B
FGD= Feature group D
           (Equal access)
FEX=Foreign exchange

TANDEM SWITCH FEATURES

Most tandem switching system features are implemented in software. Therefore, systems can be used in either public or private networks by changing the generic program. Although the architecture for private and public tandem switches is similar, feature differences between the two applications may be significant. In the discussion that follows, the features are segregated by public and private switch features, but depending on the generic program, the distinction between the two is not absolute.

Public Tandem Switch Features

Tandem switches for public telephone networks terminate large numbers of both analog and digital trunks. The primary features employed are discussed in the following sections. Private networks use some of these same features in private tandem switches as noted under the feature descriptions.

Routing

Public networks are designed to provide a high degree of facility utilization while still providing good service to customers. The competition for customers is intense

TABLE 14-1

Trunk Maintenance Test Lines

Type	Function	Purpose
100	Balance	Provides off-hook supervision and terminates the trunk in its characteristic impedance for balance and noise testing.
101	Communications	Provides talking path to a test position for communications and transmission tests.
102	Milliwatt	Provides a 1004-Hz signal at 0 dBm for one-way loss measurements.
103	Supervision	Provides connection to signaling test circuit for testing trunk supervision.
104	Transmission	Provides termination and circuitry for two-way loss and one-way noise tests.
105	Automatic transmission	Provides access to a responder to allow two-way loss and noise tests from an office equipped with an ROTL and responder.
107	Data transmission	Provides access to a test circuit for one-way voice and data testing. Enables measurement of P/AR, gain/slope, C-notched noise, jitter, impulse noise, and various other circuit quality tests.

among IXCs. Customers are unlikely to tolerate blockage just to save a few cents on each call. Therefore, tandem switches must have the ability to sense overloads and reroute calls around congestion. Tandems should provide dynamic routing control to change their routing patterns automatically when congestion occurs. They also must provide circuit utilization information to enable administrators to change routing tables quickly to respond to changes in customer usage patterns.

Testing Access

Because of their heavy reliance on trunk quality, all tandem switches require trunk test positions. Trunks are switched through the switching network to the test position for making continuity, transmission, and supervision tests. In a network of multiple tandem switches, technicians communicate between test positions by dialing a special access code, usually 101. This connects the two test positions so technicians can talk and test over the trunk. Several different codes are employed in the long-distance trunks of the IXCs, LECs, and some private networks for testing, as Table 14-1 shows. These test lines can be used for both manual and automatic tests.

To test direct trunks between two offices automatically, computer-controlled test equipment dials a *remote office test line* (ROTL) over an IMT, as Figure 14-2 shows. The ROTL seizes an outgoing trunk and dials the test line number over the trunk. A *responder* at the distant office interacts with the ROTL and the responder at the near-

FIGURE 14-2

Automatic Remote Testing System

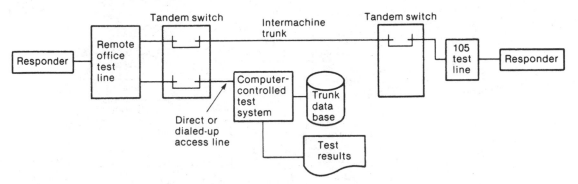

end office to make two-way transmission, noise, and supervision measurements. The test system registers the test results, automatically takes defective trunks out of service at the switching system, and marks them for maintenance action.

Signaling

Common channel switching is the rule for public toll tandem switching systems and is increasingly being employed on private systems. A common channel interface circuit connects between the processor and the data circuits that comprise the SS7 network. The switching systems select an idle path by exchanging data messages, test the path for continuity, and assign a path through all switches that are part of the connection.

Operator Service Positions

Local exchange and interexchange carriers require operator service positions (OSPs) with some of their tandem switches. Most carriers that provide operator services centralize the function with one operator center serving multiple tandems. Operator service functions include intercept, directory assistance, and toll and assistance, which helps callers complete collect, third-number, and credit-card calls. Intercept is the function of assisting customers with calls to disconnected numbers. Directory assistance provides telephone number lookup for callers.

The objective of intercept systems is to complete as many calls as possible with an interactive voice response unit (IVR), which Chapter 27 discusses in more detail. IVR systems are used for essentially all intercept functions, where callers are informed of the new number if one exists. Some calls, such as those to numbers not yet in the database or where the caller remains on the line, must be completed manually. In these cases the system connects the call to an OSP. Operators look up the number, but transfer the caller to a voice announcement unit to read out the number.

Figure 14-3 shows the components of an OSP and a tandem switch system. Incoming and outgoing digital trunks terminate on the switching network. A central

FIGURE 14-3

Components of a Tandem Switch and Operator Service System

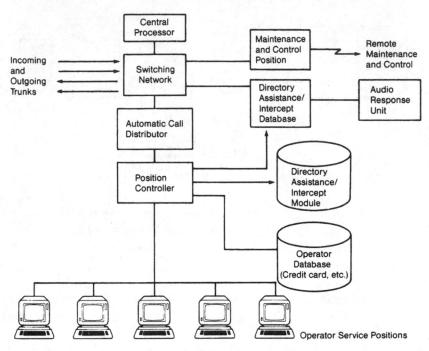

processor controls call processing. The system directly switches calls that do not require operator assistance. If the caller dials an assistance code, the processor routes the call through the switching network to the front end of the OSP, which is an automatic call distributor (ACD).

The ACD delivers calls to the appropriate position. The position controller receives calls from the ACD and supplies the circuitry to enable the operator to communicate with the various subsystems. Within limits, the larger the work group, the more efficiently positions can be staffed. The ACD delivers calls to operators in segregated groups that are called *splits.* During normal load conditions, the three types of calls—toll and assistance, intercept, and directory assistance—might constitute three splits. The ACD can be programmed to overflow calls between splits when overloads occur. During light-load periods, the splits might be combined, with the ACD routing calls to a single set of OSPs. See Chapter 25 for further information on the functions and method of operation of an ACD.

User-Dialed Billing Arrangements

Special networks that register and verify charging information handle most coin and credit-card calls. Credit-card calls are verified over a data link to a centralized database. The customer dials the desired number, then when signaled by the system, dials a credit-card number. The system sends a message to the database to verify the validity of the card number, after which it switches the call.

Coin calls are connected to a circuit that computes the rate, informs the user of the charge with a voice announcement unit, registers the values of the coins deposited, and connects the call. The equipment monitors the conversation time and reconnects the voice announcement unit when the caller is required to make an additional coin deposit.

Operator service features include:

- *Automatic call distribution.* The system routes calls to operators based on workload and queues calls when no operator is available.
- *Center shutdown.* The operator service center should be able to close operations during certain periods of the day and transfer calls to another center.
- *Centralization.* The center should be able to provide operator service features for numerous tandem switches regardless of their location.
- *Interactive voice response.* The center should provide IVR to handle intercept calls, and should route calls to a live operator for user assistance.
- *Directory assistance.* The center should act as a directory assistance center, searching on such variables as phonetics, name and address, and key word.

Authorization Codes

Tandem switches provide authorization codes to identify subscribers, determine their class of service and features, and collect call details by specific user within the subscriber's organization. Most carriers offer both verified and nonverified authorization codes. The switch accepts a verified authorization code only if it is listed in its database. This feature prevents unauthorized individuals from placing long-distance calls unless they happen upon a valid code. Most switches offer as many as seven digits for each authorization code, which makes it difficult to select a valid code by chance. An accounting code may also be required in addition to the authorization code. The system may also accept and verify bank cards and credit cards offered by the LECs and IXCs. The authorization is handled by a data link to an external center.

A nonverified authorization code relies on the subscriber to assign code numbers; the switch will accept any valid digits. Subscribers often use nonverified codes for such purposes as distributing costs among departments and to clients, but unlike verified codes, unverified codes do not offer security against unauthorized use. With either type of code the switch sends a tone to prompt the caller to enter the code. After an interval of unsuccessful or no attempts to enter the code, the switch terminates the call.

Virtual Networks

Some of the IXCs offer virtual private networks to their customers, a service that requires support from the tandem switch. A virtual private voice network is one that operates as if it is composed of switched private lines, but which, in reality, is derived by shared use of the carrier's switched facilities. Voice VPNs are not to be confused with data VPNs, a concept that is explained in Chapter 31. The database for a virtual private network is contained in a service control point, which is a computer connected to tandem switches by 64-kb/s data links. The switches in a virtual network are known as service switching points. The concept is explained in more detail in Chapter 11 under SS7.

A virtual private network handles calls in three manners:

♦ Dedicated access line–to–dedicated access line

♦ Dedicated access line–to–switched access line

♦ Switched access line–to–switched access line

A DAL-to-DAL call bypasses the LEC's access charges in both the originating and the terminating direction, reducing the cost significantly. The DAL-to-switched call is handled on a virtual private network the same way it is handled for a customer with conventional DAL service. The access charge is eliminated in the originating, but not the terminating direction. For switched-to-switched access line calls, the virtual private network handles calls like regular long-distance calls except for features and restrictions.

Virtual private networks also emulate many features of electronic tandem networks. For example, a reduced number of digits can be used to dial on-net stations. Virtual private networks offer a full restriction range such as blocking calls to overseas locations, selected area codes, central office codes, or even selected station numbers. If the virtual network is used in conjunction with account codes, calls can be restricted for certain station numbers. For example, a company could allow its accounting personnel to call the accounting department in another branch, but calls to all other numbers could be blocked.

Call Reorigination

This feature enables subscribers to place multiple calls through the network without redialing the carrier and reentering the authorization code. Manual call reorigination requires the caller to dial a digit such as * or # to place another call, after which a dial tone is returned to the user, who can continue to dial calls. Automatic call reorigination returns a dial tone automatically if the caller remains off the hook after the called party hangs up.

Accounting Information

Tandem switches provide message accounting information to allocate communications costs to the users. This information is either provided in machine-readable format for separate processing or processed by the carrier's accounting office to assemble completed message detail. IXCs distinguish themselves by the type of billing information they provide, but billing is handled by an external accounting center. The switch's role is to provide the raw call details.

Network Management Control Center

Most tandem switching systems provide either a centralized or localized network management control center (NMCC) to administer service and performance on private and public networks. The center collects all network management information in a single location. Typical NMCC functions include

◆ Manual and automatic trunk testing using the apparatus and techniques discussed previously.

◆ Statistical compilation and analysis to determine loads and service levels and to determine when circuit types and quantities should be changed.

◆ System performance monitoring, including diagnostics and maintenance control of all system features and circuits.

◆ Alarm surveillance to detect and diagnose troubles and determine the status of switching and trunking equipment.

◆ Performance and status logging to monitor and log system history, including records of trouble and out-of-service conditions.

Call Progress Tones and Recorded Announcements

Every tandem switch must be capable of inserting recorded announcements or tones to prompt callers on system usage or to inform them when the call has reached an unexpected termination. Callers are familiar with the most common progress tones such as busy, fast busy (reorder), dial tone, ringing, and ringback. Special tones such as queue tone and accounting code prompt tone are used in private systems, and users must be trained how to use the feature.

Private Tandem Switching System Features

With the exception of the lack of need for coin and operator services, private tandem switches require much the same feature set as public switches. Also, tandem switches provide other features unique to a private network. Many of these are the same as the PBX features described in Chapter 24. Circuit costs tend to drive the total network costs in a private system; therefore, tandem switches make efficient use of circuit capacity. This section covers features that are generally included in switches that use all, or a significant part, of their capacity for tandem switching.

Queuing

Public networks are designed so that blockage occurs on 0.1 percent or fewer of the calls placed. When blockage occurs, the call routes to a reorder trunk, and if the user wants to complete the call, he or she must redial. In a private network environment, circuit usage can be increased and costs controlled by queuing users for access to outgoing trunks. If calls always are backed up in the queue, trunk utilization can be increased during peak hours, but the feature must be used with care.

User dissatisfaction and lost productive time may result from queuing, so public networks, where the user can easily dial a competitor, do not use this technique. In private networks, however, the organization has control over the network and its users and may choose to pay the price of lost productive time by using queuing. An audible indication signals when the caller places a call in queue. Some systems use a tone, others use a recorded announcement, and still others use music in queue. Any network that employs queuing should collect statistical information to show the average length of queue, the number of calls abandoned from queue, and the average holding time in queue. This information indicates the amount of time that may be lost because of queuing.

Routing

Private tandem switches include least-cost routing features identical in concept to the LCR feature in PBXs, which Chapter 24 discusses. Other routing features are also available with most tandem switches and some PBXs. Code blocking prevents users from dialing certain digit combinations. With this feature an organization can block access to a given geographical area by blocking the area codes. This can be carried down to blocking individual terminating telephone numbers. For example, some organizations use this feature to block calls to 900 numbers, the cost of which is billed to the caller. The accounting information described in a later section can be sorted by called telephone number to identify heavily used numbers that might suggest abuse of communication services. Where abuse is found, the unauthorized number is blocked.

Another feature, code conversion, limits the number of digits a user must dial to make a connection. For example, a frequently used number overseas or in another area code could be dialed with seven digits, and the call completed over either a tie line or IXC facilities. If the number completes over an IXC network, the switch appends the area code before forwarding the call. Calls off-net to an IXC over a feature group A connection may require dialing a PIN that differs from the user's on-net PIN. The users can dial their own PINs, but the switch dials the PIN required by the IXC.

Time-of-day routing allows the carrier or private system administrator to select facilities based on time of day or day of week. Each day of the year is classified as a weekday, Sunday, Saturday, or special day. The routing tables indicate which route to choose based on the schedules in the database.

Restrictions

Most systems optionally provide other methods of controlling costs. For example, some users may be denied the right to place overseas calls. Some users may be permitted to access a tie-line network, but when a call is about to advance to a high-cost facility because lower-cost routes are full, a call-warning tone sounds. The call will not route to the higher-cost facility until the user dials a positive action digit to instruct the system to proceed. When the call duration exceeds a threshold set in the user's file, a time-warning signal can sound. These and other similar features are normally avoided in public networks.

Other features that are available for certain line classes include security blanking, which blanks the called telephone number on the billing record if the user wants to avoid leaving a record of calls to certain numbers. Some line classifications are given queuing priority to enable them to jump to the head of the queue when all circuits are busy. Most of these features are implemented in software and can therefore be provided for little or no cost, enabling an organization to customize a network to meet its individual needs.

Traveling Class Mark

Callers are assigned a class of service corresponding to the features and restrictions contained in the system's database. As a call advances through multiple switches, the class of service travels with the call so each switch in the chain recognizes the features to be accorded the call. This feature is called *traveling class mark.*

Remote Access

The remote access feature allows a user to dial a local telephone call to the tandem switch to complete long-distance calls over the private network. PIN identification is required to control unauthorized usage. Even with PIN control, security can be a problem with remote access. Many systems raise an alarm when they detect repeated attempts to dial with invalid PINs. It is advisable to deactivate this feature unless it is critical to company operations and is carefully policed.

Call Accounting

Tandem switches provide call details similar to the CDR in a PBX. Call details are forwarded to an outboard call accounting system where charges can be summarized by individual user, department, and accounting code, depending on the service class. For the most effective communications cost control, calling habits can be analyzed and destinations evaluated to determine whether additional private trunks should be added to reduce overflow to more expensive common carrier circuits.

Network Statistical Information

Network administrators need information about calling patterns and habits to manage a network. They use information on the disposition of originating calls to size circuit groups and switching equipment. Most systems provide the following types of information:

◆ *Trunk information* for each trunk group on the network, including peak and average number of calls, holding time of calls, and number of ineffective attempts because of blockage, cutoff, or equipment trouble.

- *Queuing statistics,* including average and peak number of calls in queue, duration of calls in queue, and abandoned calls.
- *Service circuit statistics,* including number of attempts, holding time, and overflow to service circuits such as reorder, busy, and multifrequency receivers and senders.

The amount of statistical information collected from a system is apt to be overwhelming unless the system provides some form of analysis. Some tandem switches are linked to external processors that also can analyze usage information and recommend corrective action.

APPLICATIONS

Tandem switches find their primary applications in public networks. Large companies, which formerly used private tandem switches at the hubs of their private line networks, are finding the virtual network offerings of the IXCs more attractive than private tandem networks. The tandem function can be embedded in PBXs at major switching points of all but the largest users, which means that tandem switches have limited application in most companies.

Standards

As with other types of switching systems, few standards are published with respect to tandem switching. Trunk interfaces in private network switches require FCC registration and must meet the standard technical interface information for compatibility. Most trunk connections are T1/E1 or T3/E3, which are standards that ITU and Telcordia publish. Operator service positions follow proprietary standards if they are provided at all.

Tandem Switch Evaluation Considerations

Most factors that are important for other switching systems are also important for tandem switches including reliability, capacity, compatibility of external interfaces, operational features, and internal diagnostic capability. This section covers the features that tandem switches include, primarily to control private network costs.

Queuing

Tandem switch manufacturers emphasize queue efficiency as an important way of improving circuit occupancy and controlling circuit costs. The method of handling calls during blocked circuit conditions is an important factor to evaluate in comparing tandem switches. Queuing can definitely increase circuit occupancy during busy periods, but the increase in efficiency must be evaluated. The time spent in queue is generally nonproductive and can easily outweigh the cost of the alternatives. Users may lose productivity while waiting in queue for calls to be completed. Also, the time required to administer the system is an expense that must be considered.

Three approaches can be used instead of queuing. The first is to return the call to reorder and force redialing. With a telephone that includes a last number redial feature, this approach is tolerable. The second approach is to increase the number of circuits. With adequate data from the queuing and circuit usage statistics, the cost of this option can easily be calculated. The third approach is to overflow to a higher-cost facility. IXCs design their networks to a low blocking probability. Overflow to a common carrier is usually an effective way for network managers to limit delays in private networks or voice VPNs.

Despite its hazards, queuing is an effective tool to use in managing a network. To be effective, a system should provide for variable queuing by class of service and time of day. The length of queue should be administratively variable. When a reasonable queue length is reached, additional callers should be turned back to avoid long queue-holding times. The system should provide near real-time information about queue length so system administrators can take corrective action.

Network Management Control

An effective tandem switch should provide the tools needed to manage and control the network. The system should be equipped for unattended operation from a remote location. It should have complete flexibility in changing line classifications, restriction levels, trunk classifications, queuing parameters, and other factors that affect line and trunk administration. The system should provide real-time information about trunk status. Defective trunks should be removed from service and referred to the control center for corrective action.

The system should diagnose trunk performance automatically during light-load periods. It should be equipped for transmission and supervision tests to distant tandem switches and, if permitted, to IXC and LEC responders. Direct access to individual circuits should be permitted for making transmission measurements and supervision.

A full range of statistical information should be available for evaluating service and for determining when trunk quantities should be adjusted. A method of automatically analyzing the raw statistical information should be included. The information should be formatted so the corrective action to be taken is apparent.

The system should diagnose its own troubles and direct technicians on what action to take, ideally to the point of specifying the circuit card to change. The manufacturer should provide remote diagnostic and technical assistance along with a method of keeping both hardware and software current with updates.

ISDN Compatibility

The system should be capable of supporting PRI access trunks. Basic rate is not supported on most tandem switches. The system should support ISDN features including calling line identification (CLID), call-by-call service selection, nonfacility-associated signaling (NFAS), and network ring again.

Network Modeling

Networks are sized by simulation or modeling techniques. If the vendor provides a simulation or modeling service to determine equipment and trunk quantities and to predict the effects of changes in load, tandem switch administration will be simplified. An effective tool should accept usage information from system-produced statistics and summaries of originating and terminating traffic to determine the most efficient use of equipment and facilities. The system also should accept cost information to find the best balance between options such as DALs, tie lines, and public switched networks.

Routing, Blocking, and Translations

A tandem switch should provide fully flexible routing to trunk groups based on class of service. It should have the capability of blocking area codes, central office codes, and line numbers. It also should filter calls so some users can complete calls only to selected codes. The system should block access to circuit groups to prevent unsuccessful attempts to access distant systems that are temporarily experiencing service difficulties. This capability allows the distant system to recover without being inundated with excessive call attempts. The system also should translate codes so users dial the same code to reach a destination despite the routing.

Remote Access

The value of remote access from a separate location should be considered. Security and transmission performance must be weighed against the benefits of remote access. A switch should provide an effective screen against unauthorized access and should alert the network administrator to unauthorized attempts. The transmission characteristics of the access circuits should be evaluated to predict whether service will be satisfactory.

High-Speed Switching Capability

If video conferencing, closed-circuit TV, or high-speed data transfer is anticipated, the system should be evaluated for its capability to allocate the bandwidth on an $N \times 64$ basis. The system should be capable of reserving any segment of capacity required and should preempt occupied circuits when necessary to vacate the required bandwidth.

Billing Capability

The system must generate a call-detail record for each call attempted. The record must distinguish between customer-dialed and operator-handled calls. Call details should be output to a variety of media including magnetic tape, hard disk, and solid-state storage. The system must permit the administrator to search for billing records. The system must produce billing records by ANI, personal identification number, or account code.

Operator Service Position Evaluation Considerations

A fundamental objective of operator service units is to reduce the average work time (AWT) per call to a minimum. A reduction in AWT is achieved by having automated equipment handle as much of the call as possible. For example, directory assistance positions almost universally use a voice announcement unit to read out the telephone number. The operator's function is to locate the name in the database and transfer the call to the announcement system. The more effective the search algorithm, the fewer the keystrokes the operator must make before the system finds a match. Enabling the operator to access the most frequently used functions with a single key also reduces work time. Less frequently encountered conditions may require menu access. For new operators, a Help key is important.

Signaling System Compatibility

Another important feature is compatibility with the signaling format of the central offices served. Signaling system no. 7 compatibility is usually required. Compatibility with the exchange access operator service signaling (EAOSS) protocol also may be required. The system must interface to or provide a database for intercepted calls.

Force Management Capability

An important feature of operator service systems is force management software. The force management system provides productivity statistics such as the number of calls and the average work time per operator. It provides managers with service statistics such as the number of calls exceeding the waiting time objective and the number of calls abandoned without being served. The system provides service-observing capability and enables operators to call a supervisor into the connection if necessary.

PART THREE

Transmission Systems

CHAPTER 15

Lightwave Communications

Occasionally, a development comes along that truly revolutionizes an industry. Such is the case with fiber optics. Today's boom in telecommunications would not have been possible with the old radio-based media. Without undersea fiber optics, communications would be limited to satellite with its delay deficiencies or the old copper cables with their limited capacity. Today, every major industrialized center is linked to the rest of the world with fiber-optic cable, with the resulting high-quality, low-cost circuits. Fiber has also found its way to the end-user community. The default method of linking LAN hubs is fiber, and it's a shortsighted company that installs a campus backbone without providing fiber optics. An emerging standard, Fibre Channel, provides speeds approximating 1 Gb/s for interconnecting data hosts and peripherals.

Fiber optics arrived at an opportune time in telecommunications history. It provides unlimited bandwidth in a world that was rapidly exhausting microwave frequencies. It provides interference-free communications with a level of quality that doesn't matter whether the parties to a session are next door or half a world apart. The cable is fabricated from silicon, the most abundant substance on earth, and in terms of energy consumption the electronics are far more efficient than the technologies they replace. Best of all, once the fiber-optic cable is in place, it can be expanded to many times its original capacity as the multiplexing electronics improves. Just a few years ago, 1 Gb/s was the state of the art in fiber-optic capacity. Today, OC-192 at 10 Gb/s is feasible, and the capacity of the fiber can be increased with dense wave division multiplexing.

A major controversy today is whether fiber optics on customer premises should be extended all the way to the desktop. Its proponents point out that the cost of fiber is about the same as category 5 UTP, and provides bandwidths several orders-of-magnitude higher. Opponents point to the lower cost of UTP devices and contend that UTP can handle ATM at 155 Mb/s and gigabit Ethernet, speeds that are likely to satisfy most foreseeable needs. Furthermore, the twisted-pair manufacturers are driving the bandwidths ever higher that copper wire can support.

Controversy not withstanding, the importance of fiber optics in telecommunications' future is unquestioned. As we have discussed in previous chapters, the analog network is disappearing. Coaxial cable was once the prime medium of choice in the CATV industry, but with competition entering the local network, cable companies are offering a host of services over networks that require fiber optics. Advances in fiber splicing and connectorizing techniques are bringing fiber to the point that handling skills are no longer confined to a highly trained few.

The twentieth century laced the world with fiber optics. The twenty-first century promises to bring information services that we are just beginning to glimpse, and they are all built on the need for cheap and reliable bandwidth. Fiber optics will migrate to the local loop as the economics dictate, and will bring enormous changes to the home. Education, entertainment, security, telephone, Internet, telecommuting, and a host of other services will shape the way we think, work, and learn over the next few decades.

Lightwave communication is not a complete panacea for telecommunications. Where the application needs enormous amounts of bandwidth, it is without equal, but where only a few circuits are needed it cannot compete economically with copper cable. Also, its enormous bandwidth makes it vulnerable. The natural enemy of fiber optics is the backhoe; a single cable cut can disrupt traffic to a large section of the country. It is not enough, therefore, for a common carrier to have a lightwave system. The network must be protected by diversity and automatic protection of cable routes to prevent a service disaster when a fiber route is lost. Furthermore, fiber installation is expensive. Where it is not feasible to dig up terrain or cross roads, radio is still the preferred medium.

LIGHTWAVE TECHNOLOGY

The use of light for communication is an idea that has been around for more than a century, but has become feasible only within the past two decades. Alexander Graham Bell, in the first known lightwave application, received a patent for his "Photophone" in 1880. The Photophone was a device that modulated a light beam that was focused from the sun, and radiated in free space to a nearby receiver. The system reportedly worked well, but free-space radiation of light has several disadvantages that the devices available at the time could not overcome. Like many other ideas, this one was ahead of its time. Free-space light communication is now technically feasible if the application can tolerate occasional outages caused by fog, dust, atmospheric turbulence, and other path disruptions.

Two developments raised lightwave communication from the theoretical to the practical. The first development was the laser in 1960. A laser produces an intense beam of highly collimated light, that is, its rays travel in parallel paths. The pulses from a digital signal trigger the laser on and off at the speed of the modu-

FIGURE 15-1

Block Diagram of a Typical Fiber-Optic System

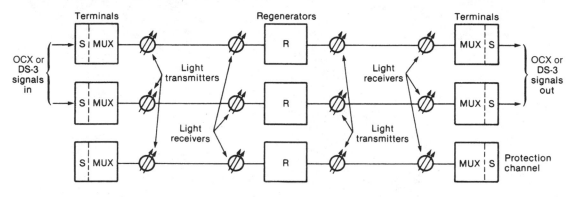

S — Protection switch
MUX — Multiplexer
R — Regenerator

lating signal. The second event that advanced lightwave was the development of glass fiber of such purity that only a minute portion of a light signal emitted into the fiber is attenuated. With a laser source that is triggered on and off at high speed, the zeros and ones of a digital communication channel can be transmitted to a detector, usually an avalanche photo diode (APD) or PIN diode. The detector converts the received signal pulses from light back to electrical pulses and couples them to the multiplex equipment. Figure 15-1 shows the elements of a lightwave communication system. Repeaters or regenerators are spaced at regular intervals, with the spacing dependent on the transmission loss of the fiber and the *system gain* at the transmission wavelength. System gain is discussed in a later section.

A standby channel, which assumes the load when the regular channel fails, protects most lightwave systems. The two directions of transmission are normally protected separately between the digital signal input and output points. If a failure occurs, the protection equipment switches the signal to a new combination of cable, terminal equipment, and repeaters.

The advantages of lightwave accrue from the protected transmission medium of the glass fiber. These tiny waveguides isolate the digital signal from the fading and interference characteristics of free space. The optical fiber attenuates the light signal, however, and as Figure 15-2 shows, the loss is not uniform across the spectrum. As Figure 15-2 shows, there are three regions or *windows* that lightwave communication can use.

The earliest fiber-optic systems used the 850-nanometer (nm) window because suitable lasers were first commercially available at that wavelength. Slower-speed LANs also use this window because LEDs are economical to operate at that wavelength. As lasers became available at 1300 nm, applications have shifted to

FIGURE 15-2

Spectral Loss for a Typical Optical Fiber: Loss Disturbances Labeled OH⁻ Result from Hydroxyl Ion Absorption

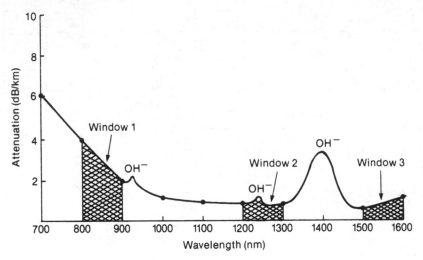

this wavelength because of its lower loss. Single-mode fiber, discussed later, exhibits slightly lower losses in its third window at about 1550 nm.

The first commercial fiber-optics system, installed in 1977, operated at 45 Mb/s (DS-3), with repeaters required at 4-mile (6.4-km) intervals. Current systems operate throughout the SONET/SDH range, up to and including OC-192, which has a line rate of 9.95 Gb/s. If this much bandwidth were populated with 192 DS-3 signals, each of which carries 672 voice channels, an OC-192 system would carry 129,024 voice channels. As discussed later, dense wave division multiplexing (DWDM) systems can multiply that capacity 40 times or more.

LIGHTGUIDE CABLES

A digital signal is applied to a lightguide by pulsing the light source on and off at the bit rate of the modulating signal, and the signal propagates to the receiver at slightly less than the speed of light. The lightguide has three parts, the inner core, the outer cladding, and a protective coating around the cladding. Both the core and the cladding are of glass composition; the cladding has a greater *refractive index* so that most of the incoming light waves are contained within the core. Light entering an optical fiber propagates through the core in *modes*, which are the different possible paths a lightwave can follow. Optical fiber is grouped into two categories, *single mode* and *multimode.* In single-mode fiber light can take only a single path through a core that measures about 9 μm in diameter, which is about the size of a bacterium. (A micrometer is one one-millionth of a meter.) Multimode fibers have cores of 50

F I G U R E   15-3

Light-Ray Paths through a Step Index Optical Fiber

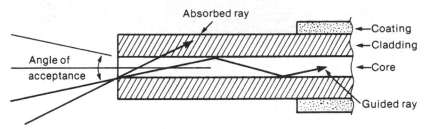

to 200 μm in diameter, with 62.5 μm the standard recommended for most applications. Multimode fiber is used almost exclusively in customer premises applications. Most LANs and high-speed networks, such as FDDI, specify multimode fiber with a 62.5-μm core. Fiber is also manufactured with a 50-μm core, but it is not standardized in EIA/TIA 568 specifications—at least yet. The gigabit Ethernet standard does mention 50-μm fiber, so it may be included in future standards.

Single-mode fiber is more efficient at long distances for reasons that we discuss later, but the small core diameter requires a high degree of precision in manufacturing, splicing, and terminating the fiber. Despite the greater precision needed, single-mode fiber is less expensive than multimode, primarily because of the vast quantities of single-mode fiber that are manufactured.

Lightwaves must enter the fiber at a critical angle known as the *angle of acceptance.* Any waves entering at a greater angle can escape through the cladding, as Figure 15-3 shows. The reflected waves take a longer path to the detector than those that propagate directly. The multipath reflections arriving out of phase with the main signal attenuate the signal, round, and broaden the shoulders of the light pulses. This pulse rounding is known as *modal dispersion.* It can be corrected only by regenerating the signal. The greater the core diameter, the greater the amount of modal dispersion. Single-mode fiber propagates only one mode of light, and therefore does not suffer from modal dispersion.

Both single- and multimode fibers are subject to another form of dispersion called *chromatic dispersion.* The term chromatic comes from the multiple wavelengths or colors of light that propagate through the core. Single-mode fiber is immune to modal dispersion because its core propagates only one path, but it is affected by chromatic dispersion. The amount of dispersion, in turn, is affected by the quality of the laser. High-quality lasers emit a narrower band of wavelengths.

Multimode fiber also is classified by its refractive index into two general types: step index and graded index. With *step index fiber* the refractive index is uniform throughout the core diameter. In *graded index multimode fiber* the refractive index is lower near the cladding than at the core so that lightwaves propagate at slightly lower speeds near the core than near the cladding. The result is pulse rounding. When pulse rounding becomes too severe, the receiver cannot distinguish ones

FIGURE 15-4

Wave Propagation through Different Types of Optical Fiber

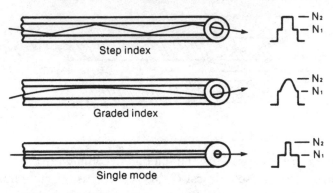

N - Refractive index

from zeros and errors result. In graded index fiber dispersion is lower and the distance between regenerators can be lengthened. Figure 15-4 shows wave propagation through the three types of fiber.

Besides the effects of dispersion, fiber-optic regenerator spacing is controlled by loss. Loss is caused by two factors, *absorption* and *scattering*. Absorption results from impurities in the glass core, imperfections in the core diameter, and the presence of hydroxyl ions or water in the core. The water losses occur most significantly at wavelengths of 1400, 1250, and 950 nm, as Figure 15-2 shows. Scattering results from variations in the density and composition of the glass material. These variations are an inherent by-product of the manufacturing process. Single-mode fiber has its lowest chromatic dispersion at the 1300-nm wavelength, but minimum loss is at 1550 nm, which has led to the development of *dispersion-shifted fiber*. Dispersion-shifted fiber shifts the minimum chromatic dispersion wavelength to the 1550-nm window to provide the lowest combination of loss and bandwidth at the same wavelength.

Most LANs operating at less than 50 Mb/s use 850-nm LEDs. Those operating between 50 and 250 Mb/s generally use 1300-nm LEDs. Applications running more than 250 Mb/s use 1300-nm lasers on single-mode fiber.

Not all fiber is made of glass. Plastic fiber, which has attenuation in the order of 160 to 200 dB/km, is also available. By comparison, glass fiber has attenuation of 2.5 dB/km or less. Plastic absorbs moisture, which increases attenuation, and it has a narrower bandwidth. Its primary application is in low-cost systems. Table 15-1 shows the loss range of different types of fiber.

Manufacturing Processes

Glass fibers are made with a process known as *modified chemical vapor deposition* (MCVD) or an alternative process called *outside vapor deposition* (OVD). The

TABLE 15-1

Typical Fiber-Optic Characteristics

Type	Core/Cladding Diameter (μm)	Attenuation (dB/km)			Bandwidth (MHz/km)
		850 nm	1300 nm	1550 nm	
Plastic	985/1000				
Multimode	62.5/125	3.0–4.0	1.0–2.0		150–800
Multimode	50/125	2.4–4.0	0.75–2.0		400–1000
Single mode	9/125		0.35–1.0	0.25–1.0	

F I G U R E 15-5

The Modified Chemical Vapor Deposition Process

Property of AT&T Archives. Reprinted with permission of AT&T.

MCVD process starts with a pure glass tube about 6 ft long and 1½ inch in diameter. The tube is rotated over a flame of controlled temperature while a chemical vapor is introduced in one end, as Figure 15-5 shows. The vapor is a carrier for chemicals that heat from the flame deposits on the interior of the glass. The deposited chemicals form a tube composed of many layers of glass inside the original tube. The OVD process deposits high-purity glass on the outside of a ceramic rod, which is removed after the process is complete. When the deposition process is complete, the tube is collapsed under heat into a solid glass rod known

FIGURE 15-6

Fiber Is Pulled through a Die into a Single Strand

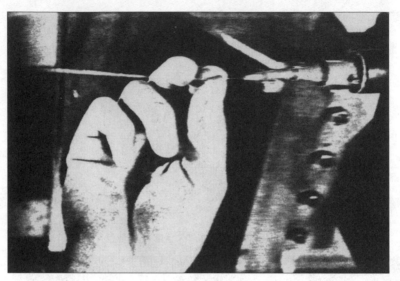

Property of AT&T Archives. Reprinted with permission of AT&T.

as a *preform.* The preform is placed at the top of a drawing tower where the fiber is heated to the melting point and drawn through into a hair-thin glass strand, as Figure 15-6 shows.

Multiple fiber strands are wound together around a strength member and enclosed in a sheath. Like copper cable, fiber cable sheaths are made of polyethylene and can be enclosed in armor to protect against damage. Fiber-optic cable is suitable for direct burial, pulling through conduit, suspension from an aerial strand, or submersion in water. Two predominate methods are used for cabling: loose tube and tight buffered. Loose-tube cabling is usually preferred for outdoor application because the fibers are loosely coupled, which allows them freedom of movement during expansion and contraction and during installation. In loose-tube construction, the fibers are placed in a buffer tube. In *tight-buffered design* the fibers are wrapped much like a copper cable. This method takes less space in conduits and raceways.

Fiber cables are spliced by adhesion or fusion. In the adhesion process, a technician places fibers in an alignment fixture and joins them with epoxy. The fusion method employs a splicing fixture that precisely aligns the two ends of the fiber under a microscope and fuses them with a short electric pulse. After splicing, the loss is measured to ensure that splice loss was acceptable. Splices are made with enough slack in the cable that they can be respliced, if necessary, until the objective loss is achieved.

Cable Connectors

In midspan, fiber cables are joined by splicing, but at terminal locations they are connectorized for coupling to terminal devices and for ease in rearrangement. The physical structure of connectors is of utmost importance because of the exceedingly close tolerances that are required to match cable to the transmission device. Connectors must be made from thermally stable materials, and have tightly locking keyed parts and highly polished mating surfaces. They also must be field-installable while maintaining factory-level performance.

Two criteria rate connector performance: the amount of insertion loss and the amount of reflection attenuation or return loss. A *reflection* is light that travels down the lightguide, strikes a discontinuity, and reflects toward the source, causing instability or errors. The amount of loss that is considered acceptable depends on the application. LAN applications, which use multimode cable almost exclusively, are more tolerant of performance. The loss of a LAN connector can usually be as much as 1.0 dB and still remain well within the loss budget. LANs can tolerate return loss as low as 20 dB, but as higher-speed applications, such as FDDI, are applied to the medium, a higher return loss is needed. A suitable connector for common carrier applications should have an insertion loss of 0.5 dB or less and a return loss of at least 40 dB.

Couplers are made either free hanging or for bulkhead mounting. Connectors use an epoxy and polishing arrangement for termination. The fiber is stripped and inserted into the connector. The ends are then polished to an optical finish. The durability of the connector is important. The connector is constructed to hold the ends of the fiber in contact, and it should remain so even under the strain of pulling or sideways motion. The types of connectors in use differ primarily in their method of latching the mating ends together. SC connectors use a push-pull type of latch with a plastic housing. They are rugged connectors that are used for high performance. FC connectors use a screw coupling. They are popular for single-mode and other high-performance applications.

ST connectors are made by Lucent Technologies, and use a bayonet-style housing. These are popular for multimode fiber. They come in both pull-proof and nonpull-proof versions. Biconic connectors have a dual cone-shaped barrel, which is the source of the name. They were one of the first types of connectors produced, and are used today primarily for additions to existing systems. FDDI connectors are a dual connector used for the separate transmit and receive fibers of FDDI.

FIBER-OPTIC TERMINAL EQUIPMENT

Fiber-optic systems have separate transmit and receive fibers, the opposite ends of which terminate in a light transmitter and receiver. The light transmitter employs either a light-emitting diode (LED) or a laser as its output element. Lasers have a greater system gain than LEDs because their output is higher and because a greater portion of the light signal can be coupled into the fiber without loss. The primary advantage of an LED transmitter is its lower cost. In applications, such as local area networks, that do not need high system gain, the cost saving can easily justify the use of LED transmitters.

The multiplex equipment connects to the input of the transmitter, and the fiber-optic cable couples to the output through a precision connector. Most fiber-optic systems use digital modulation, but analog transmitters vary the intensity or wavelength of the light signal or they modulate the pulse rate or pulse width. Although analog modulation is normally not linear enough for transmitting analog multiplex, it is suitable for transmitting a video signal, and is used in cable television systems.

The light receiver is an APD or PIN diode that couples to the optical fiber on the input end and to the multiplex equipment on the output end. The diode converts the light pulses to electrical pulses, which the receiver reshapes into square wave pulses. A lightwave regenerator has back-to-back receiver and transmitter pairs that connect through a pulse-reshaping circuit. Lightwave amplifiers, which regenerate the signal without converting it down to an electrical signal, are becoming available.

Fiber-optic systems accept standard digital signals at the input, but each manufacturer develops its own output signal rate. Error-checking and zero-suppression bits are inserted to maintain synchronization and to monitor the bit error rate to determine when to switch to the protection channel. Because of differences in the line signals, lightwave systems are usually not end-to-end compatible between manufacturers unless they meet SONET/SDH standards.

Wavelength Division Multiplexing

The capacity of a fiber pair can be multiplied by using *wavelength division multiplexing* (WDM). WDM assigns services to different light wavelengths in much the same manner as frequency division multiplexing applies multiple carriers to a coaxial cable. Different wavelengths or "colors" of light are selected by using light-sensitive filters to combine light wavelengths at the sending end and separate them at the receiving end, as Figure 15-7 shows. Because the filter introduces loss, WDM reduces the distance between regenerators, and limits the path length by the wavelength with the highest loss. When engineers design lightwave systems, they normally provide enough system gain to compensate for future wavelength division multiplexing even if it is not used initially.

WDM has gained in popularity over the past few years. As carriers exhaust their capacity in a fiber cable, they have the choice of stepping up the transmission rate or deriving additional channels over the same fiber with WDM. Products are available that modulate as many as 80 channels per fiber pair. The industry refers to these highly channelized systems as *dense wavelength division multiplexing* (DWDM). The ultimate capacity of a fiber using a combination of high-speed multiplexing over DWDM fiber has hardly been glimpsed.

FIGURE 15-7

Wave Division Multiplex

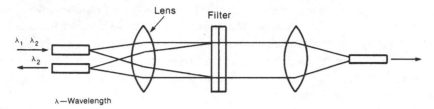

λ—Wavelength

Optical Networking

The next step forward in fiber-optic development is optical networking, in which information streams can be amplified, switched, and shifted in wavelength in light form as opposed to bringing the light back to electronic form. Just as SONET/SDH adds and drops digital bandwidth, optical networking enables carriers to add and drop light wavelengths, and permits wavelength-level routing and grooming. Although the technology to do optical networking is in its infancy, it is a logical and inevitable step to make the enormous amounts of bandwidth manageable.

LIGHTWAVE SYSTEM DESIGN CRITERIA

Fiber-optic systems are designed by balancing capacity requirements with costs for cable, cable placing, terminal equipment, and regenerators. In most systems a prime objective is to eliminate midspan regenerator points so regenerators are placed only in buildings housing other telecommunications equipment. This objective may require reducing bit rates, providing higher-quality cable, and stretching the system design to preclude future WDM. The three primary criteria for evaluating a system are

- ◆ Information transfer rate
- ◆ System attenuation and losses
- ◆ Cutoff wavelength

Information Transfer Rate

The information transfer rate of a fiber-optic system depends on the bandwidth, which in turn depends on dispersion rate and the distance between terminal or repeater points. Manufacturers quote bandwidth in graded index fiber as a product of length and frequency. For example, a fiber specification of 1500 MHz-km could be deployed as a 150-MHz system at 10 km or a 30-MHz system at 50 km. Special-purpose fiber-optic systems intended for short-range private data transmission have low bit rates, and typically use cables with considerably more bandwidth than the application requires.

System Attenuation and Losses

In any fiber system a key objective is to avoid placing repeaters between terminals, if possible, because of the expense of right-of-way and maintenance. Therefore, the system loss and attenuation, together with available bandwidth, is a key factor in determining usable range. System gain in fiber optics is the algebraic difference between transmitter output power and receiver sensitivity. For example, a system with a transmitter output of −5 dBm and a receiver sensitivity of −40 dBm has a system gain of 35 dB.

From the system gain, designers compute a *loss budget*, which is the amount of cable loss that can be tolerated within the available system gain. Besides cable loss, allowances must be made for:

- ◆ Loss of initial splices plus an allowance for future maintenance splices
- ◆ Loss of connectors used to couple fibers and terminal equipment
- ◆ Temperature variations
- ◆ Measurement inaccuracies
- ◆ Current or future WDM
- ◆ Aging of electronic components
- ◆ Safety margin

These additional losses typically subtract about 10 to 12 dB from the span between terminal points, which leaves a loss budget of about 25 dB for cable. Cable cost depends on loss, so system designers should choose a cable grade to match the loss budget.

Sample Performance Margin Calculation

Table 15-2 shows how to calculate the performance margin of a fiber-optic system. This sample is for a premises fiber-optic system, using typical values. The first step is to calculate the cable attenuation. This consists of three elements: the loss of the cable itself, the loss of connectors with which it is terminated, and the loss of any splices. These three elements are added together to get the total attenuation of the system.

The next step is to calculate system gain, which is the algebraic sum of the transmitter output power minus the receiver sensitivity. For safety sake, an operating margin is stated to allow for deterioration of the transmitter with component aging. If the manufacturer does not state a margin, 2.0 dB is typical for LEDs and 3.0 dB for lasers. If the manufacturer states a margin for the receiver, this should also be added. In addition, an allowance is made for future repair splices.

The performance margin is the system gain minus the cable loss, operating margin, and repair splice allowance. If the performance margin is not enough, the designer may have to specify lower-loss cable or higher-performance transmitter and receiver.

TABLE 15-2

Fiber-Optic Performance Margin Calculations

Cable length (km)	2.0
Fiber loss (dB/km)	1.5
Total fiber loss (dB)	3.0
Individual connector loss (dB)	1.0
Number of connectors	4
Total connector loss (dB)	4.0
Individual splice loss (dB)	0.4
Number of splices	2
Total splice loss	0.8
Total attenuation (dB)	7.8
Transmitter output power (dBm)	−17.0
Receiver sensitivity (dBm)	−30.0
System gain (dB)	13.0
Operating margin	2.0
Repair splice allowance (dB)	0.8
Performance margin (dB)	2.4

FIBER OPTICS IN THE LOCAL LOOP

Now that a substantial portion of the interexchange network is converted to fiber optics, the LECs and CATV companies are turning to the next potential application, the local loop. The rationale behind fiber in the loop (FITL) is the assumption that Internet access, telecommuting, telephone, high-definition TV (HDTV), video-on-demand, and other high-bandwidth applications will eventually require fiber. When video-on-demand develops, the user will select from a menu of educational and entertainment programs and have the program delivered to the premises over the loop. FITL could be particularly advantageous for HDTV.

Local-loop fiber will likely assume one of several architectures. The easiest application is to replace feeder cable with fiber. Fiber extends from the central office to a serving area interface point where it connects to the digital-loop carrier (DLC). The loop from the serving area interface to the customer's premises is copper cable, which simplifies the interface problem and overcomes the problem of feeding power to the customer's station. The second local-loop fiber-optic option provides fiber direct to the customer's premises. In some applications, two fibers are installed, one for voice and data communication and the other for video; in other plans a single fiber is installed, using WDM to separate the directions of transmission.

A promising method of bringing fiber to the home is the passive optical network (PON). This method places all the active equipment in the central office. A passive signal is brought to the residence, either directly to the home or to the curbside. The same fiber could be multipled into several residences, with the signals to and from the different premises multiplexed by time division multiple access

FIGURE 15-8

TAT-8 Transatlantic Fiber-Optic Cable, Shown with the Larger TAT-7 Coaxial Cable

Property of AT&T Archives. Reprinted with permission of AT&T.

(TDMA), which is similar to the method cellular radio uses to multiplex digital channels on the airwaves.

The real demand for fiber in the local loop is for business. Since local service competition came into being, the demand has soared for fiber to bring dial tone to large companies. In addition, an increasing number of companies are using DS-3 services, which cannot be transmitted for long distances over twisted-pair wire. Several AACs, in addition to the incumbent LEC, already serve all of the larger metropolitan areas in North America. Fiber optics will eventually become a dominant local-loop medium, but before that happens it must become cost-competitive with copper, and bandwidth requirements must grow to a level that cannot be economically served with alternative media.

UNDERSEA FIBER-OPTIC CABLES

Intercontinental communications services, which once were the province of satellite and conventional voice cables, are rapidly shifting to fiber optics. The first transoceanic fiber-optic cable, the TAT-8, became operational in 1988. TAT-8 can carry 40,000 simultaneous conversations. By comparison, the first undersea cable between Europe and the United States, TAT-1, could carry 36 simultaneous calls. During its 22-

year life span, TAT-1 carried 10 million calls, which TAT-8 can handle in 2 days. TAT-8 has six fiber pairs—two pairs in use and a third pair for backup, with regenerators placed at 79-km intervals. The cable is buried 1 m below the ocean floor where the water is less than 1 km deep. Figure 15-8 shows TAT-8 beside its much larger copper predecessor, TAT 7, which is a coaxial cable. The rapid growth of undersea cable will inevitably bring down the price of circuits and switched services, just as it has domestically. The availability of satellite and fiber-optic circuits between continents makes route diversity feasible for those services that must have a high degree of availability.

APPLICATIONS

Lightwave communications systems have applications in both private and public communications systems. The primary carrier applications ride on SONET/SDH. For noncarrier applications SONET/SDH is also available, as are FDDI, Fibre Channel, and LAN protocols. The following is a list of fiber applications:

- Long-haul transmission systems
- Intercontinental and undersea transmission systems
- Trunking between local central offices
- Metropolitan area backbone systems
- Digital-loop carrier feeder systems
- Local area networks
- Cable television backbone transmission systems
- Private network backbone systems
- Interconnection of PBXs with remote switch units
- Short-haul data-transmission systems through noisy environments
- Fibre Channel for high-speed computer communications

Standards

Several standard-setting bodies promulgate fiber-optic standards. The Electronic Industries Association and Telecommunications Industry Association in their Commercial Building Wiring Standards (see Chapter 7) prepare the standards for customer-premises applications. Optical transmission standards, the lack of which once held back the industry, are now published in ITU's SONET/SDH standards. These standards, which are discussed in Chapter 5, set data rates, signal formats, and performance-monitoring standards.

Application Criteria

The high cost of right-of-way often stands in the way of private fiber-optic systems, but the advantages of this medium make it attractive for private applications. A major impediment to many applications is the common carriers' refusal to offer dark fiber. Most common carriers provide bandwidth, but where the application requires dark fiber, they decline to provide it. Nevertheless, as companies are able to obtain right-of-way, they can install fiber for countless applications. The following discusses the variety of ways companies can apply fiber optics.

Campus, Intra- and Interbuilding Backbone Networks   Fiber optics is an excellent medium for a campus or building backbone. Most LANs now employ a fiber backbone. Fiber optics not only provides bandwidth, but also offers security and noise immunity that no other medium can match. Any campus or riser cable system should at least consider the potential future need for fiber optics. Either fiber pairs should be installed for future expansion or empty conduit should be installed to support future fiber. Most current applications use multimode fiber, but as speeds increase, single mode is becoming more common, particularly as applications such as Fibre Channel and gigabit Ethernet gain in prominence. Companies installing fiber today should consider installing both varieties in separate cables. At the least, subducts should be placed in conduits to provide a future pathway for single mode.

Fiber to the Desktop   The experts are in agreement about using fiber as a backbone in a building or campus network, but the question of carrying it all the way to the desktop is still controversial. Unshielded twisted-pair (UTP) is about the same price as fiber, has enough bandwidth for most applications, and is easier to install and apply. However, fiber has much greater bandwidth, and although the industry is working on higher-category UTP, the connectors are not as mature as fiber connectors are. Since fiber is not an option for telephones, UTP must be installed to every desktop; the question is whether to install fiber as well. Fiber optics is an ideal transmission medium for LANs, but the terminating equipment is twice as costly for fiber than for UTP. The fiber premium will undoubtedly decrease as the volume increases. In today's environment, fiber to the desktop can be justified only if the application has a genuine need for high bandwidth, extended range, or if there is an overriding consideration, such as security or need for noise immunity, that mandates the use of fiber.

   If fiber is not feasible today, should it be installed today and left dark to support a future application? The answer to this question depends on economics. Many buildings are difficult to wire, and placing a composite fiber and UTP cable to desktops may make economic sense because so much of the cost is in installation labor. The chief question to evaluate here is whether the location of future applications can be foreseen reliably enough to justify the expense of fiber optics.

Video Systems   Until the last few years, the lack of reasonably priced linear modulators has limited the use of fiber optics for video. Fiber is an ideal medium for digitized video, but the high cost of compression equipment has made video prohibitive for many noncommercial applications. Now, the transmission of analog television signals over fiber is technically feasible. Although fiber is more expensive than coaxial cable, it has significantly more bandwidth.

Environmental Concerns   Fiber optics has a far greater ability to survive in hostile environments than copper cable. The fiber itself is essentially immune to damage from water, caustic chemicals, and a corrosive atmosphere. In such applications, however, care should be taken that the outer sheath is equally immune to the environment. Fiber is also immune to electromagnetic interference, which may impair UTP or even coaxial cables. This makes fiber ideal in industrial environments where heavy equipment may radiate interference. The elevator shaft is an acceptable housing for riser cables in some buildings, but the motors and controls may cause noise in twisted-pair. Fiber is immune to such noise.

Security Concerns   Fiber-optic systems offer a high degree of security. They are almost impossible to tap undetected, and if properly constructed, they can meet TEMPEST standards. (TEMPEST is a Department of Defense specification that stands for Transient Electromagnetic Pulse Emanation Standard.) Equipment that meets TEMPEST standards must restrict the radiation of energy that could be picked up by nearby devices. Organizations that have sensitive information that could be compromised will find that fiber optics offers security that is unequaled by other media. It is not, however, invulnerable, so critical applications must have physically protected cable.

Evaluation Criteria

Fiber-optic equipment is purchased either as an integrated package of terminal equipment and cable for specialized private applications, or it is purchased as separate components assembled into a system for trunking between switching nodes. For the former applications, which include local area, point-to-point voice, data, and video networks, the evaluation criteria discussed subsequently are not critical. In such systems the main question is whether the total system fits the application. In all fiber-optic systems the questions of reliability, technical support, cost, and compatibility are important. Fiber-optic systems do not vary widely in their power consumption or space requirements, so these criteria may usually be safely disregarded. In longer-range trunking applications the following criteria should be considered in evaluating a system.

System Gain

In selecting lightwave-terminating equipment, the higher the system gain, the more gain that is available to overcome cable and other losses. The cost of a lightwave system relates directly to the amount of system gain. High-output lasers and high-sensitivity diodes are more expensive than devices producing less system gain. The least expensive transmitters use light-emitting diodes for output and have less system gain than lasers. When the limits of lightwave range are being approached, obtaining equipment with maximum system gain is important. For applications with ample design margin, low system gain is acceptable.

Cable Characteristics

Cable is graded according to its loss and bandwidth. The cable grade should be selected to provide the loss and bandwidth needed to support the ultimate circuit requirement. For systems operating at 100 Mb/s or more on multimode fiber, bandwidth becomes the limiting factor as opposed to loss. If the cable can support ultimate requirements, there is little reason to spend extra money to purchase a higher-grade product. In public networks, unless some compelling reason exists for purchasing multimode cable, single-mode cable should be purchased for all applications. The price of single-mode fiber is less than multimode, and its greater bandwidth and lower loss makes it considerably more valuable for future expansion. The cable composition should be selected with inner strength members sufficient to prevent damage when cable is pulled through conduits or plowed in the ground. Armoring should be considered where sheath damage hazards exist.

In private applications the core size of multimode cable is an important consideration. EIA/TIA standards specify 62.5/125-µm cable, but some applications require 50/125-µm cable. (The 62/125 designation means the cable has a core of 62.5 µm and an external diameter of 125 µm.) If the application has not been selected, and cable is being placed for future applications, the safest choice is 62.5/125-µm cable.

Wavelength

With present technology, the most feasible wavelength to choose in multimode fiber is 1300 nm. FDDI specifications call for 1300-nm cable with a bandwidth of at least 500 MHz-km. Cable should be purchased with a 1550-nm window if circuit requirements will ultimately justify the use of WDM. For most applications 850 nm should be avoided because of its greater loss. Exceptions are in local networks and private networks implemented by using leased fibers. With leased fibers, the 850-nm window can be used with WDM as a way of increasing capacity without leasing more fiber, provided the distance between terminals supports the use of 850 nm and WDM. In other applications, such as local networks, the manufacturer may predetermine the wavelength. If the total system has enough gain and bandwidth to support the application, the wavelength is of little or no concern to the user.

Light Source

The two choices for light source are laser and LED. Both are semiconductor devices that emit light when an external voltage is applied. A laser has a much higher power output than an LED, and can operate at higher bit rates. An LED is lower in cost and has a longer life, but it produces a wider beam of light and has a wider spectral width, which means that its light wavelength is broader than that of a laser.

LEDs are typically used where the distance between terminals is short, normally 10 km or less, and the bandwidth of the signal is lower than about 150 Mb/s. An LED is generally satisfactory for local networks. In long-haul networks where long repeater spacing and high bandwidth are important, a laser is the device of choice.

Wavelength Division Multiplexing

The question of whether to plan a fiber-optics system with future WDM designed into the transmission plan is a balance between future capacity requirements and costs. WDM can multiply the capacity of a fiber pair many times for little additional cost, or it can convert a single optical fiber into a full-duplex mode of operation by transmitting in both directions on the same fiber. It accomplishes this by reduced regenerator spacing, however, which is important in long systems but unimportant on systems that do not require an intermediate regenerator. On very short systems the cost of the WDM equipment may be greater than the cost of extra fibers.

CHAPTER 16

Microwave Radio Systems

$\mathbf{A}$s a communications medium, microwave had its birth during World War II. In the expansion that followed the war, microwave advanced from an experimental technology to become the workhorse of long-haul telecommunications. The North American continent was crisscrossed with networks of microwave routes, which became the information superhighways of the 1950s and 1960s. Now, most of those systems have been removed or lie dormant, replaced by the fiber-optics building boom of the 1980s. Microwave technology itself, however, is far from dead. Satellites, which we will discuss in the next chapter, are microwave repeater sites in the sky. Personal communications service, discussed in Chapter 18, is preempting some of the lower microwave frequencies and pushing the services that resided there into still-higher frequencies. Private organizations that have difficulty acquiring right-of-way for fiber routes can use microwave to bridge obstructions such as highways, lakes, and rivers. Short-haul microwave in the 18-, 23-, and 38-GHz bands has assumed increasing importance in metropolitan areas. (GHz is the abbreviation for gigahertz, which is equal to 1 billion hertz.)

MICROWAVE TECHNOLOGY

The microwave bands constitute an enormous amount of bandwidth. Figure 16-1, which is a logarithmic scale, shows how the microwave frequency spectrum fits into the total radio and light spectrum. The usable portion of microwave keeps pushing upward, with so-called wireless fiber operating at 38 GHz. The 76- to 77-GHz band is allocated in Europe and the United States for vehicular radar. Considering that the frequency spectrum below microwave occupies a total of 1 GHz of bandwidth, you can see that microwave provides at least 40 times the bandwidth that is available below the microwave bands. This submicrowave bandwidth supports all the

FIGURE 16-1

The Electromagnetic Spectrum

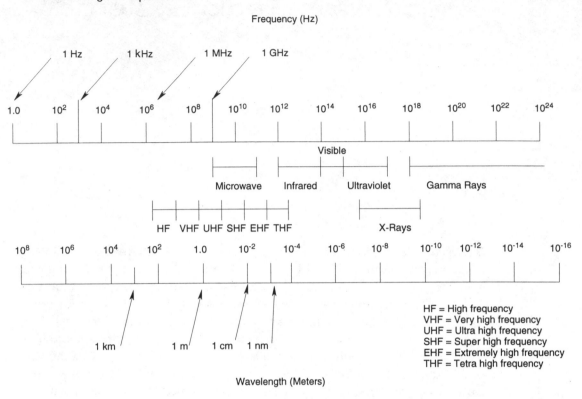

HF = High frequency
VHF = Very high frequency
UHF = Ultra high frequency
SHF = Super high frequency
EHF = Extremely high frequency
THF = Tetra high frequency

radio and television broadcast services, virtually all two-way radio, and countless other radio services.

Although the available microwave bandwidth is enormous, it is still a limited resource, and users must coordinate microwave paths to prevent interference. Because of congestion in metropolitan areas, it is often impossible to obtain frequency assignments in the lower end of the band. Table 16-1 shows the microwave frequency band assignments in the United States. Microwave services are classified as operational fixed, which are commercial and private microwave systems, government, and common carrier. Other services, such as radar, occupy the unlisted parts of the spectrum.

Different parts of the radio frequency spectrum propagate through the atmosphere by different means, as shown in Figure 16-2. Frequencies below about 30 MHz are reflected by the ionosphere, and are therefore suitable for ranges well beyond the line of sight. Very low frequencies follow the earth's surface, and may be used for extended range communications. Frequencies higher than about 30 MHz travel in straight lines, which makes them ideal for short-distance communications. The higher the frequency, the more a radio signal takes on the charac-

TABLE 16-1

Common Carrier and Operational Fixed (Industrial) Microwave Frequency Allocations in the United States—FCC Part 101

Frequency Band (MHz)	Radio Service	
	Common Carrier	Private Radio
928–929		MAS
932.0–932.5	MAS	MAS
932.5–935.0	CC	OFS
941.0–941.5	MAS	MAS
941.5–944.0	CC	OFS
952–960		OFS, MAS
1,850–1,990		OFS
2,110–2,130	CC	
2,130–2,150		OFS
2,150–2,160		OFS
2,160–2,180	CC	
2,180–2,200		OFS
2,450–2,500	LTTS	OFS
2,650–2,690		OFS
3,700–4,200	CC LTTS	OFS
5,925–6,425	CC LTTS	OFS
6,425–6,525	LTTS	OFS
6,525–6,875	CC	OFS
10,550–10,680	CC DEMS	OFS, DEMS
10,700–11,700	CC LTTS	OFS
11,700–12,200	LTTS	
12,200–12,700		OFS
12,700–13,250	CC LTTS	OFS
14,200–14,400	LTTS	
17,700–18,580	CC	OFS
18,580–18,820	CC	OFS
18,820–18,920	DEMS	OFS, DEMS
18,920–19,160	CC	OFS
19,160–19,260	DEMS	OFS, DEMS
19,260–19,700	CC	OFS
21,200–23,600	CC LTTS	OFS
27,500–29,500	CC	
31,000–31,300	CC LTTS	OFS
38,600–40,000	CC	OFS

CC = common carrier fixed point-to-point microwave service.
DEMS = digital electronic message service.
LTTS = local television transmission service.
MAS = multipoint address system.
OFS = private operational fixed point-to-point microwave service.

F I G U R E 16-2

Radio Wave Propagation

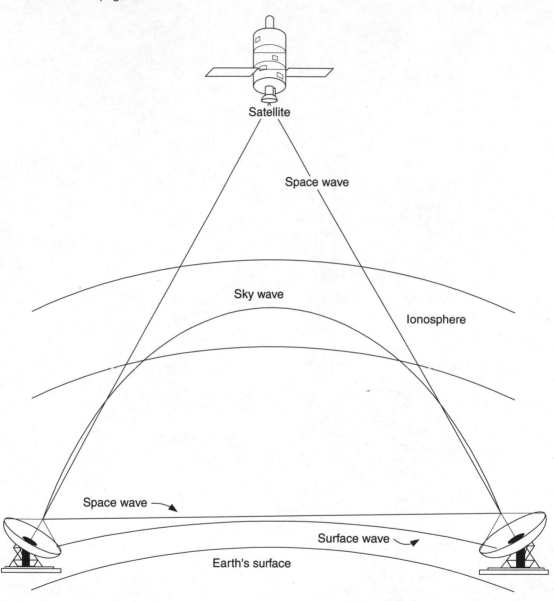

teristics of light and travels as a line-of-sight space wave. At microwave frequencies, the antenna focuses radio energy so a maximum amount of energy is radiated in the desired direction, where the receiving antenna picks them up. Provided a microwave system is properly engineered, it is a cost-effective and reliable method of communication.

When designing microwave systems, engineers take into account the following conditions that affect signals:

◆ *Free-space loss,* which is the attenuation the signal undergoes as it travels through the atmosphere.

◆ *Atmospheric attenuation,* which is closely related to free-space attenuation. Changes in air density and absorption by atmospheric particles and water density attenuate the signal.

◆ *Reflections,* which can occur when the signal traverses a body of water or a fog bank. The signal takes multiple paths, which arrive at the receiving antenna out of phase, and cause the signal to fade.

◆ *Diffraction,* which occurs as a result of the terrain the signal crosses.

◆ *Rain attenuation,* which occurs when raindrops absorb or scatter the microwave signal. The effect is greater at higher frequencies and varies with the size of the raindrops. Larger drops are more detrimental.

Both analog and digital microwave systems are available, but as with other telecommunications technologies, digital predominates in current products. A digital microwave system consists of three major components: the digital modem, the radio frequency (rf) unit, and the antenna. The modem modulates an intermediate frequency (if), which is transmitted to the rf unit over coaxial cable. The rf unit is typically connected directly to the antenna and mounted on a rooftop, tower, building mast, or tripod. At the rf unit, a signal from a microwave generator is mixed with the if signal to generate the microwave output.

Units with the rf unit separated from the antenna are also available. In such systems the antenna connects to the rf unit with a *waveguide,* which is a rectangular or round section of low-loss pipe.

The antenna focuses and radiates the signal to the receiving location. To comply with zoning restrictions that regulate appearance, the antenna is sometimes mounted indoors behind glass. The glass must be chosen to avoid loss. Loss varies with the thickness of the glass, and lead compounds in the glass result in high attenuation. The angle of incidence or the angle at which the signal penetrates the glass affects the amount of loss. Reflections also attenuate the signal.

Microwave antennas are susceptible to snow and icing. A radome can be installed on the antenna to keep ice and snow from affecting the parabolic shape of the antenna. Heaters prevent interfering elements from building up on the radome.

Microwave signals can cover only a limited range. Repeaters are used to extend the range. Repeater stations are transmitter and receiver units connected back-to-back with the frequency shifted to prevent the transmitted signal from feeding back into the receiving antenna. Passive repeaters are used in some installations where line-of-sight cannot be obtained between stations. A passive repeater can be two antennas connected back-to-back. Billboard reflectors, such as the one in Figure 16-3, are used to redirect the signal from one path to another.

FIGURE 16-3

A Billboard Microwave Reflector

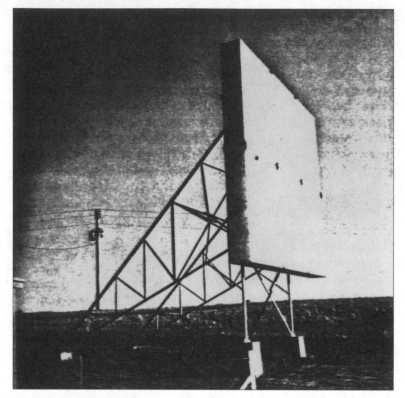

Courtesy of Gabriel Electronics Inc.

MICROWAVE CHARACTERISTICS

The general principles of microwave radio are the same as those of lower-frequency radio. A radio frequency (rf) signal is generated, modulated, amplified, and coupled to a transmitting antenna. It travels through free space to a receiving antenna where a receiver captures a portion of the radiated energy and amplifies and demodulates it. The primary differences between microwave and lower-frequency radio are the wavelength and behavior of the radio waves. For example, very high frequency (VHF) television channel 2 has a wavelength of about 6 m (20 ft). To gain the maximum efficiency, a half-wave antenna receiving element is about 3 m (10 ft) long. A 4-GHz microwave signal has a wavelength of about 7.5 cm (3 in), so an effective antenna at microwave frequencies is small compared to those at lower frequencies.

Since microwave frequencies behave similarly to light waves, they can be focused with large parabolic or horn antennas similar to the Gabriel antennas shown in Figure 16-4. Unlike lower frequencies where radio waves cannot be focused nar-

FIGURE 16-4

Gabriel TH-10 Horn Reflector Antennas

Courtesy of Gabriel Electronics Inc.

rowly enough to prevent them from radiating in all directions, microwave stations can operate in physical proximity on the same frequency without interference.

On the minus side of the ledger, microwaves have some of the undesirable characteristics of light waves, particularly at the higher frequencies. The primary problem is fading. Multipath reflections and attenuation by heavy rain cause microwave fading. Multipath reflections occur when the main radio wave travels a straight path between antennas, but a portion of it reflects over a second path, as Figure 16-5 shows. The reflected path is caused by some changing condition such as a temperature inversion, a heavy cloud layer, or reflection off a layer of ground fog. The reflected wave, taking a longer path, arrives at the receiving antenna slightly out of phase with the transmitted wave. The two waves added out of phase cause a drop in the received signal level. A second cause of fading is heavy rain,

FIGURE 16-5

Direct and Reflected Microwave Paths between Antennas

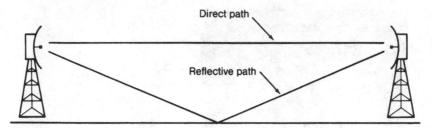

which absorbs part of the transmitted power at frequencies higher than about 10 GHz. The two primary causes of microwave path disruption, fading and equipment failures, are partially alleviated by diversity, as described in a later section.

MICROWAVE SYSTEMS

Microwave routes are established by connecting a series of independent radio paths with repeater stations. Line-of-sight is required between the transmitting antenna and the receiving antenna for all microwave systems except those that use forward scatter techniques to transmit beyond the horizon. Repeater spacing varies with frequency, transmitter output power, antenna gain, antenna height, receiver sensitivity, number of voice frequency channels carried, free-space loss of the radio path, and depth of expected fading. At the high end of the band, repeaters are sometimes spaced as close as 2 km (1.2 miles). At the low end of the band repeater spacings of up to 160 km (100 miles) are sometimes possible, but 40 to 50 km (25 to 30 miles) is more typical.

Modulation Methods

Microwave systems are modulated with either digital or with analog FM or AM signals. Most of the radio systems being installed today use digital microwave. The major advantage of digital radio results from regeneration of the signal at each repeater point. If the incoming signal is sufficiently free of interference to allow the demodulator to distinguish between 0s and 1s, digital radio provides the same high-quality, low-noise channel that T carrier provides. Unlike analog radio, which becomes progressively noisy during fades, digital radio remains quiet until it fades to a failure threshold, at which point the bit error rate (BER) becomes excessive and the radio is unusable.

Although each repeater regenerates the signal, errors are cumulative from station to station and cannot be corrected unless the radio employs forward error correction. Therefore, the errors that occur in one section repeat in the next section where additional errors may occur, until finally the signal becomes unsuitable for data transmission. For voice, however, the errors have little effect. Besides the advantage of higher quality, digital microwave offers the advantage of directly interfacing with T1/E1 carrier circuits without the use of channel banks. This is particularly advantageous for transporting circuits between digital devices such as switching systems.

Bit Error Rate

The most important measure of digital microwave radio system performance is the bit error rate (BER). BER is expressed as the number of errored bits per transmitted bit, and is usually abbreviated as an exponential fraction. Specifications are often quoted at a BER of 10^{-6}, which is one error per million transmitted bits. A BER of 10^{-6} is generally accepted as the highest that can be tolerated for digital data transmission over microwave. At a BER of 10^{-3} a radio is considered failed, although voice transmission can still take place at this error rate.

Diversity

To guard against the effects of equipment and path failure, microwave systems use protection or diversity. Engineers often design for *space diversity* by spacing receiving antennas a few meters apart on the same tower. This system protects against multipath fading because the wavelength of the signal is so short that the phase cancellation that occurs at one location will have little effect on an antenna located a few feet away.

Another protection system, permitted on common carrier bands, is *frequency diversity*. This system uses a separate radio channel operating at a different frequency to assume the load of a failed channel. When fades occur, they tend to affect only one frequency at a time, so frequency diversity provides a high degree of path reliability. The primary disadvantages of this system are the use of the extra frequency spectrum and the cost of the additional radio equipment.

FCC rules do not permit frequency diversity in most noncommon carrier frequency bands. Therefore, many microwave systems use *hot standby* diversity. In a hot standby system, two transmitter and receiver pairs connect to the antenna, but only one system is working at a time. When the working system fails, the hot standby unit automatically assumes the circuit load. Hot standby protection is effective only against equipment failure. Hot standby cannot protect against fading and absorption, which affect the microwave path between stations.

Transfer to a protection system is initiated by the received noise level in an analog radio or by BER in a digital radio. When the noise or BER becomes excessive on a protected channel, the switch initiator sends an order to the transmitting end to switch the entire input signal to the protection channel. Technicians can initiate switches manually to clear a channel for maintenance. In any protection system, some loss of signal is experienced before the protection channel assumes the

FIGURE 16-6

Microwave Diversity Systems

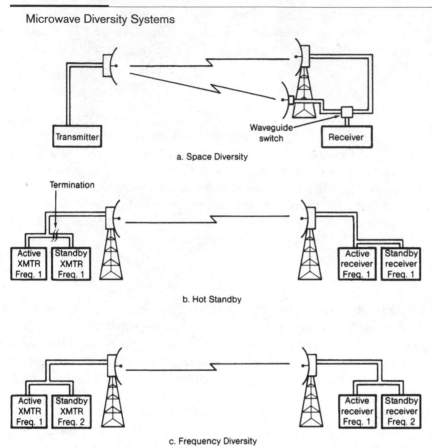

a. Space Diversity

b. Hot Standby

c. Frequency Diversity

load. This signal loss is called a *hit*. Many systems can perform a *hitless* switch when a channel is manually transferred, but if equipment fails or fades, degradation will be experienced in the form of noise, excessive data errors, or both.

Protection systems protect working channels on a one-for-one or one-for-*N* basis with *N* being the number of working channels on the route. The FCC does not permit one-for-one protection where the application requires more than one radio channel because this method is wasteful of frequency spectrum. Figure 16-6 illustrates the three applications of protection—frequency diversity, space diversity, and hot standby.

Microwave Impairments

Microwave signals are subject to impairments from these sources:

- ◆ Equipment, antenna, and waveguide failures
- ◆ Fading and distortion from multipath reflections

♦ Absorption from rain, fog, and other atmospheric conditions

♦ Interference from other signals

Microwave reliability is expressed as percent availability, or uptime, which is the percentage of the time communications circuits on a channel are usable. The starting point on a microwave path calculation is to determine the number of hours of path downtime that can be tolerated in a year. For example, 8 hours per year of path outage would equate to 99.91 percent availability from the following formula:

$$\text{Percent availability} = 1 - \frac{8 \text{ outage hours}}{8760 \text{ hours per year}}$$

Because of path uncertainties, a satisfactory reliability level is attainable only with highly reliable equipment. Fortunately, equipment reliability has progressed to the point that equipment failures cause little downtime, and those failures that do occur can be protected by diversity. Most private microwave systems require at least 99.99 percent availability. Bear in mind that microwave path failures do not usually last long. An hour per year of outage caused by rain fades is more likely to occur as 60 outages of 1 minute each than as one failure of 60 minutes.

Microwave Path Analysis

Microwave path reliability is less predictable and controllable than equipment performance. The first factor to consider in laying out a microwave system is obtaining a properly analyzed and engineered path. The path designer selects repeater sites for availability of real estate, lack of interference with existing services, accessibility for maintenance, and sufficient elevation to overcome obstacles in the path.

The first step in microwave path analysis is to prepare a balance sheet of gains and losses of the radio signal between transmitter and receiver. Gains and losses are measured in decibels (dB). The decibel is a logarithmic measure of relative power gains and losses. Absolute measures of signal level are measured in decibels compared to 1 milliwatt (0 dBm). One milliwatt is equal to 1×10^{-3} watts of power. A signal of +30 dBm is equal to 1 watt, a signal output that is typical of many microwave transmitters. The worksheet in Table 16-2 shows a sample microwave path calculation. The following explains the elements that comprise the calculation and provides information from which a similar worksheet can be constructed.

The *transmitter output power* is obtained from the manufacturer's specifications. For systems in the lower end of the microwave band, power is often 5 watts or more; for systems in the higher end of the spectrum power is a fraction of a watt. Power outputs of +10 to +30 dBm are common at 18 and 23 GHz. Remember that 1 watt = +30 dBm, so with the logarithmic nature of the decibel scale, a reduction of 10 dB is a reduction factor of 10. Therefore, +20 dBm is 0.1 watt, and +10 dBm is 0.01 watt or 10 milliwatts.

TABLE 16-2

Worksheet for Analyzing a Microwave Path

Path length (miles)	5.2
Frequency (GHz)	23
Gains:	
Transmitter output power (dBm)	20.5
Antenna gain (dB), transmit	46
Antenna gain (dB), receive	38
Total gains	104.5
Losses:	
Free space	138.2
Atmospheric	0.8
Antenna alignment	0.5
Safety factor	0.5
Total losses	140
Unfaded receive signal level	−35.5
Receiver sensitivity (dBm)	−74.5
Fade margin (dB)	39

FIGURE 16-7

Antenna Radiation Patterns

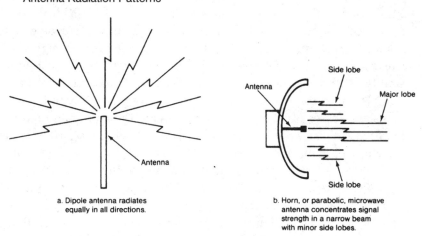

a. Dipole antenna radiates
   equally in all directions.

b. Horn, or parabolic, microwave
   antenna concentrates signal
   strength in a narrow beam
   with minor side lobes.

Antenna gain can overcome the low powers in the 18- to 23-GHz band. Although the industry commonly uses the term antenna gain, it is somewhat of a misnomer because an antenna is a passive device that is incapable of amplifying the signal. Gain is a relative term compared to the performance of a free-space–mounted dipole, or *isotropic* antenna. Figure 16-7 illustrates this concept, which shows the difference between a dipole radiating equally in all directions and a microwave antenna that focuses the signal to provide a narrower beam consisting of a major center lobe and side lobes of lesser intensity. The amount of gain is proportional to the physical characteristics of the antenna, primarily its diameter. Generally, the greater the diameter of the antenna, the greater its gain. Also, for a given diameter antenna, the gain increases as frequency increases and wavelength decreases. Because the wavelength is very short at these frequencies (1 cm, or slightly less than 0.5 in, at 30 GHz), antennas with gains in the order of 40 dB or more are readily available without the high cost of both antennas and tower structures required by large-diameter antennas.

Antenna gain is obtained from manufacturers' specifications. The size of the antenna is one variable that is reasonably easy to change to improve path reliability. Note that antenna gain operates in both transmitting and receiving directions. It is not necessary to use identical antennas for both ends of a microwave path.

The factor that has the most influence on path loss is *free-space attenuation,* which can be calculated by the formula:

$$A = 96.6 + 20 \log P_L + 20 \log F$$

where

A = free-space attenuation (dB)
P_L = path length (miles)
F = frequency (GHz)

In addition to free-space attenuation, atmospheric losses are caused by absorption of the signal by oxygen molecules and water vapor in the atmosphere. This factor should not be confused with rain attenuation, which is covered later. Generally, atmospheric losses can be estimated at 0.12 dB/mile at 18 GHz and 0.16 dB/mile at 23 GHz.

The *antenna alignment factor*—usually about 0.5 dB—is a factor that designers choose to reflect the imperfect alignment of antennas. When antennas are installed, they are aligned on major radiation lobes. With time, temperature changes and tower shifting because of wind stress may cause the signal to drift slightly. This factor is added to provide a margin of safety. Besides the antenna alignment factor, other safety factors should be added to account for other imperfections. Usually another 0.5-dB loss is added to be conservative.

Gains and losses are algebraically added to find the *unfaded received signal level.* This is the signal level that should be received at the input to the receiver in the absence of conditions, such as rain, that cause fade. The manufacturer supplies the *receiver sensitivity* figure as the minimum signal level that will provide a BER of 10^{-6} or better. If the unfaded received signal level is added algebraically to the receiver sensitivity, the result is the *fade margin,* which is the amount of fading the signal can tolerate.

If fading did not occur, it would be easy to calculate a reliable microwave path using the preceding formulas. Fading occurs, however, and the major cause at frequencies above about 10 GHz is rain. At these frequencies, the raindrop size is a significant fraction of the signal wavelength [wavelength is 3 cm (1.2 in) at 10 GHz]. The rain rate that will attenuate the microwave signal by an amount equal to the fade margin is called the *critical rain rate*. The most important factor is not so much the amount of rain that falls, but the nature of the rain. The larger the raindrops and the more intense the rainfall, the greater the attenuation and the higher the probability of outage.

Rain absorption is a most significant impairment in areas of heavy rainfall with large drop sizes such as the Gulf Coast and southeastern United States. Conventional diversity is not effective against rain absorption because rain fading is not frequency selective. The most effective defenses are frequency diversity using a lower band, such as 6 GHz, if permitted by the FCC, use of large antennas, and closely spaced repeater stations. The easiest method of obtaining rainfall data is from the microwave manufacturers, who usually can estimate the number of minutes and frequency of outage that will be caused by rain in your part of the country.

Fresnel Zone Clearance

In microwave path engineering, it is not enough to have line-of-sight communication between stations; it is also necessary to have a minimum clearance over obstacles. If insufficient clearance exists over buildings, terrain, or large bodies of water, the path will be unreliable because of reflection, or path bending.

The amount of clearance required over an obstruction is expressed in terms of Fresnel zones. A *Fresnel zone* is an imaginary elliptical zone surrounding the direct microwave beam. The first Fresnel zone is calculated by the formula:

$$FZ_1 = 72.2 \sqrt{\frac{D_1 \times D_2}{F \times D}}$$

where
    FZ_1 = the radius of the first Fresnel zone (ft)
    D_1 = the distance from the transmitter to the reflection point (miles)
    D_2 = the distance from the reflection point to the receiver (miles)
    F = the frequency (GHz)
    D = the length of the signal path (miles)

To illustrate the principle of Fresnel zone calculations, refer to Figure 16-8, in which a signal is beamed between two buildings 5.2 miles apart with an obstruction 2.1 miles from one transmitter. The first Fresnel zone is calculated to be 16.8 ft. For best results, the clearance over the obstacle should be one Fresnel zone, but satisfactory results will usually be obtained if the clearance is at least 0.6 Fresnel zone, which in this case is 10 ft. If the clearance is insufficient, multipath fading will result.

FIGURE 16-8

Fresnel Zone Clearance over an Obstruction

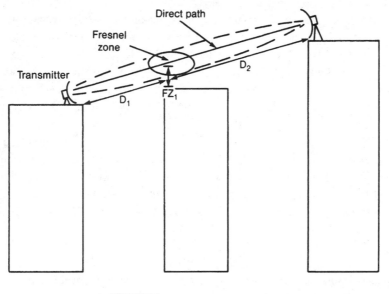

$$FZ_1 = 72.2 \sqrt{\frac{D_1 \times D_2}{F \times D}}$$

$$= 72.2 \sqrt{\frac{3.1 \times 2.1}{23 \times 5.2}}$$

$$= 72.2 \sqrt{\frac{6.51}{119.6}}$$

$$= 72.2 \sqrt{.0544}$$

$$- 16.0 \text{ feet}$$

D = 5.2 miles
D_1 = 2.1 miles
D_2 = 3.1 miles
F = 23 GHz

Multipath Fading

Multipath fading is a source of impairment in both analog and digital microwave. It is caused by conditions that reflect a portion of the signal so both the main wave and the reflected wave arrive at the receiving antenna slightly out of phase. The phase differences between the two signals cause a reduction in the received signal level. Multipath reflections usually do not affect all frequencies within a band equally, which results in signal distortion within the received passband. Distortion is of particular concern with digital microwave, which is susceptible to a higher BER under multipath fading conditions. One way of minimizing the effects of distortion is to use an *adaptive equalizer,* a device inserted in the receiver to cancel the effects of distortion within the passband. Digital radio specifications usually include the *dispersive fade margin,* which states the tolerance of the radio for the frequency selective fades that cause received signal distortion.

Both frequency and space diversity are effective defenses against multipath distortion. With a second receiving antenna mounted a few feet below the first on the same tower, the main and reflected paths do not affect the signal received in both antennas equally. The system selects the better of the two signals. Frequency diversity is also an effective defense against multipath distortion because of the frequency-selective nature of signal reflections. Frequency diversity is not, however, permitted for all types of service.

Other defenses against multipath distortion include an effective path profile study with proper site selection and sufficient tower height to provide adequate clearance over obstacles. Also, the use of large antennas focuses the transmitted signal more narrowly and increases the received signal level at the receiver. The larger the antenna, however, the more rigid the tower must be.

Interference

Adjacent channel and overreach interference are other microwave impairments. Overreach is caused by a signal feeding past a repeater to the receiving antenna at the next station in the route. It is eliminated by selecting a zigzag path or by using alternative frequencies between adjacent stations.

Adjacent channel interference is another potential source of trouble in a microwave system. Digital radios, particularly those using quadrature amplitude modulation (QAM), are less susceptible to adjacent channel interference than phase shift keying (PSK) and frequency modulated (FM) analog radios because of the bandpass filtering used to keep the transmitter's emissions within narrow limits. Multichannel radio installations usually employ cross-polarization to prevent adjacent channel interference. In this technique, channel combining networks are used to cross-polarize the waves of adjacent channels. Cross-polarization discrimination adds 20 to 30 dB of selectivity to adjacent channels.

Heterodyning versus Baseband Repeaters

Analog microwave repeaters use one of two techniques, *heterodyning* or *baseband,* to amplify the received signal for retransmission. In a baseband repeater, the signal is demodulated to the multiplex (or video) signal at every repeater point. In a heterodyne repeater, the signal is demodulated to an intermediate frequency, usually 70 MHz, and modulated or heterodyned to the transmitter output frequency. Heterodyne radio is reduced to baseband only at main repeater stations, where the baseband signal is required to drop off voice channels.

The primary advantage of baseband radio is that some carrier channel groups can be dropped off at repeater stations. Heterodyne radio has the advantage of avoiding the distortions caused by repeated modulation, demodulation, and amplification of a baseband signal. Therefore, heterodyne radio is employed for long-haul use with drop-off points only at major junctions.

Multiplex Interface

Digital microwave interfaces with multiplex equipment through either a standard or a special digital interface. Most long-haul systems provide a standard DSX interface to one, two, or three DS-3 signals. Short-haul microwave generally supports some multiple of DS-1 or one DS-3 signals. These systems usually support only standard DSX-1 interfaces directly into a channel bank or PBX.

Analog microwave connects to analog multiplex through frequency modulated transmitter (FMT) and frequency modulated receiver (FMR) equipment. The multiplex baseband signal connects to the input of an FMT, which generates a frequency modulated intermediate frequency, usually 70 MHz. This signal is applied to the input of the radio and is modulated to the final rf output frequency. At the receiver, rf and if amplifiers boost the incoming signal and connect it to the input of the FMR. The output of the FMR is a baseband signal that is coupled to the multiplex equipment.

MICROWAVE ANTENNAS, WAVEGUIDES, AND TOWERS

Microwave antennas are manufactured as either parabolic dishes or horns, and range in diameter from less than 1 m for short, high-frequency hops to 30 m for earth station satellite service.

At lower frequencies, microwave antennas are fed with coaxial cable. Coaxial cable loss increases with frequency; therefore, most microwave systems use waveguide for the transmission line to the antenna. Waveguide is circular or rectangular, with dimensions designed for the frequency range. At 18 to 23 GHz, and sometimes in lower-frequency bands, the radio frequency equipment mounts directly on the antenna, which eliminates the need for waveguide.

Multiple transmitters and receivers can be coupled to the same waveguide and antenna system by *branching filters. Directional couplers* are waveguide hybrids that allow coupling of a transmitter and receiver to the same antenna. This technique often is used in repeater stations to permit using one antenna for both directions of transmission.

Antennas are mounted on rooftops, if possible. If more elevation is needed, they can be mounted on towers. Antennas must be precisely aligned. They are first oriented by eye or calculated azimuth and then adjusted to maximum received signal level. In orienting antennas, it is important to know the calculated received signal level and to ensure that the received signal is within 1 or 2 dB of that level. Without this benchmark, it is possible that the antenna will be oriented on a minor signal lobe instead of the main lobe.

Manufacturers supply microwave towers in guyed and self-supporting configurations. Self-supporting towers require less space and must be designed more rigidly to support the antenna against the effects of weather. If enough land is available to accommodate down guys, a less expensive guyed tower can be used. The larger the antenna diameter, the more rigid the tower must be to prevent flexing in the wind. Tower rigidity is important because excessive flexing can disorient the antennas.

Entrance Links

The facility used to connect the final radio station in a route to the terminal equipment is the *entrance link.* The preferred way to terminate a microwave route is by mounting the radio and multiplex equipment in the same building. However, frequency congestion and path obstructions in metropolitan areas often make it necessary to terminate the radio some distance from the multiplex terminal. The entrance link links the multiplex to the radio. Entrance links operate at baseband or, for short distances, at intermediate frequencies. Lightwave is usually used for digital radio entrance links.

APPLICATIONS

With the availability of low-cost short-haul equipment, microwave technology has come within the reach of many companies and can quickly pay back the initial investment in savings of common carrier facilities. Microwave finds its most important applications in the following:

- ◆ Trunking between central offices
- ◆ Bypass T1 circuits from private companies to IXCs
- ◆ Studio to transmitter video links
- ◆ Wireless local loop
- ◆ Temporary or emergency restoration of facilities
- ◆ Connecting PBXs in a metropolitan network
- ◆ Interconnecting local area networks
- ◆ Providing diverse routing to protect against failure of the primary circuit route
- ◆ Crossing obstacles such as highways and rivers
- ◆ Implementing local data communications networks

Wireless Local Loop

Microwave is an effective alternative for bypassing the incumbent LEC's local loop. To that end, two different types of technology are either in use or are just coming on the market. The first, 38-GHz radio, is a point-to-point technology similar to the lower-frequency bands at 18 and 23 GHz. Many service providers refer to this as "wireless fiber," a technical misnomer, but one that expresses the bandwidth available at these frequencies. The antennas at 38 GHz are small and unobtrusive, making the service effective for residential neighborhoods.

The second service is local multipoint distribution service (LMDS), a service that is just emerging. In the United States LMDS operates in the 28- to 31-GHz band. In other countries frequencies between 25 and 40 GHz will be used. LDMS transmitters are arranged in a manner similar to cellular to provide service to surrounding nodes. They support both voice and data at rates from 64 kb/s to 155 Mb/s. The size of the cell ranges from 3 to 8 km, depending on the terrain and propagation characteristics.

The user has a small antenna mounted on the roof. The signal feeds from the antenna to a network interface unit (NIU) that interfaces the system to the application, which could be T1/E1, Ethernet, OC-3, or some other standard interface. The base stations aggregate traffic and connect it to an ISP, to the PSTN, or other destination. As the service develops, it will provide a radio alternative to applications that are difficult to justify over fiber or copper.

Standards

Microwave standards are set by the ITU internationally and by the Federal Communications Commission in the United States. The FCC licenses transmitters only after the equipment is type accepted. FCC rules and regulations list the operating rules for radio equipment within the United States. The EIA has established wind loading zones in the United States for use in radio, tower, and antenna design, and several electrical and mechanical criteria for antenna and waveguide design. The Federal Aviation Administration (FAA) specifies tower lighting requirements.

Microwave equipment made by different manufacturers usually cannot be connected at the radio frequency level. Although the frequencies and number of channels are the same, proprietary alarm and maintenance signals prevent interconnection. At a repeater station, it is usually possible to interconnect baseband signals from different manufacturers because, at this level, they conform to standard digital signal (DS) specifications.

Evaluation Considerations

In applying short-haul digital microwave, it is necessary to consider the following factors:

◆ What alternatives are available? Is microwave more cost-effective than common carrier facilities such as fiber optics and leased T1?

◆ How much bandwidth is required now and for the future? The greater the amount of bandwidth, the more expensive the system, although it is generally less expensive to purchase spare capacity with a new system than it is to add capacity later.

◆ What level of availability is needed to make the system feasible? With the spacing between terminals and the rainfall factor, is it possible to obtain the required availability factor with short-haul microwave?

◆ Is there line-of-sight between the terminal locations with sufficient clearance over intervening obstacles? If not, repeaters may be required. If repeaters are required, is the necessary real estate available?

◆ Where will the equipment be located? The most desirable location is on rooftops. If necessary, small towers can be constructed on the rooftops. Separate, ground-mounted towers are expensive and should be avoided if possible.

◆ What kind of specialized technical assistance will be required? Most companies require assistance with path surveys, license applications, and frequency coordination. Often, the equipment vendor can supply this.

The factors of reliability, power consumption, availability, floor space, and the ability to operate under a variety of environmental conditions are important with microwave as with other telecommunications equipment. Besides these considerations, which are covered in previous chapters, the following factors also must be evaluated.

System Gain   When a microwave signal radiates into free space it is attenuated by losses that are a function of the frequency, elevation, distance between terminals, and atmospheric conditions such as rain, fog, and temperature inversions. The amount of free-space loss that a system can overcome is known as the *system gain*. System gain is expressed in decibels and is a function of the output power of the transmitter and the sensitivity of the receiver. Receiver sensitivity is a measure of how low the signal level into the receiver can be while still meeting noise objectives in an analog system or BER objectives in a digital system. For example, if a microwave transmitter has an output power of +30 dBm (1 W) and a receiver sensitivity of −70 dBm, the system gain is 100 dB.

With other factors being equal, the greater the system gain, the more valuable the system is because repeaters can be spaced farther apart. Given the same repeater spacing, a microwave radio with higher system gain has a greater fade margin than one with lower system gain. System gain can be improved in some microwave systems by the addition of optional higher-power transmitters, low-noise receiver amplifiers, or both.

Spectral Efficiency   Microwave radio can be evaluated based on its efficiency in using limited radio spectrum. The FCC prescribes minimum channel loadings for a microwave before it is type accepted. Within the frequency band, the license granted by the FCC limits the maximum bandwidth. Where growth in voice frequency channels is planned, the ability to increase the channel loading is of considerable interest to avoid adding more radio channels. Spectral efficiency in both analog and digital radios is a function of the modulation method. The controlling factor is noise in analog radio and BER in digital radios.

Fade Margin   The *fade margin* refers to the amount of fading of the received signal level that can be tolerated before the system crashes. A crash in an analog radio is defined as the maximum noise level that the application can tolerate. In a digital microwave, fade margin is the difference between the signal level that yields a maximum permissible BER (usually 10^{-6}) and the crash level (usually 10^{-3}). Analog radios fade more gracefully than digital radios. As the received signal diminishes, the channel noise level increases in analog radio, but communication may still be usable over a margin of about 20 dB. The margin between acceptable and unacceptable performance of a digital radio is narrow—on the order of 3 dB. Either a digital signal is very good or it is totally unusable, and the margin between the two points is narrow.

Protection System   The user's availability objective determines the need for protection in a microwave system. Equipment failures and fades affect availability. Equipment availability can be calculated from the formula:

$$\text{Percent availability} = \frac{\text{MTBF} - \text{MTTR (100)}}{\text{MTBF}}$$

where
    MTBF = the mean time between failures
    MTTR = the mean time to repair

Availability as affected by fades can be determined by a microwave path engineering study. It is possible to calculate percent availability within a reasonable degree of accuracy for both fades and failures, but it is impossible to predict when failures will occur. Therefore, protection may be necessary to guard against the unpredictability of failures even though the computed availability is satisfactory.

Another factor weighing in the decision to provide diversity is the accessibility of equipment for maintenance. Some short-haul microwave is mounted in an office building where it can be accessed within a few minutes. On that basis it may be reasonable to provide spares and to forego diversity to save money. In a system with remote repeaters, diversity is usually needed because of difficulty in reaching the site in time to meet availability objectives.

Alarm and Control and Order Wire Systems   All microwave radios should be equipped with alarm systems that provide both local and remote failure indications. An alarm system is evaluated based on how accurately the alarm is identified. Primitive systems indicate only that trouble exists, but not what it is. Sophisticated systems provide a complete remote diagnosis of radio performance. A microwave system equipped with protection and emergency power also requires a control system to switch equipment and operate the emergency engine. An order wire should be provided so technicians can talk between units for antenna lineup and maintenance.

Standard Interfaces   Digital microwave systems should be designed to connect to a standard digital signal interface such as DSX-1, DSX-2, or DSX-3. Systems designed for the operational fixed band sometimes use nonstandard interfaces such as 12 or 14 DS-1 signals. Special multiplexers are required to implement these interfaces.

Frequency Band   Frequency availability often dictates the choice of microwave frequency band. Where choices are available, the primary criteria are the number of voice frequency channels required, the availability of repeater locations, and the required path reliability. As stated earlier, path reliability decreases with increasing radio frequency because of rain absorption. Reliability can be improved by decreasing the repeater spacing or increasing the antenna size.

Path Engineering   A microwave path should not be attempted without an expert path survey. Several companies specialize in frequency coordination studies and path profile studies, and one should be consulted about a proposed route. Sites should be chosen for accessibility and availability of real estate and a reliable power source. Engineers choose tower heights to obtain the elevation dictated by the path survey. The antenna structure must support the size of antenna in a wind of predicted velocity. Wind velocities for various parts of the country are specified by EIA.

Environmental Factors   Frequency stability is a consideration in evaluating microwave equipment. FCC rules specify the stability required for a microwave system, but environmental treatment may be needed to keep the system within its specifications. Air conditioning usually is not required, but air circulation may be necessary. Heating may be required to keep the equipment above 0°C. Battery plants lose their capacity with decreasing temperature. Therefore, in determining the need for heating, designers should remember that battery capacity is lowest during abnormal weather conditions when power failures are most apt to occur.

Test Equipment   All microwave systems require test equipment to measure frequency, bandwidth, output power, and receiver sensitivity. This equipment, which should be specified by the manufacturer, is required in addition to the test equipment needed to maintain multiplex equipment.

CHAPTER 17

Satellite Communications

Satellite communication is gaining new life. When AT&T launched the first communication satellite, Telstar 1, in 1962, it was an interesting demonstration, but otherwise it had limited impact. Orbiting the earth in about 2 hours, it was visible from the earth station for less than half an hour, and the antennas had to move to track it across the sky. For the next 35 years satellite communication was carried through geosynchronous (GEO) satellites. Orbiting the equator at an altitude of 22,238 miles (35,580 km) makes GEO satellites appear stationary to the earth station, but the low earth orbit was still a good idea because sending a radio signal up to a repeater station that far from the earth results in a delay. Even though radio waves travel at the speed of light, it still takes them about a quarter of a second to make the trip to the satellite and back again. For most data protocols this kind of delay is not significant, but for voice many people find the delay disconcerting. This limited satellites primarily to international communications, but as fiber optics came on the scene, it has largely displaced satellites for voice communications except in remote locations.

But all of that is changing. With the opening for business of Iridium in late 1998, low earth orbit (LEO) satellites have reached the practical level. Now, with a single telephone it is possible to carry on a conversation from anywhere on the surface of the earth without the delay of a geosynchronous satellite. (Unfortunately, however, Iridium encountered financial problems and at this writing is in bankruptcy.) Iridium, with 66 satellites, is aimed at the voice and paging market, but in 2002 it will be joined with another network of LEO satellites, known as Teledesic, that plans to offer data service through a network of 288 satellites. In addition, a handful of companies are offering medium earth orbit (MEO) satellites. Orbiting the earth at 10,390 km (6200 miles) ICO offers voice, data, paging, and fax service over its network of 10 satellites. Figure 17-1 shows the relative position of the three orbit classes. Of course, to provide the same amount of coverage, the lower the orbit, the more satellites needed, but the lesser the delay.

F I G U R E 17-1

Communication Satellite Orbits

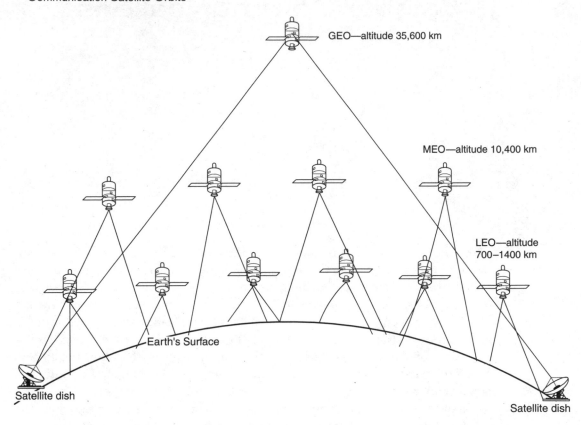

Direct broadcast television was a long time in coming, but now high-quality TV can be received, even in remote locations. Very small aperture terminal (VSAT) enables users to mount small antennas on rooftops to run a multitude of applications, such as point-of-sale, which need low-bandwidth facilities distributed over a wide range. Communications satellites are used for global positioning, communications with ships at sea, telemetering data from trucks in transit, and for many other applications where the communications device is either moving or in a remote area or both.

Conventional satellites have plenty of application left. The equatorial orbit has the advantage of covering both the northern and southern hemispheres. Except for the extreme polar regions, about one-third of the earth's longitudinal surface can be covered by a single equatorial satellite. At geosynchronous orbit, the satellite travels at the same speed as the earth's rate of spin. Geostationary satellites remain at a fixed position with relation to a point on the earth. Some satellites are launched in an orbit that inclines slightly, which makes them appear to move north

TABLE 17-1

Principal Communications Satellite Frequency Bands

Band	Uplink	Downlink
C	5925–6425 MHz	3700–4200 MHz
Ku	14.0–14.5 GHz	11.7–12.2 GHz
Ka	27.5–31.0 GHz	17.7–21.2 GHz

and south during the course of an orbit. These satellites require a moveable antenna to track them. From geosynchronous orbit, three satellites can theoretically cover the entire earth's surface, with each satellite subtending a radio beam 17° wide. The portion of the earth's surface that a satellite illuminates is called its *footprint*.

Satellites fall into three general categories—domestic, regional, and international. Domestic satellites carry traffic within one country. Regional satellites span a geographical area, such as Europe, and international satellites are intended for traffic that is largely intercontinental. Although undersea fiber-optic systems are taking much of the international voice traffic because of their lower propagation delay, international television is still a large and growing market for satellites.

International satellite communications are controlled by the International Telecommunications Satellite Organization (INTELSAT), which is an international satellite monopoly operating under treaty among its member nations and serving more than 170 countries and territories. At this writing, INTELSAT operates 20 satellites, with five more planned. Domestic satellites are owned and operated by COMSAT, AT&T, Western Union, RCA, American Satellite, and GTE.

As Table 17-1 shows, the frequencies available for communications satellites are limited. The 4- and 6-GHz C-band frequencies are the most desirable from a transmission standpoint because they are the least susceptible to rain absorption. Satellites share the C-band frequencies with common carrier terrestrial microwave, requiring close coordination of spacing and antenna positioning to prevent interference. Interference between satellites and between terrestrial microwave and satellites is prevented by using highly directional antennas. Currently, satellites are spaced about the equator at 2° intervals.

The Ku band of frequencies has come into more general use as the C band becomes congested. K-band frequencies are exclusive to satellites, allowing users to construct earth stations almost anywhere, even in metropolitan areas where congestion precludes placing C-band earth stations. The primary disadvantage of the Ku band is rain attenuation, which results in lower reliability. With identical 2° spacing for both C and Ku bands, the hybrid satellite, which carries transponders for both bands, is becoming feasible.

Ka-band satellites are becoming more feasible as the lower frequencies are used up. Ka band operates with an uplink of 27.5 to 31 GHz and a downlink of 17.7

to 21.2 GHz. Although the higher frequency of Ka band subjects the signal to a higher probability of fading, it is possible to construct satellites with smaller antennas and to use less expensive earth stations, which makes the band attractive. The Ka-band frequencies are even more susceptible to attenuation. Although considerable bandwidth is available, further development is needed before these frequencies come into general use.

The terms "uplink" and "downlink" used in Table 17-1 refer to the earth-to-satellite and the satellite-to-earth paths, respectively. The lower frequency always is used from the satellite to the ground because earth station transmitting power can overcome the greater path loss of the higher frequency, but solar battery capacity limits satellite output power.

Satellites have several advantages over terrestrial communications. These include:

- ◆ Costs of satellite circuits are independent of distance within the coverage range of a single satellite.
- ◆ Impairments that accumulate on a per-hop basis on terrestrial microwave circuits are avoided with satellites because the earth station–to–earth station path is a single hop through a satellite repeater.
- ◆ Sparsely populated or inaccessible areas can be covered by a satellite signal, providing high-quality communications service to areas that are otherwise difficult or impossible to reach. The coverage is also independent of terrain and other obstacles that may block terrestrial communications.
- ◆ Earth stations can verify their own data-transmission accuracy by listening to the return signal from the satellite.
- ◆ Because satellites broadcast a signal, they can reach wide areas simultaneously.
- ◆ Large amounts of bandwidth are available over satellite circuits, making high-speed voice, data, and video circuits available without using an expensive link to a telephone central office.
- ◆ The satellite signal can be brought directly to the end user, bypassing the local telephone facilities that are expensive and limit bandwidth.
- ◆ The multipath reflections that impair terrestrial microwave communications have little effect on satellite radio paths.

Satellites are not without limitations, however. The greatest drawback is the lack of frequencies. If higher frequencies can be developed with reliable paths, plenty of frequency spectrum is available, but atmospheric limitations may prevent their use for commercial grade telecommunications service. Other limitations include:

♦ The delay from earth station to satellite and back is about 1/4 second, or about 1/2 second for an echo signal. This delay is tolerable for voice when echo cancelers are used, but the lower delay of terrestrial circuits makes them the preferable choice.

♦ Multihop satellite connections impose a delay that is detrimental to voice communications and is generally avoided. When the distance between earth stations exceeds the satellite's footprint, multiple hops are required.

♦ Path loss is high (about 200 dB) from earth to satellite.

♦ Rain absorption affects path loss, particularly at higher microwave frequencies.

♦ Frequency crowding in the C band is high with potential for interference between satellites and terrestrial microwave operating on the same frequency.

A satellite-to-satellite radio link is one solution to the multihop limitation, but except for LEO, it still lies in the realm of future technology. The delay is greater than with a single hop, but intercontinental satellite communications will be improved when this technology becomes feasible.

The rapid growth of fiber-optic systems has had an adverse effect on satellites' share of the telecommunications market, but the technology shows no signs of dying. Although the satellites' market share may be dropping, the traffic carried by communications satellites continues to increase and will continue to do so into the future. The growth in undersea fiber-optic cables is the primary factor limiting the use of satellites for voice.

SATELLITE TECHNOLOGY

All three satellite orbits, GEO, MEO, and LEO, share much of the same technology, but they also differ in many ways. This section discusses the apparatus that is common to all three, and mentions the specifics of each of the three types.

A satellite circuit has five elements—two terrestrial links, an uplink, a downlink, and a satellite repeater—as shown in Figure 17-2. LEO systems add a third link from the satellite to the subscriber station. If the earth station mounts on the user's premises, the terrestrial links are eliminated. The satellite itself consists of the following six subsystems:

♦ Physical structure

♦ Transponder

♦ Attitude control apparatus

♦ Power supply

♦ Telemetry equipment

♦ Stationkeeping apparatus

FIGURE 17-2

A Satellite System

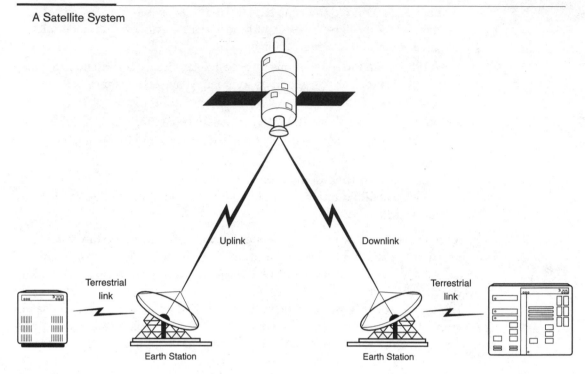

Physical Structure

The size of communications satellites has been steadily increasing since the launch of Early Bird, the first commercial satellite, in 1965. Size is limited by the capacity of launch vehicles and by the need to carry enough solar batteries and fuel to keep the system alive for its design life of 5 to 10 years. Advances in space science are making larger satellites technically feasible. Launch vehicles can carry greater payloads, and the demonstrated ability of the space shuttle to service a satellite in flight or return it to earth for maintenance is changing design considerations that previously limited satellite size.

A large physical size is desirable. Not only must the satellite carry the radio and support equipment, but it also must provide a platform for large antennas to obtain the high gain needed to overcome the path loss between the earth station and the satellite.

Transponders

A *transponder* is a radio-relay station on board the satellite. Transponders are technically complex, but their functions are identical with those of terrestrial mi-

FIGURE 17-3

Components of a Transponder

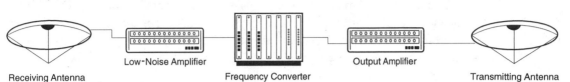

Receiving Antenna   Low-Noise Amplifier   Frequency Converter   Output Amplifier   Transmitting Antenna

crowave radio-relay stations. The diagram in Figure 17-3 shows the major elements. The receiving antenna picks up the incoming signal from the earth station and amplifies it with a low-noise amplifier (LNA), which boosts the received signal without adding noise. The LNA output is amplified and applied to a mixer that reduces the incoming signal to the downlink frequency. The downlink signal is applied to a high-power amplifier, using a traveling wave tube or solid-state amplifier as the output amplifier. The output signal couples to the downlink or transmitting antenna. Traveling wave tubes provide up to 10 W of power. Solid-state amplifiers are popular because of their high reliability. Most satellites carry multiple transponders, each with a bandwidth of 36 to 72 MHz. For example, AT&T's Telstar 6, which was launched in February 1999, contains 52 transponders—24 in the C band and 28 in the Ku band. It covers the United States, Puerto Rico, the Caribbean, and sections of Canada and Latin America from 93° W longitude. TICO's MEO satellites have an output power of 2500 W, and Iridium has a 1400-W output.

Attitude Control Apparatus

Satellites must be stabilized to prevent them from tumbling through space and to keep antennas precisely aligned toward earth. Satellite stabilization is achieved by two methods. A *spin-stabilized satellite* rotates on its axis at about 100 revolutions per minute (r/min). The antenna is despun at the same speed to provide constant positioning and polarization toward earth. The second method is *three-axis stabilization*, which consists of a gyroscopic stabilizer inside the vehicle. Accelerometers sense any change in position in all axes, and fire positioning rockets to keep the satellite at a constant attitude.

Power Supply

Satellites are powered by solar batteries. Power is conserved by turning off unused equipment with signals from the earth. On spin-stabilized satellites, the cells mount outside the unit so that one-third of the cells always face the sun. Three-axis–stabilized satellites have cells mounted on solar panels that extend like wings from the satellite body. Solar cell life is a major factor that limits the working life of a satellite. Solar bombardment gradually weakens the cell output until the power supply can no longer power the on-board equipment.

A nickel-cadmium battery supply is also kept on board most GEO satellites to power the equipment during solar eclipses, which occur during two 45-day periods for about an hour per day. The eclipses also cause wide temperature changes that the on-board equipment must withstand.

Telemetry Equipment

A satellite contains telemetry equipment to monitor its position and attitude and to initiate correction of any deviation from its assigned station. Through telemetry equipment, the earth control station initiates changes to keep the satellite at its assigned longitude and inclination toward earth. Telemetry also monitors the received signal strength and adjusts the receiver gain to keep the uplink and downlink paths balanced.

Stationkeeping Equipment

Small rockets are installed on GEO vehicles to keep them on station. When the satellite drifts from position, rockets fire to return it. The tasks that keep the satellite on position are called *stationkeeping* activities. The fuel required for stationkeeping is the other factor, along with solar cell life, that limits the design life of the satellite. With future satellites, refueling from the space shuttle may become feasible, extending the design life accordingly. MEO and LEO satellites are tracked by moveable antennas, so stationkeeping equipment is not required.

EARTH STATION TECHNOLOGY

Earth stations vary from simple, inexpensive, receive-only stations that can be purchased by individual consumers to elaborate two-way communications stations, such as the one in Figure 17-4, that offer commercial access to the satellite's capacity. An earth station includes microwave radio-relay equipment, terminating multiplex equipment, and a satellite communications controller. The earth stations for MEO and LEO satellites link to the PSTN for dial-up telephone service.

Radio-Relay Equipment

The radio-relay equipment used in an earth station is similar to the terrestrial microwave equipment described in Chapter 16 except that the transmitter output power is considerably higher than that of terrestrial microwave. Also, antennas up to 30 m in diameter in GEO earth stations provide the narrow beam width required to concentrate power on the targeted satellite.

FIGURE 17-4

An Earth Station in Jakarta, Indonesia

Courtesy of Scientific Atlanta.

Because the earth station's characteristics are more easily controllable than the satellite's and because power is not the problem on earth that it is in space, the earth station plays a major role in overcoming the path loss between the satellite and earth. Path loss for GEO satellites ranges from about 197 dB at 4 GHz to about 210 dB at 12 GHz. Also, the higher the frequency, the greater the loss from rainfall absorption. Therefore, the uplink always operates at the higher frequency where higher transmitter output power can overcome absorption, while the lower frequency is reserved for the downlink where large antennas and high-power amplifiers are not feasible.

GEO antennas are adjustable to compensate for slight deviations in satellite positioning. Antennas at commercial stations are normally adjusted automatically by motor drives, while inexpensive antennas are adjusted manually as needed. Thirty-meter antennas provide an extremely narrow beam width, with half-power points 0.1° wide. LEO and MEO antennas are moveable to track the satellite in its orbit.

Satellite Communications Control

A satellite communications controller (SCC) apportions the satellite's bandwidth, processes signals for satellite transmission, and interconnects the earth station microwave equipment to terrestrial circuits. The SCC formats the received signals into a single integrated bit stream in a digital satellite system or combines FDM signals into a frequency modulated analog signal in an analog system.

Multiplexing

The multiplex interface of an earth station is conventional. Satellite circuits use either analog or digital modulation, with interfaces to frequency division and time division terrestrial circuits of the type described in Chapter 5.

Access Control

Satellites employ several techniques to increase the traffic-carrying capacity and to provide access to that capacity. *Frequency division multiple access* (FDMA) divides the transponder capacity into multiple frequency segments between end points. One disadvantage of this system is that users are assigned a fixed amount of bandwidth that cannot be adjusted rapidly or easily assigned to other users when it is idle. Also, the guard bands between channels use part of the capacity.

Time division multiple access (TDMA) uses the concept of time sharing the total transponder capacity. Earth stations transmit only when permitted to do so by the access protocol. When the earth station receives permission to transmit, it is allotted the total bandwidth of the transponder for the duration of the station's assigned time slot. A master station controls access or the earth station listens to which station transmitted last and sends its burst in a preassigned sequence. Each earth station receives all transmissions but decodes only those addressed to it. TDMA provides priority to stations with more traffic to transmit by assigning those stations more time slots than it assigns to low-priority stations. Therefore, a station with a growing amount of traffic can be allotted a greater share of total transmission time.

Demand assigned multiple access (DAMA) is an alternative to preassigned multiple access. DAMA equipment keeps a record of idle radio channels or time slots.

Channels are assigned on demand by one of three methods—polling, random access with central control, and random access with distributed control. Control messages are sent over a separate terrestrial channel or contained in a control field in the transmitted frame from a TDMA station.

Signal Processing

The SCC conditions signals between the terrestrial and satellite links for transmission. The type of signal conditioning depends on the vendor and may include compression of digital voice signals, echo cancellation, forward error correction, and digital speech interpolation to avoid transmitting the silent periods of a voice signal.

GEO SATELLITE TRANSMISSION

Much of the previous discussion is of only academic interest to those who use satellite services. However, satellite circuits and terrestrial circuits have different transmission characteristics. Users should be aware of the differences so satellite circuits can be applied where they are both technically and economically feasible.

Satellite Delay

The 1/4-second delay between two earth stations is noticeable in voice communications circuits, but most people become accustomed to it and accept it as normal if the circuit is confined to one satellite hop. Data communications circuits are another matter. Throughput on circuits using a block transmission protocol, such as IBM's binary synchronous (BSC), drops to an unacceptably low level through a satellite because a station can transmit a block only after the receiver acknowledges the preceding block. Since the transmission and acknowledgment sequence requires two round trips, each block takes a 1/2 second. At this rate, a maximum of only two blocks per second can be transmitted, assuming other data transmission delays such as the CPU processing time are zero. Throughput on polling circuits likewise drops because a complete poll from a host computer is an inquiry and a response, requiring two earth station–to–earth station links, and a 1/2 second of propagation delay.

A satellite delay compensator can mitigate the effects of delay in data circuits, as Figure 17-5 shows. In a delay compensator, the DTE communicates in its native protocol, but communication is with the delay compensator instead of the DTE at the other end of the circuit. The delay compensator buffers the transmitted block, awaiting acknowledgment from the distant end. If it receives a negative acknowledge message, indicating an errored block, the delay compensator retransmits either the errored block and all succeeding blocks (go back N) or only the errored block (selective retransmission). Figure 17-5 lists the steps the DTEs and the delay compensator use. Throughput is somewhat lower than a terrestrial circuit because

FIGURE 17-5

Data Transmission through Satellite Delay Compensators

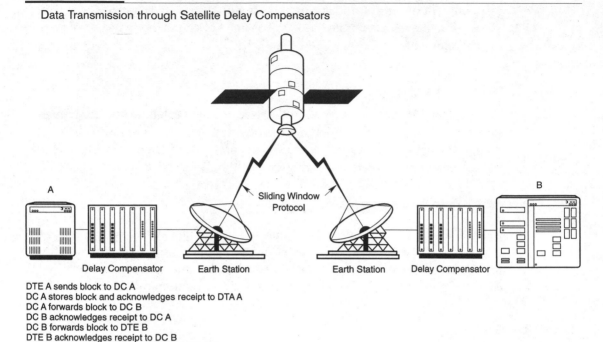

DTE A sends block to DC A
DC A stores block and acknowledges receipt to DTA A
DC A forwards block to DC B
DC B acknowledges receipt to DC A
DC B forwards block to DTE B
DTE B acknowledges receipt to DC B
DC A receives acknowledgment from DC B and removes
block from buffer

the delay compensator interrupts transmission until an error is corrected. Throughput depends on error rate as it does on terrestrial circuits, although satellite circuits react more severely to a high error rate because of delays during error correction. The alternative to using a delay compensator is to change to a protocol such as HDLC or SDLC that permits multiple unacknowledged blocks. Extensive changes needed in the host computer system may make this alternative economically unfeasible.

The TCP/IP protocol also is affected by delay. If a packet is not acknowledged within a specified interval, the transmitter assumes it has been lost and retransmits it. This is resolved in satellite networks by "spoofing," in which the satellite terminal returns a packet acknowledgment to the sender. Then, in a manner similar to the delay compensator, the satellite terminals carry on the dialogue to ensure packet delivery.

Rain Absorption

Rain absorption has a dual effect on satellite communications: heavy rains increase the path loss significantly, and they may change the signal polarization enough to impair the cross-polarization discrimination ability of the receiving antennas. Unfortunately, the greatest impairment exists at the higher frequencies where interference is less and greater bandwidths are available. Rain absorption can be countered by these methods:

- ◆ Choosing earth station locations where heavy rain is less likely
- ◆ Designing sufficient received signal margin into the path to enable the circuits to tolerate the effects of rain
- ◆ Locating a diversity earth station far enough from the main station with the expectation that heavy rainstorms will be localized

Technical considerations may limit the first two options. Transmit power and antenna gain from the satellite can be increased only within limits dictated by the size of the satellite and the transmit power available. Locations with low precipitation cannot always deliver service where required. These considerations mandate the use of earth station diversity at higher frequencies, which suffers the disadvantage of being costly.

Sun Transit Outage

During the spring and fall equinoxes, for periods of about 10 minutes per day for 6 days, the sun is positioned directly behind the satellite and focuses a considerable amount of high-energy radiation directly on the earth station antenna. This solar radiation causes a high noise level that renders the circuits unusable during this time. Solutions are to tolerate the outage or to route traffic through a backup satellite.

Interference

Interference from other satellites and from terrestrial microwave stations is always a potential problem with satellite circuits. The FCC requires all proposed licensees to conduct interference studies before it grants either a satellite or a terrestrial license.

Carrier-to-Noise Ratio

Satellite transmission quality is based on the carrier-to-noise ratio, which is analogous to signal-to-noise ratio measurements on terrestrial circuits. The ratio is relatively easy to improve on the uplink portion of the satellite circuit because transmitter output power and antenna gain can be increased to offset noise. On the downlink portion of a circuit, the effective isotropic radiated power (EIRP), which is a measurement of the transmitter output power that is concentrated into the downlink footprint, can be increased only within the size and power limits of the satellite or by using spot beams to concentrate signal strength.

REPRESENTATIVE SATELLITE SERVICES

In this section, four different types of satellite services are discussed to illustrate the versatility of communications satellites. LEO is a brand new service that avoids the delay inherent with other satellite services. Maritime radio service is an excellent example of a service that cannot be provided in any other feasible way: communication with ships at sea. VSAT replaces conventional terrestrial communications and offers the advantage of bringing signals directly to the user without requiring the last link in a communications path—the local telephone loop—that is often expensive and bandwidth limiting. The fourth service is aircraft-based satellite service, which GTE and COMSAT are offering on United Airlines planes. All four of these services are possible only because of the unique coverage characteristics of satellite service.

Low Earth-Orbiting Satellite

Iridium began operation in the fall of 1998, the first company to use LEO satellites to provide voice, paging, and narrowband data service worldwide. It uses 66 satellites. Eventually, the number of earth stations, which were 11 at system turn-up, may increase to 20. Iridium has a partnership with cellular providers so that calls use the land-based network if available, and if not, they use the satellite service. The service is expensive—in the order of US $3 per minute, but it enables callers to stay in telephone contact virtually anywhere in the world. Exceptions are countries that have not approved the use of Iridium phones within their borders. The service has not been as popular as expected, however, and the company is in serious financial difficulties at this writing.

Voice is digitized and compressed to 2.4 or 4.8 kb/s. Data can be transmitted at a maximum speed of 2.4 kb/s, although higher speeds are expected to be available eventually. Satellites are connected via intersatellite links to the four nearest neighbors. Calls can be connected to landline telephones or to other satellite phones. The satellites operate in the Ka band for earth station communications and in the L band at 1616 to 1626.5 MHz for communication with the subscriber terminals. You can receive telephone calls and pages while roaming anywhere in the world that the service is authorized.

International Maritime Satellite Service (INMARSAT)

INMARSAT is an international maritime satellite service operating under the auspices of the International Maritime Organization (IMO), a United Nations agency. The INMARSAT system has a network of 17 coastal earth stations. These stations form one terminal of a circuit; the other terminal is the ship earth station. The ship earth station mounts above decks and automatically stays in position with satellite-tracking equipment. INMARSAT type accepts and regulates shipboard equipment.

FIGURE 17-6

A Typical VSAT Network

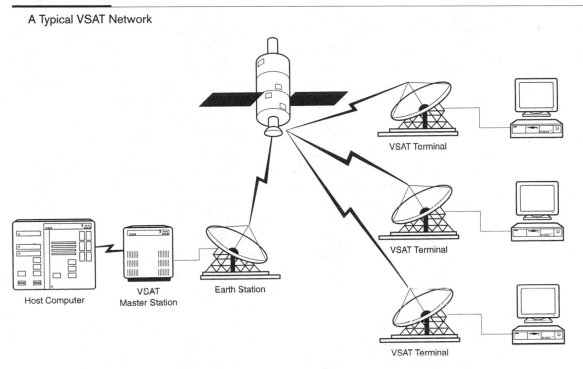

VSAT Terminal

VSAT Terminal

VSAT Terminal

Host Computer

VSAT Master Station

Earth Station

INMARSAT provides the same kinds of communications services for ships at sea that land stations can access through satellite or terrestrial circuits. In the past, the principal methods of communication from ships were telex and Morse code over high-frequency radio, which were unreliable and expensive. Now data circuits are replacing those modes of communication. Voice circuits replace the high-frequency ship-to-shore radio that often suffered from poor signal propagation reliability. In addition, services such as video and facsimile can be carried over INMARSAT. Other services that do not generally apply to land stations also can be accessed through INMARSAT. Ship locations can be monitored precisely through polling equipment. Distress calls can be received and rebroadcast to ships in the vicinity but out of radio range. Broadcasts, such as storm warnings, can be made to all ships in an area.

Very Small Aperture Terminal (VSAT)

VSATs are named for the size of the transmitting antennas, which are much smaller than those used in conventional earth stations. VSAT antennas are normally 1.8 m (6 ft) or less in diameter, which makes them easy to conceal on rooftops and in areas with zoning restrictions. A VSAT network is star-connected with a hub at the center and dedicated lines running to the host computer, as shown conceptually in Figure 17-6.

The hub has a larger antenna, often 4 to 11 m in diameter aimed at the satellite. Hubs cost from $1 million to $1.5 million to construct, so only the largest organizations can justify a privately owned hub. Usually, the VSAT vendor owns the hub, or one organization owns it and shares it with others. Not only is a shared hub more cost-effective for most companies, it also relieves the company of the necessity of managing the hub, which may require one or two people per 100 nodes. Generally, a privately owned hub is feasible only when 200 or more remote stations share the service.

The hubs control demand assignment to the satellite and monitor and diagnose network performance. Demand is allocated in one of four ways—pure aloha, slotted aloha, time division multiple access (TDMA), or spread spectrum. The first three methods generally are used on Ku band, and the last on C band. Pure aloha is an inefficient method of regulating access. Stations transmit on a free-for-all basis and when their transmissions collide, they must retransmit. Slotted aloha is somewhat more efficient in that stations can transmit only during allotted time slots. TDMA and spread spectrum are the most effective ways of allocating access. VSAT provides bandwidth as high as T1 (E1 in Europe), and as low as the customer needs to go. It is used for voice, video, and data transmission.

The remote station has an antenna and a receiving unit, which is about the size of a personal computer base unit. Figure 17-7 is a photograph showing both a master station and a remote antenna. The receiving unit contains a modulator/demodulator, a packet assembler/disassembler, and a communications controller. The remote transmitter operates with an output power of about 1 W. The receiver uses a low-noise amplifier.

The primary application for VSAT is data, although it also can carry voice and video. Typically, C-band VSATs carry 9.6-kb/s data, and Ku-band VSATs carry 56-kb/s data; some systems carry a full or fractional T1 or E1. Most applications are two-way interactive. The primary advantage of VSAT is its ability to support multiple locations. For a few locations, the terrestrial link from the host computer to the hub plus the investment in remote stations may make VSAT prohibitively expensive. As the number of remote sites increases, however, VSAT becomes more attractive.

Satellite-Based Air Telephone

COMSAT and GTE have formed a partnership that allows passengers on transoceanic flights to make telephone calls outside North America. COMSAT provides satellite telephones on more than 70 United Airlines aircraft, enabling passengers to send and receive faxes as well as telephone calls via satellite.

On United's 777 aircraft, GTE's digital service is integrated with the aircraft's interactive video system (IVS). Communication services that allow passengers to make phone calls and send and receive data and faxes via their laptop computers are initially available from six locations on the 777 aircraft. In a later phase of United's IVS, GTE will install its phone system at all seat locations so passengers

FIGURE 17-7

A Very Small Aperture (VSAT) Master Station with a 7-m Antenna and a Remote Station with a 1.8-m Antenna Terminal

Courtesy of Scientific Atlanta.

can receive calls, conduct conference calls, and call seat to seat, in addition to communicating anywhere in the world from their seat location via voice, data, and fax.

APPLICATIONS

In one sense, satellite applications will diminish as terrestrial and undersea fiber-optic circuits become more plentiful and economical. Satellite services are still uniquely suited for many applications, however, and the heavy investments the major providers are making shows that they expect satellites to survive well into the future.

Standards

The FCC in the United States and ITU internationally regulate satellite communications. Satellite carriers are free to design systems to proprietary standards and objectives, but the radio frequency spectrum and satellite positioning must conform to standards set by the FCC and international organizations. Most users obtain their services from a satellite carrier and, therefore, are not concerned with the performance of the satellite and earth station equipment, but they are concerned with circuit performance. The carrier establishes circuit performance criteria. ITU-T recommends circuit performance objectives, but compliance is voluntary.

Satellite Service Evaluation Considerations

Satellite space vehicle evaluation criteria are complex, technical, and of interest only to designers, owners, and manufacturers of satellites and on-board equipment. Therefore, this discussion omits these criteria. Likewise, common carrier earth station equipment evaluations are omitted from this discussion. Evaluation criteria discussed in Chapter 16 on microwave equipment generally apply to satellite services, except that multipath fading is not a significant problem in satellite services. Also, alarm and control systems in terrestrial microwave are different from those used in satellite systems.

The following factors should be considered in evaluating satellite services and privately owned earth station equipment.

Availability

Circuit availability is a function of path and equipment reliability. To the user of capacity over a carrier-owned earth station, equipment reliability is a secondary consideration. The important issue is circuit reliability measured as percent error-free seconds in digital services and percent availability within specified noise limits for analog services.

These same availability criteria apply with privately owned earth stations, but the carrier can quote availability based only on path reliability. Equipment availability depends on MTBF and MTTR and must be included in the reliability calculation. The frequency and duration of any expected outages because of solar radiation or solar eclipse should be evaluated. Availability figures of 99.5 to 99.9 percent are typical.

Data Bandwidths

Satellite carriers typically provide transponder bandwidth in 128-kb/s segments. The number of stations that can be supported in this amount of bandwidth depends on the amount of activity. Bear in mind that throughput is less than the data rate of the terminal. VSAT is generally cost-competitive with frame relay, and offers a similar type of service, but with somewhat lower throughput for a given bandwidth of the access facility. The applications of VSAT are similar to those for frame relay with certain exceptions. First, the cost of a frame relay access channel varies with the distance from the carrier's point of presence. VSAT is not distance-sensitive except for the cost of a backhaul circuit to carry data from the earth station to the customer's site. The backhaul circuit can be a point-to-point circuit or frame relay.

Access Method

Satellite carriers employ several techniques to increase the information-carrying capacity of the space vehicle. Techniques such as DAMA can result in congestion during peak load periods and the possibility that earth station buffer capacity can be exceeded or access to the system blocked. Users should determine what methods the carrier uses to apportion access, whether blockage is possible, and whether transmission performance will meet objectives.

Transmission Performance

The carrier's BER, loss, noise, echo, envelope delay, and absolute delay objectives should be evaluated. To support TCP/IP service, the carrier should provide spoofing. Except for absolute delay, which cannot be reduced except by using terrestrial facilities to limit the number of satellite hops, satellite transmission evaluation should be similar to terrestrial circuits.

Earth Station Equipment

Earth station equipment is evaluated against the following criteria:

◆ Equipment reliability
◆ Support for specific protocols such as TCP/IP

◆ Technical criteria, such as antenna gain, transmitter power, and receiver sensitivity, that provides a sufficiently reliable path to meet availability objectives

◆ Antenna positioning and tracking equipment that is automatically or manually adjustable to compensate for positional variation in the satellite

◆ Physical structure that can withstand the wind velocity and ice-loading effects for the locale

◆ The availability of radome or deicing equipment to ensure operation during snow and icing conditions

Network Management Capability

Network management is important in VSAT networks where many earth stations are under the control of a single hub. The service provider should be able to re-configure the network rapidly from a central location. Monitoring and control equipment should be able to diagnose problems and detect degradations before hard faults occur. The network management package should collect statistics on network use and provide information for predicting when growth additions will be required. Determine whether the network provider can service all network components including routers.

CHAPTER 18

Mobile, Cellular, and PCS Radio Systems

Wander any place on the face of the earth today, and you are apt to see people talking on tiny transceivers held to their ears. Low earth-orbiting satellites have removed the last refuge from the clutches of the telephone, and users are embracing the service enthusiastically. Cellular and personal communication service (PCS) have demonstrated that the cost and lower quality of ubiquitous telephone service are more than outweighed by the convenience.

The history of mobile radio is short compared to other voice technologies. The first documented use of mobile radio was by the Detroit police department in 1921. Mobile telephone service was introduced in 1946, 25 years after the first mobile radio system went into operation. The following year Bell Laboratories developed the concept of cellular radio, but vacuum-tube circuitry was far too bulky to make it practical, so cellular had to wait for the transistor, which removed power and size constraints. Also, the switching systems available at the time lacked the intelligence needed to control the cell sites and effect hand-off from one cell to another. It wasn't until 1965 when the first electronic switching system was introduced that cellular radio could become technically feasible.

The initial cellular growth spurt was in Europe, where the service was first widely available, while it languished in the United States because of regulatory restraints. The first issue was frequency spectrum. In 1974 the FCC designated part of the UHF television spectrum—between 800 and 900 MHz—for cellular. The concept of cellular radio had been studied for more than two decades, but the lack of FCC approval, a sufficiently large block of clear frequencies, and a suitable control technology impeded its advancement. Although the FCC allocated frequencies in 1974, they delayed approval of the service pending a lengthy hearing process, which included a solicitation of proposals for demonstration systems. A major issue in the United States was pressure on the FCC to not grant an exclusive license to telephone companies, which then had a monopoly on landline services. Finally, in 1978, Advanced Mobile Phone System (AMPS), an AT&T subsidiary, installed the first cellular radio demonstration system in the United States in Chicago. The monopoly issue was resolved by breaking the spectrum into two segments, one of which was allocated to a nonwireline carrier. Today, conventional analog cellular service is referred to as AMPS; the digital version is referred to as D-AMPS.

Meanwhile, conventional two-way mobile radio advanced rapidly. Police, taxicabs, utilities, farmers, and construction workers all rely heavily on conventional mobile and hand-held radios. Radio is one of the enabling technologies supporting vast industries that would otherwise be impractical. The airlines, public safety, and all companies that use radio dispatch are based on access to the airways.

Citizens band radio has long been available to the public at low cost, but mobile and hand-held radio connected to the PSTN was too costly for general use. As we will discuss later in this chapter, the early versions of public mobile radio shared a limited frequency resource and either manual operation or an awkward signaling arrangement. As solid-state electronics advanced, radios shrank in size, power consumption, and cost, but cellular was the development that turned mobile radio into a household utility.

Technology has not only decreased the size of radios, but it also has found ways to pack more channels into a limited frequency spectrum. Digital radio, which once required more bandwidth than its analog counterpart, now provides as much as a 20:1 channel advantage in the same spectrum. Spread spectrum technology enables transceivers to use the same frequency without mutual interference, and the push to ever higher frequencies results in more directionality, which enables channel reuse with less physical separation than the lower frequencies require.

Despite cellular radio's popularity, it isn't the only technology competing for the consumer's dollar. Specialized mobile radio (SMR) has many of cellular's characteristics, but a different network architecture. SMR, originally set up as a local dispatch service, is formed into networks that are growing rapidly in competition with cellular and PCS. Roaming capability is gradually developing, enabling SMR users to enjoy the same ubiquitous telephone service that cellular provides.

This chapter discusses voice radio services of all kinds except microwave, which is covered in Chapter 17, and private wireless, which, together with mobile data, is covered in Chapter 19.

CONVENTIONAL MOBILE TELEPHONE TECHNOLOGY

The term "mobile radio" often is used synonymously with mobile telephone. Although the two services use technology and equipment that are essentially the same, they differ in these ways:

♦ Mobile telephone uses separate transmit and receive frequencies, making full-duplex operation possible. Mobile two-way radios operate either on the same frequency in a simplex mode or on different frequencies in a half-duplex mode.

♦ Mobile telephones are connected directly to the telephone network and can be used to originate and terminate telephone calls with billing rendered directly to the mobile telephone number. Mobile radio, if connected to the telephone network, connects through a coupler to a telephone line. Billing, if any, is to the wireline telephone.

♦ Mobile telephones signal on a dialing plan that is compatible with the nation's plan. Mobile radios use loudspeaker paging or selective signaling that does not fit into the national dialing plan.

As an aid to understanding cellular radio, it is instructive to review the operation of conventional mobile telephone service. In Part 22 rules, the FCC authorizes Public Mobile service in the ranges of 35.18- to 35.69-, 43.18- to 43.69-, 152- to 152.255-, 152.495- to 152.855-, 157.755- to 162.0125-, 454- to 455-, 459- to 460-, 470- to 512-, 824- to 849-, 869- to 894-, 928- to 929-, 931- to 932-, and 944- to 960-MHz bands. Coverage in these four frequency ranges is essentially line-of-sight with the lower frequencies providing the widest coverage. Under some propagation conditions in the 35-MHz band, coverage is so broad that mobile units frequently communicate with unintended base stations. To prevent interference, channels can be reused only with a geographical buffer of 50 to 100 miles between base stations.

Conventional mobile telephone service suffers from several drawbacks as a communications medium. First, demand greatly outstrips capacity in the limited frequency spectrum, resulting in long waiting lists for service in many parts of the country. Also, a mobile telephone channel is a large party line with the disadvantages of limited access and lack of privacy. Some parts of most serving areas have only limited coverage. When a vehicle leaves a coverage area, quality deteriorates and the conversation often must be ended and reestablished on a different channel or deferred until signal strength improves. Within the coverage area, communication is apt to be sporadic or impossible.

A metropolitan mobile telephone service area has transmitters centrally located and operating with 100 to 250 W of output. Because of the difference between mobile and base station transmitter output power, common carriers often install receivers in more than one site to improve coverage, as Figure 18-1 shows. These receivers are called *voting receivers* because a central unit measures the relative signal-to-noise ratio of each receiver and selects the one with the best signal. This improves the power balance between the mobile, which has relatively low output and a low gain antenna, and the base station unit. Most coverage areas have several radio channels. Transceivers can shift between channels within the same band, but not between bands.

For the first 20+ years of mobile telephone use, the LECs operated the service manually. Users placed calls by lifting the handset and keying the transmitter on momentarily to signal the operator. The operator connected and timed the call

FIGURE 18-1

Diagram of Conventional Mobile Telephone Service

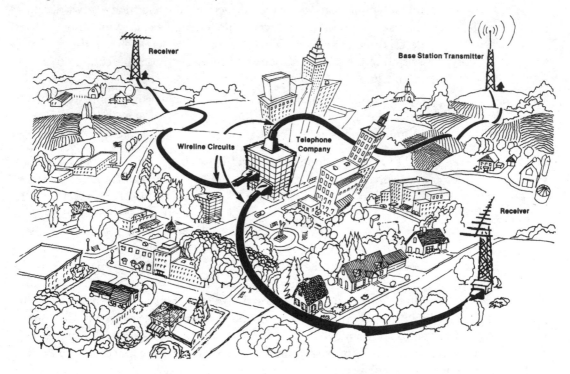

to a wireline telephone or other mobile unit. With this system the operator supervised only the wireline telephone. Mobile-to-mobile calls were manually monitored to detect the start and end of the conversation. The operator signaled the mobile telephone by multifrequency dialing. A selector inside the mobile transceiver responded to a five-digit number. To avoid the problem of frequency congestion, many users purchased multichannel sets. The greater number of channels improved the chances of finding an idle channel for outgoing service, but more channels did not improve incoming service to the mobile unit because users could be called only on the channel they monitored.

In 1964, AT&T introduced Improved Mobile Telephone Service (IMTS) to align mobile telephone service more closely with ordinary telephone service. The IMTS mobile receiver automatically seeks an idle channel and tunes the transceiver to that channel. When the user lifts the handset, the system returns dial tone, and the user dials the call like a conventional telephone. Calls from wireline to mobile units are dialed directly without operator intervention. The base station automatically selects an idle channel and signals the mobile unit over that channel. IMTS, with its idle channel–seeking capability, improved service for users by eliminating the need for manual channel changes and by making more channels available to reduce congestion.

Roamers—users who travel between serving areas—present a particular problem for mobile telephone service providers. Mobile users have a designated home channel and can be called only while they tune that channel. When they leave their home areas, they must inform potential callers of what channel they are monitoring or they cannot be called.

With both manual and IMTS systems, the base station configuration presents several disadvantages. The coverage area of a base station is more or less circular. The actual coverage area depends on the directionality of the antenna system and on the terrain. Obstructions are a problem with ordinary mobile telephone service. A hill some distance from the base station typically creates a radio signal shadow on the side away from the transmitter. When the user leaves the coverage area of the channel on which the call was established, the call must be terminated and reestablished on another channel.

PRIVATE MOBILE RADIO SERVICE

Mobile radio operates in one of three modes—single-frequency simplex, two-frequency simplex, and duplex. Both of the simplex modes use push-to-talk operation. When the transmitter button is in the talk position, the receiver cuts off. In a single-frequency mode, the mobile units and base unit send and receive on the same frequency. In a two-frequency operation, the base transmits on one frequency and receives on another; the mobile units reverse the transmit and receive frequencies.

In a duplex mode, the rf carriers of both the mobile and the base are on for the duration of the session. The base station usually uses separate transmit and receive antennas, but most mobile units use the same antenna to transmit and receive. A filter separates the transmitter's rf energy from the receiving transmission line. The transmit and receive frequencies must be separated sufficiently to prevent the transmitter from desensitizing the receiver. Duplex operation provides mobile radio units with the equivalent of a wireline telephone conversation.

To improve mobile radio coverage, which is apt to be spotty in mountainous terrain, repeaters are often employed. If a session between a mobile and a base station is set up through a repeater, two sets of frequencies are used—one between the mobile and the repeater and the other between the repeater and the base station.

The base station is often mounted at a remote location to improve coverage and therefore must be remotely controlled. Control functions, including keying the transmitter, selectively calling the mobile unit, and linking the audio path between the base station and the control unit, may be carried on over landline or point-to-point radio. Siting of the base station is a complex process. Because obstructions adversely affect mobile signals, it is advantageous to mount the antenna as high as possible. To overcome the effects of fading, it is desirable to use high transmitter power. Both of these, however, must be balanced with the objective of frequency reuse. On crowded frequencies, interference from distant stations becomes a problem, and a user may capture two base stations simultaneously.

Mobile-to-mobile communication is easy to administer in a single-frequency simplex operation because the mobiles can hear each other. In a duplex operation, the mobiles can hear only the base station unless the base station retransmits the signal from mobile units. The retransmission of the mobile signal, which is called *talk-through,* permits mobiles to communicate with one another. It is necessary for the base station to monitor a mobile-to-mobile conversation and to disconnect the path when the session ends.

Mobile Unit Signaling

The simplest form of signaling a mobile unit is voice calling. The base station calls the mobile unit's identification, and the mobile unit responds if the operator is within earshot. On a crowded radio frequency, the constant squawking of the speaker can be annoying, which leads to the need for some form of selective calling.

The simplest form of selective calling relies on the receiver's squelch circuit. The *squelch* is the circuitry that deactivates the receiver's audio in the absence of a received carrier. Several receivers can operate on the same frequency by assigning subaudio tones to break the squelch of the desired receiver.

For a few stations, the tone-activated squelch is satisfactory, but it does not permit many users to share the same channel. In channels with more users, a selective calling system similar to that used in mobile telephone can be employed. The receiver has a selector that responds to a series of audio tones or a digital code. When the user's unit is signaled, the selector rings a bell, which can also activate an external signal such as honking a horn or turning on a flashing light.

Trunking Radio

If many users are contending for a single communication channel, the channel occupancy may be high but service will be poor. As channels are added to a radio system, the number of calls that can be carried for a given grade of service increases dramatically. *Trunking radio* employs multiple channels to improve service to a group of users. The best example of trunking radio is a cellular system, but many private and public safety radio systems also use trunking to improve service. Specialized mobile radio (SMR) uses trunking radio to provide dispatch services for its customers.

A trunking system designates one channel as the calling or control channel, and all idle receivers tune to that channel. The control channel can be the next idle channel in a sequence, or it may be a channel that is designated as the control. Some loss of efficiency occurs when units must switch signaling channels, so high-usage systems, such as cellular, reach a point at which it is more efficient to have a dedicated signaling channel.

Trunking systems must resolve the occasional conflict of two stations signaling simultaneously. Two methods commonly are used—polling and contention. Both systems work the same way that channel-sharing methods in data communications systems work. In a polling system, the base station sends a continuous stream of polling messages to all mobiles on the channels. The polling messages consume signaling channel time and are therefore inefficient. In a contention system, the mobile unit listens for an idle channel before transmitting. If two mobiles transmit simultaneously, the base station recognizes the collision and informs the mobiles of it. They then back off a random time before again attempting to transmit. Cellular digital packet data (CDPD), which is discussed in Chapter 19, uses contention access.

Mobile Radio Design Objectives

Private and public mobile radio and paging systems share a common set of design objectives. The design process is not precise because of the unpredictable nature of radio waves. Obstructions and fading cause the principal disturbances. Designers of point-to-point radio systems have several tools at their disposal to compensate for the effects of disturbances. They can use high power, directional antennas, and diversity to design a reliable path. The mobile radio designer is at a disadvantage because omnidirectional antennas are needed to reach roaming users. The nature of the remote unit may make it difficult to increase power because of the resulting increase in battery drain. Also, the remote unit frequently operates in an undesirable noise environment (for example, ignition noise), and most important, the base station is attempting to communicate with a target that is constantly moving. As a result, no mobile radio system gives quality that is consistently as good as that provided by land telephones. This section discusses some techniques that designers use to generate satisfactory mobile radio service.

Wide-Area Coverage

The major objective in mobile system design is to provide coverage that allows a mobile unit to move through a coverage area without loss of communication. Cellular radio, which is discussed later, is one way of accomplishing this. Another way is *quasisynchronous* operation.

FM receivers have a tendency to be captured by the strongest signal. Quasisynchronous, which also is called simulcast, employs adjacent transmitters operating on frequencies that are slightly offset. The offset is small enough that the resulting beat frequency is inaudible.

A second method of achieving wide-area coverage is a receiver voting system. When a mobile unit initiates or responds to a call, the receivers in the coverage area compare signal strength and determine which unit has the best signal. That unit and its associated transmitter establish communication with the mobile until it moves beyond the coverage area and captures another transmitter.

Adequate Signal Strength

Mobile units live in a hostile environment of high noise, most of which is man-made, with the predominant source being auto ignition and charging systems.

Portable units often are carried inside buildings where the signal may be attenuated or other noise sources, such as elevators and industrial machinery, may interfere with the signal. These noise sources tend to be most disruptive at lower frequencies.

Another source of signal loss is fading. A primary cause of fading is a multipath signal: a signal may arrive over one path slightly out of phase with the signal over the other path, which causes a reduction in the received signal strength. A stationary user may experience a slow fade due to gradual changes in atmospheric reflection. A moving user on the edge of the coverage area is likely to experience a fast fade as the signal bounces off buildings, trees, and other obstructions. As the vehicle moves, the frequency of the fade changes. If the fade is fast enough, it can be tolerated and sounds much like a noisy signal. A fade of about 10 cycles per second has the greatest adverse effect on the user and makes communication practically impossible. A user on the fringes of the coverage area often can improve communication by stopping the vehicle and edging forward to a high signal strength location. A move of only a few inches can make a great difference in received signal strength.

Fading is often frequency-selective. If a band of frequencies is transmitted, one range of frequencies may be subjected to heavy fading while the other suffers little or not at all. The range of frequencies that are subject to similar fading effects is called the *coherence bandwidth.* Because of the frequency-selective nature of fading, designers can use frequency diversity to establish a reliable communication path.

Since VHF and higher frequencies have a short wavelength, it is often possible to counter the effects of fading by using space diversity. In a space diversity system, antennas are mounted at a distance that reduces the probability of a similar fade striking both antennas simultaneously. In a vehicular radio, for example, one antenna might be mounted on the front fender and another on the rear.

Wave Propagation

Radio waves propagate by one of three methods—the ground wave, the tropospheric wave, and the ionospheric, or sky, wave. Each of these acts differently on different frequency ranges and has a significant effect on the propagation characteristics of the signal.

The *ground wave* guides radio frequencies below about 30 MHz. The signal follows the contour of the earth and diminishes with distance. Ground-wave communication is effective for short distances and has little effect on VHF and higher frequencies.

The *tropospheric wave* is effective at VHF and higher frequencies but has little effect below 3 MHz. At microwave frequencies, the tropospheric wave can be used to communicate beyond the line-of-sight.

The *ionospheric wave* is most effective below VHF frequencies. The ionosphere reflects high frequencies in a manner that is highly frequency-selective. With ionospheric reflection, signals can travel well beyond the range of the ground wave, a condition that is called *skip*. Skip conditions can result in excellent communication capability most of the way around the world with low power, but the communication path is unreliable and difficult to predict. For mobile radio skip is generally undesirable.

CELLULAR MOBILE RADIO

In 1981, the FCC authorized 666 cellular radio channels in two bands of frequencies—825 to 845 MHz and 870 to 890 MHz. The lower half of each band, called the A band, is designated for *wireline carriers,* which are defined roughly as local exchange companies. The upper half, or B band, is designated for *nonwireline carriers,* which are non-LEC common carriers. With the mergers and acquisitions that have occurred since the original allocations were made, this distinction has all but disappeared. The FCC grants licenses in both bands to serve a cellular geographic serving area (CGSA). A CGSA corresponds to a standard metropolitan statistical area (SMSA), which is a major metropolitan area defined by the Office of Management and Budget.

The demand for cellular service grew rapidly, to the point that the carriers returned to the FCC for additional frequencies. The FCC reluctantly granted an additional 10 MHz—5 in each band. With the prospect of again running out of frequency spectrum, the carriers are shifting to digital cellular. D-AMPS uses a combination of frequency and time division multiplexing to modulate three digital channels in the spectrum occupied by one analog channel. Since neither the carriers nor the users can justify replacing all the existing analog equipment, cell sites are equipped with some analog and some digital transceivers. The subscriber units must be dual mode to communicate on either analog or digital channels. Over the next several years digital cellular with its greater channel capacity will replace analog.

In addition to dual-mode mobile phones, the industry offers dual-band phones that can communicate on either the cellular or the PCS bands. PCS, as discussed in the next section, operates in the 1900-MHz band. The process of selecting a phone is further complicated by the fact that three different modulation methods are in use throughout the world. D-AMPS uses time division multiplexing (TDM) to share the spectrum. TDM was the first digital cellular method to reach users. Several North American carriers adopted a competing technology, code division multiplexing (CDM). The FCC has elected to let the market set the standards, so both of these are in operation in North America today. In much of the rest of the world, global system for mobile communications (GSM) is the dominant digital cellular modulation scheme. PCS-1900 is the North American version of GSM, and is used for PCS. It is not, however, completely compatible with European GSM, making it impossible to use the same phone in all parts of the world. The differences between these modulation methods are discussed later.

FIGURE 18-2

Frequency Reuse in a Cellular Serving Area

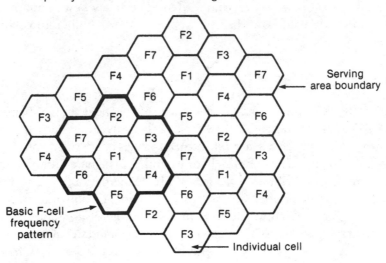

Cellular Technology

Cellular mobile radio overcomes most of the disadvantages of conventional mobile telephone. A coverage area is divided into hexagonal *cells,* as shown in Figure 18-2. Frequencies are not duplicated in adjacent cells, which reduces interference between base stations. It also allows the carrier to reuse frequencies within the coverage area with a buffer between cells that are operating on the same band of frequencies. This technique greatly increases the number of radio channels available compared to a conventional mobile telephone system, which uses a frequency only once in a coverage area.

The general plan of cellular radio is shown in Figure 18-3. The carrier selects the number and size of cells to optimize coverage, cost, and total capacity within the serving area. FCC rules and regulations do not specify these design factors; the service provider selects them. The mobile units are *frequency agile,* that is, they can shift to any of the voice channels. Channel frequency assignments are shown in Table 18-1. To operate on either digital or analog channels, the mobile units also must be dual mode. A dual-mode unit responds to a digital channel first if one is available. If not, it falls back to analog.

Mobile units are equipped with processor-driven logic units that respond to incoming calls and shift to radio channels under control of the base station. Each cell site is equipped with transmitters, receivers, and control apparatus. One or more frequencies in each cell are designated for calling and control. For incoming and outgoing calls, the *cell-site controller* assigns the channel and directs a *frequency synthesizer* inside the mobile unit to shift to the appropriate frequency.

FIGURE 18-3

Cellular Radio Serving Plan

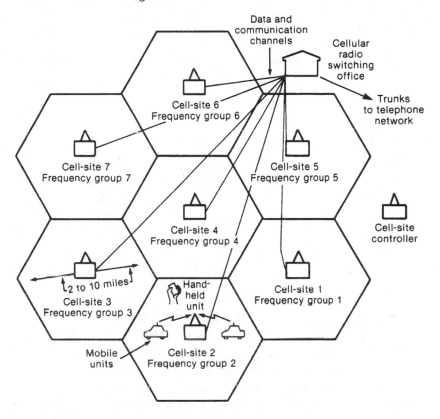

An electronic central office serves as a *mobile telephone switching office* (MTSO), and controls mobile operation within the cells. The cell-site controllers connect to the MTSO over data links for control signals, and voice channels for talking. The MTSO switches calls to other mobile units and to the local telephone system, processes data from the cell-site controllers, and records billing details. It also controls *hand-off* so a mobile leaving one cell switches automatically to a channel in the next cell.

Cellular radio overcomes a major drawback of conventional mobile telephone service: the lack of supervision from the mobile unit. Cellular radio uses the control channel to supervise the mobile station. Unlike conventional mobile telephone service, in which calls are timed on the basis of supervisory signals from the wireline telephone, cellular radio permits either the wireline or the mobile unit to control timing. This aids mobile-to-mobile calling, which closely approximates ordinary telephone service.

TABLE 18-1

Cellular Radio Frequency Assignments

System	Number of Channels	Center Frequency Mobile Transmit (MHz)	Center Frequency Mobile Receive (MHz)
A expansion	33	824.040	869.040
		825.000	870.000
A	333	825.030	870.030
		834.990	879.990
B	333	835.020	880.020
		844.980	889.980
A expansion	50	845.010	890.010
		846.480	891.480
B expansion	83	846.510	891.510
		848.970	893.970

Cell-Site Operation

A cell site has one radio transmitter and two receivers per channel, the cell-site controller, an antenna system, and voice and data links to the MTSO. The cell shape is roughly hexagonal because that shape provides a practical way of covering an area without the gaps and overlaps of circular cells. As a practical matter, cell boundaries are not precise. Directional antennas can approximate the shape, but the MTSO switches a user from one cell to another based on signal strength reports from the cell-site controllers. The hand-off between cells is nearly instantaneous, and users are generally unaware that it has occurred. The hand-off, which takes about 0.2 seconds, has little effect on voice transmission aside from an audible click, but data errors will result from the momentary interruption. As many as 128 channels per cell can be provided, with the number of channels based on demand. Most cells operate with 70 or fewer channels.

Cell sites provide coverage with the relatively low power of the cell-site transmitters. FCC rules limit cellular transmitters to 100-W output, with higher power used only if necessary to cover large cells. At the UHF frequencies of cellular radio, transmission is line-of-sight, so careful planning is needed to define the coverage area of the individual cell while minimizing the need to realign cells in the future.

A minimum of one channel per cell is provided for control of the mobile units from the cell-site controller. The cell-site controller directs channel assignments, receives outgoing call data from the mobile unit, and pages mobile units over the control channel. When the load exceeds the capacity of one channel, separate paging and access channels are used.

The cell-site controller manages the radio channels within the cell. It receives instructions from the MTSO to turn transmitters and receivers on and off, and it su-

F I G U R E 18-4

A Sectored Cell

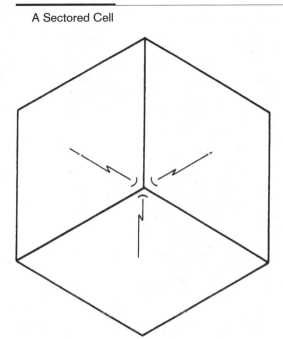

pervises the calls, diagnoses trouble, and relays data messages to the MTSO and mobile units. The cell-site controller also monitors the mobile units' signal strength and reports it to the MTSO. It scans all active mobile units operating in adjacent cells and reports their signal strengths to the MTSO, which maps all working mobile units. This map determines which cell should serve a mobile unit when handoff is required. In some second-generation systems the cell-site controllers off-load some functions from the MTSO. For example, the cell site may control power and frequency administration.

The number of users that a single cell can support depends on traffic. As cellular radio is introduced to an area, usage is low. As the prices of portable units and monthly service charges drop, the demand grows, necessitating increases in cell capacity. Cell capacity can be expanded by adding radio channels up to the maximum. When cells reach their channel capacity, they can be *sectored*, that is, subdivided into two to six sections with frequencies reused within the cells. Interference is avoided by providing directional antennas, as Figure 18-4 shows. Sectored patterns also are used near mountains, water, and other terrain obstructions to direct radio frequency energy away from areas where it is not needed.

Cells also can be split to increase capacity. One strategy for introducing cellular radio is to begin with large cells, as shown in Figure 18-5. As demand increases, a larger cell can be subdivided into smaller cells by reducing power and

F I G U R E 18-5

Increasing Capacity by Splitting Cells

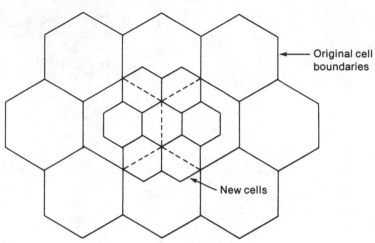

Original cell boundaries

New cells

changing the antenna patterns. A fourth method of increasing capacity is to borrow unused channels from an adjacent cell.

Supervisory audio tones (SAT tones) prevent a mobile unit from talking on the same frequency at separate cell sites. The base station sends one of three SAT tones, and the mobile loops it back. If the SAT tone returned by a mobile unit is different from the one sent by the cell site, the MTSO will not accept the call.

Mobile Telephone Switching Office

The MTSO is essentially an end-office switching system of the type described in Chapter 13 with a special-purpose generic program for cellular radio operation. Not all MTSOs are local switching systems; some products are designed specifically for cellular radio, but in most cases, MTSOs are digital switching systems that can be used for ordinary telephone service with a different program and hardware configuration. The objective of most service providers is to offer cellular radio features that are essentially identical to wireline telephone features. The MTSO's tasks can be grouped into three categories: connection management, mobility management, and radio resource management.

The MTSO links to the cell-site controller with data circuits for control purposes and with four-wire voice circuits for communication channels. When the cell-site controller receives a call from the mobile unit, the controller registers the dialed digits and passes them over the data link. The concept is similar to common channel signaling as described in Chapter 11, but X.25 protocol is used. The MTSO registers the dialed digits and switches the call to the telephone network over an intermachine trunk or to another cellular mobile unit within the system. When mobile-to-mobile calls or calls from the local telephone system are placed, the MTSO pages the mobile unit by sending messages to all cell-site controllers.

The MTSO receives reports from the cell-site controller on the signal strength of each mobile unit transmitting within the coverage area. Data is relayed to the MTSO to enable it to decide which cell is the appropriate serving cell for each active unit. The MTSO also collects statistical information about traffic volumes for allowing the system administrator to determine when to add channels. In addition, the MTSO stores usage records for generating bills.

Mobile Units

When cellular radio first was introduced, mobile units were expensive, with many units retailing for as much as $3000. The increasing demand for cellular has resulted in fierce competition and dramatic cost reductions. Hand-held units are so compact that they can easily fit into a shirt pocket or purse.

The *transceiver* is a sophisticated device that can tune all channels in an area. Unlike conventional mobile transceivers that use individual crystals for setting the frequency of each channel, cellular transceivers are frequency agile, using frequency synthesizers, which are circuits that generate the end frequency by multiplying from a reference frequency. When cellular theory was first examined in 1947, the science of solid-state electronics was undeveloped. Control circuitry was electromechanical and bulky and consumed considerable power. Transceivers of today are small enough to be contained in a housing the size of a telephone handset or smaller and are powered by rechargeable batteries.

The major components of a typical mobile unit are shown in the block diagram in Figure 18-6. The transmitter and receiver are coupled to the antenna through a *diplexer,* which is a device that isolates the two directions of transmission so the transmitter does not feed power into its own receiver. The frequency synthesizer generates transmit and receive frequencies under control of the logic unit. The synthesizer generates a reference frequency from a highly stable oscillator and divides, filters, and multiplies it to generate the required frequency.

The most complex part of the mobile unit is the logic equipment. This system communicates with the cell-site controller over the control channel and directs the other systems in the functions of receiving and initiating calls. These functions include recognizing and responding to incoming signals, shifting the rf equipment to the working channel for establishing a call initially and during hand-off, and interpreting users' service requests. The logic unit periodically scans the control channels and tunes the transceiver to the channel with the strongest signal. The user communicates with the logic unit through a control unit, which consists of the handset, dial, display unit, and other elements that emulate a conventional telephone set.

FIGURE 18-6

Block Diagram of a Cellular Mobile Radio Transceiver

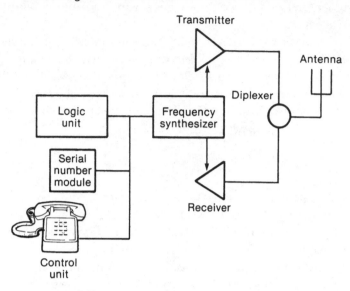

The unit also includes a power converter to supply the logic and rf equipment with the proper voltages from the battery source. FCC rules limit the transmitter to 7-W output, but many mobile units use 3 W or less, and hand-held units are a fraction of a watt to reduce battery drain. Battery drain is particularly important in hand-held or portable units. The FCC segregates mobile units into three power classes ranging from 0.6 W to the maximum power permitted.

Another module electronically generates the unit's 32-bit binary serial number, which theoretically prevents fraudulent or unauthorized use of a mobile unit. In practice, however, toll thieves intercept the electronic serial number and duplicate it so they can use the cellular phone to place telephone calls at the registered owner's expense. The serial number is communicated to the cell-site controller with each call for comparison with the MTSO's database. The unit's 10-digit calling number and a station class mark also are built into memory and transmitted to the cell-site controller with each outgoing call. The class mark identifies the station type and power rating.

Signal Enhancements

Some buildings are constructed with so much steel and concrete that cellular signals cannot penetrate. The cellular industry provides two solutions to the problem: booster amplifiers and microcells. A *booster amplifier* amplifies the frequency range of the nearest cell site, retransmitting it inside the building. The amplifier picks up signals from hand-held units and retransmits them so the cell site can pick them up. This method is the least expensive alternative, but it provides poorer security. Anyone wanting to intercept cellular conversations going on inside a building has an easy time of it because the stations and frequency range are fixed.

A *microcell* is a low-power cell site that is dedicated to a building. An antenna system is extended throughout the building to transmit and receive low-power signals. The microcell has its own set of channels, and is connected to the MTSO with a T1/E1 connection just like any other cell site. The microcell provides better security than a booster, at a higher cost and at a cost of additional administration. The microcell's transceivers must be administered for traffic load like any cell site. They also require the same balancing of analog and digital channels if the carrier has converted to digital.

Mobile Telephone Features

A full description of mobile telephone features is beyond the scope of this book. The following is a brief description of the most popular cellular radio mobile features. Among the most important features are those that improve safety by enabling the user to operate the system while driving.

◆ *Automatic answer.* This feature allows the user to program the telephone to answer an incoming call automatically after a given number of rings.

◆ *Call-in-absence indicator.* When an incoming call is unanswered, the unit displays an indicator.

◆ *Call timer.* Displays elapsed time of calls, displays accumulated time to aid in estimating billing costs, and provides a preset interval timer during a call.

◆ *Dialed number display.* The dialed number is displayed in readout on the handset. Misdialed digits can be corrected before the number is outpulsed.

◆ *Dual-mode operation.* The unit can operate on either digital or analog cellular.

◆ *Dual-band operation.* The unit can operate on either the cellular or the PCS frequency bands.

◆ *Last number dialed.* As in a conventional telephone, this feature stores the last number dialed so it can be recalled with a touch of a button.

◆ *Muting.* The handset cuts off with a button so the distant party cannot hear a private conversation from the mobile unit.

◆ *On-hook dialing.* This feature allows the user to dial a number while the unit is on-hook. If the unit has a dialed number display, the number can be pulsed into a handset and reviewed before it is sent.

◆ *Paging.* The unit has built-in paging capability.

- ◆ *Scratch pad.* This feature stores numbers entered with the keypad in a temporary memory location.
- ◆ *Security features.* An electronic lock can be programmed into the telephone so it cannot be used until the proper code is entered. Some units can be programmed to lock automatically after each use.
- ◆ *Self-diagnostics.* Internal diagnostics indicate trouble in the transceiver and control unit tso aid in rapid troubleshooting.
- ◆ *Signal strength meter.* The unit displays the strength of the received signal.
- ◆ *Speaker.* Some units include a speaker and remote microphone so others can monitor conversations and to permit hands-free operation of the unit.
- ◆ *Special signaling.* A call-in-absence indicator turns on a light when a call is received but not answered. Auxiliary signals can honk the horn or turn on the lights when a call arrives at an unattended unit.
- ◆ *Speed dialing.* The unit stores a list of telephone numbers that can be selected by dialing one or two digits.
- ◆ *Voice dialing.* The system can recognize certain voice commands including dialing from a speed-dial list.

Roaming

Every cellular operator provides a home area in which normal cellular rates apply. *Roaming* is the ability of a mobile unit to move outside its normal service area. A premium charge is levied for roamers. The cellular operator must know about a roaming user to route calls to the proper service area and to know where to send the bill. Roaming service is enabled by use of SS7 between the MTSOs. The MTSO maintains home location register and visitor location register databases. The visitor location register keeps track of visiting stations that are roaming within the MTSO's domain. The identity and location of roaming stations are validated with the home MTSO over the SS7 network. The carrier may extend roaming capability throughout a wide service area by linking its switches over SS7 networks with switches of other service providers, enabling users to roam without special procedures.

When roaming outside the carrier's network, special procedures are required to place and receive calls. Callers must know the roamer access number for the service area. After the access number is reached, dial tone is provided so the cellular number can be dialed. Outgoing calls are handled normally if your serving carrier has an agreement with the other carrier. Otherwise, it may be necessary to use a credit card to place long-distance calls. If the telephone is equipped for two-service operation, it may be necessary to switch it between the A and B bands to retain full network privileges. This can occur if your home carrier is the wireline carrier in one locality, but the nonwireline carrier in another. As the SS7 network is expanded and carriers develop interconnection arrangements, roaming will become easier, but currently it often requires knowing how the system operates.

Cellular Radio Services

Cellular radio duplicates the services of wireline carriers as nearly as possible. Carriers offer equal access to any long-distance carrier, emergency numbers, and operator services to allow users to place collect, third-number, and credit-card calls. Most carriers offer voice mail to answer calls when the telephone is off or outside the service area. An attendant service is also required so roaming users can check in when they leave one carrier's service area and enter another. Although the mobile unit automatically identifies the user, the different jurisdictions require identification and registration of the user for billing purposes.

Digital Cellular

Cellular radio design has alleviated the problems of poor coverage and congested frequencies, primarily in urban areas. The principle of cell splitting, which was supposed to reduce large cells to smaller ones as traffic increased, has not proved as technically or economically feasible as expected. The cellular carriers all agree that a gradual shift from analog to digital cellular is required in order to make the best use of the frequency spectrum. They have been unable to agree, however, on which of two competing technologies will be used. McCaw Cellular (now AT&T Wireless) began deploying TDMA systems in the early 1990s. Competing carriers, including most of the wireline carriers, have either implemented or are planning to use CDMA systems. The Telecommunications Industry Association has standardized both methods and in most of the rest of the world, GSM is the dominant method.

The three systems are not compatible with each other nor with the analog method of frequency division multiple access. To effect the transition from analog to digital, dual-mode units are required. The TDMA/CDMA controversy means that either subscriber stations must be compatible with three modulation schemes or users will be unable to roam freely or to change carriers without changing the subscriber set. The standardization of analog cellular has always been one of its major advantages. A major reason the price has dropped so dramatically is because the demand enables manufacturers to produce large quantities of a standard product.

Under the analog FDMA system, a user has exclusive use of a channel in a cell site for the duration of a session. The inherent half-duplex character of voice communications, plus the frequent pauses in most conversations, wastes much airtime, which TDMA and CDMA can utilize. TDMA effectively divides each 30-kHz analog channel into three 8-kb/s segments, tripling the capacity of the spectrum. Eventually, TDMA proponents expect to double the capacity of digital channels, providing a 6:1 improvement. The control channels remain analog, but eventually digital control channels will be used.

F I G U R E   18-7

North American PCS Frequency Spectrum

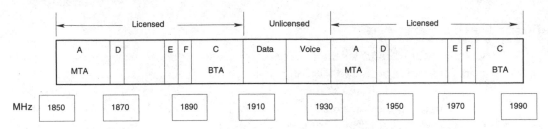

MTA = Major trading area
BTA = Basic trading area

CDMA uses spread spectrum techniques to multiply spectrum capacity. CDMA encodes 64 channels into 1.25 MHz of spectrum. Each channel uses an orthogonal code, with all channels transmitting across the same bandwidth. The CDMA receiver picks the code out of the appropriate signal and demodulates it. CDMA is not as susceptible to multipath fading as FDMA and TDMA. Another advantage of CDMA is its hand-off method, which is a make-before-break arrangement that eliminates the signal dropout that is common with TDMA and FDMA.

GSM uses a TDMA/FDMA method of dividing the radio spectrum not unlike D-AMPS, but it uses a signaling protocol that is based on OSI and ISDN standards. The call setup and teardown method is a modified Q.931 standard, which is the protocol used in ISDN. The layer 2 protocol used for transferring information across the radio channel in frames is a modified version of link access protocol for the D channel (LAPD).

PERSONAL COMMUNICATIONS SYSTEM (PCS)

The frequency spectrum allocated to PCS in the United States is shown in Figure 18-7. In Europe the service is called personal computer network (PCN). The frequency ranges are similar, but the coding methods are incompatible. Even if the North American carrier has chosen GSM as its coding method, there are enough incompatibilities that a mobile unit from one continent cannot be used in the other unless it has been designed for the purpose. PCS is similar in many ways to cellular, but with several notable exceptions, including these:

- PCS omitted the analog phase. It is a digital service from the outset.
- Its frequency range is higher—in the 1900-MHz band.
- The PCS spectrum is divided into licensed and unlicensed portions, which enables private wireless users to shift to an adjacent PCS frequency when they roam outside the bounds of the unlicensed system.

♦ The frequency spectrum for PCS in the United States was auctioned off and divided into multiple segments to avoid some of the monopolistic characteristics of cellular.

Other than these, the distinctions between PCS and cellular are technical and of little interest to users. Service differences are largely a matter of the carrier's choice rather than because of any inherent differences in the technology. The small amount of space devoted to PCS here as opposed to cellular has nothing to do with the superiority of one system over the other. The technologies and method of operation are similar enough that they are conceptually the same. With coverage, cost, service quality, and other such variables equal, the subscriber has little reason to choose one over another.

The promise of PCS is simple. Telephone numbers are associated with people, not places, and you can use the service or be reached anywhere or any time. Of course, the telephone provides features to handle calls when you don't want to be quite that accessible, and the completely portable telephone number will not be achieved across national boundaries in the foreseeable future, if ever.

The promise of PCS is improved lifestyle through a combination of easy portability and random mobility. Easy portability means the telephone instrument is a small size that fits the user comfortably. Random mobility means that subscribers can roam and use their personalized services wherever they are. For example, present nationwide paging systems approach the objective of random mobility. Except for dead spots, users can be reached easily without caller or called party being concerned about special check-in procedures as cellular sometimes requires. A nationwide signaling network is needed to identify PCS roamers and to inform the local carrier of the subscriber's personalized services. Smartcards may enable subscribers to use any telephone on the network while keeping the system informed of their identity and preferences.

In the United States, PCS licenses two 30-MHz channels per MTA (major trading area) and one 20-MHz plus four 10-MHz channels in the basic trading area (BTA) band, with a minimum of three competitors in each market. In addition, the C and D blocks in each band are reserved for protected groups: rural telephone companies, small business, and women- and minority-owned businesses. In theory at least, the additional competition should result in better coverage, more innovative services, and competitive prices. PCS has no mandatory service standards. Competition drives the cost and features included in carriers' service offerings.

APPLICATIONS

Cellular radio and PCS are rapidly becoming necessities much like ordinary telephone service. This section includes considerations that users of cellular radio service should evaluate, in terms of both the service itself and the mobile radio equipment.

TABLE 18-2

Selected Cellular and PCS Standards

Standard	Covers
IS-41	AMPS mobility managment
IS-54-B	D-AMPS TDMA
GSM 900	Original GSM standard
DCS-1800	GSM standard for 1800-GHz band
PCS-1900	North American GSM standard
IS-136	Second-generation TDMA standard
IS-95	CDMA standard

Standards

In the United States, the FCC Rules and Regulations set forth mobile radio standards. FCC rules establish the authorized frequencies, power levels, bandwidth, frequency stability, signaling formats, and other such variables in the public mobile service. Cellular radio standards are outlined in the "Cellular Mobile/Land Station Compatibility Specification" issued by the FCC and EIA. Internationally, ITU-R issues mobile radio recommendations. TIA has standardized both TDMA and CDMA protocols for digital cellular. Table 18-2 lists some of the many standards involved with cellular and PCS.

Evaluation Criteria

Cellular mobile telephone equipment is evaluated on much the same basis as other telecommunications equipment. Reliability, coverage, and the ability to obtain fast and efficient service is a paramount concern. Cost is also an important consideration. When cellular equipment was introduced, costs were high, but with the popularity of the technology, prices have dropped to the point that equipment cost is now a minor consideration. The cost of airtime, however, remains high, but some attractive pricing options effectively eliminate roaming and long-distance costs.

Security Issues

Regular mobile radio is inherently an unsecure medium. Anyone with a receiver tuned to the mobile frequency can eavesdrop on any conversation, and there is little practical means of preventing it aside from scrambling, which is impractical on public radio systems because of the need for matched scrambling devices. Cellular radio offers inherent security that may be sufficient but still is not interception-proof. If a session takes place in one cell, it is easy for someone to intercept it. If, however, the vehicle is moving, each time it is handed off to another cell, an eavesdropper may have some difficulty resuming reception of the conversation. The smaller the cells, the more frequent the hand-off, and the less likely it is that the entire session can be monitored. A vehicle following the vehicle under observation can, however, monitor the entire session.

TDMA digital cellular is somewhat more secure than analog because the equipment for monitoring is not as readily available. Anyone with the motivation and the proper equipment can still eavesdrop on a TDMA session, and since the control channels are analog, interception of the ESN is still not difficult. CDMA is inherently more secure than TDMA because an eavesdropper would have great difficulty intercepting the code or frequency-hopping pattern that the base and mobile stations are using. GSM uses a unit identification protocol that is inherently more secure from fraud. The mobile unit receives an identification number from a pool just for the duration of the session. Its voice channels are TDMA/FDMA, and with the right equipment, are subject to interception.

Coverage

The coverage area is one of the two or three primary considerations most users review in an evaluating a mobile radio system. Coverage can best be evaluated by taking a test drive and making calls from the areas you plan to drive through, paying particular attention to the fringe areas. The carriers' coverage maps are a good way to compare the home and roaming areas, but are not reliable indicators of coverage on the fringes. The two carriers in an area are unlikely to have identical coverage areas outside the urban area, which may make coverage the deciding factor. Note which areas are in the home area and which are in the carrier's service area, but for which a roaming charge is applied.

Ease of Roaming

For users who spend time outside the home area, the cost and difficulty of roaming are important selection criteria. Carriers that have an extensive SS7 network and interconnection agreements with other carriers make it easier and less costly to roam than more restrictive carriers.

Blockage

Cellular services with large numbers of cell sites are the most likely to provide satisfactory service. Large cells are likely to be sectionalized as usage increases. Sectionalization itself does not necessarily disrupt service, but the cell is apt to become crowded before the need for sectionalization is apparent. The main way of evaluating this feature is to ask other users how often they encounter a reorder signal in attempting to place calls with the carrier.

Selecting Cellular Radio Equipment

The first decision in selecting equipment is to determine whether you need vehicular or hand-held equipment. As the name implies, vehicular equipment is mounted inside a vehicle. Vehicular equipment has more power output than hand-held radios, and its car-mounted antenna provides more gain and therefore better coverage than hand-held units. A compromise is mounting a hand-held unit where it can couple to a vehicular antenna, but still be removed when leaving the vehicle. Determine whether digital or analog cellular is the best choice. Analog station equipment is less expensive, but carriers may offer more attractive pricing plans to move to digital.

Usage Charges

Cellular radio charges are based on duration of both originating and terminating calls. Carriers charge for total airtime and add on other message charges such as roaming and long distance. Therefore, both originating and terminating calls are charged to the terminating mobile number; outgoing long-distance usage is billed twice—once for the airtime and once for the wireline long-distance service. Some carriers do not charge for the first minute of incoming calls, which can make a big difference in the cost for some users.

CHAPTER 19

Wireless Communications Systems

In the beginning, the British called it wireless and the Americans called it radio, but it was the same technology, using power-hungry devices called vacuum tubes in the United States and valves in Britain. Now, the term wireless is cropping up worldwide to refer to a family of products that essentially displaces copper wire—something that mere radio is not intended to do.

To eliminate some of the ambiguity, with a few exceptions the focus in this chapter will be on wireless as a copper replacement, including in-building private wireless systems, which are practically indistinguishable from cellular and PCS phones. Wireless includes the wireless local loop, which may be a fast way for CLECs to bypass the LECs to deliver telephone and data services. It includes wireless LANs, which free users of laptop computers, personal information managers, and other such devices from the LAN patch cord. We will exclude from this definition cordless telephones, which aren't designed as a system, but rather as a device that uses wireless techniques. To muddy the distinction a bit more, we will include two other products in this chapter that aren't strictly wireline replacements: pagers and cellular digital packet data (CDPD).

These devices are all about accessibility—of the individual to coworkers, customers, and family—and accessibility of information. Devices such as 3-Com's Palm Pilot aren't telecommunications devices so much as they are miniature computers and database organizers, but they use wireless technology to marry them to electronic calendars, pagers, and information databases such as stock quotes. They, therefore, become portable communications devices. The changing styles of workers all over the world generate a demand for devices such as these that untether the individual from the confines of the wireline telephone.

The dream of not being tethered to the telephone cord has been around for many years, and spawned the cordless telephone. Wireless telephone technology is not markedly different from cellular and PCS, but the markets are different.

Wireless is intended to be confined to a building or campus. Its customers are mobile but not in a vehicular sense. Nurses and physicians, production personnel, managers, food service workers, technicians, and maintenance personnel who move about the plant and dozens of other such occupations need to be telephone-accessible, yet free from cords and pagers.

Once these people leave the confines of the plant, their needs don't change dramatically, but they move into the public communications arena. Cellular is one solution for mobility, but unless the building is equipped with a microcell, coverage may be a problem in heavily shielded buildings. Besides, the charges for extensive cellular usage are hefty. Ultimately, a person will have a single number that is reachable from anywhere at any time. He or she could use the phone at the desk, carry it about the plant, out into the parking lot, into the car, into an airplane, and have it work wherever the journey ends—and all of this at an affordable price. The ideal will not be realized immediately. For the immediate future, the hand-off from wireless to PCS will not be seamless. The ideal of a universal, transportable number will be achieved in time, but not until some technical and practical problems are resolved.

UNLICENSED WIRELESS PHONES

Most wireless voice and data products operate in frequency bands that are set aside for the purpose, and not licensed by the FCC. The industrial, scientific, and medical (ISM) band is an unlicensed spectrum in the 46- to 49- and 902- to 928-MHz ranges. The 46- to 49-MHz band is used for cordless telephones among other things. Several manufacturers produced wireless products in the 902-MHz band while waiting for the FCC to allocate frequency spectrum. Some products are still provided in this band but the risk of interference is high. The FCC states that users have no recourse if they are interfered with, and that they are prohibited from interfering with existing signals. This makes the ISM band a poor long-term choice for wireless.

When the FCC allocated space for the PCS band, it sandwiched 20 MHz of unlicensed spectrum between the two licensed portions of the band. The proximity is designed to allow frequency-agile units to hop from the unlicensed to the licensed spectrum, so wireless units can be used interchangeably for PCS communications. Although this spectrum, like ISM, is unlicensed, it is an exclusive-use segment, meaning it is used only for communications. The low-power or wireless transmitters should limit interference, or at least make it easy to find noninterfering frequencies.

A wireless installation consists of a central controller that interfaces with the office telephone system and controls a selection of remote base stations or cells. Figure 19-1 shows how the system is connected. The controller is either a standalone device that connects to analog ports on the PBX or an integrated unit that provides station features over the radio link.

F I G U R E 19-1

Business Wireless Configuration

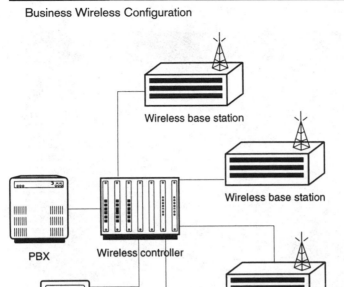

The base stations (see the example of the Nortel Companion unit in Figure 19-2) are self-contained low-power, multichannel radio transceivers. Locations are selected throughout the building to provide satisfactory coverage. A typical base station has a maximum range of about 700 ft, but less under adverse conditions such as steel and concrete in the building that limit the base station range. The base stations can be equipped with multiple radio channels, the quantity of which is chosen to support the number of simultaneous conversations expected. The base stations hand off to one another in a manner similar to cellular.

The portable instruments are either universal devices that emulate an analog telephone or they are proprietary stations that work with the manufacturer's PBX. Analog stations are the least expensive, but they suffer the drawbacks of any analog telephone: features are activated by dialing codes. Proprietary instruments offer button access to features, but the physical dimensions of the instrument may limit the number of buttons. Some products are designed so the portable device is the handset of the regular desk instrument. The user can pick up the handset and walk away from the instrument, making a seamless wire-to-wireless transition.

FIGURE 19-2

A Nortel Networks Companion Wireless Base Station

Courtesy of Nortel Networks, Inc.

WIRELESS LANS

The wired LAN is perfectly acceptable for office workers who sit at a desk all day, but many workers are mobile at least part of the day. The ideal of a wireless laptop or personal digital assistant would allow people to receive e-mail, keep their desk and portable calendars synchronized, or pop into the office file server to pick up an occasional file. All of these applications—and many more—are driving the need for wireless LANs. Students in a classroom are a perfect case in point. It is difficult for a teacher to predict where computer activities will be located, and the scene may shift from hour to hour. Warehouse workers, nurses, and retail clerks all need access to files from a portable computer or point-of-sale device. Nearly every retail establishment can profit from checking stock levels, preparing paperless pick slips, sending orders to the shipping department, and other such transactions that now take place with paper and pencil or by telephone. Much of the communication that now requires a voice call can be eliminated or simplified with inexpensive and ubiquitous wireless data.

Also driving the need for wireless LANs is the difficulty of wiring certain buildings. Historical buildings that cannot be altered, those built of masonry, and those constructed before computers were conceived pose real wiring difficulties that the wireless LAN can overcome. Wireless LANs can be divided into three application categories: mobile/portable, building-to-building, and desktop. The applications for each of these are different, as are the alternatives that the market provides.

In the past, wireless LANs were impeded by the lack of standards, but in 1997 the IEEE 802.11 committee published wireless LAN standards operating at 1 and 2 Mb/s. The 802.11 specification consists of two layers, the physical and data link, just as with wired LANs. Also in compliance with the wired LAN protocols, the data-link layer is subdivided into the 802.2 logical link control (LLC) and an 802.11 MAC layer. The physical layer provides for three alternatives:

- ◆ Spread spectrum frequency hopping
- ◆ Spread spectrum direct sequence
- ◆ Infrared

Carrier sense multiple access with collision avoidance (CSMA/CA) is used for the transmission protocol. This has some important differences compared to the CSMA/CD protocol used on Ethernet. First, CSMA/CD on a wired LAN assumes that all stations can hear one another for collision detection, which is not always the case with a wireless LAN. Second, on a wired LAN each station transmits and receives on a separate pair of wires. The equivalent on a wireless LAN would be simultaneous transmission and reception on the same frequency, which is technically difficult.

The CSMA/CA protocol used in 802.11 requires a station to broadcast a request-to-send packet containing its address and the address of the receiving station plus the duration of the information packet. If the receiving station is in a position to accept a packet, it broadcasts a clear-to-send packet. Stations on the network that receive the RTS or CTS packets set internal timers that prevent them from sending during the expected duration, thereby reducing the probability of collisions.

Spread Spectrum

Spread spectrum operates on unlicensed frequency ranges in the ISM band, with frequency ranges of 2.4 to 2.4835 and 5.1 to 5.825 GHz, although the latter is not included in the IEEE standard. The FCC requires such devices to use spread spectrum modulation with a maximum of 1 W of power. Most of the wireless LAN products on the market use the 2.4-GHz band. Since the frequencies are not licensed, interference is always a possibility. Fortunately, the spread spectrum method is robust at handling interference.

Two different methods of implementing spread spectrum are in common use in wireless LANs. In the *direct sequence method* the radio signal is broadcast over the entire bandwidth of the allocated spectrum. The transmitter and receiver both include a synchronized pseudonoise generator, which the receiver uses to detect the desired signal out of the resulting jumble. Most of the early wireless LAN products use direct sequence.

The second method is *frequency hopping* where the transmitter and receiver are synchronized to hop between frequencies, stopping on each frequency for a few milliseconds. The amount of time per hop is called the *dwell time*. The FCC requires products to use at least 75 different frequencies, and dwell no more than 400 ms. Later-generation LANs use frequency hopping, which is an excellent way of handling interference. If the equipment finds an interfering signal, it marks that portion of the spectrum as busy and skips it. Both frequency hopping and direct sequence provide excellent security. An eavesdropper would have a difficult time duplicating the pseudonoise or determining the channel-hopping sequence of spread spectrum.

Unlike infrared, spread spectrum can penetrate walls to cover a broad area in a building. The main limitation is transmission speed, which, with today's technology, is much slower than the speed of a wired LAN. Typical speeds do not exceed 1 or 2 Mb/s. Spread spectrum is normally used either for desktop or mobile/portable applications, with the latter restricted to a narrow range such as a building or campus.

Infrared

Infrared wireless products have appeal because they do not require any form of FCC licensing. Infrared products use one of three methods for distributing signals:

- ◆ *Line-of-sight.*   Uses infrared transceiver pairs set up in a manner similar to point-to-point microwave. This method is used for building-to-building communications.
- ◆ *Reflective infrared.*   Bounces the infrared signal off ceilings, walls, and floors to blanket an area.
- ◆ *Scattered infrared.*   Uses a diffused signal that also bounces off walls and ceilings to cover an area.

Scattered and reflective infrared are primarily used for desktop wireless applications. The directionality of the signal and the inability to penetrate walls generally makes infrared impractical for mobile/portable operation. Line-of-sight infrared has a wider bandwidth than spread spectrum. Reflective and scattered infrared are low-speed systems.

High-Speed Applications

Even though users sometimes exaggerate the need for speed in LANs, low speed is one of the main factors (in addition to cost) that limit the growth of wireless LANs. Several manufacturers have announced wireless LANs operating at 10 Mb/s, and proposals are in the works for LANs running up to 100 Mb/s. Nothing inherent in technology limits the speed of LANs to the current standards, and, in fact, the IEEE 802.11 committee is working on increasing the standards to higher speeds. As with other technologies, numerous proprietary protocols are on the market and will continue to come, but they may be made obsolete by additional standards activity.

Wireless Bridges

A *wireless bridge* is a radio connection between two network segments. Wireless bridges generally have a range of a few hundred yards, depending on the terrain. Most bridge products operate in the 2.4- and 5.7-GHz unlicensed bands, but some operate in the unlicensed 24-GHz spectrum, which provides for greater throughput.

WIRELESS MOBILE DATA

Mobile and portable applications require some form of technology that allows the user to link to a remote computer or server over an intermediate network. Parcel delivery companies now use wireless data extensively. Many police departments use mobile data terminals (MDT), so they can review arrest records and warrants without involving a dispatcher. Taxicab and service companies, and any company that dispatches personnel, can save time, improve accuracy, and eliminate telephone calls with mobile data terminals. Private radio systems also use mobile terminals for such purposes as linkage between a law-enforcement agency and a vehicular or law-enforcement database.

The simplest and least expensive form of MDT is the alphanumeric pager. Provided the application can get by without an answer, pagers are an effective way of sending short messages but they are slow, transmitting a limited amount of data at about 600 b/s. At the other end of the scale are two-way terminals with full QWERTY keyboards and laptop computers equipped with rf modems.

Within the narrow range of a building or campus, wireless data can be accomplished with privately owned spread spectrum radio. Broader ranges require some form of public network. The most common methods are dial-up over cellular, cellular digital packet data, or use of an SMR or private packet carrier.

Cellular Dial-Up

While cellular appears to be—and can be—a simple method of solving the mobile data problem, some precautions must be observed. First, ordinary commercial modems may not work well with cellular, particularly at high speed. The modulation methods of these modems are complex, and do not gracefully handle the vagaries of interference, fades, and signal dropout. The hand-off between cells causes a momentary interruption, and may cause the connection to drop. If a file is being

FIGURE 19-3

Mobile Data through Two Options: CDPD and Dial-Up Cellular

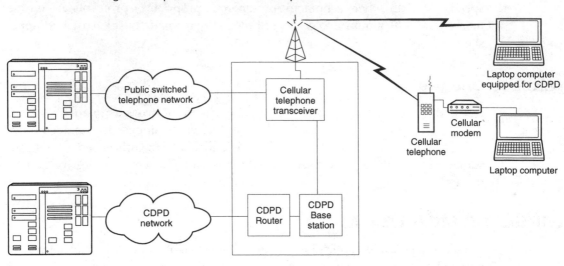

downloaded when the dropout occurs, it may be necessary to start over again. Furthermore, many modems are designed to operate only after they recognize dial tone, which cellular does not provide.

Two vendors, Microcom with its MNP-10 protocol and Paradyne with its enhanced throughput cellular (ETC) protocol, provide methods for addressing the problems. The MNP-10 protocol starts that handshake with the session receiver at 1200 b/s to negotiate the connection. The protocol then gradually increases the transmission speed to reach the point of maximum throughput. ETC takes the opposite approach. It starts at a higher speed and reduces if necessary. This method of communication is shown in Figure 19-3 along with CDPD.

Cellular is a good alternative for occasional use and mobile file transfer, but it is expensive for short messages. Most cellular operators levy a 1-min/call minimum charge, which may mean paying 30 to 50 cents for a transaction that takes only a few seconds. Also, the setup time is long compared to other alternatives. Cellular has the advantage of good coverage. In general, its applications are similar to those of the PSTN—it is good for facsimile and file transfers but poor for short, bursty messages.

Cellular Digital Packet Data (CDPD)

A major advantage of cellular is coverage, which makes CDPD an attractive alternative. CDPD is a packet-switched data service that rides on top of cellular, and uses idle analog channel time. It can be added to existing cell sites at a moderate cost. Charging is by the packet or kilobyte instead of by the minute, and the long call setup time is eliminated. This makes it good for short bursty messages such as point-of-sale, dispatch, package tracking, telemetry, and e-mail. CDPD is available in most metropolitan areas.

CDPD operates at 19.2 kb/s, using a TCP/IP type of protocol, which raises the problem of IP addressing because the subnet is mobile. To be entirely effective for some applications, a laptop user should be able to disconnect from the LAN, travel to another location while remaining in contact with the network through a wireless connection, reconnect to the LAN at the distant location, and become part of the network again. The process is possible today, but the user needs to understand how to do it. Therefore, it is not yet feasible for the true mobile laptop or PDA application.

To implement CDPD, carriers install mobile data base stations (MDBS) which retrieve packets from the wireless network, and a mobile data intermediate system (MDIS) which routes them. The subscriber device is a modem and radio. Frames are picked up by the MDBS and handed off to the MDIS. Mobile stations use a protocol called digital sense multiple access with collision detection (DSMA/CD) for access to the network. The access method is similar to Ethernet's CSMA/CD. A station wishing to transmit listens to the outbound channel to determine if a carrier is present. If not, it transmits a packet. If so, it backs off and attempts a short time later.

The main advantage of CDPD is the coverage it can offer. The main population areas of the country are well covered for cellular, and if the carrier elects to overbuild the network with CDPD, data coverage can be equivalent. It is good for short, bursty applications, but for lengthy file transfers, dial-up application over regular cellular may be less costly.

A key question to ask in setting up CDPD is what protocol to use. TCP/IP is logical, and the carriers are generally prepared to provide IP addresses. While TCP/IP is an excellent protocol for wired services, however, it isn't optimized for mobile use, particularly where a per-packet charge applies. Frequent acknowledgment packets are returned by TCP/IP, and although these are short, unless the charge is byte-oriented instead of packet-oriented, as much as one-third of the cost of a session may be taken up with acknowledgment packets. The TCP/IP protocol provides the user datagram protocol (UDP), which is a connectionless protocol, but it isn't generally robust enough for an application where the loss of link is probable. The hazards of mobile and portable communications make dropped and out-of-sequence packets likely.

Roaming may be a problem with CDPD. Unless the carrier has equipped all cell sites with CDPD, which may not always be the case, the coverage may be narrower than regular cellular. Also, roaming to nonaffiliated areas can be a problem, ranging from lack of service to lack of an interconnection agreement.

Private Packet Carrier

Private packet radio carriers serve some metropolitan areas. These services can be a good way to handle mobile and portable data, except that the service is not

FIGURE 19-4

Local Multipoint Distribution Service Architecture

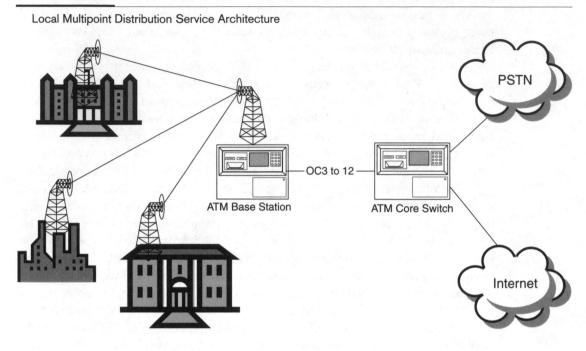

generally available everywhere. Where it is available, the coverage range may not match cellular or CDPD. The same factors must be considered in evaluating these carriers as in evaluating CDPD.

THE WIRELESS LOCAL LOOP

Incumbent LECs have a tremendous advantage—their lock on the local loop—that makes it difficult for CLECs to penetrate their territory. Their copper facilities to virtually every residence and business in the developed world are a tremendous resource that has taken decades to build, and would cost billions to replace. Into this market comes the wireless local loop (WLL), which is intended to deliver voice and data services without wire. Cost is a big motivator. While wireline local loops may cost more than $1000 per subscriber, the wireless loop costs perhaps one-third to one-half as much, and scales more readily as subscribers are added.

Despite the advantages, WLL has not taken off as its developers have hoped. One reason is the lack of common, readily available frequency spectrum that can be used in any country. Another is the lack of standards. To date, the systems are proprietary, which limits interoperability. These factors have resulted in limited production of equipment, which in turn has kept prices relatively high.

Local Multipoint Distribution Services (LMDS)

In 1998 the FCC auctioned 1.3 GHz of spectrum at 28 GHz to WLL providers. LMDS is a point-to-multipoint service where the service provider locates a hub in the center of a serving area. Subscribers are equipped with antennas and transceivers and feed data into the pipeline using an ATM-like protocol. The services range from one DS-1 to one DS-3. Figure 19-4 shows the architecture of a typical LMDS network.

RADIO PAGING

Paging is a radio application that is less sophisticated and less costly than cellular radio, but it is growing at a fast pace. Developed under the centralized transmitter and receiver plan of conventional mobile telephone service, one variety of radio paging offers dial access from a wireline telephone to a pocket receiver. The readout is a beeping sound or vibration to alert the user to an incoming message. Digital pagers allow the caller to send a callback number or numeric message to a digital readout.

Several interesting advances have been made in radio paging in the past few years. One useful feature is alphanumeric paging, in which the caller can send a text message in place of the alternative, which is either beeping the user or sending a numeric message such as a callback number. To activate alphanumeric paging the caller must have a keyboard. The message is keyed in, and it displays on the pager readout. Pagers are available with one or more readout lines. By pressing a button, the user scrolls the message in serial fashion across the readout if it is too long to fit in a single screen. Alphanumeric paging can reduce the number of cellular phone messages at a significantly lower cost. The main drawback is the need to have a keyboard and modem available to send the message. If only a DTMF telephone is available, the pager can operate in a numerical paging mode.

Alphanumeric paging is made easier with a paging server, which can be operated off a LAN. Any user on the network can access the server, send the message to it, and the server outdials to the paging system. Features available include sending messages to e-mail, screening calls, and outdialing messages from only selected stations.

Another recent innovation is answerback paging. When a message has been received, the recipient answers by pressing a button on the pager and the pager sends an acknowledgment to the sender. Because of the small size of the pager, its transmit power is low, so the service provider must have a network of receivers throughout the coverage area. Some pagers enable the user to send messages to other one- and two-way pagers, fax machines, and Internet e-mail. Combined with devices such as the personal information manager, the two-way pager can be a compact device for keeping in touch.

APPLICATIONS

Wireless is not a universal replacement for wired voice or LAN service. At the present time, the service is expensive enough to discourage all but those who have a genuine need for wireless service. Payoff can be realized in businesses such as hospitals where nurses and physicians need to be in constant contact, yet cannot be tied to a telephone. Paging can fulfill some of these needs, but some can be handled only by two-way radio.

Standards

In the United States, the FCC rules and regulations set forth wireless, PCS, and mobile data standards. FCC rules establish the authorized frequencies, power levels, bandwidth, frequency stability, signaling formats, and other such variables. A consortium of major cellular carriers established CDPD standards.

The principal wireless LAN standard is IEEE's 802.11 protocol. Even with compliance to this standard, however, users need to be wary of interoperability because the standard specifies three incompatible physical layers. In addition, the Wireless LAN Interoperability Forum developed a wireless LAN standard known as OpenAir. It is not compatible with 802.11, nor has it been adopted by any international standards organizations even though several manufacturers support it.

Evaluating Wireless Voice

This section deals with evaluation criteria for wireless voice and data. The following criteria should be considered in evaluating products.

Number of Simultaneous Calls   Within an area in the building, how many calls can be carried at once?

Frequency Band   Determine the frequency band in which the system works. Early products use the 900-MHz ISM band, which is nonexclusive to wireless and may result in interference problems. Products that operate adjacent to the PCS band are more desirable.

Coverage   Determine the coverage area of wireless cells. How well does the signal penetrate walls? Can users roam from one cell to another? The narrower the coverage range, the more cells that will be required to cover a building or campus. Evaluate coverage between floors in buildings, such as hospitals, that may have a great deal of concrete and steel in their structure. Cells with less coverage may enable more consistent reuse of the available channels since the same frequencies can be reused in a different part of the building.

Station Sets   Analog station sets are universal and connect to any analog port on any telephone system. Proprietary sets connect to proprietary ports, and offer the advantage of button access to features. Determine what features are available and whether they match the organization's needs. Determine the talk and standby time of the batteries.

Integration   How well does the system integrate into your telephone system? Are proprietary phone sets available? Are multiline sets available? Does the display show the same information that a wired set does?

Evaluating Wireless Data

The nature of the application is the first criterion to use in selecting wireless data. Is the application building-to-building, desktop, or mobile/portable? If the latter, what area must be covered? Is coverage required for e-mail or other types of messaging, calendar synchronization, file transfer, point-of-sale, or other applications? If the application is building-to-building, what bandwidth is required? Is the distance far enough or are the weather conditions, such as fog, frequent enough that interruption of infrared is likely?

Range   What is the geographical area the application must cover? Does the product have the range to allow users to roam within the required area?

Service Availability   For mobile/portable applications, what alternatives are available locally? Does CDPD cover the required area? Do specialized carriers offer packet radio? What do the various services cost?

Speed   Can the application live with the limited throughput of an 802.11 LAN? If not, are high-speed alternatives available?

Security   Can the data be intercepted easily? Is it critical? If so, is encryption available?

Robustness   How well does the system handle signal dropouts, fades, interference, and other such irregularities? How well does it handle long frames? How does it recover from interruptions? If it is interrupted in the middle of a file transfer, is it necessary to start over from the beginning? What kind of speed is available? Does it automatically adjust to optimize throughput?

Vendor Support   How many vendors are able to support the application in the local area? Do they have experience with wireless data? Be sure to check references.

Mobility   Can users move from one LAN segment to another and be automatically reregistered?

Evaluating Paging Equipment

Many of the same criteria, such as coverage and vendor service, apply for evaluating paging as listed earlier for evaluating cellular equipment. The first question is what type of service to acquire. The market offers signal-only, numeric display, alphanumeric display, and two-way paging. The coverage areas range from local to regional to national, with the cost increasing as the service area increases. The following are some factors to consider.

One-Way or Two-Way　Now that two-way paging is available, the question of whether the page was received or not can be answered.

Numeric Only or Alphanumeric　An alphanumeric pager is capable of receiving complete messages versus a numeric pager, which receives only numbers. An alphanumeric pager becomes, in effect, a mobile data receiver.

Message Capacity　How many characters of text message can be displayed? Is it easy to scroll through a multiscreen message?

Signaling Method　Most pagers have the option of vibrating to receive pages silently. All pagers have audible signal capability.

Application Program Capability　Many pagers come equipped with application programs that support signaling over the Internet and connecting to devices for alarm reporting.

Coverage Area　Does the pager cover the required area? How reliable is the reception in the fringes?

CHAPTER 20

Video Systems

Two telecommunications media serve most homes and businesses in the developed world today: telephone and television. Historically, telephone has entered buildings on wire and video over the airwaves, but that is changing. A significant percentage of urban residences are wired for cable, if for no other reason than the limited entertainment choices available on broadcast television. Cable provides at least 500 MHz of bandwidth, which is enough for plenty of entertainment choices plus room for other services such as telephone and Internet access. AT&T, with its purchases of Teleport Communications Group (TCG) and Telecommunications Inc. (TCI), has announced its intention to combine TCI's cable with TCG's telephone service and its own expertise to deliver a full range of services over cable. And that is just the beginning. The video infrastructure is limited, as we will discuss in this chapter, but as it is rebuilt with fiber optics, the availability of a broadband channel into millions of households offers an impressive potential for future services.

Video itself is poised for some interesting changes as high-definition television (HDTV) begins to test the market. Until the arrival of HDTV, television had changed little over the years. Color was added to the monochromatic signal in the late 1950s, and the quality of television equipment improved dramatically while the price dropped, but analog video today is technically the same as it was at its commercial inception. HDTV will change that, but how quickly the public will accept it will not be known until the prices drop. Meanwhile, inexpensive direct broadcast satellite television offers an alternative to cable, and wireless distribution systems may eliminate the need to wire neighborhoods for telephone.

Cable television (CATV) has been available for more than half a century. Today it is a major source of entertainment for millions of people, but its services aren't limited to traditional movies and television programs. Cable can deliver one-way services such as home shopping, news sources, educational services, stock market reports, and games, but to become a full-fledged entertainment and information medium, cable has to evolve. Most residential systems are incapable of two-way service, which is necessary if subscribers are to communicate with the information source. The bandwidth requirements are greater in the downstream or headend–to–subscriber direction than upstream, but upstream communication is essential, and requires extensive rebuilding of most CATV systems.

While entertainment is the prevalent use of video today, videoconferencing is an important facility for businesses. Distance learning for schools and telemedicine for healthcare organizations are emerging applications. As with most newer technologies, the key to expansion has been the development of standards. For years, the videoconferencing manufacturers produced equipment with proprietary standards, which meant they could not interoperate. Then, ITU-T passed H.320 standards that enabled manufacturers to design equipment that could interoperate over dial-up or dedicated digital facilities. Meanwhile, developers were working on equipment that could operate over packet networks, starting with LANs at the desktop and operating over IP or frame relay networks. This equipment too was proprietary at first, but H.323 standards, which are discussed in Chapter 38, enable video communication across a variety of networks.

While videoconferencing is costly and rare today, in the future it can be expected to become the normal way of communicating. The Picturephone, which AT&T introduced in 1964, failed to attract enough interest to make it a commercially successful product at the time. Like many other product developments, however, it was merely ahead of its time. Conferencing equipment built into desktop computers will soon be a regular feature in most companies and many homes. When digital bandwidth to the home and small business becomes readily available and economical, video telephone calls will be the accepted way of communicating.

VIDEO TECHNOLOGY

At its present state of development, video is inherently an analog transmission medium because of the method of picture generation. Video signals in North America are generated under the National Television Systems Committee (NTSC) system. In Europe they are generated under two different and incompatible standards: phase alternate line (PAL) and sequential couleur avec memoire (SECAM). A video signal is formed by scanning an image with a video camera. As the camera scans the image, it creates an analog signal that varies in voltage with variations in the degree of blackness of the image. In the NTSC system, the television *raster* has 525 horizontal scans. The raster is composed of two fields of 262.5 lines each. The two fields are interlaced to form a *frame,* as Figure 20-1 shows. The frame repeats 30 times each second; the persistence of the human eye eliminates flicker. Since the two fields are interlaced, the screen is refreshed 60 times per second.

On close inspection, a video screen is revealed as a matrix of tiny dots. Each dot is called a *picture element,* abbreviated as *pixel.* The resolution of a television picture is a function of the number of scan lines and pixels per frame, both of which

FIGURE 20-1

Interlaced Video Frame

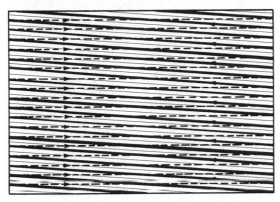

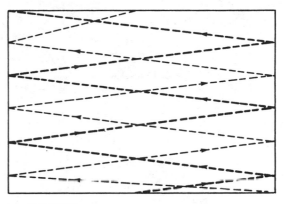

Active Fields
Heavy lines represent first field.
Light lines represent second field.
Dotted lines represent retrace lines
that are blanked out.

Inactive Fields
Heavy lines show retrace pattern from
bottom to top of screen during vertical
blanking interval. Heavy lines represent
first field and light lines the second.

affect the amount of bandwidth required to transmit a television signal. The NTSC system requires 4.2 MHz of bandwidth for satisfactory resolution. Because of the modulation system used and the need for guard bands between channels, the FCC assigns 6 MHz of bandwidth to television channels in the United States.

The signal resulting from each scan line varies between a black and a white voltage level, as Figure 20-2*a* shows. A horizontal synchronizing pulse is inserted at the beginning of each line. Frames are synchronized with vertical pulses, as Figure 20-2*b* shows. Between frames the signal is blanked during a vertical synchronizing interval to allow the scanning trace to return to the upper left corner of the screen. Teletext services transmit information during this interval, which is known as the *vertical blanking interval.*

A color television signal has two parts: the *luminance signal* and the *chrominance signal.* A black-and-white picture has only the luminance signal, which controls the brightness of the screen in step with the sweep of the horizontal trace. The chrominance signal modulates subcarriers that are transmitted with the video signal. The color demodulator in the receiver is synchronized by a *color burst* consisting of eight cycles of a 3.58-MHz signal that is applied to the horizontal synchronizing pulse, as Figure 20-2*a* shows.

When no picture is being transmitted, the scanning voltage rests at the black level, and the television receiver's screen is black. Because the signal is an amplitude-modulated analog, any noise pulses that are higher in level than the black signal level appear on the screen as snow. A high-quality transmission medium keeps the signal level above the noise to preserve satisfactory picture quality. The degree of resolution in a television picture depends on bandwidth. Signals sent through a

FIGURE 20-2

Synchronizing and Blanking in a Television Signal

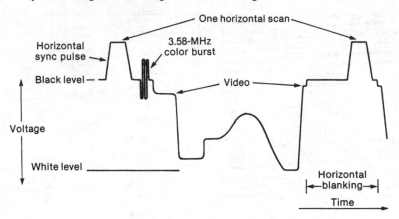

a. Voltage levels during one horizontal scan. As image is scanned, voltage varies
from reference black to reference white level.

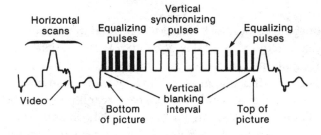

b. Vertical synchronization. Vertical blanking occurs during retrace of scanner
to top of screen.

narrow bandwidth are fuzzy with washed-out color. The channel also must be sufficiently linear. Lack of linearity results in high-level signals being amplified at a
different rate than low-level signals, which affects picture contrast. Another critical requirement of the transmission medium is its envelope delay characteristic. If
envelope delay is excessive, the chrominance signal arrives at the receiver out of
phase with the luminance signal, and color distortion results.

The four primary criteria for assessing a video transmission medium, therefore, are noise, bandwidth, amplitude linearity, and phase linearity. The primary
media used for analog video are analog microwave radio, analog coaxial cable, and,
for broadcasting, free space. Analog signals also can be transmitted over fiber optics using intensity modulation, or frequency modulation of a light carrier. Analog
signals can be carried for a limited distance over category 5 UTP by the use of video
baluns. Digital video signals can be transmitted over coaxial cable or twisted-pair
wire, as well as being broadcast, but fiber optics is the preferred medium.

FIGURE 20-3

Diagram of a CATV System

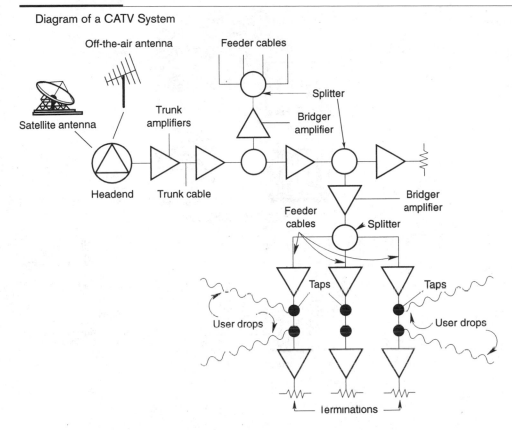

CABLE TELEVISION SYSTEMS

Cable television systems have three major components: headend equipment, trunk cable, and feeder and user drop equipment. Figure 20-3 is a block diagram of a CATV system. A characteristic of CATV systems is a lack of selectivity for the end user. All channels that originate at the headend are broadcast to all stations, which means the operator must either limit the number of channels carried or block premium channels for which the user is not paying. Except for various devices to prevent unauthorized reception of pay television signals, any receiver can receive all services on the network. This is in contrast to the telephone network, which routes lines in a star configuration to each user individually.

Headend Equipment

Headend equipment, as Figure 20-4 shows, receives and generates video signals and, in two-way systems, repeats the signal from the user on the upstream channels to

FIGURE 20-4

Headend Equipment

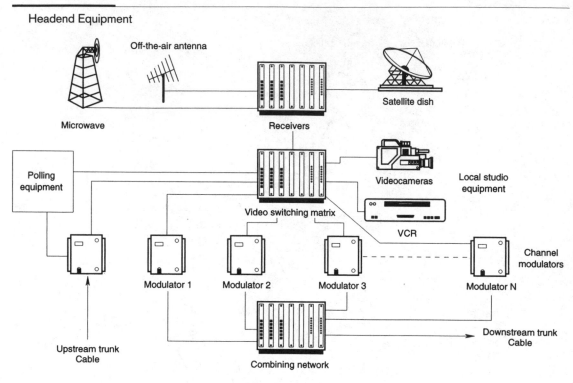

terminals on the downstream channels. Signals from the following sources are inserted at the headend:

- Off-the-air pickup of broadcast signals, including both television and FM radio
- Signals received over communications satellites
- Signals received from distant locations over fiber optics or microwave radio-relay systems
- Locally originated signals

The headend equipment modulates each television signal to a separate channel in the range of 50 to 500 MHz. Some companies use narrower bandwidth systems, but current systems support up to 80 channels over this frequency range, as Figure 20-5 shows. Some systems support a bandwidth of as much as 1 GHz. UHF television channels are remodulated into another channel within the passband. Most CATV systems use a single coaxial cable to carry signals, but some systems double their capacity by using two cables. Amplifiers and cable facilities are duplicated in a two-cable system.

FIGURE 20-5

Cable Television Frequency Bands

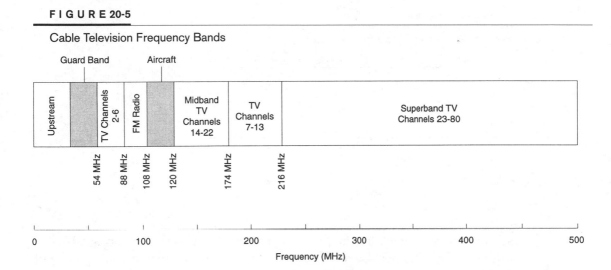

Trunk Cable Systems

Headend equipment applies the signal to a trunk to carry the signal to local distribution systems. Some systems use hub headends to distribute the signal. *Hub headends* are satellites of a master headend and have the ability to add or distribute services before sending the signal through the local feeder area. The cable between the master headend and the hubs is called a *supertrunk.* Hubs may be fed by point-to-point microwave radio operating in a band designated by the FCC as Cable Television Relay Service. Increasingly, CATV companies use fiber optics for trunks and distribute the signal to users over either coaxial cable or fiber optics.

Early CATV systems used a separate amplifier for each television channel. This technique simplified the amplifier design, but restricted the practical number of channels that could be transported. Current systems use broadband amplifiers that are equalized to carry the entire bandwidth. Amplifiers have about 20 dB of gain and are placed at intervals of approximately 500 m. Amplifiers known as *bridgers* split the signal to feeder cables.

Amplifiers contain automatic gain-control circuitry to adjust gain as cable loss changes with temperature variations. Power is applied to amplifiers over the coaxial center conductor, with main power feed points approximately every 1.5 km. Many subscribers use CATV systems for home security and alarm systems so continued operation during power outages is essential. To continue essential services during power outages and amplifier failures, the cable operator provides redundant amplifiers and backup battery supplies.

Trunk cable uses a high grade of coaxial cable with diameters of 1.9 to 2.5 cm (0.75 to 1 in). The cable often shares pole lines and trenches with power and telephone. The cable and amplifiers must be free of signal leakage. Because the CATV

FIGURE 20-6

Two-Way Cable Frequency Splitting

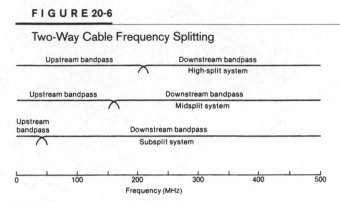

signals operate on the same frequencies as many radio services, a leaking cable can interfere with another service or vice versa. FCC regulations curtail the use of CATV in frequency bands of 108 to 136 and 225 to 400 MHz in many localities because of the possibility of interference with aeronautical navigation and communication equipment.

As with other analog transmission media, noise and distortion are cumulative through successive amplifier stages. Noise and distortion limit the serving radius of 80-channel CATV to about 8 km from the headend.

Feeder and Drop System

Bridger amplifiers split feeder or distribution cable from the trunk cable. Multiple feeders are coupled with *splitters* or *directional couplers*, which match the impedance of the cables. The feeder cable is smaller and less expensive and has higher loss than trunk cable. Subscriber drops connect to the feeder cable through *taps*, which are passive devices that isolate the feeder cable from the drop. The tap must have enough isolation that shorts and opens at the television set do not affect other signals on the cable.

Two-Way CATV Systems

Two-way communication is available on some CATV systems, but many systems do not provide enough upstream bandwidth to make them an effective alternative for two-way service. The key to a two-way system is bidirectional amplifiers. Filters split the signal into the high band for downstream transmission and the low band for upstream transmission. Figure 20-6 shows three splitting methods. The subsplit is the most common in CATV systems, with the midsplit and high-split methods often used in broadband local area networks. A guard band 15 to 20 MHz wide separates the two directions of transmission. The upstream direction shares frequencies with high-powered short-wave transmitters operating on 5- to 30-MHz frequencies, so interference from these sources is a potential problem. Cable and amplifiers must be adequately shielded to prevent interference.

Headend equipment is more complex in a two-way than in a one-way CATV system. User terminals access the upstream cable by contention or token passing or by being polled from the headend. The headend of a two-way system contains a computer to poll the terminals. Some systems use a transponder at the user end to receive and execute orders from the headend. For example, a polling message might instruct the transponder to read utility meters and forward the reading over the upstream channel.

VIDEO COMPRESSION

Analog video is an inexpensive and effective method of transmission, but it is wasteful of bandwidth. A video signal contains considerable redundancy. Often large portions of background do not change between frames, but conventional transmission systems transmit these anyway. Removing redundancy in an analog signal is difficult, but digital signal processing can compress a video signal into a reasonably narrow bandwidth. If a 4.2-MHz NTSC video signal is digitized with PCM, it requires a bandwidth of approximately 90 MHz. This signal can be compressed to occupy as little as 64 kb/s with today's technology, but the result falls short, even for videoconferences. At least T1 bandwidth is needed for a satisfactory signal that is approximately equal to the quality of a home VCR and at least two 64-kb/s channels are needed for minimally acceptable videoconferencing. Excellent quality, suitable for all but the most demanding conference applications, can be obtained on 512 kb/s, but most videoconferences settle on 384 kb/s, or six channels, as a reasonable balance between quality and cost.

Three public standards have been published for video compression. ITU's H.261 is intended for videoconferencing, and is discussed later in more detail. MPEG-1 and MPEG-2 are intended for broadcast or narrowcast video. MPEG is an abbreviation for Motion Picture Experts Group, which is the body that developed the standards. MPEG-1 compresses a video signal into bandwidths of up to 2 Mb/s. The resolution is 288 lines/frame, which is home VCR quality. It is satisfactory for most home use if the scene doesn't have too much action. MPEG-2 compresses a high-definition television (HDTV) signal, which normally would require 25 MHz of analog bandwidth, into the 6-MHz channel allocated to broadcast television.

Video compression is achieved by eliminating redundancy and by predictive coding. The equipment that encodes and decodes the video signal is called a *codec*. Flicking by at 30 frames per second, much in a moving picture doesn't change from frame to frame. *Interframe encoding* recognizes when portions of a frame remain constant, and transmits only the changed portions. *Intraframe encoding* provides another element of compression. The picture is broken into blocks of 16 × 16 pixels.

A block is transmitted only when pixels within that block have changed. Otherwise, the decoding equipment retains the previous block and forwards it to the receiver with each frame. *Predictive coding* analyzes the elements that are changing, and predicts what the next frame will be. If the transmitting and receiving codecs both use the same prediction algorithm, only changes from the prediction must be transmitted, not the complete frame. Approximately every 2 seconds, the entire frame is refreshed, but in intervening frames, only the changed pixels are transmitted.

Encoding systems are known as *lossless* or *lossy*. A lossless coding system transmits information in a manner that can be restored bit for bit. Run length encoding, used by facsimile, is a good example. If a scan line or series of lines contain a long run of zeros (white) or ones (black), it is necessary to transmit only a short message telling the receiver how many zeros or ones to insert. If the message is shorter than the original string, compression results. This method of encoding is widely used by both data and video systems.

A lossy encoding system discards information, transmitting only enough to retain intelligibility, but not enough to ensure the integrity of the received signal. Lossy systems work well for sending still scenes, but motion can cause a tiling or smearing effect as the receiving codec attempts to catch up with the transmitter. The higher the compression and the more vigorous the motion, the greater is the smearing effect. More bandwidth improves the signal quality.

VIDEOCONFERENCING

Videoconferencing can add quality to a meeting. For the cost of the telephone connection, people from locations too far away to justify the cost of travel can participate and video adds a presence that just isn't possible with a telephone conference. The cost of videoconferencing equipment is dropping, to the point that a decent unit costs about the same amount as a round-trip between the United States and Europe on the Concorde. It isn't necessary to purchase the equipment for occasional conferences. Many businesses offer videoconference facilities as a utility, leasing conference rooms and full video facilities. The cost is still substantially more than an audio conference, but it is much less than travel.

A videoconference facility has the following subsystems integrated into a unit:

- ◆ Video codec
- ◆ Audio equipment
- ◆ Video production and control equipment
- ◆ Graphics equipment
- ◆ Document hard-copy equipment
- ◆ Communications

A full description of these systems is beyond the scope of this book. We will discuss them here briefly to describe the composition of a videoconferencing facility.

Video Codec

Codec is a contraction of the term coder-decoder. It is the equipment that converts the analog video signal to digital and compresses it for transmission. At the distant end the process is reversed. Codecs must support H.261 to ensure interoperability with equipment from different manufacturers. They may also support a proprietary protocol for communication with like equipment. Proprietary codecs often have better quality and features that are missing from ITU-T standards.

Audio Equipment

Most analysts believe that audio equipment is the most important part of a videoconference facility. In large videoconferences it is often impossible to show all participants, but it is important that everyone hear and be heard clearly. Audio equipment consists of microphones, speakers, and amplifiers placed strategically around the room. Sometimes speaker telephones are used, but with generally less satisfactory results than the audio produced by the codec. The codec robs a portion of the bandwidth to transmit the audio, so some products allow the operator to reduce the amount of audio bandwidth as a way of improving the video.

Video and Control Equipment

Video equipment consists of two or three cameras and associated control equipment. The main camera usually is mounted at the front of the room and often automatically follows the voice of the speaker. Zoom, tilt, and azimuth controls are mounted on a console, where the conference participants can control them from a panel with a joystick. A second camera mounts overhead for graphic displays. The facility sometimes includes a third mobile camera that is operated independently. A switch at the console operator's position selects the camera. Monitors placed around the room can easily be seen by the participants. Usually one monitor shows the picture from the distant end and another shows the picture at the near end. In single-monitor conferences the near end can usually be viewed in a window using the monitor's picture-in-picture feature.

In a videoconference selecting the camera position can minimize the adverse effects of smearing. When the camera is positioned to encompass a passive group, smearing is generally not objectionable. It is most objectionable when there is considerable action or when the camera shows a close-up of the face of an individual who is talking.

Digitizing and encoding equipment compress full-motion video or create freeze-frames. In addition, encryption equipment may be included for security. Other equipment can freeze a full-motion display for a few seconds while the participants send a graphic image over the circuit. Sometimes digital storage equipment enables participants to transmit presentation material ahead of time so graphics transmission does not waste conference time.

Graphics Equipment

Videoconference facilities may include graphics-generating equipment to construct diagrams. Some systems provide for desktop computer input so that tools in the computer can be used for generating graphics.

Communications

Digital communications facilities are required for videoconferences. ISDN is an ideal medium. Its two 64-kb/s B channels and separate signaling channel provide enough bandwidth for an acceptable conference. BRI channels can be obtained directly from the LEC or through a PBX that has PRI connections to the LEC or IXC. If additional bandwidth is needed, some PBXs provide $N \times 64$ capability, which provides as much bandwidth as needed up to full T1. If $N \times 64$ capability is not available in the PBX, a device known as an *inverse multiplexer* can be used to aggregate the bandwidth. An inverse multiplexer accepts multiple digital input channels and combines them into a higher-speed bit stream. Videoconferences can also be conducted over switched 56-kb/s service, dedicated digital facilities, or over a packet network using H.323 protocol, as discussed later.

Justification for Videoconferencing Equipment

Videoconferencing is now becoming economically feasible—not just to reduce travel but as a way of doing business. Interest in videoconferencing is surging because costs are continuing to drop. Coder/decoders (codecs) that cost more than $100,000 in the mid-1980s are now available for a fraction of that amount, and prices will undoubtedly continue to drop as the demand increases.

Complementing the drop in codec costs are reductions in the costs of transmission and equipping conference rooms. Most LECs and the major IXCs offer switched 56/64-kb/s services, and ISDN is now available in most parts of the country. The interexchange portion of switched 56-kb/s and ISDN service is only marginally more expensive than ordinary direct-dialed telephone service. It requires a dedicated loop to either the LEC or the IXC, which adds to the fixed cost of the service, but it is still only a fraction of what it cost a few years ago.

Portable conference room facilities, consisting of audio equipment, codec, monitor, and a camera with pan, tilt, and zoom can be purchased for between $7000 and $25,000, depending on manufacturer and features. Although this is still too high to be within the reach of casual users, it is less than one-half the price of a few years ago and will undoubtedly drop further as demand increases.

ITU-T H.320 Standards

A major factor that facilitates videoconferencing is the ITU-T H.320 standards. The following standards fall under the H.320 umbrella:

◆ *G.711, G.722, and G.728 audio compression.* These standards define audio compression at bandwidths of 3.0 to 7 kHz. G.728 recommends a method of compressing 3-kHz audio into 16 kb/s. G.711 is a toll-quality audio standard. G.722 is a higher-fidelity audio standard than G.711.

◆ *H.221 data formatting and framing.* This standard outlines how bits are identified as video, audio, and control, and how they are fitted into frames.

◆ *H.230 control and indication information.* This standard defines commands for control and diagnostics.

◆ *H.233 transmission confidentiality.* This standard outlines methods for handling encrypted data.

◆ *H.242 transmission protocols.* This standard outlines call setup, transfer, and disconnect procedures.

◆ *H.243 multipoint handshake.* This standard defines communications between the codec and a multipoint control unit.

◆ *H.261 syntax and semantics of the video bit stream.* This standard defines the video coding algorithms and recommends the picture format.

◆ *H.32P video telephone standards.* These provisional standards recommend methods of videoconferencing over analog telephone lines.

Before the standards were developed, codec manufacturers used proprietary standards, which meant that they could communicate only with codecs of the same manufacturer. All codec manufacturers still have proprietary standards that, in most cases, are superior to H.261, but H.261 provides a fall-back that allows otherwise incompatible systems to communicate.

ITU-T standards are known as $P \times 64$ (pronounced P times 64). Two options are offered. The full common intermediate format (CIF) offers frames of 288 lines by 352 pixels. This is approximately one-half the resolution of commercial television, which is 525 lines by 480 pixels. The second alternative is one-fourth CIF, which is 144 lines by 176 pixels. The modulation method is the discreet cosine transform (DCT) algorithm. The amount of bandwidth supplied in the transmission facilities must be in multiples of 64 kb/s. Several proprietary algorithms on the market yield better quality, but as with many other ITU-T standards, the standardization process takes so long that it is difficult for standards to keep pace with advances in technology.

ITU-T H.323 Standards

Videoconferencing is handicapped by the inflexibility of different media for carrying the signal. Videoconferencing through the PBX has never gained acceptance for several reasons. The PBX must support basic rate ISDN for internal communications, and primary rate for external communications. The user has the choice of using three BRIs from the LEC to carry a 384-kb/s conference, but the result is usually underutilized facilities that sit idle for most of the time since they can't easily be used for something else. In addition, many of the LECs and IXCs charge a premium for ISDN trunking, which tends to discourage its use. The IXCs also charge a premium for a digital switched circuit, even though their entire network is digital anyway.

All of this tends to discourage the use of ISDN for videoconferencing. For companies that must communicate with multiple points, ISDN is still the preferred medium. For point-to-point communications, most companies have another alternative, which is to use their frame relay or IP intranet. Until recently, the equipment for videoconferencing over these facilities was developmental, but in 1996 ITU-T passed the H.323 standards, which support time-sensitive applications such as video and voice over packet networks. Chapter 38 explains H.323 in more detail.

For videoconferencing within a private network, the beauty of H.323 is its simplicity once it is set up and working. The standard RJ-45 Ethernet jack is ubiquitous, and can accept video without concern about how many channels are needed. A rollout video unit can be hooked to any jack just like a laptop computer—provided someone has done the hard work of setting IP addresses and configuring the equipment. The difficulty should not be underestimated at this stage of development. Interoperability among routers, codecs, gateways, and other equipment is far from assured, but users can count on it getting better as the standard shakes out.

One of the driving applications is desktop videoconferencing. The equipment is contained in a standard desktop computer that has a small video camera mounted on top of the monitor. The conferencing equipment is mounted on a board that plugs into a computer expansion slot, or it is an external box that plugs into a board in the computer. The computer plugs into a network that must be designed for the load that videoconferencing imposes. Since videoconferencing is full duplex, and since Ethernet is half duplex in most of its configurations, a videoconference can exercise even fast Ethernet to its limits. Therefore, the network must be built to support the load. Within the local network, LAN switches are an effective way of distributing the load.

The result is an economical method of conducting a personal videoconference. Conferences are spontaneous, with no need to schedule a conference room. The addition of a picture to the call allows the parties to pick up the nonverbal content of a session by seeing expressions. The screen is generally too small and the camera angle too narrow for group conferences, but for one-to-one conferences it is excellent. Most products permit the users to share and view computer files over the network. When desktop video equipment is widely accepted, as it is likely to be over the next few years, it will be an effective tool for enhancing the quality of telephone calls and for enabling users to collaborate on files.

F I G U R E 20-7

H.323 Video Network

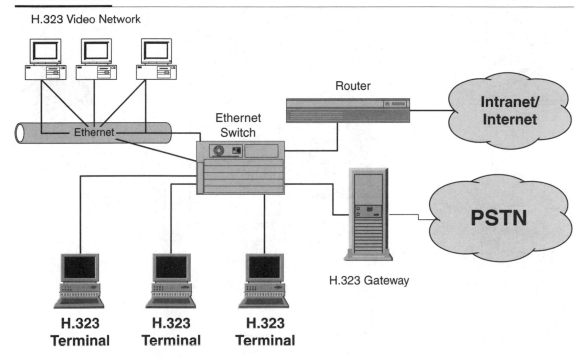

In the wide area, H.323 video can be launched through a router that has the capacity to handle the packet stream. Beyond a point, packets cannot be delayed or discarded without adversely affecting quality. Therefore, the network must be robust enough to handle the load. Frame relay is more predictable and has less overhead than IP, and therefore is the preferred medium for video, provided the committed information rate is set high enough. Private intranets running IP have higher overhead than frame relay, and are less predictable. Quality is not likely to be as high, but provided enough bandwidth is available, it should be acceptable. At this point, the Internet is too unpredictable to be usable for videoconferencing, although it may be usable for real-time applications such as enabling callers into a call center from the Internet to see and talk to an agent. Figure 20-7 illustrates the configuration of an H.323 network. The H.323-compliant terminals can carry on a videoconference across the switched Ethernet. They can conference across the PSTN through a gateway, or across an IP or frame relay intranet.

Although many H.323 products are available on the market, interoperability is likely to be a problem. Moreover, many of the features of H.320 video are not available on H.323 except as proprietary applications. For example, control of the remote end camera is not readily available. Wideband audio may be available only

F I G U R E 20-8

Video on Demand

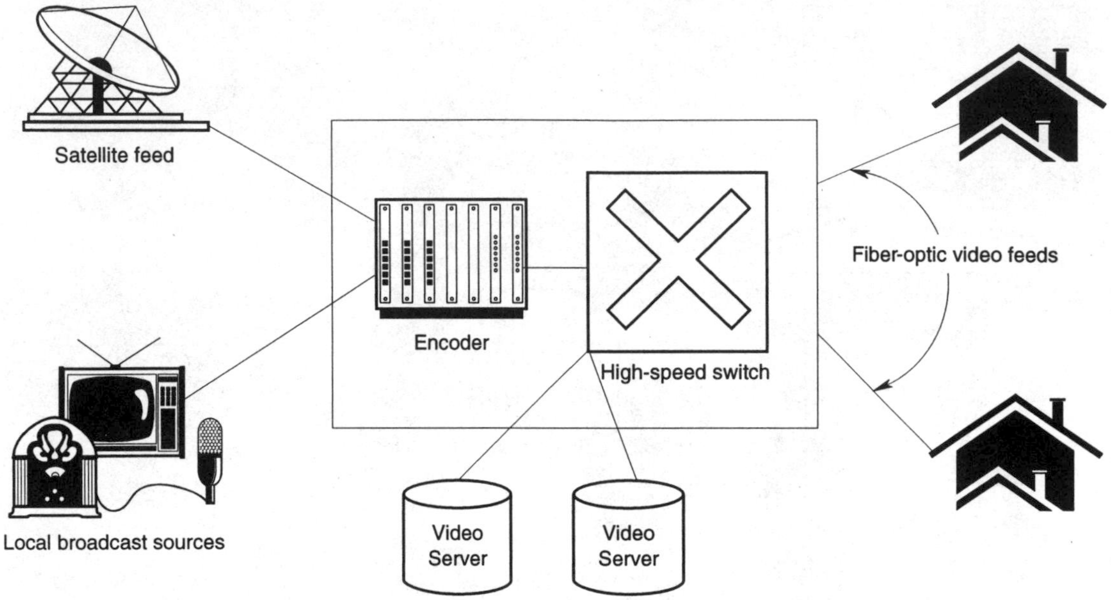

as a proprietary feature. H.323 video is about 10 years behind H.320, and needs considerable development to catch up.

DIGITAL TELEVISION

The future of analog television is limited. Although there is plenty of bandwidth in the UHF bands, the VHF bands, which offer the best coverage, are crowded. With MPEG-1 technology, as many as four compressed channels can be broadcast in the same frequency spectrum as one analog channel. Digital television can be delivered by satellite, broadcast over the airwaves, or terrestrial media such as fiber optics or asymmetric digital subscriber line (ADSL), a technology we will discuss in Chapter 32. Digital television brings the benefits that it has brought to voice: improved signal quality, reduced equipment costs, and more effective switching and multiplexing methods.

Video on Demand

A driving factor for digital television is video on demand (VOD). Today's CATV systems deliver all channels to every residence, and unwanted or unauthorized channels must be trapped out or scrambled. VOD as a concept refers to a broad spectrum of services that are delivered over the broadband medium: entertainment, information, and education services are examples of VOD services that can be ordered by dialing the service provider and arranging to have them delivered. Figure 20-8 illustrates how VOD is delivered to the end user.

Although the technologies for VOD have mostly been developed, several questions remain. A major question is how the services will be delivered. Existing coaxial cable owned by the CATV companies does not lend itself well to VOD. It is analog plant, and VOD is delivered as a digital service. Digital television sets will undoubtedly be produced in quantity before long, but for now television sets are analog, which means a converter is required. Who will pay for the converters and how much they will cost has not been determined. Video servers can also be a stumbling block. The amount of data that must be delivered to fill digital pipes to thousands of simultaneous users outstrips the capabilities of today's server technologies.

Video over Fiber

A major issue is how video will be delivered to residences in the future. Fiber optics is the obvious and unanimous choice. Although the conversion will be gradual, fiber is the only terrestrial medium that has the necessary bandwidth. It also carries a hefty price tag that prevents the carriers from leaping headlong into fiber technology.

Three different schemes for deploying fiber have been proposed:

- Fiber to the node (FTTN)
- Fiber to the curb (FTTC)
- Fiber to the home (FTTH)

FTTN, which requires the least fiber, brings the video signal to a distribution point in the neighborhood. From there the signal is delivered by wire, either twisted-pair, coaxial, or both. This method approximates the architecture of local telephone distribution plant today, but it requires more expensive electronics at the node. If the digital signal is converted to analog at this point, it can be distributed over coax but requires additional equipment in the node to do. This method of distributing signals is known as *hybrid fiber-coax* (HFC).

A second alternative is distributing the signal to an interface that serves a handful of residences. This plan, FTTC, gets the signal close enough to the residence that a coaxial drop or twisted-pair wire can distribute the signal digitally. FTTC uses less nodal equipment. The third alternative, FTTH, runs fiber directly into the home. This is the technically most elegant and expensive solution, and is the one that will most likely evolve eventually, but the applications will have to emerge to justify the cost.

As cable companies position themselves to offer telephone and Internet service over their networks, the network must be upgraded to fiber, and standards must be developed to replace the proprietary methods of current cable modems. Cable Television Laboratories is releasing a specification known as DOCSIS, which stands for data-over-cable-service interface specification. This specification for data plus voice over IP for voice will enable cable operators to offer both CLEC service and access to Internet service providers.

Asymmetric Digital Subscriber Line

Everyone agrees that, in the long run, fiber optics is the best alternative for delivering video services to residential areas, but the cost is so high that the conversion must be gradual. Meanwhile, nearly every residence is served by twisted-pair wire, which has the capability of delivering video within narrow distance and bandwidth limits. The technology is known as *asymmetric digital subscriber line* (ADSL). It is asymmetric because the bandwidth is greater in the downstream direction. A single cable pair delivers regular telephone service in the 0- to 4-kHz portion of the bandwidth. A narrow upstream channel for signaling and control is multiplexed above the voice channel, and above that is video bandwidth.

ADSL, which is described in more detail in Chapter 32, comes in two varieties: ADSL-1 and ADSL-3. ADSL-1 provides one MPEG-1 channel on subscriber loops as long as 18,000 ft. ADSL-3 provides four 1.5-Mb/s MPEG-1 or one 6-Mb/s MPEG-2 HDTV signals on loops as long as 9000 ft. The loop limitation means that it cannot be used universally. It is, however, an acceptable method of video transmission from a node.

ADSL is not a long-term solution to video on demand. ADSL-1 allows only one video signal at a time, which does not meet the needs of multiset families. ADSL-3 allows multiple channels to be watched, but only as long as they are conventional TV.

Direct Broadcast Satellite Service

Direct broadcast satellite service (DBS) has evolved from theory to reality. Viewers have long been watching video broadcast from satellites, but that service does not fall under the FCC's definition of DBS. Most of the existing services are in the 4-GHz common carrier band, and not in the 12-GHz (Ku band) DBS band that the FCC authorized in the mid-1980s for DBS.

DBS satellites are high-powered, which enables users to have small receiving antennas. The ease with which antennas can be concealed overcomes some of the zoning restrictions that have hampered satellite service in the lower-frequency bands. The new services use digital transmission, although most users convert to analog for compatibility with existing television sets. With the compression systems used, as many as 200 channels can be supported. DBS is a technically viable alternative to CATV, except that it does not offer a way of receiving local channels. It offers pay-per-view video, which subscribers order with a telephone call. DBS is a good test bed for VOD because it shows the willingness of subscribers to purchase the electronic equipment and to pay for the entertainment services that DBS delivers.

High-Definition Television

The present NTSC television standard was defined in 1941 when 525-line resolution was considered excellent quality and when such technologies as large-scale integration were hardly imagined. The standard was satisfactory for its time, but it is far from the present state of the art. Larger cities are running out of channel capacity. Although not all channels are filled, cochannel interference prevents the FCC from assigning all available channels. Large television screens are becoming more the rule than the exception, and at close range the distance between scan lines is disconcerting. The 525 scan lines of broadcast television and the 4:3 width-to-height ratio of the screen, called the *aspect ratio*, place limitations on picture quality. With wide-screen movies and the growing popularity of large-screen television sets, the definition of the current scanning system is considerably less than that of the original image. HDTV has an aspect ratio of close to 2:1 (the actual ratio is 16:9), which allows wide-screen reception.

Under the urging of the FCC's Advisory Committee on Advanced Television Service (ACATS), a consortium of seven manufacturers and research institutions joined forces in 1993 to form the Digital HDTV Grand Alliance, whose goal was to produce an HDTV system for the United States. The standard is complete, and limited HDTV broadcasts are being transmitted in the major markets. It is too early, however, to determine the extent of public acceptance because of the high costs of the equipment.

VIDEO SERVICES AND APPLICATIONS

Entertainment is likely to remain the primary driving force behind video into the future, but business, healthcare, and educational uses of television will be increasingly important. As CATV provides a broadband information pipeline into a substantial portion of U.S. households, the growth of nonentertainment services is expected. The services described next are intended primarily for residences, but business applications will follow the availability of the services.

Teletext

Teletext is the transmission of information services during the vertical blanking interval of a television signal. As discussed earlier, the vertical blanking interval is the equivalent of 21 horizontal scan lines of a television signal, during which no picture information is transmitted. Teletext services transmit information, such as magazines and catalogs, over a television channel. An adapter decodes the information and presents it on the screen.

The British Prestel system was the first widespread application of teletext. The French have introduced teletext throughout much of the country. In the United States the public broadcasting channels convey programming information and accurate time signals through their stations.

Security

Television security applications take two forms—alarm systems and closed-circuit television (CCTV) for monitoring unattended areas from a central location. Many businesses use CCTV for intrusion monitoring, and it is also widely used for intraorganizational information telecasts. Alarm services have principally relied on telephone lines to relay alarms to a center, which requires a separate line or automatic dialer. The expense of these devices can be saved by routing alarms over a CATV upstream channel, but to do so requires a terminal to interface with the alarm unit. As described earlier, a computer in the headend scans the alarm terminals and forwards alarm information to a security agency as instructed by the user. H.323 video can also be used to deliver narrowband video for security purposes.

Data Communications

Many CATV companies offer two-way data communications over their systems. An rf modem converts the digital data signal to analog for application to the cable. Bandwidths up to 10 Mb/s are available over systems equipped for two-way operation. As discussed earlier, these methods are proprietary, but data standards are just beginning to emerge. The primary driving application is Internet access.

Control Systems

Two-way CATV systems offer the potential of controlling many functions in households and businesses. For example, utilities can use the system to poll remote gas, electric, and water meters to save the cost of manual meter reading. Power companies can use the system for load control. During periods of high demand, electric water heaters can be turned off and restored when reduced demand permits. A computer at the headend can remotely control a variety of household services such as appliances and environmental equipment. CATV companies themselves can use the system to register channels that viewers are watching and to bill on the basis of service consumed. They also can use the equipment to control addressable converters to unscramble a premium channel at the viewer's request.

Opinion Polling

Experiments with opinion polling over CATV have been conducted. For example, CATV has been used to enable viewers to evaluate the television program they have just finished watching. The potential of this system for allowing viewers to watch a political body in action and immediately express their opinion has great potential in a democracy, although it has not yet been used to any extent.

APPLICATIONS

Companies that had never considered videoconferencing are investigating it more closely as the economics become more compelling. The first line of justification is generally replacement for travel, but as organizations adopt video as a way of doing business, the need for economic justification will disappear. For example, the telephone and the facsimile machine no longer need to be justified; it is unthinkable to do business without them, and neither is viewed as a replacement for doing business face to face. The same undoubtedly will happen with video, but the demand is growing more slowly than the industry had expected. However, a new group of low-cost video terminals should help generate demand.

The most obvious video application is for meetings, but other applications will develop as costs continue to decline. For example, here are some applications that show unexpected benefits of video applications:

♦ A food producer has farmers bring produce to a staging area and dump it on slabs for later redeployment. Video equipment shows the production department the types of produce and quantities on hand at plants located in three different cities.

♦ A countywide fire and rescue system uses the CATV system to administer training to firefighting crews who must remain at their present facilities to respond to emergencies. Not only is the CATV system used for sending video, it also is used as a data communications system to provide access to the host computer and to transmit location maps from the 911 center when alarms are dispatched.

♦ A company has found a secondary benefit of videoconferencing. Not only are travel costs reduced, but since conference participants must schedule video facilities, it forces managers to limit time, resulting in more efficient and productive meetings.

Videoconferencing makes it economical for more people to participate directly in events. Before videoconferencing facilities were available, the company authorized only a few people to travel. With videoconferencing, more people can obtain information firsthand.

Standards

United States television signals are generated according to standards developed by the National Television System Committee (NTSC). Rules and standards of the FCC regulate television broadcasts and CATV. EIA specifies electrical performance standards of television signals and equipment. ITU-T establishes standards for international television transmission, recommends signal quality standards, and also specifies compression standards. The principal ITU-T standards covering video-conferencing are listed in an earlier section.

Evaluation Considerations

This section discusses evaluation considerations of videoconferencing and transmission equipment. Other video services, including CATV, are provided only as—and where—available and are not usually subject to choice.

Type of Transmission Facilities

The initial issue to resolve is the degree of signal quality that is needed to fulfill the objectives. The decision is largely driven by costs, which in turn are determined by the transmission facilities available. For most business conferences over the PSTN, 384 kb/s is considered the best balance between cost and quality. Satisfactory conferences can be held at 128 kb/s, but at this speed the codecs have a difficult time keeping up with motion.

If available, BRI ISDN service offers ideal videoconferencing facilities. For higher bandwidths, inverse multiplexing may be required. Some units have the inverse multiplexer built in, while others use an external I-mux.

The following issues should be evaluated in selecting videoconferencing equipment:

- ◆ Is the compression algorithm proprietary or does it support ITU-T standards? Is H.261 available as a fallback standard?

- ◆ What level of quality is needed? Is a highly compressed signal satisfactory? Does the system offer full 30 frames per second or some lower factor?

- ◆ Can the system support multiple video formats (NTSC, SECAM, PAL)?

- ◆ Does the system support still graphics?

- ◆ Does audio ride on the video facility? Is wideband audio available?

- ◆ Is single-point or multipoint communication required? If multipoint, will the user supply the multipoint control unit or use facilities offered by the IXC?

Single- or Multipoint Conferences

Videoconferences are classed as point-to-point or multipoint. With terrestrial facilities, the distance and number of points served have a significant effect on transmission costs. Satellite facility costs are independent of distance and, except for earth station costs, are independent of the number of points served if the points are within the satellite footprint. If earth stations exist for other communications services, such as a companywide voice and data network, multipoint videoconferences can be obtained for costs equivalent to those of point-to-point conferences.

Large companies with a significant amount of multipoint conferencing can often justify the cost of a multipoint control unit (MCU). Companies that use multipoint conferencing only occasionally can use multipoint services offered by the major IXCs. The IXCs offer "meet-me" conferencing in which conferees dial into a bridge. The control unit receives inputs from all locations, and sends each location the image that has seized the transmitting channel. The transmitting channel is allocated by one of three methods: under control of the conference leader, under time control in which each location gets a share of the time, or by switching in the location that is currently talking. The latter method is the most common, but it requires a disciplined approach.

The type of transmission facility also is a function of the bandwidth required. Full-motion, full-color video requires a 6-MHz analog channel or a 1.544-Mb/s digital channel. With a sacrifice in clarity during motion, digital bandwidths can be reduced to as little as 64 kb/s. Freeze-frame video can be supported over narrower bandwidths. Digital transmission is usually less economical for multipoint or one-way broadcasts because of the cost of video compression equipment.

System Integration

Videoconference equipment is usually an assembly of units made by different manufacturers. To ensure compatibility, it is usually advisable to obtain equipment from a vendor who can assemble it into a complete system.

Security

The type of information being transmitted over the channel must be considered. Often, proprietary information is discussed during conferences. Both terrestrial microwave and satellite services are subject to interception; signals transmitted over fiber optics are less vulnerable. Scrambling or encryption of both video and audio signals often is warranted.

Public or Private Facilities

Private videoconference facilities have a significant advantage over public access systems. Public facilities are unavailable in many localities, which may preclude holding many videoconferences. The travel time to a public facility offsets some of the advantages of videoconferencing. Unless a private facility is used frequently, however, public facilities are usually the most cost-effective option.

Future Expansion

Videoconference facilities should be acquired with a view toward future expansion plans. For example, a conference facility may start with freeze-frame with plans to convert to full-motion video later. The facility should be expandable to other points if growth is foreseen.

Fixed or Portable Equipment

Portable videoconference equipment is available, and some applications require it. A roll-around unit about the size of a two-drawer filing cabinet can quickly be set up for an impromptu videoconference. Unless there is a need for portability, however, the best results will be obtained with fixed equipment. Portable satellite equipment also is used in some video services—particularly one-way broadcasts to hotels and other meeting facilities.

H.323 Evaluation Considerations

As discussed earlier, H.323 video is in its infancy, and must be evaluated carefully to determine if it will fulfill the users' expectations. The typical company in the market for H.323 video will have an existing internal network with spare capacity or one to which capacity can be added inexpensively. It will have internal video-conferences with the expectation of reducing transmission costs. The terminal equipment may be identical to that used for H.320 conferences, and in fact the equipment may be used interchangeably with the right interfaces. The vendor should be asked to demonstrate the viability of the application before committing to equipment purchase.

PART FOUR

Customer Premises Equipment

CHAPTER 21

Local Area Network Equipment

With LAN protocols, access methods, and topologies covered in Chapter 9, in this chapter we turn to equipment that makes up single and multisegment LANs and LAN internets, a topic that is covered in more detail in Chapter 37. Excellent equipment is readily available for assembling one of the many LAN configurations. No single configuration is universally best. In planning a LAN you need to understand the issues, the alternatives, and the objectives and choose the architecture accordingly. The task is not difficult in small LANs with up to two or three dozen workstations, but as the LAN expands and branches off-site the issues become complex. Unless the appropriate equipment is selected and properly configured, performance will suffer. Managing a complex LAN requires information that a management system, such as simple network management protocol (SNMP), provides, a topic we will visit in Chapter 39.

As it turns out, the arguments of the 1980s about whether Ethernet or token ring was the best protocol were largely irrelevant. Although token ring has a performance edge over the original Ethernet protocol, in most offices it makes little difference which access method is used, so the choice usually defaults to Ethernet, which is less costly and easier to implement. Now that fast Ethernet costs little more than 10-Mb/s Ethernet, it provides better throughput than the fastest token ring option. The IEEE 802.5 working group is currently working on 100-Mb/s token ring standards, and may eventually swing the nod back to token ring. The discussions about thick net, thin net, or twisted-pair have been settled in favor of UTP for all but a few specialized applications. The broadband/baseband argument has resolved itself in favor of baseband.

Now attention has shifted to higher layers in the protocol stack, which raises issues such as these:

- ◆ Performance of the network operating system
- ◆ Segmentation of the network to improve performance

- ◆ Extension of the network range limits
- ◆ Performance of the file server
- ◆ The use of VLANs to separate subnet membership from physical location

The industry uses the term *system integration* to describe the process of bringing together software and devices from multiple sources and making them operate as a unit. Network managers have three choices in the matter of system integration: turn the project over to the vendor, who usually can furnish all the components; contract with an independent system integrator; or become their own system integrator. This chapter discusses the equipment-related issues that must be addressed no matter which path is chosen. To achieve satisfactory performance from your local network you will need to gather information and address issues such as these:

- ◆ How large will the network be? Determine the number of workstations at the network's immediate and ultimate size.
- ◆ What applications will the network run? Pay close attention to database, imaging, and multimedia applications, which can impose a large load on the network. Word processing and spreadsheet, on the other hand, load the network only when users are retrieving or saving files.
- ◆ Where will software be stored? If on workstations, large workstation disks are required, otherwise, a larger server hard disk is needed.
- ◆ Where will workstations be located? Multiple locations require bridging, switching, and routing.
- ◆ What protocols will the network operate? Identify requirements for protocol conversion.
- ◆ What applications will be running that may require specialized servers, such as e-mail and print servers, and server protection features such as RAID-5 disks?
- ◆ What network operating system (NOS) will be used?
- ◆ How will the network be managed? Include such issues as file backup, trouble isolation and repair, and administration of adds, moves, and changes.
- ◆ What vendors have the resources to engineer, install, and support the network?

So many variables are involved in network design and implementation that it is impossible to generalize. The equipment considerations for a small office with a single-segment network are significantly different than those for a campus environment or for a multilocation company. In this chapter we will discuss the major families of equipment that are available and the differences between products. The purpose of this chapter is to give you an understanding of the issues surrounding equipment selection and to provide information that will help you select firms with the expertise to develop the network.

SERVERS

The network usually includes one or more *servers,* which fill the following functions:

File servers enable users to store files in a central location. The file server may contain allocated disk space for users, and it may regulate their access to shared space and files. The filer server contains the network operating system (NOS), and may also fulfill one or more of the other server functions on the network.

Print servers connect one or more printers to the network and regulate printing jobs. Print servers determine priority, send jobs to the appropriate printer, and enable the operator to manage print resources through NOS utilities.

Mail servers hold the office's e-mail software, provide storage space for mailboxes, and if the network is connected to the Internet, provide the connection for receiving and sending external messages.

Terminal servers connect nonintelligent terminals and asynchronous ports to the network.

Fax servers connect users to a pool of facsimile devices for sending and receiving faxes.

Modem servers connect users to a modem pool. The modem and fax server function makes it unnecessary for each user to have his or her own fax card or modem.

Remote access servers enable users outside the network to dial in to access network resources as if they were directly attached. The access server may also function as an outbound modem pool.

File Servers

The file server is the kingpin of any server-centric network. It serves these major functions:

- ◆ Provides storage facilities for user files.
- ◆ Provides storage facilities for application programs.
- ◆ Provides facilities for sharing common resources such as disk space and printers.
- ◆ Provides, in server-centric LANs, a residence for the network operating system.

As Figure 21-1 shows, peripherals may be attached to the network in three ways: through the file server, through a workstation, or directly to the network itself. Workstation attachments have a place for specialized devices such as plotters that are used primarily by the workstation operator. They also are effective in smaller networks where the administrator can ensure that the station user makes the peripheral

FIGURE 21-1

LAN Configuration Showing Different Methods of Peripheral Attachment

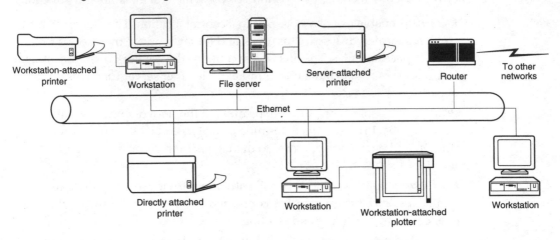

available for sharing, but in larger networks workstation attachments may create administrative problems. Direct attachment to the LAN is completely satisfactory but is not available with all NOSs and all printers. Most devices that do not support a network interface card (NIC) can be attached to an adapter. If direct attachment is available, it is the preferable method, offering the highest speed and fewest administrative problems of the alternatives. Server attachment is feasible with most server-centric networks, but it may operate more slowly than direct attachment.

The file server in a LAN is treated as a virtual drive on the users' desktop computers. A virtual drive is one that appears to be directly attached but is shared with other users. The network operating system maps the drive to the user's personal computer, intercepts calls from the personal computer's operating system, and directs them to the file server.

Factors Affecting File-Server Performance

LANs are most vulnerable in the file server. Failures can result in potentially disastrous file and productivity loss. Techniques for guarding against data loss are presented in the Chapter 9 discussion of fault-tolerant networks. This section discusses the design and administrative factors that affect file-server efficiency.

Network Data Rate   In every network, some factor limits throughput, and the data rate may be the limiting factor. The data rate is not the same as the data transfer rate or throughput; the latter is sometimes no more than one-third of the data rate because of overhead and collision recovery time. Often network inefficiencies are caused by a factor other than the data rate, but with other factors equal, a faster network will provide better response time to the users.

Number and Activity of Users   With other factors equal, the greater the number of users and the greater their activity, the slower the network's response time will be. The effect is more pronounced in a contention network, but file servers attached to deterministic networks will experience greater demand with more users and respond less efficiently to service requests.

Hard-Drive Access Time   Access time is a function of how rapidly the disk moves to the sectors where data is stored. The access time of a hard disk is composed of two factors: *seek time,* which is the time it takes for the read head to move to the proper track, and *rotation time,* which is the time it takes for the disk to rotate to the appropriate sector. Also, the design of the hard-disk controller affects access time. The shorter the access time, the more efficient the file server will be. Generally, access times greater than about 8 ms should be avoided in LANs with more than a few users.

File-Server Memory   In addition to housing operating system and application software, file servers use memory to execute read and write commands and to buffer print data. It is better to err on the side of providing too much RAM than too little because a shortage of memory will adversely affect file-server efficiency. The network operating system uses RAM for *caching* to improve network efficiency. When a user issues a read instruction to the disk, the operating system reads more data than necessary on the probability that the next read operation can be served from RAM rather than from the disk. Caching, which requires RAM, reduces the frequency of disk access, and therefore improves response time.

Network Software Efficiency   Network operating system vendors are quick to point out differences in efficiency between their products and those of their competitors. The network operating system, which is discussed later, is probably the most difficult for a LAN owner to evaluate because it is difficult to construct tests that match reality and because organizations use networks in so many different ways. The NOS provides network administrators with numerous tools for tuning the network.

Print Servers

Many printers can be connected directly to the network, with print server software loaded in one of the network servers. Printers that are not network-compatible are connected through a print server or, if the NOS permits, to a workstation. A print server may be a computer that has enough ports to host the printers, or it may be a nonprogrammable hardware device that supports multiple computers. Parallel printers must be collocated with the server or connected to an Ethernet-to-parallel print server because of distance limitations on the connecting cable. Serial printers can be located any place in a building or a campus by using line drivers if the distance exceeds the limits of a serial port.

Printers can also be attached to workstations as shared devices. Some NOSs provide for printer sharing through the workstation. If the network uses a server-centric NOS that does not permit sharing printers through the workstation, peer network operating systems and some desktop computer operating systems can be operated with the NOS to enable users to share printers, but the user may pay a performance penalty.

Mail Servers

A mail server contains the office's e-mail system. Smaller offices may be able to run e-mail on the file server if the level of activity is low enough, but off-loading the functions into a separate box is advisable. If the e-mail application hangs up for some reason, which is not uncommon, and the server must be rebooted, it is preferable not to affect a file server at the same time. The mail server contains mailboxes for all users and maps the box to the user name for ease in addressing. When users direct mail to an outside service such as the Internet, the mail server relays the message. Likewise, it receives external mail messages from the ISP and translates the Internet address to the LAN address.

Terminal Servers

Since terminals are nonprogrammable devices, they cannot be connected directly to a LAN except through a terminal server. A terminal server is a protocol converter that accepts ASCII input from terminals or computer ports, packs it into frames, and outputs it on the network. It recognizes the addresses of its attached ports, breaks down the frames, and distributes a data stream to the appropriate port. The concept of a terminal server is similar to that of a statistical multiplexer, using Ethernet as the transmission medium. Connecting an asynchronous device directly to a contention network is inadvisable because each character is individually packetized. If a host echoes the character, each keystroke generates two frames that must be padded to the minimum length. An Ethernet can support several users manually keyboarding, but the safest course is to use a terminal server that stores and packetizes keystrokes.

Fax Servers

A fax server gives all users the services of a fax machine at their desks without the need to put a fax-modem card in each PC and convert it to analog ports on the PBX. The fax server provides a pool of fax cards in a central server. The server connects to an Ethernet port on one side and multiple business lines or analog PBX boards on the output side. Users can have as many simultaneous sessions as there are fax cards in the server.

Outgoing calls are easy with a fax server. Most products have a graphical user interface, which enables the user to click on a fax icon to set up a session across the network to a fax card. Application software operates with the server to choose an idle card and set up the session through the PBX or the business lines.

Incoming calls are more difficult. Some systems are compatible with direct inward dialing (DID). The PBX detects the DID number dialed, reads it over a group of lines to the fax server, and passes the DID digits to the server so it knows the workstation to which the call should be sent. If DID is not available, calls are sent to a common pool and distributed on a conventional basis.

Remote Access Server

People who travel or work at home need access to files and services on the LAN. Options for remote access to LANs, in the order of descending cost, are remote access servers, dial-up bridges and routers, remote control software, tunneling through an intranet, and remote access capabilities of some NOSs such as Microsoft Windows NT Server.

Except for the speed of the telephone line, the remote access server provides the same functionality as a direct connection. Remote access servers fall into two categories: remote control and remote node. Remote control software enables users to operate as if they were sitting at a keyboard of a computer attached to the LAN. After satisfying the login and security requirements, users see exactly the same screens and prompts as they see with a directly attached computer. Remote control can be installed on stand-alone computers, or it is available in banks of computers that are racked to provide multiple channels. If the company has a mixture of Macintosh and IBM-compatible computers, different devices will be required in the pool. The main advantage of remote control is that users have a familiar interface. However, graphical user interfaces such as Microsoft Windows are high overhead, so applications may run slowly over a telephone line, even with V.90 modems. The throughput is generally acceptable with ISDN lines, particularly when both B channels are used.

Remote node systems can further be divided into two types: dial-up bridge/router and modem connections. The dial-up bridge operates like a remote bridge so the dial-in station is, in effect, a LAN segment connected by a telephone line. The modem alternative uses point-to-point protocol (PPP) or synchronous line interface protocol (SLIP) to establish a connection between the remote station and the LAN. Software running on a remote computer enables the user to log on as if the station were directly attached. Remote node systems are normally independent of the type of computer dialing in. Either Macintosh or IBM-compatible devices can use the ports interchangeably.

Remote access servers reside on the corporate LAN and allow remote users to be fully functioning nodes, subject only to the speed of the interconnecting circuit. Most remote access servers also provide modem pool service for outgoing calls. Remote dial-up bridges and routers are paired with a matching unit at the central site so workers can operate as if they were attached to the LAN. Remote control software is the least expensive, but its performance is not as good in graphics-intensive applications and it requires a computer for each simultaneous session.

The least costly method of remote access is built into the NOS. The file server hosts one or more modems. Client software on the distant end pairs with host software to enable properly authenticated users to access the network as if they were directly attached.

LAN SEGMENT EQUIPMENT

Many LANs, perhaps a majority of the LANs in existence, consist only of workstations, network interface cards (NICs), hubs, servers, and a network operating system. The *segment*, or *subnet* as it is called in a multisegment LAN, is common to all LANs, and the equipment chosen has a significant effect on user satisfaction.

Network Interface Cards

The choice of NIC can have a significant effect on network performance. It is tempting to buy based on price alone, but more expensive cards offer features, such as self-configuring, that can be recouped by reduced administrative costs. Network performance is affected by the speed of the NICs in both the server and the workstations. If the server has a high-speed bus such as PCI, an NIC that uses the auxiliary bus will be faster than one that fits an ISA bus alone. Server performance can also be improved in some cases by using high-speed or full-duplex cards or by using cards that plug into a 32-bit bus.

The NIC plugs into an expansion slot or PCMCIA (personal computer memory card international association) connector on the workstation. The functions of the interface card are

- *Buffering* the speed of the network to the speed of the device.
- *Packetizing and depacketizing* the information. The NIC accepts a data stream from the device and converts it to a frame. Incoming data frames are converted to a continuous data stream and presented to the device.
- *Parallel/serial conversion.* The NIC plugs into the parallel bus in the workstation and converts data into the serial form that the network requires.
- *Encoding and decoding.* LANs use a scheme such as Manchester coding for pulsing the data on the network. The NIC converts the coding on the computer bus to that required by the network.
- *Access* to the transmission medium. The NIC checks the busy/idle status of a contention network or grabs the token in a token network.
- *Address detection.* The NIC checks incoming frames to determine if it is the addressee.

FIGURE 21-2

A Nortel Networks Stackable Hub

Courtesy Nortel Networks, Inc.

NICs are specific to the type of transmission medium, and to the network access method. Ethernet cards are available with one or more of the three common interface connectors: RJ-45 for 10base T, BNC for thin net, and attachment unit interface (AUI) for transceiver connections. Buyers must pay close attention to speed. Cards are available for 10 or 100 Mb/s or they may be dual-speed cards that automatically detect the speed. In addition, of the fast Ethernet cards both 100base T and 100 VG AnyLAN cards are available. Token ring cards are available for the two transmission rates, 4 and 16 Mb/s, and for shielded and unshielded wire connections.

Hubs

Hubs come in two varieties: stackable, as shown in Figure 21-2, or modular wiring concentrators. The latter type holds plug-in modules that support different access protocols. Modules are available for Ethernet, token ring, and AppleTalk. The hub backplane may be segmented and provide for plug-in bridges or routers to connect the segments. Some hubs support switching modules and FDDI, ATM, or switching backplanes. The modular hub is more versatile and also more expensive than the stackable hub.

Stackable hubs have a fixed number of ports; 8, 12, 16, 24, 36, and 48 are common port multiples. To expand the number of ports, additional hubs are cabled to the primary hub. Although the term stackable implies shelf mounting, many stackable hubs are equipped for rack mounting. In the same rack, hubs are usually interconnected with an AUI connector or with a thin-net connection. Hubs can also be connected through RJ-45 jacks. Usually, one jack has the transmit and receive pairs reversed to interface with the RJ-45 connection on another hub. Hubs may also use fiber optics to connect to a remote hub. If hubs are fiber compatible, it is through a fiber-optic inter-repeater link (FOIRL) module that plugs into a connector in the chassis. If they are not fiber compatible, an external AUI or RJ-45 to fiber transceiver can be used.

The modular wiring concentrator hub consists of several individual components. The chassis consists of a framework that contains multiple card slots. The card slots hold different types of modules. Depending on the type of hub, individual modules may support Ethernet, token ring, AppleTalk, router, bridging, switching, FOIRL, and network management. The card slots are interconnected by a backplane.

FIGURE 21-3

Alternatives for Applying Hubs in the Enterprise Network

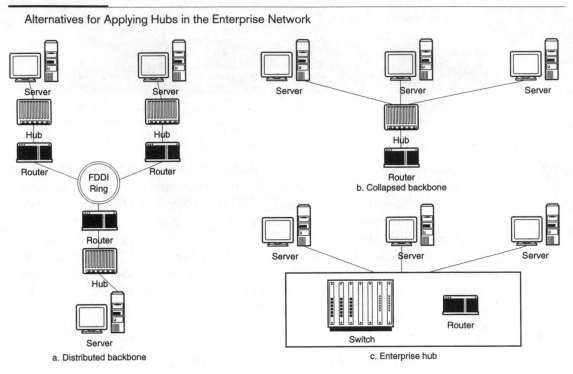

LAN segmentation is different between the two types of hub. Stackable hubs require external devices. Wiring concentrators may have bridging capability built in, or it may be added in some models with plug-in modules. Figure 21-3 shows three different methods of fitting hubs into the enterprise network environment. These methods, the distributed backbone, collapsed backbone, and switched backbone, are discussed in more detail in Chapter 37.

Port switching is a valuable feature of enterprise hubs. With standard hubs users are moved between segments by unplugging the computer from one port and moving it to another. The port switching feature allows the administrator to assign a port to any segment regardless of where it appears in the hardware. Without port switching, all of the ports in a module have to be assigned to the same LAN segment. Port switching has two advantages. First, it improves port utilization. Without this feature some ports will be unused because the segment a hub serves does not have enough stations to use all the available ports. The second value of port switching is to implement *virtual LANs* (VLANs). A VLAN is one that is composed of stations that are independent of physical location. Switching allows the administrator to connect a workstation to any LAN segment in the hub. With port switching, ports can span multiple segments, and in some products, multiple hubs. Port switching is usually confined to modular hubs, although some high-end stackables also offer this feature.

Switching backplanes are available in two versions. The *physical layer switching* backplane permits changing users from one LAN to another without moving the wire to another port. Any port can be assigned from the management terminal to any LAN served by the hub. The *MAC layer switch* is a software application that allows moving users from one segment to another by frame routing. Users can be assigned their own segment connected to a switch port or segments can be shared. Backplane speed is an important consideration. Some modular hubs have multi-megabit-per-second backplanes that enable one hub to support multiple LANs simultaneously.

As with NICs, hubs supporting the fast Ethernet protocols are available. In modular hubs separate modules may be available to support fast Ethernet. In stackable hubs the hub itself is designed to support single or dual speeds.

Network management is an important hub feature. Managed hubs can shut off defective ports or isolate ports that have a defect such as a jabbering or unresponsive workstation. Remote monitoring (RMON) support is available with some hubs, making the degree of compliance an important factor. See Chapter 39 for discussion of RMON.

The choice of hubs is easy for some companies, and difficult for others. Small companies and branch offices, including virtually all single-segment networks, use stackable hubs because of their lower cost. Modular hubs have a high getting-started cost because of the cost of the card cage and power supply. On the other end of the scale, large companies with enterprise networks may use modular wiring concentrators because of their greater capacity and ability to support multiple network media and protocols. Also, their ability to support switching, bridging, and routing in the hub makes modular wiring concentrators the preferred option.

Between size extremes, hub selection is not easy. Companies that are growing rapidly and with no capacity limit in sight will generally prefer modular hubs. Companies that are growing more slowly, particularly those with one network protocol, will find stackable hubs to be less expensive and to have growth capability comparable to many modular hubs.

REPEATERS, BRIDGES, SWITCHES, ROUTERS, AND GATEWAYS

Network designers have numerous tools, including repeaters, hubs, switches, bridges, routers, and gateways, for building complex networks. Repeaters and hubs are single-segment devices that have limited application and flexibility. When the reach of a LAN exceeds the span of a single segment, it can be extended with a *repeater.* If the capacity of a single segment is exceeded, a LAN may be broken into multiple segments that are connected by a *bridge, switch, router,* or *gateway* to form

FIGURE 21-4

Repeaters, Bridges, Routers, and Gateways as Related to the OSI Model

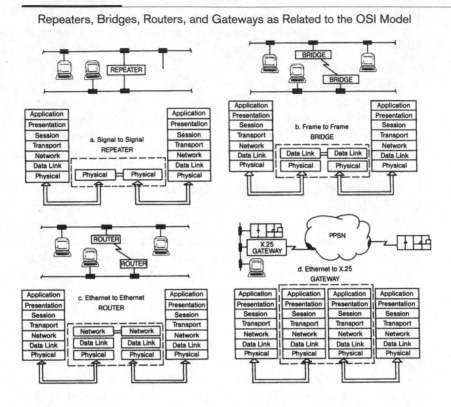

an internetwork. Figure 21-4 shows the relationship of each type of device to the OSI model. A *switch* is a multiport bridge that segments the network into smaller collision domains, providing more bandwidth at each port at a cost that isn't significantly greater than a hub. A *router* does everything a switch does, including limiting broadcast traffic, but it provides for redundant paths, firewalling, and intelligent packet forwarding. It also provides access to wide area networks such as frame relay. Routers are more expensive than switches and there is little overlap between the applications for the two. Both can be used effectively to build the scalable networks that modern enterprise networks need. This section discusses the building blocks and the considerations in their selection.

Repeaters

As signals travel along the transmission medium they are attenuated, and must be regenerated by a repeater. A repeater operates at the physical level, and can detect collisions, but it has no processing ability. The repeater's only function is to regenerate the bit stream. Its purpose is to extend the diameter of the network by linking segments. Repeaters regenerate pulses, and add to the delay across the network,

Ethernet Segments Connected with a Bridge

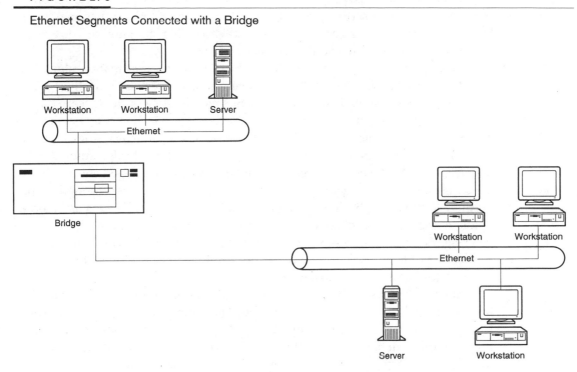

which increase the probability of collisions. Therefore, the number of repeaters in a segment is limited by the 5-4-3 rule. This rule states that no more than five segments can be joined by a maximum of four repeaters, and only three segments can be populated with devices.

Bridges

One drawback of conventional Ethernet is its method of growth. Network usage typically starts low, but as high-bandwidth applications are added, performance begins to deteriorate. The solution is to identify communities of users and break the LAN into segments using a bridge, as Figure 21-5 shows. Bridges are relatively inexpensive devices that are independent of the network protocol. A bridge fits between two network segments and reads the MAC layer addresses of frames on both segments. If the destination of a frame is the same side of the bridge as its origin, the bridge ignores it (*filtering*), but if the address is on the other segment, the bridge lets it across (*forwarding*). If the bridge doesn't have a table entry for a particular MAC address, it floods the address into all segments. A bridge is an appropriate device for dividing an overloaded network into two segments. Note, however, that unless the segment being divided has distinct communities of interest, segmentation is ineffective as a means of deloading the network. For example, if the segment has one server and all the traffic is directed toward that one device, breaking it into two segments with users still accessing the same server will accomplish nothing in terms of reducing network load.

Bridges are protocol-independent. They ignore all information above the data-link layer, so they can pass higher-level protocols such as TCP/IP and IPX. When a bridge is first put in operation, it sends broadcast messages to learn the addresses on the segments to which it is attached. By recording the responses, it builds an address table so it knows which frames belong on which side of the network. If a node moves from one subnetwork to another, the bridge automatically discovers the change and updates its table. Inactive users are aged and purged to keep the table size manageable. Bridges can be purchased as pass-through or converting. A converting bridge converts dissimilar LAN protocols such as Ethernet to token ring. The bridge cannot, however, segment frames, so the length of the token ring frame must be reduced to match that of Ethernet. Bridges can also be configured for different types of media. For example, you can bridge a twisted-pair network to coaxial cable or to a fiber-optic backbone.

Remote bridges are installed in pairs with a telecommunications circuit linking the two halves. Except for the slow-speed circuit between the halves, a remote bridge operates exactly like a regular bridge. Remote bridges usually have the ability to compress data to improve throughput. Compression ratios of from 2:1 to as much as 7:1 are possible, depending on the type of data being transmitted. Remote bridges contain buffers to hold excess frames when the capacity of the connecting circuit is exceeded. The buffer size is an important factor because if the telecommunications circuit is congested, the bridge has no choice but to discard frames.

Two types of bridging are available: transparent bridging and source routing. In a *transparent bridge* the only information used to make the bridging decision is the frame's source and destination address. The bridge ignores all other frame information. Ethernet-to-Ethernet bridges use the transparent bridging technique.

Source routing bridges, which are often used in token ring networks, are protocol-dependent, and are therefore slower than transparent bridges. The source routing algorithm allows the source to specify the route a frame will take to reach the destination. To learn the route, the source sends an explorer frame with only the destination address. Each receiving bridge forwards the explorer frame on all of its ports. As the frame travels through the network, the bridges that handle it append routing information to the MAC layer. When the explorer frame gets to the destination, the destination replies to each explorer frame showing the route the frame took to reach the destination and the route is put in the routing information field of the 802.5 frame.

A bridge is a potential failure point that can disrupt a network that lacks backup protection. Data-link protocols do not provide for alternate routing, but it is still possible to run two bridges in parallel, provided one is active and the other is standby. The bridges negotiate with each other to determine which is designated as primary and carries all traffic unless it fails, in which case the secondary bridge takes over. The IEEE 802.1d *spanning tree algorithm* is used to allow multiple bridges to communicate with each other and ensure that only one route is active at a time. Bridge ports that would create loops are put in a standby condition and the bridge forwards on the standby port only in case of failure on the primary path.

The industry's tendency is to build more intelligence into bridges. Some products that are sold as bridges provide the functions of higher-level devices such as routers and gateways. A bridge equipped for alternate routing is called a *brouter*. Also available are bridges that support multiple links and prioritize traffic. For example, some devices can block longer frames such as file transfer during periods of heavy traffic.

Compared to routers, which are discussed later, bridges have the following strengths:

+ They are protocol independent. They can pass higher-level protocols of all types.
+ They are less expensive.
+ They have higher throughput.
+ They require less effort to start up and to manage.

Limiting their use for many applications, bridges have the following weaknesses:

+ They are subject to broadcast storms that flood a network with unwanted traffic.
+ Firewalling for security is primitive compared to the capabilities of a router.
+ Because of the different frame lengths, it isn't easy to mix LAN technologies such as Ethernet and token ring.
+ Multiple routes are not permitted.
+ They lack the intelligence of higher-layer devices, so they are unable to filter specific types of frames or prevent unauthorized traffic from reaching a segment.

Switches

In effect, switches are fast multiport bridges that switch one port to another long enough to pass a frame. Each port on the switch supports the full wire speed of the network, so if a station is directly connected to a port, it has the equivalent bandwidth of a dedicated segment. A switch is an economical way to deload a network. Since ports are switched together, collisions between segments are eliminated, which increases the total network throughput. A switch port can be connected to a single station, such as a server, or to a multistation network segment. If a segment serving multiple stations is connected to the port, collisions are not eliminated in the segment but only in the path between the source and destination ports of the switch. Although the most common type of switch is the Ethernet switch, token ring switches are also available, but the broadcast scheme of Ethernet is more adaptable to switching than is token passing.

Often, when a network manager encounters congestion, the question is whether to increase the speed of the network or to segment it using switches. Usually, the latter alternative is the most cost-effective because switches can be added without making any changes at the workstations. The existing NIC cards can be used, and where contention is not a problem, existing hubs can be retained and fed into a switch port.

Switching is sometimes built into hubs, but Ethernet switches are not to be confused with port switching hubs. As discussed earlier, port switching hubs allow network managers to move users from one segment to another without reconfiguring the hub. When a port is assigned to a segment, it remains connected with all other users in the segment. When a station or segment is connected to a port on an Ethernet switch, the port is isolated from all other ports until the switch reads a MAC address intended for another port, whereupon both ports are connected together for the duration of one frame.

Switching technology uses either hardware or software to route frames. Hardware switches use application-specific integrated circuits (ASICs) as the switching element. Software switches use a high-speed processor, such as an RISC processor, to route frames between ports. Switches are distinguished by the way they connect frames. A *cut-through switch* makes the connection from the incoming to the outgoing port as soon as it reads the MAC address. A *buffered* or *store-and-forward switch* reads the entire frame and forwards it only after it determines that the frame is valid. A cut-through switch may forward invalid frames such as broadcast storms or those mutilated by collision. Buffered switches have somewhat greater latency than cut-through switches, but they have the ability to discard invalid frames.

Switches can be obtained with both conventional and fast Ethernet ports. Fast Ethernet may be a desirable option even if it will not be used initially because the network could be upgraded to fast Ethernet or it might be desirable to use fast Ethernet or full duplex on the server port to eliminate bottlenecks. Often, one or more servers can be connected to a fast Ethernet port since they are the focus of most of the traffic on the network.

Switches have the following strengths:

 ◆ They are a fast and economical way to resolve network congestion. A switch is less expensive than upgrading the speed of the network.

 ◆ The network can be reconfigured while retaining its present topology, cabling, NOS, and NICs.

 ◆ Switches are protocol-independent.

 ◆ They have low latency and a high filtering and forwarding rate compared to other alternatives.

◆ They are less difficult to configure than routers.

◆ They establish point-to-point connections between nodes, which makes it easy to move users among subnets or to form virtual LANs.

Switches have the following drawbacks:

◆ They make it difficult to measure, identify, and manage traffic. Traffic flow is not visible as it is with bridges and routers. New network management tools will probably be required.

◆ Under heavy load conditions some switches may drop frames.

◆ Compared to routers they lack the ability to filter out or firewall unwanted or unauthorized traffic.

Routers

A router works at the network layer of the OSI stack, which enables it to perform the functions of a bridge, plus routing. This gives it the capability of choosing alternate routes to the destination, but at the same time it is protocol-dependent. Therefore, routers are chosen to support the specific protocols the network uses. Routing is important when multiple segments are connected in such a way that there is more than one possible path by which a station can reach another station on the network. Figure 21-6 shows three token ring networks interconnected by routers. Station A can reach station B by the direct route or via the third ring, which both A's and B's network have in common. Source routing enables the source to specify the route that a frame should follow to its destination. Source routing requires the originating station to map the network with the location of addressees and routers. Frames originated by the source are transmitted to the destination with routing information.

A basic difference between a bridge and a router is that the router knows the route to the destination address. A bridge knows only whether the address is local or not. Furthermore, a router knows all the paths to the destination. It can consider such factors as congestion, cost of the route, and other such information that a bridge cannot. If the router can reach the destination directly, the address is contained in its routing table. If it cannot reach it directly, it knows the address of the next router in sequence, and hands the packet to it to flow to the destination.

A single-protocol router can handle only one protocol; a multiprotocol router can handle more than one. Routers may have to fragment packets to put them on the intervening network. For example, if routers are connected across a packet-switching network that has a maximum packet size of 100 bytes, the router would fragment the packets to make them fit.

Router performance is measured by packets transferred per second, the filtering rate, and the forwarding rate. Multiprotocol routers are configured to support protocols such as TCP/IP, DECnet, AppleTalk, IPX, etc., but routers do not convert protocols or allow different protocols to communicate with one

FIGURE 21-6

Token Ring Networks Connected by Routers

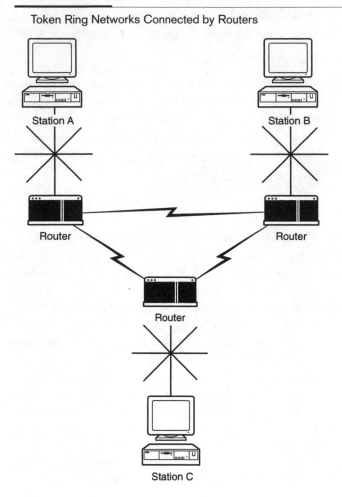

another. Routers can keep statistics on traffic in the network, and assist in managing it.

Before shopping for routers it's important to have the network architecture selected. A collapsed backbone architecture requires a single router with multiple ports and high packet-forwarding capacity. A distributed backbone requires smaller routers, fewer ports, and more devices.

The primary benchmark of router performance is its *packet-forwarding rate*, which specifies the number of packets per second it can forward from input to output ports. Although the vendors' specifications don't normally indicate it, the packet-forwarding capability will depend on packet size, and may depend on how many protocols are being supported. Routers can handle more aggregate data throughput with large packets than with small because each packet forwarded requires reading the packet header, which consumes time. To send the same number of bits with multiple small packets compared to a single large one, more processing is required and more delay results.

Many protocols are nonroutable because they do not have network addresses. A common way of handling nonroutable protocols, such as NetBIOS, is to use *tunneling*. Another term that is frequently used for tunneling is *encapsulation*. Effectively, the nonroutable protocol is fragmented, if necessary, and embedded in the data block of a routable protocol. It is sent across the network and reassembled at the distant end.

Routers operate on the edge of the LAN, and enable computers with a MAC address to communicate in the wide area. The MAC address is a nonhierarchical address, and so does not lend itself to communication outside a narrow range. The router uses a hierarchical addressing method such as IP, translating between the MAC and IP addresses by using address resolution protocol (ARP). Hosts needing to find a MAC address broadcast an ARP message with a corresponding IP address. All stations on the segment receive the broadcast. The one that recognizes its IP address responds with message containing its MAC address. The host retains the MAC address in cache memory.

Routers may use a variety of routing protocols, which are classified as interior and exterior domain protocols. An *interior domain protocol* controls the flow of information within an internetwork. Routing tables are created for each subnet within the domain. Typically, the hop count is used as the router's decision factor. A common interior protocol is open shortest path first (OSPF). Routers use a short message to test for the presence of other devices on the network. The responses enable each router to discover its neighbors and the number of hops to the destination. Tables are updated every 30 minutes or when there is a change such as failure of a router, in which case they are updated immediately. OSPF is an improved version of routing information protocol (RIP), which was one of the first protocols developed for TCP/IP. Devices on an RIP network broadcast their table updates every 30 seconds, which in itself imposes a load on the network.

Exterior routing protocols are used to connect independent domains. Two such protocols are the border gateway protocol (BGP) and exterior gateway protocol (EGP). An EGP router sends messages between domains to exchange routing information with a neighbor. Updates are transmitted every 2 minutes, which consumes bandwidth. BGP alleviates this by exchanging information only when changes occur.

Routers offer the following strengths in connecting networks:

◆ They can make routing decisions based on more criteria than address alone.
◆ They can make alternate routing decisions based on network congestion and other such conditions.

- ◆ They can be configured as firewalls to block traffic between unauthorized networks.

- ◆ They provide more information than other devices, enabling the manager to analyze traffic and congestion conditions.

Compared to other alternatives, routers have the following weaknesses:

- ◆ Routers are complex to install, configure, and manage.

- ◆ They may have a lower packet-filtering and -forwarding rate than bridges and switches because of the greater amount of processing required.

- ◆ Routing table exchanges among routers add to network congestion.

- ◆ Since they are protocol-dependent, routers may be unable to handle some protocols on your network without reconfiguration. Furthermore, not all protocols can be routed.

Firewalls

When a network is connected to another network that cannot be trusted, the connection is usually made through a *firewall*. A firewall is a device that inspects packets and determines whether to let them through to the network or not. The decision could be based on the TCP or UDP port number. For example, the firewall could block the TELNET application, which has a unique port number. The firewall can filter packets based on the originating address, blocking all packets except those from a known trusted source such as a business partner. It can also block on destination address, allowing packets to reach a Web server, for example, but not allowing them to reach a file server.

Packet filtering is the most basic function of a firewall, and can be built into either a router or a specialized firewall. The firewall inspects each packet and blocks or admits it based on address and port information built into its tables. Packet filtration is marginally effective in a firewall but is vulnerable to attack from a knowledgeable hacker. One common method of attacking a packet filter is through a technique known as *spoofing*. The hacker simply falsifies the source address in the packet, and the firewall has no way of distinguishing it from a genuine packet.

Another method of protecting a network is through a *proxy server*, which is a device that intercepts packets from originators within the network and retrieves the requested information. This shields the identity of the requesting station, substituting the address of the server instead. This protects against outsiders obtaining IP addresses deep within the network and penetrating by addressing packets to a known address. Instead, the only address that is visible to the outside world is that of the proxy server.

Gateways

The fifth device for linking networks is the *gateway*, which spans all seven layers of the OSI protocol model. A gateway is designed to link incompatible networks. For example, a gateway could link Ethernet to an SNA network. A gateway is a proto-col converter that must be specific to the network pairs it is intended to link. Gate-ways typically handle three different protocols: source network, destination net-work, and transmission path protocols.

SNA gateways are available for most LANs, which permits stations on the LAN to function as if they were terminals behind a cluster controller. Gateways are protocol-specific devices that link dissimilar networks, so they are designed for specific protocol pairs. Since they work at all seven layers of the OSI protocol stack, the activity of the gateway is processor-intensive, and the device can become a bot-tleneck. All the criteria in selecting routers also apply to selecting gateways.

APPLICATIONS

The applications for local-area networks are as varied as the organizations they serve. This section discusses some of the criteria used in selecting LAN equipment and presents a case history that illustrates the variety of configurations that LAN equipment can assume.

Case History: A School District Network

A large suburban school district with 46 schools and several administrative build-ings initiated a project to bring network technology down to the classroom level. The schools use a combination of Macintosh and IBM-compatible devices. The dis-trict started with approximately 3000 existing computers, many of which were not network-compatible. The district planned to increase this number to about 10,000 computers, or 10 computers per classroom, within the third year of operation. Two CATV channels that use a token-passing protocol for data communications link the schools. One channel is assigned to elementary schools and the other to the mid-dle and high schools.

The applications on the network are instructional software, electronic mail, In-ternet access, access to student records, and access to the district's automated library system. All computers are equipped with general-purpose works software, which provides spreadsheet, word processing, and database. Teachers also have access to student records, which, together with the library system, run on a Unix server.

The architecture chosen is shown in Figure 21-7. Each classroom is wired with four category 5 UTP drops, which are installed in pairs in two classroom locations. Each school has a main distributing frame that serves the front office plus some classrooms. Each school has one or more intermediate distributing frames that serve the remaining classrooms plus special-purpose rooms such as libraries, gym-nasiums, teachers' workrooms, counselors' rooms, and so on. Intermediate dis-tributing frame (IDF) locations are chosen to balance the cost of wire against the cost of additional electronics. Drops average about 150 ft in length. This distance allows the school to distribute video on the shorter category 5 wire runs.

FIGURE 21-7

School District Network

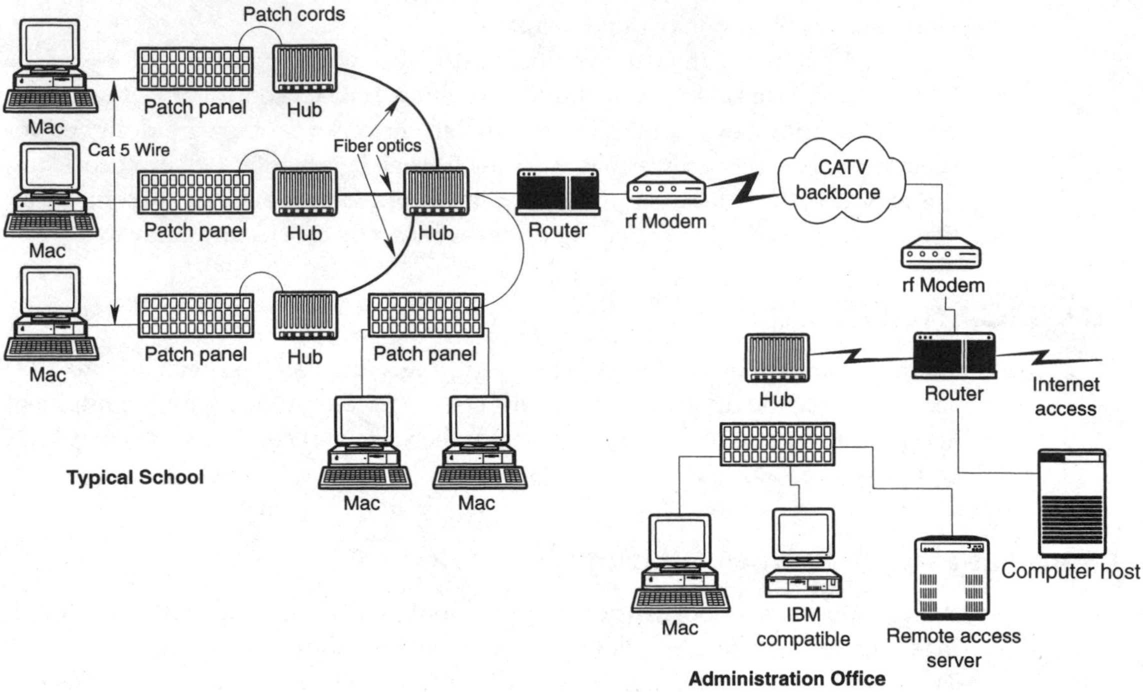

The IDFs are connected to the MDF with three types of cable: multimode fiber for connecting Ethernet hubs, 50-pair noncategory wire for telephone, and RG-11 coaxial cable for video. Hubs and patch panels are installed in relay racks in each IDF and MDF. Each classroom is supported with two 10base T ports. Eight-port minihubs are installed in each classroom. The minihubs provide ample port capacity for less money than installing additional hubs in the MDFs and IDFs and providing additional category 5 wire runs.

A remote access server in the administration building enables students and teachers to dial in from home for Internet access and, where permitted, for access to online files. It also provides dial-out modem-pool access for authorized users. All classrooms can reach applications in the administration building such as mechanized library, Internet access, and the remote access server over the backbone CATV network. The limited bandwidth of the backbone makes it necessary to provide file service capacity in each school.

This network is a good example of balancing cost with functionality. In a school district the budget is typically tight, and while the network is important, it is not mission-critical. Therefore, some features that would be detrimental to operations in a business can be tolerated in a school. The backbone bandwidth is insufficient for a commercial network of this size, but the school has fewer shared files than an organization with an equivalent number of computers.

Evaluation Criteria

This chapter has discussed the primary criteria that users consider in selecting a network. The following are the most important considerations in deciding among the many alternatives on the market.

Preferred Computer Vendor   Companies that use IBM equipment and software should consider the token ring network because IBM directly supports it. Companies that use most other computers will favor Ethernet. Other computer manufacturers may support either or both networks, but the predominant network for most manufacturers is Ethernet.

Wiring   Although it is possible to operate a LAN successfully on existing wiring that may not be intended for data applications, anytime a new building is constructed or an existing building is remodeled, the wiring should be upgraded to EIA/TIA 568 standards. Category 5 wiring should be installed for data at every workstation. With a properly designed and installed system, the wiring will support the present and any future networks that have been proposed up to now. If the present wiring system is not designed for data, it should be replaced as part of the job of installing a LAN.

Network Management   Small networks with only a few workstations do not need centralized network management, but when the size of the network expands to encompass multiple rooms, floors, and buildings, a network management system is required. Devices should be compatible with SNMP down to, and possibly including, the NIC. Consider whether the system supports RMON and version 2 of SNMP.

Access Protocol   When LANs were first introduced, there was a common belief that contention protocols would not provide enough throughput to support applications that required guarantees of data delivery. Experience has shown, however, that CSMA/CD networks are as effective in most applications as token passing, and the access protocol argument has largely disappeared. The most important reason for using token passing is that the application or manufacturer supports it.

Speed   The price of 100-Mb/s or dual-speed Ethernet NICs is little more than 10-Mb/s cards, and should probably be purchased for new networks whether the additional speed is needed or not. The cost of dual-speed and high-speed ports on switches is higher, however, and may not be required. In designing the network, pay particular attention to which segments need high speed.

Vendor Support   The choice of LAN will frequently be dictated by the degree of support offered by the vendor. Unless someone in the organization is equipped to become the systems integrator, it is usually necessary to have assurance of continued local support from the vendor. The following support features should be evaluated:

- ◆ *Implementation and installation assistance.* The design and engineering of LANs is specialized enough that vendor support will usually be required to implement a system. The vendor should have the resources to install the network operating system and debug the software.
- ◆ *Maintenance and administration support.* When a LAN fails, immediate and competent support is needed. Difficulties with the network operating system will be the most frequent. Failures of the transmission medium will be next. The vendor should employ enough technicians to cover absences and resignations. The vendor also should have the necessary test equipment to diagnose problems with the transmission medium and the operating system. The vendor should be an authorized dealer who offers warranty support on both hardware and software.
- ◆ *System integration capabilities.* Most networks do not come out of the box ready to install. It may be necessary to apply cable from one vendor, network interface cards from another vendor, and personal computers from a third. Also, most LANs require integration with existing applications programs and interfacing with hardware of diverse manufacture. Unless an organization has internal capabilities for integrating the network, it will be necessary to obtain the service from the vendor or a contractor.

Costs   LAN costs vary widely and change frequently enough that it is risky to generalize about per-station costs. Costs ranging from $20 for network interface cards to more than $1000 per device for FDDI are quoted, but it is essential to determine total costs before acquiring a network. The following cost factors should be considered:

- ◆ Design and engineering of the network, including the cost of collecting usage data for sizing it.
- ◆ Purchase price of the equipment, including spare parts, delivery, and taxes.
- ◆ Purchase price of new devices required because of incompatibilities.
- ◆ Installation costs, including labor, building and conduit rearrangements, and special permits and licenses.

♦ Software right-to-use fees, including both the operating system and upgrading applications software to operate on a network.

♦ Cost of growth when the system exceeds its capacity.

♦ Transition costs, including cutover from the old network, if any, training of users and operators, and preparation of new forms and passwords.

♦ Purchase of special test equipment, such as protocol analyzers, necessary to maintain the network (unless the vendor maintains the network).

♦ Documentation of the network, so repairs will not be delayed by lack of information.

♦ Maintenance costs, including the cost of finding and repairing trouble and lost production time during outages.

♦ Costs of periodic hardware and software upgrades.

♦ Administration costs, including usage monitoring, service monitoring, and interpretation of network statistics.

Traffic Characteristics   The volume, character, and growth rate of data traffic are important factors to consider in selecting a network. The ultimate size of the network must be considered so it can be segmented as it approaches capacity. When predicting future requirements, it is valuable to have a network that includes the ability to gather statistics on current usage. Some network operating systems provide usage information, which helps in expanding the network and assessing its health.

Bridges, routers, and gateways are potential bottlenecks in networks. It is important to understand the volume of traffic crossing these devices and to pick the device that can handle the required traffic. Capacities are usually stated in frames or packets per second. The load that devices are required to carry will depend on the demands of the application.

Reliability   The initial cost of a network often pales in significance compared to the cost of outages. The cost of lost production time can mount rapidly when people are depending on a failed network for their productivity. Networks should be as nearly invulnerable as possible to the failure of a single element. Where common equipment such as amplifiers, repeaters, and headend equipment exists, spares and duplicates should be retained. Most important, qualified repair forces must be available within a short time of failure.

When a network element or the total network fails, the more rapidly it can be restored to service, the more valuable the network. Some systems have internal diagnostics that aid in rapid trouble isolation and restoral. The network also should be designed for fault isolation. For example, a ring network should be designed to identify which node has failed. It should be designed for bypass of a failed node, and the media access controller or network control center should provide alarms indicating a loss of received signal to aid in rapid fault isolation.

Security   Both contention and token networks allow access to all traffic by all stations on the network. Although the stations are programmed to ignore messages that are not addressed to them, the potential of unauthorized reception exists. For example, a protocol analyzer can see all messages. Where security is important, it may be necessary to select a network with additional security provisions such as encryption. The transmission medium is also an important element of security. Twisted-pair wire is easy to tap. Radio transmissions can be easily intercepted. Fiber-optic cable is difficult to tap, and coaxial cable lies somewhere between fiber optics and twisted-pair wire on the ease-of-tapping spectrum. Firewall security through a router is required for networks that connect with public networks such as the Internet.

Throughput and Response Time   Ideally, a LAN should not impose response delays on the attached devices. The choice of operating system and the characteristics of the file server are the most important variables affecting throughput. For minimum delay, the file server must have a processor running at high speed, say 400 MHz or higher. The file server should have plenty of RAM for print buffering and disk caching. The speed of the network will also affect throughput.

Network Diameter   Distance limitations may dictate the choice of a LAN. When the network diameter exceeds the design limitations of the network, it must be segregated through a repeater or a bridge. To obtain the maximum diameter, a high-speed medium, such as fiber optics, may be used.

EQUIPMENT EVALUATION CRITERIA

The first step in implementing a LAN is to determine as accurately as possible how many users the network will support, where they are located, and what applications they will use. Determine what protocols the network must run. Determine how the network will be segmented and interconnected. As discussed in Chapter 37, larger networks will be developed with internetworking.

This section discusses factors in selecting the equipment that goes into a typical LAN.

Evaluation Criteria: File Servers

Both regular personal computers and special-purpose computers can be used for file servers, but the most effective servers are those designed for the purpose. The principal criteria in selecting servers includes:

Processor Type and Operating Speed   Small networks using low-demand applications, such as word processing and spreadsheet, will find slower processors are adequate for file servers provided enough memory is installed. High-end specialized servers using processors operating at 400 Mb/s or more will be needed for large networks, particularly those using high-demand applications such as database.

Amount of RAM   In general, the more RAM in the server, the better. Consider 128 Mb to be a minimum, with amounts up to the capacity of the motherboard desirable.

Amount of File Storage Capacity   It seems that network users have an insatiable appetite for storage capacity. Files keep getting larger, and will continue to grow as multimedia applications increase. The storage capacity should generally be as much as the company can afford.

Reliability   A server crash can mean disaster for the workgroup, which makes this factor the most important to evaluate. Unfortunately, it is also the most elusive. The reason is that several components may form the weakest link, with the hard disk the most vulnerable. Request comparative statistics from the manufacturer, and check experience and references carefully. Consider RAID drives and dual processors for improved reliability.

Fault Tolerance   If the NOS supports it, servers can be made fault-tolerant by duplexing or mirroring hard-disk drives. RAID drives offer large capacity with better fault tolerance than single-disk configurations. A UPS supply should always be provided to protect against power failures.

Evaluation Criteria: Remote Access Servers

Number of Ports   Servers come in cabinets with ports and, in some cases, modem cards installed. When the port capacity is exceeded, cabinets must be added. Question how the network can be expanded when the port capacity is reached. Can cabinets be appended or are they administered as separate independent devices? What is the maximum port speed supported? Does it support basic rate ISDN? Can it connect to the PSTN or to a PBX with T1/E1?

System Administration   Can the system be set up from any workstation? Is specialized client software required? If so, what is involved in setting it up?

Compatibility   What protocols does the system support? Be certain that it is transparent to any protocol you use. Also, be certain it is compatible with the LAN protocol or speed you plan to use.

Workstation Support   Is the system capable of supporting both Macintosh and IBM-compatible computers? If not, how are incoming calls recognized and routed to the appropriate port?

Dial-In/Dial-Out Capability   Does the system have the capability of both receiving calls and allowing users on the network to place out-going modem calls? Is the procedure intuitive?

Security   Any remote access server is a target for hackers, so security measures must be provided. The system should provide a password for getting into the network, after which the user can use his or her own network password to access functions. Does the system allow the network supervisor to change passwords? Can the network supervisor require a password of particular length and with special characters? Are passwords case-sensitive? Does the system disconnect after a programmable number of ineffective logon attempts?

Evaluation Criteria: Hubs

The first question in selecting a hub is how many ports are needed. The quantity of ports should equal the number of network nodes, plus known growth, plus a cushion. The next issue is whether to purchase stackable hubs or modular wiring concentrators. The choice is sometimes determined by the protocol and transmission medium. Some products require different modules for each transmission medium, while others provide multiple connectors. Stackable hubs normally do not support multiple protocols. To connect, and perhaps to bridge Ethernet, token ring, and AppleTalk, a wiring concentrator with different modules is required.

Manageability   Managed hubs support the SNMP protocol, which enables them to perform such functions as detecting and isolating defective ports, counting frames, identifying busy stations, and other such functions that are discussed in more detail in Chapter 39. Determine whether the hub supports RMON. Determine how much traffic is generated by the network management system, and whether an external port is available to diagnose troubles through dial-up when the network is down.

Expandability and Scalability   The hub must provide sufficient slots or expansion cabinets to enable it to support projected growth. Determine how many slots the chassis has. Consider whether the card slots are universal. Dedicated card slots may limit the growth capability of the chassis. Determine the number of ports added per growth increment. Is it necessary to add more ports than will be needed just to accommodate addition of one more station?

Fault Tolerance   Hubs that provide card slots for modules should provide for hot-swapping cards. Without this feature, it is necessary to turn down the hub and all stations attached to it to change modules. Some types of hubs provide redundancy of active elements and the power supply to increase reliability. Determine if the backplane is active or passive. Active backplanes are more susceptible to failure.

Protocols Supported   The most effective hubs for offices that use multiple protocols are those that support and bridge different protocols. Determine whether the hub supports switching and high-speed protocols such as fast Ethernet, 100 VG AnyLAN, isoEthernet, and so on.

Switching Capability   Intelligent hubs with a switching backplane are becoming increasingly important for support of virtual LANs. In switching hubs the bandwidth of the backplane is an important consideration.

Evaluation Criteria: Network Interface Cards

Network interface cards are specific to the transmission medium, but they are standardized to such a degree that cards from any vendor can be used with any NOS, provided the NOS or NIC manufacturer has a driver available. Drivers are software routines that reside on the workstation, and couple it to the network's MAC layer. The drivers are loaded in the workstation's startup routine. Compatibility with the operating system should be verified before purchasing cards.

Ease of Installation   Some cards come with the software stored in flash RAM, which reduces the setup time. Self-configuring cards can locate vacant interrupts and memory addresses, and set them automatically, which reduces setup time. Check the manufacturer's and vendor's technical support. The manufacturer should have technical support available on the telephone during normal business hours. It should also provide a bulletin board system (BBS) for downloading new drivers.

Fast Ethernet Support   Some cards support only 10base T, but many cards have a thin-net BNC connector as well, and some cards also include an attachment unit interface. As discussed earlier, dual speed NIC cards are only marginally more expensive than 10-Mb/s cards, and should usually be purchased unless there is a good reason to restrict their use. Purchase cards that are compatible with the hardware configuration of the computer's bus. For example, if the computer has a PCI bus, better performance will be obtained with compatible cards.

SNMP Compatibility   If you plan to use a network management system, check to be sure the card is SNMP-compatible. If the management information base (MIB) is not built into the card, you will not be able to diagnose problems with the workstation.

Evaluation Criteria: Bridges

Buffer Size   If the link between two halves of a remote bridge is congested, how much data can the bridge store before it begins dropping frames?

Filtering   Does the bridge have the ability to filter frames destined for specific addresses? What is the filtering rate?

Forwarding   What is the rate at which the bridge forwards frames to the other segment?

Spanning Tree   If multiple bridges will be used, determine whether they support the spanning tree protocol.

Ease of Setup   Consider how easy it is to change the filtering setup, the maximum frame size, and the speed of the WAN link. Also, can compression easily be disabled for testing?

Benchmarks   Check the bridge against competitors for such variables as frame filtering and forwarding and size of buffer.

SNMP Support   Is the system SNMP-compatible? Does it support SNMP version 2? Is it RMON-compatible?

Evaluation Criteria: Switches

Before applying a switch, it is necessary to know where the traffic is going. If the majority of the traffic is going to a server, for example, the port from the switch to the server can be a choke point. The solution may lie in using multiple ports or a higher-speed port between the switch and the server.

The first question to consider is the type of switch you need. Switches fall into three size ranges in increasing order of port size and complexity: desktop, workgroup, and backbone. Desktop devices are inexpensive with approximately 24 ports plus one or two high-speed ports for the server connection. All switching and filtering decisions are based on the MAC address. Workgroup switches have a larger number of ports, and support multiple addresses per port. They have the ability to contain broadcast traffic, and generally have more sophisticated network management capability than desktop devices. Backbone switches are used to connect networks or LAN segments. They have a high-speed backplane and support several thousand MAC addresses per switch. They also can route frames and do more complex filtering than lower-range products.

Quantity of Ports   How many ports does the system support? Can the system support wire-speed bridging on all ports simultaneously? If not, what happens to excess frames? How many high-speed ports does the system have?

Latency   How much delay is there between ports?

Frame Forwarding   Does the switch support cut through or store and forward? At what forwarding rate does it begin dropping frames? What is the total forwarding bandwidth?

Filtering Capability   Can the switch filter all errored frames? Does it provide destination address filtering?

Fast Ethernet Compatibility   Is the system compatible with fast Ethernet or other protocols such as 100VG AnyLAN? Does it support full-duplex Ethernet?

SNMP Support   Is the system SNMP-compatible? Does it support SNMP version 2? Is it RMON-compatible?

Virtual LAN Support   Does the switch support VLAN? Is it interoperable with products from other manufacturers?

Evaluation Criteria: Routers

Begin router selection by determining the processing power you need. Evaluate the manufacturer's record and the protocols the router supports. Be certain the router is compatible with the LAN and WAN protocols you plan to use, and that it has the necessary interface capability. For example, if frame relay will be used as the WAN, be certain that the router supports frame relay and that it has interface cards capable of the speed you plan to use.

Fault Tolerance   Mission-critical applications require fault-tolerant routers with redundant processors and power supplies. Check to be certain that cards are hot-swappable, meaning they can be changed without powering down the system.

Scalability   How well can the router meet the needs of both a high-end and a low-end network? Does it grow from low to high gracefully, or does it require a complete changeout at some growth point?

Ease of Installation   Setup menus that are easy to follow should support the configuration. SNMP compatibility is a must, and it should be possible to administer the router remotely with a local dial-in port. In a multirouter stack, is it necessary to configure each router individually, or can configuration files be downloaded from other devices in the stack? Can devices be configured on the fly without requiring network downtime during reconfiguration?

Routing Protocol   Most routers support routing information protocol. Many also support open shortest path first protocol.

Performance Benchmarks   Check the forwarding and filtering rate, the dropout rate, which is the rate at which packets are lost at the full forwarding rate of the router, and the amount of delay or latency that can be expected. Check how different traffic mixes affect throughput. Check performance in real-world conditions such as different protocols, different packet sizes, and two-way traffic.

Management   Is the router manageable through SNMP? Does it have direct terminal connection via EIA-232 ports? Is remote dial-up feasible? This is particularly important in remote offices.

Voice Support   Many companies are beginning to implement voice over IP, and routers are available equipped with voice ports. Determine the type of signaling (for example, E&M, FXS/FXO, loop start, and ground start). Determine the type of interface to the telephone system (T1/E1, analog tie line, etc.).

CHAPTER 22

Station Equipment

The least exotic and technically sophisticated element of the telecommunications system is the ordinary telephone. Yet its importance in the design of the network should not be underestimated. Because of the enormous number of telephone instruments in service, much of the rest of the network is designed to keep the telephone simple, rugged, and economical. Over the history of telephony, the telephone set has been improved, but the fundamental principles that make it work have changed little since Alexander Graham Bell's original invention. The primary changes have been improvements in three areas: packaging to make telephones esthetically appealing and easy to use, signaling to improve the methods used to place and receive telephone calls, and transmission performance to improve the quality of the talking path between users.

This chapter discusses different types of telephones, station protection equipment, and how they function in the telecommunications network.

TELEPHONE SET TECHNOLOGY

The telephone is inherently a four-wire device. Transmit and receive paths must be separate to fit the user's anatomy, but they must be electrically combined to interface with the two-wire loops that serve all but a fraction of the telephone services. Figure 22-1 is a functional diagram of a telephone set.

Elements of a Telephone Set

A transmitter in the telephone handset converts the user's voice into fluctuating direct current. The most common type of transmitter has a housing containing tightly packed granules of carbon that are energized by dc voltage. The voice waves striking the transmitter compact the granules, varying the amount of current that flows

455

FIGURE 22-1

Functional Diagram of a Telephone Set

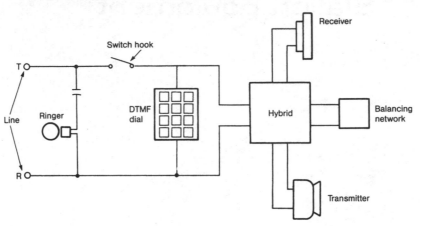

in proportion to the strength of the voice signal. This fluctuating current travels over metallic circuits to the central office. There it may be changed to a digital signal to span the office or to connect over an interoffice trunk to another central office. The terminating switch in the connection converts the signal back to fluctuating direct current to drive the distant telephone receiver, which has coils of fine wire wound around a magnetic core. The current variations cause a diaphragm to move in step with changes in the line current. The diaphragm in the receiver and the carbon microphone in the transmitter are *transducers* that change fluctuations in sound pressure to fluctuations in electrical current, and vice versa. Many new telephone sets substitute electronic transmitters for the carbon units that have been used for more than a century. Most telephone sets still use the carbon transmitter, however, because it is inexpensive and rugged.

The telephone set contains a hybrid coil that couples the four-wire handset to the two-wire cable pair. The hybrid is a passive device that couples energy from the transmitter to the line and from the line to the receiver. By design, the isolation between the transmitter and receiver is less than perfect. It is desirable for a small amount of the user's voice to be coupled into the receiver as *sidetone*, the feedback effect that regulates the volume of the user's voice. Given too little sidetone, users tend to speak too loudly; given too much, they do not speak loudly enough.

The telephone set includes a switch hook, which isolates all the elements except the ringer from the network when the telephone is idle, or on-hook. When the user lifts the receiver off-hook, the switch hook connects the line to the telephone set, furnishes the power needed to energize the transmitter, and signals the central office to connect dial tone to the line. When the telephone is on-hook, the ringer is coupled to the line through a capacitor that prevents direct current from flowing, but allows the ac ringing voltage to actuate the bell. The telephone bell is an electromagnet that

FIGURE 22-2

DTMF Dialing Frequency Combinations

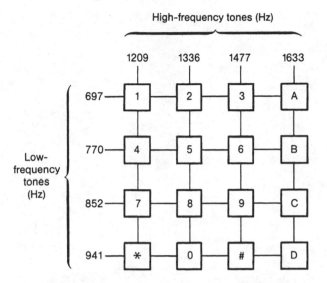

moves a clapper against a gong to alert the user to an incoming call. In many modern telephone sets an electronic tone ringer replaces the bell.

The dial circuit connects to the telephone line when the user lifts the receiver off-hook. Dial circuits are of two types: rotary dials, which operate by interrupting the flow of line current, and tone dials, which operate by sending a combination of frequencies over the line. Tone dialing, known as *dual-tone multi-frequency* (DTMF), uses a 4 × 4 matrix of tones, as Figure 22-2 shows, to transmit pairs of frequencies to the tone receiver in the central office. Each button generates a unique pair of frequencies, which a DTMF receiver detects. Ordinary telephones send only three of the four columns of DTMF signals. The fourth column can be sent by special telephones or can be electronically generated by DTMF chips that are embedded in auxiliary telephone apparatus.

The two wires of a telephone circuit are designated as *tip* and *ring*, corresponding to the tip and ring of the cord plugs used by switchboard operators. The central office feeds negative polarity talking power over the ring side of the line. When the receiver is off-hook, current flows in the line. The resistance of the local loop, which depends on the wire gauge and length, limits the amount of current flow. For adequate transmission, at least 23 mA of current are needed. If too little current flows, the transmitter is insufficiently energized and the telephone set produces too little output for good transmission. If more than approximately 60 mA of current flow, telephone output will be uncomfortably loud for many listeners. Also, DTMF dials need at least 20 mA of current for reliable operation. The telephone set, the wiring on the user's premises, the local loop, and the central office equipment interact to regulate the flow of current in the line and the quality of local transmission service.

FIGURE 22-3

Nortel Networks ADSI Telephone

Photo by James Harry Green.

Rotary dial contacts are wired in series with the loop. When the user rotates the dial to the finger stop, a set of off-normal contacts opens the loop. When the dial is released, the contacts alternately close and open to produce a string of pulses. Equipment in the central office uses these pulses to operate the switches that route the call.

Before the FCC opened the telephone network to connection of customer-owned apparatus, the LECs owned all telephone sets, and because of the large numbers of sets in service, they designed the network for reliable operation with a minimum investment in station apparatus. The basic telephone set is a rugged and inexpensive device that provides satisfactory transmission over properly designed loops. If the current flowing through the loop is sufficient to provide between 23 and 60 mA of current to the telephone set and the telephone is in good working order, satisfactory service is assured.

Caller Identification

Many central offices can send the name and telephone number of the calling party over an analog line with a protocol called *analog display services interface* (ADSI). The telephone is equipped with a display, and may include numerous other fea-

FIGURE 22-4

Diagram of a Station Protector

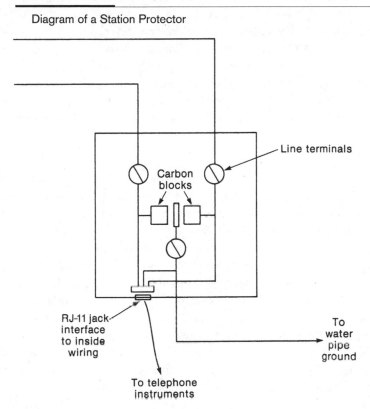

tures. The Nortel telephone shown in Figure 22-3 includes a speed-dial list, speakerphone, last-number redial, and stores the identification of the last 25 callers. Calls can be returned to any of these by selecting them from the caller list and pressing a button. Telephones such as this provide many of the same features of ISDN telephones. External caller ID boxes also provide many of the same features.

STATION PROTECTION

Telephone circuits are occasionally subject to high voltages that could be injurious or fatal to the user without electrical protection. Lightning strikes and crosses with high-voltage power lines are mitigated with a station protector, which is diagrammed in Figure 22-4. Protectors use either an air gap or a gas tube to conduct high voltage from either side of the line to the ground if hazardous voltages occur. The telephone is insulated so that any voltage that gets past the protector will not injure the user. The LEC places protectors, which also may form a demarcation point with customer-owned wiring. Protector grounds are connected to a ground rod, metallic water pipe, or other low-resistance ground.

The protector connects to the telephone set by jacketed wiring, called *inside wiring*, that is the user's responsibility to place. Inside wiring terminates on the protector on the end nearest the central office and at the telephone end on a telecommunications outlet designated by the FCC as RJ-11. Multiple lines terminate on a multiple-line connector such as the RJ-21X. FCC regulations require registration of telephone sets and other apparatus, including modems, PBXs, and key equipment, that connect directly to the network. Registration shows that the FCC approves apparatus for connection to the telephone network. For more detailed information on station protection, refer to Chapter 6.

COIN TELEPHONES

The advent of the customer-owned coin-operated telephone (COCOT) is a by-product of divestiture that is confusing to many users. In the first few years following the dissolution of the Bell System, many private companies saw COCOTs as a potentially lucrative business, which it is. The companies that ventured into this market with less-than-adequate equipment, however, quickly discovered what the LECs have long understood: the risks and administrative costs of coin telephones are high, and companies that enter the market without understanding the hazards can lose large amounts of money. The two major risks are fraud and vandalism. These can be combated with durable instruments and by building defenses into the telephone in the ways discussed here.

COCOTs have earned the distrust of many users—partly because of the inherent design of the telephone system and partly because of operator service providers (OSPs) that often charge more for long-distance calls than the major IXCs. The courts have ruled that the LECs must permit COCOT owners to choose a primary interexchange carrier, which permits the owner of the host premises to invite OSPs to bid for the highest commissions. Also, the FCC decreed that COCOT owners are entitled to compensation for calling card and toll-free calls. The IXCs generally pass these costs on to the party that is billed for the call.

It is not necessary for the owners of high-volume coin locations to own the telephones to gain commissions on long-distance calls, but for those users who do own or contemplate owning the instruments, an understanding of the features and technology is essential.

Coin Telephone Technology

A coin telephone has the following components:

◆ *Communication circuitry*, which is essentially identical with that of noncoin telephone sets.
◆ *Totalizer*, which is the device that identifies coin denominations and counts or relays the value of the money received.
◆ *Coin chute*, which is the physical channel that directs the coins from the coin slot through the totalizer and into the coin box.

- ◆ *Coin collect and control apparatus*, which controls whether coins are directed to the coin box or the refund chute.
- ◆ *Coin box*, which is the receptacle that receives and stores collected coins.

Besides these components, coin telephones may include a variety of intelligent features that substitute for centralized telephone control.

The coin telephones operated by the LECs were, until the last few years, devices with no local intelligence. All call rating, collect, and refund decisions and other such functions were handled centrally. Since the central office does not send answer supervision signals over the local loop, central office circuitry was, and for the LECs still is, used for coin control. When a caller deposits a coin, the coin chute holds it until the called party answers and then drops it into the coin box. If the caller hangs up before answer supervision signal is received, the coin is refunded. An operator or automatic apparatus rates the long-distance call, and a human or synthesized voice announces the charge to the caller. As the caller deposits coins, the totalizer returns to the central control tones that announce the denomination of the coins. Since COCOTs are not connected to central coin control apparatus, intelligence in the coin telephone handles the timing, collection, and return features.

The majority of toll calls made from coin telephones are billed to credit cards, so many coin telephones have credit card readers. Some telephones may include rating apparatus and are therefore self-sufficient. Most such telephones, however, use a centralized OSP to handle the calls and collect the revenues through agreements with the credit card companies.

Coin Telephone Features

The following are typical of features of COCOTs. The LECs also include many of these same features into their telephones.

Coin-Box Accounting   This feature enables the owner to determine the amount of money in the box without counting it. This helps prevent theft but is perhaps most important as a way of determining from a remote location when the box is ready for collection.

Alarming   Many coin telephones have reporting systems that sound a local alarm, dial a number, or both when tampering or vandalism occurs or when the coin box is near capacity.

Remote Diagnostics   The ability to dial into a coin telephone from either a manual or an automatic center and determine whether it is functioning properly is an important feature for controlling maintenance costs.

Call Timing   Most LECs measure the usage on public access lines and charge the COCOT owner accordingly. This feature times the call, requests additional coin deposit when required, and cuts off the caller when the call exceeds the time limit. Some telephones have a readout that shows the amount of time remaining so callers can feed in more coins to keep the call in progress without interruption.

Call Restrictions   The call restriction feature blocks certain codes. For example, the 976 prefix that information service providers use may be restricted because of the difficulty of rating and collecting for such calls.

Voice Store and Forward   This feature enables the caller to leave a voice message that the coin phone will attempt to deliver at certain intervals. For example, a traveler could leave a message to be delivered to a busy telephone and resume his or her trip.

Database Access   Intelligent coin telephones can retain a database of telephone numbers that users can speed dial. For example, the database might include taxi, hospital, hotel, and other such numbers. The COCOT owner may collect a fee from the called party for this service.

Facsimile Capabilities   Telephones with facsimile transmission capabilities are available in many public locations. These devices can levy a charge for facsimile service in addition to the normal long-distance charge, with the fee generally charged to a credit card.

Keypad Volume Control   The receive volume of some coin telephones can be adjusted under keypad control. This facility is valuable in noisy public locations.

Dialing Instruction Display   Given the complexity of operating some coin telephones, the need to access multiple IXCs, the need for compatibility with different kinds of credit cards, and the requirement for the user to dial unfamiliar codes, a telephone with a display and help keys helps the caller use the device.

RJ-11 Jack   To accommodate travelers who need modem access from a laptop computer, many coin phones have a built-in jack.

CORDLESS TELEPHONES

Cordless telephones are not to be confused with the wireless telephones discussed in Chapter 19. Cordless telephones have a base station that is connected to a central office line. The cordless telephone allows the user to carry the instrument within the range of the base station, which is usually limited to a few hundred feet. Wireless telephones connect to a private or public wireless network of multiple base stations. The effective range of wireless is much greater than cordless because wireless hands off from one base station to another, much as cellular phones do.

Wireless telephones are frequency agile so they seek a vacant channel out of several available frequencies. Cordless telephones are set to the frequency of the base station. Except for dual-line and channel-scanning models, they operate on a single frequency.

Cordless phones have sufficient range to cover an average residential lot. As with all radio systems, privacy can be a problem with cordless telephones. Early units were subject to interference and could be signaled by any base unit operating on the same frequency. A more serious problem is that anyone using a telephone on the same frequency can place unauthorized long-distance calls or eavesdrop on private calls.

Cordless phones operate in one of three frequency bands. Older phones operate in two channels in the 46- to 49-MHz range, with one frequency used for base-to-portable, and the other range used in the other direction. Although currently available products use the 46- to 49-MHz frequency range, many cordless units use the 900-MHz band, which provides more frequencies and guards against interference. Cordless phones are also available for the unlicensed spectrum of the 1900-MHz PCS band. These provide excellent coverage within their design range, but coverage is limited in buildings with considerable concrete and structural steel where the building structure may attenuate radio frequencies to an unacceptable degree.

In buildings where coverage or interference is a problem, some models use spread spectrum technology in the 900-MHz band. This technology transmits signals over a range of frequencies instead of just one. The receiver digs the intended signal out of the resultant complex band of frequencies.

In the 1980s the Conference European on Post and Telecommunications (CEPT) initiated work on a second-generation cordless standard that is known as the Digital European Cordless Telecommunications standard (DECT). DECT is based on OSI standards, and 32-kb/s ADPCM speech encoding.

The new generation of telephones contains safeguards against false rings and unauthorized calls. The base-to-portable link is authenticated with a code from the portable unit so the base responds only to a unit with the correct code. This prevents unauthorized calls. The ringer in the portable unit is coded to prevent false rings. Encoders affect only the signaling and do not improve privacy. Anyone who has a telephone tuned to the same frequency can listen to the call, so extended range is not necessarily an advantage. Digital cordless telephones provide better signal clarity with less noise than analog telephones.

Cordless telephones offer a variety of features, including:

- Caller identification over the radio link (where available from the central office)
- Integrated answering machine with message waiting lights
- Intercom and paging between the portable unit and the base station
- Built-in speakerphone

ANSWERING EQUIPMENT

Answering equipment varies from ordinary telephone answering sets to elaborate voice-mail equipment that provides service similar to electronic mail. Answering sets are available in a variety of quality levels, and are no more difficult to install than ordinary telephones. Many units use separate cassette tapes for recorded announcements and messages from callers. Many modern units use digitized voice for the answering function, which eliminates the moving tape and reduces wear and tear on the equipment.

Other features that many users find important include:

◆ Multiple outgoing messages

◆ Two-line capability

◆ Selective message save and delete

◆ Remote message retrieval

◆ Message time/date stamp

Because the central office does not relay answer supervision over the local loop, answering machines include timing circuitry to determine when the calling party has hung up. Most answering machines detect the caller's voice; when a silent period of more than a specified length is detected, the machine assumes the caller has hung up and disconnects. If a caller hangs up when the answering message is first heard, the machine may hold the line busy for a time while it completes the announcement and times out.

CONFERENCE ROOM TELEPHONES

An ordinary speakerphone is unsatisfactory for use in larger conference rooms because it may lack the sensitivity needed for voice pickup from all parts of the room, or it may clip parts of the conversation because it operates in half-duplex mode. Half duplex means the device switches from send to receive during conversations, with the loudest talker capturing the circuit.

Conference room telephones operate in full-duplex mode. They process the voice in a manner somewhat similar to an echo canceler to enable parties to carry on a normal conversation with few or no dead spots around the room. Some units require a separate telephone for dialing, and some include a built-in dial with all other controls such as flash and mute. Conference room telephones operate behind analog telephone lines, either directly from the central office or from a PBX.

LINE TRANSFER DEVICES

Transfer devices fall into two categories: those that operate off distinctive ring from the central office and those that answer the phone, recognize an incoming signal, and transfer the line to the appropriate terminal.

Distinctive Ring Devices

Many LECs offer distinctive ring, which provides multiple telephone numbers on a single line. Each number has a different ringing code combination. Some terminal equipment, such as facsimile machines, can be programmed to respond to a distinctive ring. Separate devices switch terminating equipment to the appropriate port based on the ringing signal. For example, a one-bell signal could ring the telephone, two-bell the fax, and a third combination could connect a modem to the line. The device recognizes an off-hook signal from any station and connects it to the line. Distinctive ring is a cost-effective method of sharing lines that otherwise have low usage.

Line Switcher

Another type of line-sharing device is the fax/modem switch. These devices have ports for telephone, fax, and may also have a modem port. These devices generally select ports by answering the call and listening for a signal from the incoming line. If a fax tone is heard, the fax port is switched to the line. If a modem tone is heard, a modem is switched to the line. If no tone is heard, the telephone is switched to the line. The device sends a ringing signal to the called equipment.

Some of these devices are not completely transparent to the calling party. For example, modem protocols normally operate with the receiving modem answering the line with a modem tone. This cannot work with a line switcher because it relies on the calling device to identify itself first. Also, the device returns answer supervision to the calling station regardless whether the line is ultimately answered or not. This may result in charges for long-distance calls that are not completed.

APPLICATIONS

The market offers two categories of analog telephone sets—general-purpose sets (known in the industry as 2500 sets) and special-purpose telephones such as ADSI display phones, COCOTs, cordless sets, and answering sets. General-purpose sets are easy to apply. They are enough of a commodity that purchase can be based on price plus special features such as speed dial, hold, and speakerphone. The price of general-purpose sets is often a clue to their quality. Many inexpensive instruments provide poor transmission quality and fail when dropped. At the high end of the scale, price usually is a function of features or decorator housings.

Since the FCC began to permit users to attach any registered device to the telephone network, the market has become flooded with special-purpose telephones. At the heart of answering machines, COCOTs, and cordless telephones is still the basic inner workings of the 2500 set, which can be evaluated by the criteria discussed in this section. In many countries the PTT owns the telephone network and prohibits connection of customer-owned apparatus.

Standards

Telephone instruments and auxiliary equipment, such as recorders and dialers, are not constructed to any standards. The FCC sets registration criteria in the United States, but these criteria relate to potential harm to the network or personnel from hazardous voltages or to interference with other services from excessively high signal levels. The FCC also sets frequency requirements for cordless telephones and regulates the amount of electromagnetic radiation that processor-equipped devices can emit. FCC rules specify the amount of internal resistance of a telephone set but otherwise do not regulate technical performance.

EIA sets certain criteria for telephone equipment, and ITU standardizes certain aspects of the telephone set and its operation. Telephone technical standards have evolved primarily from practices of AT&T that were established when it had complete network design control. Other manufacturers have adopted most of those criteria.

Evaluation Considerations

Telephone sets, key telephone equipment, answering sets, and all other equipment connected to the network in the United States must be registered with the FCC to guard against harm to the network. Other countries have similar regulations, or may prohibit connection. All telephone apparatus must be protected from hazardous voltages as Chapters 6 and 13 discuss. The LECs, at a minimum, equip their lines with carbon block protectors, which are adequate for ordinary telephone sets, but some electronic equipment may not be adequately protected. The manufacturer's recommendations should be consulted, and if necessary, gas tube protection should be provided, as Chapter 6 explains.

Telephones

The primary consideration in obtaining a telephone should be the intended use of the instrument itself. The following criteria are important in evaluating a telephone instrument:

- ◆ *Durability and reliability.* Telephone sets are often dropped, and it is often difficult to have them repaired, so the ability of the telephone to withstand wear and tear is of prime importance.
- ◆ *Type of dial.* Specialized common carriers and other telephone-related services require a DTMF dial to enter personal identification number and call details. Some telephones with push-button dials have rotary dial output and are incompatible with these services.

♦ *Number of telephone lines served.* The number of telephone lines has a significant effect on whether a single-line, multiline, or key telephone system is acquired.

♦ *Transmission performance.* Some inexpensive telephones offer inferior transmission performance and may give unsatisfactory service. They should be evaluated before purchase.

♦ *Additional features.* Such features as last-number redial and multiple-number storage are often desirable.

Special-Feature Telephones

The garden variety telephone set has gone the way of Henry Ford's Model T. Now, telephone sets can be obtained with dozens of optional features and with auxiliary equipment such as clock radios that have nothing to do with the telephone itself. Special features are available as either parts of the telephone or as add-on adapters.

Dialers   These units store a list of telephone numbers that can be outpulsed by selecting a button.

Speaker Telephones   These units provide speaker and microphone for hands-free operation. The primary considerations are range of coverage—an office or a conference room—satisfactory voice quality, and the ability to cut off the transmitter for privacy during conversations.

Cordless Telephones   These units should include circuitry to prevent false rings and to restrict call origination to authorized telephones. The range of the base station and remote should be considered. Extended range may be an advantage in some applications but may result in loss of privacy. Multiline operation is available and may be essential for some applications.

Memory   Telephones that store multiple digits and contain last-number redial capability are often advantageous. Some telephones visually display the number dialed and allow correction of dialed digits before outpulsing begins.

Calling Party Display   The calling number is displayed in an alphanumeric readout on the telephone instrument or on an outboard device.

Telephones for the Disabled   Telephones with a variety of aids for disabled users are available. These include special dials, amplified handsets, visual ringing equipment, and other such features. Of special concern are hearing aid–compatible telephones. Some hearing aids rely on magnetic pickup from the handset and are incompatible with some types of electronic handsets. Special telephone sets are equipped with keyboards and single-line readout for communication by the deaf. Compatibility between devices is important.

Answering Sets

Answering sets have many special features that should be considered before purchasing a unit. Among the most important features are

- Battery backup for continued operation during power failures.
- Call counter to display the number of messages recorded.
- Call monitoring capability so incoming calls can be screened over a speaker.
- Dual tape capability so it is unnecessary to listen to the recorded message when playing back recorded calls.
- Digital announcement and recording to eliminate the need for tapes.
- Remote control recording so the announcement can be changed from a remote location.
- Ring control so the number of rings before the line is answered can be adjusted. Some systems answer the telephone on the second ring if messages are present and on the fourth ring if they are not. This permits the owner to check for messages without paying for a long-distance call.
- Selective call erase to allow selective erasing, saving, and repeating of incoming messages.
- Multiple-line capability so one device can answer more than one line.
- Synthesized voice readout so the answering machine can announce the time and date that each call was received.

Coin Telephone Application Issues

The primary concern of most readers is how to use coin telephones, not how to evaluate them for purchase. The COCOT market is growing, however, and many companies have more than an academic interest in coin telephone applications. This section discusses the principal issues to be considered in selecting and applying COCOTs.

The first concern is physical. Coin telephones should not only have the look and feel of the traditional phones used by the LECs, they also must have the durability of traditional phones. To prevent damage by vandals and theft of coin-box contents, the housing must be made of a durable material. Coin-box locks must be sophisticated enough to deter lock pickers. The handset cord must be armored and the caps on the handset cemented in place so the transmitter and receiver units cannot be removed. The appearance of the telephone set also is important. The familiar shape and style of the single-slot coin telephone that most LECs use has been widely copied because COCOT owners have found that users prefer the look and feel of the familiar instrument.

A related issue is the instrument's ability to withstand the elements. This factor is not important in interior environments, but for outdoor installation the telephone must withstand extremes of temperatures. Cold temperatures often affect mechanical apparatus, such as totalizers and coin chutes, while hot temperatures affect the electronics.

Another key consideration is the degree of intelligence contained within the telephone. "Dumb" telephones slave off the central office and are generally used by LECs. Although the LECs have access to central office coin-control apparatus, they are beginning to retrofit telephones with intelligence to handle such features as alarming and diagnostics and to meter the number of coins in the box. Intelligent telephones can prompt users and are generally locally powered, compared to dumb telephones, which are powered from the line. The amount of intelligence is also important in handling coin collection. Coin phones should be capable of recognizing call progress signals, including ringing, reorder, and busy tones, and not collecting the coin even though time has elapsed. The phone also should be able to recognize the two-tone signal of a blocked call and not collect the coin.

The ability to read the stripes on the back of credit cards is important in locations, such as airports and bus and train terminals, where travelers concentrate. Many phones are compatible with prepaid calling cards and can read and write information embedded in them.

CHAPTER 23

Key Telephone Systems

As with all forms of telecommunications technology, key systems are evolving. New products enter the market regularly, and the older lines are adopting new features to the point that many features once exclusive to PBXs are now available in their smaller cousins. The strength of the key system lies in its simplicity. The ancestor of all modern systems is the Bell System's 1A2, which established the button pattern that is familiar to us all. Each line has an illuminated button. When the button flashes slowly the line is ringing, and the user presses it to answer. A red button holds the line, and the associated line lamp flashes rapidly.

For premicroprocessor days the 1A2 was a good product, and many are still in operation, but it has drawbacks. Each line requires control and talking pairs, so an unwieldy 25-pair cable is required for each six-button station; more buttons require more pairs and larger cable. A second drawback is the lack of features. Features everyone wants, such as speed dial and speakerphone, require add on devices and extra cost.

Today's key systems are electronically controlled, and have features that were once available only in a PBX. In fact, many systems so closely resemble a PBX that the industry has given them the name *hybrid*. The distinctions between key system, hybrid, and PBX are not always clear. Table 23-1 shows the main features that separate the three types of products, but bear in mind that many systems don't follow these distinctions.

Further blurring the distinction between key systems and PBXs is the trend of some manufacturers to make their key telephone instrument lines compatible with their PBX lines. A company can begin with a key system and grow to a PBX while retaining the same instruments. A later section further amplifies the differences between these types of systems. Key systems are even available in PC-based platforms, which enables them to communicate over nontraditional paths such as Ethernet or an IP intranet.

TABLE 23-1

Distinguishing Features of Different Classes of Customer Premises Switching Systems

	Key System	PBX	Hybrid
Program	ROM	RAM	RAM or ROM
Outgoing trunk or line selection	Push line button	Dial 9	Dial 9 or push a line button
Attendant call transfer	Attendant announces over intercom	Transfer to station from attendant console	Announce or transfer from console or telephone set
Voice mail	Sometimes available	Available	Available
Call coverage	Usually not available	Available	Usually available

KEY TELEPHONE SYSTEM TECHNOLOGY

A key system has central control equipment contained in a cabinet that is usually wall-mounted. Some cabinets have expansion slots that contain line and station cards; in others the number of lines and stations are fixed and are hard-wired in the cabinet. The central control circuitry is known as a *key service unit* (KSU). A typical key system uses from one- to three-pair cable for each station. Electronic key systems use a microprocessor to scan incoming lines. When the scanner detects an incoming ring, it signals the attendant. The attendant answers an incoming call by pressing a button—the same procedure used in an electromechanical key telephone system (KTS). Instead of directly accessing the incoming line, however, the telephone set sends a data message to the controller, which connects the incoming line to the station. Calls are held by depressing the "hold" button, which applies a flashing lamp signal to the line button. Figure 23-1 is a photograph of a Nortel Networks Norstar key system.

Electronic key telephone sets have many features that are unavailable on electromechanical systems. For example, the Norstar display telephones shown in Figure 23-1 include push-button access to special features that in other systems can be accessed only by dialing codes. A digital readout displays date and time, message waiting, called number, and other such messages. If the system is compatible with calling line identification, the calling number is displayed.

Key systems are rated according to the number of stations and central office lines they support. For example, a 6 × 12 system could terminate six telephone lines and 12 stations. Unlike 1A2, which usually has only one intercom line, most key systems have multiple intercom paths for station-to-station conversations and announcing calls. Intercom lines use either the telephone handset or a speaker/microphone for the intercom talking path.

The type and size of the switching matrix vary with the manufacturer. Manufacturers class larger systems supporting as many as 50 trunks and 200 lines as

FIGURE 23-1

Nortel Networks Norstar Key System

Courtesy of Nortel Networks, Inc.

hybrids, but the difference between hybrids and small PBXs is not distinct. The provision of processor control allows KTSs to provide many features that are similar to PBX features.

Several manufacturers produce multiline systems that do not require a KSU. Most KSU-less systems require one pair of wires per line, which limits the size of the system to four lines or fewer. Some systems employ a special signaling arrangement and use two-pair wire—one pair for talking and one for signaling. The primary advantages of KSU-less systems are low cost and ease of installation. Anyone who knows how to install a single-line telephone can install KSU-less telephones, which makes them ideal for small offices and residences.

The primary drawbacks of KSU-less systems are limited expandability and lack of features. Since the systems have no KSU, the only features available are those contained in the telephone set itself. Most KSU-less systems also lack an intercom path, which means calls cannot be announced over an intercom as they are with most key systems.

Key Telephone Systems in a PC

Several manufacturers produce small PBXs that reside in a desktop computer. These are usually available in line sizes that compete with the hybrid market.

FIGURE 23-2

PC-PBX Application

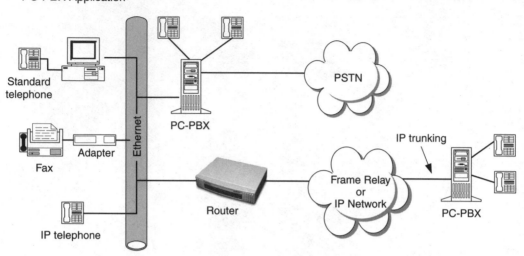

Often, PC-based systems can support H.323 connections through a router. Figure 23-2 shows one configuration.

In this configuration the PC-PBX has local trunks, but can connect to a distant PBX over an intranet. This arrangement is effective for a branch office that is connected to headquarters for data. A limited number of voice connections can be handled for minimal usage cost. The PC-PBX is, in effect, a specialized server on a LAN. Telephones can be connected directly to the PBX in some product lines. In other lines they connect to the LAN either directly or through an adapter or desktop computer. As the universal serial bus (USB) becomes more common in PCs, telephones with USB interfaces are becoming available. Chapter 38 discusses these in more detail.

Key Telephone System Features

All KTSs, including systems without KSU, have in common the following features, which are the original features of 1A2:

- ◆ *Call pickup.* The ability to access one of several lines from a telephone by pressing a line button.
- ◆ *Call hold.* The ability to press a button to place an incoming line in a holding circuit while the telephone is used for another call.
- ◆ *Supervisory signals.* Lamps that show when a line is ringing, in use, or on hold.
- ◆ *Common bell.* The ringing of a single bell to indicate an incoming call.

Most electronic systems have the following additional features:

♦ *Automatic hold recall.* After a call has been left on hold for a specified period, the telephone emits a warning tone.

♦ *Conferencing.* The conferencing feature permits a station user to bridge two or more lines for a multiparty conversation.

♦ *Data-port adapter.* A modem or facsimile machine can be connected. Without a data-port adapter or analog line cards, data stations are unable to operate through the KTS.

♦ *Direct station selection.* The DSS feature, usually combined with a busy lamp field, enables the attendant to determine if the called station is busy or idle and connects the attendant to the station at the press of a single button.

♦ *Do not disturb.* The station user can press a button that prevents intercom calls from reaching the station and silences the bell.

♦ *Hands-free answerback.* This feature permits the station user to answer the intercom or an incoming call without picking up the handset.

♦ *Intercom.* A shared path appears on all stations. By dialing the station intercom code or pressing a DSS button, users can announce calls and hold conversations.

♦ *Last-number redial.* The last number dialed can be redialed by pressing a button.

♦ *Message waiting.* A light on the telephone set shows that a message is waiting in voice mail.

♦ *Music on hold.* While a call is on hold, music or a promotional announcement is played.

♦ *Power fail transfer.* When commercial power fails, the system automatically connects the central office lines to analog station sets.

♦ *Privacy.* This feature prevents other stations from picking up a line that is in use. In some systems privacy is automatic unless the user presses a privacy release key.

♦ *Remote maintenance.* A central maintenance center can call into the system through a modem for diagnosing trouble and changing station features.

♦ *Speed dial.* Many systems have both a system speed dial, which all users share, and station speed dial, which is activated from buttons on the telephone set.

♦ *Station display.* Proprietary telephones are equipped with readouts that may display date and time, last number dialed, elapsed time on the call, etc.

♦ *Station restriction.* Although many key systems lack station-programmable features, some systems provide different classes of service for restricting long-distance calls.

◆ *Voice call.* Stations can call other stations over the speaker so the called party does not have to lift the handset to talk to the caller.

In addition to these features, many systems have features that were once exclusive to PBXs:

◆ *Call forwarding.* The station user can send calls to another station, on or off the system, or to voice mail.

◆ *Call park.* The attendant or a user can place a call in a parking orbit. The call is retrieved by dialing the park number, which is usually announced over a paging system.

◆ *Calling line identification.* If the local central office sends calling line identification with the call, the system transfers it to the station display.

◆ *Direct inward dialing.* Stations can be reached from the outside by dialing a seven-digit number that bypasses the attendant.

◆ *Automatic route selection.* The system can choose more than one route for outgoing calls, including inserting digits, such as carrier codes, for placing calls over the least expensive facility.

◆ *Station message detail recording.* A port in the key service unit puts out the details of calls for connection to a call accounting system.

◆ *T1/E1 compatibility.* The system can interface with a T1/E1 line directly.

◆ *Tie line.* The EKTS can be connected via tie lines to another KTS or a PBX. This feature gives the key system user access to the features of the other system.

◆ *Uniform call distribution.* Groups of stations can be associated to receive calls in round-robin order, with limited statistical information produced by the system.

◆ *Voice mail.* A station can be covered by voice mail when busy or not answered.

KTSs usually include one or more intercom lines. These are used for station-to-station communication—primarily for conversations between the attendant and the called party. In large systems, however, the intercom line takes on the characteristics of the intrasystem talking paths of a PBX. Most electronic key systems provide multiple intercom paths so several intrasystem conversations can be held simultaneously. Most systems provide a built-in speaker so the intercom line can be answered without using the telephone handset. Optionally, the handset can be lifted for privacy. The number of intercom lines provided is a feature that distinguishes a PBX from a hybrid. Many hybrid systems provide a limited number of intercom paths, which limits their usefulness in systems that support a large amount of intrasystem calling. Some PBXs are nonblocking, which means enough time slots are available that all stations can be talking simultaneously.

While calls can be answered from any station in many systems, a special attendant's telephone often is provided. The attendant has all the features of regular stations and also may be provided with a busy lamp field (BLF) to show which stations are occupied and a direct station selection (DSS) field, which allows the attendant to transfer calls to stations by pushing a button instead of dialing the station number. To support the attendant, many systems include paging. The paging system is accessed by pushing a button or dialing a code and can be divided into zones if the building is large enough to warrant it. Many systems provide for parking a call so a paged user can go to any telephone, dial a park number, and pick up an incoming call.

Computer-telephone integration is becoming an important issue in larger systems, and as software packages develop, it will be important for key systems as well (see Chapter 26). Some key systems provide an open application interface so a desktop computer can be connected either to the telephone instrument or to the KSU. For example, many office workers use a PC-based contact manager. To make effective use of the call-logging and out-dialing features of the contact manager, the user must either have an analog telephone set or a computer-telephony interface (CTI) to the key system.

KTSs, Hybrids, and PBXs Compared

Although the distinction between electronic key systems, hybrids, and PBXs is not clear, if an organization requires more than 100 central office line and station ports, a PBX will undoubtedly be required because of its greater line, trunk, and intercom capacity. The upper line size range of a key system is set by the size of the telephone instrument. When the organization has more than about 24 lines, it is impractical to terminate them all on the telephone, so the user must dial 9 to get an outside line and the attendant must transfer incoming calls. When a key system has these pooled trunk capabilities, it is defined as a hybrid. Many products on the market can be set up in either a key system or a hybrid configuration. The main distinction is whether central office lines are pooled or terminated on telephone buttons.

Because the cost of common equipment is distributed among all stations and because the common equipment for a PBX is more expensive, in smaller sizes a key system is more economical. Between a lower range of about 30 ports and an upper range of about 100 ports, the decision as to which type of system to buy can be based on cost, features, and technical performance.

Key systems support a limited variety of trunks. Many key systems cannot support direct inward dialing, and only a few high-end systems support tie lines. Direct T1/E1 interface is available on some hybrids but is not available for most key systems. As an option, some key systems can interface ground start lines, and others only loop start lines (see Chapter 11). Some key systems and hybrids can interface with the central office over BRI lines, a facility that is not generally available for PBXs, which use PRI trunks

PBXs generally support a wider variety of telephone sets, ranging from single-line 2500 sets to multiline display sets and ISDN sets. Most key systems have two or three telephone sets in their product range, with hybrids somewhere between the two. Some key systems do not support analog stations directly. Use of modems, fax machines, or analog stations requires an off-premises station card or a digital-to-analog adapter. Most PBXs and some hybrids have station-programmable features, compared to key systems, in which the telephone set buttons are often fixed and available for only one function.

Another distinction between the types of systems is how the program is stored. In key systems it is stored in some type of nonvolatile memory such as read-only memory (ROM). In nearly all PBXs it is stored in random access memory (RAM), which is lost and must be reloaded following power failure. Hybrids may have either volatile or nonvolatile memory.

Key systems usually have limited or no capability for call distribution so users in an incoming call center must press a button to pick up calls. This results in lost time and poor customer service because calls in progress must be interrupted to answer incoming calls, and when calls are placed on hold there is no way to tell which call arrived first. Most PBXs and hybrids offer a uniform call distribution feature, which Chapter 24 discusses.

APPLICATIONS

The variety of key and hybrid systems on the market is so vast that managers must carefully evaluate their requirements before selecting a system. The following are some general rules, but readers must realize that there are many exceptions, and product lines are changing constantly, which may invalidate some of these distinctions:

- ◆ If more than 24 central office trunks are required, favor a PBX or a hybrid.
- ◆ If fewer than eight central office trunks are required, favor a key system.
- ◆ If the system will never grow beyond three lines and about eight stations and if features are not needed, favor a system without KSU.
- ◆ If automatic call distribution or voice processing is required, favor a PBX or a hybrid.
- ◆ If one-half the total system traffic is intercom, favor a PBX or, depending on size, a hybrid.

Many more criteria should be considered in choosing a system, some of which are covered in the evaluation criteria section that follows.

Standards

There are few standards for key telephone systems beyond those that govern connection to the telephone network. Manufacturers are free to define their features and method of operation in any way they choose. Most systems have a range of standard features that operate in a similar manner regardless of product.

Evaluation Criteria

The first issue that must be addressed is whether the application requires a PBX, a hybrid, or a key system. The discussion that follows assumes that a key system is required. See Chapter 24 for PBX evaluation criteria, which also can be applied to most hybrids.

Capacity

Key telephone systems should be purchased with a view toward long-term growth in central office lines and stations. Key system capacity is specified as the line and trunk capacity of the total system. For example, a 4 × 8 system supports four central office lines and eight stations. This figure is the capacity of the cabinet, and further expansion may be expensive or impossible. Some systems can grow by adding another cabinet, but it also may be necessary to replace the power supply and main control module. With some systems it is possible to move major components, such as line and station cards, to a larger cabinet to increase capacity.

Most key systems use plug-in circuit cards. These are less costly than wired systems, which must be purchased at their ultimate size. The number of internal or intercom call paths also should be considered.

Open Architecture

An open architecture interface is important for future computer-telephony applications that will be appearing in the next few years. Determine if the key system has such an interface, and if the standards are readily available to developers. Consider that outside developers will apply the greatest amount of development effort to the most popular key systems.

Cost

The initial purchase price of a key system is only part of the total lifetime cost of the system. As with all types of telecommunications apparatus, the failure rate and the cost of restoring failed equipment are critical and difficult to evaluate. The most effective way to evaluate them on a key telephone system is by reviewing the experience of other users.

Installation cost is another important factor. One factor is the method of programming the station options in the processor. Some systems provide such options as toll-call restriction, system speed calling of a selected list of numbers, and other features that are contained in a database. If these features require a technician to program them, costs will be higher than for a system with features that can be user-programmed.

The least costly systems allow the user to rearrange telephones easily. Rearrangement costs are likely to be a function of the wiring plan the vendor uses when the system is installed. With some key systems, ports are terminated on modular jacks so stations can be rearranged by moving modular cords.

Maintenance costs may be significant over the life of the system. Cost savings are possible with systems that provide internal diagnostic capability. Some systems provide remote diagnostic capability so the vendor can diagnose the system over an ordinary telephone line. These features can offer cost savings in hybrids, but are less important in key systems.

Voice Mail

Voice mail, which was once available only in PBXs and some hybrids, is one of the most desired features among users purchasing new key systems. Most key systems are capable of voice-mail support, but as discussed in Chapter 27, the degree of integration is important. Be certain that the combination of key system and voice mail can cover unanswered telephones to voice mail, light message waiting lights, transfer to an attendant, and provide after-hours answering and access to voice mail.

Centrex Compatibility

Key systems are often used behind Centrex systems, which are covered in Chapter 28. Many Centrex features, however, cannot be activated unless the key system is Centrex-compatible. For example, call transfer requires a switchhook flash to get second dial tone. If you flash the switchhook on a key system, the dial tone you get is from the key system, not from the central office. To make a key system Centrex-compatible, it must have a special button to flash the central office line. Many key systems are provided with buttons to make them directly compatible with Centrex features.

Number of Intercom Paths

A nonblocking switching network is one that provides as many links through the network as there are input and output ports. For example, one popular key system has capacity for 24 central office trunks, 61 stations, and eight intercom lines. The system provides 32 transmission paths, which support calls to and from all 24 central office trunks. The eight intercom paths limit intrasystem conversations to eight pairs of stations. A nonblocking network provides enough paths for all line and trunk ports to be connected simultaneously. In this system, if all central office trunks are connected, of the remaining 37 stations, only eight pairs can be in conversation over the intercom paths. Although this system is not nonblocking, it meets an important test of having sufficient paths to handle all central office trunks and intercom lines.

ISDN Compatibility

ISDN is becoming an important factor in many locations, and is likely to become more so in the future as applications, such as desktop videoconferencing, develop. Consider whether ISDN compatibility is likely to be required within the life of the system, and if so, whether the system can be purchased or retrofitted to interface either BRI or PRI lines. If ISDN is not used, analog display system interface may furnish equivalent service.

Power-Failure Conditions

During power outages, a key system is inoperative unless the installation includes battery backup. Some systems include emergency battery supplies, while others are inoperative until power is restored. If no backup supply is provided, the system should at least maintain its system memory until power is restored.

The system should include a power-failure transfer system that connects incoming lines to ordinary telephone sets so calls can be handled during power outages. The method of restarting the system after a power failure is also important because the method affects cost and the amount of time required to get the system restarted. Some systems use nonvolatile memory that does not lose data when power fails. Other systems reload the database from a backup tape or disk, which results in a delay before the system can be used following restoral of power. If the system makes no provision for backup power, it can be operated from an inexpensive UPS supply of the type designed for personal computers.

Wired versus Programmable Logic

Most key telephone systems use programmable logic. Older systems including 1A2 and equivalent KTS and KSU-less systems use wired logic. The primary advantage of wired logic is simplicity. Most failures in wired logic systems are in the plug-in cards, which can be replaced by the user for minimal cost. The primary disadvantages of wired logic systems are lack of flexibility and the amount of cabling required. In stored program systems, new features can be added by changing the program, which usually is contained in ROM. Features can be added and removed to customize stations by changing the feature database.

The most important advantage of stored program systems is the wide range of features they offer. Wired logic systems offer essentially the features of the telephone system itself plus basic key features. Other features are added with outboard equipment. Stored program systems offer features that duplicate those of more expensive and complex PBXs.

Station Equipment Interfaces

Many key telephone systems support only a proprietary station interface. Therefore, inexpensive 2500 sets cannot be used except with an off-premises extension card. With some key systems, not even the OPX card alternative is available. The lack of a single-line interface is not a disadvantage in many applications, but many station users now have modems, which require analog lines. Also, some organizations prefer to have 2500 sets in areas such as lunchrooms, warehouses, and reception areas.

An important feature for many users is upward compatibility of telephone sets and line and trunk cards across the manufacturer's entire product line. This capability reduces the cost of converting from a key system to a PBX and enables users to keep their instruments, which not only reduces cost, but also minimizes retraining.

An increasingly important feature is the ability to connect a modem or facsimile machine to a key system port. These analog devices are incompatible with proprietary station interfaces, but for many organizations, the cost of providing a dedicated line is excessive. It is possible to connect modems and facsimile machines ahead of the key system and use the same line for telephone calls, but some means must be provided to prevent telephone users from barging in on a facsimile or modem session. Several manufacturers offer adapters that permit telephones and facsimile machines or modems to share lines, as discussed in Chapter 22.

Alphanumeric displays are useful additions to most key systems. A display field shows the number dialed, time of day, and station status information, such as busy or do not disturb, and in some systems the display may prompt the user in programming special features or in using features such as voice mail.

Attendant and Intercom Features

One feature that distinguishes a key system from a PBX is that in the former the attendant announces calls over an intercom path, while in the latter calls are transferred directly to the extension. The number of paths provided is important since paths are used for station-to-station communication as well as announcing calls.

Most key systems provide hands-free answer capability so a station user can answer without picking up the handset. This feature does not, however, automatically mean that speakerphone capability is available on outside calls. This often requires a special telephone set.

Many systems give the attendant the choice of announcing calls by dialing the station number or by pressing a direct station selection key. The DSS key is usually the most effective method on small key systems and may double as a station busy lamp. If a busy lamp field is not provided, the attendant hears a busy signal or receives a busy indication on a display.

Station Features

Most key telephone sets have station speed-dial capability and a common list of system speed-dial numbers. Speakerphone capability is a standard feature on many key systems, and most systems can announce calls through a built-in speaker.

Some systems have message-waiting capability, which enables the attendant to turn on a light to show that the user has a message or it lights directly from voice mail. Most systems have a privacy button, which enables the user to exclude others from the line in use or to toggle the button to permit access. A do-not-disturb button prevents others from reaching the station on the intercom, while permitting the user to make outgoing calls.

Key Service Unit versus KSU-Less Systems

Some systems provide two- or three-line capability without a KSU. For small systems these can be effective, providing the capabilities of a full key telephone system without the need for a separate central unit. Such systems have disadvantages, however, which make them inappropriate for many installations. First, they have limited capacity, so they are usable only for small locations and cannot be expanded. Second, they usually lack intercom paths, on-hook voice announcing, and other features that are essential in a multiroom office.

CHAPTER 24

Private Branch Exchanges

For years industry observers have been predicting the death of the PBX, but each year the products improve and companies keep buying them. The typical product life cycle is 7 to 10 years, but PBXs that were designed in the mid-1970s are still running, and not even the turn of the millennium brings them to a halt. Start-up companies as well as some of the traditional PBX manufacturers are producing the "un-PBX," a system that runs in a PC and uses a commercial operating system such as Unix or Microsoft Windows NT. Prospective purchasers are asking if this is the future of the PBX, and it may well be, but the traditional PBX is proving itself remarkably adaptable. While retaining its specialized platform and operating system, the new breed of PBX is adapting to resemble a server for some customers while remaining a stand-alone circuit-switched system for others. New PBXs can be equipped with Ethernet ports and connected to a LAN for voice over IP applications.

Over the next few years, PBXs will be forced to evolve, and the manufacturers appear to be well aware of the need. Historically, PBXs have been proprietary in everything from telephone instruments to operating systems. This strategy does not play well in the data industry where proprietary protocols usually don't survive, and standards are set in an open environment. Consequently, PBXs are beginning to support IP trunking, bowing to perhaps the most open of all protocols. More manufacturers are supporting Q.Sig, a protocol for networking PBXs of different manufacture. Applications are gravitating toward the LAN, and the PBX must support them or be displaced by a voice server that will.

The next few years will be critical for the future of the PBX. Sales are continuing at high levels, which appears to mean that most purchasers see the PBX's horizon as being out at least a decade. If the weakness of PBXs lies in their closed structure, this is also one of their great strengths. Call processing and feature support has evolved through decades of development, resulting in a platform that is practically bulletproof if the power doesn't fail. No commercial computer operating system can match this kind of stability. As using organizations evolve toward integrated applications on a LAN internet, the PBX will likely evolve as a voice-processing server that supports a mixed-media protocol such as H.323. The topic of packetized voice is discussed in more detail in Chapter 38.

Meanwhile, the PBX remains a strategic investment for most companies. A PBX ties your company with your customers, suppliers, the public, and other parts of the organization. The features it has and the way it is set up and administered have a significant effect on how those on the outside view your company. In this chapter we will discuss the major features of PBXs and how they are used to improve organizational effectiveness. Two of the major features, automatic call distribution and computer-telephony integration (CTI), are so important that they are treated in separate chapters. ACD and CTI can be obtained in both PBXs and stand-alone systems, and also in Centrex and key systems.

As the network evolves toward all-digital, analog interfaces for the PBX are gradually disappearing. In fact, the main impediment to the all-digital PBX trunking network is the premium prices that many LECs charge for digital or ISDN trunks, but even this is disappearing as competition enters the local network. Most LECs now offer digital trunks, either as separate two-way and direct inward dial trunks or combination trunks that can be used for either DID or outgoing service. In addition, T1/E1 and ISDN offer the advantage of relaying answer supervision from the central office to the PBX, which eliminates the problem of inaccurate call timing that plagues call-accounting systems.

The telephone station interface to the PBX is largely digital. Although a few analog telephones remain, they lack the features of digital, to the point that about all analog ports are used for is such devices as modems and facsimile, but these will eventually disappear in favor of modem and facsimile pools connected to a LAN.

This chapter discusses PBX features, and concludes with a discussion of factors to consider in evaluating PBXs.

PBX TECHNOLOGY

PBX technology has progressed through four generations. First-generation systems used wired logic and analog step-by-step or crossbar switching fabric. First-generation telephones were nonproprietary rotary-dial or DTMF analog sets. If key features were required with a first-generation PBX, a separate key telephone system was necessary. The second generation introduced stored program control processors driving reed-relay or PAM switching networks. Second-generation systems use either standard analog or proprietary telephones, most of which are analog sets, to control a limited number of key telephone features. Some second-generation systems are still in operation, but most fell by the wayside as the numbering plan changed and as manufacturers elected not to make them year 2000 compatible. The third generation, which was the first to support end-to-end digital transmission, employs PCM switching technology and both digital and analog proprietary telephones.

Private Branch Exchange Architecture

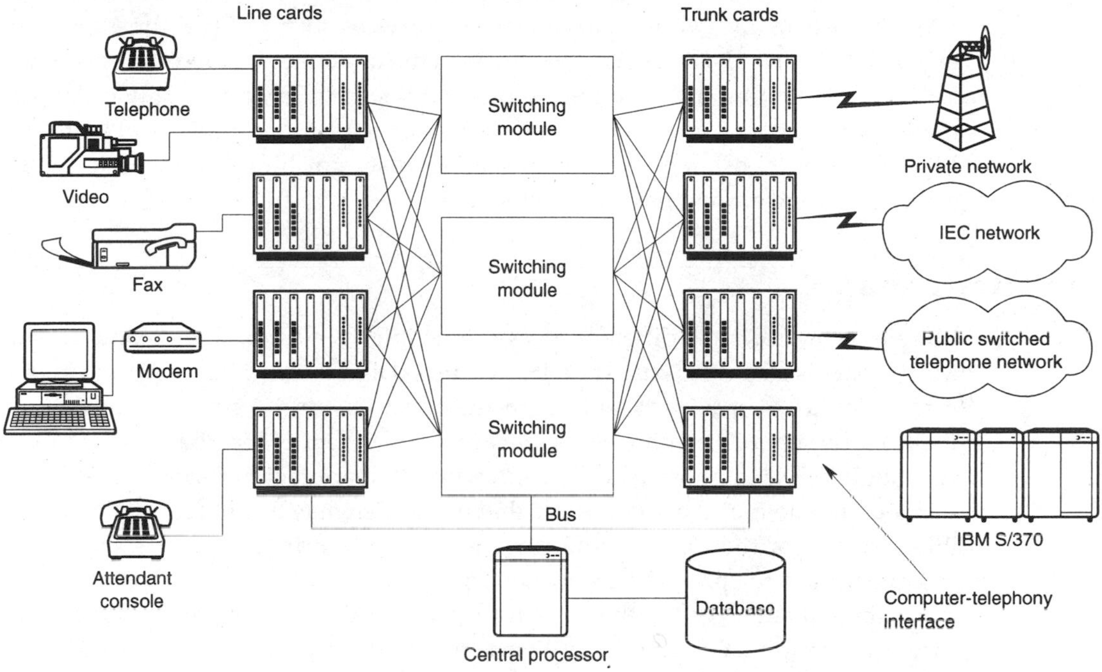

The fourth generation of PBXs is not clearly defined. The majority of the products on the market still use time division multiplexed switching, although some products are beginning to use an ATM switching matrix and others use routing. Most products can connect to an open interface, such as Ethernet, for a variety of functions such as external call control, LAN voice gateway and gatekeeper processes, and connection to external applications. Some products on the market eliminate the traditional circuit-switched architecture altogether, and embed the PBX functions in a server that uses Ethernet instead of PCM as the backbone switching fabric.

The fundamental architectures of all conventional digital PBXs are similar. As Figure 24-1 shows, a digital PBX has a switching fabric that connects to line and trunk interface circuits. A central processor operates the generic program, which is retained in memory. The circuitry is contained on cards that slide into slots that mount in modules or cabinets. The cards plug into the PBX's backplane, which ties the lines, trunks, and central control circuits to the switching fabric and busses over which the circuit elements communicate. Although the structure of PBXs is similar, significant differences exist in the products on the market and the way features are packaged and sold. Figure 24-1 shows separate line and trunk modules for clarity, but most systems have universal card slots, that is, either line or trunk cards can plug into any slot. Figure 24-2 shows a Lucent Definity G3i PBX with the cabinet doors removed. The slots holding the circuit cards can be seen.

PBXs connect to three types of external networks: local, interexchange, and private. Also, many systems support special services such as T1/E1 lines and foreign exchange trunks to local calling areas in distant cities. CTI interfaces connect PBXs to mainframes, minicomputers, or servers so the PBX can supply call information to the computer, and the computer can send routing instructions to the PBX. The variety of interface circuits is a key distinguishing feature among PBX generations and among products on the market.

Line Interfaces

PBXs have at least two different types of line interface cards, analog and digital. Most systems also offer basic-rate ISDN cards. Digital line cards support proprietary telephones that work only with that manufacturer's system. Analog and ISDN cards support telephone sets that are independent of the PBX manufacturer. Although ISDN telephones should work with any manufacturer's PBX, ISDN standards do not define all of the features that the system may be capable of. Therefore, ISDN sets from the PBX manufacturer will usually provide features that other manufacturers' telephones cannot support.

Line card density, which ranges from eight to 32 ports, is a distinguishing feature among products. High-density cards permit PBXs with a smaller cabinet size, which is usually a plus. In smaller PBXs, however, high-density cards may result in more spare ports than the owner would normally purchase. For example, if the system has 32-port cards and 33 ports are required, 64 ports must be purchased, leaving nearly half of them unused.

Another distinguishing feature is the number of cable pairs required for a proprietary telephone. All systems need only one pair for analog telephones, but some systems require two or more pairs for a digital telephone. The number of pairs needed is usually not an issue except in campuses and multistory office buildings where riser cable capacity is a concern.

PBX Trunk Interfaces

PBXs, like central offices, interface with the outside world through trunk circuits that exchange signals with other switching systems through a variety of signaling interfaces. Analog trunk circuits mount on cards that contain from four to 16 trunks per card. T1/E1 trunk cards support 24/32 circuits. Some PBXs use a single type of card for T1/E1 or PRI; others have separate card types. Analog trunk cards support two-way central office trunks, foreign exchange lines, WATS lines, and 800 lines. A separate type of trunk card is required for DID trunks in most PBXs, although some manufacturers offer universal trunk cards that will support either DID or two-way CO.

FIGURE 24-2

A Lucent Technologies Definity G3i PBX

Courtesy of Lucent Technologies

Compatibility with central office line equipment is important for proper PBX operation. The interface standard is EIA-464, which specifies technical and performance criteria for the interface between the two types of systems. The central office interfaces analog PBX trunks with the central office's local supervision; the supervision from a distant trunk is not transferred through the line circuit to the PBX. Therefore, the PBX cannot pass answer supervision through its station message detail recording (SMDR) port to an external call-accounting system. Some

LECs offer digital line and trunk connections to the central office, and these usually provide answer supervision. Supervision is also passed from the T1/E1 long-distance facilities of most IXCs.

Signaling compatibility is an important issue in connecting a PBX to a central office. If analog trunks are used, PBXs almost always use ground start trunks to prevent glare problems (Chapter 11). DID trunks are used for incoming service only, so they may be loop start from the central office, with the DID digits passed with DTMF signaling. Two-way DID trunks are normally connected to the central office as tie lines using E&M signaling. PRI trunks use the D channel for signaling, as discussed in the next section.

PBXs require an access digit, usually 9, to connect station lines to central office trunks. When the user dials 9, the PBX seizes an idle central office trunk and connects the talking path through to the station if the station is permitted off-net dialing. The station hears central office dial tone as a signal to proceed with dialing.

Integrated Services Digital Network (ISDN) Interface

Standard T1 connections to the central office signal with the in-band bit-robbed signaling that is discussed in Chapter 5. Since this type of signaling uses the least significant bit of each channel for signaling, the channel can support digital data at only 56 kb/s. For services such as high-speed data transfer and videoconferencing, use of the entire 64-kb/s channel is desirable. Clear channel transmission is a feature of ISDN, which most PBXs now support.

As discussed in Chapter 32, primary-rate ISDN provides 23 B (bearer) channels plus one 64-kb/s D (data) channel in North America and Japan. The rest of the world uses E1, which provides 32 B and two D channels. Many PBXs also support the BRI interface on the line side. BRI provides two B channels (64 kb/s) and one D channel (16-kb/s signaling). PRI channels can be used in place of analog or digital central office trunks where the LEC provides the service. Most IXCs also provide PRI service. A major feature of PRI is call-by-call service selection, which permits the PBX and the central office to determine what type of service is needed for each call. For example, if a PBX supports videoconferencing, multiple channels on the PRI will be needed to provide the desired degree of picture quality. The PBX and the central office set up the appropriate bandwidth by exchanging messages on the D channel.

BRI capability is needed in many PBXs to support desktop videoconferencing, which is an emerging service. BRI capability is also an important option for work-at-home services, which are becoming important to avoid the need for employees to commute to the office each day.

Although ISDN is not available in all locations, and is not cost-effective in many locations in which it is available, it should be considered carefully in all new PBXs. Growth of ISDN has been impeded by the high cost and lack of services to justify its application, but that is changing. The capability of obtaining both PRI and BRI ISDN interfaces should be obtained in any new PBX being purchased today.

Tie Trunks

Organizations operating multiple PBXs often link them through tie trunks, which are intermachine trunks terminating on the trunk side of the PBX. Trunk facilities may be privately owned or obtained from IXCs or LECs. They may be analog or digital, with a definite trend toward digital with the introduction of fractional T1/E1 tariffs. Tie trunks are generic, and can be set up between PBXs of different manufacture. Signaling is usually E&M.

If tie trunks terminate in a single location, they are often accessed by dialing a digit, such as 8, which connects them to the distant PBX. Many multi-PBX organizations have a separate dialing plan for each system plus a single organizationwide dialing plan. The PBX then is programmed to provide the translations necessary to reach the distant number over the tie trunk network. This feature is called *uniform dialing plan*. To avoid the need for users to understand the dialing plan, many organizations use the PBX's automatic route selection (ARS), which is discussed later, to dial the necessary codes. Users dial the number, and the PBX takes care of selecting the route and dialing any additional digits.

Special Trunks

Many PBXs have a variety of special trunks to provide access to lower-cost long-distance service. When several of these special trunks are connected to the PBX, it is impractical to expect users to select which trunk to use. Most PBXs offer ARS, which enables the system to select the most economical route, based on the class of trunks terminated, their busy/idle status, and the station line class.

Computer-Telephony Interfaces

Chapter 26 discusses CTI, which is a feature of growing importance in many companies. With CTI, the PBX is linked to a mainframe or minicomputer or to a LAN server with a two-way channel. The PBX provides call origination and call progress information to the computer, which in turn sends routing and call-handling instructions to the PBX. CTI is particularly important in call centers, where it is used to pop up an account record on the computer screen at the same time the PBX delivers a call to the workstation. CTI is also used to perform such functions as outdialing on a proprietary telephone instrument from a computer database and to store call information such as calling number, time of day, and terminating station in the database. CTI interfaces are proprietary to the manufacturer, but published as an open interface. The physical circuit may be an open standard such as Ethernet or BRI, and the programming language may be an open standard such as C, but the command structure is unique in each PBX. Therefore, CTI applications must be custom designed for each product.

Remote Switching Units

Many PBXs offer remote switching systems in which groups of lines can be contained in a module that is located away from the main switch. Connection is via T1/E1 lines or fiber-optic cable. The remote unit typically has no stand-alone capability, but many remotes are capable of terminating local trunks. If the umbilical back to the main unit is lost, the users in the remote are without service. Aside from this drawback, remote units have several advantages that make them worth considering:

♦ Only one processor and software set is needed. This is usually less expensive than maintaining separate systems.

♦ Administration is from a central site. All database changes are made on the central switch, with the remote automatically updated.

♦ Wiring costs are reduced. It is often less costly to install a remote than to cable from the central site.

♦ Total feature transparency is achieved. Users in the remote location share the same voice mail, numbering plan, and trunks as the central site, and have access to exactly the same features. Note, however, that some systems permit terminating trunks on the remote.

PRINCIPAL PBX FEATURES

This section discusses the main features that most PBXs support. Although the features are common to most PBXs, users may find differences in how they operate and how much they cost.

Direct Inward Dialing (DID)

DID offers station users the ability to receive calls from outside the system without going through the PBX attendant. The LEC's central office contains a software table with the location of the DID trunk group. When a call for a DID number arrives, the central office seizes a trunk and outpulses the extension number, usually with DTMF tones. The extra central office operations cause some delay on DID calls. DID is effective in reducing the load on PBX attendants. It also enables users to receive calls when the switchboard is closed. A separate group of trunks from the LEC is required. Most LECs charge a premium for DID trunks compared to normal central office trunks. Also, most LECs levy a charge for each DID number.

Voice and Data Integration in the PBX

Most organizations that are large enough to justify a T1/E1 line to a distant PBX have a data communications network that can also ride on the same facilities. Most PBXs provide a data adapter of some kind that connects data through a digital PBX port. This method is effective for connecting a single channel application through

F I G U R E 24-3

Sharing a T1 Circuit through an Add-Drop Multiplexer

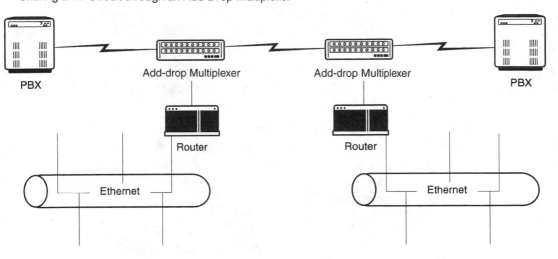

the PBX. For example, if two PBXs are connected over a digital trunk, and access to an application such as the MIS system of an ACD or the PBX's internal administration system is needed, a channel can be "nailed-up" through the PBX.

A more common method of dividing the bandwidth is to use an add-drop multiplexer to split out any required amount of bandwidth to two or more destinations. It is an excellent device for sharing a T1/E1 line between a PBX and a data application, as Figure 24-3 shows. T1/E1 cards are used in the PBXs on both ends of the connection. The PBX is programmed to access as many circuits as necessary for voice, with the remainder reserved for data. The data connection of an add-drop multiplexer is usually V.35, which matches a similar connection on the router.

A method that is increasing in importance is voice over IP (VoIP), shown in Figure 24-4. This method integrates voice and data at the packet level so they can share the bandwidth dynamically. This method, which is discussed in more detail in Chapter 38, allows voice, video, and data to share the bandwidth as needed. When one application is not using it, it is available to other applications. Since voice and video are time-sensitive, they are given priority.

Automatic Call Distribution (ACD)

Automatic call distribution is a feature that allows PBXs to route incoming calls to a group of service positions. Typical applications are the sales and service positions of any organization. Incoming calls route to an agent position based on logic programmed into the PBX or an outboard application. Calls can be routed by the 800 number that was dialed using a service called dialed number identification system

F I G U R E 24-4

Voice and Video Over IP

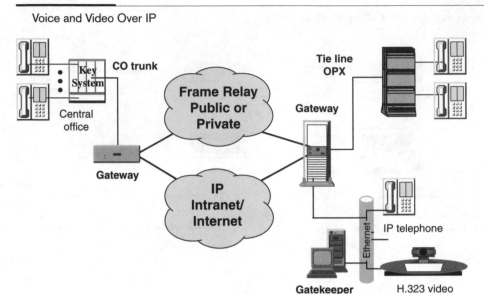

(DNIS), which is described here. The caller's telephone number may be delivered by the network and used to route calls, or the caller can be prompted by an auto-mated attendant or call prompting software in the switch to aid in identification and call routing.

When agent positions are idle, the call routes to an agent immediately. If all positions are occupied, the ACD holds calls in queue and notifies the caller by recorded announcement that the call is being delayed. Calls can be overflowed to other agent groups, routed to voice mail for a callback, or handled in a variety of different ways, which are discussed in more detail in Chapter 25. ACD is one of the most important features in a PBX, and is included in more than three-fourths of the systems shipped.

Automatic Route Selection (ARS)

Most PBXs terminate a combination of public switched and private trunks on the system. For example, in addition to local trunks, the PBX may terminate T1/E1 lines to the IXC, foreign exchange lines, and tie trunks to another PBX. Educating users about which service to use is impractical, particularly as rates vary with time of day and terminating location, and the dialing plan varies with the carrier called. It is a reasonably simple matter, however, to program route selection into the cen-tral processor of the PBX. With ARS, sometimes called least-cost routing (LCR), the user dials the number; the system determines the preferred route and dials the dig-its to complete the call over the appropriate trunk group.

The most sophisticated ARS systems can screen calls on the entire dialed number. Some simple systems can screen on only three or six digits. Three-digit screening limits the PBX to routing by area code or prefix but not both. The ability to screen on the entire number is important for many companies. With it, for example, it is possible to allow users to dial some 900 numbers but deny others. If a company has an Internet gateway that enables it to call other company numbers in an overseas location, the ARS can route those calls to the gateway and others to the IXC.

A related issue is digit insertion and deletion. Some services, such as foreign exchange (FEX), may require the PBX to insert or delete an area code for correct routing. Telephone service is easiest to use if users always dial the same way regardless of the route the call takes. For example, if the PBX has FEX trunks to another area code, the user would dial the area code, but the PBX would strip it off before passing the digits forward to the FEX trunks.

Many systems also provide a warning tone when calls are about to be routed over an expensive service so the user can hang up before the call completes. Complete flexibility in route selection is an essential PBX feature that is available on most systems, although the less costly systems are likely to have fewer capabilities than the more expensive ones.

Networking Options

Most PBXs offer networking options, which allow multiple PBXs to operate as a single system. Call-processing messages pass between PBXs over a separate data channel using some form of common channel signaling. With the networking option, call-processing information, such as a station's identification and class of service, and in most systems the calling name, travel across the network to permit features to operate in a distant PBX the same as they do in the local system.

The objective of networking is to provide complete feature transparency, which is the ability of users to have the same calling features across the network as they have at their PBX. For example, users want be able to camp on a busy station, regardless of whether it is in their PBX or in a distant system, and they want to share a voice-mail system across the network. Some features do not work across a network in some products. For example, call pickup is a feature that enables a user who hears a ringing telephone to press a button and bring the call to his or her telephone. The lack of this feature across a network is usually unimportant since users are normally in separate locations. Some companies, however, start in separate locations with separate systems and then eventually merge them. The PBXs are brought to the same equipment room and remain networked together. If features, such as call pickup, do not work across the network, users in one work group must be assigned to the same switch, which often requires moving people from one PBX to another.

Q.Sig

Until recently, networking and feature transparency between PBXs of different manufacture has been impossible, but with a protocol called Q.Sig, the capability is gradually evolving over ISDN tie trunks. Q.Sig uses a separate packet-based signaling channel to connect PBXs together and with external applications. The protocol is used more widely in Europe than in North America, where interoperability between manufacturers has not been put into practice to any significant degree. Q.Sig is intended to integrate PBXs with peripherals such as voice mail, automated attendant, and interactive voice response. These applications can theoretically work across proprietary lines, but again, the reality has fallen short of the potential. Nevertheless, Q.Sig capability is important for users who have PBXs of disparate manufacture and who wish to network them together in the future if not now.

Single-Button Feature Access

Users can access a PBX's principal features by code dialing. For example, call pickup, call hold, and call forwarding all require distinctive codes, such as *7. Code dialing has an important drawback: users often forget the dialing codes, so they do not use the features. The solution is to assign the features to single buttons on proprietary telephone sets. If users want to pick up a call in a pickup group, for example, they need only press the call pickup button to bring the call to that telephone. The number of features that can be accessed directly depends on how many buttons are on the telephone set, which, in turn, determines the cost of the instrument. Button access to features is the most important reason for using proprietary instead of analog telephone sets.

Follow-Me Forwarding

With the increasing importance of telecommuting, several manufacturers are offering this feature, which allows the user to receive telephone calls at home, on a cell phone, or in a remote location such as a conference center. The user keeps the PBX informed of his or her location, and the PBX forwards calls accordingly. With caller ID and CTI programming, the system can screen calls as well, and forward calls from only selected users. Forwarding can be selective, depending on time of day and day of week.

When a user calls in from a remote location such as a hotel room, some PBXs can download voice-mail messages as a data message so the user can play them back on a laptop computer. This is usually a feature of unified messaging, which is discussed briefly later in this chapter and in more detail in Chapter 27.

Call Detail Recording (CDR)

This feature, sometimes known as station message detail recording (SMDR), in combination with a call-accounting system, provides the equivalent of a detailed toll statement for PBX users. Most businesses require call detail to control long-distance usage and to spread costs among the user departments. The CDR port forwards this information to a call-accounting system, which, as discussed in a later section, provides this capability. CDR is limited by the lack of answer supervision over a local telephone loop, so the system cannot tell whether the called station answered or not. The determination of called station answer is based on the amount of time the calling station is off the hook. Because of the lack of answer supervision, the CDR output cannot be balanced precisely with central office billing detail. However, it is accurate enough for most organizations. As discussed earlier, this problem may be avoided by using digital trunks.

Voice Mail

Voice mail (see Chapter 27) is available as an optional integrated feature in most PBXs and can be added as a nonintegrated service to any PBX. When a station is busy or unattended, the caller can leave a message, which is stored digitally on a hard disk. The station user can dial an access and identification code to retrieve the message.

Most voice-mail systems include automated attendant, an option that enables callers with a DTMF dial to route their own calls within the system. Incoming calls are greeted with an announcement that invites them to dial the extension number if it is known, to dial a number for extension information, or to stay on the line for an attendant. This feature saves money by decreasing the amount of work required of the attendant. Most voice-mail systems also support dial-by-name for callers who reach the automated attendant and do not know the extension number.

Dialed Number Identification System (DNIS)

Offered by IXCs along with T1/E1-based 800 services, DNIS provides the equivalent of direct inward dialing for 800 calls. The call is accompanied with a number that the PBX can convert to the number the caller dialed so the PBX can route the call to the appropriate station number. DNIS enables an organization to have several 800 numbers and to route each call to a different station, uniform call distribution (UCD) or automatic call distributor (ACD) hunt group, voice mail, or any other location within the PBX. For example, if a company has different ACD groups for sales, service, and order inquiry, it can assign each of these groups a different 800 number and use DNIS to route the calls appropriately.

Direct Inward System Access (DISA)

The DISA feature enables callers to dial a telephone number and a password to gain access to PBX features. If the DISA number is restricted, callers can dial extension numbers or tie lines to on-net locations. If the DISA feature is unrestricted, callers can gain access to long-distance services. DISA helps reduce credit card calls by enabling users outside the PBX to access low-cost long-distance services.

Security is an obvious problem with DISA. It is one of the most prevalent targets for toll thieves, who use it to place calls at the company's expense. The best practice with DISA is to disable it. If it must be used, managers should change the password frequently and check the call-accounting system for evidence of misuse.

$N \times 64$ Capability

With the growth of videoconferencing, it is often desirable to dial more bandwidth than an ordinary BRI connection provides. Conference-quality video usually requires at least 384 kb/s, which requires six 64-kb/s channels. A PBX with $N \times 64$ capability enables the user to dial as many channels of contiguous bandwidth as required.

Centralized Attendant Service (CAS)

CAS enables attendants at one location to perform complete attendant functions for remote networked PBXs. Although each PBX has its own group of trunks, all calls routed to the attendant flow to the centralized location. A related feature is release-link trunk, which enables the PBX to release the attendant trunk after setting up the call. Without this feature the trunk is tied up for the duration of the call.

Power-Failure Transfer

Unless a PBX is configured to run from batteries or from an uninterruptable power supply, a commercial power failure will cause the system to fail. The power-failure transfer feature connects central office trunks to standard DTMF telephones. Since most PBXs require ground-start trunks, provisions must be made to operate from loop-start telephones. This can be accomplished by two methods: use a separate loop-start–to–ground-start converter or equip the telephones with a ground-start button. The former method is prevalent.

The power-failure transfer feature is an inexpensive and effective way to obtain minimum service during power-failure conditions. Even users of systems with battery backup or UPS should consider power-failure transfer to retain some service if the PBX itself fails. Some manufacturers offer power-failure transfer for digital or ISDN trunks, which can enable the owner to avoid analog trunks altogether.

Trunk Queuing

The trunk queuing feature enables a user to camp on a busy trunk group. Two queuing methods are in common use: callback queuing and hang-on queuing. With callback queuing, the user activates the feature by dialing a code or pressing a feature button and hangs up. The system calls back when a trunk is available.

With hang-on queuing, the user activates the feature but remains off-hook until the call completes. Some queuing features enable high-priority users to jump to the head of the queue. The system should, however, have a maximum wait, after which even low-priority users are cut through.

Restriction Features

An important feature of every PBX is its ability to restrict the calling privileges of certain stations. Even companies with an unrestricted policy normally require restricted telephones in public locations such as waiting areas and lunchrooms. The type of restriction varies with manufacturer, but it is possible with most systems to restrict incoming, outgoing, and any type of long-distance calls. Some systems can restrict down to a specific telephone number. All restriction systems should restrict selected area codes and prefixes. Area code restriction is necessary to prevent users from dialing numbers, such as 900 numbers, for which a charge is collected.

Uniform Call Distribution (UCD)

This service distributes calls evenly among a group of stations. When one or more active stations are idle, incoming calls are directed to the station that is next in line to receive a call. When all stations in the UCD group are busy, incoming calls are answered with a recording and held in queue. When a UCD station becomes idle, the call that has been in queue the longest is directed to the station. In many UCD systems, a station user can toggle between active and inactive status by dialing a code or pressing a feature button. Compared to ACD, UCD is unsophisticated, lacking the supervisory, management, and reporting features that an ACD offers. Chapter 25 discusses UCD in more detail.

Unified Messaging

This feature, which is discussed in more detail in Chapter 27, combines the PBX with voice mail, fax, and e-mail so that messages can be viewed and handled on a PC screen. The feature may also enable users to translate messages from one format to another. For example, e-mail messages may be read in synthesized voice if the user is calling from a telephone and wants them read out. Ultimately, with speech-to-text software voice-mail messages may be converted to e-mail or fax.

Data Switching Capability

Digital PBXs use a proprietary protocol that resembles BRI on their digital ports. Two information channels are sent to each station, but only one is used in the proprietary telephone. When digital PBXs first came out, manufacturers intended to use this port for data switching and for modem pooling. The theory was that the user could plug a terminal into the telephone, attach a modem from a pool, and dial out. The PBX could also serve as a data switch, providing port selection and port concentration. In the 1980s this feature was highly touted, but cheap desktop computers and modems, and the LAN with much higher speed, effectively killed data switching and modem pooling for PBXs. Recently, however, manufacturers have begun to offer data adapters and special telephones that can access this unused port and turn it into an analog channel. Users can plug in modems, faxes, answering machines, and other such devices into an RJ-11 port on the back of the telephone and obtain a second port for "free." It isn't free, of course, because the extra cost of the adapter often equals the cost of an analog port on the PBX, but it saves card slots and eliminates the need for a separate wire path.

Modem Pooling

Individual modems are cost-effective for a few connections. If data usage is extensive, however, they become expensive because of the need for separate analog ports and modems, which together may exceed the cost of a modem pool.

A modem pool has circuit cards or external data adapters in the PBX that interface with a bank of modems. When the user initiates a data call, the PBX attaches a modem and the user can dial outside the PBX as usual. A data session can be carried simultaneously with a voice session in most PBXs. The PBX requires either one or two ports per session. If an incoming data call is directed to a DID telephone number that is identified as a data device, the PBX diverts the call through the modem pool, attaches a modem, and completes the call. Although most manufacturers provide this capability, it is rarely used because most companies prefer to pool modems on the LAN.

Emergency Service Interface

Most of the developed world has adopted a special dialing code, such as 999 or 911, for universal access to emergency services. The basic service enables the public safety answering point (PSAP) to hold up the line so it can be traced in case the caller is unable to report the address of the emergency. Enhanced emergency services contain a database that associates telephone numbers with street addresses. The street address is often not a fine enough distinction, however. Users who dial the emergency code from hotels, apartments with a shared-tenant PBX, campuses, and multibuilding developments and the like may be difficult or impossible to locate. Therefore, a trend is toward reporting the station identification to the PSAP so it can be associated with the room number or building name. This is a standard feature of PRI in some PBXs, and the PSAP can receive it if the LEC passes it along. Other PBXs offer a centralized message-accounting (CAMA) trunk as an alternative. The need for this feature is particularly acute in PBXs with remote switch units that may even be located in a different PSAP's jurisdiction from the host PBX. In this case a separate trunk group to the local central office is usually provided. The ARS is programmed so it always seizes a local trunk when the emergency code is dialed.

Multitenant Service

PBXs that provide service to users from different organizations can use multitenant software to give each user organization the appearance of a private switch. Separate attendant consoles can be provided, and each organization can have its own group of trunks and block of numbers.

Property Management Interface

Hotels, hospitals, dormitories, and other organizations that resell service often connect the PBX to a computer to provide features such as checking room status information, disabling the telephone set from the attendant console, and determining check-in or check-out status. The PBX provides information to the computer, and accepts orders from the front desk via computer terminal.

Uniform Dialing Plan (UDP)

Uniform dialing plan software in a network of PBXs enables the caller to dial an extension number and have the call completed over a tie-line network without the caller's being concerned about where the extension is located. The PBX selects the route and takes care of station number translations. UDP software is effective only among PBXs of the same manufacture although it may work with Q.Sig-compatible PBXs.

Universal Card Slots

The card slots on some PBXs are designated for a particular type of card. Therefore, it is possible that a shelf or cabinet may have vacant slots but not have any available for the type of card that is needed. Except for processor and power-supply cards, which usually require dedicated slots, PBXs with universal card slots can accept any type of line or trunk card in a vacant slot. This feature lends an important degree of flexibility to the system.

Wireless Capability

Many organizations have classes of users who must roam about the building. Wireless systems are just coming on the market to allow use of the telephone anywhere in a building or within a restricted range on a campus. Two types of wireless systems are available. One type plugs into analog port on the PBX, and gives the user capabilities of analog telephones. Proprietary wireless systems provide the features of digital telephones, including button access to features, multiline capability, and other such features. Chapter 19 discusses wireless in more detail.

PBX Voice Features

As all PBXs are designed for voice switching service, they have features intended for the convenience and productivity of the users. Not all the features listed here are universally available, and many systems provide features not listed. This list briefly describes the most popular voice features found in PBXs:

- The PBX can be equipped with *paging* trunks that are accessed by an attendant or dialed from a station. An option is *zone paging,* which allows the attendant to page in specific locations rather than the entire building.
- *Distinctive ringing* enables a station user to tell whether a call has originated from inside or outside the system.
- *Speed dialing* enables station users to dial other numbers by using abbreviated codes. Speed dial is available from telephone set buttons or from a system speed-dial list that everyone within a speed-dial group shares.
- *Integrated key telephone system features,* such as those described in Chapter 20, can be integrated into the PBX software and accessed from a nonkey telephone. Features such as call pickup, call hold, call forwarding, do not disturb, and dial-up conferencing are universally available.
- The caller's name or telephone number can be displayed on special telephones equipped with an *alphanumeric display.* Systems equipped for calling number delivery show this for external as well as internal calls. When calls forward to another telephone in a coverage path, the display shows what number was dialed and why it was forwarded.
- *Call coverage* features allow the administrator to set up automatic coverage paths to determine how calls will route when the called station is busy, does not answer, or is in do-not-disturb status.
- *Forced account code dialing* is used in PBXs in which call detail must be identified by caller instead of by station number. For example, it is often used in colleges and universities where roommates share the same extension number.
- *Special dialing* features are provided in many systems. Besides digit dialing, some systems allow dialing by name from an integrated directory.
- *Executive override* allows a station to interrupt a busy line or preempt a long-distance trunk if the class of that station is higher than the class of the user.
- *Trunk answer any station* allows stations to answer incoming trunks when the attendant station is busy.

◆ *Portable directory number* allows a user on a networked PBX to move from one switch to another without changing the telephone number.

Attendant Features

Most PBXs have attendant consoles for incoming call answer and supervision. The following features are important for most consoles and represent only a fraction of the features available:

◆ *Camp-on* is a feature that allows an attendant to queue an incoming call to a busy station. When the station becomes idle, the call is automatically completed. A related feature, *automatic callback,* enables station users to camp on busy station lines.

◆ *Direct station selection* allows the attendant to call any station by pressing an illuminated button associated with the line.

◆ *Automatic timed reminders* alert the attendant when a called line has not answered within a prescribed time. The attendant can also act as a central information source for directory and call assistance.

◆ *Attendant-controlled conferencing* is available for multiport conference calls.

◆ *Computer console* integrates the attendant functions into a PC so the attendant can look up a name in a database and transfer the call by clicking a mouse button.

System Administration Features

System administration is a costly part of every PBX, so any features that ease the administrator's job are valuable. The following are some of the more popular features:

◆ *Automatic set relocation* allows users to move their telephones from one location to another without the need to retranslate. The administrator gives users a code and instructions to carry the set to the new location, plug it in, and dial the code. When this is complete, the station translations are moved to the new port.

◆ *Network move* is a feature similar to automatic set relocation, except that it works across a network, where automatic set relocation works only in the same PBX.

◆ *Ethernet connectivity* to the management terminal is a valuable feature for system mangers who move around the office. The manager can go to any computer and access the system management port without dialing in from a modem.

◆ *Integrated PBX and voice-mail update* is an external PC application that enables the voice-mail and PBX databases to be updated from a single source. The application also may permit the administrator to work translations in software in advance, and then upload them to the PBX.

CALL-ACCOUNTING SYSTEMS

All PBXs, most hybrids, and many key telephone systems include a call detail recorder (CDR) port that receives call details at the conclusion of each call. The call details can be printed or passed to a call-accounting system for further processing. The CDR output of most systems is of little value by itself because calls are presented in order of completion and lack rates, identification of the called number, and other such details that control of long-distance costs requires. Call-accounting systems add details to create management reports, a complete long-distance statement for each user, and departmental summaries. The primary purposes of a call-accounting system are to discourage unauthorized use and to distribute costs to users. They also have many other uses in some companies. For example, a supervisor may use the CDR record to check the effectiveness of an employee's outgoing sales calls.

Most call-accounting systems on the market are software programs for personal computers. Programs for minicomputers and mainframes are also available, but inexpensive PCs have largely replaced them. CDR data either feeds directly into an online PC or it feeds into a buffer that stores call details until it is polled. A buffer makes it unnecessary to tie up a PC in collecting call details. If the power fails, the battery backup in the buffer retains the stored information.

In multi-PBX environments, a networked call-accounting system may be required. These systems use buffers or computers to collect information at remote sites and upload it to a central processor at the end of the collection interval. If long-distance calls can be placed from one PBX over trunks attached to another, a tie-line reconciliation program is important. The tie-line reconciliation program uses the completion time of calls to match calls that originate on one PBX and terminate on trunks connected to another. Networked PBXs send originating station identification over the signaling channel to a remote PBX. If the remote PBX is equipped to extract the calling station from the network channel and associate it with the CDR output, the need for tie-line reconciliation is eliminated.

Most PBXs can output any combination of long-distance, local, outgoing, and incoming calls to the CDR port. The amount of detail to collect is a matter of individual judgment, but remember that sufficient buffer and disk storage space must be provided to hold all the information collected.

APPLICATIONS

Nearly every business that has more than 30 to 50 stations is in the market for a PBX or its central office counterpart, Centrex (Chapter 28). PBXs are economical for some small businesses that need features such as restriction, networking, and ARS, which most key systems do not provide. They are also economical for very large businesses that use central office switching systems of a size that rivals many metropolitan public networks. This chapter discusses an application halfway between these two extremes.

PBX Standards

Few standards exist for PBXs. The interface between a PBX and its serving local central office is standardized by EIA, and trunk interfaces follow accepted industry practices for signaling and electrical interface. Q.Sig is a standard for networking PBXs, and many systems are beginning to support H.323 for packet voice. The industry generally adopts the same PBX features, but the manufacturer may use a unique method of operating the feature. Analog telephones follow accepted industry signaling practice, but the loop-resistance range is left to the manufacturer. Proprietary station interfaces are determined entirely by the manufacturer with little uniformity among products. With only a few exceptions, proprietary station sets intended for one PBX cannot be used in another manufacturer's system.

Evaluation Considerations

In choosing a PBX it is important that you understand exactly what you want it to do. The differences between systems are often subtle, and differences in function and support aren't apparent until you have lived with the system for several months. This makes it important to check references very carefully.

The uniqueness of every organization makes a universal PBX specification impractical. Considerations that are important in some applications will have no importance in others. Therefore, the buyer should weigh them accordingly. It is, of course, essential that the system contain the required features and that it meet the requirements for quantities of line and trunk terminations. Reliability and cost are implicit requirements in any telecommunications system and are not separately discussed.

External Interfaces

Every PBX must conform to the standard EIA-464 interface to a local telephone central office and must be registered with the FCC for network connection. In addition, interfaces such as these should be considered:

♦ PRI and BRI interfaces
♦ EIA-232 or EIA-449 data set or workstation interface to telephone instruments
♦ Computer-telephony integration interface
♦ Interface to local area networks
♦ Q.Sig interface
♦ T1/E1 interface to external trunk groups or to internal devices such as remote access servers

A key consideration in evaluating a PBX is the type of terminals it supports. All PBXs have, at a minimum, a two-wire station interface to a standard analog DTMF telephone. Ordinary telephones are the least expensive terminals and because of the quantities of stations involved in a large PBX, inability to use standard telephones can add significantly to the cost. The standard analog telephone falls short, however, as a terminal in most offices.

Proprietary telephones are the most practical way of accessing integrated key telephone features. Some features tend fall into disuse because of the difficulty of using them from standard telephones. A proprietary terminal may improve ease of use for some features, such as call pickup and hold, by using buttons to replace the switchhook flashes and special codes required with standard telephones.

These features should be considered in evaluating a PBX terminal interface:

- Proprietary or nonproprietary telephone interface
- Number of conductors to the station
- Number of lines and characters on the telephone set display
- Station conductor loop range
- Integrated key telephone system features
- Message waiting or nonmessage waiting line card
- Availability of BRI interface

Universal Shelf Architecture

Universal shelf architecture permits various types of line and trunk cards to be installed in any slot. Without this feature, slots are dedicated to a particular type of card. It is, therefore, possible to have plenty of spare slot capacity in the PBX but have no room for cards of the desired type. Check to determine if all port cards are universal or whether some specialized types require dedicated slots.

Switch Network

A key evaluation consideration is whether the switch network is blocking or nonblocking. Blocking networks are acceptable, but may require additional administrative effort to keep them in balance. Also, consider the number of busy-hour call attempts the PBX is capable of supporting to determine if the processor limits the capacity of the system. Some manufacturers use the term "virtually nonblocking" to indicate that there are nearly as many time slots as stations.

Voice and Data Integration Issues

If you have enough circuits to justify a T1/E1 carrier and do not need it all for voice, it is often feasible to share the T1/E1 between voice and data.

ISDN Compatibility Issues

ISDN is not universally available yet, but the ILECs will gradually convert their central offices to ISDN over the next several years. IXCs and most CLECs offer

ISDN services now, so any company considering a new PBX must evaluate ISDN compatibility. Consider not only PRI, but also BRI so users can take advantage of desktop videoconferencing.

Administrative Interface

All PBXs have some form of administrative interface through a terminal or attached PC. The ease of use of this interface differs significantly among products. The most difficult products to use have a command-driven terminal interface. At the other end of the spectrum are systems with graphical user interfaces that allow users to make point-and-click changes.

Redundancy

Organizations that cannot tolerate PBX outages can improve reliability by purchasing redundant systems. Several levels of redundancy are available. The lowest level provides redundant processors. Higher reliability can be achieved with redundant power supplies and switching networks. Even with redundancy failures will still occur, but reliability should be much higher than with a nonredundant system.

Environmental Considerations

Most PBXs can operate without air conditioning in an ordinary office environment. The operating temperature range should be evaluated, however, because some systems do require an air-conditioned environment. Even without air conditioning, adequate air circulation will be required.

Database Updates

The ease of changing classes of service and telephone numbers is an important evaluation consideration. If the attendant console or an easy-to-use maintenance terminal can control these, it is possible to add, remove, and move stations and to change restrictions without using a trained technician. With a truly flexible system, station jacks are wired to line ports. A new station is added by plugging in the telephone and activating the line from an attendant or maintenance console.

Diagnostic Capability

The degree to which a PBX can diagnose its own trouble and direct a technician to the source of trouble is important in controlling maintenance expense. It also is important that a system have remote diagnostic capability so the manufacturer's technical assistance center can access the system over a dial-up port.

Station Wiring Limits

The station loop range of both proprietary terminals and ordinary telephones must be considered in evaluating a PBX. Most proprietary terminals and those terminals requiring an EIA interface can operate only over a restricted range. Range limits can be extended in some systems by using distributed switching, which moves the line circuits close to the stations.

Bandwidth Requirements

Bandwidth is of concern with systems that interface with high-speed digital lines. Digital voice PBXs may limit modem data speed to 9600 b/s or less. With special data ports, higher speeds are supported, including, in some systems, enough bandwidth to switch a 1.544-Mb/s bit stream. Consider whether $N \times 64$ capability is required to support videoconferencing.

Wireless Capability

Many organizations need wireless capability so the telephones of certain users are no longer tethered to the wall. Wireless systems that support analog telephones can be used with any PBX, but the ability to use proprietary telephones may be important.

Call-Accounting Evaluation Issues

Most PBXs today are purchased with a call-accounting system that is normally programmed and supported by an external company. The following are some criteria for selecting a call-accounting system.

Reports

The main reason for buying a call-accounting system is for its reports. Evaluate factors such as these:

- What kinds of reports are provided? Do they meet the organization's requirements?
- Can reports be distributed over the Internet or a company intranet?
- Are custom-designed reports possible?
- Is it possible to link report information to an external program, such as a spreadsheet or database management system, to produce custom reports?
- Are traffic reports produced? If so, are they accurate?
- Are management reports, such as inventories, provided?
- What kind of manual effort is needed to produce reports? Does it require a trained operator, or can clerical people perform the month-end operations with little or no formal training?
- Does the manufacturer support tie-line reconciliation?

Vendor Support

As with most software packages, vendor support is important for installing and maintaining the system. Evaluate the vendor's experience in supporting the package.

Determine whether the vendor has people who have been specifically trained. Evaluate the amount of support the package developer has available and what it costs. Some vendors sell ongoing support packages, and where these are available, the cost-effectiveness should be evaluated.

Call Rating

Most call-accounting packages have call-rating tables based on vertical and horizontal (V&H) tables. These divide the United States and Canada into a grid from which point-to-point mileage can be calculated. Tables must be updated regularly as rates change. Also, consider that many companies do not need absolute rate accuracy. To distribute costs among organizational units, precision is usually not required. Many long-distance rate plans use rates that are not distance-sensitive, so V&H rating accuracy is not required. Determine facts such as these:

◆ What kind of rating tables does the manufacturer support?

◆ How frequently are tables updated?

◆ What do updates cost?

◆ What IXCs' rates does the package support?

◆ How are intrastate rates calculated?

◆ Do you need to bill back with high accuracy?

Capacity

Call storage equipment is intended to maintain information on a certain number of calls. When buffer storage is full, it must be unloaded and calls processed. Usually, the system must store at least 1 month's worth of calls either directly or by uploading data to a computer. Evaluate questions such as these:

◆ How much storage space is required?

◆ What is the capacity in number of calls, both incoming and outgoing?

◆ How much growth capacity is provided?

◆ Is storage nonvolatile so if power fails calls are not lost?

CHAPTER 25

Automatic Call Distribution Equipment

Customer service is becoming the most important way that companies distinguish themselves from their competitors. Buyers have boundless choices, and the ease of shopping over the Internet means that companies must search for constant improvement in service, while trimming costs. The brick-and-mortar store is being supplemented by what might be called a virtual shopping center. Buyers can download all the information they need about a product from the Internet, and then shop for the best deal. To respond to this changing trend, the automatic call distributor (ACD) is also evolving.

At one time only the largest call centers could afford an ACD, which was a specialized stand-alone device. The ACD might integrate with the office telephone system, but often the agents or customer service representatives had separate phones on their desks. Now ACD is part of most PBXs. Major PBX manufacturers now report that more than three-fourths of their systems ship with ACD software, and stand-alone ACDs still have part of the call center market. ACD is an inexpensive addition to most PBXs, and even some hybrids. Any business with a group of agents or customer service representatives who answer incoming calls or place large numbers of outgoing calls should consider an ACD or its cousin, the predictive dialer, which is used for outbound calls.

ACDs fall into two categories: stand-alone and PBX-integrated. The former is more expensive than a PBX system and is generally effective in large call centers with sophisticated routing and reporting requirements. If the call center is a major function of a work group, a stand-alone ACD may offer features that are unavailable in a PBX. If ACD is an incidental function of a PBX that is needed for other purposes, the cost of a stand-alone system will likely be prohibitive.

Callers can so easily jump from one call center to another that managers must be prepared to respond within a holding time that the caller perceives as reasonable. When callers must wait, methods are employed to keep them informed and induced to wait, and perhaps entertained. Technology has risen to the challenge by marrying the ACD with computers and voice-processing equipment, which finds extensive application in the call center. Sophisticated algorithms predict the waiting time and announce it together with queue position to the callers while they wait. Such techniques as calling number delivery and caller-input account numbers help the equipment to recognize who is calling, what they want, and to improve their treatment while in queue. Good customers can be routed to priority queues, and given the red carpet treatment they would expect if they walked into a store. The key to effective call centers is to treat callers as individuals and handle them according to their unique needs. To do that, the equipment must obtain information without being intrusive. While it isn't perfect, call center equipment is improving every year.

A call center typically has banks of toll-free lines with different numbers associated with different product lines or promotions. Groups of agents are equipped for access to the corporate database, and a call distribution system identifies the callers and directs incoming calls to the appropriate agent. Skill-based routing is an important feature for matching callers with the agents best equipped to handle their transaction. Telemarketing centers also may use predictive dialing equipment, a technology similar to ACD that places outgoing calls automatically and delivers connected parties to a group of agents. As the Internet thrives, the ACD is married to it with technology that enables a shopper to browse an online catalog or self-help application, and connect to an agent to place an order or obtain additional information.

The opportunities for creativity are unlimited, and each new crop of equipment brings innovations that make it easier to do business through applications of technology. This chapter discusses call distribution equipment and features, but some of these features do not work without voice processing, which is discussed in Chapter 27, and in some cases computer-telephony integration, which is the subject of the next chapter.

CALL DISTRIBUTION TECHNOLOGY

An incoming call center can be set up with ordinary key telephone equipment, which is the way smaller companies handle calls to a defined work group. Calls arrive on trunk-hunting lines, and an agent pushes a button to answer the call. If incoming calls exceed the available agents, someone must interrupt a call in progress to answer it and put it on hold. If several calls are on hold, there is no easy way to know which caller has waited longest. Also, distribution of the workload depends on the action of the agents and how effectively they are supervised. Information to assess service quality and workload is in short supply. While many companies still use this method of distributing calls, any organization with more than a few answering positions finds that the cost of some form of machine-controlled call distribution pays for itself quickly. Call distribution can be effective for even a single answering position if it enables the user to avoid interrupting a call in progress.

A uniform call distribution system (UCD), which is a standard feature of most PBXs and hybrids, can improve call handling. A proprietary PBX station set serves as the agent telephone. The UCD routes incoming calls to the first available agent. If no agent is available, the UCD routes calls to an announcement, holds them in queue, and sends the call that arrived first to the first available agent. In most UCD systems, the caller hears only the initial announcement and listens to silence or music-on-hold after that. UCDs relieve agents of the need to interrupt a call in progress to answer another call and put it on hold, but they lack the ability to balance workload among agents, and they do not provide more than basic management reports.

The stand-alone counterpart of a UCD is the call sequencer. This device may work with a PBX or key telephone system or it may be connected directly to incoming lines. Unlike the UCD, a call sequencer does not direct calls. It alerts agents to the presence of incoming calls by lighting keys on the telephone or lighting an external display. It answers the call, provides a delay announcement to the callers, and provides limited statistical information.

The most sophisticated device is the automatic call distributor (ACD), which is the primary focus of this chapter. ACDs provide complex call-handling strategies that enable the call center to achieve its cost and service goals. They provide statistical information that can be used for matching the staff to the load, forecasting workload, scheduling staff, and evaluating service. The differences between ACDs, UCDs, and sequencers are significant but not always apparent without analysis. Table 25-1 lists the most important differences.

An ACD has the following major components:

- Trunks
- Switching unit
- Agent positions
- Voice-processing equipment
- Announcement equipment
- Supervisory and monitoring equipment
- Management software

The functions of an ACD are to answer calls, and, if possible, to identify callers and find out what they want. If agents are available, the ACD routes the call to the appropriate position. If no agents are available, the ACD queues the calls, provides music and an announcement while callers are in queue, and overflows queued calls to another queue or voice mail after a prescribed interval. It collects and processes call statistics, although detailed processing and reporting is usually assigned to an outboard processor.

TABLE 25-1

Comparison of Call Distribution Products

	ACD	**UCD**	**Call Sequencer**
Basis for distributing calls to agents	Based on time. Usually the next call is sent to the least busy agent. Can route based on skills.	Based on sequence. Usually top-down or circular hunt.	Does not distribute calls. Alerts agents to incoming calls by colored lamps.
Statistical information	Provides real-time information on supervisor's terminal plus standard and custom printed reports.	Limited to line utilization and other basic reports.	Provides limited reporting.
Call overflow between groups	Programmable overflow based on variables such as time, priority, workload, etc.	Does not overflow.	Overflow is not applicable.
Features	Features are virtually unlimited. Can integrate with computer for customized call treatment.	Feature set is limited. Provides practically no enhancements.	Feature set is limited, but different products provide enhancements not found in others.
Telephone system integration	Furnished as stand-alone or part of a PBX, hybrid, or key system.	Furnished as part of a PBX, hybrid, or key system.	A stand-alone device that is designed to operate with a key system.

CALL-HANDLING ELEMENTS

Every ACD call has the following elements, as Figure 25-1 shows:

- *Answering* the call.
- *Identifying* or determining who the caller is and what he or she wants.
- *Queuing* or holding the call for an agent if none is immediately available.
- *Informing,* that is, keeping callers informed as to the status of the call and providing information to callers while they wait in queue.
- *Routing,* that is, sending the call to the appropriate service agent.
- *Delivering service.*
- *Terminating* the call.

The key to successful call center operation is the sequence in which these functions are handled. If the call is identified early in the process, it can be handled more intelligently than if it is identified later. The network and the call center equipment offer several identification strategies, which are covered in more detail in *The Irwin Handbook of Telecommunications Management.* Briefly, technology can assist in several ways. The caller can be identified by calling line identification

F I G U R E 25-1

Generic Call Flow Process

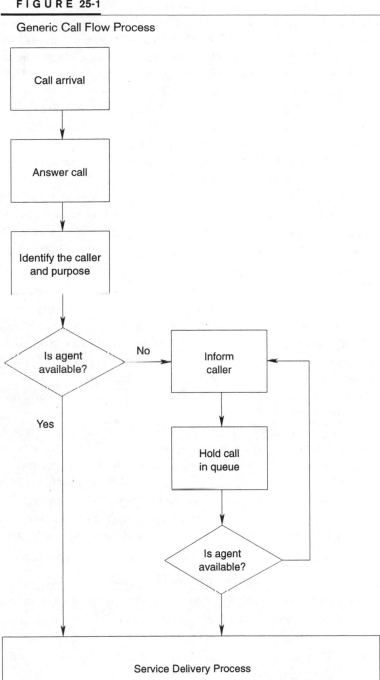

(CLID) or automatic number identification (ANI). The former applies to local trunks and the latter to toll-free lines. Callers can also identify themselves by dialing digits, such as an account number, that are captured in an interactive voice-response unit (IVR) or a call-prompting application. Callers can be identified by giving them a special DID or toll-free number to dial, with the latter captured by dialed number information system (DNIS).

Callers can be prompted to select the service they want through automated attendant or interactive voice response (IVR). Many companies provide different telephone or toll-free numbers for different services to route calls without using an automated attendant. For example, one number is sales, another customer service, another is order inquiry, and so on. The ACD uses the number to route the call. With early caller identification, calls can be routed much more effectively. The least effective strategy is to route the call directly to an agent without prescreening. If the agent receiving the call is incapable of providing the service, the call must be transferred, which contributes to added delay, customer annoyance, and extra cost.

Service Delivery

Although service delivery is the end of the call center process, considering it first can lead to some interesting alternatives. Only a human can deliver some services, and in call centers where this is the case, the objective of the process is to route the call to a qualified agent with a minimum of delay. Not incidentally, another objective is to keep the agents at a comfortable level of occupancy. (*Occupancy* in a call center is the percentage of time that agents are busy talking on calls or wrapping up after completion.)

If callers can satisfy their requests without involving an agent, they may be willing to do some of the work themselves. The IVR, which nearly every financial institution uses, is the best example of caller-directed service delivery. Account balances and fund transfers can be handled over the telephone 24 hours per day, which represents good service to customers that otherwise would have to wait for normal working hours. By thinking closely about alternatives, many forms of mechanized service delivery are possible. Here are some examples:

- Work schedules can be delivered via IVR or audiotex.
- Order status can be delivered by IVR.
- Outdialing equipment can remind patients of scheduled appointments.
- Information about job openings can be posted in an audiotex bulletin board.
- Technical service callers can be offered a trouble diagnostic tree while they wait in queue.

Callers should be offered a way of transferring to an agent after they have listened to the information available. For example, a job applicant who wants more detail should be able to press a digit to speak to a human.

Informing

Technology can improve customer satisfaction by keeping callers informed while they wait. The most basic form is through queue announcements, which can be delivered by digital announcement systems, IVR, or even by humans who can enter the queue to provide information or entertainment. Music-on-hold is one form of information—it informs callers that they are still connected in queue. Some companies provide product information through a recorded source to callers while they wait.

Some effective call centers provide intelligent queue announcements, which inform callers of their queue position and expected length of wait. An external device, usually an IVR, is needed to provide intelligent queue announcements. The outboard device obtains information about queue conditions from the ACD's management information system (MIS) channel, performs the necessary calculations, and reports it to the callers in conjunction with the regular queue announcement. The routing script may give the caller the opportunity to leave a callback message in voice mail if the wait becomes excessive. While expected wait time announcements are appealing to callers, they can also be confusing if the algorithm for predicting length of wait is deficient or if the center prioritizes certain types of calls. If callers hear a predicted wait time that is getting progressively longer instead of shorter, as it might be if other calls are moved ahead of them in queue, they may become irritated and hang up.

Routing

The objective of an ACD is to connect a caller to an available agent that has the skills to fulfill the request. To do an effective matching job, it is evident that the system needs to know something about both the callers and the agents. Agent information is readily available from the switch. Caller information is collected from a variety of sources such as caller ID, DNIS number, caller-dialed digits, speech recognition, and automated attendant menu selections.

Conditional Routing

The most flexible systems permit the administrator to write a *routing script*, or *vector*, as it is sometimes known, to vary call routing under different conditions. Typical conditions that can be programmed into routing scripts are length of time in queue, number of agents logged on in a queue, number of waiting calls, time of day or day of week, and other such variables. Writing a vector is similar to writing a simple computer program using if-and-then logic. For example, a script might read *if the number of calls in queue is greater than 10 and agents logged on are less than 8, and the length of the oldest waiting call is greater than 2 minutes, overflow to the alternate queue.*

Skill-Based Routing

The most effective ACDs maintain a skills database on each agent, match the caller's needs to agents' skills, and route accordingly. The skills could be anything from language proficiency to technical knowledge. Skill routing systems provide several levels of ability, and give the administrator tools to set up a routing algorithm. Skill-based routing software may be included in the ACD's generic program, in an IVR, or in a specialized outboard processor.

Overflow

One feature that distinguishes an ACD from a UCD or a call sequencer is its ability to overflow calls from one queue to another. An important function of all effective ACDs is the ability to route calls from one queue to another during overload conditions. *Timed overflow* routes calls based on the amount of time the user has waited in queue. For example, a queue might be programmed to play an opening announcement, hold the call in queue for 20 seconds, play a second announcement, and hold the call again. The system might loop through this set of instructions until a specified amount of time or number of loops has elapsed, and then route the call to another queue. To avoid routing a call into a condition of worse congestion, some ACDs provide *look-ahead routing,* in which the ACD looks at the next queue before overflowing. *Look-back routing* is an option in which the ACD checks to see if congestion has improved in the original queue, and if so, returns the call to its original position. Some ACDs queue the caller on both the original and the overflow queue and route the call to the first available position in either.

If the ACD has conditional routing, in addition to length of time in queue, overflow is based on one or more of the following variables:

◆   *Number of calls waiting.* For example, a routing script might check the alternate queue and overflow if fewer than a given number of calls are waiting.

◆   *Time of day.* Calls might overflow from a center in the east to one in the west after 5:00 P.M., but not during the day unless the load exceeds a threshold.

◆   *Caller priority.* Arrival on a priority trunk group or dialing a special number might entitle the caller to different treatment than callers on nonpriority groups. Calls on more expensive trunks might be afforded priority to reduce the company's expense for toll-free service.

◆   *Length of oldest waiting call.* Calls might overflow only after the oldest call in the queue has been waiting more than a given number of seconds. This keeps calls in the primary queue for service, and overflows them only when the wait is excessive.

ACDs often are equipped with an automated attendant on the front end to assist in call routing and voice mail on the back end to handle overflows and give callers the option of leaving a message instead of waiting. Chapter 27 discusses these technologies. The automated attendant can be either a front-end device that is not connected with the voice mail or part of the voice-mail system. Usually a call center is divided into several *splits* or groups. When calls are queued for a group of agents, they must have some common set of characteristics, which may be identified by the automated attendant or simply by the dialed number.

When a call arrives at the head of a queue, if an agent is available, the ACD routes the call directly to the agent unless the caller is forced to listen to an announcement before being routed. The call is delivered automatically to the agent's telephone set. The greatest amount of call-handling efficiency is gained through using larger groups. With skill-based routing, it may be possible to keep all agents in a single large group, which can improve efficiency.

ACD FEATURES AND OPERATION

To be recognized by the system, agents must log on to a particular split. In some systems agents can log on to more than one split. The act of logging on does not, however, mean the agent is available to take a call. In most ACDs the agent also must press a key on the telephone set. The system identifies agents as being in one of several states. Typically, the software recognizes the following states and tallies statistics accordingly:

- *Available.* When an agent is available, the system can deliver the next call.
- *Busy.* The busy state indicates that the agent is currently handling a call.
- *After call work or wrap-up.* Most ACDs permit the agent to spend a variable or fixed amount of time after each contact completing paper work before the next call arrives.
- *Unavailable.* This state is used when the agent is temporarily away from the position, typically during breaks.

The call center supervisor usually has a terminal to monitor the status of service and load. The terminal lists agents by name, shows their current state, and displays a summary of their production statistics. In some systems the display also shows how long agents have been in their current state, which is useful for determining when wrap-up or unavailable time is excessive. The terminal also should display information about service levels.

Most ACDs also provide supervisory monitoring capability for service observing. Monitoring may be silent or accompanied by a tone that is audible to the agent but not to the caller. Call monitoring is a sensitive issue, and company policy or state law may prohibit monitoring unless the agent is notified.

Telephone Instruments

The agent's telephone set is important to call center effectiveness. Most PBX-integrated ACDs use a specialized telephone set for the agent terminal. The set is equipped with a headset jack, and is programmed to deliver calls without the need to lift a switch hook. Multibutton digital sets provide for functions such as logging in and out and changing state without dialing the special access codes that are required with single-line sets. Display sets show the agent such information as caller identity, the trunk group on which the call arrived, length of time the caller waited, and number of calls currently in queue. In most applications, improved agent productivity justifies the extra expense of a multiline digital display set. High-end stand-alone ACDs normally are equipped with proprietary telephones. Some systems use a combined telephone and video display terminal as the agent position.

Outbound Calling

Many ACDs (also stand-alone predictive dialers) are equipped for outbound calling. A system with outbound capability dials numbers from a database and connects the called party to an agent only after dialing is complete. Some systems have answer-detection capability and connect to an agent only after the called party answers. Although answering machines and voice mail sometimes fool such systems, most systems detect busy and unanswered calls and store the numbers for later retry.

The primary hazard with outcalling systems is completing a call when no agents are available. Because so many lines are busy or do not answer, and because it takes time to set up each call, the system is placing calls when there are no idle agents. If the system waits for an agent to be idle before initiating the call, the productivity of the agents will drop. Most systems use some type of predictive calling to anticipate when an agent will become available. If an agent is not available within seconds of the time the called party answers, the party perceives the call as a nuisance call and hangs up.

ACD Reporting

A major part of an ACD's value lies in its reporting capabilities. ACD reports are either part of the generic program of the switch or they are produced in an outboard computer that attaches to the ACD's MIS channel. Reports produced in the ACD are not user-programmable, and are therefore less flexible than those produced in an outboard computer. Reports produced by most systems fall into the following categories.

Agent Reports   These reports provide statistics for individual agents, for example, amount of time logged on, number of calls handled, average talking and wrap-up time per call, number and duration of outgoing calls, hold time on calls, and amount of time in an unavailable state. Supervisors can use agent reports to determine how agents perform with respect to each other, group averages, or objectives.

Group Reports   Groups, splits, or queues, as they are variously known, are identifiable workgroups that are assigned a particular function. Group reports show group totals and averages for the variables discussed under agent reports.

They also provide information that does not apply to individual agents such as average speed of call answer, numbers of abandoned calls, average and maximum length of time to abandon, and length of longest-waiting call. Group and agent statistics together give administrators insight into service levels and information to calculate staff requirements.

Skillset Reports   Systems equipped with skill-based routing normally report results for the skillset, which may include agents that are members of multiple groups. These reports could enable a manager to determine service levels for a specific customer that has been defined as a skill, for service given to callers who speak a particular language, and other such elements that are defined as a skill.

Trunk Reports   Most large call centers have several trunk groups for which the ACD reports statistics. Reports such as call volume and length, number of abandons, trunk group usage, and so on permit administrators to determine whether service or cost trends pattern to a specific trunk group.

Routing Script Reports   These reports show information such as the stage in the routing script at which calls are abandoned. These statistics can be used to evaluate the scripts' effectiveness. A high rate of abandonment at a particular point may show that the script is confusing.

Real-Time Reporting   ACDs provide MIS channels that enable supervisors to see what is going on in real time. The screen can be switched from agent to group statistics in most systems. Group statistics show such variables as the number of calls in queue, the length of average and longest wait, number of abandoned calls, and other such variables during the current reporting period (usually 30 minutes to 1 hour). Agent reports show for each agent the current status, for example, talking, available, unavailable, wrap-up, and so on, how long the agent has been in that status, number of calls handled, and number of outgoing calls during the reporting period.

Most supervisors' terminals show alerts in different colors or screen intensity. For example, thresholds could be set for length of time in an unavailable mode, which is normally used for relief periods. The name of an agent that was within the prescribed interval would be shown in green, one that was a few minutes over would be yellow, and one that had overstayed the upper threshold would be red. Color displays aid the supervisor in monitoring staff and costs.

NETWORKED CALL CENTERS

In a company with multiple call centers, efficiency can be achieved with networking—often enough to more than pay the cost of facilities between the centers. If ACDs are connected either with PRI or a proprietary networking interface, they can exchange load and workforce information across the D channel, switching calls across a voice channel where agents are available. An ACD experiencing an overload can check other centers, reserve an idle agent, and pass the call across the network.

The major IXCs offer a call allocation service for distributing calls to ACDs that are not fully networked. In the static call allocation model, the administrator informs the IXC's signaling control point (SCP) of the percentage of calls to allocate to each center. With dynamic call allocation, the ACDs are networked together with a signaling channel or they use the PSTN to obtain status information and communicate it over a D channel to the IXC. With call-by-call allocation, the ACD informs the SCP on a real-time basis of which center should receive the next call. This application, which is often outboard of the ACD, may be a CTI device, as discussed in Chapter 26.

INTEGRATED PBX VERSUS STAND-ALONE ACD

A key question facing a prospective ACD owner is whether to select a stand-alone or a PBX-integrated system. Both systems have their applications and advantages, and the selection should be made with the factors in this section in mind. A third choice, which we will discuss in a later section, is the central office ACD (CO-ACD), which is on the LEC's premises.

The first factor to consider is the functionality needed. ACD is a processor-intensive application, and some PBXs will lack the capacity to support a large call center. The cost of a stand-alone ACD will be two to four times the cost of a PBX-integrated ACD, so small centers that are operating on a tight budget will find it difficult to justify the cost of a stand-alone system. In any call center the cost of the equipment is only a fraction of the total cost of operating the center, however. If the features or productivity gains of a stand-alone system are needed, cost should not be an overriding concern.

A second question relates to the nature of the center and the need to integrate it with regular telephone features of the rest of the organization. If the call center operates as part of a larger group, and must transfer and receive calls from the rest of the organization, a PBX-integrated ACD will be easier to set up and administer. Stand-alone ACDs can be connected via tie lines to a PBX, but full networking between the two will not be available. In either case, the Achilles' heel of some stand-alone ACDs is the difficulty of transferring calls between the PBX and the ACD. In some centers the ACD agent requires two telephones, one for the PBX and one for the ACD. The ACD usually can route calls to the voice mail on the PBX, but in a nonintegrated system there is usually no way to turn on the ACD user's message-waiting light.

Another question is how the call center is being deployed. If the company has an existing PBX and the call center is a new application that is being added to the company, it can almost certainly be added to the PBX more easily than acquiring a new stand-alone ACD. If the existing PBX is unsatisfactory and must be replaced, the cost per position of an integrated ACD will be less than the cost per position of a stand-alone ACD. If the PBX is satisfactory and can be retrofitted for an ACD package, this also will be less expensive than purchasing a stand-alone system. If, however, the PBX cannot be retrofitted, a stand-alone or CO-ACD should be considered.

Very large applications, including systems that require networking, often require stand-alone systems. In large applications, such as airline reservations systems, the ACD requirements may outstrip the capabilities of a PBX. Generally, stand-alone ACDs offer more processing power, more sophisticated software, and better reporting capabilities than PBX ACDs, but the difference is diminishing. PBXs have been increasing in processing capacity in the last few years, and networked ACD is offered by most of the major systems.

The amount of communication with non-ACD users behind a PBX is another factor that should be considered. An integrated ACD has all the features of the PBX and all the features of the ACD, which usually facilitates call transfer within the total system. If ACD and non-ACD users share central office trunks, DID trunks, and toll-free lines, the PBX attendant or the DNIS feature can route calls to the ACD. If the trunks terminate directly on the ACD and there is little intermachine communication or transfer requirement, a stand-alone ACD will be effective.

OTHER CALL DISTRIBUTION ALTERNATIVES

Although the ACD is the appropriate vehicle for most call centers, other call distribution alternatives are available. Besides UCD and call sequencers, which were mentioned in the introduction to this chapter, many LECs offer ACD from the central office.

Central Office ACD

With CO-ACD agent sets and supervisory consoles are mounted on the user's premises and extended from the central office on local loops. The user's capital investment is reduced, and the LEC takes care of maintenance. If the CO-ACD is trunk-rated, the LEC applies a software restriction to limit the number of incoming trunks. If the tariff is not trunk-rated, a CO-ACD can offer the advantage of reducing trunk costs for the user. This can, however, be a disadvantage because the user may lose some control. For example, one way of handling temporary overloads is to let incoming calls ring several times before answering and queuing them. This way, toll-free costs are reduced and the caller may be less critical of service because the length of time in queue is reduced. Another way of limiting calls is to choke down the number of trunks to return busy signal to the callers. Unless the LEC offers complete customer control of the system software, some of this flexibility will be lost.

The features of a CO-ACD are similar to the features of a stand-alone unit. The advantages and disadvantages compared to customer-owned equipment are essentially the same as those of Centrex versus a PBX, as discussed in Chapter 28.

Uniform Call Distributor (UCD)

Most PBXs and hybrids offer a uniform call distribution package as a standard or optional feature. A group of agents is defined as a UCD group. The PBX queues calls when all agents are busy, provides music or an announcement, and routes the call to the first available agent. A UCD is similar to an ACD, but it does not provide the flexible response capability of an ACD. One method of call distribution in UCDs is to route calls in sequence, starting with the agent at the head of the sequence, which means that the workload is not equalized. The agent at the head of the hunt pattern receives the largest number of calls, while the agent at the end of the sequence receives calls only when all other agents are busy.

The UCD supervisory terminal is less sophisticated than with ACDs. Most UCDs use a display telephone for the supervisory terminal, so the reports and status of agents and service that an ACD provides are not available. The routing and overflowing capabilities are also less flexible with a UCD. The flexible response features discussed earlier are generally not available with a UCD. Reports are limited to what is programmed into the system and are considerably less useful than those provided by a full ACD.

On the positive side, UCDs are much less expensive than ACDs. In most PBXs the UCD software is a standard feature, and ordinary telephone sets can be used for the agent terminals. If the company does not have an extensive call center and does not require extensive reports, UCD is an inexpensive way to improve customer service. Also, the UCD can take advantage of features that the PBX provides such as voice mail.

Call Sequencer

Call sequencers are the least sophisticated call distributors. Unlike ACDs and UCDs, which deliver calls to idle agents, sequencers require the agent to press a button to select the call. Most call sequencers do not force an agent to pick up a call. Calls are answered with an announcement, and while the caller waits, music-on-hold is played. Different colored lights show which call has been waiting the longest. Therefore, although customer service and productivity usually are improved by answering and holding calls automatically, there is no way to ensure that the workload is evenly distributed. Sequencers may be programmed to go into night mode automatically and follow a strategy such as answer the line, play a message, and hang up.

Sequencers are usually not integrated with the telephone system, so it is difficult to take advantage of features such as voice mail. It also may be difficult to transfer calls from a call sequencer to a PBX extension; frequently a complex sequence of switchhook flashes is required. Sequencers are most effective when the workgroup has other duties besides call answering. For example, a dispatch center might receive service requests from customers, make remote tests, and dispatch service people. The only portion of the job that involves answering calls is the incoming requests, which may be only a small fraction of the total process. The sequencer is valuable because it can answer calls when all agents are occupied and indicate which call has been waiting the longest.

APPLICATIONS

Selecting the correct call distribution system and applying it intelligently are critical to the success of the call center. In most applications, the arriving calls are customers or potential customers, and the objective of the organization is to treat them professionally and promptly. This section discusses some aspects of selecting and evaluating a call distribution system.

Standards

There are no call distribution equipment standards as such. External interfaces are regulated by the same standards that cover PBXs, but internal operation is governed by proprietary standards. Manufacturers use proprietary protocols for call routing, overflow, agent displays and procedures, reports, and the like. Most systems provide similar functions, but the way they go about it is proprietary.

Evaluation Criteria

Most of the criteria listed for evaluating PBXs also apply to call distribution equipment. For example, the questions of redundant processors, backup battery supply, universal port structure, cabinet capacity, and other such criteria should be evaluated. If call distribution is part of a PBX, all the criteria discussed in Chapter 24 apply along with the criteria discussed here.

Type of Call Distributor

The first issue to resolve is whether the application requires an ACD, a UCD, or a call sequencer. If an ACD is required, a second issue is whether a stand-alone unit or one integrated with a PBX is most suitable. The following is a list of generalizations, most of which have exceptions in some product lines:

- If the office is served by a key telephone system, use a call sequencer.
- If the incoming call load is handled by a pool of people for whom answering incoming calls is only one of a list of duties, choose a call sequencer.
- If handling incoming calls is a primary duty, the office is already served by a PBX, detailed reports are not important, low cost is important, and workload equalization is unimportant, choose a UCD.
- If handling calls is a primary job, detailed reports are important, and the call center must be closely integrated with non-ACD operations in the office, choose a PBX with integrated ACD.

◆ If the call center is large and needs few PBX functions, choose a stand-alone ACD.

◆ If the organization uses Centrex, consider CO-ACD.

The dividing line between call distribution applications is not distinct, and product features are constantly changing. In selecting a product, it is important to match the product to the application, bearing in mind that much of the improvement achieved with a call distributor may come from changing existing procedures.

System Architecture

The architecture of most call distribution systems is similar within a particular category, but there are important differences among systems. In sequencers, the generic program is usually contained in ROM. In ACDs and UCDs it is contained in volatile memory and loaded from a disk. These criteria are important considerations selecting the architecture.

Type of Trunk Interface   Consider the types of trunks with which the system needs to interface. The most common types are loop start, ground start, PRI, BRI, T1/E1, E&M, and DID. Also consider whether the system can interface two-way trunks when both inward and out-calling are required.

Port Capacity   Consider the number of ports in the system. Port types to be included are trunk, agent, supervisory terminal, CRT, and CTI. Also consider whether the architecture supports universal or specialized slots for ports.

Open Architecture   As Chapter 26 discusses, CTI is an important method of increasing productivity and improving call handling in a call center. Even if CTI is not planned initially, the system should provide the capability.

Traffic Capacity   ACD agent stations are designed for a much higher level of call arrivals and port occupancy than regular PBXs, and therefore consume more switch capacity. As with other switching systems, the principal evaluation criteria are expressed in terms of call completions per hour and common channel signaling (CCS) per line.

Type of Display   The type of display for both agents and supervisors can affect productivity. Color displays are less tiring for the operator, and the color can be used to display call criteria. For example, a call that has been on hold for a long time can be presented in red to the agent. Supervisory displays can show critical criteria such as low service levels in red. Supervisory graphs can be displayed with the evaluation criteria highlighted in different colors. Also consider whether the display is proprietary or whether a standard terminal or personal computer can be used. Split-screen displays permit the operator to view more than one call at a time and are particularly useful to a supervisor who monitors multiple queues.

Networking Capability   Large organizations with multiple ACDs may be interested in networking, which is the ability to connect ACDs over tie lines or PRI circuits. Networked systems should have the ability of passing call-specific information, such as caller identification, from one system to another.

Queuing and Routing Algorithms   The most flexible systems provide true ifthen-else tools to enable the administrator to program the treatment a call receives as it enters the queue. It is important to know how many steps can be programmed in the vector for a call. It is also important to know what criteria, such as time of day, day of week, number of calls in queue, and length of oldest waiting call, can be used as the test points in the script. Determine whether the system has conditional routing and if skills-based routing is available.

Switch Architecture   The architecture of the switch is just as important in an ACD as in any other type of switching system. Factors to be considered include:

- Is the switch expandable in modular increments?
- Is the ACD an integral part of the switch or are portions of it assigned to outboard processors?
- Does the switch have built-in maintenance features that improve reliability? Is it vulnerable to the failure of an outboard processor?
- Is redundancy available? If so, what elements are duplicated?
- Does the switch use open architecture to permit easy interface with another system for enabling CTI?
- Does the switch have universal port architecture?
- How many separate queues does the system support?
- How many agents does the system support?
- How many supervisory consoles does the system support? Can more than one queue be monitored from a single terminal?

External Interfaces

Most ACDs and a few UCDs and call sequencers have interfaces to external systems. For example, consider whether the system must interface with a database on a mainframe, minicomputer, or desktop computer. Callers are given several strategies for completing their calls if the system has interfaces to voice mail, automated attendant, or an interactive voice-response unit. The system may require an interface to an outbound telemarketing unit, or the outbound unit may be included as a portion of the ACD.

Features

Many of the PBX features discussed in Chapter 24 are equally important for call distributors. The following are some features that should be considered in evaluating systems.

Agent Call Access and Display   ACDs can automatically cut the call through to an agent, while some UCDs and call sequencers require agents to press a key to receive the next call. The most effective systems display for the agent such information as how many calls are waiting and, when the call is connected, how long the caller waited in queue.

Overflow Capability   Consider whether it is acceptable for callers to remain in one queue or whether they should overflow to a second queue. If overflowing is required, determine whether it can be based on length of time in queue, position in queue, trunk group over which the call arrived, caller identification, or other criteria. Also, consider whether the system provides look-ahead and look-back capability and whether the system can dynamically reassign agents to different queues to react to changes in load.

Outbound Calling Capability   Whether a feature of an ACD or of a stand-alone unit, outbound calling capability is important to companies that have telemarketing functions or other functions, such as collections, that require a volume of outgoing calls. The system should be able to interface with a user database. Other important features include computer-controlled pacing of agents, predictive dialing, some type of reliable detection of called party answer, and rescheduling of unanswered calls.

Web-Enabled Interface   With the increasing amount of business being done across the Internet, this feature enables the caller to communicate with an agent without leaving the Web browser. Generally, three options are available:

- ◆ Click a button on the Web page to leave a callback message. An agent calls immediately.
- ◆ Hold a voice-only conversation with an agent using voice over IP. The agent can guide the customer through a price list, take an order, etc.
- ◆ Hold a one-way or two-way video session with the agent using video over IP.

Wrap-Up Strategy   Many applications require time for the agent to wrap up the call after completing the transaction. For example, it may be necessary to complete an order before taking the next call. ACDs should offer one or more ways to determine the duration of wrap-up:

- ◆ *Manual.* The agent presses the available key to accept another call.
- ◆ *Forced.* The system provides a set amount of time for wrap-up, then forces the agent to available status.

◆ *Programmable.* The ACD supervisor can create a program to vary the amount of wrap-up time.

The strategy for handling wrap-up can have a significant effect on productivity. With the manual method, an agent can extend wrap-up time and reduce productivity. With the forced system, the machine fails to recognize the variability in the amount of wrap-up time needed for different types of transactions. If the system is programmable, it can vary the amount of wrap-up time allotted for each type of transaction.

Reporting Capabilities

Most companies receive as much value from the reports a call distributor creates as they do from the functionality of the unit itself. The following factors should be considered.

Record versus Status Orientation   A record-oriented system provides call status after completion. A status-oriented system provides calling information in real time. With a record-oriented system, it is possible to determine how long a caller waited in queue after the transaction is finished but not while it is in process.

Data Accumulation   ACDs have different periods of time during which they can accumulate statistical information. Hourly and subhourly information is valuable for making immediate workforce adjustments or changing switch parameters such as wrap-up time. Daily and monthly information is useful for load forecasting and making long-term workforce adjustments. Consider how the information is accumulated and displayed:

◆ Can information be extracted in some standard file format to analyze in a spreadsheet or database management system?

◆ Is information stored in a volatile medium such as random access memory, and, if so, is it lost in a power failure?

◆ Does the system collect information on how the call is handled in the second queue when it overflows?

◆ If the call is transferred or routed to give the caller an opportunity to leave a voice-mail message, are the statistics continuous or is the call treated as a fresh call and statistics counted anew?

Management Software   Many systems provide software for management analysis. These programs fall into three categories:

◆ *Scheduler.* This software, which may be combined with forecasting software, helps the supervisor prepare schedules. The program analyzes force requirements by hour of the day and day of the week and optimizes available staff to meet the requirements.

- *Tracker.* Tracking software dynamically reviews service levels, based on the number of staff logged on and the volume of calls arriving. Workforce requirements are calculated based on service objectives. The software keeps track of absences and number of agents required per hour and calculates predicted service levels based on workload and the available workforce.
- *Forecaster.* Forecasting software reviews historical data and predicts call volume, workload, and workforce requirements.

Transaction Audit Trail   A transaction audit trail may be an important feature for an ACD manager. The audit trail time-stamps each event in the transaction from start to finish. The system identifies the agent and position handling the call and leaves a trail of the times the call was transferred or put on hold. The amount of wrap-up time is registered, and any telephone numbers, such as supervisor or wrap-up position, dialed during the transaction are recorded. If the system is equipped with DNIS or DID, the system logs the number the caller dialed. If the call fails for such reasons as inadequate facilities, excessively long wait, or poor queue management, this feature helps the supervisor diagnose the cause.

Report Types   The following reports are typically produced by the more sophisticated systems:

- Percent abandoned calls
- Percent all trunks busy
- Percent calls answered in X seconds
- Percent all positions busy
- Percent position occupancy
- Longest waiting time in queue
- Average number of calls in queue

Consider whether the reports are produced in real time or only after the fact. Real-time reports should display on the supervisor's console while calls are in progress, although they may be updated at intervals of 10 seconds or so. Most call distributors include basic reports as part of the system's generic program. These are usually not user-programmable and seldom satisfy all users' requirements. Many call distributors provide a port to an outboard processor, which is usually a personal computer. The following questions should be considered:

- Are the fixed reports provided with the system sufficient? If not, does the ACD provide for download to an outboard processor?
- Is statistical information stored for some period or is it lost each time the data is refreshed?

◆ Can the user select the reporting period—for example, hourly, half-hourly, or quarter-hourly update?

◆ If agents shift between queues, do their production statistics follow them as individual agents or do the statistics remain as part of the queue? Is it possible to track both?

Call Center Supervisor's Information

A major reason for acquiring a call distributor is to provide the call center supervisor with real-time information about workload and service. Some systems use a personal computer or terminal for the supervisor's console. Low-end systems may use a display telephone or audible or visual signals or provide no information at all to inform the supervisor when certain thresholds are exceeded. The following criteria should be evaluated:

◆ What type of display is provided?

◆ Does the display alert the supervisor to critical situations with different colors, intensity, inverse video, or other means?

◆ If the display is variable, can the user change it to suit individual preference?

◆ Are thresholds programmable?

◆ How frequently is the information on the display refreshed? Can the user change the refresh interval?

◆ Is the information display programmable or fixed?

◆ Does the display show the supervisor how long each individual agent has been in the current state?

◆ Can the supervisor remotely force the agent from one state to another—for example, from wrap-up to available?

◆ Can the supervisor monitor calls without being detected?

◆ If the system provides an audible monitoring tone to the agent, does the caller hear it also?

Agent Terminals

Most call distributors will function with single-line telephones for the agent terminal. In some applications single-line sets are satisfactory, but the additional information that can be obtained from a display feature set is worth the extra cost for most call centers. The following are some criteria to use in evaluating agent terminals:

◆ What information is displayed on the agent's set? For example, does it show how long a call has waited in queue?

◆ If the agent set lacks a display, how is information, such as incoming trunk group identity or the queue from which a call overflowed, conveyed to the agent?

♦ How are agents informed in real time of critical service indicators such as waiting-time objectives exceeded?

♦ How do agents perform such functions as logging on and off, holding and parking calls, and changing to and from available state?

♦ Do the sets have enough buttons to provide push-button access to all critical features?

♦ How do agents transfer calls to one another and to an attached PBX?

Queue Management

The degree of flexibility the system offers in managing the way calls are routed to particular queues and the way agents are assigned to queues is fundamental to call center management. Low-end systems may have only one fixed queue and little or no ability for the administrator to reprogram the system. High-end systems have complete flexibility in changing routing to meet changes in workload conditions. Consider the following:

♦ Can call routing be changed? If so, is the programming language easy to understand?

♦ Is a method provided for offline testing the routing of incoming calls?

♦ Can the routing be changed in real time?

♦ If the system provides priority treatment for certain classes of callers, how is the priority recognized? How many priority classes are there?

♦ When a call is given priority treatment, how is the priority administered? For example, is the caller moved to the head of the queue, placed at the end of the first third, and so on?

♦ Can the system look ahead to evaluate congestion before overflowing to an alternate queue? If so, does the system predict waiting time in the next queue based on a dynamic evaluation as opposed to merely counting calls?

♦ After the system looks ahead to an alternate queue, can it look back to the primary queue?

♦ If a call returns to a previous queue, is it given priority treatment based on total waiting time?

♦ Can the supervisor remotely assign agents to another queue to relieve congestion?

♦ Can an agent log on to more than one queue?

♦ Can the queue routing be varied by time of day, day of week, and other such variables?

Incoming Call Handling

The least effective call distributors provide little flexibility in handling incoming calls. Calls are answered and placed in queue, and the caller may not hear anything until an agent is available. The most flexible systems offer callers a choice. These are some questions that should be evaluated:

- What does the caller hear after the initial announcement: music, promotional announcements, silence?
- Is a second announcement available? How many different announcements can be programmed in a routing script?
- Does the system offer skill-based routing? How are skill levels identified in the ACD?
- Can the system vary the announcement based on time in queue or other such variables?
- Does the system inform callers of their position in queue?
- Can the caller choose to exit and leave a message in voice mail?
- Can announcements on hold be varied by the queue or are they general across the entire system?

Case History

A state motor vehicle department operates a large call center using Nortel equipment to handle callers' inquiries about driver and vehicle licensing matters. After they are fully trained, the agents are able to handle any kind of inquiry, but they all have preferences as to which type of call they specialize in. One unique group of agents is first choice for many types of call. These are inmates in the women's state prison. They are trained to handle most inquiries, but law prohibits them from accessing the records of drivers who are under some type of disciplinary action such as a suspension. A special number is provided for these types of inquiries, but many callers dial the general information number, wait in queue for an agent, and must be transferred when the agent determines that she cannot handle the call. This results in the caller's waiting in a second queue, adding to annoyance.

The motor vehicle call center experiences large demand peaks during the day. Many calls arrive around morning relief period when citizens use their break time to clear up licensing matters. These call flurries occur at the time when agents are also on break, adding to delay times. Three supervisors used load management to shift agents between queues in an effort to reduce holding times.

Management developed a strategy for applying a new Nortel product known as Symposium to address the problems. Symposium combines three previous Nortel products that provide conditional routing, ACD reports, and computer-telephony linkage. Symposium runs on a Microsoft Windows NT server that connects to the PBX over Ethernet. The traditional call center software remains in the Meridian One PBX, but only as a backup to Symposium in case the server crashes. Symposium includes skill-based routing and expected wait-time announcements as part of the basic package.

With these new tools, the call center manager has several strategies for easing queue congestion. First, callers are asked to enter their drivers license number for identification. With a CTI link to the departmental mainframe, the computer can determine if a disciplinary suspension or revocation is in effect. If so, since this is the probable subject of the transaction, the call is routed to the main queue instead of to the prison. Skill-based routing enables the manager to direct calls to agents whose preference is driver or vehicular matters, and to keep calls away from agents who have not been trained to handle them.

Since callers are informed of expected wait time, they have the opportunity to hang up immediately if they are not willing to wait. Announcements in queue inform callers of the best times to call to avoid lengthy waits. Callers are also offered the opportunity to route to self-help devices. They can select a fax server to obtain forms and instructions on such matters as the procedure for licensing out-of-state vehicles. They can choose an IVR to learn the status of pending vehicle licenses and to schedule driver exams. The department estimated that the payback from the software upgrade and CTI programming would be approximately 2 years.

CHAPTER 26

Computer-Telephone Integration

PBXs and ACDs are marvels of flexibility and stability within the bounds of their programming, but they are limited to the features that were programmed into them. Fortunately, most of the major systems on the market provide an interface that enables an external computer to control them and obtain information that is outside the limits of their generic program. This interface is known in the industry as *computer-telephone integration* (CTI). The possibilities are still limited because switch manufacturers do not give outsiders access to their source code, but the CTI interface provides an application program interface that enables the switch to operate under external control to some degree.

For years many PBX manufacturers have offered a simplistic CTI interface known as a *hospitality package.* Used by the hotel-motel industry, a CTI package links to a program running on a central computer that enables such features as displaying room status information on the desk clerk's screen. As housekeeping personnel finish making up rooms, they dial a number that changes the room status. The hospitality package links to voice mail so mailboxes follow automatically if the guest is moved to another room. The current status of long-distance charges can be called up from the front desk. These are but a few of the features that are aimed at the hospitality industry. Although the features are useful, they are primitive compared to the total needs of the industry.

Every call center is familiar with "screen pop" even though few have it. This feature delivers the caller's database record to an agent simultaneously with an incoming call. Although screen pop saves a few seconds per call, the real payoff comes from other functions—primarily call transfers. Without CTI, when a call is transferred, the agent has two choices: a blind transfer, after which the caller must identify himself and explain everything to a new agent, or a supervised transfer to allow the first agent to explain. The supervised transfer is best from the caller's point of view, but it decreases productivity because two agents are on for part of the call.

The industry has several other CTI applications that fall under the category of "shrink-wrapped" software, but most applications require custom programming. One common application that is discussed in the next chapter is unified messaging. This feature allows voice-mail, fax, and e-mail messages to be displayed on a personal computer screen and handled with a drag-and-drop interface. The desktop computer's graphical user interface (GUI) is accepted by nearly everyone as an intuitive way to operate unfamiliar features. By integrating the telephone and the computer, a GUI screen can bring to the telephone the intelligence that it lacks. With CTI, to set up a multiparty conference call you simply open a directory, click on the names of the people you want to add to the conference, and drag them across the screen to an icon representing a conference bridge. The telephone system, under control of the computer, takes care of the rest. If you want to play a voice-mail message for someone in a different system, you can set up a telephone call, open a computer screen that displays messages, select the one you want, and click the play button on the screen.

Although the term CTI is relatively new, host computers and switch manufacturers have had interfaces available for several years. The costs have been high, and only the largest call centers have been able to justify them. Now, new products are diversifying the applications and bringing the cost within the reach of many businesses. Seeing new opportunities opening, hundreds of developers are working on new products that marry the computer and the telephone to make them both easier to use. The CTI industry is in its infancy. Most standards have proprietary origins, but many are open and available for developers to create new applications. This chapter discusses the applications and the enabling technologies that will enable CTI to be one of the next major growth industries in telecommunications.

CTI TECHNOLOGY

As with so many aspects of telecommunications, the CTI industry offers numerous ways of accomplishing the objective. Because the different approaches to CTI are rooted in proprietary software, the major vendors tout their methods as superior to those of their competitors. As a result, prospective users find it difficult to separate hype from reality. This section explains the different approaches to CTI, and suggests where they are most effective.

To cut through the competitive claims, you must first understand your application and exactly what you want to accomplish. Then the choice of architecture will narrow quickly. With the multiple combinations of switch and computer pairs, many applications will be available using only one or two approaches, which makes the choice easy. Second, if you are starting with a modest CTI application, consider where the future might lead and attempt to match the architecture of your system with applications that are likely to be programmed for it in the future. This isn't easy to do, but most vendors are willing to discuss their future directions under a nondisclosure agreement.

T A B L E 26-1

CTI Products of Principal PBX and Computer Manufacturers

PBX and ACD Manufacturers	Trade Name	Computer Manufacturers	Product Name
Aspect	Application Bridge	Digital Equipment Company	Computer Integrated Telephony
AT&T	Adjunct Switch Applications Interface (ASAI)	Hewlett Packard	Applied Computerized Telephony
Ericsson	Application Link	IBM	CallPath Services Architecture
Fujitsu	Telecommunications Computer Services Interface	Tandem	Call Application Manager
Mitel	MiTAI		
NEC	Open Applications Interface		
Northern Telecom	Meridian Link		
Rockwell	Transaction Link		
Siemens/Rolm	CallBridge CSTA		

Most of the differences in protocols are of interest primarily to developers. The using organization is concerned with the cost and functionality of the application, and which interface the developer uses is mostly of academic interest. As an analogy, in buying software the buyer usually doesn't care whether the developer has written it in C, COBOL, Visual Basic, Pascal, or any of dozens of other languages, provided it contains the features, the price is justified, and it meets performance expectations.

Every major switch and computer manufacturer provides some form of open application interface to PBXs. Table 26-1 lists the trade names of the major PBX and computer interfaces on the market. These interfaces accept some form of programming language, usually proprietary to the manufacturer, to enable computers and the PBX to carry on a dialog. This form of interface, shown in Figure 26-1, has been available for several years, and it has usually been used to link mainframe computers to the PBX. Consequently, only the largest companies have employed this form of CTI in the past.

One alternative for integrating the computer and telephone is to build the telephone into a desktop computer add-in card. Analog add-ins are easy, and have been available for several years. Digital add-in cards can either emulate a proprietary digital telephone or an ISDN telephone. Cards that interface proprietary digital ports on a switch often contain more functionality than ISDN cards because switch manufacturers have not included all the proprietary telephone functions in their ISDN interface ports.

The computer market is shifting away from mainframe computers and toward servers and desktop computers. As a result, several important new application programming interfaces (APIs) have emerged. An API is an interface that

FIGURE 26-1

Mainframe to PBX Link

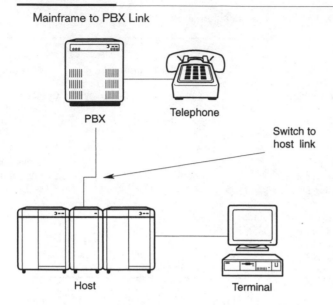

PBX

Telephone

Switch to
host link

Host

Terminal

software developers provide to enable other developers to write programs that interact with their program.

First-Party Call Control

Two terms that CTI buyers need to understand are *third-party call control* and *first-party call control.* The latter is a direct interface between the user's personal computer and the telephone system. It is called first-party or phone-oriented call control because the telephone is connected to the computer, and computer keyboard entries directly control call processing. With third-party, or switch-oriented call control, the user communicates with the application program, which controls the telephone system through a separate interface. First-party call control is generally better for small sites because less expensive hardware is needed. Switch-oriented call control is more adaptable to large sites because it isn't necessary to buy hardware and software for each desktop.

　　Microsoft's telephony applications programming interface (TAPI) is the industry's primary example of first-party call control. Figure 26-2 shows a typical architecture using TAPI software in the computer. TAPI is a link between a Windows-equipped PC and the telephone instrument. TAPI enables an application to set up and tear down calls, monitor progress, detect CLID, and activate features such as hold, transfer, conference, park, and pickup. It can redirect and forward calls, answer and route incoming calls, and generate and detect DTMF signals. TAPI enables multiple applications to share a single phone line. For example, voice mail

FIGURE 26-2

Microsoft TAPI

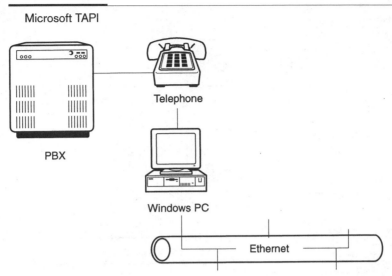

and fax can both listen for incoming calls of different types on the same line. Enabling these devices to share a single telephone line allows the user to make more efficient use of the line.

TAPI is a protocol stack that operates on IBM-compatible personal computers (at this writing it was not available on Macintosh). The interface is usually an EIA-232 connection between the telephone and the computer. The telephone can, however, be a board plugged in an expansion slot of the PC, or the telephone can plug into a jack in an expansion card.

TAPI is designed to run on the individual PC. The TAPI interface is ideal for small offices and those offices lacking Novell servers. It is independent of the telephone network type, and can interface analog, ISDN, or proprietary digital telephone ports in a PBX. A typical application is controlling the telephone from a PC screen for call logging, answering, and directory dialing.

One limitation of first-party call control is that the functions work only on certain classes of computer. For example, a function that runs under Microsoft Windows will not operate on Macintosh and vice versa. A second limitation is that telephone functions may not work if the power is turned off on the PC.

Third-Party Call Control

In third-party call control the connection between the computer and the telephone set is logical, not physical. Telephony services application programming interface (TSAPI) is a third-party control interface developed by Novell and AT&T using computer-supported telecommunications application (CSTA) standards. TSAPI is a coding standard, not an architecture or feature set. It is a Netware-loadable module

FIGURE 26-3

Novell TSAPI

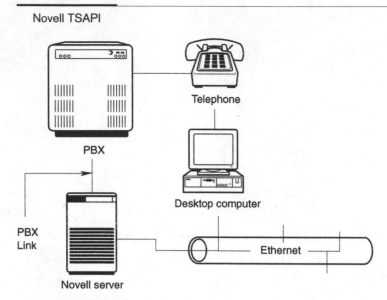

(NLM) that resides in a Novell server. The application is programmed to the TSAPI specification, and TSAPI, in turn, communicates with the PBX manufacturer's open application interface.

CSTA, on which TSAPI is based, specifies call control services that can be used by any API. Basic call control services include establishing and tearing down calls, answering calls at a device, and activating and deactivating switch features. The features specified by CSTA include, for example, call hold, call pickup, call transfer, conferencing, and consultation hold. The server sends instructions to the switch, which returns event messages to indicate the action taking place, such as completed transfers, terminated and originated calls, message-waiting indications, and so on.

TSAPI's main application at the present time is in call centers. Although TSAPI may run on servers other than Novell's, at this point its purpose is to enable Novell servers to control switches of multiple vendors. Separate drivers are needed for each type of PBX. Figure 26-3 shows how TSAPI fits into a Novell server. A card supporting the physical interface plugs in a server slot. For example, some products use a BRI interface.

Other Standards

Unfortunately for the industry, many developers have treated TSAPI and TAPI as mutually exclusive interfaces, but they are not. They are competing APIs that developers can choose to implement their applications. TASPI applies to Novell-based applications, and TAPI applies only to Windows-based applications. Although the majority of desktop computers run Microsoft Windows and a significant percentage of LANs use Novell servers, these limitations mean that the market has room for both interfaces. From the previous discussion, it can be seen that both TAPI and TSAPI perform many of the same functions. Tmap, a program developed by Nortel, translates between the two applications so that developers can write to either interface and operate with the other.

Universal Serial Bus

PCs today come equipped with one or two serial ports, which limits the number of serial devices that can be connected. The universal serial bus (USB) is an expansion scheme that replaces the serial cards in a PC. It enables CTI by providing a high-speed serial connection to the PC's bus. As many as 63 devices can be connected to the same bus. It supports a variety of applications such as printers, plotters, modems, and other such devices.

Signal Computing System Architecture

Signal computing system architecture (SCSA) is an open software model for telephony systems. It was originated by Dialogic, which manufactures voice boards for personal computers. SCSA supports multivendor-distributed applications that share a common pool of server resources. SCSA hardware consists of a digital bus supported by a switching fabric. Developers can transport and switch 64-kb/s data streams to resources in a PC.

The SCSA software model, known as telephony applications objects (TAO), defines software APIs. Because the software model is independent from the hardware model, developers can implement SCSA over different hardware models as well as over the SCSA hardware model. SCSA is a general architecture for managing real-time or time-critical resources across a network. For example, it could manage a limited pool of speech-recognition or text-to-speech engines over a network. It enables voice-mail developers to add other related applications such as e-mail and fax into their platforms.

WinSock 2

WinSock 2 is a data communications protocol that does for data circuits what TAPI does for call control. WinSock 2 provides a programming interface that allows applications to become independent of both the network and the protocol by providing a uniform interface to the application. WinSock 2 supports isochronous (time-sensitive) information such as voice and video over networks. Its quality-of-service support enables an application to request a connection with a guaranteed minimum bandwidth.

Multivendor Integration Protocols

Multivendor integration protocols (MVIP) is a series of standards to integrate telephony with computer-related functions for automating communications. MVIP is a low-level protocol for hardware interconnect that enables developers to integrate different telecommunications and voice technologies in the PC. It consists of a standard bus plus switching and operating systems.

Digital Simultaneous Voice and Data

Digital simultaneous voice and data (digital SVD) enables users to talk and exchange data simultaneously during the same session. The voice is digitized, compressed, and multiplexed with data to produce a bit stream that is transmitted over the telephone line with a special 33.3-kb/s modem. Digital SVD modems are compatible with applications that presently use conventional modems. These modems facilitate such applications as desktop conferencing and image sharing over an analog telephone line.

CTI APPLICATIONS

This section discusses some of the many applications that CTI enables. The industry has only begun to develop applications. In the next few years, managers can expect to see a flood of labor- and time-saving features such as the following.

Hospitality

The earliest application of CTI is the PBX hospitality package. Although this application was widely used before the term CTI had been accepted by the industry, it illustrates the way computers and the PBX can interact to improve productivity. In a hotel, and to some degree in hospitals, interaction between the central computer and the telephone is important. When a guest checks into a hotel, the desk clerk enters name and credit information into the computer terminal. The computer interacts with the PBX to perform functions such as these:

- ◆ Show the room as occupied in the PBX database and unlock restrictions on the telephone for placing outgoing calls.
- ◆ Show the guest's name in the PBX database so it displays on telephones, enabling staff to refer to guests by name.
- ◆ Activate the guest's voice mailbox.
- ◆ Integrate chargeable call information in the computer database so it is available for inquiry to the desk or over video display in the room.

On checkout the process is reversed. The desk clerk can inform the guest of voice-mail messages that have not been listened to and transfer them to another box. Toll calls are transferred from the call-accounting system to the guest's bill. The room phone is deactivated for outgoing calls. When the room has been cleaned and is ready for occupancy, Housekeeping can dial a code, which the PBX transfers to the computer as room ready status.

Call Centers

A major application for CTI is in call centers. Nearly every call center has three major elements: the telephone system, the computer system, and the human agents. Without CTI, the agent is the bridge between telephone and computer systems. The agent identifies the call, determines the purpose of the call, and pulls up the appropriate screen. Upon call termination, the agent manually enters information to complete the call, including data that could be furnished through direct link to the telephone system. If the call must be transferred, the caller often must repeat information that was given to the first agent. With CTI, the system enters much of the information, and the caller enters some. For example, in call centers that have an IVR the caller enters the account number and the details of the transaction. If he or she must transfer to a live agent, the purpose of the call is often evident from the details of the transaction, which are still available on the screen.

The following features are provided by most call center CTI applications. The details and equipment vary with the product, but these are the most common features and benefits.

Screen Synchronization   This feature, also called "screen pop," is the most common CTI application. It delivers a call to an agent together with the customer's account screen. Screen pop is enabled by identifying the caller from the calling telephone number, which is delivered by ANI, or from a customer-dialed account number that is captured in an IVR or call prompter. When a call must be transferred to another agent, the information on the original agent's screen is automatically sent to the receiving agent. This eliminates the need for the caller to repeat information. A similar feature enables more than one agent to share the same screen on a conference call.

Work Logging   This feature records the actions handled by CTI. Some products allow the agent to add information to the reports to create customized activity reports.

Terminal-Extension Correlation   This feature associates an agent terminal with ACD identification codes. It enables the computer to send calls to selected agents wherever they are sitting. It also may automatically log the agent onto both the computer and the ACD with a single entry.

Call Blending   In a call center that has both inward and outward dialing the system can automatically assign agents to inbound or outbound calls based on load. See the discussion of predictive dialers in the next section.

Expert Agent Selection   Once a caller is identified, the call can be routed to an agent who has the skills to handle the call most effectively. If the caller has a preferred agent, calls can be queued on that agent based on the routing algorithm and predicted waiting time. The call also may be routed to the agent who handled the customer's last call on the theory that this agent is familiar with the problem and requires less explanation. Expert agent routing can convey a feeling of personal service to customers who call frequently and are routed with each call to the same select group of agents.

Callback Request   This feature enables the caller to dial in a number for a callback in lieu of waiting in queue. If the caller indicates a desire for callback, the system prompts for a callback number. When an agent is available, the customer's screen is sent to the agent and the call is automatically outdialed. This feature saves the time it takes to transcribe callback requests from voice mail.

Automatic number identification (ANI) matching is used to identify callers and route calls. It is not, however, foolproof. Callers may call from multiple locations: home, the office, pay phones, cell phones, and so on. A list of aliases may be built in the database, but these also are not foolproof. Some ANIs may be the trunk number behind a PBX, which presents the CTI application with an impractical list of alias telephone numbers. In other cases the billing telephone number may be sent as the ANI, which makes it impossible to determine which of several customers is calling. The most effective way of identifying the caller is by capturing the account number in an IVR or call prompter.

Some CTI applications dynamically create a cross-reference file correlating customer ANIs with account numbers. A similar feature allows the agent to select the calling customer's account from a CTI screen of multiple accounts that use the same number.

Predictive Dialers

Predictive dialers are among the first of the widely accepted CTI applications. Used in telemarketing and collections, predictive dialers review the status of a group of agents and deliver calls set up and ready to talk without effort on the agent's part. The dialer selects numbers to call from a database, determines the probability that an agent will be available by the time the call is connected, and dials the number. The objective is to deliver connected calls to agents as they end the previous call, while minimizing the probability that a call will be connected before an agent is available. The system is able to recognize and reschedule calls to busy numbers, those that don't answer, and in some products, those that terminate in voice mail or answering machines.

One version of dialer connects to the PBX or ACD via T1/E1 or analog station ports and transfers calls to agents with a switchhook line transfer. The most effective dialers have a CTI connection that enables agents to log in or out from a terminal, go into wrap-up or unavailable state from the telephone, and operate as part of a call-blending operation.

With call blending agents can automatically be assigned to either incoming or outgoing calls, depending on load, agent availability, and other such factors that enter into routing decisions. Call blending needs CTI to enable the predictive dialer to see agent status and workload on incoming as well as outgoing calls. Agent statistics showing total agent performance can be shown by the switch. Unless the predictive dialer and switch are connected through CTI, outgoing statistics will be separate from those the switch produces for incoming calls.

Unified Messaging

Many products are moving toward an interchangeable and convertible in basket. As discussed in Chapter 29, unified messaging allows people to listen to, read, and create voice-mail, e-mail, and fax messages from a telephone or a computer. The office telephone system is clearly an important player. The key question is where the message center resides and how it is enabled. In the telephone-centric version of the message center, it resides in voice mail, with fax calls sent to voice mail by the switch, and e-mail messages arriving over a LAN. In the LAN-centric version, voice mail is a server on the LAN, and the universal in basket resides in a computer. In fact, in this version, the telephone switch also becomes a server on the network. The chances are high that this architecture will eventually replace the present PBX, but for the next several years the circuit-switched PBX architecture will persevere, and conflicts and incompatibilities will remain. The universal in basket will take a variety of different shapes, depending on the owner's view of the network.

JUSTIFYING CTI

CTI applications usually require custom programming. Applications are developed to match many of the popular customer contact computer packages with the most popular PBXs, but custom-programmed databases will always require custom CTI programming. As the industry matures, off-the-shelf applications will be increasingly available.

CTI is easiest to justify in a call center, where it brings the following benefits to the customer and company:

◆ Customer service in call centers is improved because customers do not have to enter or speak their account number more than once, and because calls are handled more rapidly.

◆ Revenue can be enhanced. By capturing the calling telephone number, the company builds a database of valid telephone numbers that can be correlated with buying habits and used for telemarketing. Numbers can also be used for tracing delinquent accounts.

◆ Call center agents' job satisfaction is improved by relieving them of the need to handle boring and repetitive details such as asking for and entering account numbers and waiting for response screens.

TABLE 26-2

Cost Justifying CTI in a Call Center*

Average Call Length, minutes	Calls Handled per Shift	Minutes Saved with CTI	Percent Time Saved	Dollars Saved per Shift with CTI
0.5	540	180	40.0	$60.00
1.0	270	90	20.0	30.00
1.5	180	60	13.3	20.00
2.0	135	45	10.0	15.00
2.5	108	36	8.0	12.00
3.0	90	30	6.7	10.00
3.5	77	25	5.6	8.33
4.0	67	22	4.9	7.33
4.5	60	20	4.4	6.67
5.0	54	18	4.0	6.00
5.5	49	16	3.6	5.33
6.0	45	15	3.3	5.00
6.5	41	13	2.9	4.33
7.0	38	12	2.7	4.00
7.5	36	12	2.7	4.00
8.0	33	11	2.4	3.67
8.5	31	10	2.2	3.33
9.0	30	10	2.2	3.33
9.5	28	9	2.0	3.00
10.0	27	9	2.0	3.00

*Agent cost per hour = $20; length of shift = 7.5 hours; agent occupancy = 60 percent; call setup time = 20 seconds.

◆ Agent productivity improves by eliminating the keystrokes and time it takes to query the caller and enter the account number. Average talk time is reduced and toll-free call costs are reduced because of the reduced holding time. Making more agents available to answer calls may also reduce abandoned calls.

◆ The calling number of abandoned calls can be captured, enabling agents to return them, improving customer satisfaction, and potentially reducing lost revenue.

Direct cost savings can often justify CTI. Caller identification takes 15 to 20 seconds in most call centers. The shorter the agent's talk time, the larger the number of calls they handle per shift, and the easier it is to justify CTI. The cost of CTI bears little relationship to the size of the center in many cases, so large call centers can distribute the costs among more agents than small ones, and can more quickly realize the benefits. Table 26-2 shows CTI savings at 20 seconds per call for varying call lengths, assuming a 7.5-hour shift, 60 percent agent occupancy, and a $20/hour loaded agent cost. With short calls, the setup time becomes a higher percentage of total time, so CTI is easier to justify.

Also, bear in mind that the CTI industry is in its infancy. Many developers will fall by the wayside or be absorbed by their competitors. Consequently, CTI applications should be justified on the basis of a short payback.

In other cases it isn't necessary to justify CTI based on cost savings. For example, most PC users have some form of personal information manager (PIM) that contains names, addresses, telephone numbers, and other information on client and vendor contacts. With a proprietary telephone and without CTI, the PIM cannot dial telephone numbers. Also, on incoming calls CTI can automatically bring up a contact screen so you can refresh your memory about the last call. The PIM can automatically log certain details about this call, such as the date and time, and the number from which the call was placed. The convenience of having such an interface is difficult to justify based on hard dollar savings, but the convenience is of tangible value.

STANDARDS

CTI is still in its infancy. Standards are available, but most of them are propriety standards that are either licensed by their developers or have been submitted to an open industry group that now manages their future development. Many products use standard interfaces, such as BRI, for the link between the computer and the PBX but the code sets are proprietary.

A proprietary standard isn't necessarily undesirable. For example, IBM developed the personal computer industry standard architecture (ISA) bus. Its widespread and universal acceptance as an open architecture was largely responsible for the success of the personal computer and its successors. Several major revisions such as the expanded standard industry architecture (EISA) and several successive local bus architectures have enhanced the original design. Unlike international standards that seem to move at glacial pace, proprietary standards can adapt more rapidly to technological advances. On the minus side, a proliferation of incompatible standards may be the result. Such is the case with CTI.

CHAPTER 27

Voice-Processing Systems

Many people have a love-hate relationship with voice processing. We love the convenience of getting voice messages when we are away from the office and rail at the frustration of reaching voice mail when we are in a hurry. We endure the endless prompts of miscast automated attendants, but enjoy the convenience of checking our account balance 24 hours per day. Voice-processing systems are here to stay, yet they are the most misused of telecommunications technologies. Properly designed and applied, voice-processing systems can save a great deal of time and relieve phone tag by making their users accessible while they are away from the phone, but improperly used systems generate phone tag and frustrate customers.

It is not the purpose of this chapter to discuss how to manage voice-processing technology. *The Irwin Handbook of Telecommunications Management* contains information on managing voice processing. It is worth noting, however, that managers often reject voice processing in the belief that they risk losing business by subjecting their customers to automated attendant, voice mail, and interactive voice response. While it is true that voice processing can and does result in dissatisfied customers, the bulk of the problem lies in improper system design. Properly designed and used voice-processing systems make it easier for people to interact by enabling communications outside real time and across time zones.

In the context in which we use it in this chapter, voice processing includes the following technologies:

- Voice mail
- Automated attendant
- Interactive voice response
- Digital recording
- Speech recognition

These technologies are listed in order of their maturity. Voice mail has become such a mainstream application that most new PBXs and many new key systems are purchased with integrated voice mail. Automated attendant, a close cousin of voice mail, enables callers (or forces them, depending on your point of view) to route themselves by selecting from a menu.

IVR carries the process a step further by enabling callers to converse with a computer using the DTMF pad on their telephones. As anyone who has designed or used such a system knows, however, the DTMF pad has shortcomings that limit its use. The triple-letter key combination does not make an ideal keyboard. Furthermore, although the number of rotary telephones is dropping, not everyone has a DTMF telephone. Obviously, there has to be a better way. That way is speech recognition. In time speech recognition can replace the keyboard, but the technology still has a long way to go.

Communicating with voice mail through the keypad is frustrating when there are key combinations to remember and prompts to endure. The industry solution to this problem is unified messaging, which brings voice, fax, and e-mail into the same personal computer platform. Using a graphical user interface, it's possible to select and handle any of these features on the same computer screen. The industry offers media conversion techniques, which enable users to create or retrieve messages using their choice of telephone, fax, or computer. The weak spot in media conversion today is speech recognition, which is still too primitive to support a truly universal mailbox. Unified messaging is discussed in Chapter 29.

Digital recording is required in many organizations that take orders of different kinds over the telephone. Products in this category are designed to compress and index the voice stream so a session can be retrieved for verification of what the caller and the internal individual said. The internal individual is often an agent in a call center, although digital recording has other applications besides call centers.

Speech recognition is an up-and-coming application that can be considered now for limited use. Equipment can understand simple spoken commands, and can recognize numbers, and some simple words. This makes it possible to replace automated attendant. For example, a dialog could read "for sales press or say 1, for customer service press or say 2, etc." This capability can solve the problem of directing calls for users who do not have DTMF telephones. High-end products can do an even better job of recognizing with a high degree of accuracy words spoken by random speakers. Managers should watch speech recognition closely and be prepared to adopt it when it can help them reduce costs or improve customer service.

Even given the occasional misapplication, voice-processing technologies have enormous potential for improving customer service and cutting costs. Voice mail makes it possible to leave messages across time zones, keeping voice inflections intact and avoiding the misunderstandings that so often result from passing messages through a third party. Interactive voice response makes it possible for people to receive information outside normal working hours and without enduring the delays that often occur during peak hours. The organization saves labor costs, employees are relieved of the mind-numbing task of repeatedly delivering the same information, and customers do not have to wait.

The automated attendant enables callers to route their own calls quickly to the appropriate department without lengthy oral exchanges and enables the company to eliminate the cost of direct inward dialing and attendants. Everyone benefits from voice processing if the applications are chosen carefully and administered intelligently.

This chapter discusses the elements of the five principal voice-processing technologies and describes the features available. The "Applications" section discusses typical uses and the precautions that must be observed in applying them. The chapter also covers digital announcers. Although these are not technically voice-processing devices, they have many of the same elements and are used behind PBXs and ACDs to deliver announcements to callers who dial a particular number or are placed in queue waiting for a service process.

VOICE MAIL

Voice mail has the potential for improving internal communications in most organizations. It is no secret to anyone who has worked in an office that a high percentage of telephone calls are uncompleted because the called party is away from the desk or on the telephone, and the frustrating game of telephone tag begins. Voice mail enables people to exchange messages and often serves as a satisfactory substitute for real-time communication. To apply an overworked word, this is called *asynchronous communication,* in contrast to *synchronous communication* where information exchange cannot take place unless both parties are simultaneously available. Calls can be exchanged across time zones, messages can be left and retrieved quickly when only a few minutes are available between meetings or airplanes, and the group broadcast feature enables a manager to convey information to everyone in the workgroup with a single call.

A voice-mail system is a specialized computer that stores messages in digital form on a fixed disk. In voice-mail systems, the voice is digitized and compressed to a much slower rate than the 64-kb/s signal the PBX uses in its switching network. Messages and personal greetings are stored on a hard disk that holds the voice-mail operating system and system prompts and greetings. A processor controls the compressing, storing, retrieving, forwarding, and purging of files. Voice-mail systems connect to a PBX through the PBX bus or through station ports, as shown in Figure 27-1.

Voice-mail systems are grouped into three categories:

- ◆   Stand-alone
- ◆   Nonintegrated
- ◆   PBX-integrated

FIGURE 27-1

Voice-Mail Integration with a PBX

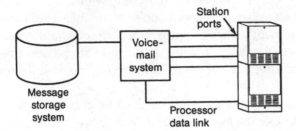

All three types share the same basic architecture, but different manufacturers design systems for different applications. Furthermore, virtually no standards for the voice-mail user interface exist, and few serious attempts have been made to develop them. Therefore, the transfer of experience from system to system on the part of both users and callers is minimal. Some manufacturers allow the user to specify prompts, which makes it easier to transition from one system to another.

Stand-Alone Voice Mail

In a stand-alone configuration, a PBX is unnecessary for voice mail. The voice-mail system can be connected directly to central office trunks or T1/E1, and used as a service bureau that offers voice-mail services to outside callers. Service-bureau voice-mail systems normally have large capacity. They are accessed through the public telephone network, and the system operator charges a flat fee plus usage. Since the incoming ports are shared by all users, the system provides a way to route calls to the appropriate mailbox. The most effective method makes use of direct inward dialing or, over toll-free lines, using dialed number identification system. These methods of called party identification are not always available, however. For example, calls may be trunked over private lines to a voice-mail system in a distant city. In such cases, the caller may be prompted to enter a code, which may be the last four digits of the telephone number or a mailbox number that the user has printed on a business card.

Service-bureau voice-mail systems are excellent for users who need a few mailboxes and cannot justify the purchase of a private system. They are also effective for users who are out of the office a great deal and have no need of message-waiting lights to indicate the arrival of a call. The lack of message-waiting lights is one of the chief drawbacks of stand-alone systems for people who are regularly in the office. Most systems can send a message to a pager to signal the arrival of a message. A second drawback may be the lack of station identification, which requires callers to know and enter the mailbox number, but this is usually handled by giving each user a private DID number. A third drawback is the dead-end nature of the medium. When a call enters the mailbox, the caller's only options are to leave a message, hang up, or possibly send a message to a pager.

Nonintegrated Voice Mail

Nonintegrated voice mail has many of the characteristics of a service bureau. The system is connected behind a PBX, as shown in Figure 27-1. A shared group of PBX ports is connected to the voice-mail system. Users can forward their calls to voice mail, but the system cannot identify the forwarding station. Therefore, the caller is prompted to enter a mailbox number, which is usually the last three or four digits the caller dialed. A caller dials the company's main listed number, asks for a user by name, and reaches an extension that has been forwarded to voice mail. If the callers hear a prompt asking for the extension number to be entered, they are confused. Users do not have message-waiting lights, so they must dial in to check for messages. Because of these drawbacks, the main application for nonintegrated systems is in older PBXs for which voice mail has not been integrated.

Integrated Voice Mail

PBX-integrated systems integrate with a specific PBX to provide features that enhance the value of the voice-mail system. A fully integrated voice-mail system offers several features that require direct communication with the PBX:

- *Return to attendant.* A caller, upon being transferred by the system into voice mail, can transfer (escape) from voice mail to a message center or switchboard operator by dialing digits on a DTMF telephone.

- *Multiple greetings.* Voice-mail users may have different greetings for internal versus external calls, or a different greeting when the phone is busy than when it is not answered. With time-of-day control, the called party can vary call coverage and personal assistance options.

- *Called party recognition.* Calls can be transferred directly into voice mail when the called PBX extension is busy or does not answer. If the called party does not answer and the call forwards to an extension that is also forwarded to voice mail, the greeting of the original called party is heard.

- *Message-waiting indication.* When a message arrives in a user's mailbox, the voice-mail system and PBX activate a message-waiting light or apply stutter dial tone to remind users to retrieve messages.

- *Alphanumeric prompts.* The voice-mail system may prompt users who have a display phone with alphanumeric instructions.

- *Security.* The telephone system and voice mail may interact to prevent would-be hackers from dialing invalid extension numbers to place fraudulent calls.

◆   *Internal caller identification.* The name of a person calling from within
      the system is inserted into the message header.

◆   *Message forwarding.* The user can forward a voice-mail message to
      another station with or without comment.

The first of these features allows the caller to escape from the voice-mail system and leave a message with a personal attendant such as a departmental secre-
tary. Without this feature, a caller can reach only the PBX attendant.

The second feature, multiple prompts, conveys valuable information to the
caller, and allows the station user to treat callers more personally. If a caller hears
a greeting that states the called party is on the telephone, the caller's action may be
much different than if he or she hears a message stating the called party is out of
the office. Furthermore, many companies are willing to have internal calls answered by voice mail, but want external calls answered by an attendant.

The third feature, called station identification, is a major flaw of many poorly
integrated systems. With full integration, if calls cover to voice mail, callers always
hear the greeting of the party they originally called, even if the call forwards to another station that is also forwarded to voice mail. With some systems the caller
hears the greeting of someone other than the called party, which is confusing.

Message-waiting light illumination is of no concern to the caller, but greatly
affects voice mail's utility to the station user. This feature turns on a message-waiting
light when a message reaches the mailbox. With an electronic telephone that displays the light on a feature button, the user may need only press the button to retrieve messages. Without the feature, the user must periodically call voice mail to
check for waiting messages, which often results in delays in returning calls. For
users who are rarely in the office, message-waiting light illumination is of little or
no value, but for users who are frequently in the office, it is an essential feature.
Some systems substitute a short burst of stutter dial tone as an alternative, which
is useful for off-premises stations or telephones that lack a message-waiting lamp.

Alphanumeric prompts on display telephones are easier to use than the audible prompts that many systems provide. Users can press buttons to replay, forward, delete, or save messages. Voice-mail security is a matter of great concern to
all companies that have it. If the proper blocks have not been installed, toll thieves
transfer through voice mail to an outside line at the expense of the company. Integrated voice-mail systems exchange information with the PBX processor to prevent such transfers.

Such features as internal caller identification, which inserts the calling party's
name into the message header, enhance voice-mail usage. If the system allows calls
to be listened to outside the sequence in which they arrived, calls can be quickly
scanned and the most important ones handled first.

Developers use three principal methods of achieving integration. The first is
through a direct data link from the voice-mail processor to the PBX processor, and
the second is through emulation of a display telephone. The third method is inte-

gration through a computer-telephony interface. This technology, which is discussed in Chapter 26, uses an open interface between the PBX and an outboard processor. The processor sends call-routing instructions to the PBX. The first method is faster and more efficient than the second, but it is usually available only to the PBX manufacturer or other manufacturers who pay a license fee. Anyone can reverse-engineer a display set to integrate voice mail with another system, but the method is slower than the data-link method. Furthermore, some features are available only through processor integration. CTI integration offers all the advantages of processor integration. Its main drawback is the expense of the PBX's CTI interface. The extra cost may be considerable unless the interface is needed for other purposes. With this configuration, the voice-mail application resides in a server. This same server may also include IVR functions and connect to the PBX over a LAN.

To achieve integration, the PBX and voice-mail system must be a matched pair. Many PBX manufacturers offer proprietary voice-mail systems, but their systems are not the only ones to achieve full integration. Most voice-mail service bureaus provide only nonintegrated service. It is, however, possible for the PBX and the service bureau voice-mail system to be integrated over private lines, which can provide the same features as a directly attached system.

Voice-Mail Capacity

Voice-mail systems are sized by number of ports and hours of storage. The number of ports limits the number of callers that can be connected simultaneously. Ports are occupied while callers are listening to prompts, leaving messages, and while the called parties are retrieving messages. The number of ports required is calculated from the number of accesses and the holding time per access during the busy hour. (See *The Irwin Handbook of Telecommunications Management* for an explanation of how to calculate voice-mail port and storage requirements.) Long-winded prompts, the inability to bypass prompts, and verbose greeting messages not only irritate callers but also consume port and hard-disk capacity. Designing the system with the correct number of ports is important. Having too many ports increases the cost of the voice-mail system; having too few restricts the ability of callers to reach voice mail and blocks users when they attempt to retrieve messages. Ports normally are added in increments of two to four at a cost of, perhaps, 10 to 20 percent of the original cost of the system.

The type of integration often affects the efficiency with which the voice-mail system uses ports. A popular feature on many systems is *outcalling*, which is the ability of the voice-mail system to dial the user's pager or cellular phone. This feature requires ports to handle both incoming and outgoing calls, and a problem may arise when a port is seized from both directions at the same time. This condition, which is called *glare* (see Chapter 11), causes the port to lock until both ends hang up. In a system in which the processors are linked together, glare is resolved by the processors without affecting the users. In a system integrated by display telephone emulation, it is often necessary to provide separate incoming and outgoing ports, which increases the number of ports required.

The amount of storage required is highly variable and depends on the number of users and the number of stored messages per user. It also depends on whether disk-storage capacity varies with the announcement messages and how efficiently the manufacturer packs the disk. Efficient packing algorithms compress the silent intervals so disk space is not wasted. As a rule of thumb in sizing voice-mail systems, the average user takes about 3 to 5 minutes of storage for greetings and messages. A system serving 100 users, therefore, would require 5 to 9 hours of storage. Heavy users or those who are not careful to purge their old messages may require more than 5 minutes of storage on the average.

The voice-mail system's purging algorithm also improves storage efficiency. The more effective systems inform the administrator when the disk is reaching capacity. Overage messages are manually or automatically purged after a specified time. Also, most systems provide for different classes of service, and can vary the amount of storage a user can have before callers receive a full-box message.

Networked Voice Mail

A large multisite operation can often bring its employees closer together with networked voice mail. A cost-effective method of networking voice mail is to terminate the voice mail on one PBX and connect other PBXs to the central PBX with networking software. This software, which Chapter 24 discusses, is an additional cost item that permits feature transparency across the network. All voice-mail functions are available to users outside the main PBX just as if the voice-mail system were attached to their PBX. The advantages of this method extend beyond voice mail because it permits automatic callback, extension-to-extension dialing without access codes, and other features that are lost in a tie-line network.

A second method is networking the voice-mail systems themselves, as shown in Figure 27-2. This method is effective when each site has many users. Messages are stored on the local voice-mail system, which reduces the tie-line traffic compared to a shared voice-mail system. Networked voice mail permits users to have a mailbox in a distant PBX and have the messages delivered to their own voice mailboxes. For example, a sales manager could provide local telephone numbers for key clients in several different cities. Managers with staffs in more than one location can maintain distribution lists and forward calls across the network.

Networked voice-mail systems use analog or digital private lines, an IP or frame relay intranet, or dial-up to flow messages between locations. Messages can also travel across the Internet. Since the data is being sent in the form of a file, the delay inherent in the Internet is not an important issue, but packet loss may be. Systems from different manufacturers can be linked through a standard known as audio message interchange service (AMIS). AMIS standards exist for both analog and digital interchange. The latter is the most effective because the digitized messages

F I G U R E 27-2

Networked Voice-Mail Systems

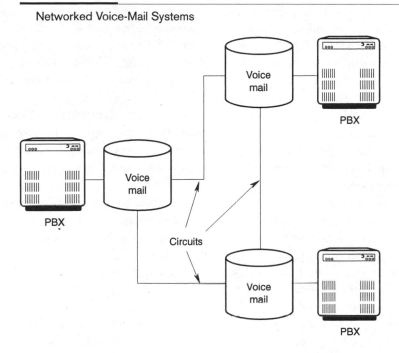

can be forwarded across the network without being converted to analog from the disk and then converted back to digital again for storage at the user's location. Note that the AMIS interface must be developed separately for each pair of PBXs, so universal networking within a company may not be possible because the interface has not been developed.

AUTOMATED ATTENDANT

The automated attendant is the most misused and maligned of the voice-processing technologies. The system answers the telephone and offers the caller a menu of choices such as "dial 1 for sales, 2 for service, 3 for engineering." A properly designed system can save time for callers, but systems with lengthy prompts and endless menus can be a source of great frustration to callers and may cause a loss of business. The automated attendant is usually a feature of a voice-mail system, but the two are separable. Automated attendant functions can also be served by IVR or digital announcer.

Many companies prefer not to have their customer calls answered by an automated attendant, in which case it is a simple matter to establish separate trunk groups for customer and employee calls. The employee calls are answered by the automated attendant, and the customer calls by an operator. In most systems, pressing 0 returns the caller to the attendant. Most systems allow callers to bypass the prompts and route directly through to the desired function.

The simplest form of automated attendant is a substitute for direct inward dialing. The system prompts the caller to enter the extension number, if known, dial by name, or to wait for an operator. This an effective tool that may reduce the extra cost of DID trunks if there is a high probability that the caller will know the extension number. When the calls are from the public, however, the extension number is less likely to be known, and the automated attendant may lengthen the average time it takes to process a call.

Name dialing can be used on most automated attendants and IVRs. The caller dials enough digits of the last name to satisfy any ambiguity. The system responds with the called party's name, often in the person's own voice. Large companies are likely to have several people with the same last name. The system may prompt for the first name or it may offer a menu of choices.

The second use of automated attendant is to enable callers to route their own calls to an answering position by dialing a code from a menu of choices. The system manager must take great care in creating the menu, because it is here that callers most frequently experience frustration. If callers are offered too many choices at a menu level, they will fail to remember them and have to start over or return to the attendant. If the menu has many levels, callers become confused or impatient with the delay. A good policy is to permit no more than four or five choices (plus return to the operator) at each menu level and no more than two or, rarely, three menu levels. The system should be set up to allow callers who know the menu to dial the code immediately without waiting for the prompt. Also, if a numbering conflict does not occur, callers may be permitted to dial an extension number.

INTERACTIVE VOICE RESPONSE

Interactive voice response is a system that prompts callers to enter information such as an account number via DTMF dialing. This information is passed to a host computer for processing, and a voice announcement unit reads the information back to the caller. Banks and credit unions use IVR to enable customers to obtain their account balances without waiting for an agent.

Besides being adopted by virtually every financial institution, IVR can be used for nearly any application where telephone service representatives receive a simple request from a caller, key it into a terminal, and read the results from the screen. The IVR enables callers to obtain the information themselves. The typical session involves, as the first step, customer identification by account number and password, after which the IVR presents a menu of choices. Within the range of choices callers can send instructions to the computer or query the database. The IVR responds with audio announcements, confirming the transaction or delivering the information to the caller. One of the earliest applications was directory assistance for LECs. After receiving a request from the customer and looking up the number, the operator transfers the call to an announcement unit, which completes the transaction. LECs' intercept services are another example. When the caller reaches an intercepted number, the system responds by announcing that the old number has been disconnected and reading the new.

The voice announcement technology of IVR falls into two categories. The most versatile method is voice synthesis, in which the characters coming from the computer are formed into words by a device that emulates the human larynx. The second form is a series of words stored in memory or on disk, which are triggered into the voice stream as needed. The synthesizer method is understandable, but the voice may sound accented. The stored voice method sounds natural, but the vocabulary is limited to what is stored, where a voice synthesizer can pronounce nearly every word.

IVR should be considered as more than just a voice-response unit. It is an outboard processor that can perform many functions that otherwise would require computer-telephony integration. Here are examples of IVR applications:

Automated Order-Entry and Status Inquiry   Callers can access databases to place an order from a catalog, check availability and price, and check the status of pending orders.

Status Verification   Callers can verify various types of information, such as credit cards, employment, insurance, and other such information, that can be delivered after the caller's right to access it has been confirmed. Frequent fliers, for example, can enter their account number to determine their current award status.

Time Reporting and Employee Information   Field personnel can report time to a system that tracks attendance, provides information on accumulated leave, and other such employee information.

Dealer Locator Service   The IVR can prompt callers to enter their ZIP code for the name of the nearest dealer.

Fax-On-Demand   The voice-response unit can lead callers through a menu of document choices. When the document is selected, the system prompts for a fax number, and sends the fax immediately.

Student Registration   Colleges and universities use IVR to enable students to register for classes from a DTMF telephone. Callers can use IVR to register for seminars and other events.

Appointment Rescheduling   Clinic patients can reschedule their own appointments by calling into an IVR and identifying themselves by patient number. Clinics can also use the outdialing capability to remind patients of appointments.

Frequently Asked Questions   Support organizations can forward callers to an IVR to listen to the answer to questions. For example, a bar association can list attorney specialties and a hospital can offer self-help information to callers.

IVRs can connect to analog or digital ports or they can connect through a CTI port for more versatility. The CTI connection is important when callers transfer from the IVR into a call center for additional transactions. The IVR should be able to send the caller's screen to the agent so it is unnecessary to ask the caller for his or her account number to pull up a screen. Also, when the agent sees the screen before the transaction begins, it offers clues about the reason for the call.

With an integrated IVR, callers can be routed in ways that they may not expect. For example, a caller with a delinquent account might automatically be routed to the collections department whenever the account is accessed through the IVR.

DIGITAL RECORDING

Many companies must record calls as a way of later confirming what was said during the session. Stock brokers, hospitals that offer advice over the telephone, catalog companies, and other such organizations sometimes need to retrieve the details of a call to resolve disputes. Instead of recording calls at the agent's position on an analog device, digital recorders provide an array of audio channels that are sampled, digitized, compressed, and stored on a disk. Usually, the disk has removable media for archiving the calls. The products also time-stamp the calls, and provide output channels that can be used to retrieve the call. Calls can be retrieved by date, time, digits dialed, and other such factors. The system may provide for time synchronization from an external source such as Global Positioning Service (GPS) or the National Bureau of Standards' radio station WWV.

SPEECH RECOGNITION

Pity the dilemma of the speech-recognition developers. Teaching a computer to recognize voices is even more difficult than training it to recognize handwriting. Dialects, accents, vocabulary, and inflection all complicate the problem. Then there are homonyms such as two, too, and to, which can be distinguished only through context. Speech recognition takes computer power, and plenty of it, but the potential rewards are enormous.

At today's state of development a computer can be trained to recognize a wide vocabulary from a single speaker or a narrower vocabulary from the public. The latter approach has the most immediate application in telecommunications. Computers can recognize numbers with a reasonable degree of accuracy regardless of dialect, and voice announcement equipment can repeat them back for verification.

Where a narrowly predictable range of words can be expected, speech recognition can substitute for an attendant. In a library, for example, the system could ask the caller to indicate the department he or she wants. If the caller says "science," the system could prompt "do you want social science or physical science?" The answer is in a predictable range, allowing the system to carry on a dialog until it is clear where the call should go or until an attendant intervenes. Speech recognition can substitute for an attendant by asking callers to say the last name of the person to whom they want to speak. The result is not infallible, but the application is improving, and will get better.

The primary uses for speech recognition today are account number recognition and call routing. As the technology improves, the applications will replace some of the mind-numbing tasks of today. Directory assistance is high on the list. Customer service centers can greatly multiply their effectiveness by doing a better job of screening and routing calls. For example, the speech-recognition system could ask several questions that enable it to route calls to an expert. By contrast, today's expert agent applications in an ACD have limited screening capability. Callers could be asked to speak the name of a preferred agent or to say what service they want.

A powerful speech-recognition application is transferring messages from a caller into an alphanumeric pager. The system should be able to accept a wide vocabulary, repeating words as they are entered, and prompting for any it does not recognize. As a fallback, the system could ask the caller to spell unfamiliar words. Although this application is not available at the time of this writing, it is one with exceptionally high payoff.

DIGITAL ANNOUNCERS

Digital announcers are the devices that play announcements over ACDs and UCDs and provide information announcements and announcements-on-hold. Unlike analog announcers that record messages on a tape, digital announcers store messages in digitized form on chips. They are, therefore, not practical for long announcements because the cost of the device increases with the length of the message.

It is important to evaluate the application carefully before buying an announcement system. As with voice mail, the primary criteria in selecting a system are the amount of message storage and the number of channels required. It is also important to decide how the message will be changed. A permanent message, such as an informational message about a company's product line, probably would be recorded professionally and changed infrequently. The message might even be encoded on a chip before it leaves the factory. Conversely, a school using an announcement system to distribute announcements about closures due to weather will want to record messages locally and, perhaps, from a remote location.

The control circuitry should determine when to connect the caller to the announcement. Some messages play only from the beginning; in other cases the listener can barge in on the message wherever it happens to be in a cycle. For example, if a promotional or informational message is being played, it would be appropriate to break in at only certain spots, and the message would play only once. Messages on hold might play repeatedly while the caller is on hold, or the system might vary the message depending on how long the caller waits.

Voice quality is another important consideration. As with voice mail, the higher the degree of compression, the lower the storage cost and sometimes the lower the voice quality. The best way to evaluate quality is to listen to a sample.

APPLICATIONS

Voice mail often is perceived as simply an expensive answering machine. It can be used as an answering machine, but a properly chosen and applied system can improve the effectiveness of the company's staff. The features, the most important of which are listed in Table 27-1, lend voice mail a flexibility that cannot be achieved without processor-driven or human intelligence. Its applications are too numerous to list and, in most cases, are self-evident. Some creative uses that are not so obvious are

- ◆ A hospital offers voice mail for its patient rooms, allowing patients to receive messages while they are asleep, in surgery, etc. and play them back at their leisure. In addition to being good for patient morale, such a system is a source of revenue for the hospital.

- ◆ A public telephone service provider allows a caller who reaches an unanswered or busy telephone the option of leaving a voice-mail message for later delivery. This is a valuable service for callers who can't afford to wait.

- ◆ A hospital posts its job openings in voice mail, segregated by licensed, nonlicensed, and office occupations. Callers can listen to descriptions of the jobs available and route themselves to the employment department to get more information.

- ◆ A school district provides its teachers with a nonintegrated voice mailbox so parents can leave messages for callback without interrupting either staff or teachers during class hours.

- ◆ A food-processing plant provides guest mailboxes for its growers to inform them of recommended planting schedules and the availability of seed and fertilizer. During the harvest season, daily tonnage quotas are left in voice mail. Not only does this system eliminate calls to farmers who are away from the telephone, it also makes it possible for the processing plant to verify that the message has been retrieved.

To gain maximum benefit from voice mail, an organization must ensure that its employees do not abuse the service. The most frequent abuse is the tendency of some users to hide behind voice mail, using it to answer all calls, which they can return at their convenience. When used this way, voice mail aggravates, instead of alleviates, the problem of telephone tag.

A second form of abuse is the verbose greeting message. Callers are annoyed by the constant repetition of a message and detailed instructions on how to use a system that should be self-explanatory. Also, verbose greetings waste ports and disk storage.

Improperly designed and applied voice-mail and automated attendant systems have led to the creation of the term *voice-mail jail*, which refers to the situation in which a caller is locked in the voice-mail system and cannot escape to get personalized assistance. A well-designed system should be brief and clear in its instructions and should give callers a choice.

T A B L E 27-1

Common Voice-Mail Features

Audiotex. A "voice bulletin board" feature that permits the caller to choose from a menu of announcements.
Automatic purge. System automatically purges overage messages to recover storage space.
Broadcast. User with this feature enabled in the class of service can send a group message to
all box holders in the system.
Class of service. Defines how a user may operate or interface with the system, including such
variables as the amount of storage allocated and the length of time messages can be stored
before they are automatically deleted.
Disk usage report. System informs administrator of percentage usage of the fixed disk-
storage unit.
Distribution lists. Permits users to establish lists of mailbox holders who receive messages
when the appropriate code is dialed.
Guest mailbox. Permits the system administrator to establish mailboxes for customers and
temporary users.
Individual user profile. Permits individual users or classes of service to establish variables such
as length of greeting, coverage for return to operator feature, and length of message retention.
Mailbox-full warning. Informs user when mailbox is close to reaching capacity.
Message priority. Permits callers to designate a message as high priority. System reads out
high-priority messages first.
Outcalling. System can call subscribers at a predetermined telephone number, cellular tele-
phone, or pager to notify them that they have received a message.

Many companies are reluctant to use voice mail with their customers because
of the impersonality of the service. The first contact a company has with a new customer usually should not be through voice mail, but when the relationship is
firmly cemented, voice mail can be as advantageous to a customer as it is to another
employee. The key is to leave the caller in control. Many companies answer outside calls with an attendant, but offer the caller the option of being transferred to
the user's voice mail. Even if messages are taken manually, the receptionist can
read them into voice mail or send them by e-mail, which is usually a more effective means of distributing messages than writing them on message slips.

Evaluation Criteria

Evaluations of voice mail, automated attendant, and audiotex systems should be
based on the features outlined in Table 27-1 and on the following criteria, which include the most important features.

Integration with a PBX

The most important consideration in evaluating and using a voice-mail system is
the degree to which it integrates with the PBX. This is not to say that integration is
always necessary; often the application needs a stand-alone voice-mail system. For

most office workers, however, an integrated system provides essential features. The most sophisticated integration is available with products that use CTI integration, but the cost may be prohibitive except in companies with call centers.

Integration with Other Voice-Processing Applications

Voice-processing equipment is available as an integrated unit containing voice mail, automated attendant, and IVR in the same package, or it is available as separate stand-alone units. The cost of an integrated unit is usually less than stand-alone units, but the separate systems may offer additional features and functions.

Compression Algorithm

All digital voice-mail systems use some form of compressed voice technology to digitize and store messages and announcements. Part of the compression is gained by pause compression and expansion, in which the duration of a pause is coded instead of the pause itself. Voice-mail systems use pause compression to speed or retard playback. If a listener wants a faster playback, the system shortens pauses; for a slower playback, it lengthens them. Also, the specific technology used for digitizing the voice affects the efficiency of the system. The more the voice is compressed, the less natural it sounds and the less storage space it occupies. Manufacturers have a choice between a natural sounding system that takes more storage space and a more efficient system that sacrifices some intelligibility. The best way to evaluate this feature is to listen to the voice quality of several different systems and compare voice quality.

Cost per Hour of Storage

The cost per hour of message storage is the most effective way of comparing costs of voice-mail systems. The cost per hour of storage is the total time on the disk less overhead for such things as system greetings and user prompts. Cost is not, however, the only criterion for evaluating systems. It is possible to reduce the amount of overhead and increase the amount of available storage by providing only a system greeting instead of personal greetings. The personal greeting greatly improves the usability of the system because it permits users to leave messages that tell callers where they are and when they plan to return.

Port Utilization

The number of ports determines how many users can leave and retrieve messages simultaneously. Not all ports are necessarily available for full voice-mail use. Some systems require dedicated ports for automated attendant. Some systems require separate ports for outgoing messages such as calls the voice-mail system places to a paging or cellular radio system. Systems that integrate through display set emulation generally cannot resolve the glare situation that arises when users seize a circuit simultaneously from both ends. Therefore, such systems may require separate incoming and outgoing ports.

System Reports

System reports can be used to determine how efficiently the system is being utilized. Reports should provide information such as the following:

- Number of messages sent and received by a specific system user.
- Average length of messages by specific user or group.
- Percentage of disk space used.
- Busy-hour traffic for various ports.
- Number of times all access ports are busy.
- Message aging by individual mailbox.
- Number of messages not deleted after specified time.

Electronic-Mail Integration

One form of electronic-mail integration permits transfer of an e-mail message from a computer into the user's voice mailbox by synthesized voice. The primary advantage is that users can retrieve e-mail messages from a telephone; there is no need to have a data device to retrieve messages. This form of integration is available only from a specific computer and voice-mail pair.

Networking Capability

This feature permits multiple voice-mail systems to act as an integrated unit. From the system administrator's standpoint, an important issue is how to maintain distribution lists across the network. Some systems exchange messages that automatically update the other machines on the network.

Another important function of networked voice mail is how systems exchange messages. In some systems, the voice-mail system can dial-up during low-cost hours to exchange messages.

Security

The voice-mail system must prevent callers from dialing invalid extension numbers, and thereby connecting through to trunks. The system administrator should be able to force password changes, and to require passwords of a minimum length.

Evaluating Automated Attendant

In applying an automated attendant system, administrators should carefully consider its effect on callers. Although the number of people who lack DTMF dialing capability is dropping continuously, some still have rotary dials and must wait through the entire menu to reach an operator. Other callers will resent the automated attendant and may avoid businesses that use them. Some automated attendants offer a confusing array of menu choices and levels. Frequent callers usually have no problem navigating the menus, but a first-time caller may be baffled by the variety of choices. Any company considering an automated attendant will be well advised to study the application carefully, design it intelligently, test it thoroughly, and listen to the comments of callers.

The disadvantages of automated attendant notwithstanding, in many applications it makes good business sense. First, it substitutes for DID in a system where DID is not available, particularly during hours when the business is closed. Second, an automated attendant is often an excellent way to enable callers on toll-free lines to reach an appropriate destination without an attendant. Although dialed number identification system (DNIS) is available in toll-free service, it is delivered only on T1/E1, and the numbering plan does not allow dailing every station on a PBX.

A third application where the automated attendant is effective is with an overloaded switchboard. Instead of installing a second attendant console, the company may find that the automated attendant offers a quick solution to customer complaints of delays in answering. Remember that it isn't necessary to require callers to listen to a voice message to get the value from an automated attendant. Employees and frequent callers can be told that when the telephone is answered they can immediately dial an extension number. Other callers simply hear a short greeting and are queued to the human attendant, whose load is reduced by the callers who dial extensions directly.

Evaluating Audiotex

The audiotex feature of voice mail is a useful means of distributing information. Callers receive a menu of choices. They can select two or three levels of menu before reaching the desired information. For example, a university might disseminate class information via audiotex by listing the major courses of study—science, liberal arts, engineering—on the first menu; the field of study—biology, botany, chemistry—on the second menu level; and class—freshman, sophomore—on a third. If the menu choices are no more than the caller can easily remember, this can be an effective way of delivering information. The system should be designed to enable callers to interrupt the menu by pressing a special key such as "#" to repeat.

The most important criteria in evaluating audiotex are the types of host interfaces, applications development tools, and local databases supported.

Evaluating Interactive Voice Response

Many of the same criteria used for voice mail can be used to evaluate IVR. A major exception is the fact that the interface between the host computer and the IVR must be programmed. So called shrink-wrapped software is available for some applications, but most require custom programming—often by a system integrator that provides the IVR hardware and the company's software application.

Voice quality, ease of programming, and quality of vendor support are important considerations in any type of voice processing. Many systems provide application development tools that provide a high-level language the developer can use. In addition, the following criteria should be considered with IVR.

Hardware Platform   The hardware platform will either be proprietary or based on a PC. The latter is less expensive to upgrade. Determine how many ports are available, what is the maximum capacity, and how much it costs to expand. When additional storage is required, can an industry standard hard disk be installed? Does the system have an Ethernet interface for connecting to an outboard computer?

Software   Check the features that the system supports. Does the manufacturer have a good record of introducing new features to keep pace with developments on the market? What is the cost of new software releases? Has the application been programmed by a third party who makes it available for a fee, or is it necessary to train or hire an application developer? If the latter, how much does the development kit cost and how easy is it to learn? What kind of debugging tools are available? Does it run an industry-standard database management system such as Informix or Oracle?

Integration   Determine how the system interfaces with the PBX or telephone system. Is it a proprietary interface that is integrated with the PBX's processor or is it a standard analog telephone interface? The former is more versatile, but the latter can be transported to other applications more easily and may integrate with any PBX. Determine how easily a caller can transfer to a live attendant. The system ideally should not require callers to reidentify themselves when transferring from IVR to an attendant.

Speech-Generation Method   Does the system synthesize speech or use stored speech fragments? How natural does the speech sound? Can words or phrases unique to your operation be added easily?

Growth Capability   How many ports does the system support? Does it have the processor power to handle as many simultaneous callers as there are ports? Are you given the tools to measure and verify performance?

Reporting Capability   Does the system provide usage statistics? What form are they in? Can they easily be translated into service-related reports? Can the statistics be extracted while the system is active?

Evaluating Speech-Recognition Equipment

The primary concern with speech recognition is its accuracy, which can be tested by observing the result with a variety of callers. Any system purchased today will undoubtedly be improved in the future, so determine the developer's commitment to continued research and development and find out how the updates are introduced, and at what cost.

Pay particular attention to the application. The best results will be achieved with simple applications that require recognizing a limited number of short words such as numbers, the alphabet, department names, and so on.

Evaluating Digital Recorders

The primary factors in evaluating a digital voice recorder are

- ◆ *Security*. Can voice sessions be kept secure from unauthorized access while still making them available to supervisors who need to review the session? Are recordings tamper-proof so they can be admitted to court sessions if necessary?
- ◆ *Accessibility*. How easy is it to find the session from the client workstation?
- ◆ *Clarity*. Is the voice-compression algorithm good enough that voice can be retrieved with a high degree of intelligibility?
- ◆ *Archiving*. How easy is it to archive the recordings onto long-term storage media such as digital audiotape?
- ◆ *Maintainability*. Is the system adequately alarmed? Does the system provide disk mirroring or other methods of fault tolerance? Is it secure against data loss during full-disk conditions?

Evaluating Digital Announcers

Digital announcers are available as stand-alone devices that can interface with any PBX or public access line and as integrated devices that fit into a card slot in a PBX. The primary criteria in evaluating digital announcement systems are

- ◆ Voice quality.
- ◆ Storage capacity.
- ◆ Number of ports.
- ◆ Method of integration with the PBX—through the bus or through a port.
- ◆ Method of storing the announcement. Is it on RAM or PROM? How is it protected against power outage?
- ◆ Method of updating the announcement—locally, remotely, or through a professional service.

Case History: Language Interpretation

Many organizations deal with people speaking a foreign language, and need to dial into a service that interprets over the telephone. For example, a physician may

FIGURE 27-3

Language Interpretation IVR and CTI Application

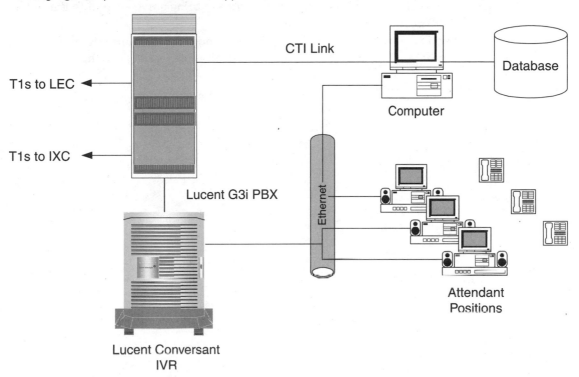

need to communicate with a patient who speaks an unfamiliar language. One company offers this service to clients who may be located anywhere in the country, using interpreters who work from their homes.

A Lucent G3 PBX is mated to a Lucent Conversant IVR to enable clients to establish a session through the IVR. Figure 27-3 shows how the equipment is connected. The client dials a toll-free number and, when prompted by the IVR, enters a credit card or account number, which is validated before proceeding. The IVR next prompts the caller for the first three letters of the language. After the client dials, the IVR repeats the language, and, when confirmed, accesses a database to determine the next available interpreters.

The client waits on hold while the IVR dials the interpreter and confirms his or her availability for this particular call. Interpreters establish their availability daily by dialing into the IVR. If the interpreter is not available or does not answer, the IVR steps to the next interpreter on the list. When the interpreter is on the line, the IVR conferences the client and the interpreter together. A CTI link to the PBX records the time of each step of the call for billing the clients and paying the interpreters. The client can press a digit at any time to bring a live agent into the call in case of difficulty.

Even considering the cost of equipment and CTI programming, this system has a payback of less than 2 years and can handle substantial growth.

CHAPTER 28

Centrex Systems

Before the arrival of microelectronics and stored program–controlled PBXs, many large companies were reluctant to place PBXs on their premises. An electro-mechanical PBX required considerable floor space and a large electrical supply. In effect, these large PBXs were the equivalent of small central offices; in fact, many of them served more stations than dial offices in small communities. The switching technology they used—crossbar or step-by-step—was nearly identical with that used in a central office, and the maintenance requirements were high. To meet this demand for complex customer switching systems, many LECs offer a central office–based service called *Centrex*.

Centrex blends the features of a PBX with those of ordinary business lines. A private partition is established in the central office, and individual lines are run to the customer's premises. Within the partition, an array of PBX-like features is defined. Early Centrex systems operating on crossbar switches had few features. As electronic central offices came into operation, features requiring intelligence in the switch were added. With electronic offices, it was possible to establish call pickup groups and provide features, such as call forwarding and speed dialing, that required a database and a processor. Today, most features that PBXs offer are available on Centrex, although not all LECs offer a full range of Centrex features.

Most LECs offer Centrex, including small-office Centrex services, which many LECs today provide with as few as two or three lines. Most of these services no longer bear the name Centrex but go by a variety of trade names, some of which are recognizable by their inclusion of the letters *cent* somewhere in the name.

With the coming of digital central offices, many LECs began offering digital Centrex services, which more closely approximate the features offered by digital PBXs. Digital Centrex extends a digital signal from the central office to the user's premises. The digital loop permits Centrex, with a proprietary feature set, to offer single-button feature access on digital lines. By contrast, features in analog Centrex are accessed by pressing a speed-dial button or pushing a flash key to get a second dial tone and dialing a code.

In both PBX and Centrex service, features that are accessible only through code dialing tend to fall into disuse. It is possible to assign the codes to speed-dial buttons on an analog set, but the features can be reprogrammed by users, so it is difficult to keep consistency in the feature pattern among stations on the system. Digital Centrex allows the administrator to assign buttons that cannot be changed by users.

In this chapter we will discuss the differences between Centrex and PBX and explore the applications for which each is most appropriate.

CENTREX FEATURES

Most features of digital Centrex are identical with analog Centrex, except digital Centrex integrates the telephone set with the central office line circuit. Digital telephones on premises provide push-button access to features. Stations equipped with single-line telephone DTMF sets have essentially the same features regardless of whether they are served by an analog or a digital central office. Digital telephone sets can access more features, but their range is limited and cannot be extended with loop extenders and voice repeaters, as can those of an analog station.

Special features, including T1/E1 to the IXC, tie lines, and toll-free lines, can be terminated on Centrex in essentially the same manner as on a PBX. Also, Centrex switches can serve as an electronic tandem switch for a company's private network.

The following are some the major features available on Centrex.

Automatic Identification of Outward Dialing   This feature records billable outgoing calls, allowing for departmental chargeback and tracking of unauthorized calls. It is similar to call detail recording in a PBX.

Call Forward   Several call-forwarding options are available to send calls from the called extension to another extension on busy, no answer, or all calls.

Call Hold   Permits the user to put a call on hold and use the line for another call. Note that the hold button on analog sets holds the line in the set, but it is not available for another call. The hold button on a digital set or the hold feature code on either type of set holds the line in the switch so it is available for another call.

Call Pickup   Enables the user to pick up calls from another station that is defined as part of the user's pickup group.

Call Transfer   Enables the user to transfer an incoming or outgoing call to another line. Off-system transfer allows transfer to a number outside the Centrex system.

Call Waiting   Indicates to the station user that another call has arrived. The user can either answer or ignore the second call.

Class of Service Restrictions   Allows the system administrator to allow or deny toll calling and access to station features.

Direct Inward and Outward Dialing   Permits station users to receive calls from outside the Centrex group and place outside calls without attendant assistance.

Distinctive Ringing   Allows users to distinguish between internal and external calls.

System Speed Dial   Permits users to use abbreviated codes for dialing numbers.

Three-Way Conference   Permits users in conference with another station to add on a third party.

Note that although the capability for these features is available in the central office, LEC tariffs may impose additional charges for some of these features.

Advantages of Centrex

Centrex service provides each user the equivalent of a personal business line. A Centrex group is defined in the central office so that members of the group have a variety of PBX-like features. The following are the primary advantages of Centrex service compared to a PBX.

Reliability

Since Centrex service is furnished from a central office, the reliability is high. Central office switching systems are inherently protected against the failure of a processor or major common control equipment item. The Centrex subscriber does not have to worry about providing battery backup, duplicate processors, duplicate power supplies, or spare equipment for service restoration. The most likely cause of Centrex failure is cable trouble, which should be rare. Local central office switching systems average 1 hour's outage or less per 40 years in service, and even if the failure rate is higher than the average, the reliability is still higher than that of most PBXs.

Integration of Multiple Locations

To link multiple small locations with a PBX, customers must use off-premises extensions (OPXs), tie lines, or a combination of both. For example, most school districts have a large central administration office and a combination of large, intermediate, and small schools. Centrex is often a less costly system for tying diverse locations together than using one or more PBXs connected with tie lines. Also, when some locations are too small to justify a PBX, they lose the features of a fully integrated system. Centrex provides uniform services to all locations, integrating them into a single system. It should be noted, however, that the range limitations of digital Centrex may preclude using digital feature sets in all locations. Also note that integrating Centrex between wire centers may carry a higher tariff rate than when all stations are in the same wire center.

Reduced Capital Investment

Station equipment for a PBX costs about the same as it does with Centrex but since the LEC owns and maintains the switching equipment, the initial capital investment required for Centrex is about half that required for a PBX. The monthly costs, however, are greater for Centrex.

Reduced Maintenance and Administrative Responsibility

The Centrex customer is relieved of maintenance and administrative responsibility except that associated with the station equipment. The LEC delivers a service and takes care of repair, recordkeeping, and system management. This factor is frequently overlooked by companies that underestimate the administrative work associated with owning a PBX.

Freedom from Obsolescence

PBXs have evolved through at least three and, by some counts, four generations, following similar evolutions in central offices. Centrex users have ridden through the evolution without feeling the impact of the technological change except insofar as it brought new features or required new telephone sets. Centrex may provide a relatively painless method of evolving into ISDN.

Virtually Unlimited Growth

PBXs grow in smooth increments up to existing shelf, cabinet, or system capacity. Growth beyond the capacity of one of these elements requires an investment that is sometimes substantial and sometimes requires changing the entire system. Centrex capacity is not unlimited, but if the LEC has sufficient notice, the user can meet most growth requirements without a major investment.

Reduced Floor Space

Centrex service requires almost no floor space other than the space required for the distributing frames. This can be important in companies that have several thousand lines. In very large PBXs, the vehicle used for switching is usually a central office switch, such as the Lucent Technologies 5ESS or the Northern Telecom SL-100, which is the PBX version of the DMS-100. Besides requiring floor space, these switches require a full-time trained staff to administer.

Short-Term Commitment

Although some LECs contract Centrex services, others offer them on a month-to-month basis. This can be important if future growth is uncertain or if the customer needs service for a short time while awaiting a more permanent type of service.

Centrex Drawbacks

Offsetting the advantages of Centrex are disadvantages that many organizations find outweigh the advantages.

Life-Cycle Cost

The life-cycle cost of a system is a composite of initial capital investment and recurring costs over the life of the investment. The cost of PBX service generally drops after the initial lease/purchase period of the equipment is over. Centrex costs continue for the life of the service and may increase with inflation. Subscriber line access charges are levied per line in a Centrex compared to a PBX where they are levied per trunk. Centrex is usually less expensive at the outset than a PBX, but many organizations find a PBX to be less costly over the long term. The key factor in determining the break-even point between a PBX and Centrex is usually the length of time it is expected to be in service. Refer to *The Irwin Handbook of Telecommunications Management* for methods of calculating the life-cycle differences between PBX and Centrex.

Features

Digital Centrex has most of the features available in a PBX. Analog Centrex has most of the important features, but they must be activated by code dialing. With either system it is difficult and costly to integrate a customer-owned voice-mail or call-accounting system. An integrated automatic call distributor (ACD) may be more costly or less effective in a Centrex system. Application program interfaces, which are available on some PBXs, may not be generally available on Centrex, limiting the ability of a company to use services such as dialed number identification service (DNIS) and automatic number identification service or calling line identification.

Feature Costs

Although features equivalent to those in a PBX may be available with Centrex, there is often an extra monthly charge for each feature. Often the additional cost makes Centrex service noncompetitive with a PBX.

Add, Move, and Change Flexibility

Customer-controlled adds, moves, and changes are an important feature of PBXs that may be unavailable or available only on a reduced level with Centrex. With Centrex, if a terminal for making customer-controlled rearrangements is provided, the LEC often posts the changes on a batch basis. Batched changes are not posted immediately, so the changes are not effective until the next working day. With a PBX, the changes can be made instantaneously.

APPLICATIONS

This section discusses the principal factors to be considered in selecting between Centrex services and in choosing between Centrex and a PBX.

Analog versus Digital Centrex   Most LECs provide a choice of analog or digital Centrex, although in a particular exchange only one or two wire centers may be equipped for digital Centrex. For most customers, the question whether an analog or a digital switching system provides the service is not relevant. The quality of service will be equivalent, and the use of Centrex to carry directly connected digital data will be rare. Differences in telephone sets, however, usually favor digital Centrex.

Analog Centrex is generally incapable of furnishing integrated key telephone service. The switch itself can provide functions such as call transfer, call pickup, and call hold, but the users must dial codes to activate the features. Attempts to train users to dial feature codes are rarely successful, so either the features fall into disuse or the enterprise installs key telephone equipment to provide the features.

Digital Centrex can support integrated key system features on proprietary telephone sets. This feature is the principal advantage of digital Centrex over its analog counterpart.

Feature Access   Many Centrex users apply key telephone systems behind analog Centrex to gain the advantages of button access to features. The equipment used behind Centrex must be designed to be compatible. It must, for example, provide a flash key to access central office dial tone for access to such features as call transfer.

Trunking Issues   In the past, one advantage of Centrex was the low probability of call blockage. LECs provided Centrex trunks to provide the same grade of service that the central office as a whole received. Compared to a PBX where the number of trunks was an economic issue determined by the customer, Centrex often provided better service.

Now LECs may offer Centrex only as a trunk-rated service, called network access restriction (NAR). In a trunk-rated service, the LEC interposes a software block that permits only the contracted number of incoming and outgoing calls to be connected simultaneously. Therefore, the quantity and cost of trunks required may be equivalent for both Centrex and a PBX.

Multiple Location Issues   Centrex allows an organization that spans an entire metropolitan area to function as if it were a single system. In a metropolitan area with only one wire center Centrex can eliminate the need for off-premises stations. In a multiwire center area both PBXs and Centrex require off-premises extensions, the cost of which may be identical, and in neither case is it possible to operate digital feature sets from remote locations. Some LECs offer a tariff for multiple location Centrex, which provides the features between central offices at an additional charge plus mileage.

Ancillary Equipment Issues   Nearly half the PBXs installed today are equipped with voice-mail, automated attendant, and call-accounting systems. These features are all available with Centrex, but they may be provided only as an extra cost option. Ancillary features may be charged per use by the LEC, which often makes

FIGURE 28-1

School District Centrex

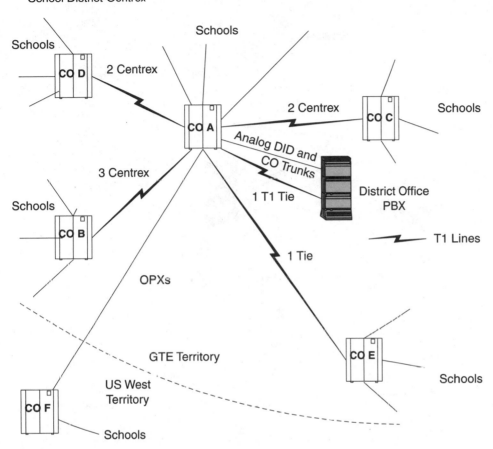

them more costly than privately owned systems. Call-accounting information may be connected back to the customer over a remote line, or it may be provided from the LEC's automatic message-accounting system and not be available on as short notice as privately owned call-accounting information.

Case History: Citywide Centrex

School districts, banks, branch retail outlets, and other organizations that are geographically spread over a metropolitan area have unique communications problems that can sometimes be solved by Centrex. The school district in question serves 41 schools and three administrative locations with conventional Centrex service. Six different wire centers, of which four are operated by GTE and two by US West, serve the buildings. The serving arrangement shown in Figure 28-1 had the advantage of connecting all schools to the district office PBX, but it also had a

FIGURE 28-2

School District Citywide Centrex

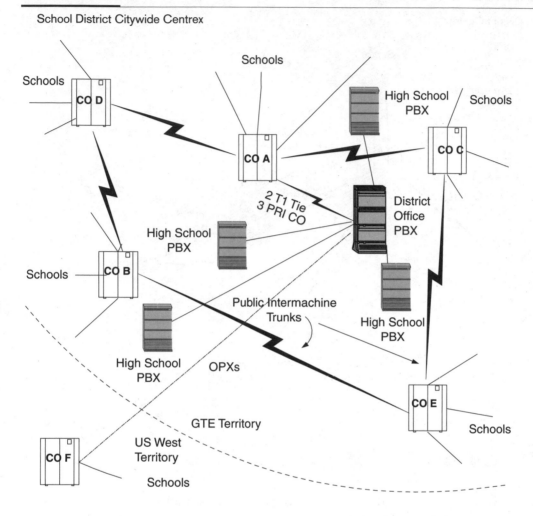

major drawback. The T1 lines from the GTE central offices to the CO serving the district office were expensive. Also, circuit utilization was poor because the trunks were not switched in the local CO. All schools received their dial tone from CO A.

GTE proposed an alternate serving arrangement, known as Citywide Centrex, that reduced costs by more than one-third. Figure 28-2 shows the new serving arrangement. The four high schools in the district have Nortel Meridian One Option 11 PBXs that are networked to an Option 61 in the district office. All high schools' incoming and outgoing calls flow over PRI trunks connected to the Option 61, except for analog trunks that are terminated on each Option 11 for E-911 access.

The middle and elementary schools located in GTE territory receive their service from the four serving central offices. The schools in US West territory are connected to the district office with OPXs. A numbering plan was chosen, using a prefix from each central office that permits four-digit dialing among all schools. Calls between the Centrex-equipped schools and the high school–district office complex flow over two tie lines. Calls between elementary schools use the public trunking network.

Citywide Centrex offers an economical and effective serving arrangement for any organization with a similar structure of a centralized administrative complex and remote branches. Banks, retail organizations, city and county governments, and such can tie the organization together with a unified dialing structure. Unfortunately, the service is not universally available. CLECs, however, which often have only a single central office overlaying an entire metropolitan area, inherently provide the equivalent of Citywide Centrex.

CHAPTER 29

Electronic Messaging Systems

*M*essaging, which is defined as the use of computer systems to exchange messages among people, applications, and organizations, has paralleled the growth of desktop computers. When nearly every user has a terminal or computer connected to a network or host, it becomes practical to communicate in ways that were previously impractical. E-mail, and its voice counterpart voice mail, are revolutionizing the way people communicate. Information can be transferred instantaneously between any locations that have access to the Internet. Messages are no longer textual in format. They can contain any type of information such as voice, video, and files. Messaging systems are inherently asynchronous, that is, they do not require users to be simultaneously available to exchange information. They are also inherently store-and-forward. Whether voice or e-mail, the message is stored for later retrieval by the user.

A few years ago sending an e-mail message meant subscribing to one of the national carriers such as MCI Mail, America Online, or AT&T Mail. These carriers provided special software for creating and sending messages. Most companies had an internal e-mail system, but sending messages between companies required a gateway to one of the national carriers, and attaching binary files was either unsupported or difficult. The Internet changed all that. Now, sending an e-mail message with an attached file is handled easily with desktop mail systems to which most companies are connected.

Most organizations today have both voice and electronic messaging. They are both capable of broadcasting to defined user groups, and either can be used for the same purpose, depending on the user's preference. With unified messaging, the two are linked together, with fax added in the bargain. For example, either voice mail or e-mail can notify each other of the existence of a message in the other medium. Voice readout of e-mail messages is feasible today, and in the future text readout of voice mail will be possible. Both types work across time zones and permit sender and receiver to communicate without being simultaneously available at the terminal device. Meanwhile, each medium has its own advantages compared to the other:

Voice-mail advantages:

◆ The telephone, which is universally available, is used for retrieving messages.

◆ Addressing is simple: the 10-digit telephone number.

◆ It covers unanswered telephones without the need for special training or equipment on the part of the caller.

E-mail advantages:

◆ A written record of the communication is produced.

◆ Simultaneous distribution to multiple users networkwide and across company boundaries is easy. Networking is inherent, not special as it is with voice mail.

◆ Messages can be dropped on a fax machine if the user lacks e-mail capability.

◆ E-mail can be used as the "envelope" for transferring a file to another user.

◆ Electronic messaging can tie the enterprise together with a fast, informal system that reduces the cost of mail, speeds the transfer of documents across departments and levels, and reduces the formality of the approval and review process. (Unless users apply this with discretion, this can be a disadvantage.)

This chapter discusses some of these applications and the protocols under which they operate. We will review the issues involved in implementing such applications as electronic mail, electronic data interchange (EDI), and data interchange between similar applications such as word processors. Voice messaging is covered in Chapter 27.

MESSAGING SYSTEMS

The terms messaging system and e-mail are often used interchangeably, but to be strictly accurate, e-mail is only one of the types of information that are communicated across a messaging system. Messaging is a transport system for delivering information. For example, scheduling, calendaring, forms, workflow, inventory, and all types of documents that are transported over electronic document interchange (EDI) are examples of messaging applications that can use the same transport system.

Types of Messaging Systems

Five different messaging system architectures are in use today:

◆   Host-based

◆   X.400

◆   Unix computer–based
◆   LAN-based
◆   Client-server

Host-Based Messaging Systems   Most major computer manufacturers provide proprietary host-based e-mail systems. These systems are expensive, difficult to set up and administer, and depend on a mainframe or minicomputer for their operation. With the decline in mainframes in favor of servers, these systems are relatively static compared to the other alternatives. Most of the growth is limited to existing systems.

X.400 Messaging Systems   X.400 is an ITU standard messaging protocol, and is the common language that many proprietary systems speak. Although it is a standard protocol, it is not used in most private e-mail systems. Public e-mail systems, such as those operated by the major IXCs plus those operated by most international carriers, use X.400.

Unix Computer–Based Messaging Systems   E-mail comes as a standard feature of the Unix operating system. Unix systems can communicate with each other using simple message transfer protocol (SMTP). The addressing systems and the protocol are used in Internet e-mail, which is the means by which many private e-mail systems communicate with each other.

LAN-Based Messaging Systems   LAN-based systems are inexpensive to purchase; some systems are even available in the public domain at no charge. Many systems run under graphical user interfaces, and are easier to use than host-based systems, which are often intended for ASCII terminals. LAN-based systems are easy to administer until several LANs are interconnected, and then routing and addressing may become complex.

Client-Server Messaging Systems   In a client-server system the e-mail application runs on a server and the user interface runs on the client workstation. These systems are similar to host-based systems except that users can choose their own client. Microsoft Outlook is a popular client since it comes with Microsoft Windows and matches well with Microsoft Exchange Server.

Messaging Terminology

The structure of a typical computer messaging system is shown in Figure 29-1. The *user agent* (UA) is used at both ends of a mail system to create, send, receive, and manage messages. The UA is the portion of the mail system that the end user contacts directly. It can limit the capabilities of the e-mail system by the features it

F I G U R E 29-1

A Messaging System

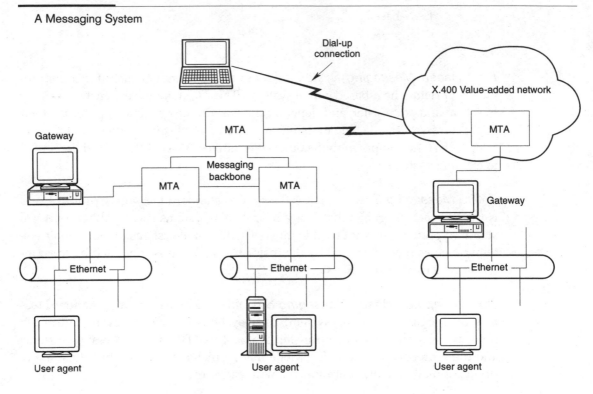

includes or lacks. For example, if the messaging system is capable of carrying voice clips, but the UA lacks that capability, the feature will be unavailable.

The *message transfer agent* (MTA) transfers messages between compatible systems over the *messaging backbone,* which is the network of circuits that interconnect the MTAs. It accepts messages from the UA, determines the route to the destination, and transfers to other MTAs based on the address. The MTA also determines messaging capabilities. For example, the UAs may be capable of handling voice and video clips, but if the MTA lacks the capability, the feature will not work. Messaging systems usually contain a directory, which lists the addresses of devices and users on the systems.

A standard protocol, such as X.400 or SMTP, or a proprietary protocol, such as Novell's message-handling system (MHS), transfers messages between MTAs. The interface from the user agent to the MTA is covered in the X.400 protocol, and the Unix operating system, but Microsoft's mail application programming interface (MAPI) is widely used.

Message transfer between incompatible MTAs must go through a *gateway,* which translates the protocols of the systems. If multiple gateways are required to translate between a multitude of incompatible systems, a *messaging switch* is used in lieu of multiple gateways.

THE X.400 MESSAGING PROTOCOL

X.400 is the ITU-T standard message-handling protocol. It is implemented by most of the major IXCs and international carriers as their standard. Such systems as AT&T Mail, MCI Mail, and SprintMail use X.400. The fact that they use the protocol for carrying messages across the network does not mean that they use all features of the protocol. For example, although X.400 includes a UA, each company is free to devise its own user interface.

The power of X.400 is procured at a sacrifice of simplicity. It is a complex system to set up and administer, which is the reason that most mail systems use their own protocol and use X.400 as a universal language across which they can exchange messages. Unlike the proprietary protocols the various messaging systems use, X.400 is an open architecture. It is impractical for LAN application, however, because of its overhead and complex addressing scheme. Each X.400 messaging system is an independent domain, and these must be connected by agreement between the carriers. Therefore, if you are an X.400 subscriber, there is no guarantee that you have connection to other X.400 subscribers. You will be able to send mail to them only if they have established an interconnection agreement.

X.400 Addressing

X.400 uses a multilevel hierarchical address, as illustrated in Figure 29-2. The character string can be daunting until one understands its structure. At the top level is the root, followed by country, which is a mandatory part of the address. The next level can be A for an administrative domain or P for a private domain. An administrative domain is usually a service provider such as AT&T Mail or MCI Mail. Large companies may use a private domain in lieu of a service provider. At the next level is organization unit (OU), which is a unique identifier referring to a company's private messaging system. Below the organization companies may identify localities and organizational units of several levels. The lowest level is the CN (common name), which can optionally be stated as given name (G) and surname (S).

The X.400 addressing system is flexible but verbose. The protocol allows for aliasing, which can jump across directory levels to provide a shortcut address. Users are unlikely to understand the addressing well enough to create their own aliases, so expert assistance may be needed. Most effective user agents provide shortcut addresses, allowing the user to substitute a short character string for a longer address.

Other messaging systems have addressing protocols that are different than X.400. The Internet, for example, has a system of user_id@hostname. domain_name. The structure of IP addresses is covered in Chapter 3. SMTP addressing, which has its origin in the Unix operating system, uses a similar structure, and is discussed later.

X.400 Addressing Structure

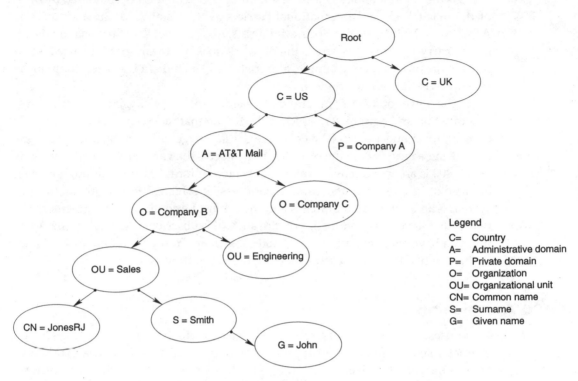

Legend

C=   Country
A=   Administrative domain
P=   Private domain
O=   Organization
OU= Organizational unit
CN= Common name
S=   Surname
G=   Given name

X.500 Directory Service for X.400

X.500 is a network of systems that hold information about X.400 addresses. Directory user agents (DUAs) are specialized user agents that can access directory systems agents (DSAs) in which the directory information is stored. DSAs communicate with each other using the directory access protocol (DAP) and the directory service protocol (DSP). The DAP is used for retrieving directory information, while DSP is used between directories for information exchange. Users who do not know the e-mail address of another user can access the DUA much as they might call directory assistance to get a telephone number. After they obtain the address, they can store it in the e-mail application or in the central directory in an enterprise e-mail system. DAP is complex for most small intracompany mail systems. These systems generally use lightweight directory access protocol (LDAP).

X.500 was first published by the ITU in 1988, and is updated regularly. It has the capability of tying e-mail systems together through gateways regardless of vendor. Within the organization, the X.500 directory serves as a single source for storing directory information about users. This makes it easier for a company to keep updated than maintaining individual departmental post offices.

F I G U R E 29-3

Simple Mail Transfer Protocol

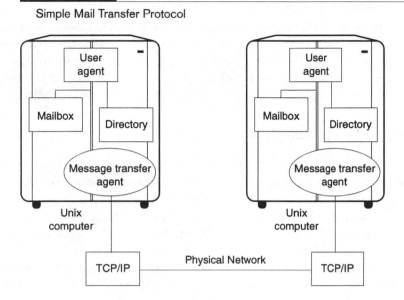

The contents of the directory are not covered by the X.500 standard. Therefore, companies can maintain any type of information desired in the database, filtering and screening to keep parts of it private. A company could, for example, publish certain e-mail addresses, but keep everything else, including telephone numbers and mail stops, private within the company. To be X.500 compliant, a system must provide four elements:

- A directory user agent for user access.
- A directory service agent that speaks the DAP and DSP protocols.
- Basic directory functions such as information storage, retrieval, and updating.
- Security, including user authentication.

SIMPLE MAIL TRANSFER PROTOCOL

SMTP is an easy and unsophisticated mail system that is used between Unix computers. Figure 29-3 shows how Unix computers transfer mail between each other. To send a message, the sender types the message into the UA, which passes the message to the MTA. Each computer contains a directory naming service (DNS) application, which contains the IP address for every user on the network. The MTA transfers the message to the other computer via a TCP/IP link. The link operates over a standard network such as Ethernet. The two MTAs carry on a simple dialog to establish communication. The message transfers to the receiving MTA, which stores it in the user's mailbox. If the addressee is unknown, the receiving MTA returns a message to that effect.

By itself, SMTP can handle only 7-bit ASCII text, which means that additional software is needed to enable a message to carry a binary file. The Internet Engineering Task Force developed a protocol known as multipurpose internet mail extensions (MIME), which converts files into a format that SMTP can handle. All mail servers that enable users to attach files to messages implement MIME.

ELECTRONIC-MAIL SYSTEMS

Most companies use some form of e-mail today. If the company started as a mainframe-oriented enterprise, the mail system probably began as a host-based system such as IBM's PROFS. As companies add LANs, the simpler forms of server-based e-mail emerge. Some of the more popular systems are Lotus Development Corporation's Domino R5 Mail Server, Microsoft's Exchange Server, and Sun Microsystem's Sun Internet Mail Server.

As e-mail becomes mission-critical in many companies, the message volume the typical worker must contend with grows, and handling becomes a problem. Intelligent e-mail systems make mail-handling decisions under user-defined criteria. Intelligent systems can make message-handling decisions, such as routing, forwarding, discarding, or prioritizing messages, based on such criteria as who sent it, what the subject is, or where it was originated. This technique, called *rules-based messaging*, enables users to filter messages that might otherwise inundate them.

Application programs, such as word processing and spreadsheets, can be designed to make use of messaging systems. The simplest configuration is a *mail-aware program*. It knows that a messaging system exists, and how to send data over it. It does not know how to process the data. A *mail-enabled* application generates e-mail messages and uses the message transfer system to transfer information through the network. A mail-enabled application can do everything that a mail-aware program can, plus it can route, receive, and authenticate messages.

UNIFIED MESSAGING

When a voice-mail system is integrated with a desktop computer, usually over a LAN, the computer becomes a message center that makes it easier to handle voice mail, e-mail, and fax. With a nonunified voice-mail system, all prompting is over the telephone. If you have saved a message and want to listen to it again, you must skip over each of the previous messages in turn. Users reach the point that they remember most prompts, but the traditional voice-mail system gives them no visibility as to the type or origin of messages. Furthermore, you must listen to messages in serial form.

With a computer-integrated system all messages are listed in a window together with the type of message (e-mail, voice mail, fax, etc.), the time of arrival, and, if available, the sender's identity. The user can tell at a glance which messages are the most important and which have already been listened to. Users can drag and drop icons to save, forward, and delete messages. Fax messages can be displayed on the screen, filed on a computer, or sent to a printer with a few mouse clicks. E-mail messages can likewise be handled, and in time the computer will be able to translate voice-mail, e-mail, and fax messages to any of the other media, making the computer a complete message-handling system regardless whether the users access it from a computer or a phone. The only thing limiting universal convertibility is the lack of reliable speech recognition.

The architecture of most unified messaging systems is similar. The voice mail connects to the PBX in the usual manner. It also has a LAN connection, as does the e-mail server. The desktop devices run client software that may be provided with the voice mail or with the e-mail. The software pulling this all together is proprietary to the voice-mail vendor, so unlike e-mail systems that can mix and match clients and servers, unified messaging is limited by the voice mail.

ELECTRONIC DOCUMENT INTERCHANGE (EDI)

Global markets are changing the way we do business. To remain competitive, businesses must know their customers and respond to their needs. In international trade it takes an average of 46 documents to move products across boundaries. Traditional mail is too slow, and facsimile is impractical to authenticate for some applications, which raises the need for electronic document interchange. EDI is the intercompany exchange of legally binding trade documents. EDI enables companies to exchange a variety of business documents, such as invoices, requests for proposals, and shipping and purchase orders, over an electronic network.

EDI offers both cost savings and strategic benefits to the trading partners. Cost savings come from reduced labor costs, reduced stock levels that result from shorter document turnaround, and savings in telephone and postage costs. Improved response time is a major advantage. Companies can respond quickly to purchase orders, requests for quotes, and other such documents. In the past, trading partners developed document formats they could use between themselves, but it was impractical to make these arrangements with multiple trading partners. An international standard set of forms was needed. EDI was conceived in the 1970s, but its acceptance has been slow. Part of the reason has been that expensive, often mainframe-based, software was required. Now EDI can be implemented on PCs at a much lower cost than mainframe or minicomputer systems. PC-based EDI can be integrated with e-mail and its user-friendlier interface.

EDI software performs two main functions. It maps the fields on EDI documents with fields in the application software, and translates the data to and from the EDI documents. EDI applications receive and prepare documents on the screen, allowing the user to fill in the fields from the keyboard. Mapping data between fields is one of the most difficult parts of implementing EDI. It may be possible to use a translation program to remap the fields from one document to another; in the worst case it may be necessary to print out the EDI document and rekey the information into the application, which defeats much of the purpose.

EDI is based on store-and-forward messaging that can be exchanged over value-added networks (VANs) such as the major X.400 or X.25 carriers provide. The networks may offer either a store-and-forward or a store-and-retrieve class function for EDI subscribers. They may also offer document validation, security functions, and special reports. VANs may also convert protocols between the trading partners if they are incompatible. SMTP has no provisions for handling EDI, which makes X.400 a better backbone choice when using EDI.

EDI Standards

Four types of EDI standards are used:

◆ Proprietary

◆ Noncompliant and industry-specific

◆ National such as ANSI X.12

◆ International such as EDIFACT (EDI for administration, commerce, and transport)

EDIFACT is a set of EDI standards developed under the auspices of the United Nations. As with many other standards, it is a compromise—an amalgamation of the desires of many agencies. Nor is it yet a fully formed standard. The following are examples of documents that have been standardized by EDIFACT:

◆ Invoice

◆ Purchase order

◆ Quality data message

◆ International forwarding and transport message

◆ Customs declaration

◆ Customs response

ANSI standard X.12 is more mature than EDIFACT, but EDIFACT is international in scope and will eventually become the single standard.

APPLICATIONS

The Internet has revolutionized e-mail, changing it from sets of internal systems that might or might not be linked to a public X.400 system into a wide-open worldwide backbone for fast and easy document delivery. It is also vulnerable, as exemplified by the Melissa virus that propagated through e-mail to thousands of computers over a single weekend in 1999. Nevertheless, there is no turning back to the days when creating and sending e-mail was hardly worth the effort. IP-based messaging enables a server to exchange mail by implementing SMTP and either post office protocol (POP) or Internet message access protocol (IMAP). POP and IMAP are protocols that enable the client to retrieve messages from the server.

In selecting an e-mail system, the following are some issues that should be evaluated.

Adherence to Standards   A messaging system may need to connect to an X.400 system for some types of communication. All mail systems support SMTP, but lack of security may preclude its use for some applications. Most systems should support LDAP, and all systems should support MIME, POP-3, and IMAP-4.

Ease of Setup   E-mail server setup is not a trivial task with most systems. In large organizations with thousands of users, some method of generating the accounts automatically should be provided. Some systems provide for importing accounts from other e-mail systems, databases, or ASCII files.

Security   Determine whether the system supports authentication and encryption methods such as secure sockets layer (SSL), which enables web clients and servers to authenticate each other. The system should provide logs that the administrator can view to detect such matters as repeated ineffective attempts to log in.

Choice of Client   The user organization may standardize on client software because it is part of a groupware application. The client and the server may, therefore, be from different manufacturers. Determine whether they support the necessary protocols to interoperate.

Disk Management   Users are often careless about purging messages, which may consume disk space rapidly, particularly when large files are attached. The e-mail system should have tools for limiting message storage space and for notifying users to purge old messages.

Additional Applications   Many mail systems provide for other applications besides mail receipt and delivery. For example, a corporate bulletin board is one popular feature. Other common features of the client are document control, calendar, and contact manager.

Usage Information   Determine whether an audit trail through the system is needed. Is message receipting necessary? Should the system provide usage statistics for charging back to users or determining which are the high-use departments?

User Interface   The user interface must be easy to use for composing, sending, receiving, and managing messages. A graphical interface in a familiar style, such as Microsoft Windows or Apple Macintosh, is most desirable. Users should be able to cut and paste to and from word processors and attach files easily and move them seamlessly across the network.

Video and Audio Clips   The ability to move video and audio clips is an essential feature. Note, however, that if this feature is enabled, storage requirements will increase, and an improved system of purging old messages may be needed.

Unified Messaging Implementation

The first issue most companies face in considering unified messaging is the need to upgrade the PBX and voice mail to the latest release, which may represent a large expense that is otherwise unneeded. Unified messaging is one of those applications that has an enormous appeal to users, but is difficult to justify based on hard savings. It is generally sold by the seat, which means that it isn't necessary to implement it across the entire enterprise. The value of unified messaging is enhanced with caller identification. Without it, external voice-mail messages are displayed simply as outside calls, so the benefits of listening to message selectively are lost.

Unified messaging integrates nicely with CTI, and, in fact, could be considered to be a CTI feature to some degree. With CTI, the calling number is captured on the PC screen, and the user can return calls with a simple mouse click.

EDI Implementation

To implement EDI, a company needs four principal elements.

User Application   This is software that generates and receives EDI documents. The major partner in an EDI exchange may furnish the software. If not, review packages on the market, looking primarily for ease of use. Programs that operate under a graphical user interface are the easiest to use.

EDI Software   This software translates the user application to EDI message formats, provides the communications protocol for accessing the network, and translates incoming EDI messages to the user application. This software may be bundled with the user application software.

EDI Hardware Platform   This is a computer for running the EDI software. In large companies it may be a mainframe or minicomputer. Most companies starting EDI implementation will run it on a PC.

Network for Accessing the Information   Most companies implementing EDI will use dial-up access to a value-added network. The trading partners store their messages in the network. The network either downloads the message to the recipient, or the recipient dials in to get the message. Companies with a large volume of messages may be directly connected to the network, or if the volume is large enough, their computers can be directly connected.

CHAPTER 30

Facsimile Systems

Few users realize that facsimile is one of the oldest forms of transmitting information electrically. It was invented in 1843, but it languished for more than a century before it was accepted in the business mainstream. Only when digital fax was developed and international standards were adopted did the technology find its way into the mainstream. The military and news agencies had always been the major users of facsimile. Machines from the middle of the twentieth century scanned a photograph or document and sent it across a telephone circuit as a continuously varying analog tone. At the receiving end, the tone was converted to an electric current that varied the heat of a stylus. The paper was mounted on a rotating drum, and as the image burned into it, a thin trickle of smoke rose from the machine.

When CCITT, now ITU-T, introduced group 3 digital fax standards in the 1980s, usage increased to the point that operating without a fax is inconceivable to most organizations and many individuals. High-quality machines are cheap, and users with V.34 modems have fax capability built in. Fax switches and distinctive ringing from the LECs make fax line sharing practical, further adding to its attractiveness.

Fax-on-demand (FOD) is a high-visibility application for many companies. Callers can request technical and product information from companies, and have it sent to their fax machines within minutes. Fax servers make facsimile available to everyone on the company network. Users can send and receive faxes without leaving their desk, and without the extra cost of a dedicated business line or an analog station port on the PBX.

These factors have converged to carve a permanent niche for facsimile. The technology has changed the way business operates. Until the last few years, converting fax to text was difficult, but now fax received in a computer can easily be converted to text with optical character recognition (OCR) software. It isn't quite as convenient as receiving a document attached to an e-mail message, but it is fast, particularly when it comes to sending documents that originate on paper.

Fax overcomes the slowness and cost of the mail. A facsimile machine can send a letter in a fraction of a minute and usually for the cost of a postage stamp or less, depending on how many pages are sent and whether the transmission is in the local telephone calling area. Facsimile quality isn't quite as good as the original letter, but recipients are willing to sacrifice quality for speed. A former Postmaster General said, "The facsimile systems and the countless other applications of electricity to the transmission of intelligence yet to be made must eventually interfere with the transportation of letters by the slower means of post." If this statement sounds prophetic, consider that its author was Jonathan Creswell, and he was speaking in 1872.

Facsimile technology has other applications that will become more important as the technology matures. Many business machines combine facsimile with a printer and scanner. The ITU X.400 standards make it easy to send documents from a computer to a facsimile machine. As discussed later, many electronic mail services offer the capability of sending a document from a computer to a facsimile machine through a value-added network.

Although facsimile got off to a slow start compared to other telecommunications technologies, its use has expanded to the point that it now is indispensable for many forms of record communication. This has happened because ITU standards are now universally accepted and machine prices have dropped to the point of affordability for nearly everyone.

FACSIMILE TECHNOLOGY

A facsimile machine has four major elements, as diagrammed in Figure 30-1: scanner, printer, controller, and communications facilities. The scanner sweeps across a page, segmenting it into multiple lines in much the same way that a television camera scans an image. The scanner output converts the image to a binary code. The digital signal is compressed and applied directly to a digital circuit or through a modem to an analog circuit. Control equipment directs the scanning rate and compresses solid expanses of black or white to reduce transmission time. At the receiving end, the incoming signal is demodulated and drives a print mechanism that reproduces the incoming image on paper.

Facsimile Machine Characteristics

Facsimile equipment is categorized by modulation method, speed, resolution, and transmission rate. Digital machines produce a binary signal that is applied to the circuit through a modem. The digital transmission speed varies from 4800 b/s to 64 kb/s. The speed of sending a page depends on circuit quality and the amount of information to be encoded. Typically a single-spaced page of text takes a minute or less, depending on factors that we will discuss later. Resolution is measured in lines per inch (lpi) and varies from slightly less than 100 to 400 lpi.

FIGURE 30-1

Block Diagram of a Facsimile System

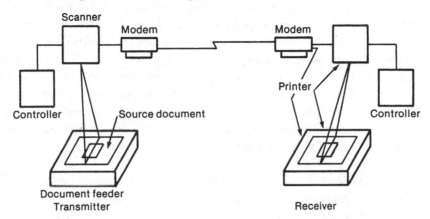

ITU divides facsimile standards into four groups. Groups 1 and 2 are analog standards that have been discontinued. The two current standards are

- *Group 3.* Compressed digital, 1-minute/page or less transmission time, 200-lpi resolution, 2400- to 33,600-b/s data rate.
- *Group 4.* Compressed digital, less than 1-minute/page transmission speed, 200- to 400-lpi resolution, data rates up to 64 kb/s.

ITU sets standards for protocol, scanning rate, phasing, scans per millimeter, synchronization, and modulation method. Facsimile machines must be both phased and synchronized. *Phasing* is the process of starting the printer and the scanner at the same position on the page at the beginning of a transmission. *Synchronization* keeps the scanner and printer aligned for the duration of the transmission.

Digital fax machines break a signal into dots, or picture elements, which are analogous to the pixels in a video signal. Unlike a video signal, which varies in intensity, digital facsimile produces a binary signal that is either on (black) or off (white) for each picture element. The number of picture elements per square inch determines the resolution of a digital facsimile and the transmission time.

Transmission times vary with the density of the information on a page. Modem speeds of 9600 b/s are standard with most digital machines. Some models, and many fax modems, are capable of transmission at speeds as high as 33,600 b/s. As with other data signals, 9600 b/s cannot always be transmitted reliably over the switched telephone network, which sometimes results in the transmission slowing to 4800 b/s or less. The 33,600-b/s systems often fail to connect at that speed and fall back to a slower speed. Even though machines may transmit at these higher speeds, the connection will step down to the speed the receiving machine is capable of. Many fax machines use memory to store the incoming signal, and therefore can receive faster than they can print.

Group 3 facsimile uses data compression to reduce transmission time. Many documents have expanses of white or black that are compressed by a process called *run-length encoding.* Instead of transmitting a string of zeros or ones corresponding to a long stretch of white or black, the length of the run is encoded into a short data message. By using run-length encoding, a digital facsimile machine compresses data into approximately one-eighth of the number of nonencoded bits, but the amount of compression depends on the character of the document. For example, a document with a border around it cannot be compressed vertically. The average typewritten document is compressed by a factor of at least 10:1.

The speed of a fax machine is often quoted in pages per minute. ITU-T publishes a standard reference page known as test chart #1 that is the standard of reference in quoting transmission speed. Four percent of the standard page is black, and the rest is white. A page with more black space will take longer to transmit.

Scanners

Document scanning converts an image to binary form. As the document moves through the feeder, the scanner detects light from the source and emits a 1 or 0 pulse, depending on whether the reflected light is above or below the threshold between black and white. The scanner output is sent to the compression circuitry where it is encoded as discussed previously.

Printing

Facsimile machines either use plain or coated electrosensitive paper. Coated fax paper comes in a roll, and is much less desirable than plain paper fax. Its major disadvantages are that it curls up, and it is not a permanent document. Plain paper fax creates documents that have the same degree of permanence as printed output, which, in effect, it is. Coated paper deteriorates over time, so it must be run through a copier to make it permanent. Plain paper fax machines are more expensive, but supplies are less costly, so for high-volume applications they are the preferable method. The principal plain paper fax printing technologies are laser and ink jet. Both technologies are identical to those used in printers.

Facsimile Handshake

When fax machines connect, they go through a handshake process to resolve such issues as the speed of transmission, compression method, and special features the machines may have. The initial handshake takes about 16 seconds for fax machines up to 14,400 b/s. They also pass messages at the end of each page to verify transmission, a process known as *retraining*. This function takes about 4 seconds per page. The G3 standard uses a compression method known as MH. Two other methods provide faster image transmission through additional compression. These are modified read (MR) and modified modified read (MMR). MMR is an advanced data encoding and compression scheme similar to group 4. Both of these still require 16 seconds for the initial handshake at lower speeds, but with V.34 modems the time is cut in half. The retraining interval is cut from 4 to 0.25 seconds.

The handshaking time has a significant effect on facsimile transmission speed. As the modem speed increases, the transmission time does not decrease in direct proportion because the handshake remains fixed. Only until the faster MMR protocol is employed does improved transmission speed become apparent.

FACSIMILE FEATURES

Some facsimile machines have features that make them complete document-communications centers, designed for attended or unattended operation. For example, stations can be equipped with polling features so a master can interrogate slave stations and retrieve messages from queue. In some machines the master polls the remote, after which the remote redials the master to send the document. Other machines have a feature called *reverse polling*, which enables the receiving machine to transmit a document on the initial poll. Most machines have automatic digital terminal identification capability and apply a time and date stamp to transmitted and received documents. Machines can be equipped with document feeders and stackers to enable them to send and receive documents while unattended. Machines using coated paper often include cutters to cut the document after each page. Some digital facsimile machines contain memory to store digitized messages and route them to designated addressees on either a selective or a broadcast basis. Memory also enables fax machines to receive documents when they are out of printing supplies. Most facsimile machines handle only standard letter or legal size paper, but some machines have a larger bed for handling oversized paper.

Besides these features, the following features are available as options on fax machines and servers.

Automatic Dial Directory   This feature is the same as speed dialing on a telephone. Direct speed-dialing buttons are available in some machines. In others the directory is stored in memory and is recalled from a list.

Automatic Redial   When a busy signal is encountered, the document can be left in the feeder. The machine continues to dial until the transmission goes through.

Confidential Transmission   The document is sent into memory in the receiving machine, and can be printed only after entering a code.

Custom Cover Sheets   This feature is common with PC fax boards and with fax servers. The system creates a cover sheet with a few keystrokes by the operator and automatically fills in details such as sender's name, number of pages, return fax and telephone number, and custom graphics.

Document Verification   The system stamps each page transmitted to enable the operator to identify misfeeds.

Duplex Transmission   The system can send and receive simultaneously over the same connection.

Dynamic Port Allocation   This feature limits fax broadcasting to certain ports so incoming ports will not be tied up with outgoing calls.

E-Mail Gateway   This feature is normally found only in fax servers. The server links to an electronic mail system and uses it to receive and deliver fax messages.

Forwarding   The system can receive a document and forward it to a different machine without the loss of resolution that results from forwarding a fax document that has been printed.

Group Fax   This feature enables the user to send the same fax to an address list.

Group 3/4 Option   The fax machine can communicate on both groups 3 and 4.

Halftone Capability   Enables the system to transmit photographs.

LAN Interface   The fax machine contains a network interface card to connect to the local area network.

Message Logging   The system logs both failed and correctly received messages. The date, time of day, received telephone number, and other significant information is logged. The log can be interrogated or printed automatically.

Phone Book   This feature enables each user to have a personal directory of fax recipients.

Priority Fax Queuing   In a fax server certain stations can be designated as high priority. Their transmissions take precedence over those of lower priority.

Receive Alerts   When a fax message is received, an alert pops up on the computer screen or telephone display to notify the user.

Transmission Scheduling   The system can schedule faxes for delivery at night when rates are lower. This feature is particularly important when large documents are sent to multiple locations. The system also can reschedule when delivery fails for some reason such as busy or no answer.

Desktop Computer Fax Boards

Personal computer users do not need facsimile machines to communicate by facsimile, particularly to transmit documents that are stored in a personal computer. Two developments, PC facsimile boards and facsimile transmission over electronic-mail networks, make it possible, with some limitations, to exchange documents between a personal computer and a facsimile machine.

Fax Boards and Modems

A board plugged into an expansion slot in a desktop computer or a fax feature in a modem allows the computer to emulate a facsimile machine. Fax-enabled application software can transmit a document via fax by treating the fax board or modem as a printer. The user does not have to go through any special steps to convert the document for transmission. The application software takes care of the conversion and dials the recipient without any special action on the user's part, except selecting the addressee.

Desktop computer fax software offers features that are available only on high-end facsimile machines. Since the file to be transmitted is retrieved from a disk, a facsimile board can transmit a document or a list of documents to a list of different telephone numbers. With a conventional facsimile machine this is possible only with memory, which is an expensive option. The fax board can store an almost unlimited number of pages, unlike the limits on the document feeder of a conventional facsimile machine. Signatures, logos, and other graphics may be integrated from a separate file, but they are difficult to authenticate. PC facsimile is also useful as a relay device. With conventional facsimile, each time a received document is rescanned and transmitted, it loses clarity. Since a PC facsimile is received and sent from a file, it can be relayed indefinitely without loss of detail.

Although a personal computer board is a satisfactory means of transmitting fax, receiving is another matter. Not all fax boards operate in background mode, and those that do may slow down the computer while a document is being received. Received documents can be displayed on either the screen or printer. Since smaller monitors are incapable of displaying an entire page in readable form, it is necessary to scroll the document, and the resolution may be too low to read the document without expanding it. When a bit-mapped document is downloaded to a printer, the quality will be good, but the speed may be less than satisfactory.

Although the cost of a fax board is much lower than a full-featured fax machine, a fax board is less convenient for users to share, more time consuming for transmitting graphics, and less than adequate for receiving documents. The strength of the desktop computer facsimile is in network applications. It makes it easy to send multiple documents to multiple recipients. The personal computer can receive a document, store it on a disk, and retransmit it without the loss of clarity that results from receiving and retransmitting a paper facsimile document.

Fax Servers

The fax modem makes it possible for multiple users to share modems through a fax server, which may also be a modem server. In most offices everyone uses fax, which results in users printing the fax and queuing at the fax machine to send it. Furthermore, when many outgoing faxes are being sent the number is busy to incoming callers. The solution to the busy fax machine is more lines and machines, or some form of fax store-and-forward capability. The latter is provided by LECs as a service, and it is available in fax servers and fax-enabled voice-mail systems. These applications can be classified as fax networking.

Fax networking offers several advantages over stand-alone fax machines. Many of the same advantages accrue from fax boards in personal computers or fax capabilities built into modems. The following are the advantages of these methods:

- It is unnecessary to print documents before faxing them, which saves cost and time.
- The quality of received documents is higher because it is unnecessary to scan them.
- It eliminates human queues at the fax machine, and therefore increases productivity.
- Automatic delivery of received documents may be possible with one of the methods discussed later.
- The system automatically redials busy numbers and those that do not answer.
- Fax lines can be left free to answer incoming calls.
- Fax documents can be sent over the company network to file in another server, eliminating the need to go outside the system, saving transmission costs.
- Fax can originate from within fax-enabled applications. Word processors, spreadsheets, and other applications treat fax servers and modems as printers.

Fax servers have some drawbacks that limit their application. Some of the principal disadvantages of a server compared to a stand-alone fax machine are

- If the document isn't already in a computer file, it must be converted with a scanner.
- Signatures are difficult to control and authenticate. Scanned signatures can be added to documents, but it is difficult to be certain someone other than the signer did not add it.

◆ Bit-mapped fax files are slow to print. They can be converted to text with OCR, but the conversion process is time consuming.

◆ Automatic routing of documents is uncertain in many network applications.

Choice of modems to use with fax servers is important. Inexpensive fax modems are readily available, but they lack the features of more expensive modems. TIA/EIA has developed standards for fax modems known as class 1 and class 2 standards. The common fax modems that are available everywhere are class 1 modems (TIA/EIA 578). They assume that most of the transmission features are built into the application software. Class 2 modems (TIA/EIA 592) build communications features into hardware. Class 2 modems have flow-control capability to enable the receiving modem to control the transmission rate. The initial handshake between the two modems, which complies with ITU T.30 standards, establishes their ability to regulate transmission rates.

Class 1 modems assume that fax timing specifications will be implemented in software. Class 2 modems handle timing from an on-board processor. The class 2 standards provide for copy quality checking, which is absent from the class 1 specification. These and other features make class 2 modems preferable for heavy fax-server applications, but at a higher price. Also, many of the devices the server communicates with will be unable to comply with class 2 standards.

Inbound reception on a fax server offers special problems that stand-alone machines do not encounter. With stand-alone machines, paper output is delivered manually, which may be time consuming and encounter delays. Theoretically, fax servers can deliver faxes directly to the desktop. This is accomplished by one of three methods. Most reliable is direct inward dialing, in which each user has his or her own DID fax number. This method is common with voice-mail systems that support fax store-and-forward. This method is the most reliable, but it may require additional expense for DID numbers and trunks.

A second method is to scan the cover page with OCR software and pick the recipient's name out of the resulting file. This method is fine in theory, but it lacks reliability because of different ways the recipient's name may be written. Users report about 75 percent reliability with this method. The third method is using additional DTMF digits for routing the document. This method is reliable, but it requires the sender to know the receiver's personal code. A common method of overcoming these problems is to use voice mail as a personal fax server. The user may have separate DID numbers for voice and fax, or the user's voice mail may prompt the caller to enter a digit to send a fax.

Delivering Facsimile via Electronic Mail

Most public electronic mail services offer fax delivery service. The user dials the electronic-mail number, usually a local telephone number in larger metropolitan areas, identifies the addressee, and transmits the document. The electronic-mail service delivers the document to the recipient's fax machine and returns a notice of delivery to the sender. The service tries several times to deliver to a busy or no-answer station before reporting nondelivery to the sender.

Electronic mail services can transmit documents with embedded graphics stored in their library. For example, a sender can furnish a logo and signature block, have them scanned and stored by the electronic mail service, and call them from storage with the transmitted document. Many of these services also offer fax broadcasting, in which documents are sent to a directory of users.

Group 4 Facsimile

ITU group 4 facsimile standards support a high-speed, high-resolution digital system operating at speeds up to 64 kb/s. Typically, either switched 56 or BRI service is used. Resolution is from 200 to 400 lpi using high compression. Group 3 fax machines code each line individually, but lines are coded in group 4 fax based on the coding of the previous line, providing higher compression. Each line becomes a reference line for the succeeding line. The G4 coding scheme is known as T.6. It achieves compression more than double that of G3 machines, so in addition to the speed improvement of the digital line, improved compression and reduced handshaking time makes G4 fax much faster than G3.

The standard for group 4 separates facsimile machines into three classes. All three classes support 100-pixel per inch resolution. Classes 2 and 3 have 300-pixel per inch resolution with options of 240 and 400 picture elements per inch. Table 30-1 lists the characteristics of the three classes of group 4 machines. The quality of group 4 fax is about as good as the quality of an office laser printer, which makes it suitable for transmitting letter-quality documents.

In addition to offering the advantages of high speed and improved resolution, group 4 standards can ease communications between word processors. Currently, memory-to-memory data transfers are a feature of communicating word processors. This feature is known as *teletex* (not to be confused with teletext, which is the transmission of information during the vertical blanking interval of a video signal). Most manufacturers now use proprietary protocols that are incompatible with the protocols of other equipment. Group 4 facsimile standards make it possible to integrate facsimile and communicating word processors. To overcome the inherent disadvantages of each type of system, class 2 and 3 machines send textual information in alphanumeric form and graphic information in facsimile form. Terminals capable of this form of communication are called *mixed mode.* Page memory is required for memory-to-memory transmission.

Group 4 facsimile standards are developed around the ISO open systems interconnection model for data communications. Currently, group 4 facsimile is not widely used for several reasons:

- ◆ Dial-up 56- or 64-kb/s circuits are not available to many companies. As ISDN becomes more common, the popularity of group 4 fax should increase.

TABLE 30-1

ITU-T Group 4 Facsimile Characteristics

Service	Class		
	1	2	3
Facsimile	Transmit/receive	Transmit/receive	Transmit/receive
Teletex		Receive	Create/transmit/receive
Mixed mode		Receive	Create/transmit/receive
	Resolution (lines/inch)		
Standard	200	200/300	200/300
Optional	240/300/400	240/400	240/400

◆ Group 4 machines cost several times as much as group 3 machines.

◆ Many documents now transmitted by facsimile do not need the higher resolution of group 4. Business culture will change to adopt group 4 quality, which approaches that of a laser printer, when machines are more widely used.

Facsimile Line-Sharing Devices

It is awkward to receive fax messages if the machine is not connected to a dedicated telephone line. Without a dedicated line, someone must answer the telephone and on hearing facsimile tones manually initiate the handshake sequence with the sending machine. Several devices on the market enable the fax machine to share the telephone line with voice. Some devices answer the telephone with synthesized voice that instructs the caller to press a DTMF key to direct the call to a person. Otherwise, the device connects to the fax machine to initiate a facsimile session.

Some line-sharing devices monitor the line for a voice signal from the calling end. If no voice is heard, the incoming line switches to the facsimile port. If no tones are heard, it transmits a voice message and monitors for voice. If a voice response is heard, it switches the call to the voice port. Other devices monitor the line for facsimile tones, and switch the line to voice if no tones are heard from the sending end. For residences and smaller businesses, a line-sharing device can save money on dedicated telephone lines.

A more effective method is distinctive ringing, which most LECs offer, and which many fax machines support. Distinctive ringing assigns more than one telephone number to the same line, with each number assigned a different ringing code. A decoding box recognizes the ring and switches it to telephone, fax, or modem as appropriate.

APPLICATIONS

Virtually every business and governmental organization has and uses fax. Its prevalence makes it reliable for many applications that previously relied on the mail. One of the most effective applications is fax-on-demand (FOD), which is a combination voice and fax service. FOD has become almost obligatory for business-to-business customer service operations. A high percentage of callers to many such operations are requesting technical or marketing information that can easily be delivered by fax. A typical FOD dialog leads callers through a menu of choices, followed by a request for the caller's fax number. Within minutes the FOD application retrieves the document from the database, seizes an outgoing circuit, and sends the document to the caller. A well-designed FOD application allows callers to obtain information 24 hours/day without human assistance.

The telecommunications aspects of FOD are not complex. FOD is an option in some voice-mail and interactive voice-response systems, or it can run in a desktop computer that is either stand-alone or connected to local exchange trunks. Call centers can make effective use of FOD. Calls arrive in the call center, where an automated attendant offers callers an FOD option. If the caller chooses FOD, the call is transferred over an analog port to the FOD server. The server may either contain the fax documents on its own hard disk, or it can be networked with a file server.

One precaution that must be observed in FOD is to design the system to prevent a new variety of fraud and personal harassment. If a caller wants to harass someone, he dials an FOD application, usually over a toll-free number, and orders documents sent to a voice telephone number. The FOD device dials the number, which fails. Unless the program has been written to prevent it, the FOD may dial the number repeatedly, trying to deliver a fax document, running up long-distance bills, and annoying the called party in the process. The FOD software must be programmed to recognize and prevent such attempts.

Standards

The principal source of facsimile standards is ITU-T, which sets the standards to which group 3 and 4 facsimile machines adhere. ITU-T's T.30 specification covers handshaking between G3 fax machines, and the T.4 protocol defines document encoding. T.6 describes the compression and handshaking between G4 machines. The TIA/EIA standards discussed earlier cover class 1 and class 2 fax modems used stand-alone and in servers. Manufacturers' specifications control other features intended to integrate facsimile into a network. Differences in storage, polling, machine identification, and other features may result in incompatibility with some machine functions, even among machines conforming to the standards of one ITU group. Fortunately, incompatibility between facsimile machines is rare.

Evaluation Criteria

The criteria discussed next apply primarily to the telecommunications aspects of facsimile. A discussion of the technical requirements and features of facsimile machines is beyond the scope of this book.

Transmission Facilities

Facsimile transmission facilities should be evaluated and selected on the same basis as voice and data circuits are evaluated. Digital facsimile can be transmitted over either analog or digital circuits, which should meet the same requirements as any other data communication service applied to the telephone network or to a public data network. The preferred medium for G4 fax is a basic-rate ISDN line.

Compatibility

When special features such as halftone transmission, networking, and polling are required, the systems should be from the same manufacturer or fully tested with systems of other manufacture. Compatibility between machines for basic sending and receiving is generally not a problem.

Document Characteristics

The primary factors in determining which group of facsimile equipment to select are the document volume and resolution required. Plain paper fax offers superior quality compared to coated paper. Of the plain paper devices, laser printers offer better quality than ink jet machines, although the difference is unimportant in most companies.

Many machines offer a high-resolution mode, which produces quality close to that of a letter-quality printer. If copy quality is important, a high-resolution machine should be selected. The need for halftones in documents also should be considered. Facsimile machines vary widely in their ability to handle halftones, with the level of gray scale varying from 0 to 64 shades of gray.

Labor-saving features, such as automatic document feed, paper cutter, automatic dial and answer, document storage, and document routing, should be considered. If confidential information is being transmitted, encryption should be considered.

Document Memory

Most high-end fax machines offer memory for document storage. This feature is useful for unattended operation. If the machine runs out of paper, received documents can be stored in memory. Multipage documents can be sent without fear of paper jams. Documents can be sent to address lists that are recalled from memory. Transmission time is often reduced because the machine receives into memory so that transmission is not paced by the speed of the printer.

PART FIVE

Telecommunications Networks

CHAPTER 31

Enterprise Networks

Private networks were once the province of large companies, but now that has changed. Several factors have contributed to bring the enterprise network down to smaller organizations. First is the networked personal computer. As users enjoy the benefits of sharing files and sending e-mail across a LAN, the demand grows to breach the bounds of the LAN and extend the network across the enterprise. No longer is a mainframe or minicomputer the center of the typical company's information flow. Although the enterprise may have a mainframe, it is the center of specialized applications such as database access. The remainder of the company is more likely to access groups of widely distributed servers for retrieving files, sending and receiving e-mail, and accessing information on the company's intranet. Where information is located has become irrelevant; the important issue is how to access it.

About the time the LAN was breaking its bonds, new network technologies were aiding the cause. Frame relay has effectively become the default choice for building an enterprise data network, but it's far from the only alternative. Organizations needing more bandwidth than frame relay supports have the option of ATM, which is available from most major carriers. They also have the option of building a private network across the Internet or a private IP network, a technique that is known as a *virtual private network* (VPN).

VPN is another of those ambiguous terms that have crept into the vocabulary. Long before the Internet became popular, the major IXCs offered virtual private voice networks. In fact, Sprint's virtual private voice network is known as Virtual Private Network or VPN. A virtual voice network, which is described in a later section, allows a large user to set up a private voice network using the same switched facilities that the IXC uses to serve its other long-distance customers. A virtual voice network allows the user organization to bypass the LEC's access circuits and therefore reduces charges. It also permits the company to use such features as dialing restrictions and abbreviated dialing that would otherwise be available on an electronic tandem network (ETN). The ETN operates over leased circuits and uses private switches to connect circuits. By contrast, a voice VPN uses private switches on the edge of the network. Public network switches and circuits form the core.

It is now possible for companies to set up a private data network by *tunneling* through the Internet. In the past few years most companies have provided Internet access to their employees. Remote offices may have a 56-kb/s circuit to an ISP. This amount of bandwidth provides plenty of capacity for remote offices to access company servers through a data VPN, a concept that we discuss later in the chapter.

Private networks bring many benefits to organizations that can justify them. The obvious reason for developing a network is cost savings, although reductions in long-distance rates over the last few years have made the public network more cost-effective than private networks unless call volumes between locations are high. A major reason for a private network is to draw the organization more closely together. Dialing extension numbers somehow seems more unifying than dialing a full 7- or 10-digit number. It's also easier to transfer calls across a private network than it is to use the PSTN. Networks are sometimes established to allow users in remote PBXs to share low-cost dedicated facilities to the long-distance carrier. If T1/E1 facilities can be shared with data, the economics are often more compelling.

Private circuits are sometimes installed to share other resources. For example, voice mail can be shared across a network or multiple voice-mail systems can be networked to enable widely distributed users to set up closed user groups, forward voice-mail messages, and retrieve messages from another office. The reasons for establishing a private voice network are often not solely economic; they relate more to the company's preferred method of operation.

The key word for any private network designer is flexibility. It is difficult to foresee what products and services will emerge in the highly competitive market that telecommunications has become, but the most effective network managers will avoid locking themselves into a single vendor or a particular architecture. The devices on today's and tomorrow's networks are intelligent and are continually getting smarter. Coupled with inexpensive circuits, networks are changing the social fabric of the world as it becomes feasible to move information instead of people.

WHY PRIVATE NETWORKS?

This chapter brings together the building blocks that previous chapters have covered and integrates them in a discussion of the shapes that private voice and data networks assume. Ultimately, both voice and data will merge in the converged networks that are discussed in Chapter 38. A few early adopters are beginning to merge voice, video, and data at the circuit level, but quality of service issues have yet to be resolved, except over closely controlled facilities such as dedicated T1/E1 and frame relay. Companies that have never considered a network beyond a few data circuits to tie remote terminals to the corporate mainframe are considering more extensive networks. The obvious motivation is saving money, but cost saving is often insignificant compared to other benefits that this section discusses. The following are some of the benefits companies realize from private networks.

Integrate the Company More Tightly   Human endeavor revolves around communication, and the more personalized the communication, the more effective the organization. Multilocation companies can be more closely knit if they have easy access to voice communication. Meetings can be made more productive with videoconferencing and presentation graphics equipment. As desktop videoconferencing becomes more universal, private networks will enable people to hold impromptu conferences and exchange or share files easily. As LANs are interconnected, workers can access remote file servers as easily as servers on their own subnet. E-mail has become an essential function within the company as well as with outsiders. Companies have developed *intranets* as a way of making information accessible over standard web browsers.

Tie the Company to Its Customers   The strategic use of telecommunications to integrate a company's business with that of its major customers has been well documented. By giving customers direct access to the company's database through the telecommunications network, companies have intertwined their businesses closely with their customers' businesses, making it easier for the customers to do business and more difficult for them to draw apart. The industry uses the term *extranet* to describe virtual networks that tie a company to its customers and suppliers, often by tunneling through the Internet.

Tie the Company to Its Major Suppliers   Businesses can become more competitive by tying their ordering procedures with those of their major suppliers using such processes as electronic data interchange (EDI). Costs drop as inventories shift from purchaser to supplier and the time between manufacture of subcomponents and delivery of completed products is reduced.

Integrate Voice and Data Communications   The single-purpose networks of the past are giving way to multipurpose networks. T1/E1 has become the default method of connecting networks, and it is usually effective to merge voice and data circuits when networks are developed. The merger is particularly effective in the loop to the IXC. The major IXCs are making T1/E1–based long-distance service increasingly attractive. The same access circuit that delivers switched voice service also can carry the local loops of data services. Frame relay services can support voice communications as well, enabling companies to share bandwidth between voice and data.

Enterprise Networks

The term industry increasingly uses to describe the network discussed here is the *enterprise network*. An enterprise network extends to the desktop where it can support a variety of devices regardless of the application or the operating system. The enterprise network recognizes that users' personal preferences dictate what kind of workstation they have. Instead of converting Apple Macintosh users to Microsoft Windows or vice versa, it is more effective to use the network to do the conversion. Instead of concerning users with routes and protocols, the network enables them to access servers wherever they are located as virtual drives on their workstations. Client-server applications are becoming more prominent. The client runs on any type of system, and the server delivers data in a format the client can understand.

The enterprise network is also multivendor. The telecommunications market increasingly is composed of niche players who happen to produce a very good device, which might be a bridge, a router, or a network operating system, that fills a particular need better than any competing product from the major manufacturers. To remain with one vendor in today's market is to pay a premium in cost or a penalty in functionality, so companies are avoiding single-vendor solutions.

The globalization of business means the enterprise network is multilocation and multinational. The strategic implications of the network also mean that it is likely to be multicompany. The multilocation/multicompany network is difficult to control. As companies do business electronically with their strategic partners, conflicts arise in protocols, governmental regulations, and standards. The enterprise network ties the parts together into a unified design and architecture.

BUILDING BLOCKS OF THE ENTERPRISE NETWORK

This section discusses the elements of an enterprise network. These have been discussed in earlier chapters and are presented here with applications to show how they fit as an integrated whole.

Terminal Equipment

Figure 31-1 shows the evolution of terminal equipment interfaces to a host computer. Many legacy networks resemble Figure 31-1*a* where a host computer superintends a network of dumb terminals. The terminals connect through a cluster controller or multiplexer to the host, which contains the database and manages the network. The dumb terminal is rapidly being replaced by the personal computer—at first emulating the terminal and then operating as a peer, as shown in Figure 31-1*b*. Even with terminal emulation, gateways, which are less expensive and more responsive, replace the cluster controller. Local area networks, usually using twisted-pair wire, replace the coaxial and EIA-232 wiring to controllers and multiplexers.

FIGURE 31-1

Evolution of Terminal Equipment Interfaces to a Host Computer

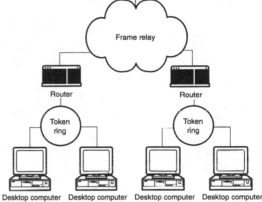

a. Dumb terminal interface

b. Desktop computer interface

Local Area Networks

The high-growth area of private networks today is LAN and internetworking equipment, and that growth is expected to continue. The basic building blocks—the network interface card, transmission medium, switches, servers, network operating system, and routers—are becoming so common as to be practically commodities. Interest is high and expected to remain so for devices such as bridges, switches, routers, and gateways that interconnect LANs over the facilities discussed in the following sections.

Circuits

The building block of the network of the past was the voice-grade analog circuit. With conditioning it supports data, and with signaling it supports voice. The limited bandwidth of the voice-grade circuit gave rise to digital data service (DDS), a fully synchronized digital service operating at speeds up to 56 kb/s. Based on the bit-robbed signaling of a T1 backbone, DDS is expensive and incapable of

FIGURE 31-2

Integrated Access Device

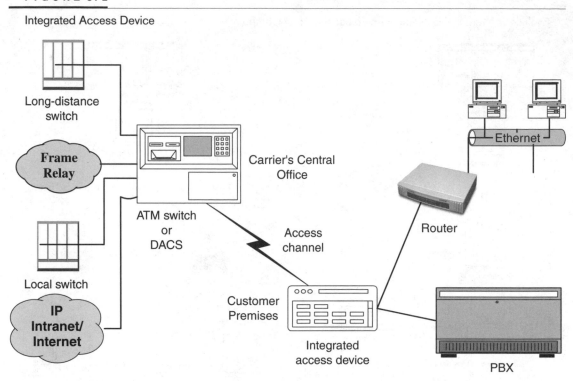

providing 64-kb/s clear channel circuits. As the demand for greater bandwidths increased, the major IXCs provided T1/E1 and fractional T1/E1 facilities and, increasingly, are delivering T3/E3 and fractional T3/E3. The trend clearly is toward providing circuits in bulk. A T1 can be leased for the price of six or seven voice-grade circuits; a T3 can be obtained for the price of the same number of T1s.

Increasingly, IXCs are beginning to offer circuits provided through *integrated access devices* (IADs). The IAD may be a standard ATM edge device, or it may be a proprietary system into which the user organization feeds various types of information. The information travels over an access circuit, which is usually T1/E1 or a multiple, to the IXC's central office, where it is separated into its component parts. Figure 31-2 shows the concept and some of the alternatives of integrated access.

Analog circuits have all but disappeared for new applications. Anyone needing fixed circuits in a network today should evaluate fractional T1/E1, which is superior to voice-grade analog circuits. Fractional T1/E1 is largely a point-to-point service between major metropolitan areas, but that limitation will inevitably disappear. Some LECs offer fractional T1/E1, but others offer digital service only in DS-0, DS-1, and DS-3 increments.

Common Carrier Switched Facilities

IXCs and LECs offer strong incentives to remain on the public switched networks. Dedicated circuits are effective for high-volume voice and most data applications, but every enterprise network makes some use of the PSTN. One of the theories behind divestiture was that competition would drive down long-distance costs, and that has proved to be true. In the past, switched long-distance networks offered two alternatives: wide area telephone service (WATS) for the heavy users and direct distance dialing for everyone else. Now, WATS has practically disappeared. T1/E1 services have replaced it for large users, and discounted long-distance is cost-effective for all but the smallest users, who will remain on the default message telephone service. T1/E1 access is particularly attractive for larger companies because the service charge is low, the usage charges are low, and the T1/E1 line can be justified by a combination of services. T1/E1 lines can support outbound, inbound, data, ISDN, and switched 56/64, which companies use for videoconferencing, group 4 facsimile, and other wideband services.

Companies obtain local switched services from the LECs as ISDN, direct inward dial, and central office trunks. For data communications, frame relay is a popular service. Packet services, such as SprintNet and intraLATA X.25 services of many LECs, are available.

Premises Switching Systems

The PBX is the most familiar kind of circuit switch in private networks. Larger networks use tandem switches, but most private networks use all or part of a PBX for the purpose. Common carrier switching services also are available and gaining increased attention. The most familiar type is the Centrex services that most LECs offer. With few exceptions, Centrex systems can support the tie lines, T1/E1 long-distance services, and special trunks that PBXs support. Although they are not switching services in the strictest sense of the word, many LECs and IXCs offer digital cross-connect services. These services do not switch one call at a time but reroute individual circuits or bandwidth on demand.

Facility Termination Equipment

Private facilities must be terminated in equipment that provides testing access, conditions the signal to meet the line protocol, and divides the bandwidth among the users. Digital facilities terminate in a channel service unit (CSU) that converts the bipolar line signal to the T1/E1 format as well as other maintenance functions. Individual channels are derived by terminating the line in channel banks or T1/E1 multiplexers, as Figure 31-3 shows. Circuits also are terminated on customer premises in digital cross-connect systems.

Time division and statistical multiplexers divide both analog and digital circuits, and increasingly the voice/data multiplexer is used to combine voice and

FIGURE 31-3

T1/E1 Line Termination Options

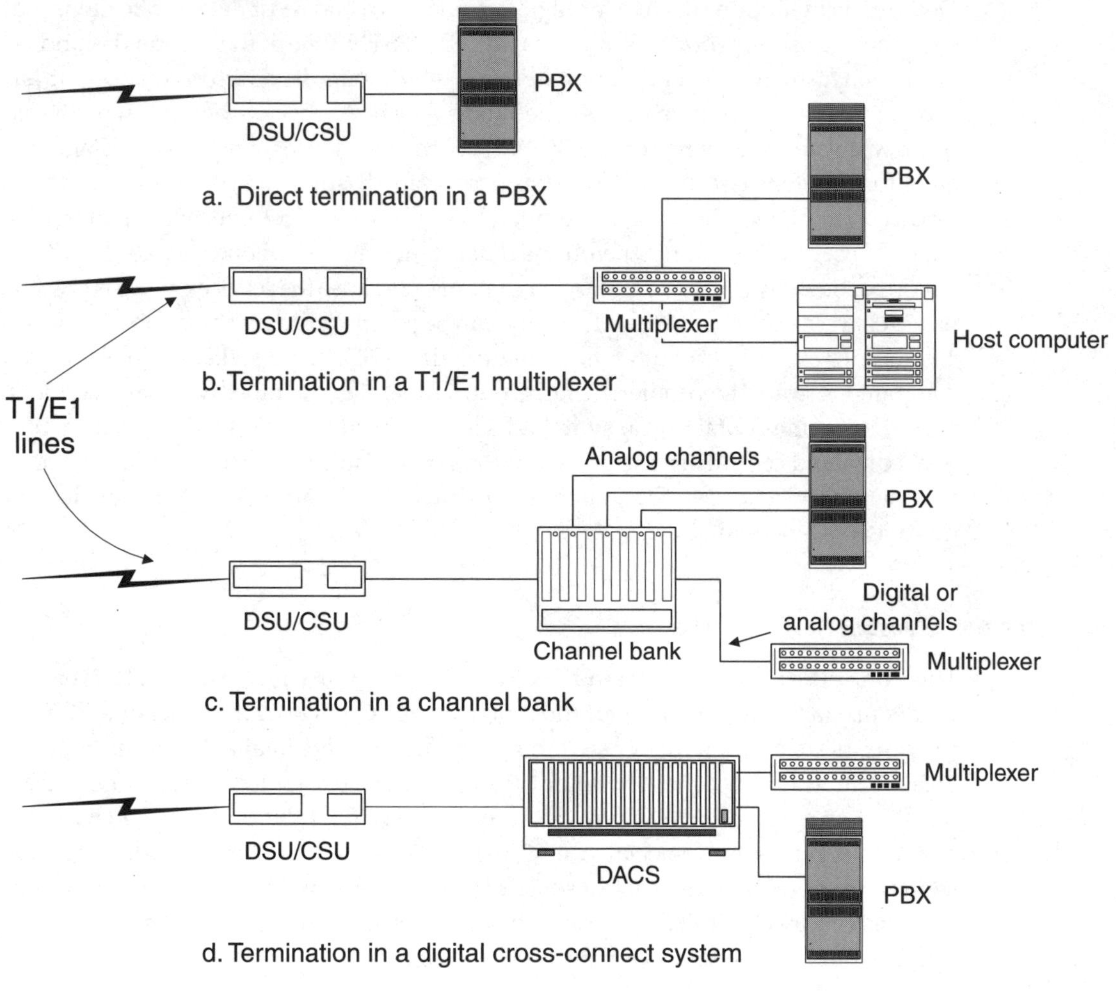

a. Direct termination in a PBX

b. Termination in a T1/E1 multiplexer

T1/E1 lines

c. Termination in a channel bank

d. Termination in a digital cross-connect system

data on the same digital facility. Where it is necessary to separate channels on a T1/E1 system, an add-drop multiplexer can divide and combine the T1/E1 routes. Figure 31-4 illustrates the use of add-drop multiplexers. The multiplexer setup can direct the amount of bandwidth desired over a serial port to the router, while the remainder of the T1/E1 is sent to the PBX. The PBX software is set up to ignore the channels that are directed to the router. Some add-drop multiplexers provide multiple serial ports so the line can be split into more than two segments.

Although the use of analog circuits is declining, families of analog network channel terminating equipment (NCTE) are still used. These devices include repeaters, signaling systems, and other devices designed to amplify, convert, and

FIGURE 31-4

Using an Add-Drop Multiplexer to Share a T1/E1 Line

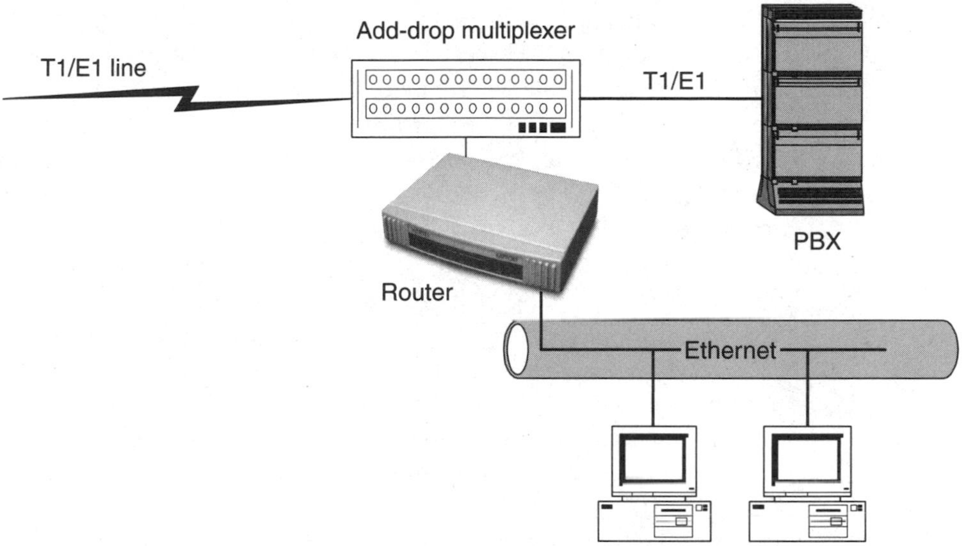

condition the line. The shift from analog has not displaced the modem, a device that continues to be used in quantity, with special emphasis on high-speed dial-up modems.

PRIVATE VOICE NETWORKS

Large organizations can develop private voice networks by one of two methods. The traditional method is to use an electronic tandem network. This arrangement connects switches together with a network of T1/E1 lines. The T1/E1 lines carry a fixed monthly rate that is independent of the amount of traffic. Since most companies are open during normal working hours, the network is underutilized at night. By running the circuits through a digital cross-connect system, the bandwidth can be directed to the data center for high-speed data transfer at night.

For companies with heavy usage, an ETN can be cost-effective. Switched long-distance costs have come down, however, to the point that it is difficult for an ETN to compete with usage-sensitive pricing from the IXCs. Of particular interest to many companies is the voice virtual private network. A voice VPN operates as if it is composed of private voice circuits, but it actually is part of the IXC's switched network. AT&T's virtual network is Software Defined Network (SDN), MCI's is V-Net, and Sprint's is Virtual Private Network (VPN). Signaling system 7, which IXCs use to connect their switches, as discussed in Chapter 11, enables VPNs. The switches are linked to computers at service control points over a high-speed data network.

The SS7 architecture enables the IXC to identify the caller and query the SCP as to features and restrictions.

Stations in a VPN are defined as off-net if they access the IXC through the LEC, and on-net if they access the IXC with a T1/E1 line, bypassing the LEC. Unlike conventional T1/E1 access to the IXC, a VPN can both terminate and originate calls over the access line. This enables the IXC to bypass the usage charges the LECs impose on the originating and terminating ends of a call. Calls placed over the network are rated in three categories: on-net to on-net, on-net to off-net, or off-net to off-net. The on-net portion of calls does not incur access charges, which reduces the cost of the call.

When the IXC's switch receives a call setup request, it sends a message to its SCP database requesting instructions. The SCP checks for restrictions and service classifications such as forced account code dialing, and returns a message to the originating switch, sends routing information to the switches in the connection, and otherwise sets up the call.

Virtual networks are economical for large companies that have a considerable amount of on-net calling. Most of the features of a dedicated private network can be provided. For example, locations can call each other with an abbreviated dialing plan, calls can be restricted from selected area or country codes, and other dialing privileges can be applied based on trunk group or location. Special billing arrangements are provided. Call detail furnished online or on a CD-ROM enables the company to analyze long-distance costs in a variety of ways.

Any company that has the following characteristics should consider a virtual network:

♦ Long-distance usage in excess of about 200,000 minutes/month.
♦ Multiple locations, at least one of which is large enough to justify one or more T1/E1 access lines.
♦ The organization needs tie-line services, such as extension number dialing, but lacks the volume to justify an electronic tandem network.

VIRTUAL DATA NETWORKS

The Internet has spawned a new class of data network known in the trade as a VPN. As discussed in the last section, a voice VPN and a data VPN are entirely different. A data VPN is a combination of authentication, tunneling or encapsulation, access control, and encryption that is designed to carry data securely over a public network, whether it be the public Internet or a private network based on frame relay or ATM technology. Other terms have cropped up to describe uses for these networks. An *intranet* is a network intended for internal company use. This use may be a connection between offices or remote access from employees' homes and branch offices. An *extranet* brings outsiders, such as suppliers and customers, into the picture. On the surface, a VPN appears to be a good way to develop a network, particularly over the Internet, which is inexpensive compared to alternatives such as leased lines and frame relay.

Users can develop their own VPN or purchase the service from a carrier. A private IP network can consist of routers connected with leased circuits, providing the private equivalent of the Internet. Such a network may be less costly than frame relay, but it adds management challenges that may exceed the benefits. A solution requiring less administrative expertise is to feed the traffic to a carrier that manages the network. Although the user typically feeds IP traffic to the network, the carrier may wrap the traffic in cells or frames and transport it across an ATM or frame relay network. Some carriers transport all or part of the traffic across the Internet with security provisions built in to prevent unauthorized access. They may use a standard tunneling protocol, such as we discuss in this section, or a proprietary protocol.

It is important to know how the carrier transports VPN traffic. If traffic is sent across a routed network, the users are generally separated by establishing closed user groups. Users can connect across the network only to stations defined in their user group. Such a network is not secure from unauthorized access, so some form of encryption is needed to keep the traffic private. Several equipment manufacturers produce access switches that integrate functions such as routing, encryption, and firewalling, plus tunneling protocols such as IP security (IPsec), layer 2 tunneling protocol (L2TP), and point-to-point tunneling protocol (PPTP) into the same package. The objective of these devices is to encrypt the traffic and tunnel it safely through the public Internet. Figure 31-5 shows a typical VPN configuration serving both branch offices and remote users.

Tunnels are of two types—end-to-end and node-to-node. An end-to-end tunnel extends from the remote PC through the network to the server. In this configuration the encryption, decryption, and session setup happen at the ends of the connection. In node-to-node tunneling the tunnel terminates at the edge of the network. The traffic connects through edge devices such as the VPN access switches shown in Figure 31-5, where it is encrypted and tunneled to a matching device at the edge of the distant network. The primary tunneling protocols in use were mentioned previously: IPsec, L2TP, and PPTP. Microsoft Windows supports PPTP, which is an end-to-end protocol based on PPP. L2TP is a node-to-node protocol. The IETF developed IPsec as either end-to-end or node-to-node. PPTP and L2TP support password authentication protocol (PAP) and challenge handshake authentication protocol (CHAP). IPsec encapsulates the original IP packet in a new IP packet that includes authentication headers.

One major purpose of an intranet is remote access. A remote user can connect to an ISP via either local dial-up or direct connection, and establish a secure tunnel back to headquarters. This avoids the need to make a long-distance call over a dial line to a remote access server. The savings are particularly attractive for overseas users. Dial-in sessions can be authenticated by the industry standard remote authentication dial-in user service (RADIUS), which provides several methods of user authentication.

FIGURE 31-5

Data Virtual Private Network

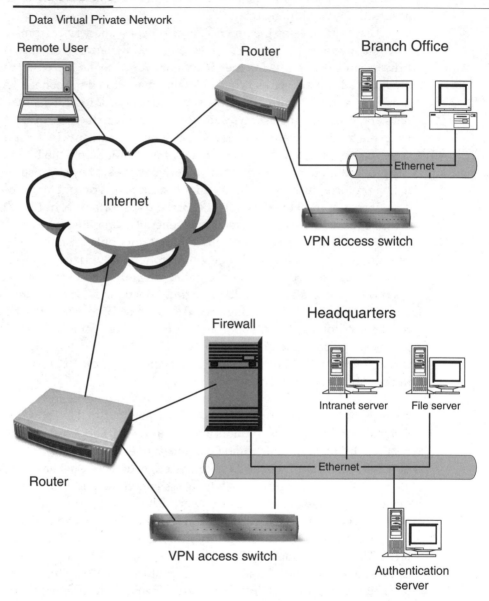

The primary reason for using a VPN as opposed to a more secure carrier service, such as frame relay, is cost savings. Many companies routinely provide Internet access for their remote offices and some remote users. This makes it possible to use the Internet for the equivalent of a directly connected network while using the access circuit for other services such as e-mail. The trade-off is increased administration to avoid security risks.

PRIVATE NETWORK DEVELOPMENT ISSUES

This overview of the building blocks of telecommunications networks shows that there is no shortage of choices. This section discusses some of the principal design issues that managers must consider in implementing networks.

The Hybrid Network

Most networks of today are not composed of any pure form of facilities or ownership. These "hybrid" networks have most or all of the following characteristics:

- *Multivendor.* In terms of circuits, equipment, and perhaps even management, the modern network involves many vendors.
- *Multiapplication.* Networks carry all of a company's applications—voice, data, video, text, graphics, and electronic mail—over the same transmission medium and possibly through the same switches.
- *Multiprotocol.* It is difficult to use a single protocol to support an enterprise network because of its multivendor characteristics. Protocol conversions or multiprotocol routers are the rule for more elaborate networks.
- *Circuit or packet switched.* The design rules are changing. In the past, packet switching was avoided for voice, and circuit switching was avoided for most data. Today's hybrid network may have a circuit-switched PBX feeding voice and data over an ATM backbone or into an IP network over a special IP trunk that packetizes the voice. Some products are available for carrying voice over frame relay.
- *Private or public.* Even the largest private networks still find it necessary to use public facilities for some applications.

Security

More and more private networks connect to the Internet, which raises security concerns for every network manager. Everyone knows of and many have experienced the hackers who find it a challenge to invade private networks. An even more subtle threat to security is the network's users, who are authorized access to the network itself, but who attempt to obtain access to unauthorized files. Network security involves the following issues:

- *Physical security.* Network and computer equipment and the circuits that connect them must be physically secure. Equipment rooms and wiring closets must be kept locked, and the keys under control. Fire prevention precautions must be taken. The facilities should be kept clean and free of debris.
- *Terminal security.* Access to the network must be controlled. Dial-up circuits should use a system such as dial-back or a hardware security

device to prevent unauthorized access. Passwords must be controlled and revised periodically. Terminals and computers should be kept physically secure, and the keyboards locked if possible.

◆ *Disaster recovery.* Every network should have a plan for restoring service in case common carrier services fail or major equipment is lost because of fire, earthquake, sabotage, or other disaster.

◆ *Data security.* It is impossible to prevent unauthorized access to many types of telecommunications circuits, particularly those that are carried over radio. An organization's telecommunications plan must include methods of preventing unauthorized people from obtaining access to the information. Often, this requires encryption of data and scrambling of voice or video. Where data is encrypted, a secure method of exchanging keys is required. Internet Society Association key management protocol (ISAKMP) and simple key management for IP (SKIP) are two common methods.

Policy-Based Networking

Policy-based networking in a data or mixed-media network is somewhat akin to restrictions in a PBX but considerably more complex. Preventing some stations from accessing certain facilities is just one of the policies that management might establish. More important in many companies is the matter of prioritization. A videoconference is far more important than casual Web surfing, both in terms of delay tolerance and value to the company. The network may be opened for web surfing at certain hours, and blocked during others. Certain web sites may be completely closed.

Policy is unique to each organization, and presupposes the availability of information and capability of control that are beyond human capacity. A rough policy of sorts can be built with a firewall and router, but these tend to be static. A dynamic policy that changes with the time of day and day of the week, and reacts to other variables such as network load, requires computer control. A policy-based network includes a policy server, which is a specialized device that monitors data flow and administers management's policies. Although hardware is available today, network administrators have much to learn about policy-based networking.

To begin with, most of the systems are designed to work only with a particular manufacturer's product and may not work well or at all with products from other manufacturers. Moreover, effective policy administration presupposes that someone has a thorough understanding of everyone's needs and knows how to translate them into computer code. The policy server gives troubleshooters yet another place to look when things go wrong. For example, a complaint about slow response time on Tuesdays could be caused by a policy that reserves a substantial part of the network's bandwidth for a videoconference. These issues will undoubtedly be ironed out as designers and managers gain more experience, but in the meantime, policy-based networking is more ideal than reality.

Network Intelligence

Networks composed of dedicated facilities tend to have static configurations because of the delays and high cost of facility rearrangements. Static networks, however, fail to meet the need for information flow in most modern organizations and may contribute to low utilization of some facilities and overloading in others. Network intelligence allows an organization to reconfigure the network based on instantaneous service demands. Products to accomplish this objective are based on digital circuit switches or on a digital cross-connect system that operates under some form of network management system. Increasingly, utilization is improved by using IP to carry all of the company's internal communications between sites. A key issue is whether intelligence is on the user's premises or at the common carrier's facility. In either case, the intelligent network provides users with a greater degree of control.

In an intelligent network a service node directs digital bandwidth where it is needed. Bit compression multiplex equipment compresses the bit stream to make the most effective use of digital facilities. The digital cross-connect system routes traffic to dedicated or switched services as needed. The network control system located on the user's premises dynamically monitors load and service and changes the network configuration in response to demand. For example, an airline reservation system extending across several time zones can be reconfigured to move calls to different answering centers as the load shifts during the day. Also, an intelligent network can give the airline the capability of offering priority treatment to their best customers when all positions in the nearest reservation center are occupied. For example, a call from a customer identified as a frequent flier could be shifted over the intelligent network to the opposite end of the country while less important customers wait in queue at the local ACD.

Network intelligence is most effective with all-digital circuits where bandwidth can be reallocated according to demand. Digital circuits that normally are used for individual voice channels can be rerouted during off-peak hours to a computer center for high-speed data transmission or reallocated to a videoconference center. The availability of low-cost bulk digital facilities has a significant impact on the demand for network intelligence.

The growth of network intelligence greatly improves the utility of information resources and demands a higher level of knowledge to use the network effectively. Users will have greater flexibility and control and will undoubtedly have to employ computer-based tools to make the maximum use of the network.

Future Compatibility

Network products and services are changing so rapidly that it is difficult to be sure a current design will be compatible with the future shape of the network. ATM and voice over IP will be an important part of many networks in the future.

Services that demand high bandwidth are here now and will gain importance in the future. Some will have a strong impact, and others may fizzle. The key to designing a network is to remain flexible—not locked into any single technology that will limit the organization's ability to follow the shifting telecommunications environment in the future.

On-Premises Distribution

Debates on the best method for distributing information on the user's premises have raged for several years. Some services are suited to coaxial cable. Others can be served on twisted-pair wire, but then the question of whether shielded or unshielded is best must be answered. Arguments can be made favoring all three media. For the most part the choice is UTP, but companies planning for the future must also decide how fiber optics fits into the distribution plan. FDDI is available, but it is too expensive to use for ordinary office applications now. But what of the future? Will FDDI, gigabit Ethernet, or another technology replace the present token ring and Ethernet networks? FDDI is not fast enough for many applications, so users are turning to gigabit Ethernet on premises and to ATM in the backbone. The relative importance of these factors is, of course, different for every company, so there are no principles to suggest except that the applications must be thoroughly understood before equipment is chosen.

Vendor Dependence or Independence

In the past, most of the components of the network were likely to be furnished by one vendor, who also probably furnished the mainframe computer at its head end. Network designers must determine whether a past vendor preference will continue into the future. The penalty for not doing so is the risk of incompatibility and difficulties in testing and clearing trouble. The penalty for remaining dependent on one vendor, however, may be a loss of performance. No vendor has a monopoly on technology, and niche players are more apt to exhibit superior performance in one family of products because their developmental efforts are more concentrated.

Network Management Issues

Chapter 39 discusses principles of testing and managing networks. The hierarchical networks of the past had a significant advantage over the peer-to-peer networks of the present and future: they were easier to manage. Vendor-specific network management products make it possible to look into the network's components and diagnose and sometimes clear trouble. As the network becomes multivendor, these management capabilities diminish.

National, International, or Proprietary Standards?

The ideal route to follow in developing a network would be to use only products that meet an international standard. As the standard develops, production costs decline, and prices drop with them. Most companies, however, will find it effective to deviate from the ideal simply because standards take too long to develop. If the payback period is short, it is often desirable to use proprietary standards to gain an immediate advantage. The course to follow depends on the company's tolerance for uncertainty.

How to Plan Networks

Many managers today face a dilemma. Control of computing budgets is moving from the management information department to the end users. Users purchase computers today as they purchased office machines in the past: they are justified on an individual basis. The arrival of stand-alone computers leads to a demand for networking, and the network manager may find it almost impossible to plan because he or she lacks control over the applications. Organizations that have control over equipment standards are in the best position to plan the network. If the information in desktop devices is of any value, someone also must plan for such factors as security, regular data backup, and network capacity.

APPLICATIONS

With the trend toward obtaining digital circuits in bulk—as either full or fractional T1/E1—the most cost-effective networks are those that integrate different applications at the transmission level; the trend is toward integration at the circuit level. Devices such as PBXs, T1/E1 multiplexers, add-drop multiplexers, and digital cross-connect systems are the means of integrating the applications onto the circuit backbone. Voice over IP trunks and routers supporting packetized voice integrate them at the circuit level. Developing a network generally involves the following:

- *Identify the applications.* Present and future applications including voice, data, video, facsimile, imaging, and all other foreseeable communications services should be identified. It is not enough to consider only present applications. Knowledge of future plans and expected growth is essential.
- *Identify locations to serve.* The geographic location of all points on the network must be identified. Although some locations are obviously too small to justify dedicated voice circuits, such locations often require data and may have enough volume to justify equipment such as voice-data multiplexers.

♦ *Determine traffic volume.* The amount of traffic, both terminating and originating should be identified at each location. Determine the volume, type, and length of data transactions from such sources as routers, multiplexers, and front-end processors. Determine the quantity of voice traffic from sources such as common carrier bills, traffic usage recorders, and call-accounting systems. Identify both on-net and off-net traffic. It is usually useful to create a matrix of traffic volumes and costs between on-net locations.

♦ *Determine network type.* Each application will have an optimum network type to support it. For example, short-range, high-speed data applications are usually best served by local area networks. Routers and remote bridges can link geographically dispersed LANs with a common interest. Companies with large amounts of intracompany voice traffic should consider a voice VPN. Companies with multiple remote offices can consider a data VPN.

♦ *Develop network topology.* The topology of the network is based on the application. Costs of alternative transmission methods are calculated, and where the volume and cost of traffic are enough to justify private circuits or a public network such as a virtual network, these are added to the design. Optimize the design by trying different combinations of circuits and by selecting alternative concentration points.

♦ *Develop security measures.* The network must be secure from unauthorized access. Develop plans to secure it physically and to prevent unwanted access. Where the public Internet is involved for private intranet and extranet communications, encryption and authentication are a must.

♦ *Determine how the network will be managed.* Most networks use SNMP and a proprietary network management system to oversee the network. See Chapter 39 for further information on selecting and applying a network management system.

CHAPTER 32

The Integrated Services Digital Network

After more than two decades of development, ISDN is finally beginning to carve a niche for itself in the telecommunications world. Other technologies, such as voice over IP, are coming on so rapidly, however, that ISDN may be consigned to remaining a niche service. The growth of ISDN has been impeded by several factors. First, the standards development process dragged on for years. Then, when standards were approved, the applications failed to emerge. Wags joked that the acronym stood for "innovations subscribers don't need," or "I still don't know." ISDN requires digital switching, and many of the LECs switches had to be replaced to offer the service. For existing digital switches, the equipment manufacturers charged high prices for the ISDN upgrade. Many LECs charged such a premium for the service that customers had a disincentive to subscribe.

Many of these drawbacks still exist, but nevertheless, several key applications are driving a demand for ISDN. For residential subscribers the incentive is dial-up Internet access without the speed restrictions of analog lines. For business subscribers, ISDN is an effective medium for videoconferencing as well as Internet access. ISDN lines are also effective for backing up routers and frame relay networks. Where the LEC tariffs are reasonable, ISDN trunking offers key advantages for PBX owners. Not only can the PBX support high-speed Internet access, but also the trunks can be used interchangeably between incoming, outgoing, and DID, which increases trunk efficiency. Another major trend is telecommuting. As more and more incentives develop for workers to spend at least part of the week working at home, ISDN can be an economical way of retaining a link to the office at reasonable speed.

The LECs now provide ISDN in a high percentage of the wire centers in many countries, but availability does not mean that users can order an ISDN line with the same degree of ease that they order analog lines. Users have to understand something of the technology to make it work, and even after it does work, the ability to place end-to-end digital calls anywhere in the world is far from assured.

One motivation for ISDN is that today's telecommunications networks give users little control over their options. Networks are circuit switched, packet switched, or private. Separate local loops are provided for every service; telephone circuits have two-wire loops, data circuits usually have four-wire loops, other special services such as alarm circuits have either two- or four-wire loops, and all services can be rearranged only with the participation of the LEC. Although the internal networks of the LECs and IXCs are largely digital, users do not realize the benefits of end-to-end digital connectivity because of the analog local loops and analog switching systems.

Both voice and data circuits can have either a digital or an analog interface, but the interface and terminating equipment are far from uniform. Public data networks have different interfaces from those of the telephone network, and video networks, such as CATV, have yet another type of interface. Furthermore, the networks are incapable of handling information interchangeably. Analog voice networks are slow and inefficient at handling data, and low-speed data networks are ineffective for voice transmission. ISDN can be the answer to all of these deficiencies.

ISDN TECHNOLOGY

ISDN lines come in two varieties, basic-rate interface (BRI) and primary-rate interface (PRI). BRI consists of two 64-kb/s B (bearer) channels plus one 16-kb/s D (data) channel. In ISDN shorthand the interface is called 2B+D. The D channel is used for signaling between the central office switch and terminating equipment, which could be a telephone set, personal computer, videoconferencing set, or other device. The B channels are used for any kind of service including voice, data, and video. Through a process known as *bonding*, the two channels of a BRI can be tied together to provide 128 kb/s of bandwidth. BRI is provided by most LECs and as a line-side option of most major PBXs. The applications behind the PBX and the customer premises are essentially the same. A special station set is required for ISDN, or, as shown in Figure 32-1, ordinary station equipment can be installed behind a terminal adapter (TA). The station equipment can be a telephone set, a card in a key telephone system, a card in a PC, or a direct interface into a group 4 fax machine or video codec.

A PRI interface is a 24/32-channel T1/E1 carrier with one or two channels reserved for signaling. A PRI can plug into any device designed to be PRI-compatible, including PBXs, routers, T1/E1 multiplexers, central office switches, tandem switches, or computers. The equipment can select 64-kb/s channels singly, in pairs, or, with some systems, in an $N \times 64$ configuration. $N \times 64$ means contiguous bandwidth equal to any quantity of 64-kb/s channels. For example, 384 kb/s is a popular bandwidth for conference-quality video, and is defined as an HO channel. The LECs provide dial tone over PRIs, and the major IXCs also provide their services over PRIs. The separate data channel allows communication between the IXC's switch and the PBX so channels can be switched at will to outgoing, 800, 900, video, data, or any other such service that can be delivered over T1/E1.

FIGURE 32-1

ISDN Architecture

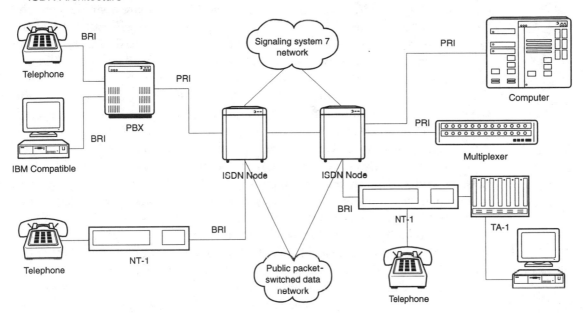

BRI=Basic rate interface
PRI= Primary rate interface
NT-1= Network termination 1
TA1= Terminal adapter

Where LECs have priced ISDN service attractively, PRI service is less expensive than analog trunks and offers the following advantages:

◆ Hardware costs are reduced in the PBX. In most PBXs a PRI card costs about the same as an eight-port analog trunk card, and uses one-third the number of slots.

◆ ISDN trunks with their call-by-call service selection provide listed directory number, outgoing, DID, and other services without the need for special trunk groups. Depending on the size of the system, trunk requirements can be reduced substantially.

◆ Transmission performance is enhanced. Digital trunks can be operated with no loss and imperceptible noise. By contrast the loss and noise of analog trunks increase with the distance from the central office.

◆ ISDN trunks can be provided over self-healing networks, reducing the vulnerability to outage.

◆ Trunks can be added up to the capacity of a PRI with no wiring work or hardware additions on the customer's premises.

The offsetting disadvantages are minimal. The signaling channel takes a substantial fraction of a T1/E1's bandwidth, but most carriers provide *nonfacility associated signaling* (NFAS), which permits multiple PRIs to share a single signaling channel. NFAS is an effective way to improve channel utilization, but if the T1/E1 carrying the signaling channel fails, access to all channels may be lost. A second disadvantage is the inability to use power-fail transfer on PBX trunks, although some products on the market support PFT on ISDN trunks.

One benefit of connecting a PBX to a PRI is call-by-call service selection. Different types of calls require different configurations, which the PBX and central office set up in response to signals received over the D channel. For example, an ordinary telephone call takes one channel, incoming or outgoing. If it is a video call, two or more channels are usually required. A data call may take one or two channels, depending on how the equipment sets up the call. ISDN can assign services to any channel in a trunk group. This eliminates the need for special circuits such as switched 56 that are used for a narrow range of purposes.

Although PRI is a good substitute for analog trunks for ordinary telephone service, it is not universally available. Most LECs have equipped their wire centers with ISDN only as the demand develops. ISDN access through the LEC to the IXC or to other LECs may be unavailable. In wire centers with multiple switching systems, ISDN is frequently available only in one system, which may mean a number change will be required to use ISDN service. The key advantage of end-to-end digital connectivity is an ideal that may be realized in the future, but cannot be depended on until the service becomes more widely available.

Whether an actual cost reduction will result from ISDN depends on the LECs' pricing policies. To implement the service, LECs must invest in improving local loops and replacing or upgrading switching systems. Furthermore, not all users need the services ISDN can provide. Residential customers can profit from having only one circuit to carry a second telephone line, but many users do not need end-to-end digital service or call-by-call service selection. Many new services that ISDN makes possible are desirable, but many residential customers will not be willing to pay for them until new services such as video telephones become common.

One advantage of ISDN is network intelligence, which allows users to instruct the network to respond differently according to time of day, day of week, or identity of the calling party. Incoming calls can be treated with the same kind of discrimination the callers would receive if they arrived in person. For example, nuisance calls can be turned away, priority callers can be shunted to trained specialists, and callers can leave voice or data messages when it is unnecessary to speak in person with someone at the receiving end. Since the calling party's identification is transmitted with the signaling message, the user has the opportunity to handle the call in a variety of ways, either manually or under processor control. The call can be selectively forwarded, rejected, sent to an answering point, or asked to hold. The central office can deliver a distinctive ring to the called party's premises, which has tremendous potential for eliminating annoyance calls and for selectively handling important calls. Most of these services can be provided by analog electronic switching systems, however, so it isn't necessary to subscribe to ISDN to obtain the service. These features fall under the umbrella of custom local area switching services (CLASS), which Chapter 13 covers in more detail.

ISDN ARCHITECTURE

The ISDN network architecture is based on standards set by ITU-T. ISDN supports any combination of voice, data, and video services over a unified network. ISDN standards are based on the ISO open systems interconnect model, which specifies physical, data-link, and network layer protocols for the physical interface, and electrical characteristics for the network. The standards specify how information is encoded and how supplementary services, such as calling features, are provided. As with present telecommunications networks, ISDN has a local and an interexchange element. An LEC usually provides the local element, and an IXC furnishes the interexchange element.

In the United States, national ISDN is evolving through three phases, NI-1, NI-2, and NI-3. NI-1 defines the most commonly needed set of features. The primary target market is small businesses and telecommuting applications. In addition, several Centrex features are included in NI-1, and can be activated by pressing a button on the telephone set. The main objectives of NI-1 are terminal portability and switch interoperability. Terminal portability enables users to move to a new location and have their telephone work without concern about the type of central office system. Switch interoperability enables switches of different manufacture to communicate over SS7.

NI-2 expands on NI-1 by defining the PRI standard and expanding BRI capabilities. In NI-1 some BRI features were proprietary. In NI-2 they are standardized. Features such as D-channel backup and nonfacility-associated signaling are introduced. NFAS permits the use of a single D channel by multiple PRIs. D-channel backup reduces vulnerability by supporting the backup of a D channel by an alternate channel.

NI-3 adds more features that are designed to enhance the revenue-generating opportunities to the carriers. It also improves the maintainability of the ISDN network.

The objectives of ISDN are

- To provide end-to-end digital connectivity.
- To gain the economies of digital transmission, switching, and signaling.
- To provide users with direct control over their telecommunications services.
- To provide a universal network interface for voice and data.

FIGURE 32-2

ISDN Standards Related to the OSI Model

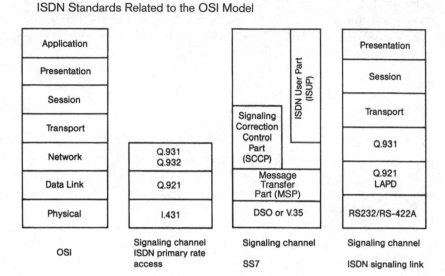

ISDN Standards

Figure 32-2 shows the major ITU standards that have been set and how they relate to the OSI model. The physical layer specifies the movement of bits over the physical medium. The data-link layer uses the distributed link access procedure (LAPD), which permits multiple terminal devices to communicate with higher-level devices in ISDN. The level 3 protocol, Q.931, is the signaling protocol that provides for call setup, supervision, and disconnection.

Network Terminations

Equipment connects to ISDN over network termination equipment designated as NT-1 and NT-2. NT-1 provides functions dealing with physical and electrical termination of the network, corresponding to the physical layer of the OSI reference model. Devices that combine the services of both NT-1 and NT-2 are called NT-12. The NT-1 functions are

- ◆ Termination of the two-wire transmission line and conversion to four-wire.
- ◆ Monitoring performance and maintenance functions.
- ◆ Timing the loop.
- ◆ Termination of the four-wire user interface and conversion to two-wire.

NT-2 terminations, which may be built into a PBX, multiplexer, local area network, or terminal controller, perform the data-link and network layer functions of the OSI model.

Connection of Devices to the ISDN Basic-Rate Service Bus

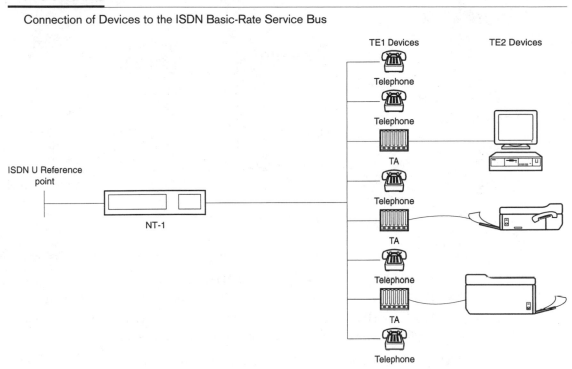

Terminal equipment that is BRI-compatible can plug directly into an NT-1 interface. In ISDN terminology it is known as TE-1. TE-2 equipment is not BRI-compatible, and must plug into a terminal adapter. Terminal adapters are required for non ISDN voice terminals and equipment with non-ISDN interfaces such as EIA-232-D, EIA-449, X.21, and V.35.

Basic-rate service permits as many as eight terminal devices to be connected to a passive bus, as Figure 32-3 shows. The passive bus is a four-wire circuit—one pair for transmit and one for receive. Since basic rate is limited to two B channels, only two of the devices connected to the passive bus can be active simultaneously, but the D channel could be used for data communications from other devices on the bus.

ISDN Interfaces

Five points of demarcation have been defined in ISDN standards, as Figure 32-4 shows.

- ◆ The R interface is a link between non-ISDN equipment and an ISDN terminal adapter.
- ◆ The S interface connects ISDN terminals to NT-2 and NT-12 devices.

FIGURE 32-4

ISDN Demarcation Points

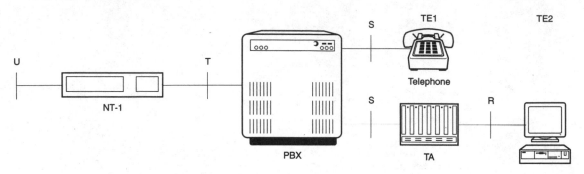

- ◆ The T interface connects NT-2 and NT-1 devices.
- ◆ The U interface connects NT-1 and NT-12 devices to the public network.
- ◆ The V interface, located in the ISDN node, separates the line termination equipment from the exchange termination equipment.

The U-V connection is the ISDN access line and replaces the local loop of pre-ISDN services. It is a single twisted-pair metallic line with a maximum length of 6500 m. NT-1 and the ISDN node obtain a full-duplex connection by using a technique called *echo cancellation.* The transmitting power of the four-wire input to the NT-1 splits between the line and an equalizing network in the NT-1. An electronic filter determines whether a line signal is original data or an echo caused by a mismatch between the line and the network. Echoes are canceled out so only the original signal remains.

ALWAYS ON/DYNAMIC ISDN

A new service called *always on/dynamic ISDN* (AO/DI) is gradually becoming available, and has considerable promise for access to service providers such as ISPs. The D channel of a BRI line is connected to the service provider through an X.25 link. It can be used alone for short messages such as e-mail. When wide bandwidth is needed, such as for a file transfer, B channels are added up to the 128-kb/s capacity of the BRI. ISDN has such fast call setup time that the lag is hardly noticeable, and on completion of a file transfer the call is torn down immediately. A standard, known as *bandwidth allocation control protocol* (BACP), lets users set thresholds so high-bandwidth applications, such as file transfer, use both B channels when needed, while using and paying for only one channel for lower-speed applications. BACP is a key protocol used in AO/DI.

TABLE 32-1

xDSL Applications

Acronym	Translation	Upstream Bandwidth	Downstream Bandwidth	Range, Feet
ADSL	Asymmetric digital subscriber line	16 to 640 kb/s	1.544 Mb/s	18,000
HDSL	Digital subscriber line	1.544 or 2.048 Mb/s	1.544 or 2.048 Mb/s	15,000
SDSL	Single-pair digital subscriber line	1.544 or 2.048 Mb/s	1.544 or 2.048 Mb/s	10,000
VDSL	Very high bit-rate digital subscriber line	1.6 to 2.3 Mb/s	13 to 52 Mb/s	1000 to 4500
RADSL	Rate-adaptive digital subscriber line			
IDSL	ISDN digital subscriber line	144 kb/s	144 kb/s	15,000

AO/DI is the solution to the problems many LECs are experiencing with long call-holding times generated by Internet subscribers. The telephone network was designed with the assumption of circuit-holding times of around 4 minutes. Calls to ISPs usually last several times that long. Packet-mode ISDN can help reduce holding times down to a more predictable model.

DIGITAL SUBSCRIBER LINE

The limitations of regular cable pairs may be overcome by the use of digital sub-scriber line equipment. xDSL (the "x" is used to denote various varieties of DSL) offers users an economical means of increasing bandwidth in residences and small offices. DSL comes in many varieties, as shown in Table 32-1. The ISDN line protocol is the foundation for most of the xDSL protocols. LECs began the quest for xDSL in the mid-1990s as a way of expanding the utility of the local loop. The amount of bandwidth the loop can carry varies with the distance from the central office, but at close ranges it has enough bandwidth to carry high-definition television signals.

The diagram in Figure 32-5 shows how asymmetric digital subscriber line (ADSL) is used for Internet access. ADSL and its cousin RADSL (rate-adaptive digital subscriber line) are asymmetric, meaning that data flow is greater in one direction than the other. Some applications such as Internet access and video require considerably more bandwidth in the downstream (receiving to the customer) direction than upstream.

In an ADSL application, the combined data and voice signal travels over ordinary copper cable pairs between the customer's premises and the central office.

F I G U R E 32-5

Using ADSL for Internet Access

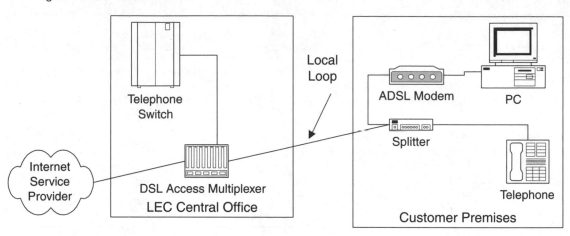

At the customer's premises, an ADSL modem connects the data application to the subscriber line. Riding under the data is the regular voice line, which is separated from data by filters in a splitter. At the central office, a similar device known as a DSL Access Multiplexer (DSLAM) combines and separates the voice and data lines. The voice line connects to a subscriber line location. The data line connects to a high-bandwidth network and is routed to the ISP.

From a technical standpoint, ADSL is a needed technology that can resolve some of the choke points in the dial-up network that limit users' ability to obtain the bandwidth they need for Internet access without reverting to an expensive alternative such as T1 or frame relay. ADSL may also be used in the future to deliver video-on-demand over copper cable. This was expected to be one of the major uses of ADSL, but Internet access now appears to offer greater potential. The LECs use HDSL extensively now for point-to-point T1, and as SDSL comes on the market it will be an important application because of its ability to carry T1 on a single pair.

DSL will also be an important facility for campus environments. Where copper cable is already in place, DSL can provide facilities for T1 and high-speed data transport at a lower cost than installing fiber optics. Fiber is much better where greater bandwidths are required, but right-of-way considerations may preclude its use in some applications where copper cable is already in place.

The highest-speed implementation of DSL that has been proposed to date is very high-speed digital subscriber line (VDSL). VDSL will support up to 52-Mb/s downstream capacity over short ranges. It will be offered in both symmetrical and asymmetrical versions. Where ADSL can operate at ranges of up to 6000 m under idealized conditions, VDSL will attain full speed only up to about 300 m. Today VDSL standards are not complete, but standards bodies are working on them, and the first standard implementations are expected sometime after 2001.

APPLICATIONS

The primary issues surrounding ISDN are cost and availability. Where the service is both available and cost-effective, managers will find little reason not to use it. Cost must be examined closely before reaching a conclusion. Even if the cost is greater than an equivalent number of analog lines, the two-way nature of ISDN means that fewer trunks will be needed for the same grade of service.

Anyone who is selecting a new PBX, or even a key system, should consider ISDN compatibility. Applications are emerging that require the digital connectivity of ISDN, and as the service becomes more ubiquitous, applications such as these will develop:

◆ Videoconferencing, primarily desktop devices

◆ High-speed access to remote databases such as the various online services and Internet

◆ High-speed remote access to LANs

◆ High-speed image applications such as group 4 facsimile

◆ Second line in the home applications driven by the development of telecommuting

◆ Dial backup for routers to restore leased line failures

Many LECs offer attractive ISDN tariff rates where facilities permit. Note, however, that in many cases only one switching system in a wire center is equipped for ISDN, which means that a number change may be needed to take advantage of the service. The major IXCs provide PRI as an alternative to the T1/E1 connections over which they offer bulk outgoing and incoming services. With call-by-call service selection the channels can be allotted to any service, which increases utilization and reduces costs.

Standards

Most of the important ISDN standards have been completed and accepted by ITU-T, and published in North America as NI-1, NI-2, and NI-3 ISDN. In the United States, ANSI's T1S1 subcommittee handles ISDN standardization work.

ISDN standards promulgated by ITU are grouped into the following categories:

◆ *I.100 series*. ISDN general concepts, methods, structure, and terminology

◆ *I.200 series*. ISDN service aspects

◆ *I.300 series*. ISDN network aspects

◆ *I.400 series*. ISDN user-network interface aspects

◆ *I.500 series*. Internetwork interfaces

◆ *I.600 series*. Maintenance principles

Evaluating ISDN Equipment and Service

In the United States the customer owns the NT-1, but in Europe it is owned by the LEC. Some equipment comes with a built-in NT-1, but this may not be advantageous. The standards permit up to eight devices to be connected to the NT-1, so built-in units may not have the required connections to support other devices. Electric power is not supplied over ISDN lines, so a backup battery will be required if the equipment is to operate through power failures. Also, not all equipment is compatible with the LEC's central office. Before purchasing equipment, get assurance from the LEC or the equipment provider that it will be compatible.

Each piece of terminal equipment has a designator called a *service profile identifier* (SPID) to define itself to the central office switch. One of the key considerations in selecting ISDN equipment is how difficult it is to set up. LECs have been slow to train their representatives on handling ISDN orders, so the user needs to know more about the technology than with most telephone services.

Here are issues to consider when selecting ISDN equipment:

◆ Does the equipment support the required physical interfaces such as EIA-232, V.35, RJ-11, RJ-45, etc.?

◆ Does the equipment have battery backup? How long will it support the application through a power outage?

◆ Does the application require bonding and, if so, does the equipment support it?

◆ Does the equipment automatically configure the SPID with the central office?

◆ Is the service available flat rate or do usage charges apply? Does the service provider offer a package including monthly cost and usage?

◆ Does the device support the required protocols such as IP and PPP for Internet access?

◆ Is the TA-1 built into the equipment or is an external TA-1 needed? If so, what other interfaces does it support?

◆ Does the LEC support NFAS or D-channel backup for PRI applications?

CHAPTER 33

Broadband Networks

New applications drive the demand for bandwidth ever higher, with no end in sight. When voice communications originate from the telephone and data from a terminal, bandwidth demands are modest. Digital leased lines and multiplexed voice-grade circuits, which have expanded from 4 to 64 kHz with ISDN, can carry all the traffic that a room full of people can generate from the keyboard, but keyboards and terminals as a data source are now the exception rather than the rule. For the price of a 1970s electric typewriter, users can purchase desktop computers with power exceeding that of super computers of a few years ago. Office workers have the ability to generate enormous quantities of data, and with such applications as imaging, CAD/CAM, desktop videoconferencing and telephony, and e-mail with voice and video clips, traffic loads are at once huge and unpredictable. Network managers must either squelch the bandwidth-hungry applications or expand the network to accommodate them.

Conventional networks are composed of fixed-bandwidth circuits, ranging from voice grade to T3/E3. When the demand exceeds the available bandwidth, something has to give. About the only alternative is to queue the data at the source, where the user sees flow control as a response delay. At other times the circuit is idle and bandwidth is wasted, even though applications on adjacent circuits may be experiencing delays. Fixed-bandwidth circuits are acceptable for many applications, but emerging services have a high ratio of peak-to-average data flow. For example, a physician examining an x-ray may need to move 10 Mb or more of data while the image is downloaded to the display, but then demand drops to zero while the image is being examined.

Contrast this to voice and videoconferencing. Voice is inherently half duplex, that is, one party transmits while the other listens. Videoconferencing is full duplex with both ends of the conference sending data simultaneously. Today's circuit-switched network is fine for these two applications, which are normally short-duration sessions to widely distributed destinations. The bandwidth requirements are fixed, but the applications have minimal tolerance for delay, and no need to correct bit errors. If voice and video are segmented into short packets, the service works fine provided the packets flow in a steady stream. If packets are delayed or lost, however, the result is jerky video or distorted voice.

Dedicated facilities are satisfactory for data applications that have reasonably constant bandwidth requirements. If the load is predictable, fixed-bandwidth circuits are satisfactory, provided they terminate at a single destination. If the bandwidth requirements are variable, the user pays a penalty, either in slow response during high-bandwidth periods, or in wasted circuit time during low-bandwidth periods. If one device must communicate with a variety of destinations, the setup time of dial-up circuits is a handicap. ISDN was expected to solve some of the problems. With SS7 signaling, setup time is faster, and its two B channels can provide appreciable bandwidth for some applications, but ISDN still suffers from being a fixed-bandwidth circuit-switched service. It is unsatisfactory for services such as multimedia and imaging, which require variable bandwidth on demand. For these services, broadband ISDN (B-ISDN) is the industry's answer. B-ISDN uses ATM, which is discussed in Chapter 36, as a method of multiplexing multiple media types onto the same medium.

The term broadband covers a gamut of alternatives for handling high-bandwidth traffic. The industry does not have a clear definition for broadband. Broadband in the ITU's definition of B-ISDN is bandwidth in excess of primary rate, which would even include standard Ethernet. ATM clearly qualifies as a broadband technology, but its speeds range from 25 to 1200 Mb/s, and at the low end it isn't as fast as fast Ethernet protocols. These local area network products generally aren't classified as broadband even though their 100-Mb/s speed matches FDDI, which is considered a broadband backbone protocol. The picture is further muddied by lumping together services and protocols. For example, switched multimegabit data service (SMDS) and ATM are both lumped under the broadband umbrella, but SMDS is a service that happens to use the IEEE 802.6 protocol. SMDS could, and someday probably will, use ATM's connectionless option, although 802.6 and ATM are designed to interoperate, so both protocols may survive.

A key issue in broadband is how far into the network the protocol penetrates. ATM is the one protocol that can be used end to end without conversion. The signal can originate in a desktop card, traverse the network, and terminate on a distant desktop without undergoing a protocol conversion. This distinguishes it from the Ethernet protocols, which are bound by distance limitations and must ride a transport protocol to traverse a fixed-bandwidth public network. It is also distinguished from FDDI, which is distance-limited, although it spans a much greater diameter than Ethernet. SMDS is generally limited to the metropolitan area, and is not intended to go to the desktop.

Many broadband protocols and services have been proposed, but some are destined to fall by the wayside as others build momentum. This chapter will focus on four alternatives. Fibre Channel has promise as a broadband alternative and forms the basis for gigabit Ethernet. FDDI is the most fully developed of the broadband alternatives, but it may have a short horizon in the future. SMDS is discussed because it is the LECs' broadband vehicle and has reasonable availability. The fourth protocol, gigabit Ethernet, has the support of all major vendors and is destined for widespread application.

These four protocols have little in common except for their ability to pass broadband data. These four protocols also differ widely in the distance they can span. Gigabit Ethernet is strictly a LAN protocol. FDDI is also a LAN since it operates under the standard 802.2 logical link control interface, but it has the range to operate in the metropolitan network. Although its payload is less and its protocol is much different than SMDS, applications for the two may overlap in some instances. Fibre Channel is a completely different protocol, with a range of up to 10 km at a variety of different speeds.

FIBRE CHANNEL

Fibre Channel almost falls outside the definition of a telecommunications technology. Its primary objective is to provide high-speed communications between computers and peripherals, primarily mass storage. It has so much bandwidth and flexibility, however, that it may carve out a role for itself in the local to metropolitan broadband arena. Furthermore, it supports speeds up to 1 Gb/s over distances of up to 10 km, which puts it in the metropolitan broadband network camp.

Fibre Channel is designed around a five-layer protocol model that permits communication over shielded copper wire, coax, or fiber optics. All three media support data transfer rates of up to 100 Mb/s, but only single-mode fiber can go the full 10-km route. Multimode fiber with 62.5-μm core is limited to 1 km; 50-μm fiber can go twice that distance. Video coax and shielded twisted-pair wire can span 100 m.

Fibre Channel's name also suggests a computer channel, which generally means a high-speed connection between a mainframe and its peripherals or other computers, but these channels normally have much shorter distance spans than Fibre Channel supports. Channels are also usually parallel, contrasted to Fibre Channel, which is serial. Note that the transfer rates are expressed in megabytes, not megabits as is usual in networks. This is because the primary purpose of Fibre Channel is connecting to mass storage or printers, where volumes are expressed in bytes.

Fibre Channel connects devices through a switching fabric that supports interconnection of multiple devices. This makes it ideal for a campus environment where several computers need to share access to multiple storage devices, printers, and other peripherals without being permanently and directly attached. The switched configuration supports up to 16 million devices, which should be more than enough for anyone. The protocol is not limited to switched connections, however. It also supports point-to-point, loop, and switched topologies, as Figure 33-1

FIGURE 33-1

Fibre Channel

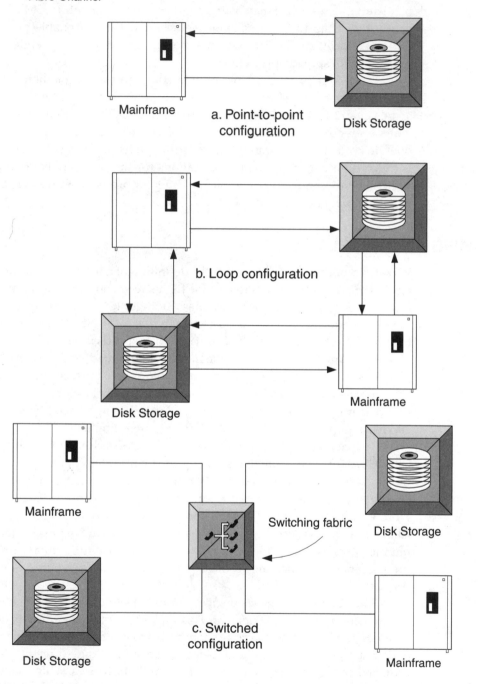

Mainframe   a. Point-to-point configuration   Disk Storage

b. Loop configuration

Disk Storage   Mainframe

Mainframe   Disk Storage

Switching fabric

c. Switched configuration

Disk Storage   Mainframe

shows. In the arbitrated loop configuration up to 126 devices can be daisy-chained in a closed loop.

The five-layer protocol is loosely based on the OSI model. The bottom layer, FC-0, is the physical layer. The fiber-optic connections use a special duplex SC connector. Coax uses BNC connectors, and shielded wire uses a nine-pin D-type connector. FC-1 is the transmission protocol, which covers byte synchronization, serial encoding and decoding, and error control. Fibre Channel uses an 8B/10B coding scheme in which every 8 bits are encoded into 10 bits. The method is similar to the 4B/5B scheme used by FDDI, which is covered in the next section and shown in Table 33-1.

FC-2 defines the frame format and specifies how data is transferred between nodes. Each node has at least one node port (N_port), which is the hardware interface. The protocol calls for four classes of service. Class 1 is a connection-oriented switched circuit. Class 2 is a connectionless service without guaranteed delivery, but with frame acknowledgement. Class 3 is a connectionless nonacknowledged datagram service. Data travels in frames, which are up to 2148 octets in length with a payload of 2048 octets. The frame has 100 octets of overhead, of which 36 are used for error detection, addressing, and framing, and the remainder used for optional overhead.

Layer 4, FC-3, handles some of the functions of the OSI transport and session layers, and several functions that are not defined in OSI. One such function is *striping*, which enables multiple N_ports to operate in parallel to obtain additional bandwidth. The multicast function allows the same data to be sent to multiple destinations. The protocol also provides for hunt groups, which enable incoming frames to hunt for an idle N_port.

FC-4 is the application layer, which provides buffering, synchronization, and prioritization of data. It also specifies methods for using other protocols over Fibre Channel. It can map Fibre Channel data to other protocols such as IP, ATM's AAL-5 (ATM adaptation layer 5), SCSI (small-computer systems interface), HPPI (high-performance parallel interface), and the logical link protocol of IEEE 802.

Fibre Channel has not been widely applied to date, but its future looks bright, particularly in campuses that have distributed computing resources. Traditional protocols, such as SCSI, are approaching an equivalent data transfer speed, but their distance limitations prevent them from competing with Fibre Channel. Once Fibre Channel is installed, its application layer enables it to carry other media such as IP or ATM. This could make it an effective vehicle for using the bandwidth of existing fiber-optic facilities.

FIBER DISTRIBUTED DATA INTERFACE

Fiber distributed data interface (FDDI) is a standard 100-Mb/s network that operates on either single-mode or multimode fiber. On multimode fiber the stations must be no more than 2 km apart. With single-mode fiber, they can be as far apart

FIGURE 33-2

FDDI Topology

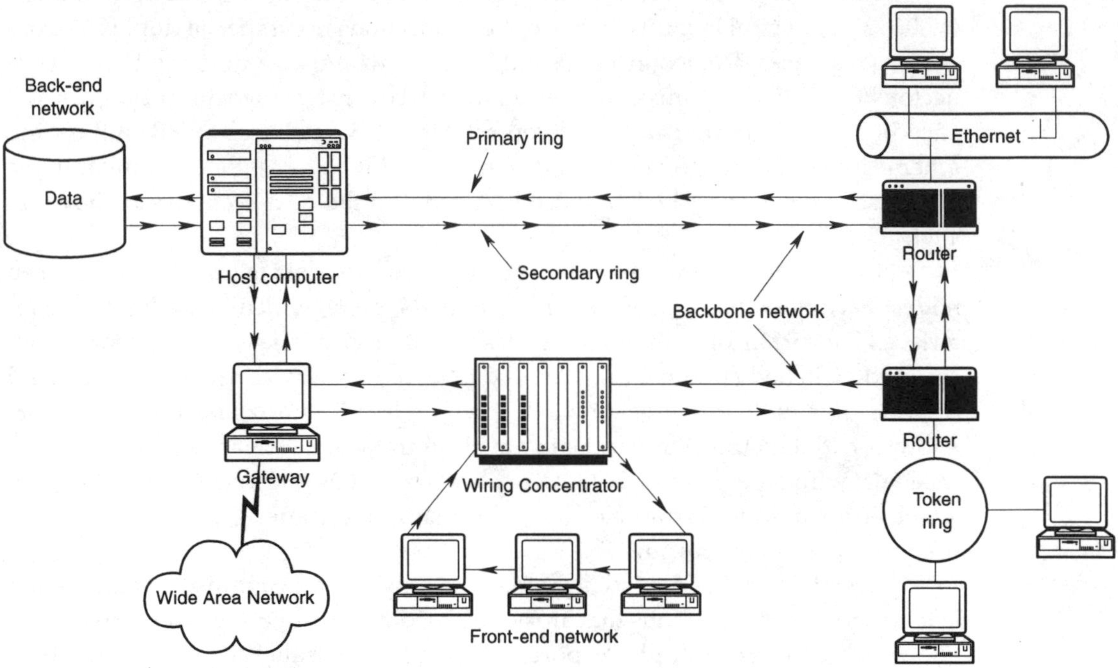

as 60 km, which is sufficient to span a metropolitan area. FDDI can also ride on category 5 UTP wire, which has a maximum length of 100 m. The UTP application is sometimes called copper distributed data interface (CDDI), although the standard is called twisted-pair physical medium dependent (TP-PMD). The specification supports as many as 500 stations in an FDDI network. FDDI operates over counterrotating token rings; one ring is designated as primary and the other as secondary. The primary ring carries data, while the secondary ring is in hot standby.

The FDDI standard specifies two classes of stations. Dual-attachment stations (DAS) connect to both rings, while single-attachment stations (SAS) connect only to the primary ring through a wiring concentrator. In addition, concentrators, which are FDDI devices that can support non-FDDI stations, can also be single or dual attachment. The dual-ring appearance of DAS stations permits double the throughput since the station can send on both rings simultaneously, but the second ring is usually reserved for backup. The FDDI network supports three types of networks (see Figure 33-2):

♦ *Front-end networks.* These are networks connecting workstations through a concentrator to a host computer or other peripherals over the FDDI network.

◆ *Back-end networks.* These allow connections from a host computer to peripherals such as high-speed disks and printers to be connected over FDDI to replace parallel bus connections.

◆ *Backbone networks.* These are connections between the main nodes on the network.

The dual-ring architecture provides an effective measure of protection. If a link or a station fails, the stations go into an automatic bypass mode to route around the failure. Stations on either side of the break loop the primary ring to the secondary ring to form a single ring of twice the diameter. The possibility of a failed station or link must be considered when designing the network to stay within the interstation and total length limitations.

FDDI operates much like 802.5 token ring, with some important exceptions besides the obvious difference in speed. First, multiple frames can circulate simultaneously on an FDDI network. When a station completes sending a frame, it reinserts the token on the network. A second station on the ring can seize the token and send a frame while the first frame is still making the trip back to the originating station. As the frames circulate, each station checks for errors and if it detects one, sets an error indicator. The network protocol does not, however, attempt to correct errors. It leaves them to higher-level protocols to resolve.

Another difference is the dual-ring configuration of FDDI, while token ring supports only a single ring. Yet another difference is in the line-coding format. Token ring uses differential Manchester coding, while FDDI supports a 5-bit encoding system that is discussed later. The FDDI protocol includes a reliability specification, while token ring provides none. Clocking on 802.5 is centralized, while in FDDI each station has a stable autonomous clock that synchronizes to incoming data.

The FDDI Protocol

The FDDI protocol fits into the OSI model in a manner closely paralleling the 802 protocols. Figure 33-3 shows the two-layer protocol with its sublayers that connect the physical ring to the higher protocol layers. Station management (SMT) handles management of the FDDI ring. Functions include fault detection and reconfiguration, insertion and removal of stations from the ring, neighbor identification, and traffic statistics and monitoring.

The physical layer uses a 4-bit out of 5-bit (4B/5B) coding scheme. The code, shown in Table 33-1, is encoded on the ring using a nonreturn-to-zero inverted (NRZI) signal, in which a transition between on and off in the light wave represents a 1, and no transition represents a 0. The 100-Mb/s signal is therefore coded into a line signal of 125 MBd. With the 5-bit code, there are at least two transitions in each 5-bit code, and never more than three 0s in sequence, which maintains clocking on the ring. Each station provides its own clocking in FDDI, in contrast to token ring, in which the active monitor provides a master clock.

F I G U R E 33-3

FDDI Protocol Layers

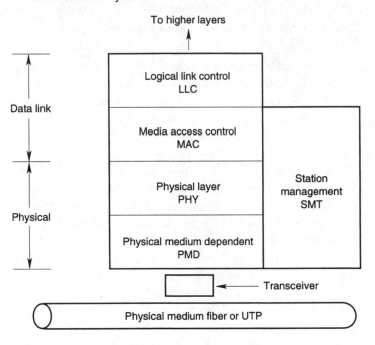

TABLE 33-1

FDDI 4B/5B Code

Hexadecimal	4-Bit Binary	5-Bit Binary
0	0000	11110
1	0001	01001
2	0010	10100
3	0011	10101
4	0100	01010
5	0101	01011
6	0110	01110
7	0111	01111
8	1000	10010
9	1001	10011
A	1010	10110
B	1011	10111
C	1100	11010
D	1101	11011
E	1110	11100
F	1111	11101

The protocol supports a mixture of bursty and continuous stream traffic by defining two types of traffic: synchronous and asynchronous. Each station is allocated part of the capacity of the ring. During a station's allocated transmission time, the frames it sends are referred to as *synchronous frames*. Frames using nonallocated or unused times are referred to as *asynchronous*.

The MAC layer of the protocol defines a maximum token rotation time (TRT), which measures the time between successive receipts of the token. When the ring is initialized each station bids for a target token rotation time (TTRT). The value of the TTRT establishes the amount of bandwidth the station can use per rotation of the token. The value in the station's token-holding timer (THT) determines how long it can transmit synchronous traffic before relinquishing the token. If the token arrives before its expected TRT, it indicates that upstream stations have not used their total allocation, so a station can transmit traffic up to the value of THT.

If the token fails to arrive after an interval determined by the protocol, a station initiates a claim token mode, which regenerates the token. If a station does not see its claim token frame return, it assumes that a ring failure has occurred. If the ring fails, the stations enter a beacon mode that is used to isolate the failure. In the beacon mode, a station sends a continuous string of beacon frames until it receives a beacon frame from an upstream neighbor. When a station receives an upstream beacon frame, it quits sending its own beacon frames, and begins repeating frames from the neighbor. All stations repeat this process until the only station left beaconing is the one immediately downstream from the fault. That station connects the primary ring to the secondary ring, a process known as *wrapping*. When the network wraps, the two rings are initialized as a single ring, and traffic resumes. The self-healing process in FDDI ensures a high degree of reliability and effectively insulates most stations from loss of service if the ring or a station fails.

SWITCHED MULTIMEGABIT DATA SERVICE

SMDS is a high-speed connectionless data service that is deployed by LECs and others for linking applications within a metropolitan area. Bellcore developed the SMDS concept, using portions of the IEEE 802.6 metropolitan area network (MAN) protocol. SMDS is a service, not a protocol in itself, so it can use any transport mechanism, including ATM. In fact, as discussed in Chapter 36, ATM provides a connectionless class of service option that is capable of supporting SMDS. The major objective of SMDS is to transport data with the any-to-any connectivity that we get from telephone or fax service.

The major difference between SMDS and other services, such as frame relay and ATM, is that permanent virtual circuits are not used, which eliminates the need for the LEC to provision a channel between locations. Wideband data connectivity is offered at a generally attractive price. Most LECs charge a flat-rate price per month, with no additional cost for distance or usage. SMDS speeds in the United States range from 1.5 to 34 Mb/s, the latter being the effective throughput of SMDS over a T3 access circuit. Access to SMDS is generally via an SMDS-compliant router or through host computers equipped with SMDS adapters. T1/E1, fractional T3/E3, or full T3/E3 is used as access circuit.

SMDS supports the most common protocols including IP, OSI, IPX, SNA, and AppleTalk, and it provides multicast addressing. SMDS maintains a database of addresses that are validated to communicate with receiving stations. This ensures that receiving sites get messages only from valid points of origin, which improves security. Its similarity to telephone service is a major advantage because with a connectionless service like SMDS you can reach any device that will accept the transmission. SMDS is, however, far from ubiquitous, so partners who wish to communicate must subscribe to the service, which is not available everywhere in ex-Bell companies, and seldom in independent telephone companies.

The principal application for SMDS is LAN interconnection, although it can be used for any data transport. It is attractive for companies with multiple sites that are interconnected with T1. Both frame relay and ATM offer the same type of connectivity as SMDS, but they require permanent virtual circuits for each pair of nodes, which may make them economically unattractive for full mesh connectivity. For uses such as Internet access, frame relay has the edge because of its lower access speed, which makes it more attractive for smaller sites. Some LECs, however, are offering 56- or 64-kb/s access to SMDS, which competes favorably with frame relay for low-speed access.

In summary, SMDS offers the following services and advantages:

◆ High-speed, low-delay, connectionless data transport providing bandwidth on demand.

◆ Robustness because data can take the least congested route to the destination.

◆ Any-to-any or full mesh connectivity, sometimes called dial tone for data, without incurring the extra cost of permanent virtual circuits. ITU-T E.164 addressing similar to standard telephone numbers is used.

◆ Multicasting or group addressing, which enables users to send traffic to multiple points.

◆ Support for multiple protocols, including TCP/IP, IPX, AppleTalk, SNA, and OSI.

◆ Network management capability.

◆ Security and privacy provided by call blocking, validation, and screening.

◆ Scalability—you can keep pace with network growth. To add a node you pay only the port connection charge.

SMDS Service Characteristics

SMDS services are unique with each LEC. Although Bellcore developed the service characteristics, pricing and service features are developed by each LEC, so the services discussed here are typical. Readers can expect local variations.

SMDS Architecture

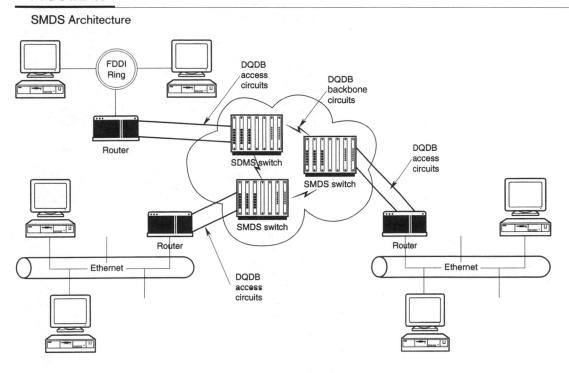

SMDS is designed to operate over a dual-bus fiber-optic network using the 802.6 protocol, which is also known as dual queued dual bus (DQDB). The protocol, which is discussed later, was developed in Australia to be a robust, low-latency protocol. Figure 33-4 shows a typical SMDS network. The SMDS switches are located in LEC central offices, with fiber-optic access circuits operating in a dual-bus arrangement to the subscribers. Multiple subscribers are bridged across the dual-bus arrangement as discussed in the next section.

The backbone switching system is a high-speed packet switch. The protocol places a limit on the amount of sustained information that the subscriber can send across the subscriber network interface to the switching system. SMDS uses the term *sustained information rate* (SIR) as the maximum guaranteed rate at which data can transit the network. SIR is similar to the committed information rate concept discussed in Chapter 35 under frame relay. SMDS supports five classes of service with SIRs running from 4 to 34 Mb/s. As with frame relay and ATM, the subscriber can send bursts of data up to the speed of the access circuit, but the access class limits the average rate of information that can be sent. The switch contains a credit manager that keeps track of the amount of data sent across the network and compares it to the amount permitted by the access class.

FIGURE 33-5

802.6 Metropolitan Area Network Architecture

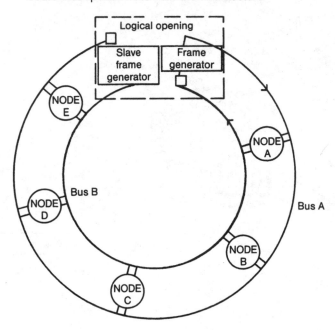

If the subscriber has a credit, the traffic is accepted; if it doesn't have credit, the traffic is rejected.

SMDS has a three-tier architecture. The switching system consists of SMDS-compatible high-speed packet switches. The delivery system is made up of subscriber network interfaces, and the third tier, the access control system, enables subscribers to connect to the switching system. The level 3 protocol data unit (PDU) accepts packets up to 9188 octets in length. These are segmented into a level 2 PDU, which uses 53-octet cells with 44 octets of payload and 9-octet headers. The cells cross the network to the destination, where they are reassembled. Since the protocol is connectionless, the cells do not follow a predefined path through the network, so a user in one site can dial up a link to a user in another site without establishing a virtual circuit. The nodes are constructed with side legs into the subscriber's premises. Traffic always passes on LEC premises, but traffic belonging to one subscriber never passes through another subscriber's premises.

The SMDS cell structure is similar to ATM, which is described in Chapter 36, except the cells contain an address in the header, which is necessary in a connectionless system. The connection-oriented ATM, by contrast, uses a virtual path and virtual connection identifier instead of addresses. The address fields in the SMDS header use a 10-digit number following the E.164 numbering plan.

F I G U R E 33-6

The 802.6 MAN Shifts Logical Break to Point of Failure to Close Ring

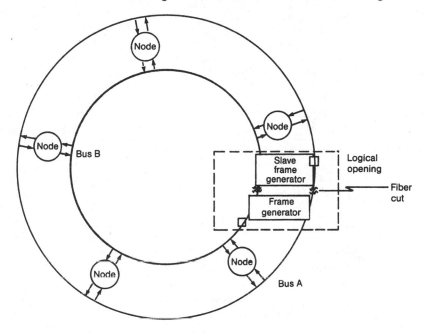

The 802.6 DQDB Protocol

The 802.6 architecture, shown in Figure 33-5, is similar to FDDI in that it uses two counterrotating rings, which permits full-duplex communication between any of the nodes. Each node has two attachments to each bus. One attachment reads bus slots and the other writes bus slots. Busses are managed by a head end, which generates slots for use by the downstream nodes. A logical break, at which clocking is introduced, is located between two of the nodes. The network is self-healing if the fiber is cut. As shown in Figure 33-6, if the fiber breaks between two of the nodes, the logical break shifts to the point of failure and the ring closes to form the logical break at the point of the physical break.

A frame generator at the master station emits 125-μs frames, which is the length of a T1 frame. Each frame can contain a fixed number of fixed-length time slots. The number of slots depends on the bit rate of the bus, which, in turn, depends on the transmission medium. In a freestanding configuration the network contains its own synchronization. When connected to a public network, however, the network must derive its synchronization from the public network.

Although the dual-ring architecture of DQDB appears to be a pair of rings, it is a logically looped dual bus, with each node appearing on each bus. Usually the transmission medium is fiber optics, but the standard permits the use of coaxial cable.

FIGURE 33-7

Queued Arbitrated Access to the 802.6 Bus

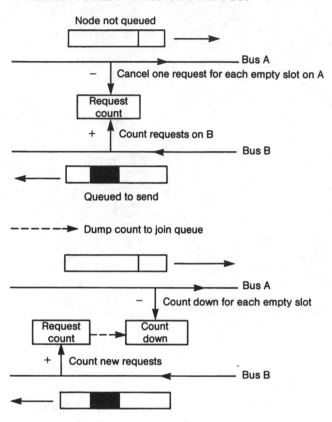

Twisted-pair wire does not have enough bandwidth for the backbone network, but it can be used for the access network.

Isochronous services, such as digitized voice and video, must be transmitted across the network with minimum delay. DQDB has two classes of service, prearbitrated (PA) and queued arbitrated (QA). PA service is for voice and video, which require a fixed amount of bandwidth. QA provides service on demand for bursty applications such as data transmission.

DQDB uses an ingenious method of allocating QA access to the bus. Each node is equipped with a request counter and a packet countdown, as Figure 33-7 shows. When a node has a packet ready for transmission, it transmits a request upstream to the head end. As the request passes the upstream nodes, each node increments its request counter by one, so each node knows at any time what its place in queue is, based on the number in its request counter. As empty slots flow downstream, each node decrements its request counter, knowing that downstream nodes with unfilled requests will fill these slots. Each node has a record, therefore, of how many slots were requested and how many were filled by passing slots intended for downstream stations. If a node's request counter is set at n, when the nth slot goes by, its counter has reached zero, so it can send on the next empty slot.

With this method of allocating bandwidth, upstream locations have a better chance to seize empty slots than downstream locations. To avoid this problem, the protocol forces stations to pass empty slots, depending on their physical location. This scheduling method provides a high degree of efficiency. Slots are never wasted while a station has traffic to send, and no station can monopolize the network.

GIGABIT ETHERNET

Since Ethernet was developed at Xerox in the 1970s, its speed has twice increased by an order of magnitude. Gigabit Ethernet was standardized as 802.3z in June 1998, only 2 years after the formation of a task force to develop the standard. The protocol has great promise because it extends technologies that many manufacturers support and users trust. Gigabit Ethernet builds on two other network technologies. From the data-link layer up, it uses the same logical link control as 802.2. The media access control is a scaled-up version of the CSMA/CD MAC used in 802.3 and operates in either half-duplex or full-duplex mode. For the physical layer it borrows the 8B/10B encoding of Fibre Channel. Since these were already well entrenched and tested, gigabit Ethernet was brought to the market much faster than other protocols, which had to prove themselves, and in several cases were never accepted.

Gigabit Ethernet supports four different media, as shown in Table 33-2. The multimode standard supports both long-wave and short-wave lasers. Only long-wave lasers, which span greater distances, are supported for single mode. Multimode fiber is supported in both the 62.5- and 50-μm sizes, with the latter providing better performance. The shielded twisted-pair wire is a new type designed for short-haul data center applications. The UTP standard uses all four pairs of category 5 cabling, and uses a different encoding scheme than fiber optics.

Gigabit Ethernet uses the same 8B/10B coding scheme as the FC-1 in Fibre Channel, but operates at a slightly different baud rate. The FC-1 layer receives octets from the FC-2 layer and maps them to a 10-bit pattern. This method improves the ability of receiving devices to recover clocking from the transmitted signal. Above the physical layer, gigabit Ethernet uses the standard 802.3 frame format, which enables slower-speed devices to communicate over gigabit Ethernet without translation. The protocol provides a flow control mechanism, whereby a receiving station can send a frame to throttle back a sending station. Flow control operates only in a point-to-point mode, not through a switch.

TABLE 33-2

Gigabit Ethernet Characteristics

Medium	Range	Abbreviation
Shielded copper wire	25 m	1000base CX
Category 5 UTP	100 m	1000base T
62.5-μm multimode fiber optics	260 m	1000base SX*
50-μm multimode fiber optics	550 m	1000base SX*
Single-mode fiber optics	3 km	1000base LX

*Multimode also is available in LX versions.

APPLICATIONS

The four products discussed in this chapter have some overlap in their range of applications, but in most cases the choice is clear. This section discusses typical applications for each, and discusses the future outlook for the protocols.

Fibre Channel

The application for Fibre Channel is clearly designed for linking high-speed devices in a campus environment. Its switching capability enables it to create exclusive nonshared channels between devices for the duration of a session, which has always been the benefit of the PSTN for low-speed applications. Figure 33-8 shows the typical application of Fibre Channel. In addition, with its high-speed switching capability, it could be used to set up paths for other functions in a campus environment where a full-time connection is not required.

SMDS has some of the same objectives as Fibre Channel, but bear in mind that it is a service, not a protocol in itself, and that it is intended for use in the public network. While Fibre Channel could fulfill some of the same functions as SMDS, it is not designed with the data-security provisions that would make it suitable as a public protocol. Furthermore, to apply it in the metropolitan environment as a private network would mean obtaining dark fiber, which is not readily available.

Fiber Distributed Data Interface

FDDI has carved a niche for itself as a backbone protocol. It is widely used for linking LAN segments through routers in a private internet, as we will discuss in Chapter 37. FDDI is theoretically a LAN alternative, but its major drawback is the cost of adapter cards, which makes it unable to compete with fast Ethernet to the desktop. In the backbone its major competitor is Ethernet switching, which is less expensive. Fast Ethernet cards are on the market at a fraction of the cost of FDDI,

FIGURE 33-8

Fibre Channel Application

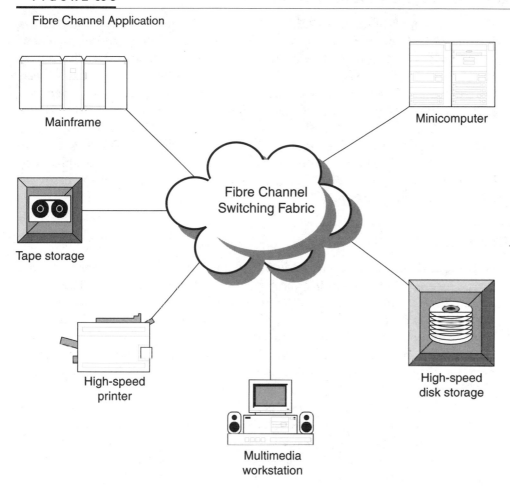

Mainframe

Minicomputer

Fibre Channel
Switching Fabric

Tape storage

High-speed
printer

Multimedia
workstation

High-speed
disk storage

but they fall far short of FDDI's span of 200 km. Gigabit Ethernet, however, with its 3-km range over single-mode fiber, has much greater throughput, and will be more readily accepted than FDDI because it is an extension of protocols that are widely used and understood.

FDDI's primary advantage is its maturity. It has been available since it received ANSI approval in 1988, and is a proven and stable technology. Its dual-fiber ring architecture makes it a robust backbone that can survive fiber cuts and station loss. Running on fiber, FDDI is immune to electromagnetic interference, which may affect copper-wire alternatives in some industrial applications. As a campus backbone, FDDI is currently a viable alternative, but in the future it is likely to be displaced by gigabit Ethernet. Some activity is directed toward increasing the speed of FDDI, but it does not have a strong impetus behind it, and many observers believe FDDI will not survive long as a backbone technology.

Switched Multimegabit Data Service

The primary application for SMDS is LAN interconnection. As the FCC and courts free the LECs from intraLATA restrictions, SMDS may become more prominent over a wider range. Its main drawback now is lack of universal availability. Where SMDS is available, it can be a cost-effective way of connecting LANs or high-speed computer connections. Its major advantage is its ability to deliver traffic between sites in a manner similar to dialed connections on the telephone network. A major unknown factor is the impact that ATM will have on SMDS. ATM may replace DQDB in the metropolitan network, or SMDS may interconnect with ATM carriers for longer hauls. Such uncertainties should not affect the use of SMDS, however, because the investment to enable companies to use SMDS is modest and easily recoverable in a few years of use.

Gigabit Ethernet

Of the four technologies discussed in this chapter, gigabit Ethernet has by far the rosiest future. The initial application for gigabit Ethernet is in the backbone connecting 10/100 Ethernet switches. When LANs first came into general use, most of the traffic was confined to the segment, with only a small percentage in the backbone. Now, however, such features as VLANs and desktop video and audio have loaded considerably more traffic onto the backbone. Also, although the requirement for gigabit bandwidth to the desktop has not yet arrived, it is only a matter of time, and when it does, gigabit Ethernet will be the logical protocol to carry it. When ATM was developed, it was expected to fill the backbone role and eventually migrate to the desktop, but its use is retarded by its complexity. Gigabit Ethernet, as a natural evolution of fast Ethernet, which managers already understand and trust, suffers from no such impediment. It can be shared, switched, and routed using the same topology as the slower-speed products.

CHAPTER 34

Wide Area Data Networks

Wide area network architectures are shifting radically. The architectures of legacy networks were developed at a time when voice-grade analog circuits ran on facilities with an error rate that was several orders of magnitude higher than today's fiber optics. Conventional networks are characterized by fixed-bandwidth point-to-point circuits and single applications. Protocols are proprietary and equipment sources may be limited to the network developer. The host controls communications, and direct communications among peers may not be supported. Terminals on a legacy network can run only the applications supported by the host computer, but over the past decade desktop computers that have an unlimited source of application software have largely replaced dumb terminals. The host connection is no longer the coaxial cable or EIA-232 connections of a terminal network; these have replaced by LANs. The hierarchical networks of the past are evolving into nonhierarchical or flat networks driven by the following trends:

- Personal computers are replacing dumb terminals.
- Workstations have processing power greater than mainframe computers had a few years ago.
- Most personal computers are networked, and the company is connected with an internet or an intranet.
- Applications, such as multimedia, imaging, and CAD/CAM, demand greater bandwidths. Voice and video are riding on networks once reserved for data.
- An abundance of low-error-rate high-speed digital fiber-optic facilities results in reduced transmission costs.
- Processing is evolving from centralized to distributed facilities.
- Compression technology squeezes voice, video, and data in ever-smaller bandwidths.

FIGURE 34-1

The Enterprise Network Permits Any Desktop Device to Connect to Any Data Source

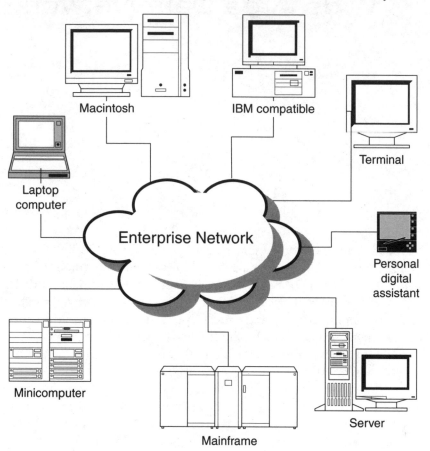

Even though many networks are evolving toward broadband, voice-grade data circuits will remain for years to come because some applications do not require greater bandwidth. For example, the bandwidth requirements for automatic teller machines and point-of-sale terminals are so low that dozens of them can be supported on a single voice-grade circuit.

The network architecture of interconnected LANs is completely different from that of wide area terminal networks. Many companies are in a transition involving both legacy networks and LAN internets, which raises a special problem for network managers. An easy and expensive solution is to leave the two types of networks separate. The logical solution is to combine networks, but then issues of handling multiple protocols are raised. A complete examination of such issues is beyond the scope of this book, but we will briefly discuss the alternatives.

New networks are constructed on the enterprise network model shown in Figure 34-1. This model assumes that users can choose applications and the terminal devices on which they run, and that they can communicate any place in the network provided they have permission. The circuits are multilocation, and, within limits, able to deliver bandwidth on demand. Applications reside on servers that may be distributed throughout the network and accessed by any authorized station. Circuits are high quality and digital with at least 56 kb/s of bandwidth, more if needed. Peers can communicate freely, and error correction is left to the end devices.

Although the enterprise network on this model is emerging, legacy wide area networks have not disappeared, and are likely to survive for as long as they meet the needs of the applications. Increasingly, however, they are riding on newer networks such as frame relay or an IP intranet, using tunneling or encapsulation to enable a frame-based or cell-based network to carry the legacy protocol transparently. A tunneling application chops the legacy protocol into segments that are carried as the data block of a PDU and reassembled at the terminating end.

In this chapter we will discuss both conventional and newer networks. This chapter will focus on facilities and common carrier alternatives that are used for both legacy networks and LAN internets up to T1/E1 bandwidth. Chapter 35 discusses frame relay and Chapter 36 covers ATM, both of which are wide area network services that support bandwidth on demand more effectively than the fixed circuits discussed in this chapter.

DATA NETWORK FACILITIES

The data communications designer has several key decisions to make in selecting network facilities. This section discusses the primary network choices the designer must make in implementing a data communications network. Decision points such as these must be considered:

- ◆ Will facilities be privately owned, leased, or a combination of both?
- ◆ If facilities are leased, will a single vendor furnish the circuits?
- ◆ Are digital or analog facilities required?
- ◆ Will facilities be terrestrial, satellite, or a combination?
- ◆ Does the application require switched or dedicated facilities?
- ◆ Is the application inherently point to point or multipoint? Full duplex or half duplex?
- ◆ Is there an opportunity to share bandwidth with other applications such as compressed voice and video?

Private or Public Ownership   Private ownership is the rule with local area data networks, but in wide area networks the cost of right-of-way usually precludes private ownership. Wide area networks are feasible for private ownership by only the largest companies. Most networks today are evolving toward a combination of private and public ownership. Such networks are one form of the hybrid networks discussed in Chapter 31.

Digital or Analog   Digital versus analog decisions are mostly resolved in favor of digital circuits. Tariff offerings, such as fractional T1/E1, are driving the network from analog to digital, to the point that the major application of analog facilities is growth of existing analog networks.

Common Carrier or Value-Added Carrier   A common carrier delivers data communications circuits to an interface point on the user's premises. The carrier transports the signal but does not process the data. A *value-added carrier* not only transports data but also may process it or add other services such as store-and-forward, error correction, and authentication. The carrier also may provide other message-processing services such as filing, electronic mail, electronic data interchange, and message logging and receipting. The value-added carrier furnishes the user with a dial-up or dedicated interface and provides the equivalent of a private network over shared facilities.

Switched or Dedicated Facilities   The nature of the application determines whether it requires a switched or dedicated network service. If multiple users communicate over distances greater than a few miles and send a few short messages, switched services tend to be most effective. If messages are long and the number of points limited, dedicated or private line services are most economical. Four types of switched services can be obtained.

> *Circuit switching* connects channels through a centralized switching system. The public switched telephone network is an example of a circuit-switched network. Its primary advantage is worldwide access to any location with telephone service over a well-known addressing scheme. Messages are highly secure, and have exclusive use of the bandwidth. Its disadvantages are cost, limited bandwidth, and inefficient use of the bandwidth.

> *Message switching,* or store-and-forward switching, is a service that accepts a message from a user, stores it, and forwards it to its destination later. The storage time may be so short that forwarding is almost instantaneous, or messages may be stored for longer periods while a receiving terminal is temporarily unavailable or while awaiting more favorable rates. The primary advantage of store-and-forward switching is that the sender and receiver do not need to be online simultaneously. If the receiving device is unavailable, the network can queue messages and release the originating device. If instantaneous delivery is not important, the store-and-forward technique can make maximum use of circuit capacity. Its primary disadvantages are the added cost of storage facilities in the switching

device and the longer response time compared to circuit or packet switching.

Packet switching controls the flow of packets of information through a network by routing algorithms contained in each node. Stations interface the packet nodes on a dedicated or dial-up basis and deliver preaddressed packets to the node, which routes them through the network to the destination. Packet switching is flexible. During temporary overloads or circuit outages, service can be maintained by the dynamic routing capability of the network. Packet switching is also good for overseas applications because many network vendors have interconnection agreements that permit delivering packets worldwide. Its primary disadvantages are its cost and the latency that packet nodes introduce.

Cell switching is an emerging technology that is discussed in more detail in Chapter 36. The data stream is broken into 53-octet cells and routed through the network over a path that is set up for the duration of the session. Cell switching, or ATM, is capable of providing bandwidth on demand.

Terrestrial or Satellite Circuits   Communications satellites offer a cost-effective alternative to terrestrial circuits, particularly where the end points are widely dispersed and located some distance from a frame relay rating point. Because the tariff rates of terrestrial circuits are distance-based, terrestrial circuits are less expensive over shorter routes unless the network has many terminal locations. Beyond a break-even point, satellite circuits are less expensive because their cost is independent of distance within the coverage field of a single satellite. Satellite circuits are also the most effective way of data transmission for mobile applications such as ships at sea and long-haul transportation.

Circuit Sharing   Most data applications do not use the full bandwidth of a circuit, so circuits can be multiplexed with a variety of methods. As discussed later, the host polls multidrop circuits. Multiplexers enable multiple devices to share the same circuit. By using add-drop multiplexers on T1/E1 lines, voice and data can share the same transmission medium. As discussed in Chapter 38, the trend is for voice, video, and data to share the same bandwidth at the circuit level.

Point-to-Point Network Facilities

Point-to-point circuits can be obtained through dial-up or dedicated connections. They can be analog or digital, with digital dedicated circuits replacing analog in most applications. Circuits are billed in three elements, as shown in Figure 34-2. The local access channels are obtained from the LEC or an AAC, and the interoffice channel is obtained from an IXC. Normally, the IXC obtains the local channel, bills the circuit as a single entity, and accepts end-to-end responsibility for

FIGURE 34-2

Billing Elements of an Interexchange Leased Circuit

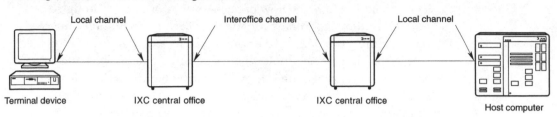

clearing trouble. The cost of the IOC portion of the circuit is distance-sensitive. The cost of the local access channel is not distance-sensitive within a wire center, but between wire centers a mileage charge applies.

Dial-Up Circuits

The public switched telephone network carries a significant portion of the data that is transported in the world. Circuit switching isn't an ideal way of handling data, but it has one major advantage: it is available nearly everywhere in the world with a universal numbering plan. Wherever telephones are found, data can be transported with respectable speed, reasonable cost, and easy setup. Dial-up data is effective under the following conditions:

- ◆ Data is exchanged among multiple terminating points.
- ◆ The application does not require an online connection.
- ◆ The use of data is occasional for limited periods each day.
- ◆ The time required to set up a data connection is not a limiting factor.

Facsimile is a data application that fits these conditions perfectly. As a result, most facsimile is sent over the PSTN because of its universal availability. The same is true of the countless dial-up sessions into Internet and public databases. Circuit switching is not ideal for these types of sessions. The transmissions are largely one-way, so bandwidth is wasted in one direction while transmission is taking place in the other and the limited bandwidth slows the session. Ideally, data would be sent over a data network with switched virtual circuits, but such a network with ubiquitous connections is not yet available. Therefore, although the PSTN may be less than ideal, most users have no alternative for the moment.

Dial-up data has become a great deal more effective in the last few years with the introduction of fast modems with data compression and error correction. V.34 modems running at 33.3 kb/s with data compression and error correction are a commodity. For Internet access, V.90 modems may provide data downstream at 56 kb/s, but it doesn't always work at top speed. The handshake for setting speed and other variables is practically automatic, which makes dial-up an attractive option for many applications.

Switched 56-kb/s Service

The major IXCs and LECs offer switched 56-kb/s services, which allow users to set up 56-kb/s connections between locations equipped for the service. Switched 56 is intended for applications that need a digital connection for a time too short to justify the use of a dedicated channel—generally 3 hours per day or less. Examples are videoconferences, high-speed facsimile transmission, graphics, and part-time extensions to existing digital networks. As with other switched services, switched 56 charges are based on usage time and carry a rate higher than an ordinary voice connection.

Point-to-Point Analog Facilities

In the past analog facilities and modems were the default private circuit, but with the introduction of fractional T1/E1 services, networks are rapidly converting to digital. Analog private lines have a nominal bandwidth of 4 kHz, with a usable bandwidth of approximately 300 to 3300 Hz. The error rate should be in the order of 10^{-5} or better.

Point-to-Point Digital Facilities

Digital facilities are available in a variety of configurations from common carriers. AT&T has offered Dataphone Digital Service (DDS) for many years. Similar types of service are available from other carriers. DDS service objectives are 99.99 percent error-free seconds and 99.96 percent availability. The carriers transport most digital circuits on lightwave and extend service to the end user over four-wire nonloaded cable facilities furnished by the LECs. Increasingly, the IXCs deliver digital services over T1/E1 facilities that the customer can use for both voice and data services. Figure 34-3 shows how a T1/E1 can provide entrance facilities for both voice and digital data.

DDS uses a bipolar signaling format that requires the user's data signal to be converted from the usual unipolar output of terminal equipment. A data service unit (DSU) located on the user's premises does the conversion. If the user's equipment can accept a bipolar signal and provide timing recovery, the data signal is coupled to a channel service unit (CSU) in a unit that is sometimes called a CSU/DSU. Both units provide loopback facilities, so the local cable can be tested by looping the transmit and receive pairs together. The signal is fully synchronized from end to end. A DDS hub office concentrates data signals from multiple users and connects them to the long-haul network. The hub is also a testing point.

T1/E1 and Fractional T1/E1

Most IXCs and LECs offer bulk digital T1/E1 transmission facilities at prices that are more attractive than those of multiple analog lines. The major interexchange carriers and some LECs also offer fractional T1/E1 services. Fractional T1/E1 is economical up to some crossover point with full T1/E1, after which a full T1/E1 is more cost-effective. Fractional T1/E1 can support analog service as well as digital.

FIGURE 34-3

Sharing T1/E1 between Voice and Data

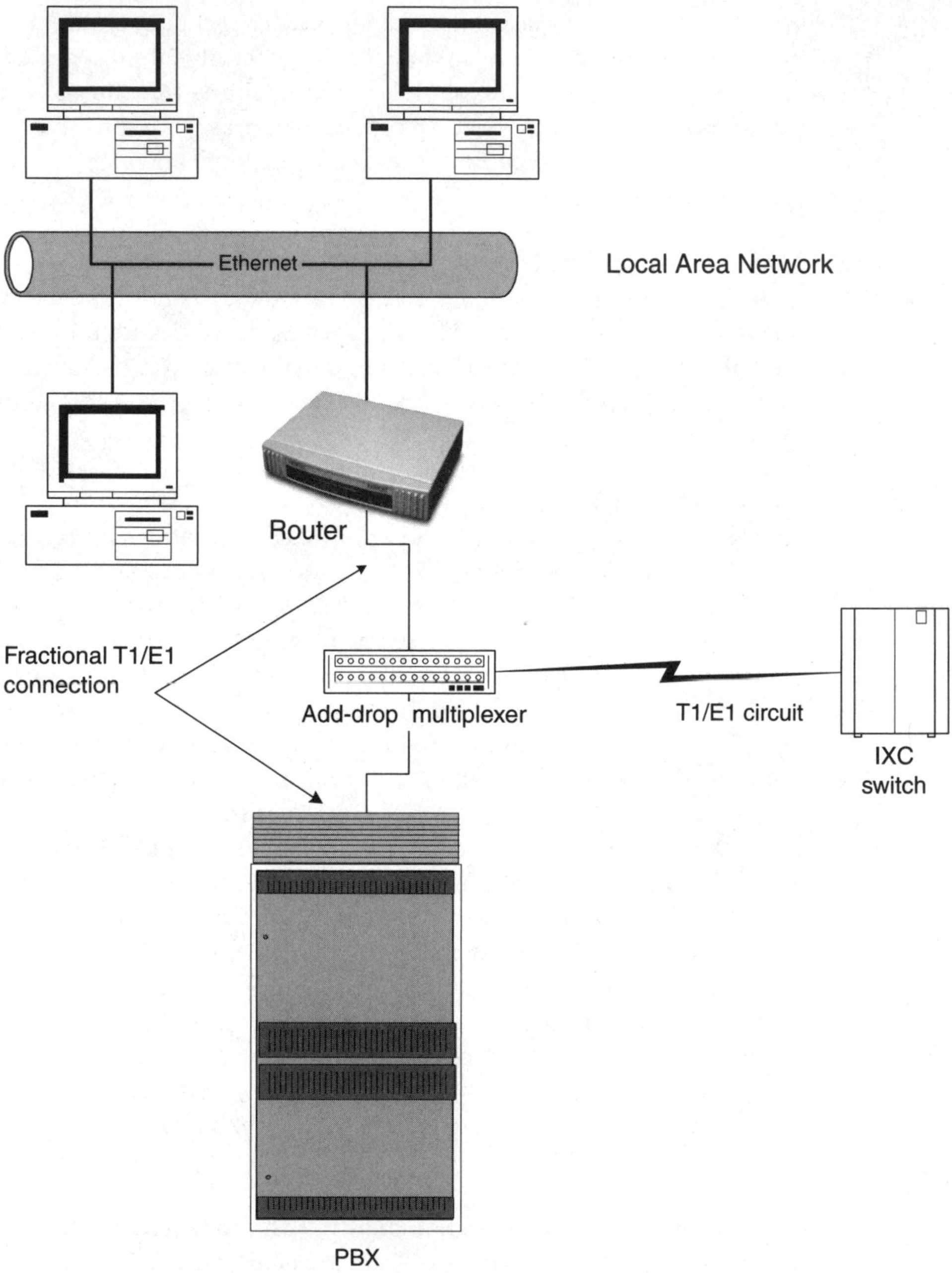
Ethernet
Local Area Network
Router
Fractional T1/E1 connection
Add-drop multiplexer
T1/E1 circuit
IXC switch
PBX

Multidrop bridging is also available. This type of service has replaced analog 3002 circuits in most cases. LECs and AACs can deliver the local access portion of T1/E1 over fiber-optic or copper facilities.

If the local access circuit permits, T1 and fractional T1 can be offered as clear channel 64-kb/s service. E1 is always clear channel. Some carriers provide central office multiplexing and service protection measures such as diversity routing and routing exclusively over fiber-optic facilities.

T3/E3 and Fractional T3/E3

Where multiple T1/E1 circuits are needed between two points, T3/E3 or fractional T3/E3 becomes economical. T3 service is a full 28 DS-1s operating at 45 Mb/s. Fractional T3/E3 is at submultiples of T1/E1. The interoffice channel of fractional T3 must be routed over the same DS-3, or the DS-1s may arrive at slightly different times. Local channels may be routed over microwave or fiber-optic facilities provided by the customer or an access carrier.

MULTIDROP NETWORKS

Point-to-point circuits are cost-effective when there is enough traffic on the network to justify the cost of a dedicated circuit between two devices. Where the traffic flows in bursts or short transmissions, some method of sharing the circuit among multiple devices is needed. Such a method, used in IBM's SNA network, is *polling*. If a polling protocol is used, a multidrop circuit is often the choice. As discussed later, however, SNA, which represents the most widespread use of polling, can be applied to packet switching and frame relay circuits. The choice of the polling protocol does not, therefore, necessarily dictate the use of multidrop circuits.

The advantage of multidrop is in the ability of multiple devices to share the same backbone circuits. For example, a bank that has multiple automatic teller machines in an area can obtain local loops to the machines and bridge them in the central office to share a single circuit to the *front-end processor*, which is a computer equipped for telecommunications. The front-end processor's role is to relieve the host computer of teleprocessing chores. Each station is assigned an address. The host polls the stations by sending short polling messages to the controller. If the controller has no traffic from any of its attached terminals, it responds with a negative acknowledgment message. If it has traffic, it responds by sending a block of data, which the host acknowledges. Before sending data to the distant devices, which are usually terminals or printers, the host sends a short message to determine whether the device is ready to receive. If it is ready, the host then sends a block of data.

Multidrop networks are designed as full duplex or half duplex. In half-duplex networks, the modem reverses after a poll or response. In full-duplex networks, the devices can send data in both directions simultaneously. Polling is an efficient way of sharing a common data circuit, but it has high overhead compared to other alternatives. The overhead of sending polling messages, returning negative acknowledgments, and reversing the modems consumes a substantial portion of the circuit time. Throughput can be improved by using *hub polling*. In hub polling, when a station receives a poll, it passes its traffic to the host and passes the polling message to the next station in line. Hub polling is more complex than *roll call* polling and is not as widely used.

IBM Systems Network Architecture

The most prominent example of multidrop architecture is IBM's original Systems Network Architecture. SNA is a tree-structured hierarchical architecture, in which a mainframe computer serves as the network host. The architecture was first published in 1974 at a time when processing was controlled by an expensive mainframe computer that communicated with remote 3270 terminals over a network built of voice-grade circuits. This network was designed to provide error-free communications over a phone network that had narrow bandwidth circuits that were subject to errors, while still providing the data integrity needed for corporate transactions such as bank transfers, reservations, payroll, and the like. In this original network a mainframe computer runs a control program known as advanced communications function/virtual telecommunications access method (ACF/VTAM), usually abbreviated VTAM. VTAM maintains a table of every device and circuit in its domain. Communications with these devices are handled through minicomputers known as front-end processors, which in turn communicate with cluster controllers and terminals. Figure 34-4 is a diagram of the logical and physical elements in SNA. SNA establishes a logical path between network nodes and routes each message with addressing information contained in the protocol. The SNA data-link protocol is synchronous data-link control (SDLC).

Network Addressable Units

The major components in the network are called network addressable units (NAUs). SNA defines four types:

- ◆ *Type 1.* Terminals
- ◆ *Type 2.* Controllers
- ◆ *Type 4.* Front-end processors
- ◆ *Type 5.* Hosts

The host NAU is categorized as a system service control point (SSCP). Each network contains at least one SSCP, which resides in an IBM mainframe computer. The SSCP exercises network control, establishing routes and interconnections between logical units. The end user interfaces the network through a logical unit (LU). The LU, generally a terminal or a personal computer, is the user's link to the network. The next higher unit in the hierarchy is a physical unit (PU). Although its

FIGURE 34-4

Physical and Logical View of IBM Systems Network Architecture

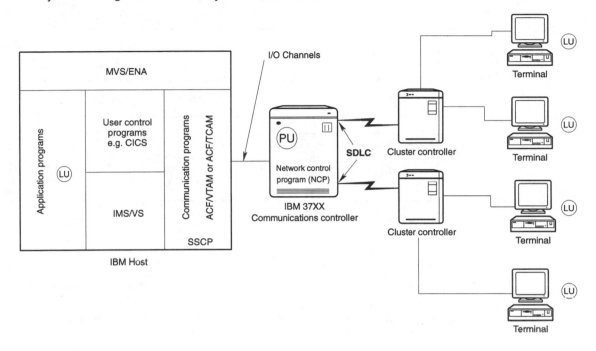

name implies that it is a piece of hardware, a PU is a control program executed in software or firmware.

Network Control Program

The network control program (NCP) resides in the front-end processor. Its purpose is to control information flow in the network. It polls the attached controllers, handles error detection and correction, establishes circuits under control of the SSCP, and handles other functions that deload the host computer.

SNA's Layered Architecture

SNA is defined in layers roughly analogous to the layers in ISO's OSI model. SNA was first announced in 1974 and is the basis for much of the OSI model, but it differs from OSI in several significant respects.

Level 1, physical, is not included as part of the SNA architecture. The physical interface for analog voice-grade circuits is ITU V.24 and V.31. The digital interface is X.21.

Level 2, data-link control, uses the synchronous data-link control (SDLC) protocol. Figure 34-5 shows the SDLC frame, which has 6 octets of overhead. The first

FIGURE 34-5

Synchronous Data Transmission (IBM SDLC Frame)

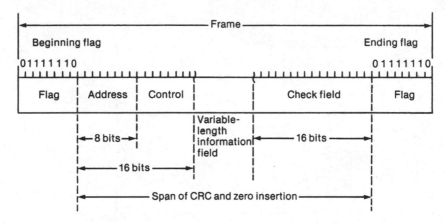

octet is a flag to establish the start of the frame. This is followed by a 1-octet address and a 1-octet control field. Next is a variable-length data field followed by a 2-octet cyclical redundancy check field and an ending flag. The control field contains the number of packets received to allow SDLC to acknowledge multiple packets simultaneously. SDLC permits up to 128 unacknowledged packets, which makes it suitable for satellite transmission. This layer corresponds closely to ISO's data-link layer and the LAPB protocol used in X.25 networks.

   Level 3, path control, is responsible for establishing data paths through the network. It carries addressing, mapping, and message sequencing information. At the start of a session, the path control layer establishes a virtual route, which is the sequence of nodes forming a path between the terminating points. The circuits between the nodes are formed into transmission groups, which are groups of circuits having identical characteristics—speed, delay, error rate, and so on. The path control layer is also responsible for address translation. Through this layer, LUs can address other LUs by terminating address without being concerned with the entire detailed address of the other terminal. This layer is also responsible for flow control, protecting the network's resources by delaying traffic that would cause congestion. The path control layer also *segments* and *blocks* messages. Segmenting is the process of breaking long messages into manageable-size pieces so errors do not cause excessive retransmission. Blocking is the reverse—combining short messages so the network's resources are not consumed by small messages of uneconomical size.

   Level 4, transmission control, is responsible for pacing. At the beginning of a session the LUs exchange information about factors, such as transmission speed and buffer size, that affect their ability to receive information. The pacing function prevents an LU from sending more data than the receiving LU can accept. Through this layer, SNA also provides other functions such as encryption, message sequencing, and flow control.

Level 5, data flow control, conditions messages for transmission by chaining and bracketing. *Chaining* is the process of grouping messages with one-way transmission requirements, and *bracketing* is grouping messages for two-way transmission.

Level 6, function management data services, has three primary purposes. Configuration service activates and deactivates internodal links. Network operator services is the interface through which the network operator sends commands and receives responses. The management services function is used in testing and troubleshooting the network.

Level 7, NAU services, is responsible for formatting data between display devices such as printers and CRTs. It performs some functions of the ISO presentation layer, including data compression and compaction. It also synchronizes transmissions.

SNA lacks an applications layer as such, but IBM has defined standards that allow for document interchange and display between SNA devices. Document interchange architecture (DIA) can be thought of as the envelope in which documents travel. DIA standards cover editing, printing, and displaying documents. The document itself is defined by document content architecture (DCA), which is analogous to the letter within the envelope. The purpose of the DIA/DCA combination is to make it possible for business machines to transmit documents with formatting commands such as tabs, indents, margins, and other format information intact. Documents containing graphic information are defined by graphic codepoint definition (GCD), which defines the placement of graphic symbols on printers and screens.

Advanced Peer-to-Peer Network

A drawback of the original version of SNA was the requirement that all data flow through the host. This condition was reasonable when terminals lacked intelligence, but as the terminal of choice evolved from dumb to intelligent, it became undesirable to have the host control every session between intelligent devices. PU type 2 cluster controllers could support only one SDLC link and could not communicate among themselves.

IBM developed a cluster controller modification known as PU 2.1, which enabled two controllers to be linked across an SDLC or dial-up connection without requiring a path through the communications controller. Although PU 2.1 supports the physical connection, it does not provide all the logical functions necessary for peer-to-peer communications exclusive of the host computer.

Advanced Program-to-Program Communications

The original SNA protocol was built on the assumption that devices, such as terminals and printers, had no processing capability. As microprocessors dropped in price and increased in power, the processing capabilities were built into the end devices. To enable device-to-device communications, IBM introduced the LU 6.2 advanced program-to-program communications (APPC) protocol. LU 6.2 eliminates the SNA master-slave relationship between devices and instead permits communication between peers. Either device can manage the session, establishing and terminating communications and initiating session error recovery procedures without the involvement of an SSCP. APPC permits direct PC-to-mainframe communications, which enables the PC to transfer files without consuming excessive mainframe processing power.

The new SNA is called *advanced peer-to-peer network* (APPN). APPN uses two kinds of nodes, network nodes and end nodes. An end node, as the name suggests, can send and receive traffic, but data is not routed through it. A network node handles through traffic, and acts as the concentration point for end nodes. Devices on the network are named. To communicate with another device, an end node sends a bind message to its network node, which, in turn, broadcasts a query that passes through the network. The node that hosts that name responds to the query with a message that establishes the session and route.

PACKET SWITCHING

Unlike circuit-switched networks, which provide a circuit between end points for the exclusive use of two or more stations, packet networks support *virtual circuits*, which share many characteristics with switched circuits. The difference is that the circuits are time-shared rather than dedicated to the connection. As Figure 34-6 shows, a packet network has multiple nodes that are accessed through dedicated or dialed connections from the end user. The nodes control access to the network and route packets to their destinations over a backbone of high-speed data circuits.

Access to public data networks is provided by one of three methods:

◆ A dedicated X.25 link between the user's host computer and the data network.

◆ A dedicated link between the data network and a PAD on the user's premises.

◆ Dedicated or dial-up access over the telephone network into a PAD provided by the network vendor.

In the first option, the user's host computer performs the PAD functions. The second option requires either a PAD provided by the vendor on the user's premises or a user-owned PAD that the vendor certifies is compatible with the network.

The third option, dial-up access, is the least complex and is the only method economically feasible for small users. It does, however, have several disadvantages. The first problem is the loss of end-to-end error checking and correction.

F I G U R E 34-6

X.25 Packet Network Showing Access Options

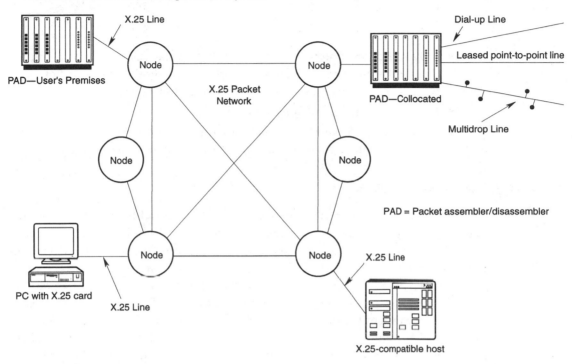

Modems with a built-in error-correcting protocol are an effective method of error correction.

The packet assembler/disassembler (PAD) creates a packet when one of three events occurs:

- ◆ A predetermined number of bytes is received.
- ◆ A specified time elapses.
- ◆ A particular bit sequence occurs.

Packet networks are effective in both public and private implementations. The primary advantages of packet switching are

- ◆ *Ready availability.* Most computer manufacturers support the X.25 protocol.
- ◆ *Reliability.* Alternate paths between packet switches minimize the effect of a switch or circuit failure.
- ◆ *Ease of crossing international boundaries.* Public data networks cover the major countries in the world. Time-consuming circuit setups are not required to begin sending data.

♦ *Economy of multiple sites.* Since costs are usage-based, small sites that often cannot justify fixed private lines can justify a connection to the nearest node.

Disadvantages are

♦ *Latency.* Packet switches are subject to both packetizing and switching delays; the more nodes on the network, the longer the delay. Packet nodes check errors on each link, which adds to latency.

♦ *Packet overhead.* The X.25 protocol adds headers that reduce throughput.

♦ *Probabilistic performance.* The response time of a packet network depends on load. During heavy load periods, response time deteriorates.

Packet Switching Nodes

The packet switching nodes are processors interconnected by backbone circuits. High-speed digital facilities are usually employed between nodes. Data flows through the network in packets consisting of an information field sandwiched between header and trailer records. Figure 34-7 shows the packet used by ITU's X.25 protocol. The X.25 packet is enclosed in a frame consisting of a 1-octet flag having a distinctive pattern that is not repeated in the data field. The second octet is an address code that permits up to 255 addresses on a data link. The third field is a control octet that sequences messages and sends supervisory commands. The X.25 packet has three format and control octets and an information field that contains the user data. The final 3 octets of the trailer are a 16-bit cyclical redundancy check field and an end-of-frame flag.

Packet Assembly and Disassembly

A packet assembler/disassembler slices the message into packets. The PAD communicates with the packet network using a packet network protocol, X.25, which is an ITU protocol recommendation that describes the interface to a packet switching node. Even though a packet network is often called an X.25 network, the protocol between nodes is proprietary. The packet network uses the address field of the packet to route it to the next node on the way to the destination. Each node hands off the packet following the network's routing algorithm until it reaches the final node. At the terminating node, the switch sequences the packets and passes them off to the PAD. The PAD strips the data from the header and trailer records and reassembles it into a completed message.

Error checking takes place in each link in the network. If a block is received in error, the node rejects it and requests a replacement block. Because errors require resending blocks and because blocks can take different paths to their destinations, it is possible for blocks to arrive at the destination out of sequence. The receiving node buffers the message and delivers the data blocks in the proper sequence.

FIGURE 34-7

Level 2 Frame Enclosing X.25 Packet

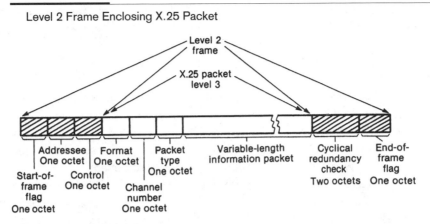

A special type of message known as a *datagram* is available in some packet networks. A datagram is a single packet that flows through the network to its destination without acknowledgment. An alternative to the datagram is the *fast select* message, which is a single packet and response. A typical application for fast select messages is the credit-checking terminal that transmits the details of a transaction from a point-of-sale terminal and receives an acknowledgment from a credit agency's database.

The network designer specifies packet size to optimize throughput. Because each packet has a fixed-length header and trailer record, short packets reduce throughput because time must be spent transmitting overhead bits in the header and trailer. On the other hand, long packets reduce throughput because the switching node cannot forward the packet until it receives all bits, which increases buffer requirements at the node. Also, the time spent in retransmitting errored packets is greater if the packet length is longer. Most packet networks operate with a packet length of 128 to 256 octets.

Virtual Circuits

Packet networks establish two kinds of virtual circuits, switched and permanent. *Permanent virtual circuits* are the packet network equivalent of a dedicated voice circuit. A path between users is established, and all packets take the same route through the network. With a *switched virtual circuit*, the network path is set up with each session.

Packets consist of two types, data and control. *Control packets*, which contain information to show the status of the session, are analogous to signaling in a circuit-switched network. For example, a call setup packet would be used to establish the initial connection to the terminating device, which would return answer packets. The network uses control packets to interrupt calls in progress, disconnect, show acceptance of reversed charges, and other such functions. Switched virtual circuit operations use these control packets to establish a session. In permanent virtual circuit operation, the path is preestablished and no separate packets are needed to connect and disconnect the circuit.

X.25 Protocol

X.25 is an example of an important protocol built on the OSI model. X.25 specifies the interface between DTE and a packet-switched network. It forms a network from the physical, link, and network layers of the OSI model. The physical layer interface is the X.21 standard. Another version of the standard, X.21 *bis*, is nearly identical with EIA-232-D and is more commonly used.

The link layer uses a derivation of HDLC called *balanced link access procedure* (LAPB) to control errors, transfer packets, and to establish the data link. The network layer establishes logical channels and virtual circuits between the PAD and the network. The X.75 protocol recommends the interface for gateway circuits between packet networks.

Value-Added Networks

Public data networks, also known as *value-added networks,* provide an alternative to the telephone network for long-haul data communications. The term "value added" derives from processing functions that are added to the usual network functions of data transport and switching. The value-added services include such features as error checking and correction, code conversion, speed conversion, and storage.

Public Packet-Switched Data Networks

Packet switching service can be obtained with private network equipment or through a public data network such as Sprint's SprintNet. Several other networks offer packet switching service, and most larger LECs provide packet switching within their LATAs. Because of the nature of the applications, most users require interLATA connections. These can be provided by the user as private lines, or the user can obtain a connection to a long-haul packet network for the interLATA connection.

Public packet-switched networks have developed more rapidly in Europe where it is more difficult to obtain private network facilities from the postal telephone and telegraph agencies. Public data networks in the United States can often transport data overseas by interconnecting through a gateway to a data network in another country.

VERY SMALL APERTURE TERMINAL (VSAT)

VSAT is an excellent medium for a widely dispersed operation. Its pricing is not distance-sensitive, and it is particularly effective in remote locations that are not

FIGURE 34-8

VSAT Network

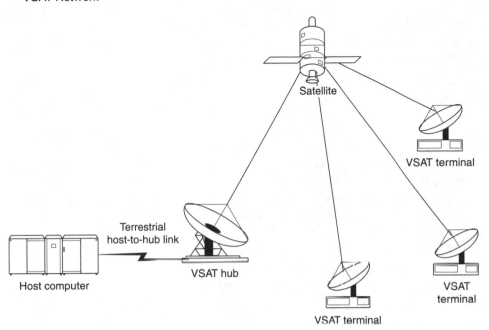

close to a frame relay point-of-presence. A typical application is point-of-sale with widely dispersed terminals, many of which are located in rural areas and small towns where a service such as frame relay is not cost-effective because of the access circuit cost. Another application for which VSAT is admirably suited is telemetering from mobile devices such as trucks, ships, and trains.

Figure 34-8 shows a typical VSAT arrangement. As discussed in Chapter 17, the VSAT terminal is a small device with a 1- or 2-m antenna. Transponder space is leased from the satellite provider or obtained from the hub provider. Large companies may be able to justify the cost of the earth station and hub, but smaller companies will lease capacity from a service provider. Added to the cost of the transponder is a terrestrial extension from the hub to the host computer. VSAT bandwidth can range from as low as 1200 b/s to T1/E1 speeds.

With all else equal, terrestrial circuits are more effective for data than satellite circuits. At longer distances, however, the greater cost of terrestrial circuits often offsets the disadvantages of a satellite. The primary disadvantage of a satellite circuit is the round-trip propagation delay, which is approximately 0.5 seconds. Some protocols, such as IBM's bisync, will not operate well with this much delay. Other protocols function with reduced throughput because of error retransmission time. Satellite delay compensators can alleviate some protocol problems, but they add latency. IBM's SDLC allows the protocol to acknowledge as many as 128 packets at a time, which enables it to operate effectively on satellite circuits. Throughput is also reduced by the access method, which is typically slotted Aloha. Multiple terminals are sharing the same frequency spectrum, but they cannot hear one another's signal. Therefore, within a time slot, stations with traffic to send may transmit simultaneously. If their signals collide, they must be retransmitted. The more heavily loaded the network, the higher the probability of collision.

APPLICATIONS

Data network applications can be separated into the following general types.

Inquiry/Response   This is typical of information services where a short inquiry generates a lengthy response from the host. Because the data flow is greater in one direction than in the other, half-duplex facilities generally offer the greatest throughput on a dedicated private line. On digital facilities, the connection is inherently full duplex.

Typical inquiry/response applications are airline reservations and online database sessions such as the World Wide Web. The operator keys a few characters into the terminal, and the host computer responds with a lengthy message that might be confirmation of a reservation, a printed ticket, or an information dump.

Conversational   This mode, typical of terminal-to-terminal communication, is characterized by short messages that are of approximately equal length in both directions. Throughput is improved by using full-duplex operation. Conversational mode is typical of LAN connectivity via remote bridges or routers. Users log on to remote file servers and send approximately equal amounts of data in each direction when files are retrieved and periodically saved. Voice and video can share a network, integrated with data at the circuit level.

Bulk Data Transfer   This is typical of applications such as mainframe-to-mainframe communications where large files are passed, often at high speed, in only one direction. This method is often used when a local processor collects information during the day and makes daily updates of a master file such as an inventory on the host. Bulk data transfer is usually a half-duplex operation because large amounts of data flow in one direction with the line reversed periodically to return an acknowledgment.

Remote Job Entry   This is typical of applications in which terminals send information to a host. The bulk of the transmission is from the terminal with a short acknowledgment from the host. Half-duplex circuits may be the most effective form of transmission because the bulk of the information flows from remote to host. Dedicated facilities, either leased lines or frame relay, are almost invariably needed for this kind of application. Many remote terminals, each of which is used only occasionally, share a higher-speed line to the host.

T A B L E 34-1

Selected ITU Packet Standards

X.21 or X.21 Bis	Physical connection between X.25 UNI and network
LAPB	Link access procedure balanced; X.25 data-link protocol
PLP	Packet layer protocol; X.25 network layer protocol

Standards

ITU-T sets international data network standards, with supporting standards set by ANSI, EIA, and major equipment vendors whose products take on the character of de facto standards. For example, in data communications, IBM's Systems Network Architecture (SNA) is so widely used as to constitute a de facto standard. The primary ITU standards that affect packet switching networks are shown in Table 34-1.

Evaluation Considerations

The criteria used to evaluate data networks differ significantly from those used to evaluate voice networks. For example, the short length of many data messages makes setup time, which is of little concern in voice networks, an important factor. Also, error considerations are important in data networks, but unimportant in voice. Circuit noise that is merely annoying in a voice network may render the channel unusable for data. Also, because many data networks' billing is not distance-sensitive and because billing is based on volume rather than connect time, cost evaluations are significantly different for the two types of network. For data networks, the primary factors are reliability, standards compliance, manageability, and cost. This section elaborates on these and other factors as they apply to the different facility alternatives.

Private Line Services

Digital or Analog Facilities   In both metropolitan and long-haul circuits, digital facilities have effectively replaced analog except for additions to existing networks.

Reliability and Availability   Data circuit reliability is the frequency of circuit failure expressed as mean time between failures (MTBF). A related factor is circuit availability, which is the percentage of time the circuit is available to the user. Availability depends on how frequently the circuit fails and how long it takes to repair it. The average length of time to repair a circuit is expressed as mean time to repair (MTTR). The formula for determining availability is

$$\frac{(\text{MTBF} - \text{MTTR}) \times 100}{\text{MTBF}}$$

For example, a circuit with an MTBF of 1000 hours and an MTTR of 2 hours would have an availability of

$$\frac{(1000 - 2) \times 100}{1000} = 99.8 \text{ percent}$$

It is important to reach an understanding with the supplier of the conditions under which a circuit is considered failed. When the circuit is totally inoperative, a failure condition clearly exists, but when a high error rate impairs the circuit, it is less clear whether the service is usable. The error rate in a data circuit is usually expressed as a ratio of error bits to transmitted bits. For example, a data circuit with an error rate of 1×10^{-5} will have 1 bit in error for every 100,000 bits transmitted. Reliability and error rate have a significant effect on throughput. Most error-correction systems initiate retransmission of a block and retransmission of blocks reduces throughput.

Costs   Cost comparisons between public data networks are difficult to make because of differences in the way data is handled. Cost depends on how the network handles data and renders bills for usage. The geographic area to be covered has a significant effect on the cost of public data network services. Costs are higher in low-density areas. With dial access, the cost of measured local telephone service or long-distance charges to the node when none is available in the locality must be considered.

Session Setup Time   Setup time is critical to most data applications. When using dial access over a public data network, setup time is significant—often longer than message transmission time. Dedicated access to a public data or frame relay network eliminates the dialing, answer, and authentication routines, greatly reducing call setup time. The time it takes to establish a session through the network to the terminating station remains a significant factor and is comparable whether dial or dedicated access to the public data network is used.

X.25 Services

Features Supported   Data communications features should be examined and compared to the services available from the different data communications network alternatives. Features to be considered include:

- *Virtual circuit or datagram service.* Users with very short messages may require a datagram or fast select service.
- *Type of message delivery.* Consider whether message delivery is to be automatic or delayed awaiting a busy or unattended terminal.
- *Message storage or electronic mail services.* May be offered by the network or a value-added service on the network.
- *Multidestination message service.* Consider whether it is important to broadcast messages to many stations simultaneously.

- *Billing service.* Consider whether detailed call accounting is required or whether message charges are bulked to a user number.
- *Security.* Networks should offer password security and also should offer encryption and a private storage facility that can be unlocked only with an additional private code.
- *Closed user groups.* These are private networks within the network that are designated for the exclusive use of users who gain access only with proper authentication. They are used either for terminal-to-terminal communication or for privately accessed store-and-forward service.
- *Protocol conversion.* The network may support communication between terminals using unlike protocols.
- *Disconnect of idle stations.* This feature should be provided.
- *Abbreviated or mnemonic addressing.* May be provided, with the system generating the data network number from a simplified address.

Very Small Aperture Terminal

The most important factors in evaluating VSAT services are network availability and throughput. Availability varies by geographical region. Areas with heavy rainfall will be subjected to more outage than drier areas, and will have lower availability. MTTR is calculated on the same basis as discussed previously, and is affected by the distance of the terminal from the nearest repair center. Dial backup can be used to improve availability. Throughput is affected by how heavily loaded the channel is. Since stations are unable to hear signals of other stations, collisions will mutilate packets and require retransmission.

Capital Investment   Capital investment is a consideration in many networks. Some VSAT carriers will carry the entire investment, charging only for the service at a rate that is independent of distance.

Network Management Capability   Network management capability should cover not only the VSAT terminal equipment, but may also extend to the customer's equipment. To compete with frame relay carriers, which often offer management of the customer's router, VSAT vendors may provide the same service.

Network Capacity   The method of quoting transponder capacity varies with the VSAT carrier. A typical method of quoting rates is based on a dedicated in route (remote to hub) and a portion of an out route (hub to remote). The amount of capacity allocated to the customer will affect response time.

Interface Type   Interface type may range from interface with both Ethernet and token ring LANs to serial interfaces. The remote unit should be configurable over the network.

Hub Location   The hub location is important because it may affect the cost of the back-haul circuit to the customer's network. Some VSAT vendors can connect to nondistance-sensitive services such as frame relay for the back-haul circuit. The customer should also inquire about the degree of redundancy in the hub.

Protocol Support   The network should be capable of supporting multiple protocols. For time-sensitive protocols such as IP, the network should support spoofing.

CHAPTER 35

Frame Relay

$\mathbf{T}$he protocols and services we discussed in the last chapter are based on the assumption that data transmission lives in a hostile environment. Protocols such as packet switching carry on the error mitigation dialog between each pair of nodes. A packet can't advance until the receiving node pronounces it pure. Moreover, these protocols are based on the bandwidth of voice-grade circuits, which is not unreasonable. After all, 64 kb/s is a lot of bandwidth when users are sitting at terminals and pecking at keyboards. At 9600 b/s, a screen fills with ASCII characters far faster than anyone can read them, so these older protocols are quite satisfactory for yesterday's data communications environment.

In the late 1980s, several factors developed that rendered these older protocols and services inadequate for the new applications. The first was the rapid and dramatic shift of transmission facilities from analog cable and microwave to digital fiber optics. Error rates dropped by three or four orders of magnitude and wide digital bandwidths suddenly became feasible. No longer was it necessary to delay packets while each node checked for errors. The error rate on fiber is so low that it's easier to let the two ends of the circuit take care of error checking and retransmission.

The nature of applications has also changed to demand a new type of circuit. The bandwidth requirements on terminal-based applications are easy to calculate, but as local area networks, remote bridges, and routers became common, bandwidth requirements lost their predictability. A circuit linking a pair of LANs may sit unused until someone decides to move a massive file, and then we reach the classic trade-off between bandwidth and speed of download. Even docile applications like e-mail suddenly become bandwidth hogs when it's easy for users to attach files and voice and video clips. Even topology changes began to drive the need for a different service. A fully meshed network provides protection against circuit failure, but it requires circuits between each pair of nodes. As the number of nodes increases, circuit costs increase proportionately. With the old applications most of the traffic was headed for a central computer at headquarters, so the mesh configuration wasn't necessary. With today's applications such as voice, node-to-node traffic is more common.

FRAME RELAY TECHNOLOGY

The new network paradigm of bandwidth on demand between peer nodes over high-quality circuits demands a new network model. X.25 is on the right track, but its node-by-node error checking is unnecessary when only one bit out of a billion is in error. By eliminating the network layer functions of X.25, we are left with a network that is similar in topology, but one that has lower latency. A frame relay network allows the customer to feed data into an access node with the amount of bandwidth that the application requires. The frame relay network, which is usually depicted as a cloud, is actually a complex of high-speed circuits and backbone processors that are often ATM switches. As with X.25, the internal workings of the network are proprietary to the service provider. Consequently, each service provider specifies its own service level agreements and establishes its own policies for carrying or discarding traffic.

From a customer's standpoint, frame relay is a simple concept. Each location connects to the network over an access circuit. This can be obtained from an LEC, a CLEC, or an AAC. Access speeds up to T1/E1 are common. Some vendors offer T3/E3 access. Often, the access circuit can be bandwidth that is split from a T1/E1 circuit that is used to access the IXC's voice network. The access circuit is terminated on a router or a frame relay access device (FRAD). The customer selects a port speed, which establishes a ceiling on the transmission rate. The customer also requests a permanent virtual circuit (PVC) between points on the network. The PVC sustains a committed information rate (CIR) that establishes the guaranteed transmission rate. If the carrier has enough capacity, it allows the customer to send bursts up to the port speed, with frames above the CIR marked as discard eligible. If the network doesn't have the capacity, the carrier can discard frames and the customers' end points recognize the failure and arrange retransmission. Some carriers offer asymmetric PVCs in which the bandwidth is greater in one direction than the other.

Another difference between frame relay and other alternatives is the method of charging. Private line circuits are distance-sensitive, so the longer the connection, the more it costs. X.25 is not distance-sensitive, but most value-added networks charge by the kilopacket. The huge quantities of data that flow across an internet would render X.25 prohibitively expensive. Frame relay, by contrast, is not distance-sensitive. Instead of metering traffic, the pricing is based on capacity. Frame relay has three pricing elements:

♦ *Committed information rate.* The throughput the carrier guarantees will be transported.

◆ *Port speed.* The speed of the access port into the carrier's network. It is in multiples of 64 kb/s.

◆ *Access circuit.* The cost of the access circuit provided by the LEC or AAC. It ranges from 56 kb/s up to T1/E1 or multiples thereof. Some carriers offer T3/E3.

The prices of the CIR and port speed are both based on the bandwidth the customer selects. The access circuit is a dedicated private line from the customer's premises to the carrier's point of presence. As with other private lines, the cost of the access circuit is determined by its length.

The difference between the CIR and port speed is the key to frame relay's method of operation. If the carrier's backbone capacity permits, the network will transport data up to the port speed. This makes the service ideal for applications with bursty data because the network can carry the average data the applications require while handling short-term bursts up to the port speed. Customers can prioritize their traffic in some networks by marking their own discard-eligible frames. This way the customer can be sure the high-priority frames are not the ones that exceed the CIR.

The network service provider manages the internal network to avoid congestion and to statistically multiplex the traffic of its customers throughout the busy periods. Customers can take advantage of the nature of frame relay by scheduling operations that are not time-sensitive during off-peak hours. For example, large file transfers can be scheduled at night when the carrier's network has plenty of spare capacity, and even though many frames may be well above the CIR, the chance of discard is small.

A typical frame relay network might resemble the one in Figure 35-1. Customers contract with the carrier for permanent virtual circuits between end points. These are shown as dashed lines in the figure. Note that all locations feed into location A and that D and E also feed into location B. The need for node-to-node traffic is determined by the customer based on the amount and type of traffic. This type of network is typical of a headquarters with several branch offices. A network such as this is frequently used for e-mail and file transfers. Increasingly, companies are adding voice capabilities to the router or FRAD and using spare capacity to link branch offices to headquarters. In a network such as this, the branch offices use 56-kb/s access circuits with a low CIR; 16 kb/s is common, but some branches with higher traffic volume or priority would use a higher CIR. Some carriers offer a zero CIR, which can be acceptable for light applications such as e-mail. The access circuit and port speed at the headquarters location would be higher than the speeds at the branches. A 256-kb/s CIR would support several branch offices. Typically, a frame relay network costs from 25 to 50 percent less than an equivalent dedicated digital network. The cost difference depends on tariffs, distance of the nodes from the carrier's frame relay POP, and span of the network. The wider the network's span, the more attractive frame relay becomes because pricing is not distance-sensitive.

FIGURE 35-1

A Frame Relay Network (Access circuits and committed rates are shown in brackets.)

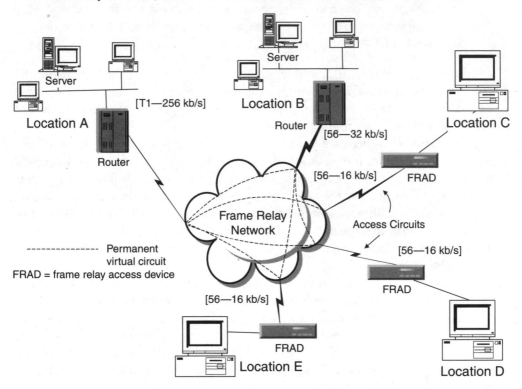

Frame relay is a robust service. The most likely point of failure is in the access circuits. Once the traffic reaches the carrier's backbone network, disruption is unlikely although not impossible. If the carrier loses a circuit or even a node, the traffic can be rerouted. To get the same degree of protection in a dedicated private line network would require full mesh architecture, which is too costly for many companies to justify. If all the traffic is destined for a single headquarters location, the access circuit and port speed for that location will need higher bandwidth and port speed than satellite locations. If satellite locations need to communicate with one another, they can communicate through the central location or they can set up virtual circuits between themselves. For light and occasional traffic, communicating through the central site is the most economical.

The major LECs offer frame relay in their serving areas. While court restrictions on providing long distance exist, LEC frame relay must connect to an IXC to bridge LATA boundaries. Their service areas may be further curtailed by exchange boundaries with independent telephone companies. Some LECs and IXCs have worked out network-to-network interface (NNI) arrangements to make the service-area boundaries transparent to the customer. In other cases dedicated circuit ex-

FIGURE 35-2

Frame Relay Frame Format

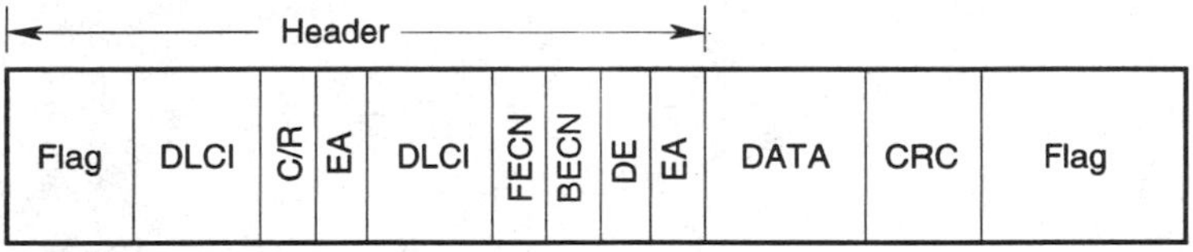

|←————————————— Header ——————————————→|

| Flag | DLCI | C/R | EA | DLCI | FECN | BECN | DE | EA | DATA | CRC | Flag |

DLCI = Data link connection identifier
EA = Address extension bit
C/R = Command/response bit
FECN = Forward explicit congestion notification
BECN = Backward explicit congestion notification
CRC = Cyclical redundancy check

tensions across exchange boundaries may be required. Most frame relay services offer both dedicated and dial-up access.

The Frame Relay Protocol

Frame relay is a connection-oriented service with a variable-length packet that can range as high as 4000 octets. Figure 35-2 shows the frame structure used by frame relay. Each frame has a 10-bit field known as the data-link connection identifier (DLCI), which identifies the connection. The 10-bit DLCI number theoretically yields 1024 connections, but the numbers 1–15 and 1008–1022 are reserved, and 1023 is used for local management interface, as discussed later. The DLCI can be expanded by two more octets, but this option is not often used. The DLCI is significant only between nodes, so the same DLCI number can be reused as shown in Figure 35-3. The combination of DLCIs forms the virtual circuit number. If the DLCI is not defined for a link, the frame is discarded. The protocol uses the frame check sequence block to review frame integrity. If the frame is in error, it is not corrected. It is discarded and left to higher-layer protocols to recover.

Congestion Control

The frame relay protocol allows the carriers to mark any frames over the CIR as discard-eligible. If the network becomes congested, the carrier buffers frames up to its buffer capacity. After the buffers are full, it can discard frames, which the end devices must detect and retransmit. A partial solution to buffer overflow is flow control, which both the frame relay switch and the router must support. The frame relay protocol includes forward explicit congestion notification (FECN) and backward explicit congestion notification (BECN) bits as a flow control mechanism. When frames begin to encounter congestion in the forward direction, the FECN bit is set. Downstream nodes detect the FECN bit and set the BECN bit in frames

FIGURE 35-3

DLCI Assignment in Frame Relay

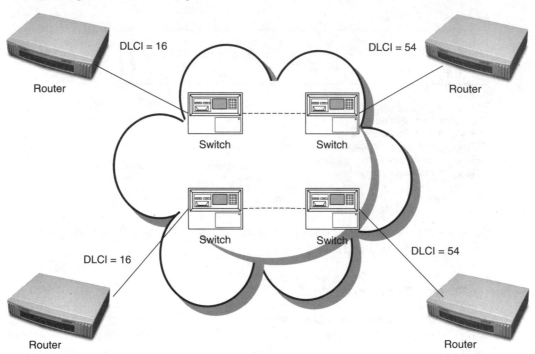

traveling in the opposite direction. If the router implements BECN, it slows the rate at which it is feeding frames into the network. Not all carriers and routers support FECN/BECN, however, so it is generally not an effective way of reducing congestion. As backbone networks become more heavily loaded, packet loss may become a problem.

Frame Relay Access

Frame relay users have a choice of using routers or FRADs for access to the network. A router is a versatile device that has the capability of routing packets to a variety of destinations based on address. A router also can handle multiple protocols. A FRAD, by contrast, is much less expensive than a router, but it has a single output port and is capable of handling only the frame relay protocol. A FRAD may be suitable for small offices that have a single connection into the frame relay network.

Quality of Service Measurement

Frame relay has several measurements of service quality that may or may not be specified by all service providers. The principal measurements and their abbreviations are

Committed rate measurement interval (T_c). The time increment used to measure information flow.

Committed burst size (B_c). The maximum number of bits the network will guarantee to deliver for the user measured over the interval T_c.

Excess burst size (B_e). The maximum number of bits the network will attempt to deliver for the user measured over the interval T_c.

Data delivery rate (throughput). The percentage of frames that are delivered per unit of time.

Availability. The percentage of time the network is available. Note that this figure should be measured end to end, which includes the access circuits on both ends of the connection.

End-to-end delay. The one-way time, in milliseconds, as measured by a router ping.

Local Management Interface

Some frame relay carriers implement LMI, which is a dedicated DLCI (1023) that is used for reporting connectivity status to the customer. If a DLCI is removed or lost for some reason, the LMI message reports the loss to the customer. LMI may also be used for sending congestion notification to the customer. The customer's router can poll the frame relay network to ensure that the PVC is active using the LMI protocol.

Network-to-Network Interface

Unlike the Internet, where practically all networks are interconnected by some means, frame relay networks are generally isolated. Some, but not all, carriers provide network-to-network interfaces (NNIs) between their networks. This means that a customer has little choice but to use the same carrier for all of its frame relay service unless it has one location of its own that connects to separate carriers to provide a bridge between them. Most of the LEC networks do provide NNI connections, if not with the major IXCs, at least to their own networks where the customer needs service across multiple LATAs. This situation will exist as long as the RBOCs are prohibited from transporting interLATA traffic.

Users need to review what provisions may be lost with NNI connections. Many of the features, such as LMI, usage reporting, congestion control, network management information, and the like, may be blocked at the NNI and provide less than a complete picture of network operations.

Switched Virtual Circuits

Although many carriers offer only permanent virtual circuits, switched virtual circuits are standardized by the Frame Relay Forum and are offered by some carriers.

SVCs are a good way of making any-to-any connections between organizations that offer dial-up access to a frame relay node. SVCs overcome some of the disadvantages of PVCs. Carriers' provisioning processes typically cannot respond quickly enough to meet customers' needs. Technically, the main difference between an SVC and a PVC is who sets up the circuit. Occasional connections between offices do not justify a PVC, but an SVC connection may be an effective way of enabling an occasional file transfer. SVCs are also effective for connections to multiple sites.

On the surface, it appears that SVCs would be an effective alternative to voice communications. In some cases, they may be, but many carriers charge per megabyte for SVCs. Therefore, switched virtual circuits may be effective only with highly compressed voice. Before using voice over SVCs, it pays to calculate the difference and cost compared to a telephone call. If the pricing is attractive, SVCs can enable a large organization to set up a fully connected network, that is, any location can connect to any other location. With PVCs, the cost of setting up this many virtual circuits is usually cost-prohibitive so that users route traffic through the main node.

VOICE OVER FRAME RELAY

Frame relay is a stable and predictable medium that is suitable for voice provided the carrier holds end-to-end delay and jitter within acceptable bounds. Some carriers provide separate service classes for delay-sensitive traffic. Sprint, for example, provides three classes of frame relay to support normal LAN applications, voice, and SNA. Each of these has progressively tighter delay specifications.

Users have several alternatives for connecting voice over frame relay. One of the most common is to use special routers or FRADs that are equipped to accept voice input in the form of tie lines, foreign exchange channels, or loop start trunks. The access device compresses the voice signal and packetizes it for transmission. Voice over frame relay can be cost-effective for companies that have enough traffic to justify the additional cost of the routers plus the equipment to terminate the voice channels on tie lines or other voice channel terminating equipment.

The primary caution when using voice over frame relay is to ensure that voice frames are not marked discard-eligible. This means that voice must be given priority over data traffic. If not enough bandwidth within the CIR is provided, data frames may experience excessive discard, which slows response time for users. Therefore, it is essential to provide a CIR that is high enough to accommodate all voice traffic at peaks plus enough to handle all data traffic that cannot be delayed. This additional cost reduces the cost-effectiveness of using voice over frame relay.

Support for fax and modem traffic is also an issue for some users. This traffic generally cannot be compressed because the terminal equipment has already compressed it to the maximum. Therefore, the equipment should be capable of recognizing fax and modem traffic and forwarding it without attempting to compress it further. The equipment should allocate enough bandwidth to a fax or modem signal to forward it at an appropriate rate.

FIGURE 35-4

Alternatives for SNA over Frame Relay

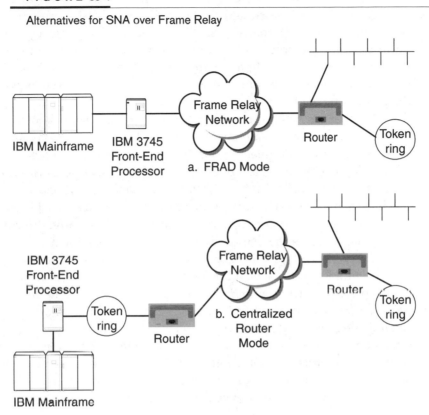

SNA OVER FRAME RELAY

The majority of large companies still run mission-critical applications over SNA networks. They also use desktop computers connected by LANs for access to the front-end processor. Since SNA is not a routable protocol, this raises the issue of whether to connect the enterprise with separate networks, one for business applications and the other for host computer applications, or to try to combine SNA and business traffic on a single network. The industry has developed two general approaches to enabling SNA to run over frame relay. In the first approach, known as the FRAD mode, the router or FRAD communicates directly with the front-end processor, as shown in Figure 35-4a. In the centralized router mode, shown in the Figure 35-4b, a router at the processing center is connected to the front-end processor through a LAN connection.

To send SDLC or LLC2 frames over a frame relay connection, the SDLC frames are encapsulated in a frame relay frame, which adds to the overhead. One technique for doing this is known as data-link switching (DLSw), which uses TCP/IP for transport. The DLSw protocol adds 52 octets of overhead to each frame, which is significant in applications with short data payloads.

DLSw blocks the frequent acknowledgement and synchronization frames that traverse an SDN network and it minimizes broadcast storms that sometimes characterize other alternatives. DLSw supports data compression, which can improve response time, and all protocols on the network can share the same PVC. The central router handles the traffic at the central site, so that the only traffic reaching the front-end processor is frames addressed to it, which reduces the processing load.

Another protocol for running SNA over frame relay is known as RFC 1490, which is also known as boundary network node (BNN). BNN is a standard developed by the Internet Engineering Task Force for encapsulating other protocols onto frame relay. RFC 1490 has less overhead than DLSw. It establishes a connection between the branch office and the host, which makes the response time more predictable than the less structured routing of IP packets used by DLSw. Note, however, that some DLSw products can encapsulate SNA traffic directly into frame relay, which reduces the overhead. A similar protocol known as boundary access node (BAN) uses the RFC 1490 specification for bridged token ring.

Several issues must be addressed in handling SNA over frame relay. One is the need for prioritization of SNA data so it isn't subjected to delay and discard. SNA can survive an occasional frame discard, but if the data is consistently exceeding the committed information rate, the SNA network may bog down under a condition of excess packet discard. The solution is to ensure that the routers recognize and prioritize packets containing SNA data. Another issue is end-to-end delay. SNA is designed for point-to-point networks that have minimum delay. If LLC2 frames encounter excessive delay, the session can be dropped.

APPLICATIONS

Frame relay has been accepted more rapidly than almost any service in existence. From the first meeting of the Frame Relay Forum in 1991, the service has developed from a curiosity that few people understood into the default protocol for most data applications. All router vendors support frame relay and the major IXCs offer the service both domestically and internationally.

Standards

The Frame Relay Forum, which is an industry group dedicated to promoting acceptance and implementation of frame relay, sets frame relay standards. The forum deals with such issues as quality of service considerations in voice over frame relay, interoperability with ATM, multiprotocol encapsulation, bonding multiple access channels, and binding frame relay and IP networks. The forum has four standing committees: Technical, Market Development, Intercarrier, and Interoperability and Testing. Table 35-1 lists the principal frame relay standards.

TABLE 35-1

Selected ITU Frame Relay Standards

LAPF	Link access procedure frame; frame relay data-link protocol
I.233	Frame architecture and relay service description
I.370	Congestion management
Q.922	Frame relay core aspects
Q.933	PVC management procedures and access signaling for SVCs

Evaluation Considerations

Frame relay services are not all equal. Each carrier publishes its own service level agreements and provides its combinations of CIR, access, and port speed. This section discusses some of the issues that should be evaluated when applying frame relay and selecting a carrier.

Access Circuit and Port Speed   Determine the required speed of the access circuit and port speed into the carrier's network. Determine if 56- or 64-kb/s service offers enough bandwidth or if T1/E1 or fractional T1/E1 is required at each location. Determine if access can be shared with some other service routed to the same carrier. For very high bandwidth applications, determine whether the carrier offers T3/E3 access speed.

Network-to-Network Connections   Some of the major IXCs and LECs have signed NNI agreements that make local access to IXC frame relay networks more economical. For example, a company with both inter- and intraLATA connections on the same network can often obtain local access circuits from the LEC's frame relay network at a lower cost than using dedicated line extensions. Note, however, that some features may be lost across the NNI. Inquire closely about service level reports and features between two carriers.

Point-of-Presence   The location of the carrier's POP is of concern to designers. In locations without a POP in the same city, the cost of the local access circuit can be high enough that frame relay is not cost-effective. If international service is required, determine what countries the carrier covers.

Committed Information Rate   Selection of the CIR is one of the most important factors in determining the success of frame relay. If the wrong choice is made initially, the carrier can change CIR in a short interval. Review the expected maximum data throughput requirement of your network and the times of day that bursts of data are likely to occur. Review how the carrier handles bursts over the CIR. Determine the degree to which they buffer or discard packets when congestion occurs.

Network Information   A major advantage of frame relay over fixed networks is the amount of network information the carrier provides. Determine what reports are available, how often they are produced, and how they are obtained. For example, does the carrier provide data online over the frame relay network?

Access Method   Determine whether frame relay access can be shared over existing T1/E1 lines, or if access can be obtained from LECs or AACs. Is dial-up access required in some locations, and if so, is it available from the carrier? Is X.25 access available? Determine whether a router or FRAD will be used as the access device.

Congestion Control   Does the carrier implement FECN and BECN to handle congestion? What method does the carrier use to set the discard-eligible bit on frames transmitted at a rate above the CIR? Does the carrier implement any discard prioritization? Discuss the conditions under which frames are discarded.

Service Level Agreement   What guarantees of availability does the carrier make? What is their guarantee of frame delivery within the CIR? What is the average end-to-end latency? How long does it take to reconfigure the PVC and CIR? The carrier should quote end-to-end availability and data delivery rate or throughput. If the carrier fails to meet its SLAs, what credits does it provide?

Local Management Interface   Some carriers have implemented LMI, which may be used to provide status information about the network. Determine whether the carrier has implemented LMI, and if so, what functions are available for such functions as automatically initiating restoral over the PSTN.

Automatic Dial Backup Initiation   The network should provide a reliable method to signal the customer's router of a loss of connectivity, including both loss of the link and end-to-end network connectivity through drop of LMI. Determine whether LMI is dropped if PVC connectivity is affected, caused either by the end nodes or any intermediate node in the network.

Disaster Recovery Plans   The carrier should have a clearly documented plan discussing what disaster conditions are covered and how the carrier minimizes the probability of lengthy service failure.

Service Alternatives   Does the carrier provide both SVC and PVC or only PVC? Is SVC service billed on connect time or quantity of data transferred? Does the carrier provide separate networks for time-sensitive applications such as voice and SNA?

Access Coordination   The carrier should coordinate access with the LECs in all locations. Most carriers provide total access coordination in which the carrier bills for the access circuit in addition to handling provisioning and trouble reports.

Backup PVC   Many frame relay carriers offer a backup PVC option so in case of failure, customer locations can be rerouted to an alternate site.

Excess Information Rate   Some carriers provide credits for information sent under the committed information rate. When frames exceed the CIR, the carrier checks to determine whether credits are available, and, if so, these excess information frames are sent without being marked as discard-eligible.

Frame Relay Access Devices

One of the first questions a manager encounters is whether to use a router or a FRAD for frame relay access. A router is a more versatile box. Generally, a FRAD sends data over only one route. The device must have large enough buffers to accommodate incoming data. The device should also have the ability to hold low-priority traffic in buffers while passing through high-priority traffic. If you plan to run voice over the frame network, a router must be able to support voice. Determine how many voice ports it provides.

Determine what protocols the device supports. Compare your requirements for LAN and WAN interfaces to the number that the device handles. Most routers can interface multiple Ethernet or token ring connections on the LAN side. They also will provide multiple WAN interfaces that automatically sync to the speed of the network. Determine whether the device supports legacy WAN networks. Determine what network management systems the device supports.

Backup and recovery in case of network failure are important considerations. Most routers and FRADs provide automatic dial backup over ISDN or the PSTN. Determine from the network vendor what variable initiates the backup. Determine whether backup can be initiated through LMI.

CHAPTER 36

Asynchronous Transfer Mode

So far in this book we have looked at a variety of networks and found them all less than ideal. Traditional TDM facilities have fixed bandwidth and do not scale well. Circuit switching offers high-quality service, but it's wasteful of bandwidth and is usually charged by the minute. Also, many applications do not lend themselves to circuit switching. Legacy data networks are designed for special-purpose applications and are not adaptable to time-sensitive applications such as voice and video. IP networks lack quality of service guarantees, and are not seamless between the local and the wide area. Networks such as frame relay are optimized for data and are limited in bandwidth. Wouldn't it be elegant to have a general-purpose network that could scale from the desktop to the wide area; carry voice, data, and video; deliver bandwidth on demand; and offer a guaranteed quality of service matching that of the circuit-switched network?

Such was the promise of asynchronous transfer mode (ATM). Although its original design intent was for the carrier backbone, designers planned to run it to the desktop so data could flow seamlessly from device to device without a media conversion, delivering whatever bandwidth and service quality the application and the network negotiated. That vision is still technically possible, but as with so many protocols, ATM has missed a large part of the market, and now appears to be relegated to the backbone. What happened? The answer is several things. First, ATM has proven to be unexpectedly complex and costly for a general-purpose protocol. Second, other alternatives have stolen a march on ATM. Ethernet switching and fast Ethernet have effectively captured the battle for the desktop. They are cheap, fast, and easy to implement, so much so that ATM to the desktop is all but abandoned, at least for now.

The next potential market is the building or campus backbone, where ATM should certainly prevail with its ability to scale to OC-3 at 155 Mb/s and on up to OC-12 at 622 Mb/s. The problem here again is cost and complexity. When this market was being developed, gigabit Ethernet was not on the horizon, but it gained acceptance even before the standards were complete. Gigabit Ethernet came on strong because of users' familiarity and its simplicity, which are two powerful arguments in its favor.

So what role does that leave for ATM? The answer is the carrier backbone, where ATM is alive and well. To be sure, it is threatened by enhancements to IP, but the standards for delivering quality on IP are still evolving, while quality of service (QoS) is inherent with ATM. Although protocols such as multiprotocol label switching (MPLS) are coming online to bring QoS to IP networks, their introduction is complex. Routers must be replaced or updated, and datagrams still flow over multiple hops. ATM can provide a shortcut between source and destination that eliminates many of the multihop drawbacks such as jitter.

With the backbone network in mind as its turf, let us turn to a high-level understanding of ATM, its method of operation, and its classes of service.

ATM TECHNOLOGY

The term "asynchronous" is overworked in telecommunications, and it is perhaps an unfortunate choice of terms for a protocol that started out to be broadband ISDN (B-ISDN). ISDN is also a misleading term, however, because it has connotations of circuit switching. While ATM can behave like circuit switching in that a call is set up across the network and enjoys high-quality service, ATM is not circuit switched. It is a form of switching, however, in that short PDUs, known as cells, find a switched path from source to destination.

In an ATM network, an information stream is segmented into cells that are 53 octets long. Each cell has a five-octet header and a 48-octet payload. Note that the header, which is shown in Figure 36-1, does not carry addresses of the source and destination. Instead, it carries a virtual path indicator (VPI) and a virtual channel indicator (VCI). These correspond to ATM's two types of circuits: virtual paths and virtual channels. Virtual channels are groups of channels between ATM devices, and virtual paths are groups of virtual channels.

Circuits are set up either by provisioning through the carrier to establish permanent virtual circuits (PVCs) or by switching and signaling to establish switched virtual circuits (SVCs). Virtual channel connections (VCCs) are concatenations of virtual channels to support an end-to-end connection. When the virtual circuit is defined, the VCC control assigns a VCI and a VPI. As the connection is set up through the switch serving a particular node, the switch must simply connect a VPI and VCI from an input port to a VPI and VCI from an output port of the switch. Figure 36-2 should help clarify this concept. The VPI is actually eight octets long, and the VCI is 16 octets instead of the two octets shown in the figure, but the principle is the same. The VPI and VCI are selected at the switch to keep track of the connections, and have no end-to-end significance.

F I G U R E 36-1

ATM Header

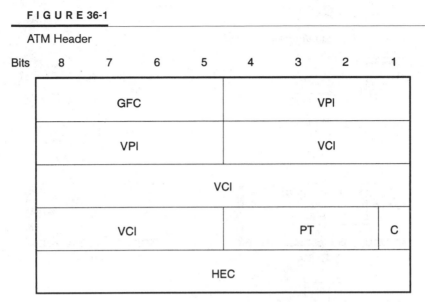

GFC = generic flow control
VPI = virtual path identifier
VCI = virtual channel identifier
PT = payload type
C = cell loss priority
HEC = header error control

ATM Switching Techniques

The next issue is how the connection is made through the switch. Two common methods are shared memory and a self-routing switch such as the banyan switch that is shown in Figure 36-3. A banyan switch is a two-state device that takes its name from the many branches of the banyan tree. The device switches a full cell at a time. The header finds a path through the switch, and the path remains intact for the transit time of the cell, after which it is torn down and reused. The header directs the packet through each of the bidirectional switching stages. A "1" in the header causes the switch to connect to the upper path and a "0" to the lower. The remainder of the cell follows the header through the path. Figure 36-3 shows a three-stage banyan switch, which can handle a 3-bit address. If two cells converge on the same output, one is buffered and sent through later. A banyan switch is fast and, therefore, ideally suited to switching the high speeds of ATM. It is also inexpensive and can be implemented easily in large-scale integration.

Shared memory switches connect input and output circuits through a large memory module. A shared access bus ties the input and output circuits to a single high-speed bus. If the speed of the bus is higher than the combined speed of the

FIGURE 36-2

Virtual Path and Virtual Circuit Indicators

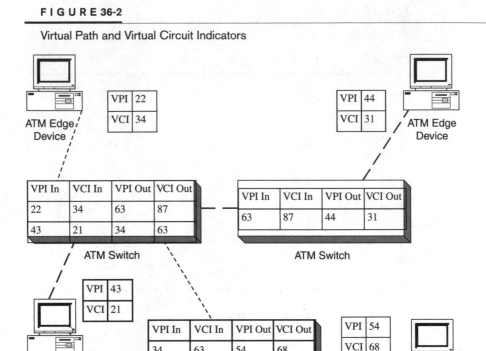

VPI = Virtual Path Indicator
VCI = Virtual Circuit Indicator

input circuits, cells can coexist without collision. Input circuits put cells on the bus with the address of the output port. All ports read the cell address, but only the destination port copies it.

Why ATM Is Asynchronous

The reason ATM is considered asynchronous is best understood by comparing cell flow to a synchronous protocol such as T1/E1. In a TDM circuit, data is multiplexed into time slots. Each time slot is assigned to its circuit in turn. If no information is being transferred, the time slot is empty. In ATM, the cells are multiplexed onto the physical facility, which is preferably, but not necessarily, SONET/SDH. Cells can occupy the capacity of the facility provided they live within the variables that the application and the network agree on when the connection is set up. This last statement indicates that ATM is a connection-oriented service. In this respect, it is analogous to the telephone network, and, in fact, it can

F I G U R E 36-3

A Banyan Switch

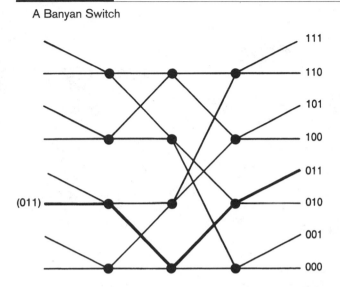

use the E.164 addressing scheme that ITU-T recommends for ISDN. It can also use a 20-byte address modeled after the OSI network service access point (NSAP) address. Addressing is discussed later.

Permanent and Switched Virtual Circuits

A PVC, whether implemented over ATM or another service, is analogous to a private line. It is set up or "provisioned" by the carrier and remains set up until disconnected by service order. An SVC is set up by the application, and is charged like a telephone call. In the time division–multiplexed world the same concepts of provisioning and switching apply, except that a digital private line is not switched through the same switching system that is used for switching calls. It is connected straight through the network from end to end. It may, however, connect through a digital cross-connect system (DCS), which is nothing more than a time division switch that establishes a permanent circuit through provisioning. Note that the circuit through a DCS is not virtual—it has dedicated time slots.

Rationale for the Short Cell

The reason for the short cell size in ATM networks isn't intuitively obvious. With 5 out of 53 octets devoted to the header, this represents almost a 10 percent overhead—as bad as ASCII transmission. Why not double or triple the payload to cut down on the amount of payload? In fact, there is nothing magic about 48 octets of payload. That cell size was arrived at through compromise, not through scientific

F I G U R E 36-4

Cell Size Alternatives

a. Variable-length cell

b. Fixed-length short cell

c. Fixed-length long cell

analysis. When ATM was being designed in the 1980s, the data faction wanted a payload size of 64 octets, while voice advocates held out for 32 octets. They split the difference. Nevertheless, both groups recognized the value of short cells of fixed length even though variable cell size is more efficient.

To understand the rationale for short cells, let's use a transportation analogy. Suppose we want to design a people mover to route various types of payloads from random sources to random destinations. (The automobile is such a device but not very efficient.) To design our system, we have a choice of using small-capacity vehicles, large-capacity vehicles, or vehicles of varying capacity. These are analogous to short payloads, long payloads, or variable-length payloads. One objective of our transportation system is to accommodate a wide variety of loads, ranging from people to freight. The freight obviously fits best in a large vehicle, but it can be boxed and spread across multiple carriers. The highway system consists of feeder routes and backbone routes over which any destination can be reached from any source. Some of the traffic is time-sensitive. Commuters, for example, cannot afford to be delayed, while shoppers, vacationers, and parcel post packages are willing to sacrifice some time predictability for lower cost.

Figure 36-4 shows what happens with the short payload, long payload, and variable payload scenarios. One of our objectives is to keep the backbone highways (the interstate) filled with traffic and to speed traffic along without delay. When delay is inevitable, another objective is that it be predictable and controllable.

Now assume the size of the payload and the speed of the vehicles are constant—completely independent of transportation. In Figure 36-4a the vehicles are of random length. This means that when a long vehicle is entering the backbone, we have to back up other vehicles that are attempting to enter by delaying or buffering other vehicles in the feeder roads. To carry the analogy a step further, it should be evident that it is much easier to calculate how much traffic to admit to the backbone if the vehicles are all the same physical lengths. In ATM this calculation or process can be done in hardware at a faster rate than it would be if it were necessary to read every header to determine the packet length.

It should be clear that it is easier to pack vehicles on the freeway with a constant speed and spacing if the vehicles are all exactly the same lengths, as in Figure 36-4b. But isn't it better to have a larger vehicle as in Figure 36-4c (that is, larger packet) than a smaller one simply because of the overhead involved in segmenting the payload, packing it into a cell for the journey, and unpacking it at the other end? If the payload is small, say one person per vehicle, a larger vehicle is less efficient than a small one because you are sending it out with a lot of empty space. If the payload is large—multiple people going to the same address—the large vehicle is more efficient. ATM is called upon to carry payloads of differing lengths.

In some cases the 48-octet payload is too long and in other cases it is too short so the data must be segmented. In any case, the efficiency of the media is improved by having short, predictable cell lengths. This is particularly important with video and voice transmissions where the cells must arrive with a constant amount of delay. The ATM protocol permits it to discard cells under congestion conditions, which makes the short cell more effective than a long one. Within limits, the cell loss can be tolerated for voice and video because either the lost data is insignificant from an intelligibility standpoint, or the end devices can process in information to make the loss transparent to the user.

ATM Protocol Layers

Like all modern protocols, ATM is a layered protocol, but greatly simplified compared to others. Figure 36-5 shows the logical layers of ATM. User applications communicate with the ATM adaptation layer (AAL). The AAL is divided into two sublayers, the segmentation and reassembly (SAR) and the convergence. The SAR is responsible for segmenting the user's data stream on outbound traffic and reassembling it inbound. The convergence sublayer protocols are different for the various types of information such as voice, video, and data. The AAL supports five different classes of traffic:

   ◆ Class A traffic is constant bit-rate, connection-oriented traffic such as voice and video. Timing between the source and destination is required.

FIGURE 36-5

ATM's Layered Architecture

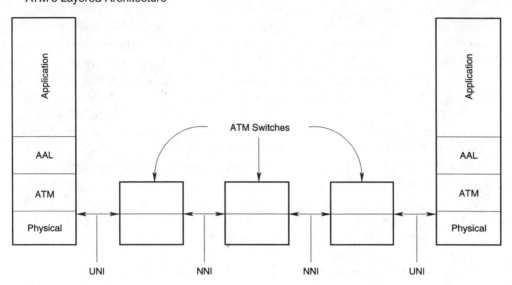

AAL = ATM adaptation layer
ATM = ATM layer
UNI = user network interface
NNI = network-to-network interface

◆ Class B traffic is variable bit-rate, connection-oriented traffic such as packet video. Timing between the source and destination is required.

◆ Class C traffic is variable bit-rate, connection-oriented traffic such as bursty data. A timing relationship between source and destination is not required.

◆ Class D traffic is variable bit-rate, connectionless traffic such as datagram services. Timing between the source and destination is not required.

◆ Class X allows user-defined traffic and timing relationships.

The protocol treats the different classes of traffic differently, which is the key to ATM's ability to handle mixed applications more effectively than other protocols. Voice and video experience constant delay, compared to class C and D data traffic, which does not require timing between source and destination. The various classes of service use different PDUs with different sized data blocks. Fields are robbed from the data block to perform such functions as sequencing, time stamping, and cyclical redundancy check of the data block. As discussed later, the header is always checked for errors.

The ATM layer moves traffic from the AAL to the switch. The user connects to the network through the user network interface (UNI). Two types of UNI are de-

F I G U R E 36-6

The ATM Layers

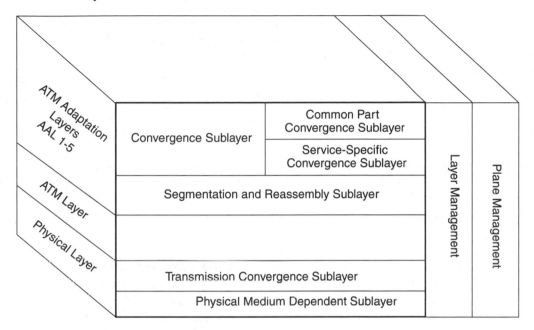

fined. A public UNI defines the interface between the user and a public ATM switch, and a private UNI defines the interface between the user and a private ATM switch. ATM switches interconnect through network-to-network interfaces (NNIs). The public NNI defines the interface between network nodes. Private network-to-network interface (PNNI) is a routing protocol that enables different manufacturers' ATM switches to be integrated into the same network. PNNI automates routing table generation, which enables any ATM switch to determine a path to another switch.

ATM uses a layered protocol that is shown in Figure 36-6. The physical layer is designed to operate over a variety of services such as DS1, DS3, SONET/SDH, fiber, twisted-pair, or even radio. The ATM layer multiplexes and demultiplexes cell streams onto the physical layer. It is media independent.

The ATM adaptation layer recognizes that different classes of traffic have different bit rates, and provides for four classes: constant bit rate (CBR), variable bit rate (VBR), available bit rate (ABR), and unspecified bit rate (UBR). CBR is the highest class of service, providing the ATM equivalent of a T1 or T3 private line. It is connection-oriented and designed for time-sensitive applications such as voice and video. VBR is also connection-oriented, and is designed for any application, such as LAN interconnection and frame relay, that requires a variable amount of bandwidth. ABR is offered as a discounted service to take advantage of the bandwidth that is left over after CBR and VBR traffic have been accommodated. Figure 36-7 illustrates the

F I G U R E 36-7

Utilization of Network Capacity

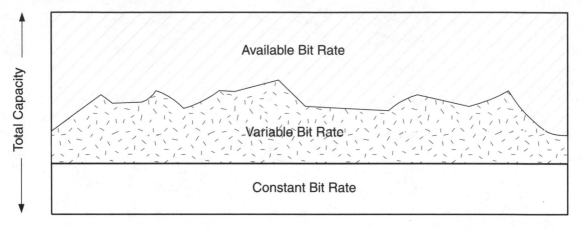

concept. Here, the solid block at the bottom of the figure represents traffic the network is committed to handling, and which requires a constant amount of bandwidth. Above it is VBR traffic that the network is also committed to handle, but which varies because of the nature of the application. The bandwidth left over is available, and can be provided at a lower cost because it does not involve a firm commitment from the carrier that it will be delivered with a specified amount of delay.

UBR is a laissez-faire class of service providing best-effort delivery. It is less complex to set up than the other service classes, and is therefore often what the carrier provides. It does not have the guaranteed QoS of CBR and VBR service, and cannot be depended upon for these applications.

Corresponding to traffic classifications, the AAL is divided into four categories. AAL-1 is designed to meet class A service requirements. It is intended for video, voice, and other constant bit-rate traffic. AAL-2 is for class B requirements. AAL-3/4 is for connectionless data service. AAL-5 is for data communications, including services such as frame relay, LAN emulation (LANE), and multiprotocol over ATM (MPOA). The AAL service differentiation is not used to support QoS. It is actually used only between the end systems. QoS is not based on the AAL designation of the cells. The user determines what QoS is required and informs the carrier. The AAL layer allows the network to provide different classes of service to meet the requirements of different types of traffic.

ATM Call Processing

When an ATM connection is set up, the calling station asks for a connection to the called station. The calling station and the network negotiate bandwidth and QoS classifications, whereby the ATM network provides the QoS and the station promises not to exceed the requirements that were set up during the establishment of the connection. Traffic management takes care of providing the users with the QoS they requested, and enables the network to recover from congestion.

Calls are established under ATM with a setup message that contains a call reference number, addresses of called and calling parties, traffic characteristics, and a QoS indicator. The destination returns a call-proceeding message that contains the same call reference number plus a VPI/VCI identifier. A series of setup and call-proceeding messages are exchanged while the network determines such matters as whether the called party is willing to accept the call. Public networks use an addressing system of up to 15 digits following E.164 standards. Private networks use a 20-octet address modeled after OSI NSAP addressing.

Cells flow through an ATM network based on the VCI and VPI identifiers contained in the header. A virtual path can be thought of as bundle of virtual channels, with each bundle having the same end points. To avoid long setup time by the carrier, the user can contract for a virtual path between end points, after which virtual channels can be set up within the path without placing service orders with the carrier.

The generic flow control (GFC) field, which is currently undefined, will be used for flow control on the UNI interface. It is not used with NNI. The payload type (PT) indicator identifies the type of traffic the cell contains. This field is also used to carry congestion information to the receiving end of the connection. The cell-loss priority indicator notifies the network if the cell is subject to being discarded. Cells that are transmitted in violation of the traffic management contract or cells with a low quality of service can be discarded.

The header error control (HEC) field in the header is a combination cyclical redundancy check and forward error-correction field. If the header experiences a single bit error, the HEC field can correct it. In case of multiple bit errors, the cell is discarded. Data applications detect the cell loss with end-to-end error correction. Voice and video applications do not detect the lost cell, and are minimally affected by it.

LAN EMULATION

ATM was designed as an end-to-end protocol that accepts a data stream from the source and delivers it to the destination. As the demand has developed, however, ATM has become a backbone between frame-based networks. IP networks are connectionless, and use an addressing scheme that is either a hardware-based MAC address, or a hierarchical software address such as IP or IPX. It is evident that the transition from frame-based networks to ATM is anything but seamless. Some method is needed for mapping IP addresses onto ATM addresses or VCIs. The industry has two techniques for accomplishing this. The Internet Engineering Task Force (IETF) developed the classical IP over ATM specification. The ATM Forum developed the LAN emulation (LANE) specification.

LANE enables an ATM network to act as a LAN backbone for hubs, switches, and routers that are acting as bridges. LANE enables the establishment of VLANs with an ATM backbone. It functions by using a LAN emulation server to translate MAC addresses into ATM addresses. The LANE address resolution operation binds the MAC address with the physical address of the ATM port. A broadcast and unknown server (BUKS) sends broadcasts to all devices within an emulated LAN to locate unknown stations.

The LAN emulation configuration server (LECS) contains tables on the VLANs to which the end station can belong. Many connectionless networks, such as Ethernet, use address resolution protocol (ARP) to locate other stations on the network. ARP was designed for a connectionless network. To place a connection-oriented ATM station on the network, the capability of broadcasting to all stations is lost, so LANE allows end systems to map the MAC address to ATM addresses. LANE has no capability for communicating a request for different QoS, so it cannot use this capability of ATM.

Multiprotocol over ATM

LANE operates at the data-link layer, and therefore enables ATM to operate as a bridge between LANs. The ATM Forum's multiple protocol over ATM (MPOA), which is in progress at this writing, operates at the network layer to enable routed networks to take advantage of ATM's low latency and scalability. MPOA is a standard protocol that the industry refers to as layer 3 switching; it is similar to proprietary protocols such as Ipsilon's IP switching and Cisco's tag switching. The objective of MPOA is to identify a flow between two network end points and affix a label to it that can be directly tied to an ATM virtual circuit. The network nodes, then, can forward packets based on labels rather than on IP address. The labels can be VCIs or frame relay DLCIs. Each flow is related to a specific path through the network that makes IP behave as if it were connection-oriented. In effect, MPOA assigns a flow between end points to a tunnel through the network. Since it reduces router hops and processing, the routers can handle significantly more throughput and networks can behave in a more predictable manner.

MPOA assigns two functions to the router. The host functional group deals with direct communication to the end-user devices. The edge device functional group deals with functions such as virtual circuit mapping, route determination, and packet forwarding. A protocol known as next hop resolution protocol (NHRP) enables routers to determine IP to ATM address mappings so the edge device can establish a shortcut path to the destination. This limits router processing and improves performance.

MPOA consists of three components:

- ◆ Route servers, which perform the routing function for hosts and edge devices. The route server appears to other routers in the network to be a normal router, but it connects the session to an ATM virtual circuit. The route server can be embedded in the ATM switch.

◆ Edge devices connect traditional LANs to the MPOA network. They can forward packets between LAN and ATM interfaces.

◆ ATM hosts are MPOA-enhanced LANE hosts that are directly connected to the MPOA network.

MPOA allows layer 3 protocols to communicate across an ATM network without using routers. The network handles the routing function. The MPOA function can be compared to the way toll-free calls are handled in the voice network. When a user places a toll-free call, the end office does not know the location of the toll-free number. Instead, it sends a query message over the SS7 network to the SCP to determine the directory number corresponding to the toll-free number. In MPOA the SCP function is handled in the route server.

MPOA is in many ways similar to LANE. At start-up time, devices contact a configuration server that knows which devices are assigned to virtual networks. As devices are turned on to connect with the network, they register themselves with their servers so they can acquire address information and begin communicating. MPOA maps network layer addresses to ATM addresses.

APPLICATIONS

Although the predominant use of ATM is for carrier backbones, it is also used as a LAN backbone for large users. Routers can be configured with an ATM backbone, a configuration that will become more prominent as voice and video are fed over high-speed routers. This section discusses standards and some of the considerations in implementing ATM in a private network.

Standards

The ATM Forum, which is a consortium of interested parties—including manufacturers, users, LEC/PTTs, and others—develops ATM standards, which ITU-T publishes. ATM standards are nearing completion, but development work remains to be done. Readers can keep touch with the latest developments in ATM by reviewing the notes and publications in both the ATM Forum's and the ITU-T Web pages, the addresses of which may be found in Appendix A.

Table 36-1 shows a correlation between service definitions used by ITU-T and the ATM Forum.

Evaluating ATM Services

In choosing an ATM carrier, here are some considerations:

◆ Does the carrier offer both PVC and SVC? Is the charging based on usage, bandwidth, connect time, or some other standard?

◆ Can the carrier provide the necessary bandwidth? Can it handle peaks in compliance with the service agreement?

T A B L E   36–1

Correlation between ITU-T and ATM Forum Services

ATM Forum	ITU-T I.371
ATM service category	ATM transfer capability
Constant bit rate (CBR)	Deterministic bit rate (DBR)
Available bit rate (ABR)	Available bit rate (ABR)
Unspecified bit rate (UBR)	Not defined
Real-time variable bit rate (RT-VBR)	Not defined
Nonreal-time variable bit rate (NRT-VBR)	Statistical bit rate (SBR)
Not defined	ATM block transfer (ABT)

- What are the bandwidth increments? Does the carrier offer inverse multiplexing to increase the bandwidth?
- Which of the four service classes does the carrier support?
- Are volume and term pricing available?
- What is the carrier's geographic coverage?
- Can you internetwork between ATM and frame relay?
- What kinds of network management reports does the carrier provide?
- Does the carrier support MPOA? PNNI?
- What can you expect with respect to end-to-end delay, delay variation, cell-loss ratio, and other such QoS measurements? How does the carrier measure the service, and what kinds of quality reports does the user receive?

Addressing procedures and policies are also important to consider when selecting a carrier. Unlike the voice network, number portability is not implemented with ATM. Some considerations, which are not unlike the kind of problems you have with DID numbers, include:

- Will the carrier give you an address base large enough to support anticipated growth?
- Can you get a contiguous range of numbers?
- If you change carriers, will you have to give back the numbers?
- What happens if you have an address conflict with an adjoining network?

Evaluating ATM Equipment

Queue management is one of the primary factors distinguishing products on the market. Determine whether a switch is blocking or nonblocking (nonblocking means the switching fabric can handle the capacity of all the input ports without cell loss). Look also at scalability and upgradability. Is the switch capable of keeping pace with changes in ATM technology? What kind of switching architecture does it use—shared memory or self-routing? How does it handle output link contention?

- Look at bandwidth scalability. For example, can you upgrade a DS-1 link to an OC-12 link, and does this require rebooting the switch? In other words, can you add bandwidth without disrupting other services?

- Ease of setup is important and one of the distinguishing factors among products. Determine whether the equipment can be set up for all classes of operation from UBR to CBR.

- Interoperability will be important if the equipment is not all furnished by the same manufacturer. Insist on demonstrated interoperability of all required features from the network interface cards through the network of switches.

- Determine the degree of fault tolerance the equipment has. Are critical components such as processors and power supplies redundant? Are modules hot-swappable?

- How do the switches handle congestion? If congestion occurs, can the switch distinguish between high-priority traffic, such as video, and give it priority over traffic, such as data, that can be discarded with less penalty?

- What is the process for rerouting around trouble? Does it implement PNNI to reroute around failures or congestion?

- What management tools are provided? Is the equipment SNMP-compatible?

CHAPTER 37

Internetworking

The Internet, which was a dim concept to most people only a few years ago, has become a household word. Schoolchildren access information worldwide on the Internet, businesses use it to keep in touch with customers and branch offices, and families use it as a source of entertainment. The Internet is reshaping society in a major way. This chapter is not, however, about the Internet; it is about internets, the LAN interconnections that have become the glue binding together departments, branch offices, and work-at-home employees. In earlier chapters we have discussed the building blocks: the LANs, routers, bridges, switches, hubs, and protocols. This chapter discusses how these are connected to form an internet.

The older networks, assembled from fixed circuits, modems, controllers, multiplexers, and the like, were better behaved than today's internets. The traffic volumes were predictable within a reasonable range, and the origins and destinations were more or less fixed. Design algorithms made the process of network configuration routine, and network performance could be modeled mathematically.

Internets, like the LANs they connect, don't behave so predictably. It's impossible to predict when a user somewhere on the network will decide to move a multimegabit file. It's also difficult to determine when relationships will change and what effect the changes will have on traffic patterns. This leads to the need for network probes, protocol analyzers, and network management systems, which are the subjects of Chapter 39.

On the brighter side, however, just as internets need more flexibility, they are easier to reconfigure than the older hierarchical networks. Network management tools provide more visibility into the network than older systems did. The old paradigms about circuit types and cost are also changing to simplify things. Fixed analog and digital circuit costs increase with bandwidth and distance. Except for the access circuits, frame relay and ATM are distance-insensitive and provide variable bandwidth within the limits of the access ports.

Internets have the following objectives:

- Provide adequate bandwidth in a scalable fashion between nodes to meet the demands of internodal traffic.
- Provide multiple paths so the network is robust enough to survive individual circuit failures.
- Maintain a high level of network availability.
- Prevent unauthorized stations from accessing the network.
- Keep facilities at a high level of utilization consistent with service level and affordable cost.
- Provide a flexible structure that is easy to administer, maintain, and troubleshoot.
- Preserve investment in existing resources such as NICs, hubs, and other devices.
- Obtain information that can be used for evaluating service and sizing and reconfiguring the network.

As with all networks, the results are affected by the architecture, the quality of the equipment, the administrative structure, and the accuracy of the information that went into the design. The design, in turn, is heavily influenced by the applications. In this chapter, we will focus on bringing these elements together into an internet design.

THE INTERNET DESIGN PROBLEM

When LANs first rose to prominence, the applications were, within reasonable limits, predictable. Applications such as word processing, database, and spreadsheets communicate with the file and print server. By knowing something of the users, the amount of traffic could be estimated and the size of the segment could be adjusted accordingly.

Conventional database applications were, and remain, a wild card in network design. If the database runs on the workstation, the file server delivers the database across the network to the workstation where the actual work of file searches and updates is done. A few stations working in this mode can overload the network. The solution is a client-server type of application in which the client, which runs on the workstation, requests the search, but the search is actually done on the server. The server delivers the results of the search to the client, sending only a few kilobits instead of megabit-sized files. With a client-server database, the network again returns to predictability—until peer-to-peer applications emerge.

Peer applications such as desktop videoconferencing and voice over IP again throw the network into a chaotic situation for the network manager. When groups of workstations can begin to communicate within and between segments, the network load increases and the route is unpredictable. Furthermore, groups of stations that were once generating a modest traffic volume can suddenly begin dumping multimegabit traffic on the network. Not only is the amount of bandwidth required by these stations important but they also need a predictable grade of service. A few discarded or delayed packets can be tolerated in conventional data applications—the user sees them as delay, which is tolerable, within limits. Delay and jitter impair time-sensitive applications such as video, however, to the point that they become unusable.

Some of the chaos can be controlled. Network designers can place servers strategically so their traffic remains on their segment, and stays off the backbone. Other applications, however, e-mail for example, are inherently centralized for a workgroup or even the enterprise. In its conventional mode e-mail is modest in terms of bandwidth demands, but e-mail packages permit users to add voice and video clips, which suddenly consume bandwidth in an unprecedented and unpredictable manner. The same is happening to other docile applications such as word processing and spreadsheets, which can be annotated with voice notes. Even when the database is tamed with client-server architecture, the addition of images can make even simple screens consume vast amounts of bandwidth. In Chapters 33 to 36 we discussed the broadband facilities that enable the network to handle these bandwidths. In this chapter we will discuss the architectures and equipment that feed these networks.

INTERNET ARCHITECTURES

When the collision lights begin to wink too often in an Ethernet or if the network begins to show signs of congestion such as slow response time, a logical solution is to segment the network, a process that requires finding the high users and what devices they communicate with. Segmenting or subnetting isn't always an effective strategy, however, because everyone on a segment may be aiming for the same server, and breaking the network in two doesn't reduce traffic. A handful of users may be accessing the server heavily and contributing to its congestion, a situation that isn't easily solved by installing a bridge. One approach is to bump the network speed, but this can be expensive because it requires replacing the NICs and hubs, and in some cases the cabling. The fastest and least expensive solution may be to use a switch, which we will discuss later.

Segmentation with Bridges

Segmentation with inexpensive bridges, as shown in Figure 37-1, works on small networks, but bridges have limitations. As the network is further segmented, segments handling transit traffic can become overloaded. The only way a device on segment A can communicate with a device on segment C, for example, is to transit segment B, which adds to the load on B. A bridge can be added between segments A and C, but that provides two potential paths between them, a situation that

FIGURE 37-1

Bridging between Segments

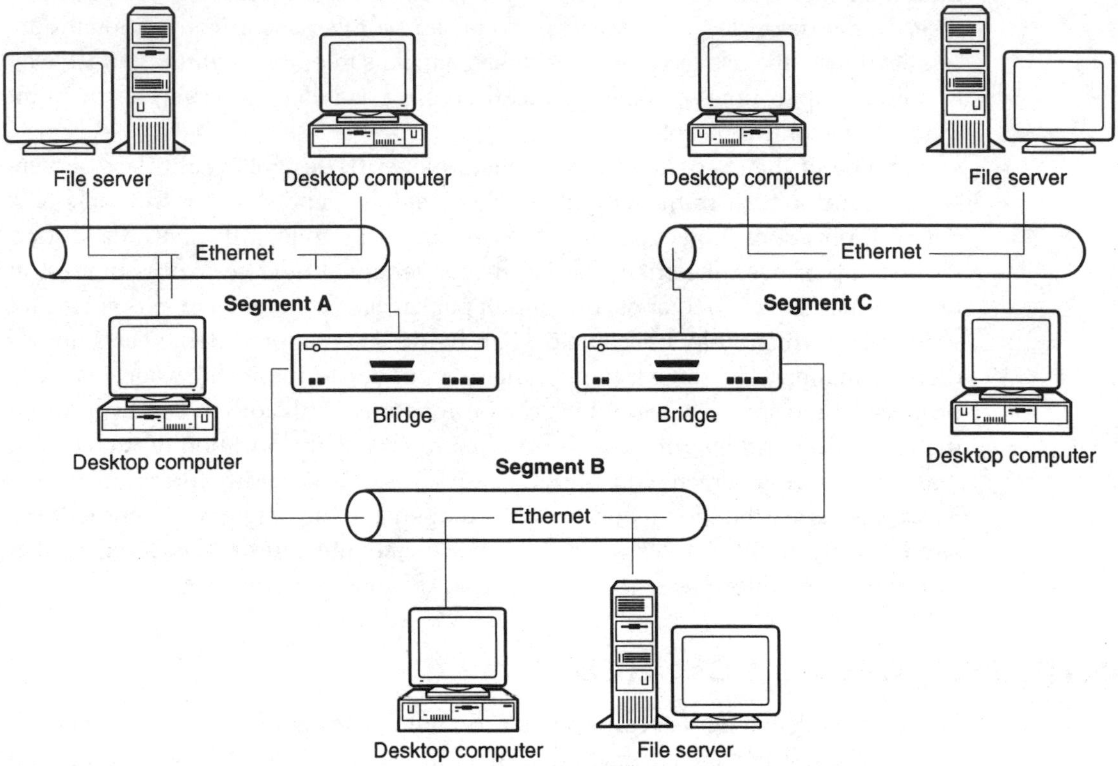

bridges cannot handle because they lack routing capability. The spanning tree algorithm allows the network administrator to define two paths across bridges to provide redundancy, but only one path must be active with the other on standby. In the spanning tree algorithm, bridges exchange information to establish a subnet that contains no loops, but which links the LANs. If one bridge fails, the standby bridge takes over. Token ring networks often use source routing, in which a route discovery process is used to develop a single path through the network. With source routing, the bridges exchange messages to establish a route from source to destination.

Segmentation with Routers

A typical solution for bridges' shortcomings is to substitute routers. These devices, operating at the network layer, contain route information in addition to addresses. With routers connected between all three segments, as shown in Figure 37-2, segment A can reach segment C by either of the two paths. As the network continues

FIGURE 37-2

Routing between Segments

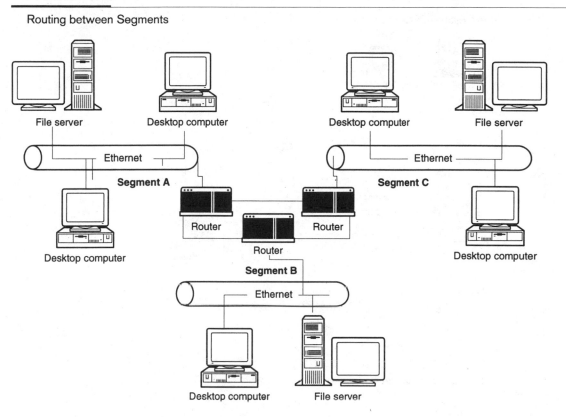

to grow, however, the router connections become complex. If they use public networks for the connection, they can be expensive as well. In a simple configuration, such as Figure 37-2, only three circuits are required for complete connectivity. As routers are added, however, the number of circuits grows, which means that one or more routers must be configured to handle transit traffic. A good solution, as discussed in Chapter 35, is to use frame relay. Each router then has a single direct connection into the carrier's frame relay network and nodes can be added by adding an access circuit and PVCs to the appropriate stations.

If the network consists of multiple segments carrying a significant amount of traffic, the routers may be connected using a high-speed backbone such as FDDI or ATM. The routers are designed with Ethernet or token ring connections at the LAN and a high-speed connection on the backbone. If the physical layout is such that all three networks can be terminated in a central location, the network can use a multi-port router to form a *collapsed backbone*. Figure 37-3 shows a collapsed backbone in which all the segments attach to a single router, with the router's backplane acting as the backbone. The collapsed backbone introduces a single point of failure, which may be mitigated by equipping routers with redundancy.

FIGURE 37-3

Collapsed Backbone Internet

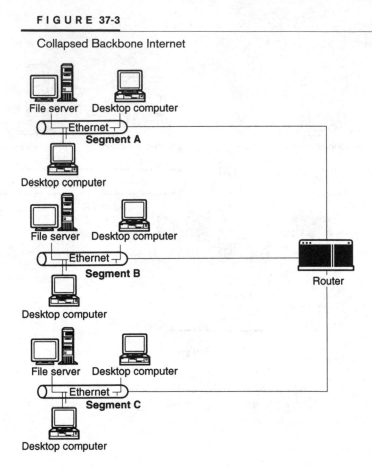

Segmentation with Switches

The network managers in many companies must cope with frequent rearrangements. Organizations may split and centers of interests may shift, but the workstation users' locations do not change. Conversely, users may move, but their community of interest does not change, which means more load on the router backbone. Port switching hubs make it possible to assign users to any segment regardless of location. A *port switching hub* is a chassis that has a backplane with multiple segments. Any port can be assigned to any segment, which offers the advantage of improved port utilization. Without port switching, if all users in a single card in the hub must be assigned to the same segment, some ports will necessarily go unused. The downside to this segmentation is that the more segments created, the more routers or bridges needed to interconnect them.

An increasingly important variation is the Ethernet switch, which is, in effect, a multiport bridge. It reads the destination MAC addresses of incoming frames, determines which segment the node resides on, and forwards the frame to the appropriate port. If the address of a frame is on the same segment, the switch ignores it. If the switch doesn't know where the destination address is, it forwards the frame to all ports and learns the addresses as it goes. As Figure 37-4 shows, the switch ports can carry traffic from a segment, or stations can have exclusive ports if they need the bandwidth. In the extreme case each device on the network can have the full wire-speed bandwidth, with the switch eliminating collisions.

The switching fabric is usually some type of shared memory. Unlike conventional bridges, which read and store the entire frame before forwarding it, some Ethernet switches use a cut-through technique to speed throughput. As soon as the switch has read the destination address, it connects the frame through to the destination port so the frame header is leaving the switch before the CRC enters it. As a result, the switch does no integrity checking of the frame, which means that invalid frames such as runts and jabbers are propagated through the network. Buffered switches read the entire frame and connect it through after they have verified its validity. Buffered switches filter out invalid frames but at the price of lower throughput. Without invalid frames, the cut-through technique substantially reduces latency, but it can propagate bad packets and collisions through the network.

A conventional Ethernet switch opens the way for the virtual LAN. A virtual LAN provides each user with a connection to a switch hub, which enables users to be assigned to the same workgroup without regard to their physical location. The network manager defines the LAN segment by grouping a number of ports together as a logical unit. Users can move physically without the need to change IP addresses.

Switching is not confined to Ethernet. Token ring switches, while less common than Ethernet switches, are also available, and offer the same advantages.

BACKBONE NETWORKS

As the network grows, the number of LAN segments and the amount of traffic between them increases to the point that a backbone network is needed. Backbones can be constructed from high-speed shared-media network, such as FDDI, or they can be composed of switching products such as Ethernet and token ring switches or ATM. In this section we will examine the ways of deploying a backbone network and the pros and cons of the different alternatives.

Distributed Router Backbone

As networks grow, a common design is to install a high-speed backbone. FDDI is a popular protocol for the purpose, with gigabit Ethernet and ATM following on rapidly. Figure 37-5 shows the layout of Ethernets connected by an FDDI backbone. In a simple network such as the one shown in Figure 37-5, this architecture works well. It is robust: the failure of a single router affects only that segment, provided the FDDI ring bypasses the failed device. Its main drawback is that traffic between

F I G U R E 37-4

Switched Ethernet Backbone

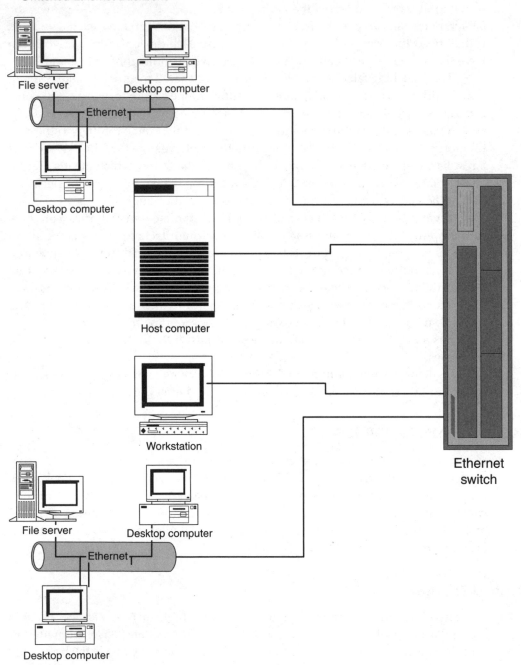

File server

Desktop computer

Ethernet

Desktop computer

Host computer

Workstation

Ethernet switch

File server

Desktop computer

Ethernet

Desktop computer

FIGURE 37-5

Distributed Router Backbone

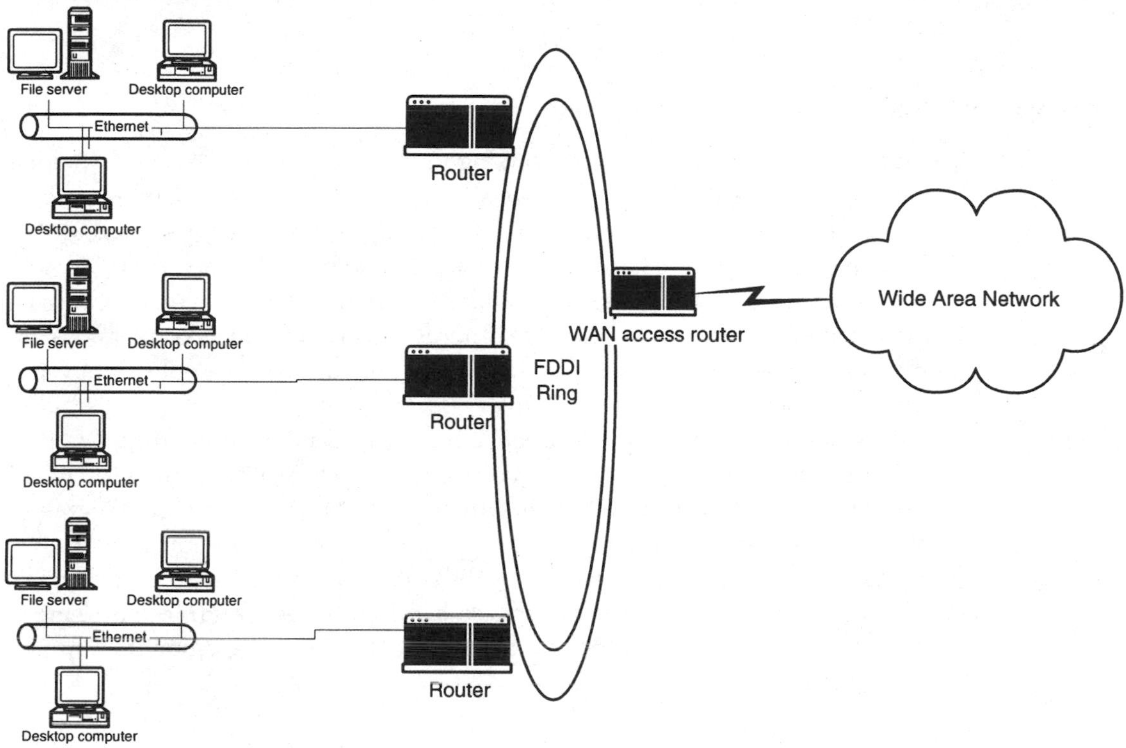

segments passes through at least two routers. The routers must convert the back-bone protocol to Ethernet for every packet that crosses the backbone, which takes a finite period of time. The latency of two routers is usually acceptable, but as the network expands into multiple rings, the number of routers increases as does la-tency. If the distances between stations permit, gigabit Ethernet eliminates the pro-tocol conversions between segments.

A second drawback of this architecture is the difficulty of rearranging sta-tions. If a station moves from segment A to segment B, a change of IP address is needed. The virtual LAN concept does not work well with this architecture be-cause traffic on the backbone increases to the point that it may become overloaded. Even though 100-Mb/s FDDI has considerable bandwidth, overloads with some applications are inevitable. Substituting an ATM backbone for FDDI increases the bandwidth to 155 Mb/s or more, but current ATM devices are significantly more expensive than FDDI, which in itself is not cheap.

A third drawback is the lack of scalability. As more segments are added, the load on the backbone increases to the point that parallel backbones are required.

Multiple routers also increase network management complexity. With routers distributed throughout the building, additional effort is required to monitor status, distribute software upgrades, keep routing tables updated, and other such administrative tasks.

Collapsed Backbone

The latency problems caused by traversing multiple routers can be solved with a collapsed backbone, as shown in Figure 37-3, but at the expense of a more powerful router. The LAN segments are brought to multiple ports in a high-speed router, usually over fiber optics. This configuration is less expensive than an FDDI backbone because the expense of the FDDI nodes is eliminated. It is faster than the distributed router architecture because the Ethernet-to-FDDI protocol conversions are eliminated. Management is easier on this type of network because only a single device must be monitored.

It is not as robust as an FDDI backbone, however, because a router failure can disrupt the entire network. By contrast, the self-healing nature of FDDI makes it less likely that a single failure will do more than isolate a single segment. Availability can be improved by using redundant processors and power supplies. As with the multirouter backbone, the collapsed backbone does not lend itself well to a virtual LAN. The backplane bandwidth is enough in many high-performance routers, but moving stations logically between segments requires changing the IP address.

Switched Backbone

If a switch is substituted for the router in Figure 37-3, the switched network shown in Figure 37-4 results. Each port on the network has a full wire-speed bandwidth, which can be dedicated to a segment or a station as the need dictates. Collisions are eliminated, and a significant increase in capacity for moderate cost is the result. Stations can be assigned to any LAN segment to create a VLAN, which simplifies rearrangements. The performance of such a network is excellent. The switch backplane is constructed with plenty of bandwidth to handle that required for all the ports transmitting simultaneously. This architecture is excellent for peer-to-peer traffic such as videoconferencing, but if all the traffic is sent to a server, the bandwidth of the server port may not be enough to carry the traffic volume. The solution may be ports supporting fast or gigabit Ethernet.

Despite its economy and bandwidth advantages, switching introduces some challenges for the network manager. The main drawback is network management. Network management systems (Chapter 39) can see individual segments, but systems to monitor all segments simultaneously have not been developed at this writing. Virtual LANs, for all their advantages, are not a standard application, so interoperability between products may be limited.

Choice of Internetworking Facilities

The primary factor affecting the choice of backbone is the proximity of the workstations. Where all LAN segments are located in the same building, cabling between them, usually with fiber, is inexpensive. In this case a collapsed backbone terminating in a switch is usually the least expensive and offers the greatest performance. Ethernet switches can be equipped with fast Ethernet or gigabit Ethernet ports, which provide plenty of bandwidth for most backbones.

A second important factor in the choice of backbone is the amount of traffic flowing between segments. If the traffic is mostly confined within the segment, a slower-speed backbone is sufficient. When the segments are located in different buildings as in a campus environment, some form of switched or shared media backbone is usually warranted. FDDI is an effective medium, although it may be too slow for some applications. When the users begin to employ multimedia applications such as desktop video, the traffic is likely to flow across the backbone, and considerable bandwidth may be needed. In this case ATM will probably be required. ATM switches can be connected with fiber optics to offer OC-12 backbones (622 Mb/s) or higher. If pathway space permits, point-to-point fiber can be installed between buildings and terminated in a collapsed backbone, but the service protection is not as great.

When the distance between segments extends into the metropolitan area and on into the wide area, some of the technologies discussed in Chapters 33 to 36 will be required. SMDS is available in some metropolitan areas, and is a cost-effective solution in some cases. Most LECs offer frame relay, which is also an effective solution up to T1/E1 bandwidths. Frame relay is also effective in the wide area, and, as discussed in Chapter 31, a VPN may be cost-effective, particularly to branch offices where bandwidth requirements are modest.

APPLICATIONS

The trade press has been predicting that switching will ultimately replace routing as the preferred means of connecting internets. In the long run, this prediction is probably true. All major vendors are supporting ATM as the next generation of switching technology. As its price comes down in the next few years, it may well replace routing, but in the near term, routing has an important role in enterprise networks, and this role is not likely to be displaced soon. Routers have capabilities that cannot be matched in bridges, which switches are. Among these are

- ◆ Routers can administer network security and create firewalls against unwanted intrusion.
- ◆ Routers can control traffic flow, including broadcast and stray packets. Switches, on the other hand, tend to propagate such packets through the network.
- ◆ Routers provide LAN-to-LAN connections in both the local and wide area.

♦ Routers do a better job of filtering protocols.

♦ Routers can provide dynamic rerouting.

For the next few years, corporate internets are likely to employ combinations of routing and switching. Switching is an excellent way of solving immediate bandwidth problems, using routing to segment the network for reasons other than just bandwidth improvement, security for example. Routing increases network complexity, while switching reduces it, so apply routers where the additional complexity is worth adding. Switches don't do any processing, but routers do, so they have greater latency, but this can be controlled by judicious placement of switches. In the next generation of products, routing capability will be embedded in devices such as servers and switches.

The key to any network development is to ensure that the design is driven by business needs, not technology. Technology is important only insofar as it assists business in meeting its goals. In deciding on which technology to implement, consider the following:

♦ Understand the timing and technical requirements of new applications such as desktop video and voice over IP and what affect they will have on the network.

♦ Understand the applications of networking technologies such as ATM and the timing and method for introducing them.

♦ Get experience with the new technologies through controlled introduction trials and by using such services as frame relay as a prelude to ATM.

♦ Plan changes in the network infrastructure. Migrate at your own pace.

♦ Carefully evaluate suppliers' capabilities and standards adherence.

♦ Focus solutions on known and standards-based products.

Case History: Switched Backbone Network

A state agency occupies a four-story building that covers a city block. The state's IS department operates a mainframe computer that is connected to all agencies over multiple FDDI backbones. Within the individual agencies, selected users must access the mainframe for common functions such as payroll and accounting. Users who are not required to access the mainframe are excluded within the agency by filtering in the router that is used to access the backbone. All agencies share the backbone for access to the Internet, which is furnished by two separate ISPs over DS-3 connections.

Figure 37-6 shows how the internetwork is configured. The building is divided into two sections on each floor. A telecommunications closet on the north and south halves of the building feed the work areas with category 5 UTP. Ethernet switches are rack mounted in each telecommunications closet and connected to

State Agency Internet

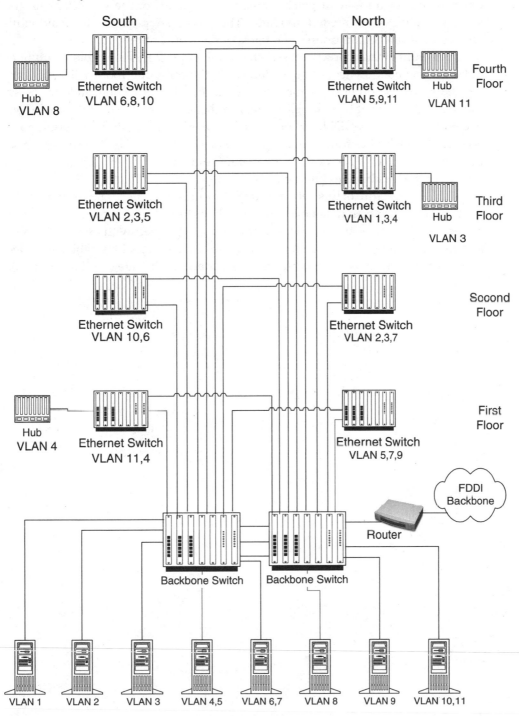

South

North

Ethernet Switch
VLAN 6,8,10

Hub
VLAN 8

Ethernet Switch
VLAN 5,9,11

Hub
VLAN 11

Fourth
Floor

Ethernet Switch
VLAN 2,3,5

Ethernet Switch
VLAN 1,3,4

Hub

VLAN 3

Third
Floor

Ethernet Switch
VLAN 10,6

Ethernet Switch
VLAN 2,3,7

Second
Floor

Hub
VLAN 4

Ethernet Switch
VLAN 11,4

Ethernet Switch
VLAN 5,7,9

First
Floor

FDDI
Backbone

Router

Backbone Switch

Backbone Switch

VLAN 1   VLAN 2   VLAN 3   VLAN 4,5   VLAN 6,7   VLAN 8   VLAN 9   VLAN 10,11

Server Farm

patch panels or hubs with patch cords. Some stations are fed directly into the switches, while others are fed into hubs. The decision depends on the bandwidth requirements and communities of interest of the workstations.

All eight of the workgroup switches on the four floors are cabled with fiber optics to backbone switches that are located in the computer room. All servers are located in the computer room for security, backup, fire protection, and other such functions that cannot be handled reliably in the work areas. The network is connected to the state's FDDI backbone with a router. The only stations permitted to access the state's mainframe are assigned to one of the VLANs. The router blocks packets from other VLANs from accessing the mainframe, but permits them to flow over the backbone to Internet.

The architecture of this network simplifies administration, and provides a degree of service protection that many organizations lack. The computer room is kept as secure as the typical mainframe room, and is equipped with air conditioning and fire protection. The same room also houses the agency's PBX, which is cabled to the same wiring closets with riser cable to connect to the category 3 wiring to the work areas.

CHAPTER 38

Voice and Data Convergence

The hottest buzzword in telecommunications today is *convergence*. While convergence has different meanings to different people in the industry, we'll define it as simply meaning the integration of multiple media at the circuit level. Media can be any combination of voice, data, video, graphics, fax, or any other digitized information form. The circuit can be any bandwidth ranging from a single voice-grade circuit to gigabit Ethernet or wider bandwidths as they become available.

Voice and data integration is nothing new. It's been done for years, but usually by channelizing the transmission medium. Companies regularly split a T1/E1 with a multiplexer that divides the bandwidth among applications. The problem with bandwidth division is that it's difficult to make idle capacity of one application available to another. The answer to improved utilization is to mix the information and inject it into a single transmission pipe. Then we have convergence. To simplify this discussion, we will often use the abbreviation voice over IP (VoIP) to signify mixed-media converged communications. The information media may include video, graphics, fax, sound clips, or whatever can be digitized. The protocol does not have to be IP. Although that is the predominant protocol in use today, another routable protocol, such as Novell's IPX, can support VoIP.

This tendency of the industry to abbreviate can result in blurred concepts that must be kept separate if we are to evaluate the technology. For example, VoIP can use several different types of transmission media with results to the user ranging from acceptable to unsatisfactory. Five types of media that can support VoIP are listed here in the approximate order of control and predictability of performance:

- Point-to-point digital circuit
- Local area network

- Frame relay
- Corporate intranet
- Internet

Besides a variety of transmission media, the industry offers several different ways of mixing the information media and pumping them into the network. A personal computer can be equipped with voice and video cards, and signals transferred over a LAN connection. Another option is to connect voice and video devices directly to the LAN. The company PBX can become a server on the LAN and control call flow as usual, directing it to the IP network when that is more effective than the PSTN. The PBX connection can be directly to IP through an Ethernet connection or through traditional tie lines to a router that is equipped with voice ports. Some companies are producing a so-called un-PBX, which is generally voice switching functions programmed into a personal computer. In considering VoIP, it is important to understand what combination of network architecture and equipment is being proposed because the results will differ dramatically.

In evaluating the effectiveness of these various convergence combinations, designers must keep a close eye on performance from the standpoint of the users. Technologists can easily become so fascinated with the technical possibilities that they forget that most users are disinterested in the technology but are critical of performance. In voice applications the user's standard is the ordinary telephone connection. Everyone knows how to operate its main features, it is dependable, and for the most part, quality is excellent. In the residential environment many users will give up some of the quality to save money, but in the corporate environment, users will be unimpressed with cost savings if quality drops much below their expectations. One possible exception is in calls to expensive overseas locations. There it is possible to convey the magnitude of cost savings to users, but with the cost of long-distance calls approaching that of local calls, users will be intolerant of subpar quality.

Nevertheless, VoIP is here, and while it isn't the universal answer to all types of mixed-media communications, and is unacceptable in some of its forms, it fulfills definite niches in the market that must be understood. In this chapter we will examine some of the standards that enable VoIP and will discuss the application considerations in some detail.

MIXED-MEDIA REQUIREMENTS

As discussed briefly in Chapter 3, voice, video, and data have significantly different characteristics and requirements, which makes conventional packet switching unsatisfactory for guaranteed quality of service (QoS). The differences are somewhat of a paradox until they are examined closely. Data transmission requires absolute accuracy, but it is tolerant of *latency*, which is defined as end-to-end delay, and *jitter*, which is defined as variations in delay. Voice, and to an even greater degree video, have contrasting requirements from data. When voice and video are digitized, users can tolerate a bit error rate (BER) that would devastate a data network, but delay and jitter can render the connection unusable.

Readers must be careful to distinguish between the industry's use of jitter to describe two different phenomena. In one case, the term means a difference in the arrival rate of individual bits. See Figure 5-7 for an illustration of this type of jitter. This type of jitter may be devastating to data because, in extreme cases, it can result in a high BER, but with respect to voice transmission, this form of jitter is irrelevant. In voice and video transmission we are concerned with the second type of jitter, which is variations in packet arrival rate.

Each time a packet traverses a router, some latency occurs. When routers experience congestion, they begin to queue packets, which results in packet delay. When the router's buffers fill up, they may flush out excess packets, either by discarding them or letting them through without buffering against jitter. Packet discard causes additional delay for data packets since the TCP protocol causes the routers to resend the packets. UDP, which is used for VoIP, is an unreliable protocol that does not call for packet retransmission.

Data requirements can be stated with a great deal of precision. A single bit error causes a packet to be rejected. When the BER exceeds a particular threshold, the circuit is unusable because throughput drops and results in a response time that users consider intolerable. Voice requirements, on the other hand, are subjective. We have all experienced circuits that are annoyingly noisy or that have volume that is so low that it is hard to hear. We can easily set thresholds for noise level and end-to-end transmission loss, but not everyone will concur with the standards. Hearing-impaired people will have difficulty communicating over a circuit that some people with acute sensitivity may find annoyingly loud. Consequently, transmission standards, as explained in *The Irwin Handbook of Telecommunications Management*, are based on subjective criteria. Combined noise and loss objectives are specified so that at least 80 percent of the users would rate a connection with those characteristics as good or better.

Effects of Delay

With voice and video over packet networks, loss and noise are mostly irrelevant today because the connection is end-to-end digital. In fact, an H.711 circuit, which has 56 or 64 kb/s of bandwidth, is used as the reference standard in subjective evaluation of voice compression algorithms. In packet networks, however, latency and jitter creep in to impair quality. Studies discussed in ITU-T G.114 have evaluated user satisfaction against round-trip delay. Figure 38-1 shows that when round-trip delay exceeds 500 ms, nearly 20 percent of the users have difficulty. Since this is the inverse of our 80 percent satisfaction criteria, it is clear that we should shoot for less than 500 ms of round-trip delay.

FIGURE 38-1

Effect of Long One-Way Transmission Times on Voice Transmission

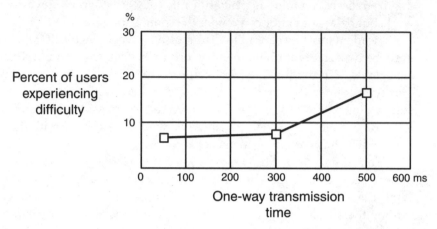

Delay in a packet network has two elements: fixed and variable. The fixed delay results from the propagation speed of the medium and the delay in packetizing the analog signal. The variable delay results from processing and routing packets through the network. Propagation delay is the same for circuit-switched and packet facilities. A 5000-km connection has a fixed delay of around 15 ms. This, added to the packetizing delay, results in a fixed delay of about 200 ms, which leaves 200 to 300 ms for the variable delay before users begin experiencing difficulty.

Here is where the differences in transmission media begin to show up dramatically. As discussed later in this chapter, frame-relay networks are reasonably predictable. Intranets are less predictable than frame relay, with a variable delay that is generally proportional to the size of the network (the larger the network, the more routers the connection can traverse, and therefore the greater the delay). When the public Internet is involved, the delay is unpredictable, although it is easy to measure. At this stage of Internet development, it should be avoided for voice transmission unless the savings potential is enough to offset user dissatisfaction. Rarely is it worth considering on domestic calls.

Fax uses the T-30 protocol, which is more critical of delay than voice users are. Too much delay in the initial handshake between fax machines may cause the connection to drop. Excessive delay during the transmission may cause the connection to lose synchronization and drop prematurely.

Latency in a controlled packet network is reasonably easy to determine by setting up a computer to measure packet delay using the ping protocol. If enough readings are taken at random throughout the business day, a good sample distribution of round-trip delay and packet loss can be recorded. If it is within the limits discussed here, the network should be acceptable from a delay standpoint.

Effects of Packet Loss

A second impairment in a packet network is packet loss. As discussed previously, when router buffers overflow, they discard packets. The IP protocol launches each packet with a time-to-live indicator. When this time is exceeded, the packet is discarded. The codecs used in VoIP can process the lost information to bridge across lost information up to a threshold of about 10 percent packet loss. Beyond that, the gaps begin to distort the transmission. Fax is more sensitive to packet loss than voice. Loss of a packet may result in loss or corruption of a line or several lines.

Effects of Jitter

In an ideal network, the packets will arrive at the destination in a precise order with interpacket intervals evenly spaced. Jitter results when packets take different paths through the network, resulting in different arrival intervals. Buffering packets and releasing them at regular time intervals can compensate for the effects of jitter, but this has two potential adverse effects. First, excessive buffering results in excessive latency, and may result in the ill effects described earlier. Second, when the buffers overflow, packets may be discarded. The effects of jitter, therefore, can theoretically be handled, but only up to a point. Beyond that point, voice or video quality can be impaired by any of the triple effects of letting jitter though, discarding packets, or excessive latency. The main way of avoiding jitter is to provide plenty of capacity in the network.

It should be clear from this discussion that VoIP must be approached with conservative expectations. If service quality is to be maintained, and if users are to be satisfied, VoIP packets must be launched into a predictable and controlled transmission medium. Enough bandwidth and router capacity must be provided to permit orderly and assured packet arrival. Obviously, for VoIP to be practical, standards are needed. Equipment should be interoperable between manufacturers. Since the protocols, call control, and signaling of packet- and circuit-switched networks are vastly different, some means of communicating between them is necessary. That is the role of the ITU-T H.323 standard.

THE H.323 STANDARD

ITU H.323 is the standard that enables mixed-media communications over packet-based networks that do not provide QoS. For devices implementing H.323, voice support is mandatory. Data and video are optional. Communications can be carried over point-to-point connections, single-segment LANs, or a multisegment internet. Communications can be point-to-point, multipoint, or broadcast. H.323 operates with a multitude of other standards, many of which are listed in Table 38-1. H.323 supports applications such as Internet telephony, desktop videoconferencing, LAN telephony, conference calling, and mixed-media conferences such as

T A B L E 38-1

Selected ITU Standards Supporting Mixed-Media Communications

	H.320	H.321	H.322	H.323	H.324
Purpose	Narrowband ISDN	Broadband ISDN, LAN, ATM	Guaranteed bandwidth packet networks	Nonguaranteed bandwidth packet networks and Ethernet	Analog PSTN telephone system
Audio	G.711, 722, 728	G.711, 722, 728	G.711, 722, 728	G.711, 722, 723, 728, 729	G.723
Video	H.261, 263	H.261, 263	H.261, 263	H.261, 263	H.261, 263
Multipoint	H.231, 243	H.231, 243	H.242, 243	H.323	
Control	H.320, 242	H.242	H.231, 243	H.245	H.245
Interface	I.400	AAL	I.400, TCP/IP	UDP/IP, TCP/IP	V.34

voice, video, and whiteboard. The data standard supported across the board for all of these protocols is T.120.

For VoIP to be successful, products from different manufacturers must interoperate, and products must operate over standard networks including both LANs and WANs. Interoperability is one of the key functions of H.323. It is intended to compensate for the instabilities in packet networks to make the voice or video connection approach the predictability of circuit switching. To accomplish this, the standard establishes call setup and control procedures and interfaces to permit call timing, charging, and other control functions. It provides bandwidth management features so that voice and data networks cannot swamp each other because of their inherently different characteristics. It supports multipoint conferencing and broadcasting or multicasting. The standard allows LAN-based mixed-media communications to operate within the LAN or to connect to outside resources including the PSTN, either as a POTS or an ISDN connection.

When H.323 operates over TCP/IP, it uses the reliable, connection-oriented service of TCP for call setup and control. It uses the unreliable service of IP packets operating under user datagram protocol (UDP) for voice packets. A signaling channel called the registration, admissions, and status (RAS) channel provides for communications between devices. For conferences, H.323 uses IP multicast and real-time protocol (RTP), which operates on top of IP multicast. This capability enables it to use the Internet's multicast backbone (Mbone) for conferences. RTP also sequences packets, compensating for the lack of this capability in UDP. Real-time control protocol (RTCP) monitors QoS.

H.323 defines four functions for packet network communications: terminal, gatekeeper, gateway, and multipoint control unit. The standard does not specify the hardware configuration, so they should be considered as functions, some of which may be contained in the same box.

Terminals

Terminals are the clients on the network. They are also referred to as end points. The terminal must support audio, and therefore contains a microphone, speaker, coder-decoder (codec), and audio compressor. In addition, the terminal contains call setup and control functions complying with H.245, including a dual-tone multifrequency (DTMF) dial and the equivalent of switchhook control. The terminal also must support Q.931 for call setup and signaling, RAS to communicate with the gatekeeper, and an RTP for sequencing packets.

Optionally, the terminal may also include video equipment such as a camera and monitor and a video codec. Since the video terminal for desktop conferencing is normally built into a desktop computer, the monitor will be the computer's monitor. The optional data interface will normally be built into a desktop computer. As the universal serial bus (USB) becomes common on PCs, USB-compatible phones will become available.

Gatekeepers

The gatekeeper is the central controller that manages the call flow within a *zone*, which is a collection of end points. The gatekeeper in an H.323 zone can be compared conceptually to a PBX in a circuit-switched network, except that it is not the interface to the outside world. That function is assigned to the gateway. The gatekeeper has two major functions. First, it manages bandwidth within the zone to ensure that a hungry application, such as a multipoint videoconference, does not consume all the available resources. Second, it translates addresses for terminals and gateways to IP addresses. In addition, the gatekeeper serves as a call router. If an end point is busy or if all paths from a gateway are occupied, the gatekeeper can reroute to another destination. Gatekeepers are not mandatory on H.323 systems, but if they are provided, the terminals must subordinate themselves to its management functions.

Gateways

As the term implies, the *gateway* is the interface from a closed local network to the outside world, normally over the PSTN or over a private network such as an intranet or the Internet. The gatekeeper functions can be included in a gateway. In some configurations the gatekeeper is mandatory, such as for translating PSTN addresses to segment hardware addresses for those terminals that are incapable of responding to E.164 addresses. The gateway performs call setup and supervision

FIGURE 38-2

H.323 System

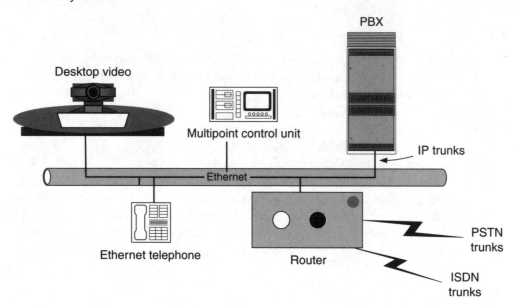

between the packet network and the circuit-switched network. If the H.323 system does not communicate with another network, the gateway is not needed since terminals can connect with each other directly. The gateway function is analogous to trunks to the outside world in a PBX. Figure 38-2 shows conceptually how an H.323 system is configured.

Multipoint Conferencing

Other functions include the multipoint control unit (MCU), which is an optional device that manages conferences between three or more terminals. An MCU consists of a multipoint controller and, optionally, multipoint processors. The controller controls conferencing resources, while the processor, which is not required, processes audio, video, and data packets. The purpose of the MCU and associated components is to facilitate multimedia conferences over a network. Participating terminals can see and talk to one another, transmit images, and share files over the network. This enables users to operate at a distance much as they would in a conference room. Some conferees may be on the local network, while others are participating at a distance. Some may have full audio and video, while others may be audio only. The character of the conference depends on the way the designer has set up the application, using H.323 as the supporting mechanism.

FACILITIES FOR MIXED-MEDIA TRANSMISSION

The discussion up to this point should have made it clear that a disciplined approach to VoIP transmission is needed. The most reliable medium for carrying packetized voice is either a direct digital line or frame relay. Carriers will provide a quality of service guarantee that removes much of the uncertainty when it comes to latency and packet loss. A typical domestic frame relay network guarantee is 140 ms of end-to-end delay and packet loss of less than 1 percent. The customer can easily calculate how large the access circuit and the committed information rate must be to stay within the quality range that users need for satisfactory service. Until the service begins to bump above the CIR ceiling, the network should behave in a disciplined fashion. Frame relay does not provide for prioritizing packets, so some carriers offer separate frame relay networks for time-sensitive traffic.

A major advantage of frame relay for voice is its low overhead compared to an IP network. If voice is compressed to 6.3 kb/s in accordance with G.723.1, a 25-octet block results in 30 ms of voice. A 38-octet frame carries this block with a total of 6 octets, or 19 percent of overhead. By contrast, if the same voice signal is carried in an IP packet over an intranet, the IP and UDP headers increase the overhead to 34 octets or 58 percent. Increasing the size of the voice payload block can reduce the overhead percentage, but the block must remain within the limits of the size of the jitter buffer.

A private IP network is a satisfactory medium for voice, although less so than frame relay. Here, carrier services are obtained to provide the bandwidth and robustness needed to assure service quality. The larger the network, however, the more routers it is likely to have, and the more routers and different circuits the packets must traverse. This increases the probability of packets arriving out of sequence since as routers sense congestion, they may divert traffic to a less congested path. The Unix protocol trace route can be used to determine how many routers a packet traverses. The congestion protocols in an IP network are not as well developed as they are in a frame relay network, so VoIP is less effective over intranets.

The least predictable path is the Internet. The variation in packet arrival and loss of packets can be predicted reasonably well by pinging a distant source and measuring the response time. Tests have shown that packet delays approaching a full second are not unusual, depending on the ISP, how it accesses the backbone, and how fully loaded the network is. At this point, voice over the Internet is fine for hobbyists, and may be acceptable for intracompany overseas traffic, but beyond that it has little place in an enterprise network.

Of course, although the Internet is the lowest quality, it has the advantage of ubiquity that the other types lack. Frame relay is essentially a point-to-point network. Although PVCs can be set up to multiple points, that complicates the network, and SVCs are rare. Intranets can flow packets among locations with fewer restrictions than frame relay, but they can't compete with the simplicity and price performance of the Internet. If the Internet could be made more predictable, say, by reserving resources for real-time traffic, it could, perhaps, deliver the QoS that enterprise networks require. If the devices on the network were unable to provide the resources, the sender could be notified to set up an alternate path. Such is the purpose of resource reservation protocol (RSVP).

Resource Reservation Protocol

RSVP compensates for the connectionless nature of the Internet by establishing paths or flows between end points. The sender sets up a flow by sending a path message to the receiver. The receiver responds with a reservation message so both the sender and intermediate routers can learn the receiver's requirements. RSVP defines two service levels, controlled load and guaranteed service. The former system provides prioritization through the network. Guaranteed service reserves a specific amount of bandwidth for voice and video. Reservations are made on a router-by-router basis. The protocol guarantees that the service will not drop packets unless the bandwidth exceeds the reserved capacity. RFC 2205 covers the details of RSVP's operations.

In addition to RSVP, two other protocols assist with maintaining QoS on IP networks. DiffServ sets up "traffic conditioners" in the network to indicate requirements for packet traffic. DiffServ is more scalable than RSVP and requires less processing. Multiprotocol label switching (MPLS) requires routers to read additional information in labels that are attached to packet headers to assign packets to specific paths. This enables the network to set up virtual circuits similar to frame relay. MPLS has its origins in proprietary protocols such as Cisco's tag switching and Ipsilon Networks' IP switching.

As these protocols and equipment implementing them reach the market, and as quality improves, the amount of Internet telephony will undoubtedly increase. A major unknown, however, is the impact of future regulatory decisions. Much of the economics of Internet telephony comes from the fact that ISPs are exempt from many of the regulatory restrictions of conventional carriers. The Internet can bypass the high costs of access charges imposed by PTTs in many countries and by the FCC in the United States.

SYSTEM CONFIGURATIONS

The market offers a glut of VoIP products of different types. Since the technology is in its infancy, it is difficult to tell which products will survive and which will pass by the wayside. The result will depend, to a large degree, on the applications and the reasons for using VoIP. This section discusses some of the configurations that are now available.

VoIP through a Router

Several manufacturers offer routers with voice ports, as Figure 38-3 shows. The PBX connects to the router over T1/E1 or with analog tie trunks. In either case, the

FIGURE 38-3

VoIP through a Router Gateway

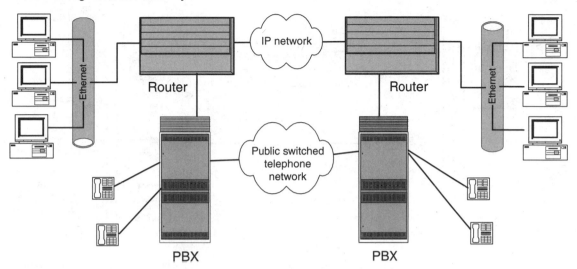

gatekeeper function is contained in the router. A gateway is usually not required because the PBX handles access to the PSTN. The automatic route selection (ARS) in the PBX recognizes when the distant end is accessible over the IP network, and routes the call to the router, which completes it over the IP network. This approach to VoIP has several advantages:

- If a PBX already exists, it makes maximum use of existing resources.
- The service is completely transparent to users.
- The connection can be completed over any available packet network. For example, the router could be connected to both an intranet and the Internet, completing different classes of calls over each.
- Blockage of voice calls should be rare since the PBX can complete the call over the PSTN.

If a router is being purchased for a new network, the incremental cost of adding voice ports to the router is small. This can be an effective way of sharing limited frame relay or dedicated bandwidth between a headquarters and a remote site. Where the traffic volume is heavy between sites, this is not the preferred method.

LAN Telephones

Telephones and video terminals can be connected directly to the LAN under this configuration, which is illustrated in Figure 38-4. Analog telephones can be connected through an Ethernet adapter through a PC. The latter method is particularly

F I G U R E 38-4

Ethernet Telephones

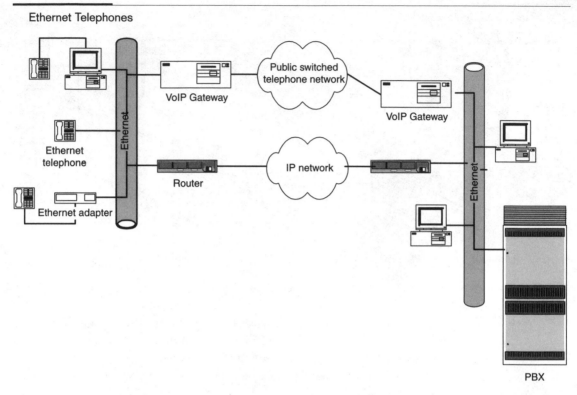

advantageous because the versatility of the PC can substitute for the telephone's button interface. For example, functions such as conferencing, which are often obscure on a proprietary telephone, can be handled by dragging and dropping icons on the PC screen.

This type of system has no PBX as such. Calls within the zone are controlled by the VoIP gateway, which includes gatekeeper functions. Calls to the PSTN are converted in the gateway. When the bandwidth of an Ethernet segment approaches overload because of this architecture, it can be deloaded by connecting devices through an Ethernet switch. This can be an inexpensive way to provide service to a small branch office or to a telecommuting employee. The branch office–to–main office implementation may be proprietary, so that the same vendor must furnish all equipment with the possible exception of the router.

IP PBX

Several manufacturers are producing systems that are sometimes referred to as an un-PBX. The PBX hardware and software functions mount in a PC, usually

FIGURE 38-5

IP PBX

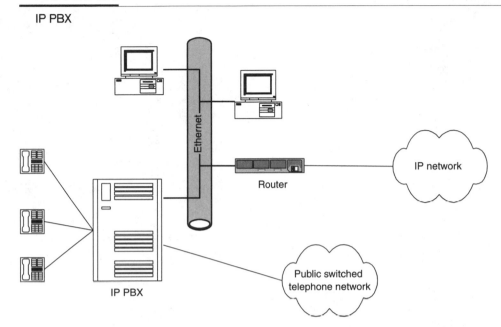

running Microsoft Windows NT operating system. The various cards mount in expansion slots in the PC, and the generic call-processing program runs under NT. Figure 38-5 shows how this PBX connects to the network. Generally, it has direct PSTN trunks, although ISPs can provide the gateway function to the PSTN, leaving the PBX to handle only internal traffic, routing all external traffic to the ISP.

One precaution that users must consider is the robustness of a PC and its operating system compared to that of a PBX. PBXs have internal diagnostics and self-monitoring capability that may make them less vulnerable to failure than a PC-based device. Network operating systems occasionally have to be rebooted to clean out accumulated garbage, which is rarely if ever required of a PBX.

VoIP through a Gateway

A third possibility is to install a gateway on an existing LAN and use the PBX to route calls to the IP network through the gateway. This arrangement, shown in Figure 38-6, is similar to the configuration in Figure 38-3, except that here the IP circuitry is in the PBX. A special trunk card in the PBX does the packetizing and connects directly to an Ethernet network. The gateway shown in Figure 38-6 may be built into the PBX trunk card or it may be a separate device.

This configuration is dependent on the products the PBX manufacturer offers. Some manufacturers such as Lucent and Nortel provide IP trunk cards, but

FIGURE 38-6

VoIP through a Gateway

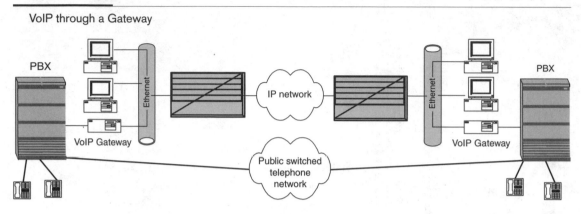

others do not, in which case the PBX would connect to either the router or the gateway through standard T1/E1 or analog tie trunk cards.

APPLICATION CONSIDERATIONS

Contrary to what some manufacturers would have you believe, IP is not the only protocol you will ever need. To be sure, it is possible today in some companies to operate with an IP-based telephone system, carrying all internal communications over a LAN internet, with communication to the PSTN carried through a gateway. LAN-based telephone systems are in their infancy, however, and are not a universal substitute for a PBX. This is not to say that it is impossible to program all PBX functions into a LAN-based system, but PBX development has progressed over many decades to a stable and reliable platform that LANs cannot yet emulate. In considering VoIP solutions, users need to consider the factors discussed in this section. For the first few years of the twenty-first century, VoIP applications will fit into selected niches, but they are unlikely to displace circuit switching in its entirety.

Economics

The driving force behind VoIP is financial. If technology does not repay its investment, some compelling reason must be found to justify it. In fact, the primary reason for packetizing voice is to conserve bandwidth. Logically, then, the greatest benefit will come where bandwidth is the most costly. Within the office, bandwidth is nearly free, and the farther from home communications travel, the more it costs. The typical office today has a dual wiring system—one for voice and one for data. The cost of wiring can be reduced if voice and data share the LAN, but a major part of wiring cost is labor. When a work area is wired, the incremental cost of added wire runs is significantly less than the first wire run, so wiring costs are not cut in half by eliminating a separate voice wire run.

In the local network the economics of VoIP are not likely to be compelling, except that some manufacturers are promoting PC-based PBXs that are designed to operate over the LAN. These may result in lower prices, but the PC platform is not the technical equal of a PBX in terms of stability.

The economics of VoIP are easy to calculate. First is the cost of the telephone system, which includes not only the initial cost but also the administrative cost. Second is the cost of trunking. If access lines are shared between voice and data, the reduced cost is easy to determine. Where VoIP offsets long-distance costs, the reduction in usage-sensitive traffic volume can be determined easily.

Productivity

A major reason for implementing VoIP for many organizations will be a productivity improvement. The value of this is closely related to the applications that are beginning to emerge. Users at different parts of the country can use VoIP to handle meetings over the network and to do multipoint broadcasts. A network meeting may be enhanced with data applications such as a computerized whiteboard, which enables all participants to see data on a whiteboard as it is being drawn. Desktop video can be added to the conference for some or only a part of the participants, and generally at a much lower cost than dial-up video, which requires digital data channels through the IXC. By integrating the telephone and the data device into the same box, productivity is also enhanced by the applications. One example that every office worker experiences is outdialing from a database. With proprietary PBX telephones, either expensive computer-telephony integration is required or the user looks up the number in the database and dials manually. When the two types of instrument are integrated, the barriers are lowered.

Closely related to productivity is telecommuting, which enables employees to work at home all or part of the time. VoIP is an excellent medium for telecommuting. The remote worker is equipped with an H.323 terminal, which can connect to the main office over ISDN, xDSL or other point-to-point circuit, or frame relay.

Branch offices can be tied to the main office through H.323. It is practically axiomatic in organizations today that unity is improved by tying branch offices to headquarters. Frame relay offers an excellent method for data applications, but voice remains dial-up. Today, with voice over frame relay, the branch office may be networked at a minimal usage cost. At some usage point long-distance savings offset the cost of the equipment.

Customer Accessibility

Within the next several years nearly every customer service or sales call center will need to convert to a Web-enabled call center. The customer may be browsing the company's Web site and have a question or want to place an order. By clicking an icon on the screen, the caller can set up a voice call. The call can route to a dedicated set of agents, or, with the right application software, it can be queued with voice calls and transferred to the agent's screen and telephone simultaneously. By adding a camera, the parties can see each other as well. The key is making the company accessible through the caller's medium of choice.

Obviously, for this kind of call center to work, the caller must have voice equipment ready to make the connection. Callers with such equipment are rare today, but in the future they will increase, and will favor the companies offering the convenience. The company profits by not only using the service as a customer magnet; it also enables a representative to converse with a customer who may be in a buying mood.

Staffing Advantages

Within the typical large organization, the numbers of people who are involved with and understand data networks outweigh the people who are voice-conversant. Furthermore, the responsibility for voice support is increasingly gravitating toward the information systems department. This means that supporting voice through LAN switches and routers puts the support people in a more comfortable position. Where they are equipped with protocol analyzers and network management systems, the support staff can use the same devices and techniques to support voice, at least to some degree.

APPLICATIONS

We have mentioned several niches into which VoIP fits nicely in today's environment. Many equipment manufacturers believe that packetized voice will eventually replace circuit switching. They may be correct, but circuit switching has a great deal of momentum, and will be difficult to dislodge. Meanwhile, however, VoIP has four principal applications that should be considered:

Branch Office   Since the branch office is already equipped with a router or FRAD, adding voice may be a natural outgrowth of the existing network. For distant branch offices, the existing frame relay network may be used. For local branches, it may be feasible to replace off-premises extensions with VoIP.

Telecommuting   Similar in architecture to the branch office, telecommuters may use VoIP to provide them a dual voice and data channel back to the main office.

Toll Bypass   Carrying long-distance traffic for next to nothing is attractive, particularly when the distances are great. The ability to send large quantities of fax messages, which tend not to be time-sensitive, over the Internet can be particularly attractive.

Web-Enabled Call Center   Callers can browse the company's Web page by computer, and then click an icon to talk to a live agent. Costs are reduced and customer convenience is enhanced.

Evaluation Considerations

In acquiring equipment and systems to support VoIP, numerous factors must be considered. The following is a list of issues to discuss and questions to ask of the vendors.

Prioritization   To what degree does the system provide priority for time-sensitive packets? How are these recognized? Can the system as designed deny throughput to lower-priority packets?

Scalability   As the company's network grows, will the network scale with it? In what increments does the system grow? What is the maximum number of voice stations it supports?

Interoperability   Does the system support only international standards? Has interoperability been tested with other manufacturers' equipment? If so, which products? Are any of the protocols proprietary?

Existing Infrastructure   Does the existing LAN/WAN infrastructure support VoIP? Will it be necessary to upgrade to a faster LAN, add switching to the existing LAN, add bandwidth to access circuits, etc.?

Emergency Services   Does the application support emergency dialing such as E-911/999? Is the calling station ID sent to the public safety answering point?

Robustness   How many simultaneous connections does the product support to the PSTN? What reroute provisions are made?

Security   How are network calls secured? Can anyone with access to the network and an H.323 protocol analyzer intercept voice conversations?

Fax and Modem Recognition   Can the system recognize fax and modem signals and provide them dedicated bandwidth?

Diagnostics   What kind of diagnostic tools are required and provided for troubleshooting? What kind of statistical information does the system provide for evaluating service and calculating trunking needs?

Architecture   Does the system have a separate codec board or does it use software to do the digitizing and compressing?

CHAPTER 39

Network Management Systems

As mission-critical operations migrate from mainframes to LANs and distributed servers, the need for a comprehensive network management system becomes compelling, and, at the same time, becomes more difficult. Mainframe manufacturers have long provided proprietary network management systems for their networks and equipment, but interoperability was, and remains, uncertain. A company with equipment from multiple vendors may have to settle for multiple network management systems with separate management workstations for each or accept reduced surveillance capability. Protocols such as ATM and switched Ethernet further complicate the picture. With regular Ethernet, a management probe can monitor an entire segment, but with switching each workstation becomes its own segment, requiring a probe for each station. Distributed communication systems do not map well to the older network management systems, which are hierarchically structured.

As networks become more complex and skilled labor to maintain them climbs in cost and shrinks in supply, it becomes attractive to mechanize network management to the greatest degree feasible. Network equipment can support automation to an ever-increasing degree. Management agents built into such devices as hubs, routers, channel banks, multiplexers, and even modems can report status and accept orders to reconfigure themselves. As the equipment becomes capable of reporting status and accepting orders, it becomes feasible to control the network from computers. Humans are needed to make decisions that cannot easily be formulated into yes and no choices, but computers can react faster and weigh and discard alternatives at a speed that humans cannot match.

As the science of artificial intelligence develops, it will support the needs of network managers. The uniqueness of every network makes it difficult to adopt standard rules and procedures, but some of the expertise of managers who know how the network is to function and the relative importance of its different elements can be captured in an artificial intelligence program and used to expand the abilities of the staff.

Local area networks present a special management challenge because they are so closely integrated with the end users' operations. The requirements for managing a LAN are not a great deal different from the management of a data center. This means the following functions, which are typical of data centers, must be provided:

- ◆ Capacity planning
- ◆ Change management
- ◆ Disaster planning and recovery
- ◆ Fault management
- ◆ Power conditioning
- ◆ Security management
- ◆ Service management
- ◆ Storage medium backup and recovery

The proprietary network management systems of the past are giving way to open systems. Simple network management protocol (SNMP) and common management information protocol (CMIP) are the two predominant nonproprietary network management systems in existence today. SNMP is based on TCP/IP, and CMIP is based on OSI. All major manufacturers support SNMP in most of their products. It is inexpensive to implement, but it has deficiencies that limit its effectiveness. Replacements, however, have been slow in coming. Version 2 of SNMP made its way through the IETF's standardization process, but bogged down because of security concerns and had to be supplemented with SNMPv3. CMIP is even slower to gain acceptance because of its complexity. Its primary use to date has been in common carrier networks where the additional complexity is accepted in exchange for its versatility.

This book does not attempt to explain the administrative aspects of network management. For information on how to use and administer network management products, refer to the companion text *The Irwin Handbook of Telecommunications Management*. This book discusses the technical aspects of network management, including how representative protocols operate and how the managed devices are configured.

NETWORK MANAGEMENT AND CONTROL

Network management is essentially a specialized client-server application that filters and correlates alarms, alerts, and statistics to either make or assist humans in making decisions that maximize network performance. *Technical control* is a term often applied to centralized network management and control systems that monitor status and manage capacity in large networks. These systems include provisions for accessing data circuits by jacks or computer-controlled switched access.

Besides providing testing capability, technical control centers include alarm reporting, trouble history, and, usually, a mechanized inventory of circuit equipment. Regardless of the type of network management system, network control center operations can be divided into the following classifications:

◆ *Configuration management.* Retains records and, where possible, configures network equipment remotely. Retains a complete record of users, assignments, equipment, and other records needed to administer the telecommunications system. The function discovers nodes on the network and detects changes in configuration and operational status.

◆ *Accounting management.* Tracks vendor bills and distributes costs to organizational units relative to resource usage.

◆ *Fault management.* Receives reports from users, diagnoses trouble, corrects trouble, and restores service to the users. Fault management also detects disorders or deterioration before users report trouble.

◆ *Performance management.* Monitors service levels and measures response time, throughput, error rate, availability, and other measures of user satisfaction. Also collects network statistics such as packet quantities, runts, jabbers, and other trouble indications.

◆ *Security management.* Ensures that network and files are accessible only to authorized personnel. Assigns passwords and user numbers and detects unauthorized attempts to penetrate the network. Controls access through authorization and authentication.

Generically, a network management system consists of managed devices connected to a management workstation over the managed network. The heart of the system is network management software that resides on a management workstation. The workstation can be a PC running management software under Microsoft Windows, or in high-end systems it may be a UNIX-based workstation running an application such as Hewlett-Packard's OpenView. Figure 39-1 shows a threshold events browser screen from an OpenView workstation. Technically, both PC and workstation devices are often called the manager, but this nomenclature is easily confused with the humans that run the system. In this chapter the manager is the human administrator of the network management system, and the management workstation, whether a PC or a workstation, is the hardware and software that support the manager.

Each managed device contains an *agent*, which is software that communicates with the management workstation. The agent collects information about its environment, responds to management workstation commands, and provides that information to the management workstation, either when polled or in response to an event. Management workstations are capable of communicating with agents, drawing network maps, and forming the interface between the managed devices and the operator. The workstation software stores and presents network information for the

FIGURE 39-1

Threshold Events Browser Display from a Hewlett-Packard OpenView Workstation

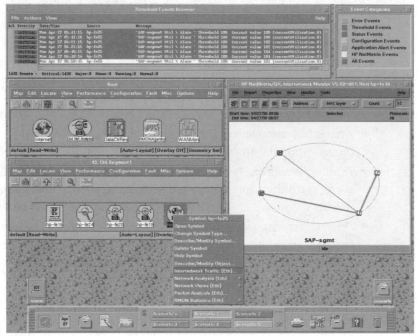

Courtesy of Hewlett-Packard Company

use of the manager. In most cases the management workstation sends requests to the agents and receives responses over the managed network, but when the network is down, it may be necessary to access certain devices over the dial-up network. As a result, some devices allow access to the agent over a dial-up connection.

The network management protocol includes a set of rules known as the *structure of management information* (SMI). The SMI defines relationships between management elements, organizes the network management data, and assigns identifiers to the variables.

Network devices often contain internal statistics that can be used to monitor the configuration, health, and activity in the network. For example, a device may contain static information about itself, such as its defined type; operational status such as up, down, or testing; and it may count statistics such as frames sent, received, and discarded as errors. This information may be stored in tables, counters, or as switch settings. This logical base of information is called a *management information base* (MIB). The MIB determines what the agent collects and stores, for example, packets sent and received, errored packets, etc. Each MIB consists of a set of *managed objects*. For example, system description, packet counts, and IP addresses are all examples of managed objects. A managed device may contain mul-

FIGURE 39-2

Elements of a Network Management System

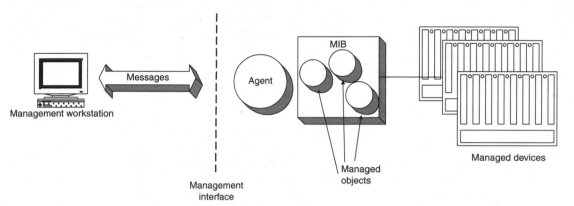

tiple managed objects. Figure 39-2 shows a functional view of a network management system.

The structure in Figure 39-2 is common to most types of network management systems. SNMP is the preferred network management method with LANs, but many WANs still retain a proprietary network management system, and many common carriers use CMIP.

SIMPLE NETWORK MANAGEMENT PROTOCOL

SNMP is a protocol for the exchange of information or objects. SNMP is developed and supported by the Internet Engineering Task Force. It was developed with the objective of being a fast and easy network management system to implement, and it has achieved that objective admirably. SNMP can perform the following operations:

- ◆ Identify devices
- ◆ Aggregate traffic measurement
- ◆ Control devices
- ◆ Detect unreachable devices

SNMP uses user-defined protocol (UDP) as its transport mechanism. UDP is a connectionless counterpart of TCP, either of which can be used as the transport mechanism for IP. SNMP is not a complete network management specification because it lacks any kind of presentation interface. That is left to the developers of the management systems that use SNMP as their foundation.

Network management systems use two techniques for obtaining information from the managed devices: polling and interrupts. SNMP supports both methods. A management workstation polls agents for information that they have collected such as performance statistics and status information. Management agents wait to be polled in all cases except for messages known as *traps,* which they send when triggered by thresholds and events. A trap message might, for example, be triggered when the number of error packets during a specified interval exceeds a threshold or when an alarm occurs. Trap messages are simple in many managed devices, which means the management workstation must poll to get the additional information needed to interpret the trap. Polling is one of the major drawbacks of SNMP. As the size of the network grows, the amount of capacity devoted to polling overhead increases. The usual response is to increase the polling interval, which limits the timeliness of information.

A key issue in network management is fault correlation. When multiple alarms are received, the manager must determine which is the major fault and which are sympathetic alarms that other devices initiate as a result of the major fault.

MIB-I, from the first implementation of SNMP, includes information such as the following:

- ◆ The number and type of interfaces the device has.
- ◆ The IP address of each interface.
- ◆ Packet and error counts.
- ◆ System description of the managed device.

SNMP's MIBs are defined in an English-like text using abstract system notation 1 (ASN.1) syntax. The MIB represents or describes the managed device, containing static information such as the vintage of the managed device or dynamic information such as the number of packets handled. MIBs are defined with a minimum of computation. Instead, computations are done at the management workstation where processing power resides. MIBs consist of basic information defined by the standard, plus proprietary extensions that most manufacturers add. These proprietary additions limit the management system's ability to collect and digest information in a multivendor network.

The SNMP protocol provides for six message types:

- ◆ *Get request.* Retrieves specific MIB objects.
- ◆ *Get response.* Sends the value of specific MIB objects in response to a get request.
- ◆ *Get next request.* Used to traverse the MIB tree or to get the next sequential MIB object.
- ◆ *Set.* Allows the management workstation to modify an MIB object to a new value.
- ◆ *Trap.* Messages sent from the managed device to the management workstation in response to some triggering event or threshold.
- ◆ *Inform.* Messages sent between management workstations.

Figure 39-3 shows how the SNMP protocol operates. The managed device responds to commands from the network management station with a get response.

F I G U R E 39-3

SNMP Command Protocol

When it needs to report an event in response to a trigger, it initiates a trap message to the workstation. Trap types include the following:

- ◆ *Cold start.* The device has done a complete reboot, which may result in reconfiguration.
- ◆ *Warm start.* The device has done a warm reboot, which retains the existing configuration.
- ◆ *Link down.* A link connected to the device is inoperative.
- ◆ *Link up.* A previously failed link has been restored.
- ◆ *Authentication failure.* A workstation attempting to communicate with the device has failed to authenticate itself properly.
- ◆ *EGP neighbor loss.* A device linked with the exterior gateway protocol has been lost.

The protocol uses an identifier called a *community string* in combination with IP addresses to authenticate set and get requests. The community string is not encrypted, and is easy to duplicate, which leaves SNMP vulnerable to security violations. Any management workstation could intercept messages, duplicate them, and use them to send its own messages to a managed device. The security weakness in the system is the chief drawback of SNMP version 1.

Each managed device contains agent software. The agent receives commands from the network management system, executes the request, and returns a response. It may also initiate a trap message when an alarm or event occurs. A *proxy agent* is one that does not reside in the same system as that which holds the MIB data. For example, a proxy agent can be configured to enable older non-SNMP devices to interface with an SNMP network management system. The proxy agent acts as a protocol translator to talk to the managed device and convert it to SNMP. Managers have an objective of managing the entire network from a single console, which may mean converting the WAN to SNMP. This can be done with proxy agents, but proxy agents often do not implement all the information in the proprietary protocol. Furthermore, proxy agents may not implement all the SNMP functions.

MIB-II

MIB-II was devised to augment and provide information that was omitted from MIB-I. It is organized into the following groups:

- *System group.* Required for every device. It includes basic system information that enables nodes to identify and describe themselves. A management station can poll a device to extract its system information.
- *Interfaces group.* Describes the configuration and status of any type of interface to the managed device. Interfaces could include any type of network such as frame relay, X.25, Ethernet, FDDI, ISDN, or any other network type. The MIB provides information about the status of the interface and pertinent data such as traffic statistics and error counts.
- *Address translation group.* Maps the IP address to the physical address of the managed device. A table may be created manually or by using a protocol such as address resolution protocol (ARP).
- *Internet protocol group.* Provides configuration and management information for hosts and routers. It contains such information as the default time-to-live counter by which misrouted IP datagrams are deleted. It includes IP routing, address translation, and forwarding tables. It also collects statistical information on IP traffic and errors.
- *Internet control message protocol (ICMP) group.* Provides information back to the source about unreachable destinations, redirected messages, time-out information, and invalid information in IP headers. ICMP provides special service requests and responses such as echo request that forms

the ping function, which allows the workstation to determine the operational status of a device.

◆ *Transmission control protocol group.* Enables the workstation to detect TCP variables such as traffic and error statistics and TCP connection statistics. The group allows the network management station to view active TCP connections to see which applications are being accessed.

◆ *User datagram protocol group.* Enables the management station to view UDP traffic statistics and to determine which UDP services are active.

◆ *Exterior gateway protocol group.* Provides information such as message counts and the identity of EGP neighbors.

◆ *SNMP group.* Keeps count of SNMP variables such as the number of traps and get and set responses that occur.

Remote Monitoring MIB (RMON)

RMON, and the updated version RMON2, is an SNMP MIB that enables a network management workstation to monitor remote devices much in the same way a protocol analyzer would be used locally. The management workstation can communicate with RMON over TCP/IP to tabulate statistics in a flexible manner. Networks using protocols other than IP cannot use RMON. RMON allows probes or agents embedded in managed devices installed on the LAN segment to collect as many as nine types of information:

◆ *Statistics.* Measures such variables as numbers of packets, octets, broadcasts, collisions, errors, and distribution of packet sizes. These variables are accumulated from the start of the monitoring session.

◆ *History.* Collects statistics based on user-defined sampling intervals.

◆ *Host.* Discovers what hosts are active on the network and tracks statistics for each of them.

◆ *Host top N.* Selects the hosts that had the largest traffic or error counts based on statistics from the host group.

◆ *Alarm.* Allows managers to set alarm thresholds based on absolute or delta values. Alarms trigger other actions through the events group.

◆ *Events.* Operates with alarms to define an action that will be taken when the condition occurs. The event may write a log entry or send a trap message.

◆ *Matrix.* Logs statistics by pairs of nodes.

◆ *Filter.* Allows the manager to define the criteria that trigger an event.

◆ *Capture.* Stores captured packet data for protocol analysis.

Although RMON is not quite as versatile as a local protocol analyzer, it provides much more complete information than SNMP does by itself. Note, however,

FIGURE 39-4

Hewlett-Packard Internet Advisor

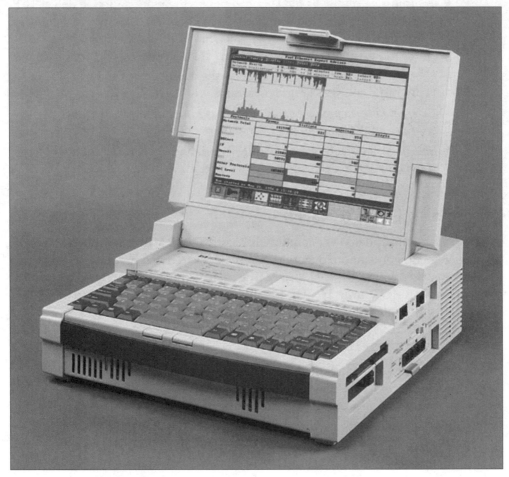

Courtesy of Hewlett-Packard Company

that RMON compliance does not mean that all nine categories are implemented, so it pays to inquire which categories a product supports. RMON is limited to looking at layer 2 protocols. RMON2 can monitor all seven layers of the OSI model, which enables agents to track activity such as quantities of packets of different types. RMON2, therefore, can provide information that would otherwise require a protocol analyzer such as the Hewlett-Packard Internet Advisor shown in Figure 39-4.

SNMP Version 2

SNMP has numerous weaknesses that led to proposals for SNMPv2. Chief among these is its lack of authentication and privacy provisions. The community string serves as a password in each protocol data unit. A hacker monitoring the network with a protocol analyzer would be able to intercept SNMP messages, determine the community string, and communicate with agents to wreak mischief. For example, a hacker might send a message to a mission-critical device such as a hub or router telling it to disable its ports or shut itself down. As a result, many network managers disable the set command to prevent malicious interference.

SNMPv2 introduced several changes to improve security, but they were never widely accepted. Several subversions were published, but they eventually culminated in a new working group that was chartered in 1997 to develop consensus on a new version, which would be called version 3. SNMPv3 is not a stand-alone management system. It adds essential security features that were missing from version 1 and never widely implemented in version 2.

The SNMPv2 inner PDU supports the five original commands from SNMP version 1, plus two new operations: inform-request and get-bulk-request. Inform-request enables management workstations to pass information between themselves. Inform-request is similar to a trap message in that the network management workstation sends the message without being polled. Unlike trap messages, however, the receiving station responds with a confirmation so the sender can be certain the message was received. Inform-request messages can be more complex than the trap messages ordinary devices send. Since the management workstation has intelligence, it can receive, digest, and report complex events that may be a summarization of many events sent from the managed devices.

A further deficiency with version 1 is its inability to retrieve large blocks of data, such as a large router table, without multiple requests. If the agent is unable to respond to the entire get-request, it responds with nothing. The get-bulk-request enables the management workstation to retrieve a collection of variables, perhaps an entire table.

SNMPv2 adds several other enhancements. Here are some of the differences between versions 1 and 2:

♦ The word "get" is dropped from responses. Instead of responding to a get-request with "get-response" the station simply returns "response."

♦ A manager-to-manager MIB is added to enable management workstations to exchange information.

♦ SNMP can be mapped to a variety of different transport protocols in addition to UDP.

♦ The data types in MIBs are expanded.

♦ MIB definitions allow the vendor to specify which of the MIB variables it supports.

A major problem with SNMPv2 is that to implement it all devices must be updated to the new version, which can be expensive if the upgrade is available, which it often is not. Second, the management workstations themselves must be updated to SNMPv2. Proxy agents can be used to translate between versions if they are available. Another alternative is to use a bilingual network management workstation that supports both SNMP 1 and 2.

SNMP Version 3

As mentioned earlier, SNMPv3 is intended to provide the security that SNMPv1 and SNMPv2 lack, but it is not a complete management system itself. Either a version 1 or a version 2 PDU is encapsulated in a version 3 message. SNMPv3 introduces a security model that is designed to control access to managed devices and to provide message-level security through authentication, encryption, and timeliness checking. The access control system operates on SNMP PDUs, while the security system operates on SNMP messages. The details of version 3 can be found in RFCs 2271 through 2275, which are available on the IETF's web site.

Version 3 uses a modular architecture to allow the standard to evolve easily. The major elements are an SNMP engine containing subsystems for message processing, security, and access control. The engine accepts outgoing PDUs from the SNMP applications, encrypts them, inserts authentication codes, and sends them out on the network. The process is reversed on incoming messages. RFC 2271 discusses the security threats the model is designed to prevent:

◆ *Modification of information.* Prevents an unauthorized entity from altering in-transit SNMP messages, including falsifying the value of an object.

◆ *Masquerade.* Prevents an unauthorized entity from assuming the identity of an authorized entity.

◆ *Message stream modification.* Prevents an unauthorized entity from reordering, delaying, or replaying a message.

◆ *Disclosure.* Prevents unauthorized eavesdropping on exchanges between SNMP engines.

Since security functions require authentication and encryption, the engine requires authentication and encryption keys for both local and remote users. The keys are generated from the user's password. As an additional security precaution, the protocol checks for the timeliness of messages. The device responding to a message inserts clock time so the receiving device can determine elapsed time between message transmission and reception. A delayed message could indicate that an unauthorized station has intercepted a message and delayed it while it was being modified.

Desktop Management Interface

Another problem with SNMP is that it extends only to the network interface card, and not down to the level of the computer itself. DMI is a three-layer protocol from the Desktop Management Task Force that is designed to act as a management framework for PC products. The objective is to do for desktop systems what SNMP does for network devices. It provides an interface between desktop components such as application software and peripherals and SNMP agents.

Within the DMI structure is the management information format (MIF) database, which defines the standard managed attributes of desktop products. The remote management application program connects over a network to the top layer of the protocol, which is the management interface (MI). The MI, in turn, communicates with the service provider (SP), which communicates with the managed components through the lower layer, which is the component interface. The SP collects information from the managed components and the MIF database, and passes the information upward to the management workstation. The DMI system can track elements such as these:

- ◆ Processor performance
- ◆ Motherboard
- ◆ Physical and logical memory
- ◆ Basic input/output system (BIOS)
- ◆ Serial and parallel ports

Currently, few desktop devices support DMI, but in the future it should become an important tool for managers attempting to control a diverse network of computers and applications.

COMMON MANAGEMENT INFORMATION PROTOCOL

CMIP is the other contender for the title of a universal standard network management protocol, but like the contention between OSI and TCP/IP for the network architecture standard, it is losing out to SNMP. The principal reason is that while SNMP is alive and well and supported by nearly every manufacturer in North America, CMIP is bogged down in complexity, at least as far as non-common carrier networks are concerned. CMIP maps an MIB to each of the OSI layers, as Figure 39-5 shows.

The functions defined so far for CMIP far outstrip SNMP's limited functions:

- ◆ Access control
- ◆ Accounting meter
- ◆ Alarm reporting
- ◆ Event reporting
- ◆ Log control
- ◆ Object management
- ◆ Relationship management
- ◆ Security audit trail
- ◆ Security-alarm reporting
- ◆ State management

FIGURE 39-5

OSI Network Management

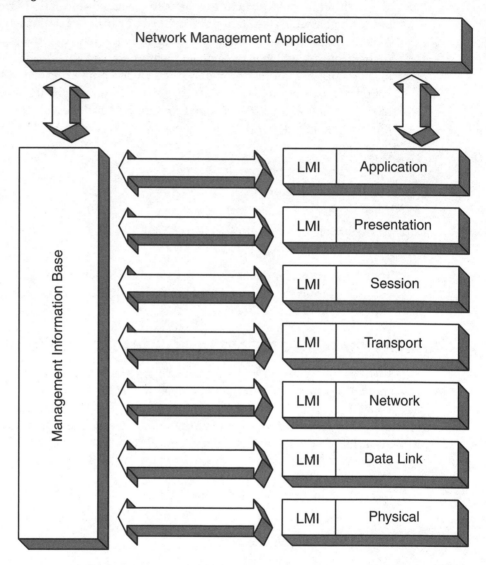

LMI = Layer Management Interface

- ◆ Summarization
- ◆ Test management
- ◆ Workload monitoring

Although its complexity has held its development back so far, CMIP is an international standard that will undoubtedly grow in the future. One factor that is expected to push CMIP into the mainstream is the expansion of ATM, which is too complex to be managed by a protocol as basic as SNMP. Some of the major advantages of CMIP over SNMP include the following:

- ◆ Unlike SNMP, which manages devices, CMIP manages relationships between devices.
- ◆ CMIP uses a connection-oriented transmission medium. With SNMP's datagram transmission method, data can be lost without the sender being notified.
- ◆ CMIP has more comprehensive automatic event notification. It has a larger number of alarm indications.
- ◆ Polling is reduced or eliminated with CMIP.
- ◆ Improved event filtering reduces the number of event messages (corresponding to SNMP's traps) that are sent to the management workstation.

CUSTOMER NETWORK MANAGEMENT

The major IXCs offer CNM to their customers. CNM gives users the ability to access information on usage, accounting, fault, and performance on a near-real-time basis. Through a CNM interface, customers can order new services and reconfigure existing ones in less time than it takes to order them through regular channels. Network managers can use the service to determine if their facilities are being used efficiently, and also to determine just what they have in the way of service. Without CNM, telephone bills are about the only source of information on what services a company has. Extracting information on private lines, frame relay circuits, access circuits, and the like from bills is often a daunting task, and getting the information from the carrier is difficult. CNM enables the user to extract the information from the carrier's database without going through conventional channels.

CNM is an MIB that enables the service to work through network management systems. Some network management systems are available with a CNM interface, but the lack of standards may make it difficult to obtain the desired result immediately. The initial implementations of the service for most users will likely be through vendor-provided application software.

APPLICATIONS

Single-segment networks and networks that reside within a single building can be managed effectively without a network management system, but when these boundaries extend into other buildings and other cities, network management becomes vital. Ideally, managers would have a single system that manages the entire network from a single group of consoles, but that is rarely possible today except when all equipment is from a single manufacturer. Managers are faced with conflicting alternatives. Proprietary network management systems are available for proprietary networks, but they cannot be expanded to encompass LANs. Simple management systems are available for LANs, but they lack security, may overload the network with overhead traffic, and are not easily extensible to proprietary WAN architectures. More secure and robust systems are becoming available, but these are not backward-compatible with legacy equipment, and they increase the complexity and resources needed to manage the network.

Faced with these alternatives, most managers will be forced to live with network management systems that are less than ideal for the next several years. If networks migrate into ATM, management will take on a different flavor than it has today, but the problems will not diminish. To minimize management difficulties today, the best approach is to obtain all equipment from a single vendor, or at least to require interoperability among the equipment you purchase. That too, however, is an ideal that few networks can realize in practice. As a result, network management will remain one of the major challenges that managers face.

Centralized versus Decentralized Network Management

Hard and fast rules about centralization or decentralization of a network management system cannot be given. The benefits of centralization depend on the character of the network, the types of services being carried, the penalty for outages, the availability of trained people to administer the system at remote locations, and the nature of the organization that owns the network. If centralization can be justified, it is usually the most effective method of managing a network because diagnosing network trouble requires information that often can be analyzed more meaningfully from a central site. The people on the spot, however, are usually the best equipped to take corrective action when problems occur. Some of the most complex networks in the world, the telephone networks, are administered locally with central sites monitoring traffic flow and dealing with congestion. The issue of centralization is one that must be dealt with as part of the fundamental network design and reexamined as new services and equipment make it feasible to change the basic plan.

A parallel issue to that of centralization is whether testing will be done manually or automatically. As networks gain intelligence, automatic testing becomes more the rule than the exception. The network must be large enough, however, to justify the cost of automatic testing before it can be considered. Equipment to do automatic tests is advancing rapidly, and network management strategies should be reexamined periodically in the light of new developments.

Multiple Vendor Issues

With the demise of the end-to-end service responsibility of the LECs, network users increasingly must obtain their equipment from multiple vendors. Although this offers opportunities for cost saving, it thrusts a much greater responsibility on the network manager to monitor service and develop techniques for dealing with multiple vendors. Compatibility problems become the user's responsibility—a responsibility that can be exercised best by preparing precise procurement requirements and specifications when acquiring equipment and services.

An allied issue is the degree of internal network management expertise that an organization develops. Although it is possible to turn the problem of network administration over to an outside contractor, to do so is to incur both a risk and an expense. The risk and the expense may be preferable to developing internal resources, but this is a decision that should be made only after an analysis of the alternative of developing internal staff.

Organizational Considerations

Many companies have not yet aligned their internal organizations with the realities of the new telecommunications networks. In many companies data-processing people administer the data network, and a separate staff administers the voice network. The information resource that both support may be managed by yet a third group. In the future the integration of voice and data networks is inevitable for most large organizations. Though the two may be separated at the source, bulk circuit procurement is more economical and flexible than obtaining individual circuits. When failures occur, a single organizational unit will be the most effective in dealing with the problems of restoring services and rerouting high-priority circuits over alternate facilities. In most organizations, the most effective structure will separate the information-generating entities from the information-transporting entities. As this is contrary to the way most companies are organized, this issue should be dealt with as the character of the network becomes more integrated.

Another issue that must be dealt with is flexibility of network planning. Changing tariffs and rates of long-distance carriers, access charges, and measured local service of local telephone companies make it essential that managers continually reexamine network plans. Plans should be flexible enough to enable the organization to react quickly as changes in tariffs and grades of service occur.

Standards

As discussed earlier, two standards, ISO's common management information protocol and the IETF's simple network management protocol, are the two major standards in existence today.

Evaluation Criteria

As networks grow increasingly complex, network management systems likewise grow in complexity. Also, as networks are continually changing, network management systems must have the flexibility to accommodate the growth and rearrangement of the network without becoming so complicated that only experts can administer them. Network management can be simplified by using computers, and as with any mechanized system the user interface is essential to keeping it understandable. The primary issues in evaluating a network management system are as follows.

Interoperability   Ideally, the system should operate with equipment from several different manufacturers. In practice, manufacturers include functions in their MIB implementations that may reduce interoperability with network management systems from other manufacturers to only basic functions.

Multiprotocol Support   The most effective systems are able to operate over the common transport protocols.

Security   The system should provide adequate security to prevent unauthorized persons from deactivating equipment, intercepting confidential information, duplicating commands, or other such potentially harmful functions.

Ease of Configuration   The administrator should be able to configure the key elements in the network from a management workstation. The workstation should be capable of performing all the desirable functions without requiring a visit to the managed device to set switches, check light status, and other items of status and configuration.

Scalability   As the network grows, the management system should grow with it without overloading the network with additional management overhead traffic.

MIB Definitions   The management workstation should provide MIB definitions on demand.

Out-of-Band Management   In addition to in-band management, the system should be accessible over the dial-up network to aid in diagnosing and restoring troubles during circuit failure conditions.

Alarm Correlation   The system should aid the manager in determining which of multiple alarms is the primary fault and which are sympathetic alarms. For example, a hardware alarm should be diagnosed as the cause of a group of circuit failures. The system should aid the operators in determining appropriate action for alleviating symptoms.

Manager-to-Manager Capability   The system should provide for management workstations to communicate with one another. Subordinate workstations should be able to summarize and condense information, and report it to workstations higher in the hierarchy.

Platform Performance   The platform on which the management workstation runs must be powerful enough to handle the volume of traffic and overhead. Microsoft Windows–based workstations are less powerful and the software is not as complete as that running on UNIX-based workstations with RISC processors.

Mapping Capability   The management workstation should be able to interrogate all devices on the network and compile a network map showing information such as IP addresses, system status, and alarms in color. The network layout records should be readily accessible and easily understood.

Output Data   The system should provide output data summarized and sorted for analysis or should provide a port to an external system to accomplish the same objective. A complete trouble and event log should be provided. The system should be able to correlate events relating to a single case of trouble. The system should be able to export data to spreadsheets or other applications.

Web Implementation   The system should be capable of extending management functions over the Internet to devices located on intranets and extranets.

CHAPTER 40

Future Developments in Telecommunications

Telecommunications is destined to have a dynamic future as far in advance as the eye can see. People have an insatiable desire to communicate and the means are becoming more varied and more available, so there is nothing much on the horizon to slow the growth of technology. This chapter is a look into what the next few years are likely to bring. The breakup of the Bell System, the passage of the Telecommunications Act of 1996, and eventual deregulation promised a flood of new innovations, reduced price, and better service. The innovations have certainly occurred. Hundreds of new developments reach the market every year, some of which survive to provide more choices than ever before in this marriage between the computer and the network. As for improved service and lower prices, those have yet to occur for most customers. While large businesses enjoy reduced long-distance rates, most residential and small-business users have yet to enjoy the fruits of competition.

Nevertheless, the pace of change is dramatic. Many developers are predicting nothing less than a complete technology revolution as the traditional circuit-switched network bows to its eventual replacement by packet-switched services. That change will not, however, occur as rapidly as many believe because the immense investment in telecommunications plant will not be replaced quickly in the absence of some compelling advantages. Except for a few niche applications, those advantages are not on the horizon.

Fueled by the same techniques that are expanding computer applications and bringing prices down, telecommunications and computers together are improving productivity and making possible applications that were only a dream a few years ago. Human ingenuity is boundless in its ability to examine the way people work and develop new ways to improve the process. The transition to new methods of doing things isn't always easy. We adapt techniques and styles to work around the technical obstacles, and even when the obstacles are removed some of the old ways persist.

763

Social as well as technical forces are extending the reach of the traditional office. Telecommuting is a growing trend and one that seems likely to continue as companies face mandates to help relieve traffic congestion. Telecommunications makes it possible for people to choose where they work and live, so at least in some occupations the fixed office environment will give way to a dispersed office, which, at least part of the time, is in the home or in the neighborhood. This, in turn, will drive the need for broadband facilities. As the carriers move fiber optics into residential areas, a trend that will presumably be driven by entertainment as well as voice and Internet access, facilities for broadband communication will become available, although the cost is impossible to predict.

Predicting changes of the future telecommunications system is a risky proposition. No one can foresee the rate of technological development, but several clear trends will shape the network of the future. Some of these are

- Processor speeds will continue to increase, and prices will continue to drop, at least as measured by MIPs per dollar. This will spawn new applications in voice processing, multimedia, imaging, and other bandwidth-hungry services.

- Electronic commerce will grow dramatically as industries change their method of delivering service. Traditional retailing and business-to-business services will either adapt to doing business over the Internet or be left behind.

- Competition, which has already reshaped the network, will continue to have a significant impact. The local network is the current battleground, but the effects of competition there are slight so far. This will not last as carriers compete for the most lucrative customers.

- The future of regulation, which is competition's recourse, is in the hands of Congress and the courts, and the outcome is anything but certain. Deregulation is not only an American trend; it is happening worldwide.

- Traditional circuit switching will be supplemented by packet technologies as new niche applications begin to develop for carrying voice and video over packet networks.

- Cable networks will begin to compete with traditional telephone networks for carrying voice and Internet access. Telephone companies will respond as rapidly as they can with digital subscriber lines to provide more bandwidth to access the Internet.

- Voice recognition technology has left the laboratory and is ready for prime-time service. With it new applications will assist companies in providing a higher quality of customer support at lower cost.

The telecommunications industry is poised on the threshold of dramatic change that will reshape services over the next few years. This chapter is more a projection than a prediction. In it, we will look at some of the fundamental forces reshaping the telecommunications industry, and discuss the impact they are likely to have during the next few years. We are specifically excluding technologies such as photonic switching and super conductivity, which have yet to emerge from the laboratories and carve a role for themselves.

INTERNET

Nothing in the memory of most of us has caught hold as quickly as the Internet, which has leaped into public consciousness over the past few years. Where communicating ends and computing begins is irrelevant to users. They are concerned only with the ability to access information wherever it resides, and to communicate with others effortlessly, with the network making distance and protocol irrelevant.

The Internet has emerged in the last few years as one of the major forces shaping telecommunications. The momentum behind the Internet will ensure its role for the future. It is the only medium that provides universal worldwide connectivity without the bandwidth restriction and usage-sensitive pricing of the dial telephone network. It provides connectivity between carriers that traditional data networks do not support, which opens users to the concepts of intranets and extranets. These are the networks that open information flow between users in the same company and externally with their suppliers and customers.

The deluge of the World Wide Web has submerged the original concept of the Internet as a means of open information interchange among government, universities, and contractors. Access to the Internet is a necessity in most businesses. It is also essential for businesses to keep in touch with their publics and customers. All of this leads to increased demand for bandwidth. Dial-up access is suitable for SOHO (small office/home office), but larger businesses need direct connectivity, which inevitably leads to security problems.

Electronic commerce is another significant trend that the Internet enables. Most of the publicity to date from e-commerce has revolved around consumer business. The success of Amazon.com in retailing has been nothing short of phenomenal, and is prompting hundreds of imitators to follow its example. E-commerce isn't simply about retailing, however. The business-to-business aspects of e-commerce are just beginning to emerge, and will forever reshape the way business is done. Companies are growing to expect that information will be accessible on the Web, and they will communicate with their customers and suppliers over the Internet. E-commerce will reshape advertising, education, insurance, health care, law, and virtually every other profession. In addition, costs will be reduced. Airlines, for example, have found that issuing an e-ticket over the Web costs a little more than 10 percent of the cost of traditional tickets and banking by personal computer cuts the cost of a transaction by almost 90 percent compared to using a teller.

As e-commerce catches on, dial-up access to the Internet will be a thing of the past for most businesses. Residences will continue to use dial-up access except for those for whom Web-surfing is a hobby that justifies the extra cost of a dedicated connection. If cable access catches on, this picture could change, but in the United States today, 40 percent of the households do not have cable. For businesses, cable will have little impact for Web access. ADSL will be satisfactory for smaller companies, but most businesses will migrate to frame relay or point-to-point access. Speed is of the essence in e-commerce applications. Studies have shown that most Web users will wait no more than 30 seconds for a page to load and 2 minutes for information to return. Those thresholds will only get tighter as users become more demanding.

A world where most businesses are directly connected to the Internet will have a monumental impact. The main thing hampering connectivity between trading partners now is good facility for doing so. Frame relay is an excellent medium, but the world has multiple frame relay carriers and they are not interconnected to any appreciable degree. This means that a business with multiple trading partners must have multiple frame relay accounts, which is not a palatable situation. Internet overcomes that. Even though there are multiple Internet backbones, they are interconnected and use universal IP addressing, which makes it easy for companies to communicate regardless of who their ISP is or what carrier the ISP uses.

The importance of this connectivity cannot be overestimated. It enables any-to-any connectivity anywhere in the world with bandwidth that is limited by the access circuit. The clock doesn't limit the connection. That kind of connectivity is possible only with the telephone system, but not with the cost and bandwidth that the Internet provides. Computers keep businesses open for 24 hours per day, bypassing the limitations of multiple time zones. Of course, if security is a concern, the ease of connectivity drops quickly. Organizations can't afford to let just anyone through the firewall, but tunnels will be built for trading partners. E-commerce is a trend that has barely started, but it promises to reshape not only the Internet, but also the very manner in which business is conducted.

CONVERGENCE

We have devoted a chapter to this subject, but it belongs in the future because it will be one of the major driving forces of telecommunications. Despite the hype, convergence isn't about replacing the infrastructure we now have. Although that may happen sometime over the next few decades, the economics of displacing circuit-switched devices aren't there and won't be for general use. Even AT&T, which is investing immense sums on cable television as a way of distributing local services, is still investing heavily in circuit-switched central offices. AT&T will deliver packet voice to homes over cable, but its large business services and connections to the PSTN will continue to be traditional circuit switching for years to come.

Convergence isn't about displacing what we have now, it is about applications. People choose their method of communication, whether it is dialing on the telephone or surfing the Web, and it isn't good business to require customers who have been browsing a Web-based catalogue to hang up and dial a toll-free number if they can reach a representative over the Web. Branch offices are likely to have a frame relay connection in place for low-bandwidth applications such as an occasional file transfer and e-mail. The spare bandwidth can carry voice conversations and where there is enough traffic to justify the extra equipment cost, voice rides free. Telecommuting will be enhanced as companies have the option of displacing expensive office space with low-cost telecommunications facilities.

Voice over IP will start with niche applications. These will gradually expand into interesting products that aren't feasible with separate voice and data networks. Several driving forces make this trend inevitable. The first is a tremendous technology push. Countless developers are looking for market niches and are working on products that are enabled by voice over IP. Working with them are data professionals inside corporations who have voice responsibility but understand data networks better than they do voice. They generate a demand-pull for voice over IP in advance of any pressing need. Economics isn't always the driving force. Many users are purchasing VoIP products because of an advantage that will prove more illusory than real.

Voice over the Internet will also gain some credibility as new protocols emerge to provide some quality of service predictability. Here, some businesses will use gateways to reduce the cost of calls, but most people will be unwilling to accept a reduction in quality except in such applications as a Web-enabled call center. An exception will be people who tolerate poor voice quality to gain cost saving and in some cases convenience.

THE FUTURE OF CIRCUIT SWITCHING

Many observers are predicting the demise of circuit switching, contending that packet switches can do everything circuit switches can, and do it better. It would appear that the major manufacturers agree because all of them are bringing packet switching facilities into their circuit switching systems. Although the PBX and carrier switches will undoubtedly evolve over the next decade or so, they will not disappear altogether. Circuit switching is still a high-quality low-cost way of connecting voice sessions, and voice still makes up a substantial part of daily communications. Only with difficulty can packet switches approach the service quality that circuit switches provide inherently. Consequently, circuit switching will be around for many years to come.

The CLECs are good evidence of the expected longevity of circuit switching. In building their networks, they place conventional central office switches at the heart, but this doesn't mean that they won't have need for a packet interface. As carriers begin to offer voice service over cable, for example, voice will ultimately be packetized at the customer premises and routed to a circuit switching interface into the PSTN.

PBXs will still retain conventional circuit-switched trunk interfaces to the PSTN and these will be augmented by IP trunking. Increasingly, the PBX will become a voice server on the corporate network. Some applications will connect over a packet network, while others remain circuit-switched. Users will have more flexible options than ever before as they can choose how to interface the various networks.

The trend is also definitely toward off-loading special applications such as voice mail, call distribution, and the like to servers. This makes a lot of sense because servers, while lacking the reliability of a PBX, are more flexible and have open interfaces that permit owners to customize their applications without compromising the stability of basic voice services. The PBX of the future will have multiple port interfaces. Today most PBXs offer standard analog, proprietary digital, and semiopen BRI interfaces on the line side, and standard analog, T1/E1, and PRI on the trunk side. In the near future, nearly every manufacturer will provide IP trunks. Some switches will offer ATM interfaces and many will provide gateway services for H.323 voice and video applications. Ethernet interfaces will be offered in addition to station ports so users have the choice of accessing the network via H.323 or circuit switching.

Computer-telephony integration will offload many of the functions of the PBX to outboard processors. Initiatives by major manufacturers, such as Microsoft and Novell, are leading numerous developers to produce CTI products. Although the quantity of applications won't equal the flood of software products inspired by inexpensive desktop computers, the fact remains that everyone has a telephone, and the user interface is deficient. The next few years should bring hundreds of new CTI products, not just for call centers, but also for PBXs, key systems, and ordinary telephones. Will the products be a computer with a telephone inside or a telephone with a computer inside? We can expect both kinds of products.

CTI will also augment nearly every call center. Functions that are considered leading edge today will become commonplace tomorrow. Screen pop is just the beginning of CTI applications for the call center. Personalized treatment for callers will be enhanced by caller recognition and call routing based on callers' personal preferences. Voice-processing adjuncts, including speech recognition, will aid the call center in determining who the callers are and what they want. Computers will also assist callers in fulfilling their requests without human assistance.

MULTIMEDIA OVER CABLE

While the local exchange market migrates into the hands of a few major players, the same thing is happening with cable. No longer eyed as just an entertainment medium, cable can become an information channel into households. AT&T is the 2-ton gorilla in the cable marketplace. They purchased TCI in 1998 for a price that was around $3000 per household. Together with Time Warner, these two giants have about one-half of the American market. Comcast, which is another player, attempted to acquire MediaOne's 5 million subscribers at a price of $4000 per household, but in the final analysis AT&T outbid them. However this bidding war comes out, it is obvious that investments of this magnitude will not pay off at the rate of $25 to $40 per month per subscriber, which is the range that cable television commands for entertainment alone. Additional revenues will have to be generated, and these are expected to come from Internet access and local telephone service.

The cable companies have a massive rebuilding job to do because coaxial cable is unsuitable for the information delivery job in the future. Billions more must be invested to upgrade cable to bring fiber optics to nodal distribution points, but once this is accomplished, new markets will open. The cable providers are betting billions of dollars that new facilities will attract new revenues. Supplementing entertainment, they believe, will be revenues from Internet access and local and long-distance telephone service. At the same time, their markets are being threatened by direct broadcast satellite services.

To be successful, cable must become a digital medium, at least from the node back to the headend. Analog cable systems have a limited capacity, and analog Internet and telephone systems have transmission and bandwidth problems over cable. To overcome these limitations, cable carriers must use packetized voice and fiber optics in the backbone. As discussed earlier under "Convergence," they have technical obstacles to overcome, but there is little doubt that with the stakes as high as they are these obstacles will soon be removed. In opposition to the digital trend in voice and Internet access, however, broadcast video is analog and millions of television sets and VCRs would have to be replaced to change that.

The large cable companies, such as AT&T and Time Warner, are not having a smooth ride, however. In addition to enormous investments that may have an exceptionally long payback period, they are being besieged by other would-be competitors who are petitioning the FCC and local regulators to require the cable carriers to open their networks to equal access. So far, the FCC has declined to get involved.

MERGERS AND ACQUISITIONS

One trend that seems destined to continue is mergers and combinations of the telecommunications giants into even larger companies. SBC Corporation has been the most vigorous of the RBOCs in combating the effects of divestiture and the Telecommunications Act by a combination of mergers and court actions. First, they merged with Pacific Telesis, which serves California and Nevada. They have filed several court cases seeking to overthrow the restrictions they operate under. They have merged with Southern New England Telephone Company to extend their reach into Connecticut, and with Ameritech, the RBOC that serves the upper midwestern states.

Meanwhile, Bell Atlantic merged with Nynex to establish an RBOC powerhouse along the northeastern seaboard, and with GTE, which extends its territory across the nation. US West announced plans to merge with Global Crossings, but Qwest raised the ante and is seeking approval of the acquisition as this book goes to press. These mergers leave Bell South as the only one of the original seven RBOCs that has retained its original boundaries.

The IXCs have likewise been busy expanding their influence. MCI, which was the second largest IXC in North America, merged with WorldCom to form WorldCom, still the second largest carrier. As this is written, WorldCom is seeking approval to acquire Sprint, which is the number three carrier. The largest carrier, AT&T, acquired TCI in one of the largest deals of the century. Overseas companies have not been idle while these combinations have been occurring. British Telecom has been one of the most aggressive of the expanding companies and in mid-1999 Deutsche Telekom and Telecom Italia announced that they are merging.

This trend of mergers and acquisitions will continue. The critical question is whether consumers will benefit. Theoretically, the combinations could reduce overhead expenses, but cultural clashes and mass layoffs are the more probable result, and the consumer will pay the price.

SPEECH RECOGNITION

Speech recognition is the beneficiary of both faster computers and improved technology. Several manufacturers are now shipping their voice-mail products with speech recognition capability. This is a boon to users who can never remember the keystrokes for forwarding and deleting messages, and for mobile users who can't let go of the steering wheel to key in responses to prompts. Also affecting telecommunications will be major changes in automated attendants, and the possibility of replacing many conventional console attendant duties by enabling callers to access the company directory and transfer to extensions by voice command. Many such products are available today. The results aren't flawless, but the potential demand for future products is enormous.

Today's DTMF keypad is a poor substitute for a keyboard. It is slow, limited in scope of coverage, and requires eye contact for its operation. Speech recognition overcomes all of these difficulties, and can make the telephone (or microphone) a universal input device. The ability to convert speech to text enables the universal mailbox, which allows an unrestricted exchange among e-mail, voice mail, and facsimile messages. Telephone operator and console attendant functions will be revolutionized. The challenge managers face is in preventing the functions from being objectionably dehumanized.

When systems reach the point of recognizing a large vocabulary from a wide variety of speakers, numerous applications will be possible. Applications that can have a large effect on telecommunications include:

- Automated attendant replacement
- Replacement of directory operators
- Voice-driven commands to perform operations such as conferencing, outdialing, transferring, and so on

WIRELESS

The radio spectrum is a marvelous and underutilized resource. Technologists are discovering how to cram an increasing amount of information into a limited amount of spectrum. This enables more efficient use of cellular frequencies, and equally important, enables personal communications service (PCS) to develop. Wireless also enables the mobile data terminal, which solves numerous problems such as portable and desktop calendars that are often out of sync, and the ability to retrieve a file without the worry of cabling, ports, and protocols. It solves some of the problems of connecting workstation users to LANs, particularly in buildings that are difficult to wire.

Wireless PBX stations will likely have a significant impact in the future. Many people, such as healthcare workers, retailers, manufacturing personnel, and others who work on their feet most of the day, have learned to work around the confines of the telephone cord. Wireless will change the working styles and probably improve the productivity of such people. Wireless data can have a similar effect on workers. The keyboard-equipped mobile data terminal has applications in law enforcement, dispatch operations, and any class of workers who carry a laptop to meetings. The wireless personal digital assistant will have a large effect on working styles and productivity if the service is cost-effective. The wireless local loop is also likely to have an impact on users as it brings information to the household without the need to run copper wire, coaxial cable, or fiber optics through the neighborhood.

The transition from wired to wireless will not happen overnight, and many years will pass before copper wires are eliminated, if they ever are. Being tied to a telephone cord doesn't matter for many people, but for those who must roam, the implications of wireless are important. Easy portability will change professions such as medicine, retail, education, construction, and other occupations that today are currently able to receive calls only in fixed locations that they occupy for short intervals during the day. Whatever form it takes, wireless will have a significant impact on the way we work and live. Whether the change is a convenience or an intrusion will depend on how the cultures of those professions adapt.

COMPETITIVE LOCAL SERVICE

Local circuit competition is just getting started in the United States. The major cities all have multiple CLECs, and companies with enough line requirements to justify a T1 can make some excellent deals on local dial tone. So far, however, the innovation in local service that the Telecommunications Act of 1996 set as one of its ideals has yet to happen. The competition is on price, and while local service isn't yet a commodity, the time will come when there isn't much to distinguish local exchange carriers except price and service.

One major negative impact of competitive local service is already beginning to occur: rural areas are in danger of being left out of the benefits of the information revolution. Competitive carriers are in no hurry to provide service to small towns because they can't reach the critical mass of lines needed to make the service profitable. As the LECs that serve these towns lose revenues to competition in the metropolitan areas, service will inevitably decline, cost will increase, or both. The incumbent local exchange carriers are, for the most part, not freed from regulation, so they are trying to compete with carriers that are free to set their own prices and service conditions. Congress' attempt to deal with the problem by establishing subsidies is doomed to failure. Moreover, the carriers are passing on the costs the act imposes on them to consumers who are paying for it in higher rates. It can be argued that residential and rural users have always been subsidized by business and metropolitan users, which is true, but in the past the class lines have not been so clearly drawn. The fruits of long-distance competition have been enjoyed by large users, while rates of small users have increased as the carriers ratchet up their prices for incidental long-distance calls.

Competition in the local exchange network bodes even worse for small consumers. Many states have authorized LECs to charge a fee, typically 50 cents per line per month, for local number portability. IXCs and LECs alike are passing through the PICC fees and contributions to the Universal Service Fund. These fees have the effect of raising the cost of local service without corresponding benefits, all in the name of competition, which the vast majority of subscribers cannot enjoy.

Over the next few years, local service competition will cause some significant dislocations for consumers. Businesses using more than a dozen lines or so will enjoy savings of close to 50 percent on their local service bills when compared to the rates the ILECs have been charging. These savings translate into a loss of revenues for the ILECs, which must keep earnings up by cutting costs or finding other revenues. Since divestiture, the ILECs have demonstrated that cutting costs means service reductions, and more of this is undoubtedly yet to come. Rural areas, which cannot attract the competition to keep rates down, will suffer in particular. Utility commissions will be faced with the unenviable task of presiding over deregulation, declining service, or both.

The ILECs have, for the most part, not garnered much sympathy from their customers as their service quality has deteriorated. The ex-Bell companies are all petitioning the FCC and the courts for permission to carry long-distance outside the LATA boundaries. So far, several state utility commissions have recommended that the RBOC serving their state be granted this permission, but the FCC has continued to deny its approval. This situation will not last long, however, because RBOCs are losing market share to competitors that can undercut their prices while the RBOCs are refused permission to deviate from their tariffs. None of this is in consumers' long-term best interests because the country needs healthy ILECs during the evolution to local exchange competition.

The United States is leading the world in the transition to a competitive local exchange market. It is to be hoped that the rest of the world learns from the mistakes of American regulators and politicians, who have, so far, neither accomplished a free local exchange market nor achieved the promise of greater innovation and reduced costs.

COMPETITION AND REGULATION

In the United States, competition in the interexchange network is mature and large users are enjoying its fruits. One of the major trends is the movement away from distance-sensitive pricing. Practically all domestic long-distance calls for large businesses today are based on connect time alone. In fact, long-distance rates are approaching the rates that some LECs charge for metered local service. Other countries that have privatized and deregulated their networks are seeing similar effects on domestic calls. Competition has not yet had a similar effect on international calls, however. The restraints are artificial. Governments and protected groups have become accustomed to subsidies and keep the cost of international calls artificially high.

Several forces are converging, however, to bring international calls closer to cost. Voice over IP is one such force, the effects of which have hardly been felt yet. Another is the more subtle pressure resulting from the need governments have to be competitive, not just in telecommunications, but in their economic development. Countries that maintain restrictions on the free flow of information will not be able to compete in the world economy.

While competition in the long-distance market has worked well for large users, the same cannot be said for small users and users of services such as pay telephones and hotel phones, at least in the United States. Small users are being hurt by surcharges that many IXCs apply. For example, AT&T announced a $3 per line minimum charge for users, and they levy USF and PICC charges on top of the minimum. Users who never place a long-distance call are still required to pay or switch to another carrier with more liberal policies. Users cannot escape the costs of regulation by declining to pick an IXC because in this case the FCC mandates that the LEC levy a charge—a curious case of users in a presumably free market being charged for not using a service! The FCC has decreed higher access charges for users with multiple residential lines in the same premises. These apply even in group homes where only one user is entitled to the lower primary line charge.

The United States is currently in a curious state of paradox when it comes to the issue of allowing the free market and competition to substitute for regulation. The Telecommunications Act of 1996 contains these words in its preamble:

> To promote competition and reduce regulation in order to secure lower prices and higher quality services for American telecommunications consumers and encourage the rapid deployment of new telecommunications technologies. *Be it enacted by the Senate and House of Representatives of the United States of America in Congress assembled, . . .*

In the face of this, the FCC has consistently failed to promote competition and reduce regulation. For example, pay phone providers complained to the FCC about lack of compensation for toll-free calls. The FCC responded by decreeing that IXCs would reimburse the pay phone providers even though the IXC often has no good way to identify which carrier is entitled to reimbursement. The IXCs promptly began passing these charges through to the toll-free customer, often marked up to a level higher than the fee they paid. Clearly, pay phone providers entered a competitive business knowing how it was structured. Had the FCC been following a consistent set of principles, it would have elected to let the market resolve the issue.

As this book is written, the FCC is considering rules that would impose airtime charges on the originator of cellular calls instead of the cell phone user. The problem with this, of course, is that the callers have no way of knowing that they are calling a cell phone and will be charged for the call. This issue is one in which the FCC can best discharge its duties by letting the market deal with the problem itself. With respect to cell phones, the FCC has elected to let the service providers decide what coding scheme they will use for digital cellular, with the result that in the United States three separate and incompatible methods are available.

As deregulation occurs, it is inevitable that some groups will be hurt, since perfect competition in the local exchange market is impossible at this juncture. The FCC, which should provide some stability, has acted with no perceptible consistency in their approach. As discussed earlier, they have, on the one hand, acted to protect the interests of pay phone providers, which many users believe are among the least deserving participants in the deregulated world. On the other hand, they have turned a deaf ear to the LECs requests to apply access charges to operators providing long-distance over the Internet. Meanwhile, the United States is entering a phase in which the simplicity of use of the telephone is being lost. The issue of whether to split area codes has been left to the states. Consequently, some have chosen overlay area codes in preference to area code divisions. As a result, users who travel to different parts of the country no longer instinctively know how to use the telephone.

Anyone attempting to predict the course of deregulation will be ill advised to examine the past too closely. Regulators on both a state and federal level are following no observable consistency in deciding which frays to enter and which to ignore. The only safe prediction to make is that the United States, at least, seems destined to follow a course of regulatory inconsistency that is shaped more by political pressure than by either technical foundation or guiding principle.

World Wide Web Addresses of Selected Telecommunications Manufacturers, Carriers, Vendors, and Organizations

This collection of Web addresses provides a way of reaching companies and organizations referenced in this book plus many others in the telecommunications industry. The author apologizes for any errors or omissions in this list. This directory is kept updated on the Pacific Netcom Inc. Web site. Corrections and additions can be e-mailed to *directory@pacificnetcom.com*.

Manufacturers

3Com	*www.3com.com*
3M	*www.3m.com*
ABL Canada	*www.abl.ca*
Accelerated Networks	*www.acceleratednetworks.com*
ACT Networks, Inc.	*www.acti.com*
Active Voice	*www.activevoice.com*
ADC Kentrox	*www.kentrox.com*
Adtech	*www.adtech-inc.com*
Adtran, Inc.	*www.adtran.com*
Adva Optical Networking	*www.advaoptical.com*
Advanced Fibre Communications	*www.fibre.com*
AG Communication Systems	*www.agcs.com*
Aironet Wireless Communications, Inc.	*www.aironet.com*
Alcatel Network Systems, Inc.	*www.alcatel.com*
Allen Telecom	*www.allentele.com*
Allied Telesyn International	*www.alliedtelesyn.com*
American Power Conversion	*www.apcc.com*
Amp, Inc.	*www.amp.com*

Antec	*www.antec.com*
Array Telecom	*www.telecom.array.ca*
Asanté Technologies	*www.asante.com*
Ascend Communications	*www.ascend.com*
Ascom Timeplex	*www.timeplex.com*
Aspect Telecommunications	*www.aspect.com*
Astarte Fiber Networks	*www.starswitch.com*
Atronics	*www.atronics.com*
Avanti Technology	*www.avanti-tech.com*
Axent Technologies, Inc.	*www.axent.com*
Aydin Communications	*www.aydin.com*
Bay Networks	*www.baynetworks.com*
Belden Wire and Cable Co.	*www.belden.com*
Berk-tek	*www.berktek.com*
Best Power	*www.bestpower.com*
Bicc Cables	*www.bicc-brandrex.com*
Bookham Technology Ltd.	*www.bookham.com*
BreezeCOM	*www.breezecom.com*
Brooktrout Technology	*www.brooktrout.com*
Cable Systems International	*www.csi-cables.com*
Cable Television Laboratories	*www.cablelabs.com*
CableData, Inc.	*www.cabledata.com*
Cabletron Systems	*www.cabletron.com*
Callware	*www.callware.com*
Canoga Perkins	*www.canoga.com*
C-COR Electronics, Inc.	*www.c-cor.com*
Centigram Communications	*www.centigram.com*
Check Point Software Technologies	*www.checkpoint.com*
Ciena Corp	*www.ciena.com*
Cisco Systems	*www.cisco.com*
Clarion	*www.clarionwireless.com*
Com21	*www.com21.com*
Comdial	*www.comdial.com*
CommScope, Inc.	*www.commscope.com*
Compaq Computer Corporation	*www.compaq.com*
Comverse Information Systems	*www.cis.comverse.com*
Concord Communications	*www.concord.com*

Convergys Corporation	*www.convergys.com*
Corning Fiber	*www.corningfiber.com*
Cortelco	*www.cortelco.com*
CSG Systems, Inc.	*www.csgsys.com*
Cubix	*www.cubix.com*
Cylink	*www.cylink.com*
Data Fellows Ltd.	*www.datafellows.com*
Datacom Technologies	*www.datacomtech.com*
Dialogic	*www.dialogic.com*
DiCon Fiberoptics Inc.	*www.diconfiberoptics.com*
Digi International	*www.digi.com*
Digital Equipment	*www.digital.com*
Digital Telecommunications Inc.	*www.dticorp.com*
Digital Voice Technologies	*www.dvsinc.com*
DSC Communications	*www.dsccc.com*
DTI Corporation	*www.dticorp.com*
Efficient Networks	*www.efficient.com*
E-Fusion, Inc.	*www.efusion.com*
Eicon Technology	*www.eicon.com*
E-Net	*www.datatelephony.com*
Ennovate Networks	*www.ennovatenetworks.com*
Equinox Systems	*www.equinox.com*
Ericsson, Inc.	*www.ericsson.com*
Excel	*www.xl.com*
Executone Information Systems	*www.executone.com*
Extreme Networks	*www.extremenetworks.com*
Faxback, Inc.	*www.faxback.com*
FlowPoint	*www.flowpoint.com*
Fluke	*www.fluke.com*
Fore Systems	*www.fore.com*
Foundry Networks	*www.foundrynet.com*
Franklin Telecommunications Corporation	*www.ftel.com*
Fujitsu Business Communications Systems	*www.fujitsu.com*
Gandalf Technologies	*www.gandalf.com*
General Cable	*www.generalcable.com*
General DataComm	*www.gdc.com*

General Instrument Corporation	*www.gi.com*
Genesys Telecommunications Laboratories, Inc.	*www.genesyslab.com*
Glenayre Technologies	*www.glenayre.com*
Globalstar	*www.globalstar.com*
Greenlee Textron Inc.	*www.greenlee.textron.com*
Harris Communications Products	*www.harris.com*
Harris Farinon Division	*www.farinon.harris.com*
Hewlett-Packard	*www.hp.com*
Hitachi	*www.hitel.com*
Hubbell	*www.hubbell-premise.com*
Hughes Network Systems, Inc.	*www.hns.com*
Hybrid Networks	*www.hybrid.com*
Hypercom Network Systems	*www.hypercom.com*
IBM	*www.networking.ibm.com*
ICG Telecom Group, Inc.	*www.icgcomm.com*
Infinite Technologies	*www.infinitemail.com*
Innosoft International, Inc.	*www.innosoft.com*
Intecom	*www.intecom.com*
Intel Corporation	*www.intel.com*
Intelect Network Technologies	*www.intelectinc.com*
Internet Telephony Exchange Carrier Co.	*www.itxc.net*
Inter-tel, Inc.	*www.inter-tel.com*
Ipsilon Networks	*www.ipsilon.com*
Ipswitch, Inc.	*www.ipswitch.com*
Iwatsu	*www.iwatsu.com*
KVX	*www.kvx.com*
LANcast	*www.lancast.com*
Larscom	*www.larscom.com*
Larus Corporation	*www.laruscorp.com*
Leviton Telecom	*www.levitontelecom.com*
Linkon Corporation	*www.linkon.com*
Loop Telecom	*www.looptelecom.com*
Lotus Development Corporation	*www.lotus.com*
Lucent Technologies	*www.lucent.com*
Lynk Ltd.	*www.soholynk.com*
MacroTel International	*www.macrotel.com*

Madge Networks	*www.madge.com*
Maxtech Company	*www.maxtech.com*
Memotec Communications	*www.memotec.com*
Micom Communications Corporation	*www.micom.com*
Microcom	*www.microcom.com*
Microsoft Corporation	*www.microsoft.com*
Microtest	*www.microtest.com*
Microwave Radio Communications	*www.cm-mrc.com*
Mitel	*www.mitel.com*
MOD-TAP	*www.mod-tap.com*
Mohawk/CDT	*www.mohawk-cdt.com*
Motorola	*www.mot.com*
Multilink Technologies Group	*www.multilinkinc.com*
Multi-Tech Systems	*www.multitech.com*
Natural Microsystems	*www.nmss.com*
NBase Xyplex	*www.nbase-xyplex.com*
NBX	*www.nbxcorp.com*
NEC America	*www.cng.nec.com*
Neo Networks	*www.neonetworks.com*
NetCentric	*www.netcentric.com*
NetPhone	*www.netphone.com*
Netrix Corporation	*www.netrix.com*
Netrue	*www.netrue.com*
NetSpeak Corporation	*www.netspeak.com*
Network Associates	*www.nai.com*
Network Equipment Technologies	*www.net.com*
Network General	*www.ngc.com*
Network Peripherals	*www.npix.com*
Newbridge Networks	*www.vivid.newbridge.com*
Nitsuko Telecom Division	*www.nitsuko.com*
Nokia	*www.nokia.com*
Nordx/CDT	*www.nordx.com*
Nortel Networks	*www.nortelnetworks.com*
Novell	*www.novell.com*
Nuera Communications	*www.nuera.com*
Nynex	*www.nynex.com*
Octel Communications	*www.octel.com*

Oki Network Technologies	*www.oki.com*
OpenBSD, Inc.	*www.openbsd.org*
OpenCon Systems, Inc.	*www.opencon.com*
Optical Cable Corporation	*www.occfiber.com*
Orbcom Global LP	*www.orbcomm.net*
Orion Network Systems, Inc.	*www.orionnetworks.net*
Ortronics	*www.ortronics.com*
Osicom Technologies, Inc.	*www.osicom.com*
Panduit	*www.panduit.com*
Philips Broadband Networks, Inc.	*www.be.philips.com/pbn*
PictureTel Corporation	*www.picturetel.com*
Preformed Line Products	*www.preformed.com*
Premier Metal Products Company	*www.premiermetal.com*
Prestolite Wire Corporation	*www.prestolite.com*
Proteon	*www.proteon.com*
Racal Data Group	*www.racal.com*
Racon	*www.racon.com*
RAD Data Communications, Inc.	*www.rad.com*
Radguard Ltd.	*www.radguard.com*
RadioLAN	*www.radiolan.com*
Radvision Ltd.	*www.radvision.com*
Raptor Systems	*www.raptor.com*
Redcom Laboratories, Inc.	*www.redcom.com*
Rockwell Telecommunications	*www.nb.rockwell.com*
Scientific Atlanta	*www.sciatl.com*
Selsius Systems	*www.selsius.com*
Sentient	*www.sentient.com*
Shiva	*www.shiva.com*
Shoreline Teleworks	*www.shoretel.com*
Siecor	*www.siecor.com*
Siemens Corporation	*www.smi.siemens.com*
Siemens Stromberg Carlson	*www.ssc.siemens.com*
Siemon Company	*www.siemon.com*
Simplex Wire and Cable Corporation	*www.simplextech.com*
SmartBits Netcom Systems	*www.netcomsystems.com*
Sonoma Systems	*www.sonoma-systems.com*
SpectraLink	*www.spectralink.com*

SRX	*www.srx.com*
Stentor Alliance	*www.stentor.ca*
Sumitomo Electric	*www.sel-rtp.com*
Summa Four	*www.summa4.com*
Sun Microsystems	*www.sun.com*
Superior Modular Products	*www.superiormod.com*
Switchcraft, Inc.	*www.switchcraft.com*
Sycamore Networks, Inc.	*www.sycamorenet.com*
Tadiran Telecommunications, Inc.	*www.tadiran.com*
Tektronix	*www.tek.com*
Telco Research Corporation	*www.telcoresearch.com*
Telcordia Technologies	*www.telcordia.com*
Telehub Technologies	*www.telehub.com*
Telephony Experts	*www.t-experts.com*
Teligent	*www.teligent.com*
Telinet Technologies	*www.telinet.com*
Tellabs Operations, Inc.	*www.tellabs.com*
Telology Networks	*www.telology.com*
Teltronics	*www.teltronics.com*
Telular Global Data	*www.global-data.com*
Telxon Corporation	*www.telxon.com*
Timestep Corporation	*www.timestep.com*
Toshiba Telecommunications System Division	*www.telecom.toshiba.com*
TTC	*www.ttc.com*
Tut Systems	*www.tutsys.com*
Unisys	*www.unisys.com*
US Robotics, Inc.	See 3Com
VCON, Inc.	*www.vcon.com*
Verilink Corporation	*www.verilink.com*
Vicorp	*www.vicorp.com*
Vienna Systems	*www.viennasys.com*
Viking Electronics	*www.vikingelectronics.com*
Vina Technologies	*www.vinatech.com*
VocalTec Communications	*www.vocaltec.com*
Vodavi	*www.vodavi.com*
Voice Ware	*www.voiceware.net*

VoxWare	*www.voxware.com*
Vyvx Inc.	*www.vyvx.com*
Wandel & Golterman	*www.wg.com*
WaveAccess	*www.waveaccess.com*
Wavespan Corporation	*www.wavespan.com*
Wavetek	*www.wavetek.com*
Western Telematic, Inc.	*www.wti.com*
Williams Communications Group	*www.willtales.com*
Winncom Technologies	*www.wincom.com*
WinStar Wireless	*www.winstar.com*
Wiremold	*www.wiremold.com*
Wygant Scientific	*www.wygantsci.com*
Xircom	*www.xircom.com*
Xylan Corporation, Inc.	*www.xylan.com*

Standards Agencies and Associations

ADSL Forum	*www.adsl.com*
American Facsimile Association	*www.afaxa.com*
American National Standards Institute	*www.ansi.org*
ATM Forum	*www.atmforum.com*
Building Industry Consulting Service International	*www.bicsi.org*
Canadian Standards Association	*www.csa.ca*
Conference European on Post and Telecommunications	*www.thk.fi*
Corporation for Open Systems	*www.ora.com*
Desktop Management Task Force	*www.dtmf.org*
Electronic Computer Telephony Forum	*www.ectf.org*
Electronic Industries Association	*www.eia.org*
Electronic Messaging Association	*www.ema.org*
European Telecommunications Standards Institute	*www.etsi.fr*
Federal Communications Commission	*www.fcc.gov*
Frame Relay Forum	*www.frforum.com*
Institute of Electrical and Electronics Engineers	*www.ieee.org*

Insulated Cable Engineers Association	*www.electricnet.com*
International Telecommunications Union	*www.itu.com*
Internet Engineering Task Force	*www.ietf.org*
National Emergency Number Association	*www.nene9-1-1.org*
National Exchange Carriers Association	*www.neca.org*
National Fire Protection Agency	*www.opc.com*
North American Numbering Plan	*www.nanpa.com*
Telecommunications Industries Association	*www.tiaonline.org*
Underwriters Laboratories	*www.ul.com*
US Telephone Association*	*www.usta.org*
Voice over IP Forum	*www.imtc.org*
Wireless LAN Alliance	*www.wlana.com*

Local Exchange Carriers and Interexchange Carriers

Ameritech	*www.ameritech.com*
AT&T	*www.att.com*
Bell Atlantic	*www.bell-atl.com*
Bell Canada	*www.bell.ca*
Bell South	*www.bellsouth.com*
British Telecom	*www.bt.com*
Cable & Wireless	*www.cw-usa.net*
Comsat Corporation	*www.comsat.com*
Deutsche Telekom	*www.dtag.de*
GE Capital Spacenet Services, Inc.	*www.gespacenet.com*
Global Crossing	*www.globalcrossing.com*
GST Telecommunications, Inc.	*www.gstcorp.com*
GTE	*www.gte.com*
Helsinki Telecom Company	*www.hpy.fi*
Intelsat	*www.intelsat.int*
Iridium World Satellite Service	*www.iridium.com*
Nippon Telephone and Telegraph Company	*www.ntt.co.jp*

*This site has links to the public utilities commissions of the 50 states.

Pacific Bell	*www.pacbell.com*
Pacific Telesis	*www.pactel.com*
Panamsat Corporation	*www.panamsat.com*
PTT Telecom (Netherlands)	*www.ptt-telecom.nl*
Qwest Communications	*www.qwest.com*
SBC Communications	*www.sbc.com*
SkyTel	*www.skytel.com*
Southwestern Bell	*www.swbell.com*
Sprint	*www.sprint.com*
Swisscom (Swiss Telecom)	*www.telecom.ch*
Tampere Telephone (Finland)	*www.tpo.fi*
Tele Danmark	*www.teledanmark.dk*
Telecom Eireann (Ireland)	*www.telecom.ie*
Telecom Finland	*www.tele.fi*
Telecom Italia	*www.telecomitalia.it*
Teledesic LLC	*www.teledesic.com*
Teleport Communications Group	*www.tcg.com*
Telesat Canada	*www.telesat.ca*
Telkom SA (South Africa)	*www.telkom.co.za*
Telstra Corp. Ltd. (Australia)	*www.telstra.com.au*
US West	*www.uswest.com*
UUNet Technologies	*www.uu.net*
WorldCom	*www.wcom.com*

Miscellaneous Companies and Associations

Canadian Telecommunications Consultants Association	*www.ctca.ca*
Computer Telephony Institute	*www.ctinstitute.com*
Eastern Research	*www.erinc.com*
Education and Library Networks Coalition	*www.itc.org*
Pacific Netcom, Inc.	*www.pacificnetcom.com*
Society of Telecommunications Consultants	*www.stcconsultants.org*

Telecommunications Acronym Dictionary

The telecommunications industry is as expansive in its use of acronyms as the computer industry. The following is a list of acronyms used in this book, without definitions. Definitions for most acronyms are indexed by their full name in the Glossary.

AAC	Alternate access carrier
AAL	ATM adaptation layer
AC	Alternating current
ACD	Automatic call distributor
ACP	Action control point
ACTS	Automatic coin telephone system
ADM	Add-drop multiplexer
ADPCM	Adaptive differential pulse code modulation
ADSI	Analog display services interface
ADSL	Asymmetric digital subscriber line
AF	Audio frequency
AIN	Advanced intelligent network
AIS	Automatic intercept system
ALI	Automatic location information
AM	Amplitude modulation; active monitor
AMA	Automatic message accounting
AMI	Alternate mark inversion
AMIS	Audio messaging interchange specification
AMPS	Advanced mobile phone system
ANI	Automatic number identification

AO/DI	Always on/dynamic ISDN
AOS	Alternate operator service
APD	Avalanche photo diode
API	Application program interface
APPC	Advanced program-to-program communications
ARP	Address resolution protocol
ARQ	Automatic repeat request
ASCII	American standard code for information interexchange
ASIC	Application-specific integrated circuit
ASN	Abstract system notation
ATM	Asynchronous transfer mode
AUI	Attachment unit interface
AWG	American wire gauge
B8ZS	Bipolar with 8-zero substitution
BACP	Bandwidth allocation control protocol
BBS	Bulletin board system
BCD	Blocked calls delayed
BCH	Blocked calls held
BCR	Blocked calls released
BECN	Backward explicit congestion notification
BER	Bit error rate
BERT	Bit error rate test
BGP	Border gateway protocol
BHCA	Busy-hour call attempts
BIOS	Basic input/output system
BLER	Block error rate
BOC	Bell operating company
BRI	Basic-rate interface
BSA	Basic service arrangement
BSC	Binary synchronous communications (bisync)
BSE	Basic service element
BTA	Basic trading area
BUS	Broadcast and unknown server
CAC	Carrier access code
CAD	Computer-aided dispatch; computer-aided design
CAMA	Centralized automatic message accounting
CAS	Centralized attendant service

CATV	Community antenna television
CBX	Computer branch exchange
CCIS	Common channel interoffice signaling
CCITT	Consultative Committee on International Telephone and Telegraph
CCS	Centum call seconds; common channel signaling
CCTV	Closed circuit television
CDDI	Copper-distributed data interface
CDO	Community dial office
CDPD	Cellular digital packet data
CDR	Call detail recorder
CELP	Code excited linear prediction
CEPT	Conference European on Post and Telecommunications
CGSA	Cellular geographic serving area
CHAP	Challenge handshake authentication protocol
CIF	Common intermediate format
CIR	Committed information rate
CLASS	Custom local area signaling services
CLEC	Competitive local exchange carrier
CLID	Calling line identification
CMIP	Common management information protocol
CNM	Customer network management
CNS	Complementary network services
CO	Central office
CO-ACD	Central office automatic call distributor
COCOT	Customer-owned coin telephone
CODEC	Coder/decoder
CPE	Customer premises equipment
CPU	Central processing unit
CRC	Cyclical redundancy checking
CSMA/CD	Carrier sense multiple access with collision detection
CSTA	Computer-supported telecommunications application
CSU	Channel service unit
CTI	Computer-telephony integration
CTS	Clear to send
DAL	Direct access line
DAMA	Demand assigned multiple access

D-AMPS	Digital advanced mobile phone system
DAP	Directory access protocol
DAS	Dual attachment station
dB	Decibel
DBS	Direct broadcast satellite
DC	Direct current
DCA	Document content architecture
DCE	Data circuit-terminating equipment
DCO	Digital central office
DCS	Digital cross-connect system
DCT	Discreet cosine transform
DDD	Direct distance dialing
DECT	Digital European Cordless Telecommunications
DES	Data encryption standard
DHCP	Dynamic host configuration protocol
DIA	Document interchange architecture
DID	Direct inward dialing
DISA	Direct inward system access
DLCI	Data-link connection identifier
DLSw	Data-link switching
DMI	Digital multiplexed interface; desktop management interface
DNIC	Data network identification code
DNIS	Dialed number identification system
DNS	Domain name service; directory naming service
DOC	Dynamic overload control
DOCSIS	Data over cable service interface specification
DOV	Data over voice
DQDB	Distributed queue dual bus
DSA	Directory systems agent
DSI	Digital speech interpolation
DSMA/CD	Digital sense multiple access with collision detection
DSP	Directory service protocol
DSX	Digital service cross-connect
DTE	Data terminal equipment
DTMF	Dual-tone multifrequency
DUA	Directory user agent
DWDM	Dense wavelength division multiplexing

E-911	Enhanced 911
EAOSS	Exchange access operator service signaling
EAS	Extended area service
EBCDIC	Expanded binary-coded decimal interexchange code
EDI	Electronic data interchange
EDIFACT	EDI for administration, commerce, and transport
EF	Entrance facility
EFS	Error-free seconds
EGP	Exterior gateway protocol
EIA	Electronic Industry Association
EIRP	Effective isotropic radiated power
EMF	Electromagnetic force
EMI	Electromagnetic interference
ER	Equipment room
ERL	Echo return loss
ESF	Extended super frame
ESP	Encapsulating security payload
ESP	Enhanced service provider
ESS	Electronic switching system
ETC	Enhanced throughput cellular
ETN	Electronic tandem network
FCC	Federal Communications Commission
FDDI	Fiber distributed data interface
FDMA	Frequency division multiple access
FEC	Forward error correction
FECN	Forward explicit congestion notification
FEX	Foreign exchange
FM	Frequency modulation
FOD	Fax on demand
FRAD	Frame relay access device
FTP	File transfer protocol
GCD	Graphic codepoint definition
GEO	Geosynchronous earth orbit (satellite)
GFC	Generic flow control
GOS	Grade of service
GUI	Graphical user interface
HDTV	High-definition television

HEC	Header error control
HFC	Hybrid fiber-coax
IC	Independent company
ICMP	Internet control message protocol
ICSA	International Computer Security Association
IDF	Intermediate distributing frame
IETF	Internet Engineering Task Force
if	Intermediate frequency
IKE	Internet key exchange
IMAP	Internet message access protocol
IML	Incoming matching loss
IMTS	Improved mobile telephone service
INMARSAT	International Maritime Satellite Service
INWATS	Inward wide area telephone service
IP	Internet protocol
IPng	IP next generation
IPsec	IP security
IPv6	IP version 6
ISAKMP	Internet society association key management protocol
ISDN	Integrated services digital network
ISM	Industrial, scientific, medical
IVR	Interactive voice response
IVS	Interactive video system
IXC	Interexchange carrier
KTS	Key telephone system
L2F	Layer 2 forwarding
L2TP	Layer 2 tunneling protocol
LAMA	Localized automatic message accounting
LAN	Local area network
LANE	LAN emulation
LAPD	Distributed link access procedure
LATA	Local access transport area
LCR	Least-cost routing
LDAP	Lightweight directory access protocol
LDP	Label distribution protocol
LEC	Local exchange carrier; LAN emulation client
LECS	LAN emulation configuration server

LED	Light-emitting diode
LEO	Low earth orbit (satellite)
LES	LAN emulation server
LIS	Logical IP subnet
LIT	Line insulation test
LLC	Logical link control
LMDS	Local multipoint distribution service
LMI	Local management interface
LNP	Local number portability
LSR	Label switch router
LTD	Local test desk
LU	Logical unit
MAC	Media access control
MAP/TOP	Manufacturing automation protocol/technical and office protocol
MAPI	Mail application programming interface
MAU	Multistation access unit
MCU	Multipoint control unit
MCVD	Modified chemical vapor deposit
MDBS	Mobile database station
MDF	Main distributing frame
MDIS	Mobile data intermediate station
MDT	Mobile data terminal
MEO	Medium earth orbit (satellite)
MHS	Message-handling system
MIB	Management information base
MIF	Management information format
MIME	Multipurpose Internet mail extensions
MLN	Main listed number
MPEG	Motion Picture Experts Group
MPLS	Multiprotocol label switching
MPOA	Multiprotocol over ATM
MSS	Multiprotocol switch services
MTA	Message transfer agent; major trading area
MTBF	Mean time between failures
MTS	Message telephone service
MTSO	Mobile telephone switching office

MTTR	Mean time to repair
MTU	Maximum transfer unit
MVIP	Multivendor integration protocol
NAR	Network access restriction
NAS	Network access server
NAT	Network address translation
NAU	Network access unit; network addressable unit
NBMA	Nonbroadcast multiaccess network
NCP	Network control program; network control point
NCTE	Network channel-terminating equipment
NDIS	Network device interface specification
NEXT	Near-end crosstalk
NFAS	Non-facility-associated signaling
NHRP	Next hop resolution protocol
NIC	Network interface card
NID	Network interface device
NIU	Network interface unit
NLM	NetWare-loadable module
NMCC	Network management control center
NNI	Network-to-network interface; network node interface
NPA	Numbering plan area
NRZ	Nonreturn to zero
NRZI	Nonreturn to zero inverted
NSAP	Network service access point
NSC	Network services complex
NSN	National significant number
NT1	Network termination 1
NT12	Network termination 1–2
NT2	Network termination 2
NTN	Network terminal number
NTSC	National Television Systems Committee
OCR	Optical character recognition
ODI	Open data-link interface
ONA	Open network architecture
OPX	Off-premises extension
OSI	Open systems interconnect
OSP	Outside plant; operator service provider

OSPF	Open shortest path first
OSS	Operations support system
P/AR	Peak-to-average ratio
PA	Prearbitrated
PABX	Private automatic branch exchange
PAD	Packet assembler/disassembler
PAL	Phase alternate line
PAM	Pulse-amplitude modulation
PAP	Password authentication protocol
PBX	Private branch exchange
PCM	Pulse code modulation
PCS	Personal communication service
PDU	Protocol data unit
PIC	Primary interexchange carrier
PIN	Personal identification number
PKI	Public key infrastructure
POP	Point-of-presence; Post office protocol
PPP	Point-to-point protocol
PPTP	Point-to-point tunneling protocol
PRI	Primary rate interface
PSAP	Public service answering point
PSK	Phase-shift keying
PSTN	Public switched telephone network
PT	Payload type
PU	Physical unit
PVC	Permanent virtual circuit
QA	Queued arbitrated
QAM	Quadrature amplitude modulation
QoS	Quality of service
RADIUS	Remote authentication dial-in user service
RARP	Reverse address resolution protocol
RAS	Remote access server
RCF	Remote call forwarding
rf	Radio frequency
RFC	Request for comment
RIP	Routing information protocol
RISC	Reduced instruction set computer

RMATS	Remote maintenance and testing system
RMON	Remote monitoring
rms	Root mean square
rn	Reference noise
ROM	Read-only memory
ROTL	Remote office test line
RSL	Received signal level
RSVP	Resource reservation protocol
RTCP	Real-time control protocol
RTP	Real-time protocol
SAR	Segmentation and reassembly
SAS	Single-attachment station
SCC	Satellite communications control
SCP	Service control point
SCSA	Signal computing system architecture
SDLC	Synchronous data-link control
SDN	Software-defined network
SECAM	Sequential coleur avec memoire
SF	Single frequency
SIP	SMDS interface protocol
SIR	Sustained information rate
SIT	Special identification tones
SKIP	Simple key management for IP
SLIP	Synchronous line interface protocol
SMDR	Station message detail recording
SMDS	Switched multimegabit data service
SMI	Structure of management information
SMR	Specialized mobile radio
SMS	Service management system
SMSA	Standard metropolitan statistical area
SMTP	Simple mail transfer protocol
SNA	Systems network architecture
SNMP	Simple network management protocol
SOHO	Small office–home office
SONET	Synchronous optical network
SP	Signal point
SPC	Stored program control

SPID	Service profile identifier
SRL	Singing return loss
SSB	Single sideband
SSCP	System service control point
SSI	Switch-switch interface
SSL	Secure sockets layer
SSTDMA	Spacecraft-switched time division multiple access
STP	Signal transfer point
SVC	Switched virtual circuit
SVD	Simultaneous voice data
SVN	Switched virtual networking
TACAS	Terminal access controller access system
TAO	Telephony application object
TAPI	Telephony applications programming interface
TC	Telecommunications closet
TCAM	Telecommunications communication access method
TCM	Trellis-coded modulation
TCP/IP	Transmission control protocol/internet protocol
TDM	Time division multiplexing
TDMA	Time division multiple access
TDR	Time domain reflectometer
TE1	Terminal equipment type 1
TE2	Terminal equipment type 2
TEMPEST	Transient electromagnetic pulse emanation standard
THT	Token-holding timer
TIA	Telecommunications Industry Association
TLP	Transmission level point
TMGB	Telecommunications main grounding busbar
TRT	Token rotation time
TSAPI	Telephony systems applications programming interface
TTRT	Target token rotation time
TUR	Traffic usage recorder
UA	User agent
UCD	Uniform call distribution
UDP	User datagram protocol
UNI	User-to-network interface
UPS	Uninterruptable power supply

USB	Universal serial bus
USF	Universal service fund
VAN	Value-added network
VC	Virtual channel
VCC	Virtual control channel; virtual channel connection
VCI	Virtual channel identifier
VF	Voice frequency
VLAN	Virtual LAN
VNL	Via net loss
VOD	Video on demand
VPI	Virtual path identifier
VPN	Virtual private network
VRU	Voice response unit
VSAT	Very small aperture terminal
VTAM	Virtual terminal access method
VU	Volume unit
WA	Work area
WAN	Wide area network
WATS	Wide area telephone service
WDM	Wavelength division multiplexing
WG	Workgroup
WLL	Wireless local loop
XPD	Cross-polarization discrimination

GLOSSARY

A bit: In T1 carrier, the signaling bit that is formed from the eighth bit of the sixth channel.

A law: The coding law used in the European 30-channel PCM system.

Absorption: The attenuation of a lightwave signal by impurities or fiber-core imperfections, or of a microwave signal by oxygen or water vapor in the atmosphere.

Access tandem: An LEC switching system that provides access for the IXCs to the local network. The access tandem provides the IXC with access to more than one end office within an LATA.

Adaptive differential pulse code modulation (ADPCM): A method approved by CCITT for coding voice channels at 32 kb/s to increase the capacity of T1 to either 44 or 48 channels.

Adaptive equalizer: (1) Circuitry in a modem that allows the modem to compensate automatically for circuit conditions that impair high-speed data transmission. (2) A circuit installed in a microwave receiver to compensate for distortion caused by multipath fading.

Add-drop multiplexer (ADM): A device that extracts channels from a digital bit stream and inserts other channels into the bit stream.

Address resolution protocol (ARP): A protocol that translates between IP addresses and Ethernet addresses.

Addressing: The process of sending digits over a telecommunications circuit to direct the switching equipment to the station address of the called number.

Advanced intelligent network (AIN): An interface between the LEC switching system and an external computer that can provide special and custom services to subscribers independently of features offered by the switch manufacturer.

Aerial cable: Any cable that is partially or completely run aerially between buildings or poles.

Agent: In ACD an agent is a customer contact person, also known as a telephone service representative. In network management an agent is software that resides on the managed device and communicates with the network management workstation.

Alerting: The use of signals on a telecommunications circuit to alert the called party or equipment to an incoming call.

Alternate access carrier (AAC): A common carrier that builds a local access network, usually of fiber optics, to provide access service to the IXCs in competition to the LECs.

Alternate mark inversion (AMI): See Bipolar coding.

Alternate routing: The ability of a switching machine to establish a path to another machine over more than one circuit group.

Always on/dynamic ISDN (AO/DI): An ISDN service that keeps the D channel actively connected to a service provider. B channels are called in as needed.

American standard code for information interexchange (ASCII): A 7-bit (plus 1 parity bit) coding system used for encoding characters for transmission over a data network.

Amplitude distortion: Any variance in the level of frequencies within the passband of a communication channel.

Analog: A transmission mode in which information is transmitted by converting it to a continuously variable electric signal.

Angle of acceptance: The angle of light rays striking an optical fiber aperture, within which light is guided through the fiber. Light outside the angle of acceptance escapes through the cladding.

Antenna gain: The increase in radiated power from an antenna compared to an isotropic antenna.

Armored cable: Multipair cable intended for direct burial that is armored with a metallic covering that serves to prevent damage from rodents and digging apparatus.

Aspect ratio: The ratio between the width and the height of a video screen.

Asymmetric digital subscriber line (ADSL):   A technology for multiplexing a high-speed data or compressed video signal above the voice channel in a subscriber loop.

Asynchronous transfer mode (ATM):   A broadband connection-oriented switching service that carries data, voice, and video information in fixed-length 48-octet cells with a 5-octet header.

Asynchronous transmission: A means of transmitting data over a network wherein each character contains a start and stop bit to keep the transmitting and receiving terminals in synchronism with each other.

Atmospheric loss: The attenuation of a radio signal because of absorption by oxygen molecules and water vapor in the atmosphere.

Audible ring: A tone returned from the called party's switching machine to inform the calling party that the called line is being rung.

Audio frequency: A range of frequencies, nominally 20 Hz to 20 kHz, that the human ear can hear.

Audio messaging interchange specification (AMIS):   A standard that permits networking of voice-mail systems from different manufacturers.

Audiotex: A voice-mail service that prompts callers for the desired service, and delivers information in audio form.

Automated attendant: A feature of voice-mail and stand-alone systems that answers calls, prompts callers to enter DTMF digits in response to menu options, and routes the call to an extension or call distributor.

Automatic call distributor (ACD):   A switching system that automatically distributes incoming calls to a group of answering positions without going through an attendant. If all answering positions are busy, the calls are held until one becomes available.

Automatic coin telephone system (ACTS):   A coin telephone service that rates calls, collects coins, and completes other types of calls without intervention by an operator.

Automatic location information (ALI):   Emergency equipment that enables a 911 center to determine the location of a caller using a table lookup function.

Automatic message accounting (AMA):   Equipment that registers the details of chargeable calls and enters them on a storage medium for processing by an offline center.

Automatic number identification (ANI):   Identification of the calling line that is delivered from the calling station to the IXC for the purpose of billing the call. ANI is similar to calling line identification (CLID) and comes from the same source, except that CLID may be blocked by the caller where ANI, which is used on long-distance and 800 calls, cannot be blocked.

Automatic repeat request (ARQ):   A data communications protocol that automatically initiates a request to repeat the last transmission if an error is received.

Automatic route selection (ARS):   A software feature of PBXs and hybrids that selects the appropriate trunk route for a call to take, based on digits dialed and the caller's class of service.

Avalanche photo diode (APD):   A light detector that generates an output current many times greater than the light energy striking its face.

B bit: In T1 carrier, the signaling bit that is formed from the eighth bit of the twelfth channel.

B channel: The 64-kb/s "bearer" channel that is the basic building block of ISDN. The B channel is used for voice and circuit- or packet-switched data.

Backbone cable: Cabling connecting a main distributing frame to intermediate distributing frames located in telecommunications closets.

Backoff algorithm: The process built into the media access control of contention network to determine when to reattempt to send a frame.

Backplane: The wiring connecting the sockets of an equipment cabinet.

Balance: The degree of electrical match between the two sides of a cable pair or between a two-wire circuit and the matching network in a four-wire terminating set.

Balancing network: A network used in a four-wire terminating set to match the impedance of the two-wire circuit.

Balun: A device that converts the unbalanced wiring of a coaxial terminal system to a balanced twisted-pair system.

Bandwidth: The range of frequencies a communications channel is capable of carrying without excessive attenuation.

Banyan switch: A high-speed switching system that takes its name from the many branches of a banyan tree. A banyan switch is bidirectional and chooses its path from the address contained in the header of an incoming packet. If an address bit is a 1, the upper path of the switch is taken. Otherwise the switch takes the lower, or 0, path.

Baseband: A form of modulation in which data signals are pulsed directly on the transmission medium without frequency division.

Basic-rate interface (BRI):   The basic ISDN service consisting of two 64-kb/s information or bearer channels and one 16-kb/s data or signaling channel.

Battery: A direct current voltage supply that powers telephones and telecommunications apparatus.

Baud: The number of data signal elements per second a data channel is capable of carrying.

Beacon: In a token ring network, beacons are signals sent by stations to isolate and bypass failures.

Bearer channel: A 64-kb/s information-carrying channel that furnishes integrated services digital network (ISDN) services to end users.

Bell Operating Company (BOC):   One of the 22 local exchange companies (LECs) that were previously part of the Bell System.

Binary: A numbering system consisting of two digits, zero and one.

Binary synchronous communications (BSC or bisync):   An IBM byte-controlled half-duplex protocol using a defined set of control characters and sequences for data transmission.

Bipolar coding: The T carrier line coding system that inverts the polarity of alternate 1s bits. Also called alternate mark inversion (AMI).

Bipolar violation: The presence of two consecutive 1s bits of the same polarity on a T carrier line.

Bipolar with 8-zero substitution (B8ZS):   A line-coding scheme used with T1 clear channel to send a string of eight zeros with a deliberate bipolar violation. The 1s bits in the bipolar violation maintain line synchronization.

Bit: The smallest unit of binary information; a contraction formed from the words BInary digIT.

Bit error rate (BER):   The ratio of bits transmitted in error to the total bits transmitted on the line.

Bit rate: The speed at which bits are transmitted on a circuit, usually expressed in bits per second.

Bit robbing: The use of the least significant bit per channel in every sixth frame of a T1 carrier system for signaling.

Bit stream: A continuous string of bits transmitted serially in time.

Bit stuffing: Adding bits to a digital frame for synchronizing and control. Used in T carrier to prevent loss of synchronization from 15 or more consecutive 0 bits.

Block error rate (BLER):   In a given unit of time, BLER measures the number of blocks that must be retransmitted because of error.

Blocking: A switching system condition in which no circuits are available to complete a call, and a busy signal is returned to the caller.

Bonding: The permanent connecting of metallic conductors to equalize potential between the conductors and carry any current that is likely to be imposed. Also, combining two ISDN B channels to increase the bandwidth. The process of combining the operational support systems of an LEC with those of a CLEC.

Bootp: A boot protocol that dynamically assigns IP addresses to nodes.

Branch feeder: A cable between the distribution cable and the main feeder cable that connects users to the central office.

Branching filter: A device inserted in a waveguide to separate or combine different microwave frequency bands.

Breakdown voltage: The voltage at which electricity will flow across an insulating substance between two conductors.

Bridge: Circuitry used to interconnect networks with a common set of higher-level protocols.

Bridged tap: Any section of a cable pair that is not on the direct electrical path between the central office and the user's premises, but which is bridged onto the path.

Bridger amplifier: An amplifier installed on a CATV trunk cable to feed branching cables.

Broadband: A form of LAN modulation in which multiple channels are formed by dividing the transmission medium into discrete frequency segments. Also, a term used to describe high bandwidth transmission of data signals.

Broadband ISDN (B-ISDN):   A broadband service based on the use of ATM and SONET.

Broadcast: A transmission to all stations on a network.

Brouter: A local area network bridge that is capable of routing.

Bus: A group of conductors that connects two or more circuit elements, usually at a high speed for a short distance.

Byte: A set of 8 bits of information equivalent to a character. Also called an octet.

C message weighting: A factor used in noise measurements to describe the lesser annoying effect on the human ear of high- and low-frequency noise compared to midrange noise.

C-notched noise: A measurement of C message-weighted noise in a circuit with a tone applied at the far end and filtered out at the near end.

Cable racking: Framework fastened to bays to support interbay cabling.

Caching: The use of memory in a file server to read more information than is requested, storing it so the next information request can be served from memory instead of from the disk.

Call detail recorder (CDR):   An auxiliary device attached to a PBX to capture and record call details such as called number, time of day, duration, etc.

Call progress tones: Tones returned from switching systems to inform the calling party of the progress of the call. Examples are audible ring, reorder, and busy.

Call sequencer: An electronic device similar to an automatic call distributor that can answer calls, inform agent positions of which call arrived first, hold callers in queue, and provide limited statistical information.

Call store: The temporary memory used in an SPC switching system to hold records of calls in progress and pending changes to permanent memory.

Call-by-call service selection: An ISDN feature that lets more than one service be assigned to a single channel. ISDN-compatible switching systems communicate across the D channel to select the appropriate service.

Called party control: The provision in a 911 system for the called party to supervise a call and to hold it up for tracing.

Calling line identification (CLID):   A service offered by LECs in which the calling line number is delivered with the call.

Carbon block protector: A form of electrical protector that uses a pair of carbon blocks separated from the ground by a narrow gap. When the voltage from the block to the ground exceeds a specified value, the blocks arc across to ground the circuit.

Carrier: (1) A type of multiplexing equipment used to derive several channels from one communications link by combining signals on the basis of time or frequency division. (2) A card cage used in an apparatus cabinet to contain multiple circuit packs. (3) A company that carries telecommunications messages and private channels for a fee.

Carrier access code (CAC):   A seven-digit code consisting of the digits 101 plus a four-digit carrier identification code. For example, the CAC for MCI is 1010222.

Carrier sense multiple access with collision detection (CSMA/CD):   A system used in contention networks where the network interface unit listens for the presence of a carrier before attempting to send and detects the presence of a collision by monitoring for a distorted pulse.

Carrier-to-noise ratio: The ratio of the received carrier to the noise level in a satellite link.

Cell: A hexagonal subdivision of a mobile telephone service area containing a cell-site controller and radio frequency transceivers. Also, a group of octets conditioned for transmission across a network.

Cell relay: A data communications technology based on fixed-length cells.

Cell-site controller: The cellular radio unit that manages radio channels within a cell.

Cellular geographic serving area (CGSA):   A metropolitan area in which the FCC grants cellular radio licenses.

Central office (CO):   A switching center that terminates and interconnects lines and trunks from users.

Central processing unit (CPU):   The control logic element used to execute instructions in a computer.

Centralized attendant service (CAS):   A PBX feature that allows the using organization to route all calls from a multi-PBX system to a central answering location where attendants have access to features as if they were collocated with the PBX.

Centralized automatic message accounting (CAMA):   An LEC message-accounting option in which call details are sent from the serving central office to a central location for recording.

Centrex: A class of central office service that provides the equivalent of PBX service from an LEC switching machine. Incoming calls can be dialed directly to extensions without operator intervention.

Centum call seconds (CCS):   See *Hundred call seconds.*

Channel: A path in a communications system between two or more points, furnished by a wire, radio, lightwave, satellite, or a combination of media.

Channel bank: Apparatus that converts multiple voice frequency signals to frequency or time division multiplexed signals for transmitting over a transmission medium.

Channel service unit (CSU):   Apparatus that terminates a T1 line providing various interfacing, maintenance, and testing functions.

Chrominance: The portion of a television signal that carries color-encoding information to the receiver.

Circuit: A transmission path between two points in a telecommunications system.

Circuit pack: A plug-in electronic device that contains the circuitry to perform a specific function. A circuit pack is not capable of stand-alone operation but functions only as an element of the parent device.

Circuit switching: A method of network access in which terminals are connected by switching together the circuits to which they are attached. In a circuit-switched network, the terminals have full real-time access to each other up to the bandwidth of the circuit.

Cladding: The outer coating of glass surrounding the core in fiber optics.

Class 5 office: The former designation for an end office in the AT&T/BOC switching hierarchy that directly serves end users. See *End office.*

Class of service: The service classification within a telecommunications system that controls the features, calling privileges, and restrictions the user is assigned.

Clear channel: A 64-kb/s digital channel that uses external signaling and therefore permits all 64 kb/s to be used for data transmission.

Clock: A device that generates a signal for controlling network synchronization.

Closed circuit television (CCTV):   A privately operated television system not connected to a public distribution network.

Cluster controller: A device that controls access of a group of terminals to a higher-level computer.

Coaxial cable: A single-wire conductor surrounded by an insulating medium and a metallic shield that is used for carrying a telecommunications signal.

Code-excited linear prediction (CELP):   A speech-encoding algorithm that enables speech to be digitized at 8.0 kb/s.

Coder/decoder (codec):   The analog-to-digital conversion circuitry in the line equipment of a digital CO. Also, a device in television transmission that compresses a video signal into a narrow digital channel.

Coherence bandwidth: The bandwidth of a range of frequencies that are subjected to the same degree of frequency-selective fading.

Coin-free dialing: The ability of a caller from a coin telephone to reach an emergency or assistance operator without using a coin to place the call.

Collimate: The condition of parallel light rays.

Collision: A condition that occurs when two or more terminals on a contention network attempt to acquire access to the network simultaneously.

Collision window: The time it takes for a data pulse to travel the length of a contention network. During this interval, the network is vulnerable to collision.

Committed information rate (CIR):   In a frame relay network the CIR is the speed the carrier guarantees to provide. Frames above the CIR are carried on a permissive basis up to the port speed, but are marked discard-eligible.

Common carrier: A company that carries communications services for the general public within an assigned territory.

Common channel signaling (CCS):   A separate data network used to route signals between switching systems.

Common control switching: A switching system that uses shared equipment to establish, monitor, and disconnect paths through the network. The equipment is called into the connection to perform a function and then released to serve other users.

Communications controller: See *Front-end processor.*

Community antenna television (CATV):   A network for distributing television signals over coaxial cable throughout a community. Also called cable television.

Community dial office (CDO):   A small CO designed for unattended operation in a community, usually limited to about 10,000 lines.

Compandor: A device that compresses high-level voice signals in the transmitting direction and expands them in the receiving direction with respect to lower-level signals. Its purpose is to improve noise performance in a circuit.

Competitive local exchange carrier (CLEC):   A company offering local service in competition with the incumbent local exchange carrier.

Complement: A group of 50 cable pairs (25 pairs in small cable sizes) that are bound together and identified as a unit.

Computer-telephony integration (CTI):   Marriage of the PBX with a host computer or file server. The PBX provides call information to the computer, and accepts call-handling instructions from the computer.

Concentration: The process of connecting a group of inputs to a smaller number of outputs in a network. If there are more inputs than outputs, the network has concentration.

Concentration ratio: As applied to CO line equipment, it is the ratio between the number of lines in an equipment group and the number of links or trunks that can be accessed from the lines.

Concentrator: A data communications device that subdivides a channel into a larger number of data channels. Asynchronous channels are fed into a high-speed synchronous channel via a concentrator to derive several lower-speed channels.

Conditional routing: An ACD feature that routes calls based on variables such as number of agents logged on, length of oldest waiting call, etc.

Conditioning: Special treatment given to a transmission facility to make it acceptable for high-speed data communication.

Conference European on Post and Telecommunications (CEPT):   The European telecommunications standards-setting body.

Connectionless: A data transmission method in which packets are launched into the network with the sending and receiving address, but without a defined path. For example, LANs use connectionless transmissions.

Connection-oriented: A circuit that is set up over a network so that the originating and terminating stations share a defined path, either real or virtual. For example, a telephone call uses a connection-oriented circuit.

Connectivity: The ability to connect a device to a network.

Consultative Committee on International Telephone and Telegraph (CCITT): An international committee that sets telephone, telegraph, and data communications standards. Now known as the International Telecommunications Union (ITU-T).

Contention: A form of multiple access to a network in which the network capacity is allocated on a "first come, first served" basis.

Control equipment: Equipment used to transmit orders from an alarm center to a remote site to perform operations by remote control.

Converter: A device for changing central office voltage to another dc voltage for powering equipment.

Core: The inner glass element that guides the light rays in an optical fiber.

Coverage path: In a PBX the coverage path determines where the call will be routed if the called telephone is busy or does not answer.

Critical rain rate: The amount of rainfall where the drops are of sufficient size and intensity to cause fading in a microwave signal.

Cross: A circuit impairment where two separate circuits are unintentionally interconnected.

Crossbar: A type of switching system that uses a centrally controlled matrix switching network consisting of electromechanical switches connecting horizontal and vertical paths to establish a path through the network.

Cross-connect: A wired connection between two or more elements of a telecommunications circuit.

Cross-polarization: The relationship between two radio waves when one is polarized vertically and the other horizontally.

Cross-polarization discrimination (XPD): The amount of decoupling between radio waves that exists when they are cross-polarized.

Crosstalk: The unwanted coupling of a signal from one transmission path into another.

Custom local area signaling service (CLASS): A suite of services offered by LECs. Examples are calling line identification (CLID), distinctive ringing, automatic callback, etc.

Customer premises equipment (CPE): Telephone apparatus mounted on the user's premises and connected to the telephone network.

Cutover: Any change from an existing to a new telecommunications system.

Cyclical redundancy checking (CRC): A data error-detecting system wherein an information block is subjected to a mathematical process designed to ensure that errors cannot occur undetected.

D channel: The ISDN 16-kb/s data channel that is used for out-of-band signaling functions such as call setup.

Daisy chain: A local area network configuration in which nodes are directly connected in series.

Data: Digitized information in a form suitable for storage or communication over electronic means.

Data circuit–terminating equipment (DCE): Equipment designed to establish a connection to a network, condition the input and output of DTE for transmission over the network, and terminate the connection when completed.

Data compression: A data transmission system that replaces a bit stream with another bit stream having fewer bits.

Datagram: An unacknowledged packet sent over a network as an individual unit without regard to previous or subsequent packets.

Data link: A circuit capable of carrying digitized information. Usually refers to layer 2 of the OSI protocol stack.

Data network identification code (DNIC):   A 14-digit number used for worldwide numbering of data networks.

Data service unit (DSU):   Apparatus that interfaces DTE to a line. Used with CSU when DTE lacks complete digital-line interface capability or alone when DTE includes digital-line interface capability.

Data terminal equipment (DTE):   Any form of computer, peripheral, or terminal that can be used for originating or receiving data over a communications channel.

dBm: A measure of signal power as compared to 1 mW (1/1000 W) of power. It is used to express power levels. For example, a signal power of -10 dBm is 10 dB lower than 1 mW.

dBrn: A measure of noise power relative to a reference noise of -90 dBm.

dBrnc: A measure of noise power through a C message weighting filter.

dBrnc0:   A measure of C message noise referred to a zero test level point.

Decibel (dB):   A measure of relative power level between two points in a circuit.

Dedicated access: The interconnection of a station to an IXC through a dedicated line.

Dedicated circuit: A communications channel assigned for the exclusive use of an organization.

Delay: (1) The time a call spends in queue. (2) The time required for a signal to transit the communications facility; also known as latency.

Delta modulation: A system of converting analog to digital signals by transmitting a single bit indicating the direction of change in amplitude from the previous sample.

Demand assigned multiple access (DAMA):   A method of sharing the capacity of a communications satellite by assigning capacity on demand to an idle channel or time slot from a pool.

Demarcation point: The point at which customer-owned wiring and equipment interfaces with the telephone company.

Demodulation: The process of extracting intelligence from a carrier signal.

Dense wavelength division multiplexing (DWDM):   The process of multiplexing fiber optics with multiple wavelengths—up to 40 with today's technology.

Dialed number identification service (DNIS):   A service offered by most 800 carriers that reports to the PBX which 800 number was dialed. The PBX can then use the 800 number to route the call. DNIS on 800 circuits is equivalent to DID on central office trunks.

Dial-up: A data communications session that is initiated by dialing a switched telephone circuit.

Digital: A mode of transmission in which information is coded in binary form for transmission on a network.

Digital access cross-connect system (DACS):   A specialized digital switch that enables cross-connection of channels at the digital-line rate.

Digital service cross-connect (DSX):   A physically wired cross-connect frame to enable connecting digital transmission equipment at a standard bit rate.

Digital switching: A process for connecting ports on a switching system by routing digital signals without converting them to analog.

Digroup: Two groups of 12 digital channels integrated to form a single 24-channel system.

Diplexer: A device that couples a radio transmitter and receiver to the same antenna.

Dipole: An antenna that has two radiating elements fed from a central point.

Direct broadcast satellite (DBS):   A television broadcast service that provides television programming services throughout a country from a single source through a satellite.

Direct control switching: A system in which the switching path is established directly through the network by dial pulses without central control.

Direct distance dialing (DDD):   A long-distance calling system that enables a user to place a call without operator assistance.

Direct inward dialing (DID):   A method of enabling callers from outside a PBX to reach an extension by dialing the access code plus the extension number.

Direct trunks: Trunks dedicated exclusively to traffic between the terminating offices.

Directional coupler: A device inserted in a waveguide to couple a transmitter and receiver to the same antenna. Also a passive device installed on a CATV cable to isolate the feeder cable from another branch.

Discard-eligible: In a frame relay network, frames above the committed information rate are marked discard-eligible. In case of congestion the carrier can discard such frames to preserve network integrity.

Dispersion: The rounding and overlapping of a light pulse that occurs to different wavelengths because of reflected rays or the different refractive index of the core material.

Dispersive fade margin: A property of a digital microwave signal that expresses the amount of fade margin under conditions of distortion caused by multipath fading.

Distortion: An unwanted change in a waveform.

Distributed control: A switching system architecture in which more than one processor controls certain groups of line ports.

Distributed processing: The distribution of call-processing functions among numerous small processors rather than concentrating all functions in a single central processor.

Distributed queue dual bus (DQDB):   The protocol used in the 802.6 metropolitan area network.

Distributed switching: The capability to install CO line circuits close to the served subscribers and connect them over a smaller group of links or trunks to a CO that directly controls the operation of the remote unit.

Distributing frame: A framework holding terminal blocks that interconnect cable and equipment and provide test access.

Distribution cable: Cable that connects the user's serving terminal to an interface with a branch feeder cable.

Diversity: A method of protecting a radio signal from failure of equipment or the radio path by providing standby equipment.

Domain name service (DNS):   Translates host names to IP addresses.

Downlink: The radio path from a satellite to an earth station.

Download: To send information from a host computer to a remote terminal.

Downstream channel: The frequency band in a CATV system that distributes signals from the headend to the users.

Drop wire: Wire leading from the user's serving terminal to the station protector.

Dual-tone multifrequency (DTMF):   A signaling system that uses pairs of audio frequencies to represent a digit. Usually synonymous with the Lucent Technologies trademark Touch-tone.

Dumb terminal: A terminal that has no processing capability. It is functional only when connected to a host.

Dwell time: In frequency hopping spread spectrum radio dwell time is the time the system stays on one frequency before changing to another.

E&M signaling: A method of signaling between offices by voltage states on the transmit and receive leads of signaling equipment at the point of interface.

Earth station: The radio equipment, antenna, and satellite communication control circuitry that is used to provide access from terrestrial circuits to satellite capacity.

Echo: The reflection of a portion of a signal back to its source.

Echo canceler: An electronic device that processes the echo signal and cancels it out to prevent annoyance to the talker.

Echo cancellation: A protocol used to obtain full-duplex data communication over a two-wire line.

Echo checking: A method of error checking in which the receiving end echoes received characters to the transmitting end.

Echo return loss (ERL):   The weighted return loss of a circuit across a band of frequencies from 500 to 2500 Hz.

Echo suppressor: A device that opens the receive path of a circuit when talking power is present in the transmit path.

Effective isotropic-radiated power (EIRP):   Power radiated by a transmitter compared to the power of an isotropic antenna, which is one that radiates equally in all directions.

Electromagnetic interference (EMI):   An interfering signal that is radiated from a source and picked up by a telecommunications circuit.

Electronic data interchange (EDI):   The intercompany exchange of legally binding trade documents over a telecommunications network.

Electronic mail: A service that enables messages and file attachments to be transferred across a communications network.

Electronic tandem network (ETN):   A private telecommunications network that consists of switching nodes and interconnecting trunks.

Emergency ringback: A feature that enables a 911 center to connect a caller to the appropriate Public Service Answering Point (PSAP) and to enable the PSAP to rering the circuit if the caller disconnects. This enables the PSAP to connect to the caller to get additional emergency information.

End office: The central office in the LEC's network that directly serves subscriber lines.

End-to-end signaling: A method of connecting signaling equipment so it transmits signals between the two ends of a circuit with no intermediate appearances of the signaling leads.

Enhanced 911 (E-911):   An emergency service in which information relative to the specific caller, such as identity and location, is forwarded to the 911 agency by the serving central office.

Enterprise network: A private network of both switched and dedicated facilities that enables users to connect to services wherever they are located without concern about how to establish the session.

Entrance facility (EF):   The physical structure and cable connecting the main equipment room to the common carrier's facilities.

Entrance link: A coaxial or fiber-optic facility used to connect the last terminal in a microwave signal to multiplex or video terminating equipment.

Envelope delay: The difference in propagation speed of different frequencies within the passband of a voice channel.

Equal access: A central office feature that allows all interexchange carriers to have access to the trunk side of the switching network in an end office.

Equipment rooms (ER): Building areas intended to house telecommunications equipment. Equipment rooms also may fill the functions of a telecommunications closet.

Error: Any discrepancy between a received data signal from the signal as it was transmitted.

Error-free seconds: The number of seconds per unit of time that a circuit vendor guarantees the circuit will be free of errors.

Ethernet: A proprietary contention bus network developed by Xerox, Digital Equipment Corporation, and Intel. Ethernet formed the basis for the IEEE 802.3 standard.

Extended superframe (ESF): T1 carrier framing format that provides 64-kb/s clear channel capability, error checking, 16-state signaling, and other data transmission features.

Extranet: A virtual network tying a company to outside organizations, often through the Internet, but also through frame-relay and other such network services.

Facility: Any set of transmission paths that can be used to transport voice or data. Facilities can range from a cable to a carrier system or a microwave radio system.

Facsimile: A system for scanning a document, encoding it, transmitting it over a telecommunications circuit, and reproducing it in its original form at the receiving end.

Far-end crosstalk (FEXT): The amount of crosstalk measured at the distant end of a receive circuit when a signal is applied at the near end.

Fax on demand (FOD): Equipment that prompts a caller to enter digits from the dial pad identifying information needed and a fax number. FOD equipment retrieves the information from a database and automatically faxes it to the caller.

Fibre Channel: An ANSI standard protocol for connecting high-speed devices that are located too distant to use a protocol such as small-computer system interface (SCSI).

File transfer protocol (FTP): A protocol used by TCP/IP networks to transfer files from one system to another.

Firewall: A device that protects the connection between a network and an untrusted connecting network such as the Internet. The firewall blocks unwanted traffic from entering the network and allows only authorized traffic to leave.

Flow control: The process of protecting network service by slowing or denying access to additional traffic that would add further to congestion.

Foreign exchange (FEX): A special service that connects station equipment located in one telephone exchange with switching equipment located in another.

Four-wire circuit: A circuit that uses separate paths for each direction of transmission.

Frame relay: A data communications service that transports frames of information across a network to one or more points. Cost is based on three elements: committed information rate (CIR), access circuit, and port speed.

Front-end processor: An auxiliary computer attached to a network to perform control operations and relieve the host computer for data processing.

Full duplex: A data communications circuit over which data can be sent in both directions simultaneously.

Gas tube protector: A protector containing an ionizing gas that conducts external voltages to ground when they exceed a designed threshold level.

Gateway: Circuitry used to interconnect networks by converting the protocols of each network to that used by the other.

Gauge: The physical size of an electrical conductor, specified by American Wire Gauge (AWG) standards.

Generic program: The operating system in an SPC central office that contains logic for call-processing functions and controls the overall machine operation.

Glare: A condition that exists when both ends of a circuit are simultaneously seized.

Grade of service: (1) The percentage of time or probability that a call will be blocked in a network. (2) A quality indicator used in transmission measurements to specify the quality of a circuit based on both noise and loss.

Ground start: A method of circuit seizure between a central office and a PBX that transmits an immediate signal by grounding the tip of the line.

Half duplex: A data communications circuit over which data can be sent in only one direction at a time.

Handshaking: Signaling between two DCE devices on a link to set up communications between them.

Heat coil: A protection device that opens a circuit and grounds a cable pair when operated by stray currents.

High-usage groups: Trunk groups established between two switching machines to serve as the first choice path between the machines and handle the bulk of the traffic.

Holding time: The average length of time per call that calls in a group of circuits are off-hook.

Horizontal wiring: The wiring from the equipment rooms or telecommunications closets to the work area.

Hundred call seconds (CCS):   A measure of network load. Thirty-six CCS represents 100 percent occupancy of a circuit or piece of equipment.

Hybrid: (1) A multiwinding coil or electronic circuit used in a four-wire terminating set or switching system line circuits to separate the four-wire and two-wire paths. (2) A key telephone system that has many of the features of a PBX. Such features as pooled trunk access characterize a hybrid.

Impedance: The ratio of voltage to current in an alternating current electric circuit.

Impulse noise: Short bursts of high-amplitude interference.

Incumbent local exchange company (ILEC):   The traditional telephone company that serves a particular franchised area.

Independent telephone company (IC):   A non-Bell ILEC.

Inside wiring: The wiring on the customer's premises between the telephone set and the telephone company's demarcation point.

Integrated services digital network (ISDN):   A set of standards promulgated by ITU-T to prescribe standard interfaces to a switched digital network.

Integrated voice/data: The combination of voice and data signals from a workstation over a communications path to the PBX.

Interactive voice response (IVR):   Also known as voice response unit (VRU), equipment that acts as an automatic front end for a computer system, enabling callers to conduct their own transactions. The IVR prompts the caller to dial identification digits plus digits to complete transactions such as checking account balance, transferring funds, etc.

Interexchange carrier (IXC):   A common carrier that provides long-distance service between LATAs.

Interface: The connection between two systems. Usually hardware and software connecting a computer terminal with peripherals such as DCE, printers, etc.

Intermediate distributing frame (IDF):   A cross-connection point between the main distributing frame and station wiring.

Intermodulation distortion: Distortion or noise generated in electronic circuits when the power carried is great enough to cause nonlinear operation.

International Telecommunications Union (ITU):   An agency of the United Nations that is responsible for setting telecommunications standards.

Internet protocol (IP):   A connectionless protocol used for delivering data packets from host to host across an internetwork.

Intranet: A network linking a company's offices together and making information accessible, usually with a web browser.

Inverse multiplexer: A device that combines multiple 64- or 56-kb/s channels into a higher-speed bit stream. It is often used to combine multiple switched 56 or ISDN channels for videoconferencing.

Jabber: A single or steady stream of Ethernet frames longer than the maximum.

Jitter: (1) The phase shift of digital pulses over a transmission medium. (2) The variation in arrival intervals of a stream of packets.

Jumper: Wire used to interconnect equipment and cable on a distributing frame.

Key telephone system (KTS):   A method of allowing several central office lines to be accessed from multiple telephone sets.

Latency: The time it takes for a bit to pass from origin to destination through the network.

Leased line: A nonswitched telecommunications channel leased to an organization for its exclusive use.

Least-cost routing (LCR):   A PBX service feature that chooses the most economical route to a destination based on cost of the terminated services and time of delay.

Level: The signal power at a given point in a circuit.

Line conditioning: A service offered by common carriers to reduce envelope delay, noise, and amplitude distortion to enable transmission of higher-speed data.

Link: A circuit or path joining two communications channels in a network.

Loading: The process of inserting fixed inductors in series with both wires of a cable pair to reduce voice frequency loss.

Local access transport area (LATA):   The geographical boundaries within which Bell Operating Companies are permitted to offer long-distance traffic.

Local area network (LAN):   A narrow-range data network using one of the nonswitched multiple access technologies.

Local automatic message accounting (LAMA):   An LEC message-accounting option in which call details are recorded in the serving central office.

Local exchange company (LEC): Any local exchange telephone company that serves a particular area. An LEC may be an incumbent LEC (ILEC) or a competitive LEC (CLEC).

Local multipoint distribution service (LMDS): A microwave-based service that serves multiple voice and data users from a central base station hub.

Loop start: A method of circuit seizure between a central office and station equipment that operates by bridging the tip and ring of the line through a resistance.

Loopback test: A test applied to a full-duplex circuit by connecting the receive leads to the transmit leads, applying a signal, and reading the returned test signal at the near end of the circuit.

Loss: The drop in signal level between points on a circuit.

Low earth orbiting satellite (LEOS): A global personal communications service technology using a constellation of satellites orbiting the earth at a few hundred miles for communications with hand-held units.

Main distributing frame (MDF): The cable rack used to terminate all distribution and trunk cables in a central office or PBX.

Management information base (MIB): A database contained in an SNMP-compatible device that defines the object that is managed.

Mean time between failures (MTBF): The average time a device or system operates without failing.

Mean time to repair (MTTR): The average time required for a qualified technician to repair a failed device or system.

Message switching: A form of network access in which a message is forwarded from a terminal to a central switch where it is stored and forwarded to the addressee after some delay.

Message telephone service (MTS): A generic name for the switched long-distance telephone service offered by all interexchange carriers.

Message transfer agent (MTA): In a messaging system the MTA transfers messages between the user agents and other MTAs.

Messaging: The use of computer systems to exchange messages among people, applications, systems, and organizations.

Messenger: A metallic strand attached to a pole line to support aerial cable.

Microwave: A high-frequency, high-capacity radio system, usually used to carry multiple voice channels.

Milliwatt: One one-thousandths of a watt. Used as a reference power for signal levels in telecommunications circuits.

Mobile data terminal (MDT): A wireless terminal that permits one-way or two-way data communications. The MDT may be vehicular or hand-held.

Mobile telephone switching office (MTSO): The electronic switching system that switches calls between mobile and wireline telephones, controls handoff between cells, and monitors usage. This equipment is known by various trade names.

Modeling: The process of designing a network from a series of mathematical formulas that describe the behavior of network elements.

Modem: A contraction of the terms MOdulator/DEModulator. A modem is used to convert analog signals to digital form and vice versa.

Modem pool: A centralized pool of modems accessed through a PBX or LAN to provide off-net data transmission from modemless terminals.

Modulation: The process by which some characteristic of a carrier signal, such as frequency, amplitude, or phase, is varied by a low-frequency information signal.

Multicast: A transmission that includes multiple selected stations on a network.

Multidrop: A circuit dedicated to communication between multiple terminals that are connected to the same circuit.

Multiline hunt: The ability of a switching machine to connect calls to another number in a group when other numbers in the group are busy.

Multiple access: The capability of multiple terminals connected to the same network to access one another by means of a common addressing scheme and protocol.

Multiplexer: A device used for combining several lower-speed channels into a higher-speed channel.

Near-end crosstalk (NEXT):   The amount of signal received at the near end of a circuit when a transmit signal is applied at the same end of the link.

Network: A set of communications nodes connected by channels.

Network access restriction (NAR):   A software restriction built into Centrex systems to limit the number of simultaneous trunk calls the subscriber can place.

Network administration: The process of monitoring network loads and service results and making adjustments needed to maintain service and costs at the design objective level.

Network channel-terminating equipment (NCTE):   Apparatus mounted on the user's premises that is used to amplify, match impedance, or match network signaling to the interconnected equipment.

Network design: The process of determining quantities and architecture of circuit and equipment to achieve a cost/service balance.

Node: A major point in a network where lines from many sources meet and may be switched.

Noise: Any unwanted signal in a transmission path.

Non-facility-associated signaling (NFAS):   The capability in a primary-rate ISDN network of using one 64-kb/s D channel to control the signaling of multiple PRIs.

Octet: A group of 8 bits. Often used interchangeably with byte, although a byte can have other than 8 bits.

Off-hook: A signaling state in a line or trunk when it is working or busy.

Off-premises extension (OPX):   An extension telephone that uses LEC facilities to connect to the main telephone service.

On-hook: A signaling state in a line or trunk when it is nonworking or idle.

On-net: In a virtual network, an on-net call is one that uses a dedicated access line (DAL).

Open network architecture (ONA):   A telephone architecture that provides the interfaces to enable service providers to connect to the public switched telephone network.

Open systems interconnect (OSI):   A seven-layer data communications protocol model that specifies standard interfaces which all vendors can adapt to their own designs.

Overflow: The ACD process in which a call is routed to a queue other than the original one.

Overhead: Any noninformation bits such as headers, error-checking bits, start and stop bits, etc., used for controlling a network.

Packet: A unit of data information consisting of header, information, and error-detection and trailer records.

Packet assembler/disassembler (PAD):   A device used on a packet-switched network to assemble information into packets and to convert received packets into a continuous data stream.

Packet switching: A method of allocating network time by forming data into packets and relaying it to the destination under the control of processors at each major node. The network determines packet routing during transport of the packet.

Parity: A bit or series of bits appended to a character or block of characters to ensure that either an odd or even number of bits are transmitted. Parity is used for error detection.

Patch: The temporary interconnection of transmission and signaling paths; used for temporary rerouting and restoral of failed facilities or equipment.

Peak-to-average ratio (P/AR):   An analog test that provides an index of data circuit quality by sending a pulse into one end of a circuit and measuring its envelope at the distant end of the circuit.

Peg count: The number of times a specified event occurs. Derived from an early method of counting the number of busy lines in a manual switchboard.

Permanent virtual circuit (PVC):   In a data network a PVC is defined in software. The circuit functions as if a hardware path was in place, but the path is shared with other users.

Personal communications service (PCS):   A radio-based service that allows subscribers to roam anywhere, using a telephone number that is not associated with a fixed location.

Personal identification number (PIN):   A billing identification number dialed by the user to enable the switching machine to identify the calling party.

Point-of-presence (POP):   The point at which a carrier meets the customer-provided portion of a circuit. For LECs the POP is usually on the customer's premises. For IXCs the POP is usually on the carrier's premises.

Point-to-point circuit: A telecommunications circuit that is exclusively assigned to the use of two devices.

Poll cycle time: The amount of time required for a multidrop data communications controller to make one complete polling cycle through all devices on the network.

Polling: A network-sharing method in which remote terminals send traffic upon receipt of a polling message from the host. The host accesses the terminal, determines if it has traffic to send, and causes traffic to be uploaded to the host.

Postalized rates: A method many IXCs use for billing long-distance calls. With postalized rates the cost is sensitive to talking time but not to distance.

Power-fail transfer: A unit in KTS that transfers one or more telephone instruments to central office lines during a power failure.

Primary-rate interface (PRI):   In North America a 1.544-Mb/s information-carrying channel that furnishes integrated services digital network (ISDN) services to end users. Consists of 23 bearer channels and one signaling channel. In Europe a 2.048-Mb/s channel consisting of 30 bearer and two signaling channels.

Private automatic branch exchange (PABX):   A term often used synonymously for PBX. A PABX is always automatic, whereas switching is manual in some PBXs.

Private branch exchange (PBX):   A switching system dedicated to telephone and data use in a private communications network.

Propagation delay: The absolute time delay of a signal from the sending to the receiving terminal.

Propagation speed: The speed at which a signal travels over a transmission medium.

Property management system (PMS):   A computer application used in the hospitality industry to handle functions such as check-in/check-out, room status, etc. The PMS is often linked to the telephone system to provide such functions from the PMS terminal.

Protector: A device that prevents hazardous voltages or currents from injuring a user or damaging equipment connected to a cable pair.

Protocol: The conventions used in a network for establishing communications compatibility between terminals and for maintaining the line discipline while they are connected to the network.

Protocol analyzer: A data communications test set that enables an operator to observe bit patterns in a data transmission, trap specific patterns, and simulate network elements.

Protocol converter: A device that converts one communications protocol to another.

Protocol data unit (PDU):   A formatted data message, the size and structure of which depends on its position in the protocol stack. For example, a frame is a data-link layer PDU, a packet a network layer PDU, and an X.400 message is an application layer PDU.

Public data network (PDN):   A data transmission network operated by a private telecommunications company for public subscription and use.

Public switched telephone network (PSTN):   A generic term for the interconnected networks of operating telephone companies.

Pulse code modulation (PCM):   A digital modulation method that encodes a voice signal into an 8-bit digital word representing the amplitude of each pulse.

Q.Sig: A protocol for networking PBXs of different manufacture.

Queuing: The holding of calls in queue when a trunk group is busy and completing them in turn when an idle circuit is available.

Redundancy: The provision of more than one circuit element to assume call processing when the primary element fails.

Reference noise (rn):   The threshold of audibility to which noise measurements are referred, −90 dBm.

Remote access: (1) A family of products that allow users who are away from the office to dial into the LAN and access its resources. (2) The ability to dial into a switching system over a local telephone number in order to complete calls over a private network from a distant location.

Remote call forwarding (RCF):   A service offered by most LECs that allows a user to obtain a telephone number in a local calling area and have calls automatically forwarded at the user's expense to another telephone number.

Remote maintenance and testing system (RMATS):   A service offered by PBX manufacturers and vendors that enables the vendor to access a PBX over the PTSN and perform testing and administrative functions.

Remote MONitoring (RMON):   A network management function that enables the manager to monitor network functions from a remote management workstation.

Reorder: A fast busy tone used to indicate equipment or circuit blockage.

Repeater: A bidirectional signal regenerator (digital) or amplifier (analog). Repeaters are available to work on analog or digital signals from audio to radio frequency.

Response time: The interval between the user's sending the last character of a message and the time the first character of the response from the host arrives at the terminal.

Restriction: Limitations to a station on the use of PBX features or trunks on the basis of service classification.

Return loss: The degree of isolation, expressed in decibels, between the transmit and the receive ports of a four-wire terminating set.

Ring: The designation of the side of a telephone line that carries talking battery to the user's premises.

Riser cable: In a building, riser cable runs between the main distributing frame and telecommunications closets on other floors. In a campus environment riser connects the MDF to TCs in other buildings.

RJ-11:   A standard four-conductor jack and plug arrangement typically used for connecting a standard telephone to inside wiring.

RJ-45:   A standard eight-conductor jack and plug arrangement typically used for connecting a telephone or data terminal to inside wiring.

Routing: The path selection made for a telecommunications signal through the network to its destination.

Rules-based messaging: An e-mail feature that enables a user to screen messages based on criteria that the user specifies.

Runt: An Ethernet frame shorter than the 64-byte minimum.

Segment: See *Subnet*.

Serial interface: Circuitry used in DTE to convert parallel data to serial data for transmission on a network.

Server: In a telecommunications network servers are the trunks or the service process, such as call center agents, that fulfill the users' service requests. In a LAN servers are devices that provide specialized services such as file, print, and modem or fax pool services.

Service level: In a call center service level is defined as the percentage of calls answered within an objective time interval.

Service profile identifier (SPID):   A unique number that ISDN equipment uses to identify itself to the central office.

Short: A circuit impairment that exists when two conductors of the same pair are connected at an unintended point.

Sidetone: The sound of a talker's voice audible in the handset of the telephone instrument.

Signaling system no. 7 (SS7):   An out-of-band signaling protocol between public switching systems.

Signal-to-noise ratio: The ratio between signal power and noise power in a circuit.

Simple mail transfer protocol (SMTP):   A protocol for delivering messages across a TCP/IP network.

Simple network management protocol (SNMP):   A management protocol for monitoring and controlling network devices.

Simulation: The process of designing a network by simulating the events and facilities that represent network load and capacity.

Singing: The tendency of a circuit to oscillate when the return loss is too low.

Skill-based routing: An ACD function that routes calls based on a table containing the skills of each agent.

Split: A designated group of answering stations in an automatic call distributor (ACD).

Spread spectrum: A radio modulation method that transmits its signal over a broad range of frequencies (direct sequence method) or rapidly jumps from one frequency to another (frequency hopping). Spread spectrum provides excellent security and resists interference.

Station message detail recording (SMDR):   The port in a PBX that provides information such as called and calling station, time of day, and duration on long-distance calls. The SMDR port is usually connected to a call-accounting system to produce the necessary reports.

Station range: The number of feet or ohms over which a telephone instrument can signal and transmit voice and data.

Statistical multiplexing: A form of data multiplexing in which the time on a communications channel is assigned to terminals only when they have data to transport.

Store-and-forward: A method of switching messages in which a message or packet is sent from the originating terminal to a central unit where it is held for retransmission to the receiving terminal.

Striping: In an RAID disk, striping is the process of parceling a file across several disks. In Fibre Channel it is the method of aggregating multiple N_ports to obtain greater bandwidth.

Structure of management information (SMI):   The framework that defines network management variables in a network management system.

Subnet: A group of workstations in a LAN that is separated from other groups by a bridge or, more frequently, a router.

Subscriber carrier: A multichannel device that enables several subscribers to share a single facility in the local loop.

Subscriber loop: The circuit that connects a user's premises to the telephone central office.

Supervision: The process of monitoring the busy/idle status of a circuit to detect changes of state.

Sustained information rate (SIR):   The maximum guaranteed rate at which data can transit an SMDS network. SIR is similar to committed information rate (CIR) in a frame relay network.

Switched multimegabit data service (SMDS):   A high-speed connectionless data transport service offered by LECs and some IXCs.

Switched virtual circuit (SVC):   A logical link between points on a carrier network that is set up and disconnected with each session.

Synchronous: A method of transmitting data over a network wherein the sending and receiving terminals are kept in synchronism with each other by a clock signal embedded in the data.

System integration: The process of bringing software and equipment from different manufacturers together to form an operational unit.

Systems network architecture (SNA):   An IBM data communications architecture that includes structure, formats, protocols, and operating sequences.

T1 multiplexer: An intelligent device that divides a 1.544-Mb/s facility into multiple voice and data channels.

Telecommunications: The electronic movement of information.

Telecommunications bonding backbone: A backbone cable run between equipment rooms and telecommunications closets and the building's telecommunications main grounding busbar.

Telecommunications closet (TC):   In a telecommunications wiring plan, a satellite closet containing a junction between backbone and horizontal cable.

Telecommunications grounding busbar: A grounding point for telecommunications services and equipment in each telecommunications equipment room and closet.

Telecommunications main grounding busbar (TMGB):   The central grounding point for telecommunications equipment rooms and closets. The TMGB is bonded to the electrical ground and to the building's metal framework.

Telephony applications programming interface (TAPI):   A programming interface developed by Microsoft that connects PCs to telephone instruments to enable computer-telephony applications.

Telephony services applications programming interface (TSAPI):   A programming interface for Novell servers that enables developers to write computer-telephony software for applications that work on Novell servers.

Terminal: (1) A fixture attached to a distribution cable to provide access for making connections to cable pairs. (2) Any device meant for direct operation over a telecommunications circuit by an end user.

Text messaging: The use of a computer-based network of terminals to store and transmit messages among users.

Thermal noise: Noise created in an electronic circuit by the movement and collisions of electrons.

Throughput: Information bits correctly transported over a data network per unit of time.

Tie trunk: A privately owned or leased trunk used to interconnect PBXs in a private switching network.

Time division multiplexing (TDM):   A method of combining several communications channels by dividing a channel into time increments and assigning each channel to a time slot. Multiple channels are interleaved when each channel is assigned the entire bandwidth of the backbone channel for a short period of time.

Time slot: In a TDM system each byte is assigned a unit of time sufficient for the transmission of 8 bits. This unit of time recurs at the same instant of time in a transmission frame.

Timed overflow: In an ACD this feature allows a call to overflow to an alternate queue after it has waited in the original queue for a specified period of time.

Tip: The designation of the side of a telephone line that serves as the return path to the central office.

Token: A software mark or packet that circulates among network nodes.

Token passing: A method of allocating network access wherein a terminal can send traffic only after it has acquired the network's token.

Topology: The architecture of a network, or the way circuits are connected to link the network nodes.

Traffic usage recorder (TUR):   Hardware or software that monitors traffic-sensitive circuits or apparatus and records usage, usually in terms of CCS and peg count.

Transceiver: A device that has the capability of both transmitting and receiving information.

Transducer: Any device that changes energy from one state to another. Examples are microphones, speakers, and telephone handsets.

Translations: Software in a switching system that establishes the characteristics and features of lines and trunks.

Transmission: The process of transporting voice or data over a network or facility from one point to another.

Transmission control protocol (TCP):   A protocol for providing reliable end-to-end delivery of data across an internetwork, usually used with IP.

Transmission level point (TLP):   A designated measurement point in a circuit where the designer has specified the transmission level.

Trap: A message sent by an SNMP-managed device to indicate that a threshold or alarm has been reached.

Traveling class mark: A feature of switches used in electronic tandem networks to carry the class of service of the user with the call so downstream tandems know what features and restrictions to apply.

Trunk: A communications channel between two switching systems equipped with terminating and signaling equipment.

Tunneling: The process of encapsulating one protocol in another for transport across a network.

Uplink: The radio path from an earth station to a satellite.

User agent (UA):   In a messaging system the UA is the user's interface to the system. The UA provides for message composition, receipt, sending, and handling.

Utilization: The ratio of the time a resource is used to the total time it is available. For example, if a circuit carries 25 CCS of traffic during the busy hour, its utilization is $25/36 =$ 69.4 percent.

Value-added network: A data communications network that adds processing services, such as error correction and storage, to the basic function of transporting data.

Vector: A series of routing and call-handling instructions in an ACD.

Video on demand (VOD):   The delivery of video services to customers in response to their specific request. VOD is contrasted to conventional cable television where all channels are delivered over the medium.

Videotex: An interactive information retrieval service that usually employs the telephone network as the transmission medium to provide information with text and color graphics.

Virtual circuit: A circuit that is established between two terminals by assigning a logical path over which data can flow. A virtual circuit can either be permanent, in which terminals are assigned a permanent path, or switched, in which the circuit is reestablished each time a terminal has data to send.

Virtual LAN (VLAN):   A LAN composed of users that are attached to different hubs. Users can be assigned to a LAN segment regardless of their physical location.

Virtual network: A switched voice network offered by interexchange carriers that provides service similar to a private voice network. Virtual networks offer reduced rates for on-net calling, which is available from stations with a direct T1 connection from the user to the IXC.

Virtual private network (VPN):   A private data network that is deployed by tunneling through the Internet and/or by using dedicated data facilities.

Voice mail: A service that allows voice messages to be stored digitally in secondary storage and retrieved remotely by dialing access and identification codes.

Voice response unit (VRU):   See *Interactive voice response.*

Wide area telephone service (WATS):   A bulk-rated long-distance telephone service that carries calls at a cost based on usage and the state in which the calls terminate.

Wireless: A radio or infrared-based service that enables telephone or LAN users to connect to the telecommunications network without wires.

Wiring closet: See *Telecommunications closet.*

Work area: In the EIA/TIA 568 specifications the work area is the area in which the station jack is located to feed the terminating devices.

BIBLIOGRAPHY

Black, Uyless. *Advanced Internet Technologies.* Upper Saddle River, NJ: Prentice Hall, 1999.

Black, Uyless. *ATM,* Vol. I. Upper Saddle River, NJ: Prentice Hall, 1999.

Black, Uyless. *Emerging Communications Technologies,* 2d ed. Upper Saddle River, NJ: Prentice Hall, 1994.

Black, Uyless. *Second Generation Mobile and Wireless Networks.* Upper Saddle River, NJ: Prentice Hall, 1999.

Blumenthal, U., N. Hien, and B. Wijnen, *SNMPv3 Handbook.* Reading, MA: Addison-Wesley, 1999.

Cole, Marion. *Telecommunications.* Upper Saddle River, NJ: Prentice Hall, 1999.

Goralski, Walter J. *SONET.* New York: McGraw-Hill, 1997.

Green, James H. *The Irwin Handbook of Telecommunications Management,* 2d ed. Burr Ridge, IL: Richard D. Irwin, 1996.

Held, Gilbert. *Ethernet Networks,* 3d ed. New York: John Wiley, 1998.

Kuruppillai, Rajan, Dontamsetti Mahi, and Fil J. Cosentino. *Wireless PCS.* New York: McGraw-Hill, 1997.

Minoli, Daniel, and Andrew Schmidt. *Network Layer Switched Services.* New York: John Wiley, 1998.

Oppenheimer, Priscilla. *Top-Down Network Design.* Indianapolis, IN: Macmillan Technical Publishing, 1999.

Sportack, Mark A., et al. *High Performance Networking.* Indianapolis, IN: Sams.net, 1997.

Stallings, William. *High Speed Networks.* Upper Saddle River, NJ: Prentice Hall, 1998.

Stallings, William. *SNMP, SNMPv2, SNMPv3, and RMON 1 and 2,* 3d ed. Reading, MA: Addison-Wesley, 1998.

Taylor, Ed. *Encyclopedia of Network Blueprints.* New York: McGraw-Hill, 1998.

INDEX

ABOUT THE AUTHOR

James Harry Green is president of Pacific Netcom, Inc., a telecommunications consulting firm that helps its clients apply technology to solve their business problems. He founded Pacific Netcom in 1983 following a 28-year career with the Bell System, one which encompassed all telecommunications engineering and operations aspects from switching through transmission and network design. A popular speaker, Green is the author of numerous articles and books on telecommunications including *The Irwin Handbook of Telecommunications Management,* and he is a member of the Society of Telecommunications Consultants.